Agricultural and Environmental Resource Economics

Biological Resource Management Series

Wayne M. Getz, Editorial Adviser

Agricultural and Environmental Resource Economics

Edited by Gerald A. Carlson,
David Zilberman, and John A. Miranowski

Agricultural and Environmental Resource Economics

Edited by

GERALD A. CARLSON

DAVID ZILBERMAN

JOHN A. MIRANOWSKI

New York   Oxford
OXFORD UNIVERSITY PRESS
1993

Oxford University Press

Oxford   New York   Toronto
Delhi   Bombay   Calcutta   Madras   Karachi
Kuala Lumpur   Singapore   Hong Kong   Tokyo
Nairobi   Dar es Salaam   Cape Town
Melbourne   Auckland   Madrid

and associated companies in

Berlin   Ibadan

Published by Oxford University Press, Inc.,
200 Madison Avenue, New York, New York 10016

Oxford is a registered trademark of Oxford University Press

Library of Congress Cataloging-in-Publication Data
Agricultural and environmental resource economics / edited by Gerald
A. Carlson, David Zilberman, and John A. Miranowski.
p.   cm.—(Biological resource management series)
Includes bibliographical references and index.
ISBN 0-19-507651-6
1. Agriculture—Economic aspects.
2. Agriculture—Environmental aspects.
I. Carlson, Gerald A.
II. Zilberman, David, 1947–
III. Miranowski, J. A.
IV. Series.
HD1433.A353   1993
338.1—dc20   92-21524

9 8 7 6 5 4 3 2 1

Printed in the United States of America
on acid-free paper

Preface

A growing concern for environmental quality and resource scarcity has led to numerous policy debates regarding resource utilization around the world. This is especially true when it comes to resource utilization in agriculture. Some of the issues stem from increased demand for water and land for urban and recreational uses, while others appear in rural or remote areas of the world from deforestation, by increased use of agrichemicals, and in association with cropland expansions to feed growing populations. Local and international external costs, together with growing demand for a cleaner, safer environment, bring these agricultural resource and environmental problems to the front pages of newspapers and to research journals on a regular basis.

The Consortium for Integrated Crop Production Systems—a group of fourteen individuals from U.S. universities, Resources for the Future, and the U.S. Department of Agriculture—met several times to plan, write, and critique this book. For those of us teaching resource economics there was no textbook that adequately brought together economic theory and resource-specific problems of agriculture. Those responsible for policy evaluation saw that traditionally trained resource and environmental economists needed exposure to the institutions and physical-biological linkages in agriculture. There was no comprehensive book for economists in other fields to review recent developments in agricultural resource economics. This book is intended to fill these gaps.

This is not a book of readings but rather a set of chapters developed as a comprehensive treatment of resource economics. It includes aggregate and micro level models and examples for most resource and environmental issues in agriculture. Technical and institutional changes are modeled and included in the range of possible policy changes. Renewable and nonrenewable resource models are presented in depth with numerical examples. The emphasis is on cropland agriculture, but examples from livestock, poultry, grazing, fisheries, orchards, and forestry fit our broad view of agriculture. Although there are specific chapters on water, pesticides, and land, evaluations of other resources appear in several chapters. Policy analysis is treated in most chapters but especially Chapters 4 and 10.

The book can be used in several ways and at several levels. As a textbook for a graduate course in resource economics it assumes that students already have microeconomic theory, calculus and some familiarity with statistics. The theory chapters (2–6) progress from familiar constrained optimization to more advanced methods. Many sections of the book are suitable for advanced undergraduate courses in resource economics. Instructors at several universities who tried most of the chapters in graduate and undergraduate classes found selectivity is needed as all of the models in the book cannot be covered in one semester. The book should also be useful in graduate level professional programs in resource management or resource policy. Economists, policy analysts, and researchers from other disciplines can use some of the key models and empirical examples of the resource-specific chapters to develop expertise in dealing with particular environmental or resource problems. Most of the chapters have vignettes, tables, and figures to provide comparisons across models and brief reviews of other studies.

This book reflects the perspectives and work of many individuals. Fourteen authors provide more breadth and experience than most textbooks, yet more contributors will bring other obstacles for readers. Multiple authors cannot reach a consensus on all controversial policies, emphasis of topics, or writing style. However, to simplify the reader's task, notation and definitions of key concepts were standardized, and models and concepts are referenced across chapters. When there is a change in notation this is explained, for example, derivatives may appear as $f'(x)$, f_x, and $\partial f / \partial x$. Some conceptual differences across chapters remain. Students and scholars who must read journal papers gradually learn that one benefits from exposure to multiple authors; additional insights are gained from reviewing several ways to characterize a particular issue.

We wish to acknowledge financial support for this effort by the Resources and Technology Division of the Economic Research Service, USDA. In addition the Land Grant Colleges of Alabama, Arkansas, California (Davis and Berkeley), Florida, Georgia, Illinois, Maine, Montana, New Mexico, North Carolina, Texas, and Virginia and Resources for the Future provided time and travel support. Earl Swanson gave us a comprehensive review of most chapters and added many valuable suggestions from his experience in this area. Finally, numerous graduate students and colleagues at several universities deserve special attention for their critical reviews of various versions of chapters.

Raleigh, N.C.   G.C.
Berkeley, Calif.   D.Z.
Washington, D.C.   J.M.
September 1992

Contents

Contributors

John Antle, Montana State University, Bozeman, Montana

William Boggess, University of Florida, Gainesville, Florida

Gerald A. Carlson, North Carolina State University, Raleigh, North Carolina

Mark Cochran, University of Arkansas, Fayetteville, Arkansas

Richard Howitt, University of California, Davis, California

Randall Kramer, Duke University, Durham, North Carolina

Ronald Lacewell, Texas A & M University, College Station, Texas

Thomas McGuckin, New Mexico State University, Las Cruces, New Mexico

Michele Marra, University of Maine, Orono, Maine

John A. Miranowski, U.S. Department of Agriculture, Washington, D.C.

Katherine Reichelderfer, U.S. Department of Agriculture, Washington, D.C.

C. Robert Taylor, Auburn University, Auburn, Alabama

Michael E. Wetzstein, University of Georgia, Athens, Georgia

David Zilberman, University of California, Berkeley, California

Agricultural and Environmental Resource Economics

1

Agricultural Resource Economics: An Overview

JOHN A. MIRANOWSKI AND GERALD A. CARLSON

In recent years there has been growing concern over surface and ground water quality, mounting public apprehension over the ecological and human health effects of agricultural chemicals, increasing conflicts over water supplies, spreading resistance to pesticides, and much debate about wetland losses and the consequences of global warming. These developments have highlighted the fragility of the natural resource base of U.S. agriculture and, hence, the importance of understanding the impacts of government policies, changes in consumer demand, and shifts in production possibilities from technical changes on this resource base. There is a need for developing effective, socially desirable strategies for managing the resources. Moreover, current trends suggest that the importance of these topics will continue to grow as resource scarcities and environmental concerns come to play an increasingly critical role in policy debates relating to agriculture.

These considerations suggest that government agencies (federal, state, and local) primarily concerned with agriculture will need to enhance their capacity to address agricultural resource management issues. This need is becoming increasingly acute as other public and private entities concerned with agriculture, the environment, and food safety become increasingly active in this arena. The Alar case for apples and the "Big Green" initiative in California are recent examples. It is becoming obvious that we need to improve policy-making analysis with respect to environmental and resource management. The problems in agriculture are shared with other sectors of the economy because agriculture is a major user of land, water, and agrichemicals, and these resources affect environmental quality, recreation, wildlife, urban water supplies, and human health. Therefore, agricultural problems are a very important part of overall environmental and resource issues.

The ability of economists to improve both the understanding and the practical management of the natural resource base of agriculture rests on three foundations: 1) an adequate data base that can be used to define problems, describe how they have changed over time, and indicate what incentives have caused change; 2) a coherent body of knowledge synthesizing the findings of the research undertaken by the agricultural, resource, and general economics professions; and 3) well-trained applied economists and policy analysts addressing these issues in public agencies and private firms. Unfortunately, none of these foundations is sufficiently well developed to allow rapid advances in research, training, or policy analysis in the near future. There are only a few research programs emphasizing agricultural resource issues, no specific publications devoted to these issues, and no comprehensive textbooks. Students and analysts interested in the field are typically trained in mainstream natural resource and environmental economics with emphasis on industrial pollution control, timber, fisheries, energy, and recreation. Others are trained as agricultural economists with minimal appreciation of resource scarcity, environmental, or applied welfare issues.

Agricultural and natural resource issues have received considerable attention by economists, biologists, and physical scientists, but the concepts, models, and data are widely scattered. Agricultural resources have unique market, property right, and physical features that set them apart from conventional production inputs (capital and labor). Models for evaluating natural resources such as petroleum, minerals, fisheries, wildlife, and forestry are similar, but usually not directly usable for many agricultural resource issues.

Because research on agricultural resources has been diffused and conducted by individuals and small groups of researchers, there has been limited cross-fertilization of ideas between these individuals and small groups, and little effort to develop general theories and unified methodologies. This book is an attempt to remedy this state of affairs by summarizing the current state of the art in agricultural resource economics research.

The book has two principal focuses. First, analytical models and concepts common to all areas of agricultural resource economics are reviewed. Second, economic issues relating to specific agricultural resources such as pesticides, water, and soil are explored as applications of the analytical concepts. The theory chapters include critical evaluations of the usefulness and potential of major techniques in agricultural resource analysis. Each resource-specific chapter attempts to describe the physical, biological, and economic aspects of managing the resource. We contend that basic technical knowledge is essential to relevant and practical analysis.

SPECIAL FEATURES OF AGRICULTURAL RESOURCES

The particular nature of agricultural resources and past developments in resource economics provide an outline for what issues are critical in our study of resource problems. There is a long history of the study of *land economics* dealing with tenure, ownership, land value, and farm size issues, which also argued the role of government programs in reducing soil erosion (Ciracy-Wantrup, 1952; Ely and Wehrwein, 1990). During the 1950s analysis of water and fertilizer production functions was an active research area for agricultural economists (Heady, 1952). Subsequently, studies on water-based recreation brought attention to water quality and the valuation of nonmarket goods, as well as to the conflicts between rural and urban uses of limited water quantities. Analysis of pesticide productivity and the value of information in pest management gradually increased during the 1970s. Although the environmental legislation of the early 1970s was primarily directed at urban pollution (autos and point sources of air and water pollution), pesticide and point source agricultural run-off were included in amendments to federal legislation. The large expansion in U.S. crop output during the 1970s helped draw attention to the potential conflicts between commercial agriculture and a wide array of other interests. In the early 1980s, Crosson and Brubaker (1982) projected output and resource use for four major U.S. crops to the year 2010. They concluded that soil erosion would be the major form of agricultural pollution with sedimentation doubling between 1977 and 2010. However, growing public demand for food safety and water quality, together with heightened concern for endangered species, deforestation, and global warming associated with agricultural activities around the world, are currently more frequently mentioned than is soil sedimentation (Bockstael and Just, 1991).

This book emphasizes an *integrated* treatment of all major resources and purchased inputs in agriculture. We believe that such an integrated framework is necessary for assessment of resource adequacy, for understanding critical resource linkages, and for identifying agricultural, resource, environmental, and policy tradeoffs. It is usually inappropriate to evaluate the adequacy of a particular agricultural resource while abstracting from other resources and technological change. For example, the adequacy of our soil resource is dependent on the supply of water, energy, and current and future technology. Alternatively, this approach may be viewed as emphasizing opportunities for substitution between inputs, outputs, and technologies. If the substitution opportunities are large, then a single resource may not be constraining. A treatment of technical change as it relates to resource adequacy and other issues is a unique feature of our view of agricultural resource economics (Chapter 5).

One key dimension of agricultural resources is their intertemporal or long-run nature and the need to select an optimal time path of use. Owners and managers will make a series of annual use or allocation decisions that will ideally follow an optimal time path of consumption of resources. Consider, as examples, managing the development of pest resistance to a particular pesticide, the erosion of cropland, or the depletion of an aquifer—each of these processes happens gradually over many years. Generally, these processes are surrounded by much uncertainty because of our limited knowledge of resource stocks, future demands for agricultural outputs, and the potential contribution of technology and productivity growth to satisfying future needs. Without a proper understanding of the risky and dynamic nature of agricultural resource decisions, we are possibly solving nonproblems, ignoring real problems, and making misguided policy decisions (Chapters 2 and 3).

This discussion does not suggest that short-run concerns are not important, but rather, that we may not be treating agricultural resource decisions in the proper context. For example, if the media succeeds in convincing the public that we have a soil erosion or ground water problem, the typical reaction is to solve that "short-run" problem and move on to the next issue. Hopefully, the chapters that follow will convince the reader of the importance of utilizing a dynamic framework in making intertemporal agricultural resource decisions.

A unique characteristic of agricultural resource problems is the close linkages with the physical and biological sciences, hence the need to capture physical and biological phenomena in developing the associated economic framework. For example, the current focus on sustainable agriculture really is an attempt to capture these linkages. *Sustainable agriculture* is defined as a production system that can be maintained over the long run while ensuring profitability, productivity, and environmental quality. Such a system may involve the substitution of more farm-source inputs for purchased chemicals and the substitution of crops that enhance nutrients and contribute to pest control for more conventional crops, as well as the substitution of technology and information for conventional practices.

To capture the linkages between biological systems and human welfare, a broad definition of agriculture to include forestry, livestock, fisheries, newly discovered crops, and other managed, living resources is used in this book. Even though most of the examples come from the United States, a comprehensive set of concepts and institutions is evaluated that applies to worldwide agriculture. International agriculture is increasingly linked by transfers in technology as well as commodity trade. Some see critical food shortages while others emphasize progress in global food production (Avery, 1991; Brown, 1991). Chapter 11 will demonstrate that the results and analyses of this book apply to resource problems in developing countries and to new agricultural commodities.

Another characteristic of agricultural resources is that if managed judiciously, their services are *renewable* over the long run. Simultaneously, critical resources such as land may have a relatively fixed stock. Thus, profligate use of the land resource, for example, unmitigated soil erosion or salt accumulation, could ultimately result in exhaustion. The same case could be made for pest resistance to particular pesticides. Other agricultural resources that exhibit slow or no recharge are finite in nature, and any consumption might deplete and eventually exhaust the economic supply. A similar argument can be made for ground water that is rendered useless for human, animal, or irrigation use because it is contaminated by a particular chemical. Unless there is an economically viable way of removing the contaminant, that particular ground water supply is for all intents and purposes exhausted in an economic sense. Renewable and exhaustible resources are defined and evaluated in detail in Chapter 3.

The *environmental economics* literature devotes attention to the concept of a closed "spaceship earth" popularized by Kenneth Boulding (1966). According to this concept, we live in a closed system and by the "law of conservation of matter" what goes in must come out, although usually in altered form. All production and consumption processes produce unwanted residuals. Agricultural production and food consumption are no exception to the law. For example, using conservation tillage to reduce the runoff of soil particles and agricultural chemicals into surface water may encourage the percolation of these chemicals into ground water. Short of not using the chemicals, it is impossible to eliminate residuals; managers can only shift the location of deposition or the method of decomposition. There is a clear tradeoff between environmental media. The authors attempt to recognize these important environmental tradeoffs in developing their analytical frameworks and in discussing particular agricultural resource issues. A comprehensive description of concepts and models for evaluating pollution generation and pollution abatement is presented in Chapter 6 and is developed further in the resource-specific chapters.

Land, pesticides, and water are used at much higher levels in agricultural production relative to production in most other economic sectors. Land and water are both important productive inputs in agriculture and media for holding agrichemicals. Land, air, and water have absorptive and regenerative capacities that degrade inorganic as well as organic residues. The pollution control models for industrial pollution often do not fit the heterogeneous spatial, or nonpoint, nature of agricultural resources. Fortunately, the spatial nature of agricultural production sometimes makes separation of conflicting activities easier than it would be in concentrated urban areas. Farmers and others are interested in both a profitable and a safe rural environment. Evaluating and fostering development of institutions and technologies to enhance these objectives for rural and urban populations is part of the challenge of this book (Chapters 7–9).

Lastly, we want to focus on *analytical policy evaluation.* Policy analysts make a much more important contribution to the process if they can clearly articulate or demonstrate tradeoffs. Although opinions may be important in the policy process, they are not the focus of this book. Likewise, we have attempted to avoid currency and instead focus on relevant, generic examples that illustrate the important underlying economic concepts, linkages, and tradeoffs. If we can convey how to account for the key tradeoffs in an integrated framework, we will have accomplished our objective. In order to accomplish this objective, the chapters use economic theory to construct a solid analytical framework, drawing heavily from the resource, environmental, agricultural, and general economics literature. The analytical framework is then used to evaluate the economic, as well as agricultural, environmental, and resource tradeoffs dictated by different policy options. Applied welfare theory is utilized to help measure consumer and producer gains and losses for both market and nonmarket goods. When possible, the analytical framework is used to integrate across all agricultural resources, commodities, and production regions in order to draw comprehensive policy implications. When major parts of markets are affected, output and input prices are altered and the effects on multiple commodities become important. Aggregate evaluation methods and models are reviewed in Chapter 4, and general policy analysis is reviewed in Chapter 10.

Agricultural resource use and *externality generation processes* should be specified in models that account for variability in resource availability and a wide range of institutional settings. *Heterogeneous* endowments in resources such as soil qualities, climate, water stocks, human capital, and pest densities affect the use of water, pesticides, and land in agricultural production. Externality generation is also affected by resource endowments and institutional factors such as ownership characteristics, legal constraints, and commodity program requirements. The resource endowments change slowly, such as when new equipment or genetic materials become available from research, farmers receive training in pest management thresholds, or physical barriers are built to reduce soil erosion. The effects of *institutional changes* are difficult to detect because they are infrequent and experimentation is usually not possible. Evaluating institutional changes is a critical challenge for resource economists.

To obtain a perspective on the themes of this book, here are some of the questions that run through several of the chapters:

1. To what extent might farmers gain from policies that limit resource use and increase commodity prices?
2. Why have markets not developed more rapidly to allocate resources such as water or wetlands?
3. To what extent will new technologies be developed to reduce agricultural externalities as they have been to enhance crop yields?
4. Are farmers attempting to prevent off-farm movement of resources (pesticides, fertilizer) because in doing so they will increase their own health and agricultural output?
5. To what extent can information subsidies reduce pesticide use or food contamination risks?
6. Will biotechnologies help reduce agricultural chemical use and increase farm sustainability?

These and many other economic questions loom ahead for research directors at universities and policy makers in the U.S. Department of Agriculture, the Food and Drug Administration, the U.S. Environmental Protection Agency, and agencies dealing with international agriculture. The economic models, concepts, data collection framework, and other ideas that will help economists play their role in answering these questions can be found in the subsequent chapters.

HISTORY AND INCENTIVES FOR AGRICULTURAL RESOURCE USE

It is impossible to analyze agricultural resource issues without specific data on the institutions, property rights, and availability of inputs over time. The data bases for agricultural resource evaluation, as incomplete as they are, are nevertheless often better than those for urban or nonmarket resources. There are some time series data on land allocation, water supply, and even pesticide use. With such data sets and through coordination with agricultural scientists, empirical analysis of resource and pollution problems in agriculture is possible without sole reliance on theoretical models.

An important argument for emphasizing agricultural resource issues is that this category of resources has been receiving increased scrutiny from public interest, legislative, and administrative bodies. Recent media and other attention to food safety, ground water quality, irrigation water recontracting, and environmental impacts of agricultural commodity programs are a manifestation of the public concern. Even though the factual evidence concerning the human and ecological risks may show that they are small, the perceived risk frequently exceeds the scientific evidence. We could be defensive, as the agricultural establishment is

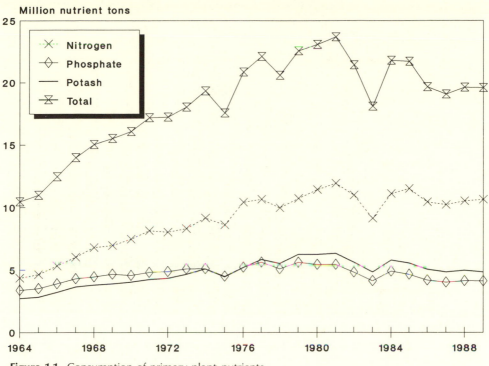

Figure 1.1. Consumption of primary plant nutrients.

sometimes prone to be, or we can present the best possible economic evidence of the risk/benefit tradeoffs. Policy analysts have a professional responsibility to do the latter.

Another motivation for the increasing concern for agricultural resources is the fact that they have received less scrutiny than other resource and environmental concerns during the 1970s and 1980s. With the exception of pesticides, much early attention by the EPA and other regulatory agencies centred on industrial, municipal, and transportation pollutants and energy resources. Additionally, point source pollutants received primary emphasis in both legislation and programs of the executive branch. Recently, the emphasis has shifted to nonpoint source residuals and agricultural resources, assuming that point source residuals, energy, and minerals are being controlled by existing laws.

To obtain a better understanding of the use of agricultural resources and also the potential generation of agricultural residuals, a number of graphs and maps are reviewed. (Most of this information is compiled and updated by the Economic Research Service of the U.S. Department of Agriculture.) Figure 1.1 (Tennessee Valley Authority, 1991) illustrates the growth in the consumption of nitrogen, phosphate, and potash. As can be seen, nitrogen has accounted for much of the growth in the use of fertilizer nutrients. It is also interesting to note that total nutrient use has been decreasing slightly since roughly 1980. Figure 1.2 (Unpublished EPA data) provides an indication of the increase in total and agricultural

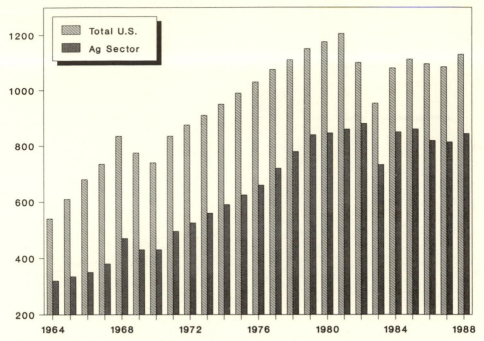

Figure 1.2. U.S. conventional pesticide usage, total and estimated agricultural sector share.

pesticide use in millions of pounds of active ingredients. Additionally, Figure 1.3 (U.S. International Trade Com., 1989 and earlier years) divides pesticide expenditures into herbicides, insecticides, and fungicides, and displays their use per acre of cropland. Much of the increase in pesticide use can be attributed to the widespread adoption of herbicides in field crop production, but again there is a slight downward trend in the late 1980s.

Witnessing significant increases in agricultural chemical use, an obvious question is "why did it occur?" Figures 1.4 and 1.5 (U.S. Dept. of Agriculture, 1991 and earlier years) provide a strong economic argument for substitution among inputs or resources and the responsiveness of input use to relative prices. Throughout most of the early part of the period, pesticides were becoming relatively less costly and being substituted for machinery, fuel, land, and labor. Since pesticide market prices reflect most farmer costs in using these materials (but not the potential externality costs), producers have strong incentives to reduce total costs and increase returns by substituting pesticides for other inputs and using pesticides to enhance yields. The slow down and possible reversal of the long-term downward trend in agricultural chemical prices relative to those of other inputs in the 1980s may mean less use of the chemicals in the future. Although little more than casual empiricism, these figures illustrate a powerful economic story with important implications for the design of agricultural resource policies; relative prices and markets *do* matter. Other public and private incentives and information, if they alter relative agricultural resource costs, could have similar impacts (U.S. Dept. of Agriculture, 1991a).

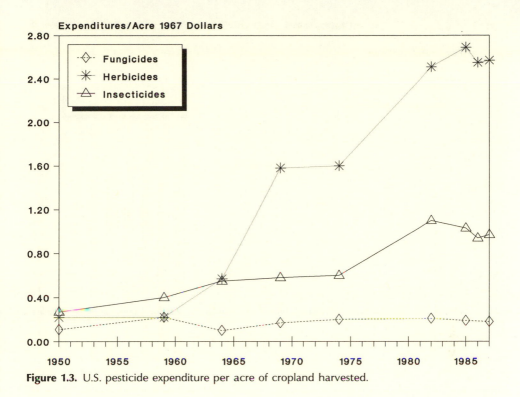

Figure 1.3. U.S. pesticide expenditure per acre of cropland harvested.

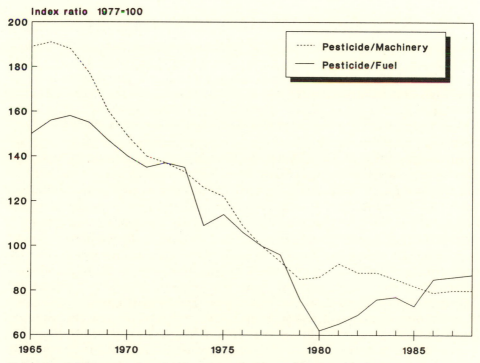

Figure 1.4. Relative cost of pesticides compared with machinery and fuel costs.

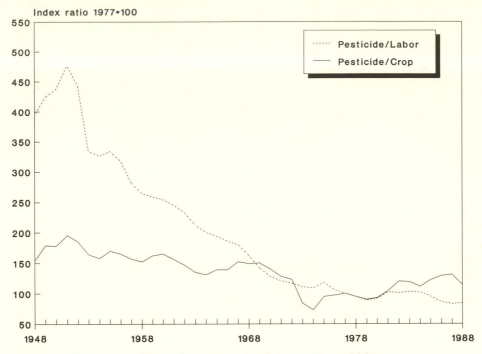

Figure 1.5. Relative costs of pesticides compared with crop prices and labor costs.

Other resource use patterns are presented for background information. Figure 1.6 (U.S. Dept. of Agriculture, 1991b) shows data on several types of farm fuel use in recent years, while Figure 1.7 (Daugherty, 1991; U.S. Dept. of Agriculture, 1992a) displays information on cropland utilization. One can easily distinguish the reductions in cropland and power inputs in the 1980s relative to the 1970s. Part of the reduction in cropland in the late 1980s is related to the Conservation Reserve Program. Irrigated acreage is shown in Figure 1.8 (U.S. Dept. of Commerce, 1987); it illustrates one of the agricultural inputs that has continued to expand in the 1980s, but conflicts with urban, recreational, and other uses of water are expected to increase in the future.

The total factor productivity index and its components are reported in Figures 1.10 and 1.9, respectively (see also Chapter 5). Agricultural productivity has continued to grow over the past 20 years as farmers have substituted chemicals, knowledge, and new technology for labor, capital, fuel, and land. Further regulatory constraints on the use of particular agriculture resources would provide incentive to substitute other inputs currently used less intensively and may also reduce agricultural productivity growth. Figure 1.10 again illustrates the importance of viewing agricultural resources in the aggregate production function context when considering resource adequacy, resource use tradeoffs, environmental implications, and policy choices (U.S. Dept. of Agriculture, 1992b).

In addition to reviewing agricultural resource use and productivity, it is equally important to assess the potential environmental impacts of residuals produced in

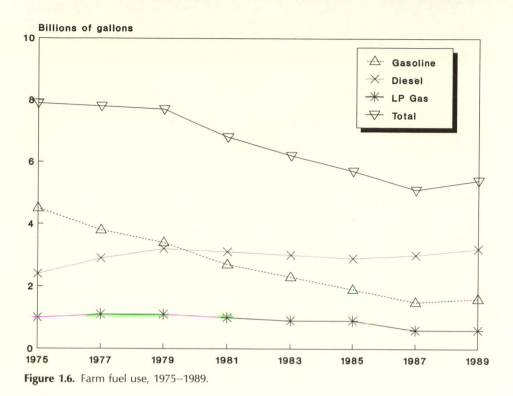

Figure 1.6. Farm fuel use, 1975–1989.

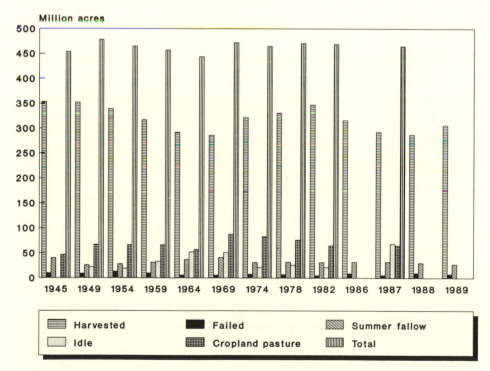

Figure 1.7. Major uses of cropland, 1945–1989.

Million acres

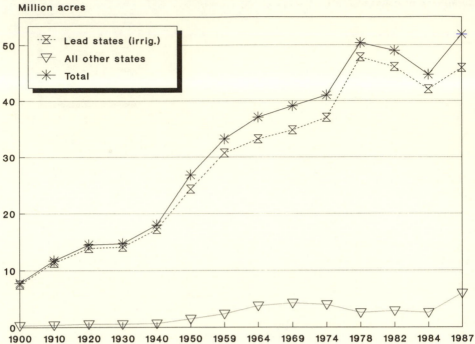

Figure 1.8. Irrigated farmland, 1900–1987.

Index ratio 1977=100

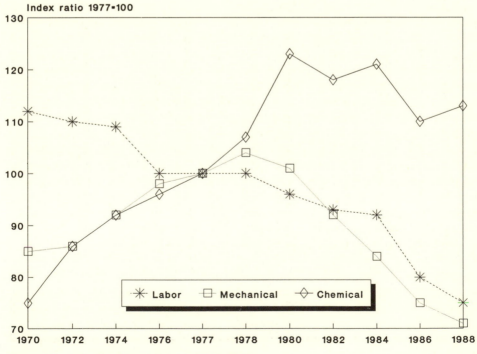

Figure 1.9. Agricultural input indexes, 1970–1988.

14

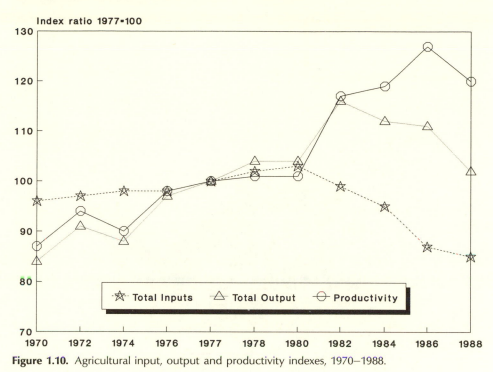

Figure 1.10. Agricultural input, output and productivity indexes, 1970–1988.

using agricultural resources in the production process. Unfortunately, given our limited knowledge and information gaps pertaining to natural processes as well as human and environmental risks, we have a data base that is incomplete, not statistically reliable, and somewhat speculative. In spite of these data base deficiencies, we believe that it is important to gain some sense of the problem as long as the reader does not attempt to attribute too much significance to specific estimates or details. Figure 1.11 indicates geographical regions that have a higher potential for ground water contamination from nitrates and pesticides. The potential for contamination is based on state level chemical use levels and county level soil and ground water characteristics. It is *not* tied to actual evidence of chemical residues in ground water but rather to higher potential for chemicals to percolate to ground water. The Southeast Coastal Plain has a high potential for ground water problems because of shallow water tables and sandy soils. Figure 1.12 shows that the river basins in the Corn Belt and Northern Plains are ones in which surface water quality is most affected by agriculture (Nielson and Lee, 1987; and unpublished U.S. Dept. of Agri. data).

Part of *water quality degradation* is related to erosion of cropland topsoil. Figure 1.13 (U.S. Dept. of Agriculture, 1987) shows the recent decline in average wind and water erosion. The locations of different types (sediment, phosphorus, and nitrogen) of surface water pollution are indicated in the maps in Figure 1.14a–c. Finally, major areas with chronic ground water mining are depicted in Figure 1.15. Determining efficient ground water utilization is an important

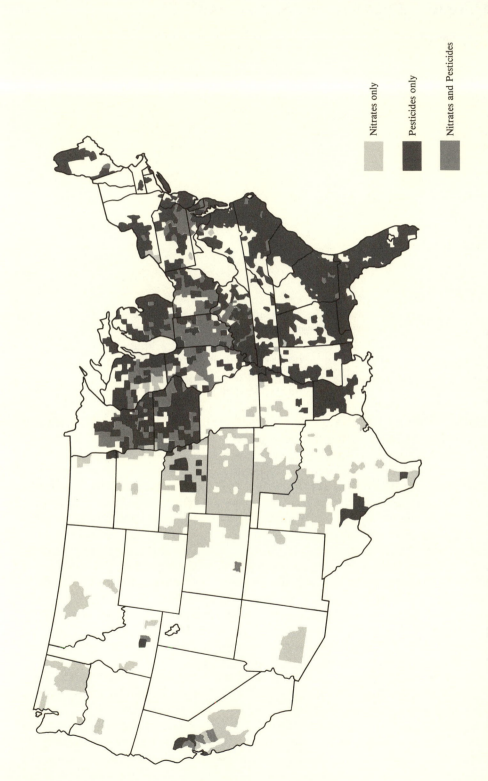

Figure 1.11. Areas vulnerable to ground water contamination from agricultural chemicals.

Nitrates only

Pesticides only

Nitrates and Pesticides

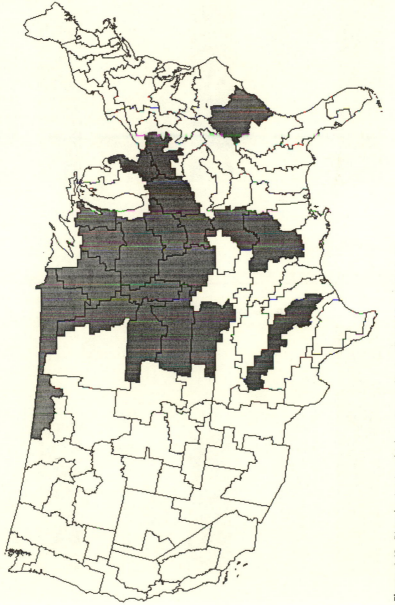

Figure 1.12. River basins in which water quality is affected by agriculture.

Cropland Sheet and Rill Erosion

Average annual tons per acre

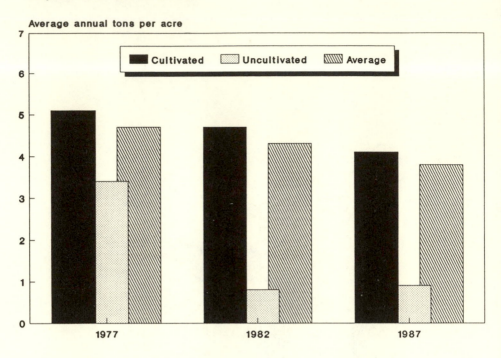

Cropland Wind Erosion

Average annual tons per acre

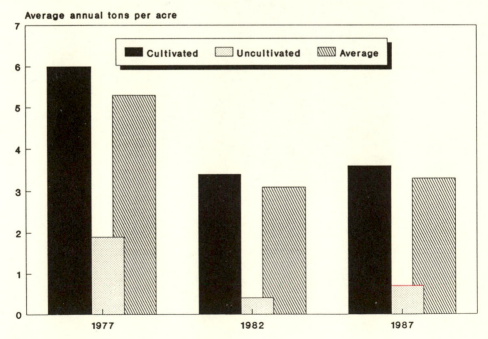

Figure 1.13. Cropland erosion, 1977–1987.

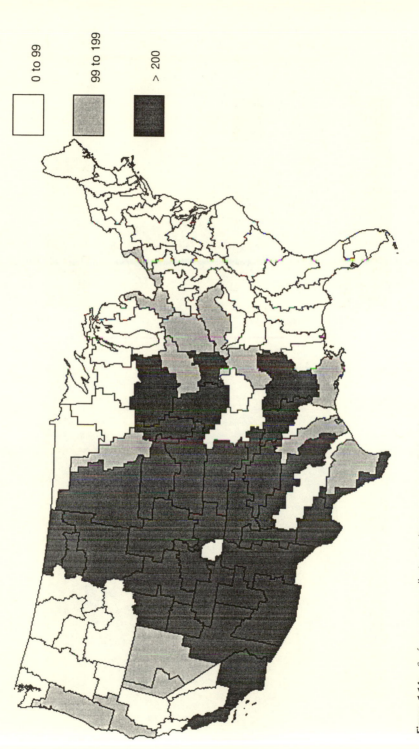

Figure 1.14a. Surface water pollution indicators: suspended sediment.

Concentration (mg/l)

☐ 0 to 99

▨ 99 to 199

▧ > 200

19

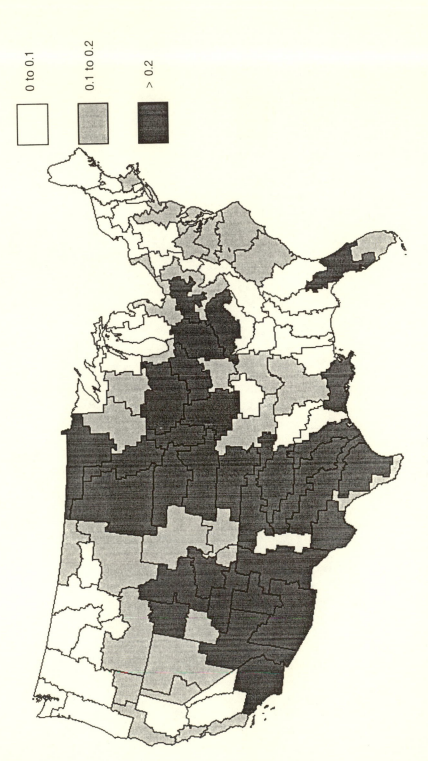

Figure 1.14b. Surface water pollution indicators: total phosphorus.

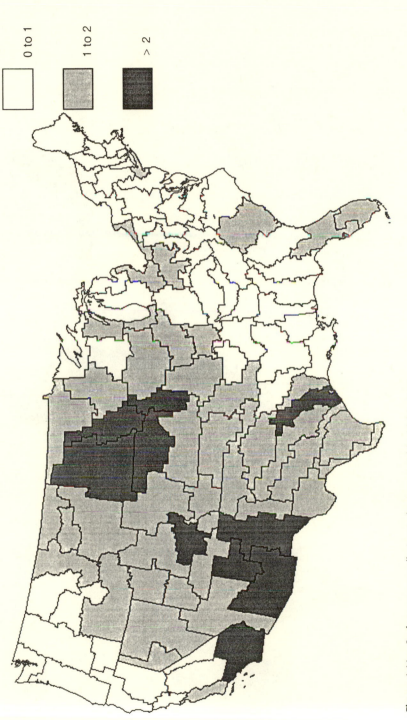

Concentration (mg/l)

☐ 0 to 1

▨ 1 to 2

■ > 2

Figure 1.14c. Surface water pollution indicators: total kjeldahl nitrogen.

21

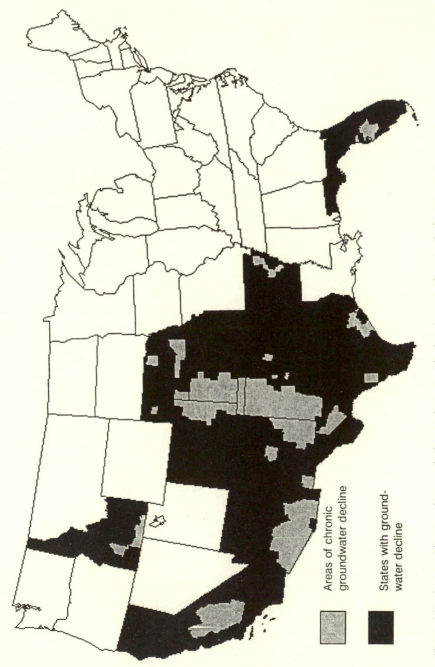

Figure 1.15. States with ground water decline and areas with chronic ground water decline.

Areas of chronic
groundwater decline

States with ground-
water decline

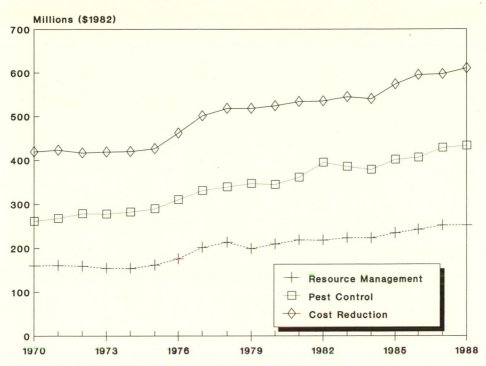

Figure 1.16. Public research expenditures by research problem area.

example of both resource use over time and efficiency in use of shared resources. Comparisons across locations help highlight the diversity in resource stocks and pollution potential in the U.S., and the possible role of agriculture (Unpublished U.S. Dept. of Agri. data).

Given the importance of technology in mitigating many of the agricultural resource and environmental concerns, *agricultural research* has played a critical role in technological development. Figures 1.16 and 1.17 (Friswold, 1989) indicate recent upward trends in public research and development for pest control, resource management, and cost-reducing technologies. At the same time, public research on environmental quality as related to agricultural resources was declining in the 1980s.

The presence of ground water mining, pesticide, and fertilizer contamination potential, and decreased expenditures on environmental research does not mean that progress in environmental quality has not been made. Changes in agricultural legislation and federal and state regulations, together with information and technical innovations, have changed agricultural pollution in the past several decades. For example, many persistent pesticides have been banned, and worker exposure to pesticides has been reduced by safety regulations and the adoption of safer compounds. Almost 60 million acres of marginal land have contributed to wildlife habitat by the commodity set-aside requirements and the Conservation Reserve Program. These adjustments and others not enumerated are costly to

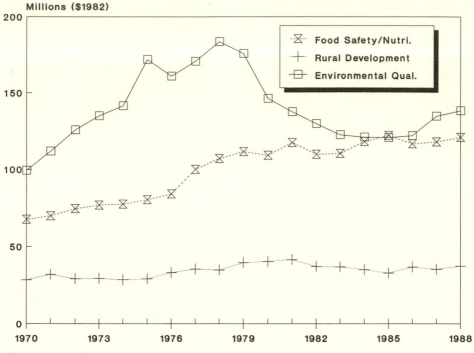

Figure 1.17. Public research expenditures by research problem area.

some groups, but they benefit consumers and some agriculturalists. Evaluation of these policies and related agricultural adjustments is one of the major tasks for economists.

We have presented a significant amount of historical background information on agricultural resources, potential environmental and resource problems, and the directions of public research and development expenditures. These numbers should be useful in putting the more resource-specific issues into perspective in the following chapters.

A PREVIEW OF SOME AGRICULTURAL RESOURCE CONCEPTS

There are a number of important economic concepts used throughout this book that are critical in addressing agricultural resource issues. A few of the more important concepts need to be defined before we proceed with development of an analytical framework.

Property Rights. The way in which producers and consumers use natural resources depends on the underlying set of property rights. Property rights refer to a bundle of entitlements that convey to the owner certain privileges and constraints. They can take the form of property rules, liability rules, or inalienable entitlements (Calabresi and Melamed, 1992). In order for markets to lead to an efficient allocation of natural resources, the property rights to the resources generally must have some degree of four characteristics: ownership, exclusivity, transferability, and enforcement. Ownership is a legal device that assigns the right to use a resource to a private owner. Without an assurance for the right to use, there is no economic incentive for efficient resource management. If exclusivity is present, all benefits and costs from the use of the resource will accrue only to the owner. If the odor from a poultry farm causes a neighbor's property value to decline, the test of exclusivity fails. The absence of exclusivity is the main distinction between a private property resource and an open access resource. Transferability implies that property rights are fully transferable between people through trade. Restrictions on water transfers are a major source of inefficiency in water resource policy. Finally, to be effective, a system of rights must be enforceable. Private ownership of forested land means little to owners if they are not able to prevent others from cutting timber on the land without compensation to the owner. Well-defined property rights coupled with competitive markets can lead to a set of incentives for efficient market exchange.

Externalities. Having argued that well-defined property rights lead to efficiency, we now consider what happens when property rights are not well defined. One broad class of violations of appropriate property rights is referred to as externalities. An externality exists whenever the welfare of a firm or household is directly affected by the activities of others. Obviously, this is a broad concept since almost every activity involves externalities. The presence of an externality can lead to economic inefficiency. In the case of agricultural nonpoint source water pollution, the nonpriced use of water bodies as a waste sink causes too much of the product generating pollution to be produced and at too low a price. This outcome indicates that an externality is a form of market failure.

One of the most direct ways to overcome the effects of an externality on efficiency is through private negotiations (Coase, 1960). This will work best when the number of affected parties is small. For most externality problems related to pollution, negotiation is an unfeasible solution since the number of agents generating the pollution is very large, as is the number of parties adversely affected by use of the polluted water. Government intervention potentially can correct the inefficiency through a variety of policy tools. These tools include taxes, subsidies, quotas or standards, and marketable pollution permits.

Public Good. The economics literature frequently deals with private or excludable goods where consumption can be rationed by the market and the consumer cannot obtain the good without paying the price. However, when consumption by one consumer does not exclude or reduce the utility another individual receives from consuming the same good, we have what is known as a public good. A pure public good, if produced, will be consumed by all and thus a positive price cannot be extracted from each consumer through the market. A variety of examples can be used to illustrate the concept—national defense, clean air, and scenic views. Because individual preferences cannot be registered through the marketplace, an alternative avenue to express individual preferences for some resources such as environmental quality is needed. In the case of public goods, a freely competitive economy will fail to achieve optimality (Randall, 1972).

Common Property Resources. A common property resource is one for which there is mutual use of a resource by a specific group of individuals. Exclusivity is defined for the user group relative to nonmembers. Important examples are common grazing lands, some water resources, and wildlife under controlled access. Generally, a particular institutional arrangement has evolved that determines the common use of these resources. Property rights are so defined to give both obligations of the group and use rights to the resource (Bromley, 1989).

Open Access Resources. When users of a scarce resource are not excluded by the property rights, then the resource is an open access resource. Open access is a characteristic found in many resource systems: mineral deposits in public lands, fisheries in international waters, and congestion in wilderness areas to name a few. Open access resources impacted by agriculture include ambient air and water systems. Ground water supplies sometimes suffer from two open access problems: they may be overpumped as a source of irrigation water, and their capacity as a waste sink may be exceeded. The economist's policy prescription for open access resources is regulation, marketable permits, or taxes to offset the inefficiencies inherent in private management. Taxes are generally considered a more cost-effective policy tool, although regulation is more widespread in practice.

Optimal Rates of Resource Use. To define what is meant by optimal use of resources, one must consider resource use over time. The most widely used criterion for determining optimal resource use is dynamic efficiency. This criterion assumes that society's objective is to maximize the present value of net benefits from use of the resource. The dynamically efficient allocation must satisfy the condition that the present value of the marginal net benefit from using the resource must be equal in each time period. When the use of the resource in one time period increases the degree of scarcity in later time periods, the optimal time path of use must take into account marginal user cost. Marginal user cost is simply the opportunity cost of foregone future resource use. If producing more output this year causes more soil erosion and less output in future years, then the discounted value of the future output foregone is the user cost incurred by this year's production decision.

These concepts give us a taste of the complexities of resource use in the broadly defined agricultural setting. In some cases there will be familiar market transactions in well-behaved input markets. In other cases there will be institutions, transaction costs, and resource endowments that lead to complex allocations and policy formulations. In this chapter the maps illustrated the highly localized pollution potential in agriculture, while the time plots indicated some significant changes in agricultural input use. We first turn to a more formal treatment of analytical models and then to the specific features of agricultural resources.

REFERENCES

Avery, D.T. *Global Food Progress 1991.* Indianapolis, Indiana: Hudson Institute, 1991.

Bockstael, N. and R.E. Just (eds.) *Commodity and Resource Policies in Agricultural Systems.* New York: Springer-Verlag, 1991.

Boulding, K.E. "The Economics of the Coming Spaceship Earth." In H. Jarrett (ed.): *Environmental Quality in a Growing Economy*. Baltimore, MD: Johns Hopkins Press, 1966.

Bromley, D.W. *Economic Interests and Institutions*. New York: Basil Blackwood, 1989.

Brown, L. *State of the World 1991*. Washington, D.C.: Worldwatch Institute, 1991.

Calabresi, G. and A.D. Melamed. "Property Rules, Liability Rules and Inalienability: One View of the Cathedral." *Harvard Law Review* 85:1089–1128, 1972.

Ciracy-Wantrup, S.V. *Resource Conservation*. Berkeley, CA: Univ. of California Press, 1952.

Coase, R.H. "The Problem of Social Cost." *The Journal of Law and Economics* 3:1–44, 1960.

Crosson, P.R. and S. Brubaker. *Resource and Environmental Effects of U.S. Agriculture*. Washington, D.C.: Resource for the Future, 1982.

Daugherty, A.B. *Major Uses of Land in the United States: 1987*. AER-643. U.S. Dept. Agr., Econ. Res. Serv., Washington D.C., January 1991.

Ely, R.T. and G.S. Wehrwein. *Land Economics*. New York: Macmillan and Co., 1940.

Frisvold, G. "Trends in Public and Private Research Investment." *Management of Biological Resources: Roles and Responsibilities for Agricultural Research*. Sixth Working Conference of Directors of Agricultural Research, Organization for Economic Cooperation and Development, Paris, France, October 9–13, 1989, pp. 59–69.

Heady, E.O. *Economics of Agricultural Production and Resource Use*. Englewood Cliffs, NJ: Prentice-Hall, 1952.

Nielsen, E.G. and L.K. Lee. *The Magnitude and Costs of Groundwater Contamination from Agricultural Chemicals: A National Perspective*. AER-576. U.S. Dept. Agr., Econ. Res. Serv., Washington D.C., October 1987.

Randall, A. "Market Solutions to Externality Problems: Theory and Practice." *American Journal of Agricultural Economics* 54:175–183, 1972.

Tennessee Valley Authority. *Commercial Fertilizer Consumption*. National Fertilizer and Environmental Research Center, Muscle Shoals, AL, December 1991 and earlier issues.

U.S. Dept. of Agriculture. *Agricultural Resources. Cropland Situation and Outlook Report*. AR-27. Washington D.C., September 1992a and earlier years.

U.S. Dept. of Agriculture. *Agricultural Statistics*. Washington D.C., 1991a and earlier years.

U.S. Dept. of Agriculture. *Economic Indicators of the Farm Sector. Production and Efficiency Statistics, 1990*. ECIFS 10-3. Econ. Res. Serv., Washington D.C., May 1992b.

U.S. Dept. of Agriculture. *Farm Production Expenditures*. National Agriculture Statistics Service, Washington D.C., 1991b and earlier years.

U.S. Dept. of Agriculture. *National Resources Inventory*. Soil Conservation Service, Washington D.C., 1977, 1982, and 1987.

U.S. Dept. of Commerce. *Census of Agriculture and Special Farm and Ranch Irrigation Surveys*. Bureau of the Census, Washington D.C., 1987 and periodic years.

U.S. International Trade Commission. *Synthetic Organic Chemicals: United States Production and Sales*. USITC pub. No. 2009. Washington D.C., 1989 and earlier years.

2

Some Microeconomics of Agricultural Resource Use

RICHARD HOWITT AND C. ROBERT TAYLOR

This chapter focuses on the microeconomics of an agricultural firm that employs natural resources in its production process. Traditionally, economists envisage natural resources as stock or flow factor inputs such as land, air, or water. However, the use of natural resources for byproduct disposal in agricultural and industrial production has become increasingly important in both biological and policy terms. Both types of resource use will be addressed in the microeconomic specifications.

Microeconomic optimization conditions are an essential precursor to empirical or policy work. By comparing optimal, microeconomic conditions under alternative policy options a behavioral hypothesis can be proposed, which is then empirically tested. For instance, what changes, if any, would small profit-maximizing firms make in the intensity of their input use if the input were transformed from a common property (open access) grazing area to one with exclusive rights specified for each firm? The qualitative properties of common property allocations have been known for centuries and encapsulated in country sayings such as "Everybody's property is nobody's property." Resource economists should strive to be more precise than folklore in their qualitative conclusions, or at least be able to use economic theory to identify and analyze the appropriate folklore saying.

Resource economic theory is distinct from the conventional firm microtheory in that it addresses cases of market failure and success concerning use of natural resources. These market failures invariably involve externalities, uncertainties, and intertemporal allocation. Externalities and public good aspects of agricultural natural resources are covered in Chapters 3 and 6. The first section of this chapter introduces the static deterministic model of the resource-using firm. The remaining two sections address uncertainty and intertemporal allocation of the resource-using firm.

Agricultural resource property rights are measured in the form of *stocks* of potential wealth or *flows* of value. In some cases a single resource yields values based on both. A large water reservoir can yield flow benefits in the form of irrigation water, hydroelectric power, and instream values. Clearly, the stock of water in the reservoir has value in terms of the flow of benefits when released. In addition to these capitalized flow values, many reservoirs generate benefits based on the existence of the stock over time. Wildlife habitat, hunting, and water-based recreation are common stock benefits generated by water storage projects. In some cases these nonmarket stock benefits conflict with flow benefits. Drawing down the reservoir to a low level in the summer increases the flow benefits from power generation and irrigation, increases the stock benefit of flood control, but decreases the recreation and habitat stock benefits. Resource inputs to the firm cannot be assumed to have a simple supply curve based on factor market equilibrium. The timing and balance of the resource stocks and flows determines the availability and cost of the resource input to a firm. We will show below that equilibrium in a natural resource market requires that both the stock and flow markets are in equilibrium. If complete markets are established for both stocks and flows such as those found in the oil industry, the interdependent equilibria can be observed and predicted with some success. An oil company owns certain oil reserves that can be extracted at a projected cost. Given the price of oil on the "flow" market for the product, the stock value of the oil company reserves is reflected in the traded share price of the company. Changes in the price of oil or the cost of extracting it will be reflected as changes in the stock value of the company. Likewise, changes in the proven reserves held by a major oil company will be reflected in current oil prices.

The interactions of the stock and flow markets are greatly complicated if markets only reflect some of the stock and flow values. This is often the case where full markets are not established. In many cases of environmental pollution some of the resources are nonmarket goods, such as recreational or aesthetic values; in other cases resource stocks are owned by the public, but private producers have rights to use the flows. The latter situation is typical of the law governing ground water in many states. These brief examples illustrate that, in terms of property rights, values, and timing, natural resources are considerably more complicated to analyze than the traditional neoclassical factor market of purchased inputs with stable supplies.

The conventional neoclassical supply function and its associated producer's surplus is based on input costs and technologies, which are often assumed equal across firms. An early resource economist, David Ricardo (1903) realized that heterogeneous natural resource stocks facing a common market for their flows of produce acquired differential rents, which are immediately capitalized into their value. Ricardo first proposed his rental analysis using the distance to market as a measure of costs of producing agricultural commodities at a specific location. Differing rental values for natural resources are driven by their *heterogeneity* in space, quality, extraction cost, and risk. For example, for a resource such as land with constant supply price c_j, Figure 2.1 shows that higher quality land will have rent R_j^*, while a lower quality plot has rent $\bar{R}_j$, primarily because of the lower marginal product (VMP_{xj}).

A deterministic static analysis of resource use by a firm is used as a foundation for the microeconomics of natural resource use. The analysis is then extended to include firm reactions under risky and dynamic specifications.

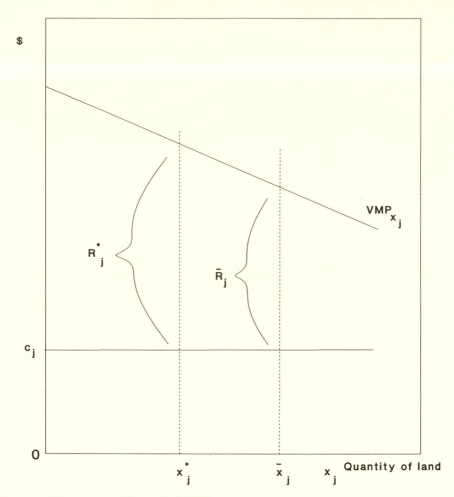

Figure 2.1. Ricardian rent for land of differing qualities.

STATIC DETERMINISTIC FIRM MODEL

As an introductory model, a firm is defined as producing a single product for a known price. The production process uses flows of inputs from a natural resource and other variable inputs. A simple theoretical framework will show the effects of input substitution, joint output production, multiproduct production, and the effect of resource scarcity on the allocation and rental value of a fixed but allocatable resource used in production. We will use pollution generation to illustrate joint production in the next section.

The *production function* is defined as

$$y = f(x_k, x_j) \tag{1}$$

where y is a single output sold for price P; x_k is a vector of k variable inputs (examples would be labor, fuel, pesticides, and fertilizer); x_j is a vector of j flows of inputs from natural resources, such as land, water, and drainage capacity. The distinction between inputs from natural resources and purchased variable inputs is sometimes needed, because, while natural resource inputs can be varied, their costs often cannot. The production function has the usual properties of a positive, but nonincreasing *marginal product* from the inputs x

$$\frac{\partial f(\cdot)}{\partial x} > 0 \quad \text{and} \quad \frac{\partial^2 f(\cdot)}{\partial x^2} \tag{2}$$

These properties can be generalized to negative resource effects by defining the x_j values in terms of pollution abatement as we will see below.

The *nonresource variable inputs* x_k have a vector of factor prices v_k, while the *resource input flows* x_j often have an associated cost of c_j. We should stress here that v_k is a price in the factor market for labor or fertilizer, whereas c_j is a cost of using the resource flow, which is usually firm and location specific. For many natural resources, such as sunlight, the cost to the firm c_j approaches zero or it is capitalized into the cost of other resources such as land.

Given these definitions, the firm's direct profit function π, can be defined as:

$$\pi = Pf(x_k, x_j) - v_k x_k - c_j x_j \tag{3}$$

First-order conditions for profit maximizing input use require that x_j and x_k be used until their price or cost equals their value of marginal product

$$\frac{\partial \pi}{\partial x} = 0 \quad \text{implies} \quad \left. \begin{aligned} P\frac{\partial f(\cdot)}{\partial x_k} &= v_k \\[2ex] \text{and} \quad P\frac{\partial f(\cdot)}{\partial x_j} &= c_j \end{aligned} \right\} \tag{4}$$

Note that we assume that all input levels can be controlled, and that conditions (4) hold simultaneously for all inputs. Also, these conditions assume that the resource flows are available to the firm at cost c_j in quantities sufficient to enable the firm to use the resource until its value marginal product equals the marginal factor cost. This assumption often does not hold and will be relaxed later.

Simultaneous solution of these conditions for all inputs gives the (unconditional) *factor demand equations* $x_j^*(P, v_k, c_j)$. Substitution of these factor demand equations into the production function (1) gives the product supply equation $y^*(P, v_k, c_j)$. Rearranging (4) yields the condition that the input price ratio is equal to the rate of technical substitution (RTS):

$$\frac{v_k}{c_j} = \frac{\dfrac{\partial f(\cdot)}{\partial x_k}}{\dfrac{\partial f(\cdot)}{\partial x_j}} = RTS_{x_j, x_k} \tag{5}$$

This relationship has two consequences for natural resource allocation. First, if

c_j, the cost of the resource, does not reflect all costs, the resource will be overused. Second, changes in factor market prices, v_k, or changes in the ability to substitute inputs will change the use of natural resources. Technical change can modify resource costs, quality, or degree of substitutability (Chapter 5).

The micromodel defined above is not fully satisfactory for analyzing some resource use problems in agriculture. Agricultural production is characterized by multiproduct production processes, with several crops being produced by the same resource base and management unit. However, farm output can be adequately defined by nonjoint production processes for each crop, linked by a common resource base such as land. The recognition that the resource base is usually fixed in the short run, but can be allocated among crops, results in these resources (x_j) being termed allocatable inputs. Agriculture is thus characterized by multioutput, multi-input firms, whose inputs comprise variable and fixed, but allocatable, factors. We also may have some nonallocatable factors not directly considered here.

For simplicity, assume a multioutput specification with no jointly produced external effects. The farm firm profit function is then defined as

subject to

$$\left. \begin{array}{c} \pi = \displaystyle\sum_{i=1}^{n} P_i f_i(x_{ik}, x_{ij}) - \sum_i v_k x_{ik} - \sum_i c_j x_{ij} \\ \\ \displaystyle\sum_i x_{ij} \le \bar{b}_j, \qquad \text{for all } j \end{array} \right\} \tag{6}$$

In equation (6), the farm firm produces n crops with production function $f_i(\cdot)$. Each crop uses a different mix of variable inputs (x_{ik}) and allocatable inputs (x_{ij}), and all allocatable inputs are subject to a finite stock, $\bar{b}_j$. The production functions for different crops are assumed to be nonjoint, but the constraint on the total amount of allocatable inputs makes the decisions on all inputs interdependent. Sometimes the multiple-output production process can be described by fixed proportions of inputs. The optimal input and output mix can then be examined by Linear Programming (see Box 2.1).

Joint Output Production—Pollution Generation

The classical static model of firm behavior can be modified to show joint production of a "bad" output (market or nonmarket) such as pollution by introduction of a *pollution generation function* (*h*), which is similar in concept to the classical production function:

$$z = h(y, x_k, x_j) \tag{7}$$

where z can be thought of as the flow (quantity) of the "bad." The general notation used for (7) allows for the bad to be generated directly by output, y (and thus indirectly by inputs), generated directly by variable or purchased input usage, x_k, or be generated directly by natural resources x_j. Henceforth, we will generically refer to production of the "bad" as pollution (Whitcomb, 1972).

Box 2.1. Modelling Farm Resource Use

Farm production has been defined as producing several different outputs from fixed, but allocatable resources. If the production process can be adequately approximated by fixed proportion input requirements in the neighborhood of the optimal output, the farm production problem can be modeled by Linear Programming (*LP*). The *LP* modeling method defines the feasible set of production alternatives by a set of linear constraints and assumes that input allocation and crop production decisions are made in a way that maximizes profit.

A greatly simplified illustrative example of a linear programming problem can be given in terms of two crop choices with three constraints. The three constraints represent land and seasonal labor restrictions and a rotational proportionality constraint between the two cropping activities x_1 and x_2. This simple example can be written as

$$\text{Max} \qquad x_1 + 3x_2$$

$$\text{Subject to} \begin{cases} 2x_1 + x_2 \leq 4 & \text{(Land)} \\ 2x_1 + 4x_2 \leq 8 & \text{(Labor)} \\ -x_1 + x_2 \leq 1 & \text{(Rotation)} \\ x_1 \geq 0 \\ x_2 \geq 0 \end{cases}$$

The feasible solution set is formed by the intersection of the linear inequality constraints. The fundamental theorem of linear programming shows that the optimal solution will be one of the extreme (corner) points of the convex solution set formed by the constraints.

The problem is solved by the simplex algorithm that optimizes by searching over the extreme points. A graphical representation of the problem is shown in Figure 2.2. The extreme points of the feasible solution set at the vertexes *A*, *B*, *C*, *D*, and *E*. The objective function is also linear in x_1 and x_2 and is a line with the slope of x_1 to x_2 as 1:3. This slope yields an "iso profit" line. For the *LP* maximization problem, the optimal solution is the extreme point that is tangent to the highest objective function value. In this example, the optimum is at the extreme point *C*. This point represents a mix of the x_1 and x_2 cropping allocation with 0.66 units in x_1 and 1.66 units of land in x_2, and an objective function value of 5.66.

The advantage of the linear programming model of production is that it can be constructed with a minimum of data. The fixed proportion input assumption and the linear costs and revenues are often reasonable approximations for relatively small shifts around the base year production levels. Another advantage of linear programming models is that they yield the imputed values of the fixed, but allocatable resources found in all types of agriculture. In addition, the linear constraints are able to model policies that are imposed through constraints or ratios. This type of policy is frequently used in agriculture; a common example is the proportional "set aside" required to participate in government crop price support programs. Further reading on the application of linear programs to agricultural models can be found in Q. Paris (1991), and there is a detailed discussion of aggregate modeling issues in Chapter 4.

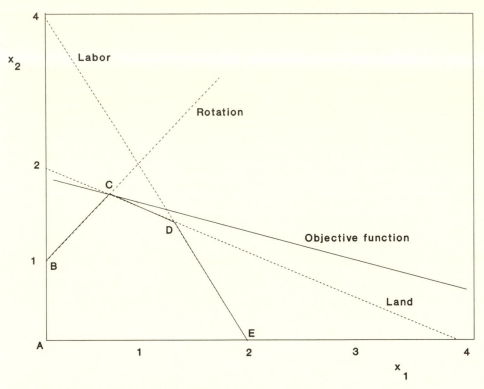

Figure 2.2. Diagram of optimal LP solution.

Purchased and natural resources can either increase or decrease pollution generation

$$\frac{\partial z}{\partial x_k} \gtreqless 0 \quad \text{and} \quad \frac{\partial z}{\partial x_j} \gtreqless 0 \tag{8}$$

Similarly, the second derivative can be of either sign since increased input use can accelerate or abate pollution generation.

In resource economics, we often compare the case of unregulated pollution (i.e., the classical state model of firm behavior, appended with the pollution generation function, equation (7)), to various means for correcting the bad effects; that is, we compare resource allocation and firm profits for the case where there is a market (i.e., penalty) or nonmarket (i.e., regulation) correction for the lack of well-defined or appropriately defined property rights.

We first consider the unregulated case appended with the pollution generation function, then consider the case of a regulation on the amount of pollution generated, and finally the case of a penalty for generation of the pollution. In all cases, we simplify the analysis by assuming that all pollution is external to the firm (i.e., the pollution does not affect the firm). To further simplify the analysis, we assume that the firm is a price taker in the product market and all factor markets.

Unregulated Pollution

If we let the optimal solution to the classical static firm problem (4) be denoted by x_j^* and y^*, with input prices v_k, c_j and output price P, the amount of pollution generated is obtained by substituting these choice functions into the pollution generation function, (7), to give

$$z \equiv h[y^*(P, v_k, c_j), x_k^*(P, v_k, c_j), x_j^*(P, v_k, c_j)] \qquad \text{or} \qquad z^* = h(P, v_k, c_j) \quad (9)$$

Since pollution generation is ancillary to the mathematical optimization that leads to first-order conditions, (4), we do not need to make *any* assumptions about the curvature of the pollution generation function. For example, we can allow for the case in which the change in input use accelerates the change in pollution flows once the natural assimilative capacity of the environment is exceeded, or we can allow for the case of decreasing marginal effect on pollution accumulation.

Pollution Penalty

Now suppose that property rights are defined in such a way that there is a (negative) price for pollution generated by the firm, or that legislation establishes a *penalty* (tax) on pollution, denoted by pb, which the firm must pay. The profit function for the firm with two variable inputs (x_1, x_2) now becomes

$$\pi = Py - v_1 x_1 - v_2 x_2 - pb \cdot z \qquad (10)$$

Substituting the production function for y into (10) gives

$$\pi = Pf(x_1, x_2) - v_1 x_1 - v_2 x_2 - pb \cdot z \qquad (11)$$

Since there are no constraints on profit maximization not implicitly reflected in (11), the first-order conditions for profit maximization with marginal products $\partial f/\partial x_k$ written as f_k are

$$\frac{\partial \pi}{\partial x_k} = Pf_k - v_k - pb \cdot \frac{\partial z}{\partial x_k} = 0, \qquad k = 1, 2 \qquad (12)$$

Simultaneous solutions of these first-order conditions will give the factor demand equations, $x_k^b(P, pb, v_1, v_2)$. Substitution of these equations into the production function will give the product supply equation, $y^b(P, pb, v_1, v_2)$. The product supply equation (y^b) and factor demand equations (x_k^b) can be substituted into the pollution generation function, (7), for appropriate quantities (y, x_k) to show how optimal (from the firm's perspective) pollution is related to prices, $z^b(P, pb, v_1, v_2)$. Note that the per unit penalty, pb, is an argument in these behavioral equations and makes them different from usual factor demand and supply equations. Cases with natural resources (x_j) generating pollution $(\partial z/\partial x_j > 0)$ or both resources and variable inputs affecting the h function are mathematically equivalent for (9)–(12).

Second-order conditions are that the profit function (11) be strictly concave. Note that these conditions will be satisfied if the production function is strictly concave *and* if the pollution generation function is strictly convex; however, the individual functions (1) and (7) need not meet these requirements as long as the term $[Pf(\cdot) - pbh(\cdot)]$ is strictly concave. To avoid getting bogged down in mathematics, derivation of second-order conditions in this general case is left to the interested reader. Appropriate mathematical concepts for deriving the second-order conditions are given in Chiang (1974, Chapter 11).

It is instructive to rearrange the terms in (12) to give

$$Pf_k = v_k + pb \cdot \frac{\partial z}{\partial x_k} \tag{13}$$

From (13) it can be seen that if input use increases pollution (i.e., $(\partial z/\partial x_k) > 0$), then penalizing pollution is conceptually similar to increasing input price, v_k, which results in decreased use of that input. On the other hand, if the input helps reduce pollution (i.e., $(\partial z/\partial x_k) < 0$), then the pollution penalty will increase use of that input for the profit maximizing firm.

Further insight into how a pollution penalty or tax affects firm behavior can be obtained by expanding the partial derivative $\partial z/\partial x_k$ in (12) and (13). Although this terminology is rarely used, the term $(\partial z/\partial x_k)$ should be viewed as *partial-total* derivative (cf. Chiang, 1974, p. 202). It is a total derivative in the sense that z depends directly on x_k (input usage per se causes pollution) and, in general, depends directly on y (output per se causes pollution), but it is partial in the sense that all other arguments of the function (e.g., all other input levels) are not allowed to change. Hence:

$$\frac{\partial z}{\partial x_k} = \frac{\partial h}{\partial y} \cdot \frac{\partial y}{\partial x_k} + \frac{\partial h}{\partial x_k} = h_y f_k + h_k \tag{14}$$

where subscripts refer to derivatives of the pollution and production functions. If changes in output per se do not cause changes in pollution, then $h_y = 0$. If input use per se causes increases in pollution, then $h_k > 0$, while if input use reduces pollution, then $h_k < 0$.

Full comparative statics (i.e., analyzing how parameter changes, such as a change in the penalty, will influence the direction of changes in factor usage and output as related to partial derivatives of the production function and pollution generation function) of this model can be developed along the lines given in Chiang (1974, section 11.7) or Beattie and Taylor (1985, section 3.2).

Pollution Restriction

Consider now the case of a "regulation" that limits pollution to a certain amount, say z^r. Maximization of the profit function, (3), must be done subject to this constraint. In general, we should set the problem up as an *inequality* constrained maximization problem, but this would require us to use the Kuhn–Tucker conditions to characterize the solution (see the Box 2.2). These conditions are mathematically complicated, but can be simplified by assuming that z^*, from the unregulated case presented above, always exceeds z^r. Then we can convert the

Box 2.2. Complementary Slackness, Tractor Dealers, and Imputed Values

The Kuhn Tucker complementary slackness conditions can be intuitive, and they are the basis of several jokes. One of the better known ones is about the tractor or car salesman, who when asked by a customer how he can sell "below factory invoice," explains that "What we lose on each tractor, we make up on the extra volume." Over a wide range of cultures, the claim that a product is being knowingly sold below its imputed or shadow value is greeted with disbelieving grins, yet this is simply what the complementary slackness conditions state.

The complementary slackness conditions for the basic production or primal linear programming problem (Box 2.1) can be written using a condensed notation. The linear programming problem is

$$\text{Max } px$$

$$\text{subject to } Ax \leq b$$

where p is the vector of net returns, x is a vector of production activities, A is a matrix of input requirements per unit of x, and b is the vector of available resources or other "policy" constraints.

The primal complementary slackness (CS) conditions that are derived by putting the problem in Lagrangian form and applying the Kuhn-Tucker first-order conditions are

$$\lambda_i \left(b_i - \sum_{j=1}^{n} a_{ij} x_j \right) = 0 \qquad \text{for} \qquad i = 1, \ldots, m$$

The CS conditions express the basic concept of scarcity values for resources or policy constraints in this production or primal problem. λ_i is the dual variable associated with the ith input. "Dual" is the terminology used to represent a price or imputed value problem, and λ_i is the marginal "value" of another unit of b_i. The primal CS states that if the input b_i is fully used ($b_i - \sum_j a_{ij} x_j = 0$), then the input can have a nonzero scarcity value. Conversely, if the input is not fully used, additional units have no scarcity value. For example, in Box 2.1, labor was not fully utilized at the solution C, and additional units of labor (b_2) have no value. Alternatively, if the objective function had a higher value for x_2 so that the solution was at D, then there is slack in the b_3 (rotation) constraint and λ_3 has zero value.

The dual density complementary slackness conditions derived by applying Kuhn-Tucker conditions to the dual problem Lagrangian are

$$x_j \left(p_j - \sum_{i-1}^{m} a_{ij} \lambda_i \right) = 0 \qquad \text{for } j = 1, \ldots, n$$

For an illustrative example we return to the tractor dealer. Suppose that the dealer buys a given tractor x_j from the factory for a cost of p_j. In selling the tractor, the dealer prices the different components ($i = 1, \ldots, n$). The components such as the basic chassis, motor size, auxiliary equipment, etc., are related to the tractor by a_{ij}. If you offer a set of prices $\lambda_i, i = 1, \ldots, n$ for the components, under what conditions will the dealer accept your offer? The dual CS conditions say that the dealer will only sell you the tractor, that is x_j can be positive, if the terms in the parentheses sum to zero. The terms $p_j - \sum_{i=1}^{m} a_{ij} \lambda_i$ are the dealer cost minus the sum of the offer prices when incorporated into a tractor by summing a_{ij} over i. In short, if your offers of λ_i do not cover the dealer cost p_j he will not sell the tractor to you.

Tractor or car dealers are famous for advertising that they are selling "below the factory invoice." Truth in advertising usually requires that they note in much smaller print that "invoice amount may exceed actual dealer cost." Even car dealers are bound by the complementary slackness conditions.

problem into an *equality* constrained maximization problem, which allows us to use calculus in a more straightforward manner to characterize the solution to the problem.

We can convert the equality constrained optimization problem into an unconstrained optimization by using a Lagrangian approach. With this approach, the unconstrained profit equation (15) is *augmented* with a term defined to be the product of a Lagrangian *multiplier* (λ) and the equality constraint written in implicit form. The profit function (3) including variable inputs and natural resources is

$$\pi = Pf(x_k, x_j) - v_k x_k - c_j x_j \tag{15}$$

The pollution constraint in the implicit form is

$$h(f(x_k, x_j), x_k, x_j) - z^r = 0 \tag{16}$$

From a mathematical standpoint, the multiplier is introduced as a "trick"; however, from an economic standpoint the Lagrangian multiplier has a meaningful interpretation. The trick is to define the Lagrangian objective function ($L\pi$) as the original objective function (profit) augmented with a Lagrangian term for the pollution constraint

$$L\pi = Pf(x_k, x_j) - v_k x_k - c_j x_j - \lambda[h(f(x_k, x_j), x_k, x_j) - z^r] \tag{17}$$

With this Lagrangian approach, the Lagrangian multiplier is treated as a choice variable along with the input rates. First-order conditions for maximization of (17) where subscripts for the functions f and h are derivatives are

$$\left. \begin{array}{l} \dfrac{\partial L\pi}{\partial x_k} = Pf_k - v_k - \lambda(h_y f_k + h_k) = 0 \\[4mm] \dfrac{\partial L\pi}{\partial x_j} = Pf_j - c_j - \lambda(h_y f_j + h_j) = 0 \end{array} \right\} \tag{18}$$

$$\frac{\partial L\pi}{\partial \lambda} = -h(f(x_k, x_j), x_k, x_j) + z^r = 0 \tag{19}$$

Note that condition (19) is simply a restatement of the equality constraint, which is why, in a loose sense, the Lagrangian trick works. Second-order conditions for this specialized problem can be derived using the framework given in Chiang (1974, Chapter 12).

Simultaneous solution of the ($n + 1$) first-order conditions in (18) and (19) gives the factor demand equations $x^r(P, v_k, c_j, z^r)$ and the Lagrangian multiplier as a function of the parameters $\lambda^r(P, v_k, c_j, z^r)$. Substituting the factor demand functions into the production function gives the product supply equation $y^r(P, v_k, c_j, z^r)$. Carefully note that if the constraint, (19), is satisfied, the Lagrangian term [the last term in (17)] is zero for all values of λ; therefore, (16) is maximum (constrained) profit when $z^* > z^r$.

For this problem, the Lagrangian multiplier has an important economic interpretation. Some insight into this interpretation can be gained by noting from (17) that $(\partial L\pi/\partial z^r) = \lambda$, and noting that $L\pi = \pi^r$, when π is evaluated at the optimum values of the variables. λ^r shows the effects on profit of an infinitesimal change in the level of the pollution constraint, z^r, holding variable inputs and natural resources constant. Thus, λ^r can be thought of as the shadow value of a small change in the pollution constraint. (See the discussion of shadow values in Box 2.2.) Readers desiring a formal proof of this assertion can appeal to the envelope theorem or carry out a full comparative static analysis of this model, focusing on how λ changes in response to parameter changes (see, e.g., Chiang, 1974, Chapter 12).

There is an equivalent between the pollution constrained profit maximization model and the previous model of a pollution penalty. If the pollution constraint is set equal to the solution value (z^r) from the penalty model, the value of the Lagrangian multiplier, λ, will exactly equal the pollution penalty, pb. Conversely, if the pollution penalty is set equal to the solution value, λ^r, the solution to the penalty model will give a pollution level equal to z^r. This comparison establishes the resource allocation equivalence of taxing pollution (at a rate of pb to achieve a pollution level of z^r) and imposing a pollution standard.

The concept of λ as a shadow value is also useful when considering the effects of finite stocks of a resource available to a firm to allocate among the firm's various outputs. In this case, λ is more aptly described as the marginal opportunity cost, or rental value of using the resource in the production of one output, as opposed to the others. (See Box 2.2 on stock resources and shadow values.)

A Pollution Disposal Firm

The profit maximization model given by equation (6) was used to address behavior of a firm that generates pollution. A slightly different interpretation of this classical static model also gives insight into behavior of a firm that is engaged in disposing of (rather than generating) pollution. For this case, we assume that the firms generating undesirable byproducts (i.e., pollution) are willing to pay other firms to dispose of or clean up the pollution. For example, poultry production generates poultry wastes that, because of their nutrient content, may be water pollutants. Although the poultry wastes have a value to a corn producer, the poultry producer may pay the corn producer to dispose (by application to corn fields) of the wastes. Thus, from the perspective of the corn producer, poultry wastes, which can be an input to corn production, can have a *negative* price.

The most interesting aspect of this situation is that the profit maximizing corn producer will, because of the negative price for poultry waste, operate in stage III [i.e., negative marginal physical product (MPP)] of production with respect to plant nutrients. This effect can be seen by examining the first-order condition [taken from (4)] for that factor:

$$Pf_k = P \cdot MPP_k = v_k \tag{20}$$

From (20) it can be seen that if product (corn) price is positive, and factor price (v_k) (poultry wastes) is negative, then marginal physical productivity of that factor must be negative in order to satisfy the first-order condition (20). Thus, the firm will operate in state III of the production function with respect to that factor. Note that it does not mean that the firm will operate in stage III of production for other factors with positive prices.

The micromodels defined above to include pollution can be extended in a straightforward way to the general case of multiproduct, multifactor production such as shown in equation (6). The case of imperfect competition in one or more markets can be introduced by defining appropriate price functions (such as output price as a function of output level), then recognizing this dependency when deriving first-order (marginal) conditions. Since many resource markets have imperfectly competitive elements, the reader is encouraged to consider these cases, especially compared to the competitive case emphasized in the above derivations.

So far we have assumed that we can accurately measure and predict resource stocks and the flows of factor inputs from them. A fundamental characteristic of natural resource supplies is that they are uncertain. Uncertainty occurs in supplies in one or more ways. The total resource stock may be uncertain as in mining and extractive industries. The linkage between the stock and flows may be very variable between years as in rainfall run-off and effective yields from a dam. In many cases, the cost of extracting or cleaning up a natural resource varies substantially owing to annual fluctuations or ignorance about the resource. All these changes are reflected in changes in the price per unit of the resource. Fluctuating prices add risk to the operations of a profit maximizing firm. The next section will return to a simple model to examine the effects of risk on output level and resource allocation.

THE FIRM RESPONSE TO RISKY RESOURCES

The deterministic comparative static model is modified below by considering a risk averse decision maker who is facing a risky supply of resource inputs from a given resource base. The first development takes the basic production model using resource inputs and derives the effect on resource use when resource supply fluctuates. More specific definitions of risk preference are then specified. If a particular utility function is specified, more precise conclusions can be drawn. The section ends with a brief review of some methods by which risk has been empirically incorporated into production decision models.

Using the case of a variable water supply as an illustration, the profit equation (3) is simplified to a single resource or vector of resource inputs x. The firm's cost of x is assumed to be c, its shadow value. For example, a farmer may have water rights (riparian) on a river that can be diverted at minimal cost for irrigation. The

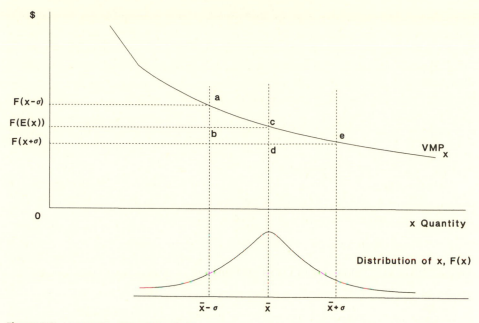

Figure 2.3. Uncertain resources values.

farmer could also have a small hydroelectric generator downstream of the irrigation diversion point that provides an opportunity cost for undiverted water. The resource base in the riparian rights is constant, but the actual flows in the river and consequent diversions and power outputs fluctuate from year to year. These stochastic river flows have a known distribution that results in a random rental value with a known distribution.

Figure 2.3 shows the effect of an uncertain supply of resource flows x on the rental value of the resource. The curvature of the value marginal product function is due to decreasing short-run marginal productivity of the resource. The distribution of the resource is graphed below the horizontal axis, and the vertical axis measures cumulative probabilities of marginal values, $F(x)$. Two points are notable. First, owing to the decreasing productivity, the value of flows above the mean does not offset the loss of flows in dry years. This can be seen in Figure 2.3, where the benefits of above average flows, area cde, is smaller than the losses from below average flows, area abc. Thus the average value of fluctuating flows is less than the value of the average flow. In short, uncertainty is costly. The second conclusion that can be drawn from Figure 2.3 is that quantities that are more certain to be delivered have a higher rental value. This can be seen by picking a resource quantity to the left of the mean of the distribution, say $\bar{x} - \sigma$, which has a better than average chance of being available. That is, in most years one would expect to have at least $\bar{x} - \sigma$ available for use. The rental value of this quantity $\bar{x} - \sigma$ exceeds that of the less reliable quantity $\bar{x} + \sigma$.

A practical illustration can again be drawn from water prices in California. The State Water Project defines its water into "firm" supplies that are designed to be delivered in all but 1 year in 50. "Surplus" water supplies are available in years with above average water capacity. The firm supply price is approximately twice the surplus price, which is based on the variable costs of delivering the water.

The profit function with x representing both variable and natural resources with cost c is

$$\pi = Pf(x) - cx - FC \tag{21}$$

where $f(x)$ is the production function ($f'(x) > 0$, $f''(x) < 0$, in which f' and f'' are the first and second derivatives); P is the output price; c is the stochastic imputed rental value of the resource, distributed as a normal variable, $N(\bar{c}, \sigma_c^2)$, and FC is a fixed cost of production.

This development parallels that of Sandmo (1971) who analyzes a stochastic output price and known cost function. Assume that the firm has a utility function in profits, maximizes expected utility, and is risk averse.

$$\text{Max } E[u(\pi)], \qquad u'(\pi) > 0, \qquad \text{and} \qquad u''(\pi) < 0 \tag{22}$$

Substituting (21) into (22), the expected utility is

$$E[u(Pf(x) - cx - FC] \tag{23}$$

Taking the first-order conditions of (23) with respect to the resource allocation x yields

$$E[u'(\pi)(Pf'(x) - c)] = 0 \tag{24}$$

The second-order conditions are likewise

$$E[u''(\pi)(Pf'(x) - c)^2 - u'(\pi)(Pf''(x))] < 0 \tag{25}$$

The first-order condition is used in Appendix 2.1 to derive the qualitative result on resource allocation by a risk averse firm. The derivations show that (24) implies that

$$E[(u'(\pi)(Pf'(x) - \bar{c}] > 0 \tag{26}$$

where $\bar{c}$ is the expected value of the stochastic rental value c. Since $u'(\pi)$ is nonnegative by assumption and intuition, equation (26) implies that the firm's optimal resource allocation is characterized by

$$Pf'(x) > \bar{c} \tag{27}$$

The optimal allocation by a risk averse firm requires that the value marginal product of a resource exceed its expected rental value. Given the production function, this condition implies that risky resources are allocated with less intensity. The level of input use and output produced is lower when resource availability is uncertain than when resources are priced at their expected scarcity price. In Figure 2.2, the rental value $F(E(x))$ exceeds $E(F(x))$ evaluated at $\bar{x} + \sigma$ since, as previously noted, area cde is less than area abc.

From his development of price uncertainty, Sandmo draws additional comparative static results. From the parallel development of input price uncertainty in Appendix 2.1, and some definitions of risk aversion, the following qualitative conclusions can be drawn. The standard definitions of *risk aversion* are the

Arrow-Pratt measures:

$$
\left.
\begin{array}{l}
\text{Absolute Risk Aversion:} \quad r_A(\pi) = -\dfrac{u''(\pi)}{u'(\pi)} \\[2em]
\text{Relative Risk Aversion:} \quad r_R(\pi) = -\dfrac{u''(\pi)\pi}{u'(\pi)}
\end{array}
\right\}
\tag{28}
$$

and

These are local curvature properties of the utility of profit functions $u(\pi)$ with more curvature meaning more risk aversion. The absolute risk aversion measure can be thought of as a measure of curvature of the utility function that is not changed by positive, linear changes in profit. However, relative risk aversion $r_R(\pi)$ is weighted by the level of profits. Constant absolute risk aversion ($CARA$) is shown in the negative exponential utility function

$$
u(\pi) = 1 - e^{-r_A \pi}
\tag{29}
$$

where r_A is the absolute risk aversion coefficient. This form of utility function is found widely in empirical risk applications due to its convenient properties.

Sandmo's qualitative conclusions can be summarized under three headings: 1) the effect of risk on fixed cost effects; 2) the influence of shifts in the mean of the random variable, but not the distribution, on output supply; and 3) the effect of changes in a tax rate on input use. In deterministic comparative statics, the fixed cost component does not influence the first-order resource allocation decisions. However, if the profit function (21) is substituted into the first-order condition (24), we see in (23) that the equilibrium resource use level x^* derived from (24) is changed by changes in the fixed cost component FC. Specifically, Sandmo (1971) shows that decreasing absolute risk aversion ($DARA$) is a necessary and sufficient condition for the derived demand for resource inputs to be reduced by increases in the fixed cost of the resource. The fluctuations in resource use are generally driven by natural resource phenomena, and the average level of resource use is often defined by property rights or institutions. Thus, based on these conditions, Sandmo (1971) concludes that $DARA$ is a sufficient condition for the supply to respond to shifts in the mean of the distribution. Positive shifts in the mean result in positive supply response. The effect of tax rates is shown to depend on whether the relative rate of risk aversion is increasing, constant, or decreasing. Increases in tax rates move the output level in the same direction as the relative risk aversion. This leaves the effect of taxation on resource use somewhat uncertain, since the evidence of decreasing relative risk aversion is not conclusive.

An approach that leads to empirical analysis of production with resources under risk is developed in Anderson et al. (1977). Specifying a function form for the utility function, a Taylor series expansion is taken around the mean, which enables the utility level to be approximated by the moments of the expansion in what is called a "mean-variance" approximation.

Defining a general form of a utility function as $u(\pi)$ and the expected profit as

$E(\pi)$ a Taylor series expansion is:

$$u(\pi) = u(E(\pi)) + u'(E(\pi))[\pi - E(\pi)] + \frac{u''(E(\pi))[\pi - E(\pi)]^2}{2!}$$

$$+ \frac{u'''(E(\pi))[\pi - E(\pi)]^3}{3!} + \cdots + r \tag{30}$$

Taking the expectation of $u(\pi)$ removes the second term since $E[\pi - E(\pi)] = 0$. Therefore, the expected utility can be approximated as

$$u(\pi) = u(E(\pi)) + u''(E(\pi))E(\pi - E(\pi))^2/2 + u'''(E\pi))E(\pi - E(\pi))^3/6 + \cdots + r \tag{31}$$

It is usually sufficient for most applied work to approximate the function by the first two terms.

If sufficient accuracy is achieved by truncating after the second term the expected utility can be expressed in terms of expected profit $e(\pi)$ and its variance $e(\pi - E(\pi))^2$, the "mean-variance approximation":

$$u(\pi) \approx u(E(\pi)) + \frac{u''(E(\pi))}{2} \operatorname{Var}(\pi) \tag{32}$$

where $\operatorname{Var}(\pi)$ is the variance of profits.

A source of risk when using resources as productive inputs could be specified as uncertain yields from the production function. Using the earlier definition of output $y = f(x)$, the profit function is:

$$\pi = Py - cx - FC \tag{33}$$

Using the mean variance approximation to the utility function $u(\pi) = u(E(\pi))$, and $\operatorname{Var}(\pi)$ written as $V(\pi)$ described above, the first-order condition is

$$\frac{\partial u(\pi)}{\partial x} = \frac{\partial u(\cdot)}{\partial E(\pi)} \frac{\partial E(\pi)}{\partial x} + \frac{\partial u(\cdot)}{\partial V(\pi)} \frac{\partial V(\pi)}{\partial x} = 0 \tag{34}$$

which implies that

$$\frac{\partial E(\pi)}{\partial x} + \left[\frac{\partial u(\cdot)}{\partial V(\pi)} \bigg/ \frac{\partial u(\cdot)}{\partial E(\pi)} \right] \frac{\partial V(\pi)}{\partial x} = 0 \tag{35}$$

The term in square brackets is the ratio of the marginal effects of profit variance and expected profit on utility—that is, the rate of substitution in utility terms of expected profit, for profit variance. In graphical terms, this is the negative of the slope of an isoutility curve in EV or mean-variance space. It is also the negative of what Magnusson (1969) has called the "risk evaluation differential quotient" (*REDQ*).

Substituting in expressions for $\partial E(\pi)/\partial x$ and $\partial V(\pi)/\partial x$, Anderson et al. (1977) show that the optimal input allocation equation reduces to

$$c = P\frac{\partial E(y)}{\partial x} - REDQ\left(P^2\frac{\partial V(y)}{\partial x}\right) \tag{36}$$

This qualitative conclusion agrees with that from equation (27), in that the optimum is not achieved when mean input price is equated with the expected value of the marginal product, but when expected value marginal product exceeds the input price by an amount determined by the $REDQ$, the marginal variance of output, and the output price squared. This difference between the factor cost and expected value marginal product is sometimes termed the marginal risk deduction.

The effect of stochastic factor prices has also been analyzed by Turnovsky (1969) and Just and Pope (1979) who indicate that factor demand is reduced by increases in expected factor price, variance of factor price, and risk aversion by the decision maker. Empirical applications of risk to production decisions have used a wide range of approximations based on the method of moments. Many applications have used the mean/variance approximation for empirical reasons.

An empirical approach that has a different utility specification is one in which the utility function is lexicographic. The intuition behind these specifications is that utility functions are not continuous, but that some levels of profit have high, but discontinuous levels of utility. For instance, the probability of large negative profits and the consequent danger of going out of business may have a dominating disutility to a family farmer. The "safety first," "focus loss," or "maximin" decision rules all share this condition. These approaches are usually implemented by discrete optimization approaches that maximize net return subject to a constraint that the probability of some event such as negative profits does not exceed a prespecified level. A useful text for this approach is Roumasset et al. (1979).

OPTIMAL RESOURCE USE OVER TIME

In the previous analysis of the firm's use of natural resources the profit function is specified for a single time period, and the resource inputs are defined as a measurable flow quantity in that period. A few oblique references were made to the resource stock that underlies this flow of services. This stock/flow relationship of natural resources is a characteristic that distinguishes them from some variable inputs. Many resources have the physical property that if the flows used in production in a given time period are reduced the stock will grow, and thereby result in proportionally larger flows available in the future. The previous model specifications have indicated that an optimal static solution trades off between resources, other factors, products, and risk. With the stock flow relationships the optimizing resource user also has to trade off resource use among time periods. A two-period example of ground water allocation for irrigation can illustrate this dynamic linkage. Consider ground water as a stock that is recharged by annual inflows at a prespecified rate. If more ground water is pumped out than flows in, the stock will be drawn down and the greater depth of pumping will increase extraction costs in the next time period. When deciding the optimal level of water use in the first year, the firm must consider the cost of the marginal pumping in the following years. This is called "user cost" and it generally changes over time. The user cost is influenced by the change in stock, the discount rate, and the value put on the resource stock at the end of a planning horizon, this latter value is usually called the terminal value. In some cases, there are not well-defined property rights on the future stock. This is a case of a dynamic externality which may cause excessive resource use in the current period. Environmental damage from agricultural production is often in the form of a dynamic externality where current markets are sufficient, but intertemporal market failure exists.

Until recently, the comparative dynamics of the firm was an area with limited investigation by economists. Generally, articles and books on dynamic economics approach the necessary and sufficient conditions from the rigorous, but daunting, perspective of calculus of variations and the maximum principle, which have limited appeal to many economists. Alternatively, dynamic programming, while having numerical advantages, does not yield as many analytic insights. We take the view here that anyone who can do comparative statics can also derive simple comparative dynamic conditions. In addition, we hope to show that the comparative dynamic conditions such as the arbitrage relationship can be intuitive, and are practiced in a general way by careful decision makers.

In the previous sections, production and pollution generation were assumed to take place instantaneously. However, many production, investment, and even pollution generation activities take years to occur. For example, a water supply project that provides irrigation, flood control, and recreation benefits takes several years to complete and has benefits and operation costs that extend over many years. The timing as well as the level of costs and returns is critical in determining optimal resource use.

There are several basic concepts that are essential for understanding resource use over time. These include 1) time preferences or discount rates, 2) growth and decay processes, and 3) resource inventories or stocks.

To induce individuals to delay consumption some premium must be paid. This payment per period is referred to as the *discount rate*. By discounting future streams of income we can directly compare these to current income or consumption values. For example if you have a 3 year project that costs C dollars today and has a net benefit stream of B_1 in 1 year, B_2 in 2 years, and B_3 in the last period, then the project has a current or present value of

$$-C + B_1/(1 + r) + B_2/(1 + r)^2 + B_3/(1 + r)^3$$

The interest rate r reflects the opportunity cost of money or the discount rate per time period. If there is a large number of time periods with small intervals, the discounting processes $(1 + 1/(1 + r) + 1/(1 + r)^2 + \cdots)$ can be approximated by the continuous form e^{-rt}, where e is the base of natural logarithms and t is the time period. Notice from both the discrete and continuous form of this process, that a larger r will lead to a lower net present value. In addition as r increases there is less investment because the net present value should be positive for investment to profitably take place. Different individuals and business firms have different discount rates which depend upon risk, expected inflation, taxes, and transaction costs (Howe, 1971). The practical problem is to find a real (nominal rate − expected inflation rate) cost of funds that is relevant for all individuals who both pay for and benefit from a particular investment. (See Box 2.3 on water project evaluations.)

The second basic component of dynamic problems are growth and decay processes. In what follows this will often be summarized as an equation of motion. This explicitly states how the resource stock changes over time. Resource economists need to understand the technical nature of the resources well enough to specify these relationships. For many nonrenewable resources this will be a simple accounting of amounts withdrawn or added to starting stock levels. For example, the change in the level of water in a ground water aquifer between two periods is the amount withdrawn for irrigation and other purposes plus the amount added by infiltration. For renewable resources the equation of motion is equal to the growth rate per period less the amount harvested (see Chapter 3). In some cases the quality of resources change over time and an appropriate adjustment is required. Care must be taken in determining how various management or control variables augment growth or change the harvest rates or quality.

Finally, all dynamic problems involve issues of resource stocks. Optimal use over time for resource situation with high stocks will be different from those with low stocks. This occurs because low stock levels can directly influence growth rates, and can affect harvest or mining costs. In addition when borrowing is involved, higher stocks will usually lower borrowing costs because more collateral is available. Stocks can also interact with the discounting process to influence optimal timing of resource use. These time concepts will appear in most dynamic problems throughout this book.

Comparative dynamic first-order conditions in this chapter are first derived using a two period graphical example. In the graphical example the problem is allocation of a fixed resource quantity between two periods. The second problem shows optimal use of fertilizer when fertilizer affects yield in two periods. Next, the Lagrangian approach is applied to more general discrete time systems including long-term external effects. We then move to continuous time first-order conditions in terms of the Hamiltonian and Pontryagin conditions.

The Two-Period Model of Optimal Resource Use

The dynamic concepts of optimal intertemporal allocation of agricultural or natural resources is illustrated in Figure 2.4 (McInerney, 1976). The graphical model relies on a two-period intertemporal analysis. Two periods may appear an unrealistic representation of resource allocation over time, but this framework does illustrate the important economic concepts before attempting a more general mathematical development. The fixed stock of the agricultural resource (e.g., cropland, pest susceptibility, environmental capacity) is the length of the horizontal axis, OS. The marginal social benefits from utilizing the resource stock in periods

Box 2.3. Federal Water Supply Investments

The history of agriculture and resources in the Western United States is closely linked to irrigation. Early, private irrigation was augmented by federal tax support following the passage of the Reclamation Act of 1902. Congressional support for the subsidies came from the desire to "provide a release of overpopulated areas of the East and for conserving the nation's natural resources" (Rucker and Fishback, 1983). Money to build the projects was mostly obtained from federal land sales, and levels of subsidies were affected by the interest costs and repayment schedules.

Farmers receiving the irrigation water were asked to repay the construction costs, but the repayments were scheduled over long periods. With the time value of money ignored, the Bureau of Reclamation and taxpayers were subsidizing development of water supplies. The size of the subsidy is sensitive to the length of the repayment schedule and various factors affecting the discount rate. The initial policy in the 1902 Act was to allow equal annual payments over 10 years. By 1910 there were defaults on the payments and the repayment schedule was extended to 20 years in the 1914 legislation. Finally, to accommodate settlers' ability to pay when they first arrived the 20-year schedule included a 5 percent down payment, followed by a 5-year grace period with no payments, then annual payments of 5 percent for 5 years and 7 percent for each of the final 10 years.

What is the size of the subsidy for each of these three payment schedules? Risk-free government bonds in the early 1900s paid interest at about 3 percent. However, inflation was about 2 percent per year and risk could easily increase farmer costs of borrowing to about 10 percent. We might see what the size of the subsidy is for three discount rates and three repayment schedules (Table 2.1).

The basic subsidy of 3 percent discount rate and 10 year repayment schedule is 14.7 percent because the present value of annual payments for each $1,000 construction cost would be $853. If the basic inflation rate is 2 percent then the nominal rate is 5 percent (real = 3, inflation = 2). For the 10 year repayment scheme this leads to a 22.8 percent subsidy. Finally, column 3 shows the subsidy level for a 10 percent discount rate. Since farmers and others experience high levels of risk because of weather and other calamities, 10 percent was not an unreasonable cost of borrowing. This rate leads to a 38.6 percent subsidy for the 10 year repayment schedule. The 1914 extension of the repayment schedule to 20 years with payments increasing after 10 years, but no payments until after 5 years further increased the size of the subsidy. Most of the increase is due to the time extension to 20 years (row 2), but the repayment schedule 3 leads to subsidies of about two-thirds of the capital costs for the 10 percent discount rate.

The complete story on the western water investments involves the size of the benefits that flowed from these investments, the distribution of the subsidies among farmers, and values of alternative use of water for urban and industrial purposes. Clearly, the settlement of the West was enhanced by these subsidies. Most of the projects provided recreation, power, flood control, and other benefits that expanded rapidly in later years. What we need to appreciate from the small part of the story here is that timing of payments and discount rates can greatly change investment subsidies.

Costs and benefits

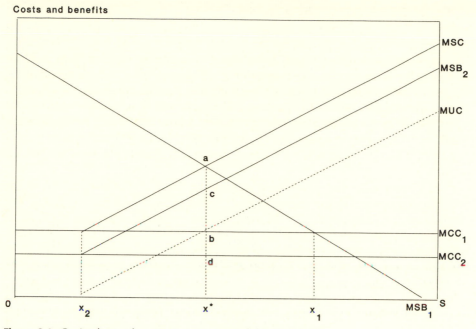

Figure 2.4. Optimal use of water or pest susceptibility over time.

t_1 and t_2 are represented by curves MSB_1 and MSB_2. MSB_2 is reversed (measured from right to left) to illustrate that resource use in period t_2 is limited by the resource stock remaining after period t_1 (e.g., if Ox_1 were used in t_1, then x_1S would remain for use in t_2). The marginal costs of using the resource in periods t_1 and t_2 are represented by MCC_1 and MCC_2. MSB_2 and MCC_2 have been discounted, and thus MSB_2 lies below MSB_1, and MCC_2 below MCC_1. By expressing all costs and benefits in present value terms, direct comparisons can be made over time.

Table 2.1. Percent Water Subsidies in Western United States[a]

	Discount rate (percent)		
Repayment schedule	3	5	10
10-year, equal installments	14.7	22.8	38.6
20-year, equal installments	22.5	37.7	57.5
20-year, graduated with 5-year grace period	30.7	44.8	66.7

[a] Based on the present value of annuities of 10 and 20 years for rows 1 and 2, respectively. The repayment schedule in row 3 is for 5 percent down payment, 5 percent payment in each of years 6–10 and 7 percent in years 11–20 (Rucker and Fishback, 1983). The percent subsidy is construction cost minus present value of repayments divided by construction costs. Present values of equal payments for years 10 to 20 can easily be found by subtracting the present value of a 1 dollar annuity for 10 years from that for 20 years.

Figure 2.4 illustrates why a dynamic model is critical in analyzing many resource allocation decisions. In a static model, the decision maker would set $MSB_1 = MCC_1$, and x_1 would be the optimal level of resource use in period t_1. The resource allocation decision becomes more complex in a dynamic analysis assuming the resource stock is constraining. (If the resource stock is nonlimiting, i.e., the stock is sufficient to satisfy both current and future demands, then the static solutions will prevail in t_1 and t_2.) The static solution, $MSB_1 = MCC_1$ and x_1 as the optimal use, results in an insufficient stock of resource in t_2 to satisfy $MSB_2 = MCC_2$, which requires the quantity $(x_2 S)$ (Fig. 2.4). To achieve optimality in a dynamic context requires reallocating the existing stock, OS, between periods t_1 and t_2.

The opportunity cost of using a natural resource in the first period is the foregone net benefits in the second period, or the *marginal user cost* (MUC). The marginal user cost in period 1 is the marginal cost of a unit reduction in the stock of a resource available in period 2; in this example it is the difference between MSB_2 and MCC_2. Thus, the marginal social cost (MSC) of using the resource in period t_1 is the sum of MUC and MCC_1. The optimal intertemporal allocation of the stock of the resource, say water, is where $MSB_1 = MSC$, or at x^*. So Ox^* of the resource is used in period t_1 and x^*S in period t_2. By allocating the water resource such that $MSB_1 = MSC$, the present value of the marginal net benefits at x^* are equal in periods t_1 and t_2, or $ab = cd$. The concepts of MUC and resource allocation in the two period setting are developed further in Chapter 3.

The farmer has no incentive to conserve the ground water or pest susceptibility to pesticides in the common property case because it will be depleted by other farmers irrigating their crops or using pesticides to control "their" pests. The common stock of the resource will be overexploited in the earlier period(s), from society's point of view, leading to a smaller stock of water or greater pest resistance in the later period(s). To achieve a socially optimal allocation of x^* in the common property case will require incentives or regulations that are both difficult to implement and administratively complex.

A Two-Period Optimal Carryover Problem

Comparative dynamic first-order conditions can be illustrated by extending our previously analyzed static model of firm behavior [given by equations (1) through (6)] to a two-period dynamic example that allows for carryover of fertilizer in the soil from one growing season to the next. In this model we add a stock variable S_t, which is a plant nutrient that changes over time t. Future plant nutrients available for plant growth can be varied indirectly by changing the amount of fertilizer (or poultry wastes) applied in the current season, x_t.

Suppose that the production function in general notation is:

$$y_t = y_t(x_t, S_t) \tag{37}$$

where y_t is production of the crop in period t. Now assume that carryover of nutrients from one time period to the next is modeled by the equation:

$$S_{t+1} = \theta(x_t + S_t) = \theta x_t + \theta S_t \qquad 0 < \theta < 1 \left.\right\}$$

$$S_0 \quad \text{given} \tag{38}$$

where S_0 is a given "initial" condition. In dynamic optimization terminology, the variable S_t is called a "state" variable (because it described the state of the system at time t), and equation (38) is referred to as the "equation of motion" or the "state transition" equation. x_t is the control variable in each period t. The coefficient θ is the percent of the total nutrients (applied and stock available in the soil) that is carried forward to the next period or year. For real plant nutrient carryover problems, the state transition is likely more complex than (38), but the simple model suffices to illustrate dynamic optimization.

The objective function for this problem is assumed to be maximization of the discounted present value of profit for the two-period planning horizon. To further simplify the analysis, we assume no *terminal value*. That is, we assume that carryover nutrients have no value past the end of the two-period planning horizon. Discounted present value, PV, is defined as

$$PV = \pi_1 + \beta \pi_2 \tag{39}$$

where β is the discount factor, defined to be $(1/1 + r)$, and where r is the discount rate used to discount future returns. The one-period profit function, π_t, is defined as

$$\pi_t = P_t y_t - v_t x_t \tag{40}$$

where P_t is output price and v_t is factor price. For simplicity, prices at any future time are assumed to be known, and there is only one input.

Substituting the one-period profit equation for π_t (40) into (39) gives

$$PV = P_1 y_1 - v_1 x_1 + \beta(P_2 y_2 - v_2 x_2) \tag{41}$$

To maximize (41) using an ordinary calculus approach, it is imperative to recognize that input levels at *each* time period are treated as separate choice variables. That is, we treat x_1, x_2, y_1, y_2 are choice variables. In optimizing (41) we must also account for the production function constraint, (37), and account for the state transition equation, which can be viewed as a constraint on dynamic optimization.

Much like we did in converting the constrained static optimization problem into an unconstrained optimization problem, we first eliminate output levels as explicit choice variables by substituting the production function for y_t in (41), which gives

$$PV = P_1 y_1(x_1, S_1) - v_1 x_1 + \beta(P_2 y_2(x_2, S_2) - v_2 x_2) \tag{42}$$

Characterizing a Solution to the Dynamic Problem

In optimizing (42) we must also account for the state transition constraint, (38). To *characterize* a solution to this problem, we need only account for this constraint *conceptually* by recognizing the dependence of S_2 on x_1. For formal optimization and for numerically solving such a problem, we must explicitly account for the state transition equation, which we can do by using the Lagrangian approach. However, before using the Lagrangian approach, we gain economic insight by simply conceptually recognizing the state transition equation.

From a conceptual standpoint, the first-order conditions for optimization are given by equating to zero the partial derivatives of (42) with respect to the choice variables in time periods 1 and 2 (x_1 and x_2), recognizing that the choice of x_1 influences S_2 via (38):

$$\frac{\partial PV}{\partial x_1} = P_1 \frac{\partial y_1}{\partial x_2} - v_1 + \beta P_2 \frac{\partial y_2}{\partial S_2} \cdot \frac{\partial S_2}{\partial x_1} = 0 \qquad (43a)$$

$$\frac{\partial PV}{\partial x_2} = \beta P_2 \frac{\partial y_2}{\partial x_2} - \beta v_2 = 0 \qquad (43b)$$

In deriving (43a) we recognized the dependence of S_2 on x_1, which gives the last term in this equation.

To give an economic interpretation to these two first-order conditions, first inspect (43b), which implicitly gives the optimal rate of applied fertilizer in the last period, conditional on the amount of carryover nutrients from the previous year. Rearranging terms in (43b) and noting that the discount factor, β, cancels from the expression gives

$$P_2 \frac{\partial y_2}{\partial x_2} = P_2 \frac{\partial y_2(x_2, S_2)}{\partial x_2} = v_2 \qquad \text{or} \qquad P_2 \cdot MPP_2 = v_2 \qquad (44)$$

Equation (44) simply states that, given carryover nutrients into the second period of the two-period planning horizon, set output price times marginal physical product (MPP_2) equal to factor price. This is exactly the same marginal condition we obtained in the static model in this planning horizon.

Now refer back to first-order condition (43a), which refers to choice in the first period of the two-period problem. Rearranging terms in (43a) and noting from (38) that $\partial S_2/\partial x_1 = \theta$, gives

$$P_1 \frac{\partial y_1}{\partial x_1} + \beta P_2 \theta \frac{\partial y_2}{\partial S_2} = v_1 \qquad (45)$$

Notice that the first term in (45) is the value of the marginal product (in the first period) of fertilizer applied in the first period, given by initial (condition) value of S_1. Consider now the economic interpretation of the second term (carryover effect) on the left-hand side of (45). The expression $(\partial y_2/\partial S_2)\theta$ shows the *future* (next period) crop yield consequences of fertilizer applied in the first time period for the part (θ) that is carried forward to the second period. That is, this partial derivative can be defined as the future marginal physical productivity of fertilizer applied in the first period. Since this partial derivative is multiplied by price and the discount factor, β, raised to the first power, the second term on the left-hand side of (45) is the discounted future value of marginal productivity of fertilizer applied in the first period.

The full economic interpretation of (45) is that we equate the current value of marginal productivity plus the future value of marginal productivity of the current decision to the factor price. That is, we equate first period factor price to the marginal benefits in the first period plus the discounted carryover effect. Ignoring the carryover component would lead to under-application. Extending this model to longer planning horizons would give similar results, except that the stream of discounted benefits would continue for more than one time period.

Dynamic Conditions Using Lagrangians

To simplify notation, assume that a firm produces a single product in time t, whose quantity is defined as y. The product sells for a price P_t. The production function for y_t has as arguments a vector of variable inputs x_t, the stock of capital k_t, and the stock, or level, of externalities z_t. Variable z_t can be thought of as the accumulated level of pollution in the system. Notice this is a slight change in notation in that pollution z_t is an argument of the production function rather than an output or byproduct as in (7):

$$y_t = f(x_t, k_t, z_t) \tag{46}$$

where increases in x or k increase output, but z_t may decrease output when it reaches high levels.

The firm's cost is determined by the variable input level and the rate of capital investment I_t

$$c(x_t, I_t) \tag{47}$$

External costs of the pollutant stock level z_t may affect other producing firms through their production functions if the pollution has common property characteristics. The external costs may also directly influence the utility of other consumers in time t. These general effects are represented by the social cost function

$$q(z_t) \tag{48}$$

For the firm, pollution level is not a choice variable, social costs are not included, and the static profit function for the firm is therefore

$$\pi_t = P_t f(x_t, k_t, z_t) - c(x_t, I_t) \tag{49}$$

This departs from a general externality specification used in Chapter 6 in that the current externality is assumed to be caused by the level of externality z_t and not the current marginal pollution discharges from production in time t. This describes the build-up process for some resource externalities for which the time delay of current decisions on future stocks is considerable. For example, for some ground water contaminants the time delay or "memory" may be over 20 years.

Despite the possible detrimental influence of the externality level z_t on current production, static short-run profit maximization may not internalize the effect. This extreme case of intertemporal failure may sometimes be as widespread in agricultural externalities as the common property effect. Static, first-order conditions on π_t show that the producer does not take into account either the common property effects $q(z_t)$ or the intertemporal impacts:

$$\frac{\partial \pi_t}{\partial x_2} = P_t \frac{\partial f(\cdot)}{\partial x_t} - \frac{\partial c(\cdot)}{\partial x_t} = 0 \tag{50}$$

The short-run impacts of capital investment are also influential:

$$\frac{\partial \pi_t}{\partial I_t} = P_t \frac{\partial f(\cdot)}{\partial k_t} - \frac{\partial c(\cdot)}{\partial I_t} = 0 \tag{51}$$

Equation (51) shows a myopic view of investment in which the marginal cost of investment $[\partial c(\cdot)/\partial I_t]$ has to be justified by its immediate payoff $P_t[\partial f(\cdot)/\partial k_t]$.

This short-run view of firm decision making can be improved by assuming that the firm recognizes and uses two sets of dynamic equations of motion for stocks of pollution and capital, and a finite time horizon. The equation of motion for capital depends on the changes in capital stocks or levels, and the physical rate of deterioration over time ($\delta < 0$) expressed in financial terms:

$$k_{t+1} - k_t = \delta k_t + I_t \tag{52}$$

The pollution stocks z_t are assumed to have some natural rate per unit of time of degradation or absorption α ($\alpha < 0$) and to be augmented by annual pollution discharge (d_t). To simplify the dynamic specification, the time delay for current input use to change resource stocks is assumed to be one period:

$$z_{t+1} - z_t = \alpha z_t + d_t \tag{53}$$

where

$$d_t = d(x_t, k_t), \qquad \partial d/\partial x \geq 0, \quad \text{and} \quad \partial d/\partial k \geq 0$$

Now z_t is implicitly a choice or control variable through d_t. Define a discrete firm decision horizon for the t periods and a discount factor of β_t where

$$\beta_t = \frac{1}{(1 + r)^t} \qquad \text{and } r \text{ is the firm discount rate} \tag{54}$$

The intertemporal firm problem is

$$\text{Max } J = \sum_{t=0}^{T-1} \beta_t \pi(x_t, I_t, k_t, z_t) + \beta_T \pi_T(x_t, k_t, z_t) \tag{55}$$

subject to

$$k_{t+1} - k_t = \delta k_t + I_t$$

$$z_{t+1} - z_t = \alpha z_t + d(x_t, k_t)$$

$$k_0 = \bar{k} \qquad z_0 = \bar{z}$$

The pollution discharge function $d(x_t, k_t)$ recognizes that the level of discharge of pollution by a producing firm is not in constant fixed proportions to output, but is a function of the variable input mix and the capital stocks available for both production and pollution abatement. Considering nitrogen pollution from crop or animal production, the quantity of nitrogen reaching the ground water declines as more precisely applied or costly forms of nitrogen fertilizer are used, or as nitrogen is applied with improved timing or equipment.

The terminal value function, π_T, is singled out from the other time periods because it has different arguments and parameters. Investment level I_T is absent since a profit maximizing firm would not invest for future returns that are beyond the planning horizon (T). The valuation parameters are also different for the terminal value function. Function $\pi_T(\cdot)$ has to reflect the value of capital and pollution stocks on the capitalized value of the firm, such as the market price of assets such as land. (See Chapter 9 for an application to soil erosion.)

The intertemporal problem (55) can be expressed as a Lagrangian by introducing two sets of multiplier variables (one for each period t) for the two sets of equations of motion. The multipliers λ_{t+1} are added to the capital dynamic equation (52) and likewise multipliers γ_{t+1} to the pollution equation of motion (53). The resulting Lagrangian is

$$L = \sum_{t=0}^{T-1} [\beta_t \pi(x_t, I_t, k_t, z_t) - \lambda_{t+1}(k_{t+1} - k_t - \delta k_t - I_t)$$

$$- \gamma_{t+1}(z_{t+1} - z_t - \alpha z_t - d(x_t, k_t))] + \beta_T \pi_T(x_t, k_T, z_T) \qquad (56)$$

The Lagrangian specified in (56) contains three types of endogenous variables: state variables k_t, z_t, control variables I_t, x_t, and multipliers λ_{t+1} and γ_{t+1}. *State variables* are defined as the minimum set of variables that describe the system at any point in time. That is, the level of pollution or capital investment. *Control variables* are those variables that the decision maker can use to change the objective function and state variables.

The first set of dynamic, first-order conditions define the control levels. The now unconstrained control decisions on variable inputs and investment reflect the long- and short-run effects of the decisions on the firm's profit

$$\frac{\partial L}{\partial x_t} = \beta_t \frac{\partial \pi(\cdot)}{\partial x_1} + \gamma_{t+1} \frac{\partial d(\cdot)}{\partial x_t} = 0 \qquad (57)$$

The discounted net marginal effect on profits of an additional unit of variable input such as nitrogen is now balanced by the long-run cost of the externality on the firm in the second term of (57). The long-run cost $\gamma_{t+1}[\partial d(\cdot)/\partial x_t]$ reflects the marginal effect of an input x_t on the pollution level and the marginal cost of the pollution z_t on the firm. This cost is transmitted through the multiplier γ_{t+1}, which has a negative impact on the firm's profits in the future. If the social cost function $q(z_t)$ was internalized into the firm's decisions as was the case for the penalty in (10) or (13), the long-run cost of the externality would include both the private and social costs.

A comparison with the static first-order conditions is shown by removing the dynamic components from equation (57). A static version of (57) would have a discount factor $\beta_t = 1$, and the marginal effect on future stocks $\partial d(\cdot)/\partial x_t$ would be zero by definition. Under this situation, equation (57) reduces to $\partial \pi(\cdot)/\partial x_t = 0$, which is identical with the first-order condition in equation (50).

The first-order condition for optimal investment balances the current net return on capital plus the marginal value of the future capital stock through λ_{t+1}:

$$\frac{\partial L}{\partial I_t} = \beta_t \frac{\partial \pi(\cdot)}{\partial I_t} + \lambda_{t+1} = 0 \tag{58}$$

The last set of first-order conditions are

$$\frac{\partial L}{\partial \lambda_{t+1}} = k_{t+1} - k_t - \delta k_t - I_t = 0 \tag{59}$$

$$\frac{\partial L}{\partial \gamma_{t+1}} = z_{t+1} - z_t - \alpha z_t - d(x_t, k_t) = 0 \tag{60}$$

The partial derivatives of (56) with respect to the multipliers λ_{t+1} and γ_{t+1} ensure that the equations of motion describing capital and pollution changes over time are satisified in all time periods. It is important to note that this problem incorporates both the financial dynamics of capital and investment in equation (52) and the physical or biological dynamics in equation (53). This explicit incorporation of a physical stock flow relationship in the economical model is the key to deriving economic policies that are consistent with the physical response and constraints of the system. Traditional biologically oriented resource managers are more likely to accept economic conditions that directly incorporate critical biological relationships.

The two sets of first-order conditions in (57) and (58) are dynamic analogs to the static Lagrangian first-order conditions. The conditions that result from setting the derivative of the Lagrangian with respect to the state variables equal to zero also has a uniquely dynamic interpretation:

$$\frac{\partial L}{\partial k_t} = \beta_t \frac{\partial \pi(\cdot)}{\partial k_t} - \lambda_t + \lambda_{t+1} + \lambda_{t+1}\delta + \gamma_{t+1} \frac{\partial d(\cdot)}{\partial k_t} = 0 \tag{61}$$

Notice that the $-\lambda_t$ term comes from the preceding term in the sum in the Lagrangian. Rearranging the terms results in

$$\lambda_{t+1} - \lambda_t = -\beta_t \frac{\partial \pi(\cdot)}{\partial k_t} - \lambda_{t+1}\delta - \gamma_{t+1} \frac{\partial d(\cdot)}{\partial k_t} \tag{62}$$

Since λ_t is the marginal value of the capital stock over the remaining time horizon at time t, equation (62) shows how the marginal value of capital changes over the time interval t to $t + 1$. The first term on the right-hand side of (62) is the present value of the effect of the capital stock on the profit function over the interval t to $t + 1$. The second term is the cost of the depreciation per unit of capital over the period, while the third term is the marginal cost of the externality stock times the change in externality stock that a unit change in capital investment causes.

The changing value of the externality stock has a parallel interpretation

$$\frac{\partial L}{\partial z_1} = \beta_t \frac{\partial \pi}{\partial z_t} - \gamma_t + \gamma_{t+1} + \gamma_{t+1}\alpha = 0 \tag{63}$$

or rearranging terms

$$\gamma_{t+1} - \gamma_t = -\beta_t \frac{\partial \pi}{\partial z_t} - \gamma_{t+1}\alpha \tag{64}$$

The change in marginal cost of the externality stock is equal to the discounted marginal effect on profit of a marginal change in the externality stock, less the rate of assimilation of the externality times its marginal value.

The three sets of Lagrangian relationships above illustrate three key aspects of dynamic resource allocation. First, the biological and financial dynamics of the resource and capital equations (59) and (60) must be explicitly modeled. Second, the long-run and short-run impacts of current decisions must be considered in equations (57) and (58). The long-run effects are a combination of biological dynamics and marginal stock value. Third, the marginal value or cost of stocks is shown to change in a systematic manner over time in equations (62) and (64).

A simplification of the Lagrangian conditions is possible by noticing that a mathematical expressions called a *discrete time* Hamiltonian is embedded in the Lagrangian conditions. Defining a discrete time Hamiltonian at t as

$$H_t(x_t, I_t, k_t, z_t, \lambda_t, \gamma_t) = \beta_t \pi(x_t, I_t, k_t, z_t) - \lambda_{t+1}(-\delta k_t - I_t)$$
$$- \gamma_{t+1}(-\alpha z_t - d(x_t, k_t)) \tag{65}$$

the Lagrangian (56) can now be written as

$$L = \sum_{t=0}^{T-1} (H_t(x_t, I_t, k_t, z_t, \lambda_t, \gamma_t) - \lambda_{t+1}(k_{t+1} - k_t)$$
$$- \gamma_{t+1}(z_{t+1} - z_t) + \beta_T \pi_T(x_T, k_T, z_t) \tag{66}$$

For simplicity, the three types of endogenous variables are grouped and redefined as

States	$k_t, z_t \equiv s_t$
Controls	$x_t, I_t \equiv u_t$
Multipliers	$\gamma_t, \lambda_t \equiv \phi_t$

The Hamiltonian on the left-hand side of equation (65) can now be more compactly written as $H_t(s_t, u_t, \phi_t)$ using this condensed notation.

The Lagrangian first-order conditions can now be written in terms of the discrete time Hamiltonian:

$$\frac{\partial H(\cdot)}{\partial u_t} = 0 \tag{67}$$

which is equivalent to (57) and (58), and

$$\frac{\partial H(\cdot)}{\partial \phi_{t+1}} = g(s_t, u_t) = s_{t+1} - s_t \tag{68}$$

equivalent to (59) and (60), where $g(s_t, u_t)$ is a general equation of motion. Finally,

$$-\frac{\partial H(\cdot)}{\partial s_t} = \phi_{t+1} - \phi_t \tag{69}$$

is equivalent to equations (62) and (64).

The multipliers ϕ in the model differ from the usual Lagrangian multipliers, in that the first-order conditions (69) show that they are linked over time by the difference equation. As the biological or capital equations are the physical linkage of the system over time, the difference equation linking ϕ_t over time is the intertemporal value linkage. Thus the multipliers ϕ_t have been given a particular name; they are called costates or sometimes adjoint variables. Since the original problem (55) is defined as maximizing the present value in discrete time, ϕ_t are called discrete time present value costate variables. The costate variables are widely used in resource economics and generally termed *user costs*.

The costate equation (69) indicates how dynamic market failure may occur. Equations (67) and (57) indicate that the level of an externality generating input depends on current profits and the long-run costs reflected through the costate variable associated with the externality stock. If the costate variables accurately reflect future externality costs back to the present, optimal intertemporal internalization will result. Examination of the costate variables reflects the three situations that cause dynamic market failure. Rewriting (69) for the externality stock z_t using (64) yields

$$\phi_t = \phi_{t+1} + \beta_t \frac{\partial \pi}{\partial z_t} + \phi_{t+1}\alpha \tag{70}$$

The current marginal value (ϕ_t) is equal to the future marginal value (ϕ_{t+1}) plus the additional discounted costs in the current period $\beta(\partial\pi/\partial z_t)$, and is adjusted for the marginal value of any physical change in the externality stock $\phi_{t+1}\alpha$ that happened during the period. By successive substitution or solving the difference equation (69) we could determine that the current marginal cost of the externality stock is the discounted sum of the profit lost from all future discrete time periods, modified by changes in the physical stock from accumulation or assimilation. However, in some cases common property features of d_t make firm decisions difficult. For example, pesticide use that builds up future pest resistance is an example in which the optimal dynamic conditions in equation (70) are usually violated. Owing to the common property nature of pesticide resistance in a cropping region, a grower will not experience the full marginal future cost of resistance ϕ_{t+1}, but rather his fraction of increased resistance ϕ_{t+1}/n, where there are n growers in a given pest region. As the number of growers, n, gets large, the future value of marginal change in the common pesticide resistance gets very low, and the optimizing grower applies pesticides in a short-sighted socially suboptimal manner. (See the elaboration in Chapter 7.) There are many other examples in which the common property rights of agricultural resources cause their use to differ from the dynamic optimal allocation.

The time sequence ends in this model with the terminal value function $\pi_T(x_T, k_T, z_T)$. Optimal dynamic resource allocation requires three conditions. The private and social discount factor β_t should not differ. The firm must have full information on the future physical changes of the externality stock and the effect of controls on them. The firm must use a terminal value function at the end of its planning horizon that accurately reflects the future value of the externality and capital stocks. With uncertainties and long lags associated with many resources and externalities, the pervasiveness of dynamic and common property externalities is not surprising.

A CONTINUOUS TIME SPECIFICATION OF RESOURCE USE OVER TIME[1]

Theoretical dynamic problems are usually posed in continuous time, since the comparative dynamic properties are easier to derive than in discrete time. The firm problem in equation (55) is defined in continuous time over a finite horizon by replacing the summation of periodic profits by an integral over time. Likewise the discount rate is continuous, and the equations of motion for the states, stocks or pollution, and capital are expressed as continuous rates of change. The present value firm problem in continuous time is specified using condensed notation. A widely used shorthand for a time derivative is $\dot{s} \equiv \partial s_t / \partial t$. Using this notation,

$$\text{Max} \int_{t=0}^{T} e^{-rt} \pi(s_t, u_t)\, dt + e^{-rt} F(s_T) \tag{71}$$

subject to

$$\dot{s} = g(s_t, u_t), \qquad s_{t_0} = \bar{s}$$

where $F(s_T)$ is the *terminal value function*, s_t is the set of state variables, u_t is the set of controls, and g is a general equation of motion. The corresponding Hamiltonian is (Pontryagin et al., 1962)

$$H_t(s, u, \phi) = e^{-rt} \pi(s_t, u_t) + \phi_t g(s_t, u_t) \tag{72}$$

The resulting first-order conditions, which are part of the Pontryagin maximum principle, are analogous to equations (67), (68), and (69). More specifically, they are the derivatives of the Hamiltonian in (72) with respect to the control variables u_t, the *costate variables* ϕ_t, and the negative of the derivative with respect to the

---

[1] This section is optional and not necessary to understand most dynamic problems in this book, except the last part of Chapter 3.

state variable:

$$\frac{\partial H}{\partial u_t} = e^{-rt}\frac{\partial \pi(\cdot)}{\partial u_t} + \phi_t\frac{\partial g(\cdot)}{\partial u_t} = 0 \tag{73a}$$

$$\frac{\partial H}{\partial \phi_t} = g(s_t, u_t) = \dot{s}_t \tag{73b}$$

$$-\frac{\partial H}{\partial s_t} = -e^{-rt}\frac{\partial H(\cdot)}{\partial s_t} - \phi_t\frac{\partial g(\cdot)}{\partial s_t} = \dot{\phi}_t \tag{73c}$$

and

$$s_{t_0} = \bar{s}, \qquad \phi_T = \frac{\partial(e^{-rt}F(s_T))}{\partial s_T} \tag{73d}$$

The three unconstrained maximum principle first-order conditions have analogous interpretations to the discrete time conditions (57)–(64) derived from the Lagrangian specification.

If the discrete-time difference between any $t + 1$ and t is defined as Δt, then the continuous time case follows when Δt gets very small (formally $\Delta t \rightarrow 0$). While empirical examples are invariably measured in discrete time units such as days, months, or years, the continuous time specification makes theoretical derivations using calculus much easier.

Equation (73a) is the continuous time control condition. The discount rate r is now an instantaneous rate and the costate is now defined at every time period t, rather than the discrete future point of $t + 1$. The interpretation of (73a) is exactly the same as (57), in that the condition balances the long- and short-run impacts of the control action. In the continuous time case, the marginal value of the state variable ϕ_t is changing continuously; thus the future cost of the control is continuously updated, and the impact on future levels of states is continuously measured through the equations of motion. The control variables u_t can be thought of as a vector with x_t and I_t as elements. Thus both equations (57) and (58) have their continuous time equivalents in equation (73a).

Equation (73b) is the continuous time equation of motion. Since s_t is a vector of state values at time t, the equation is equivalent to equations (59) and (60), which are in discrete time. Thinking of the states as vectors enables a more general simultaneous specification among the state (s_t) and control (u_t) variables to be specified.

Equation (73c) is the continuous time costate equation. Since the equation of motion, the objective function, and the discount rate are all measured in continuous time, the costate value that depends on them must also be continuously changing. Equations (62) and (64) are discrete time equivalents of (73c), but the parallels can be seen more closely between the more general discrete time statement in equations (69) and (73c). In the latter equation, the marginal value of the costate is continuously changing. The negative sign on the Hamiltonian derivative comes directly from Pontryagin's maximum principle, but has a strong intuitive basis. Since the Hamiltonian is defined in terms of positive values from the impact of states and controls on the profit function, the value of a stock depends on the future stream of profit flows. The problems considered here are finite, that is, they have a well-defined ending point in time T. Thus as time progresses in the problem, the potential stream of benefits from a given stock (or state) is shorter, and ceteris paribus, one would expect the marginal value of the stock to diminish as one got closer and closer to the problem end point.

Simplifying the problem by ignoring the capital stock, the change in value of the stock of pollution can be clarified by following an exposition used by Dorfman (1969) and Kamien and Schwartz (1981). The maximum value (J^*) to the firm of producing while generating internalized pollution stocks z_t over the horizon is

$$J^* = \int_{t=0}^{T} [\pi(x_t, z_t) + \phi_t g(x_t, z_t) - \phi_t \dot{z}_t] \, dt \tag{74}$$

Separating the integral on the third term and integrating by parts results in

$$-\int_{t=0}^{T} \phi_t \dot{z}_t \, dt = -\phi_t z_t \Big|_{t=0}^{T} + \int_{t=0}^{T} \dot{\phi}_t z_t \, dt \tag{75}$$

where $\dot{\phi}_t = d\phi_t/dt$ is the instantaneous change in the costate value. Substituting (75) back into (74) yields

$$J^* = \int_{t=0}^{T} [\pi(x_t, z_t) + \phi_t g(x_t, z_t) + \dot{\phi}_t z_t] \, dt - \phi_T z_T + \phi_{t_0} z_{t_0} \tag{76}$$

where x_t and z_t are at their optimal levels.

The cost of a stock of pollution at any time is the product of the number of units of pollution and the marginal cost per unit. That is, $\phi_t z_t$ is the current valuation of the stock. Equation (76) thus states that the difference between the initial and ending pollution costs $\phi_{t_0} z_{t_0} - \phi_T z_T$ is the integral in the square brackets. Since $\dot{z}_t = g(z_t, x_t)$ is an identity we can substitute it into (76). Thus the rate of change of externality cost at time t is

$$\pi(x_t z_t) + \phi_t \dot{z}_t + \dot{\phi}_t z_t \tag{77}$$

Since the total capitalized cost of the pollutant stock at t is $\phi_t z_t$, the change in total cost is

$$\frac{d(\phi_t z_t)}{dt} = \phi_t \dot{z}_t + \dot{\phi}_t z_t \tag{78}$$

Equation (77) says that the change in total capitalized cost of a pollution stock can occur from three influences, the current profit foregone at t, $\pi(x_t z_t)$, the value of a change in the physical quantity of pollution $\phi_t \dot{z}_t$, or the change in the cost or asset value of a given stock of pollution $\dot{\phi} z_t$.

So far the Lagrange and Hamiltonian specifications have been proposed in terms of present value from the viewpoint of a forward-looking planner. In many cases it is more useful to pose testable hypotheses of behavior in current value terms. The *current value Hamiltonian* can be viewed as the present value Hamiltonian (which discounts values back from time t to time t_0), compounded forward to time t. Defining the current value Hamiltonian as $\hat{H}$,

$$\hat{H}_t(\cdot) = e^{rt} H_t(\cdot) \tag{79}$$

or using (72)

$$\hat{H}_t(s, u, m) = \pi(s_t u_t) + m_t g(s_t u_t) \tag{80}$$

where the current value costate variable m_t is defined as

$$m_t \equiv e^{rt} \phi_t \tag{81}$$

Of the three maximum principle conditions, the following two are unchanged by the shift from present to current values:

$$\left.\begin{aligned} \frac{\partial \hat{H}_t}{\partial u_t} &= 0 \\ \frac{\partial \hat{H}_t}{\partial m_t} &= \dot{s}_t \end{aligned}\right\} \tag{82}$$

The costate condition does change because the current value costate variable m_t is a product of the change in discount factor and the change in costate. Taking the time derivative of equation (81)

$$\dot{m}_t = r e^{rt} \phi_t + e^{rt} \dot{\phi}_t \tag{83}$$

Since in present values $\dot{\phi}_t = -(\partial H_t / \partial s_t)$ from equation (73c), and using equation (81), (83) can be rewritten now using (79)

$$\left.\begin{aligned} \dot{m}_t &= r m_t - e^{rt} \frac{\partial H_t}{\partial s_t} \\ \dot{m} &= r m_t - \frac{\partial \hat{H}_t(\cdot)}{\partial s_t} \end{aligned}\right\} \tag{84}$$

or rearranging terms

$$-\frac{\partial \hat{H}_t(\cdot)}{\partial s_t} = \dot{m}_t - r m_t \tag{85}$$

Thus, balancing current values between time periods requires that the marginal value of a stock is changed by the opportunity cost of money over a time instant as well as changes in the other marginal values. Rearranging (85) and expanding $\hat{H}(\cdot)$, we obtain the basic *arbitrage relationship* for dynamic equilibrium in a capital market

$$\dot{m}_t + \frac{\partial \pi_t(\cdot)}{\partial s_t} + m_t \frac{\partial \dot{s}_t}{\partial s_t} = r m_t \tag{86}$$

Recall that $\dot{s}$ in the condensed notation of (86) is the physical change in resource or pollution stocks over time. Equation (86) states that the sum of capital appreciation, $\dot{m}_t$, current value of marginal value product, $[\partial \pi(\cdot)/\partial s_t]$, and the value of marginal rates of change in the capital stock $[m_t(\partial \dot{s}_t / \partial s_t)]$ are equal to the opportunity cost of the capital value $(r m_t)$ at all points on the dynamic equilibrium path.

Alternatively, the key relationship in equation (86) can be considered as the conditions under which one would be indifferent to holding or selling a unit of resource over a period t. The costs of holding the asset are the opportunity cost of the asset and the physical depreciation. At an opportunity cost interest rate r, and a current marginal value of m_t, the opportunity cost is rm_t. During the time period, the stock of resource may physically depreciate; this change in the rate of depreciation is represented by $\partial \dot{s}_t / \partial s_t$. The unit cost of this depreciation change is $m_t(\partial \dot{s}_t / \partial s_t)$. Returns from owning the resource come in two ways, current profits shown here as $\partial \pi_t(\cdot)/\partial s_t$ and capital appreciation of the resource stock $\dot{m}_t$. Equation (86) states that the dynamic equilibrium exists when one is indifferent between holding the stock of resource s_t, or its value in some other interest earning asset such as a bond paying r percent interest

$$\dot{m}_t + \frac{\partial \pi(\cdot)}{\partial s_t} = rm_t - m_t \frac{\partial \dot{s}_t}{\partial s_t} \tag{87}$$

Simply put, if net returns plus capital appreciation equal the cost of depreciation plus opportunity cost, the capital stock s_t is in dynamic equilibrium. This relationship explains many situations in which an investment in an agricultural resource shows a negative current cash flow, but the investor relies on capital appreciation to balance the opportunity cost over time.

In terms of resource allocation in production this explains many cases that appear irrational in a comparative static specification. Under dynamic conditions, counterintuitive decisions on crop production and long-term pollution are usually rational given high opportunity costs of capital, low rates of accumulation, and uncertain terminal cost functions. Two agricultural resource examples illustrate this point.

Equation (87) is the basis for the economic theory of crop rotations. Most forms of agriculture rotate crops of differing profitability on the same land area. For simplicity consider two crops, a high value "cash" crop that depletes the soil fertility and a low value "rotation" crop, possibly leguminous, that improves the soil fertility. How much land should be assigned to the rotation crop? The answer lies in equation (87). Define the stock of land s_t to be an acre. Ignoring soil erosion, we can set the change in land $\dot{s}_t = 0$ in a given year. The opportunity cost of the land is determined by its net revenue in the profitable cash crop and the discount rate, shown in equation (87) as rm_t. The current profit from the rotation crop is $\partial \pi(\cdot)/\partial s_t$. In a static analysis the rotation crop would only be grown when the yield of the cash crop was reduced by low fertility, so that the VMP of the cash crop equalled the VMP of the rotational crop. This holds when

$$\frac{\partial \pi(\cdot)}{\partial s_t} = rm_t \tag{88}$$

Clearly this ignores the benefits from the rotation crop in the future. The optimal dynamic decision is to equate the sum of current net revenues $\partial \pi(\cdot)/\partial s_t$ and the value of future fertility increases $\dot{m}_t$ to the opportunity cost of the cash crop. This leads to

$$\frac{\partial \pi(\cdot)}{\partial s_t} + \dot{m}_t = rm_t \qquad (89)$$

That is, the dynamic optimal solution leads to a greater proportion of land in rotation than the static analysis.

The arbitrage relation in equation (87) also explains supply response behavior in the cattle and other livestock industries. In this example s_t is the breeding herd stock. Assume that the net reproductive rate is fixed, and for simplicity we ignore genetic improvement by culling, although this can also be analyzed by equation (86). Given stable price expectations for cattle and the culling assumption, $\dot{m}_t = 0$.

The general equation of motion, $\dot{s} = g(s_t, u_t)$ can be interpreted in this cattle example as representing the effect on the herd of mortality, birth, and sales. The derivative $\partial g(s_t, u_t)/\partial s_t$ is the net per unit reproductive rate. Since this can be assumed to be positive, setting $\dot{m} = 0$, equation (87) can be rewritten as

$$\frac{\partial \pi}{\partial s_t} = \left(r - \frac{\partial \dot{s}_t}{\partial s_t} \right) m_t \qquad (90)$$

The short-run returns to the herd ($\partial \pi / \partial s_t$) are constant, and in steady state under two conditions. Dynamic expectations equilibrium, $\dot{m} = 0$, and equilibrium between the biological discount rate $\partial \dot{s}_t / \partial s_t$ and the financial discount rate r. Under these conditions the opportunity cost of capital in the herd is balanced by its net reproductive rate.

Since the herd can only expand by reducing sales of cattle, $\partial \pi / \partial s_t$ is negative. The reduction in sales will reduce short-run profits. This condition is in dynamic equilibrium if the net reproductive rate exceeds the discount rate, and the right-hand side of (90) is negative. Conversely, if the financial discount rate exceeds the biological rate, the optimal financial action is to sell down the herd, possible to extinction. This occurs with Blue whales and other slowly reproducing biological resources.

An interesting extension of the idea is to consider a cattle price increase. The current net returns $\partial \pi(\cdot)/\partial s_t$ increase, but since m_t, the current value costate, depends on the stream of future prices (equation 70), m_t will also increase making it more desirable to expand the herd. If the price increase leads the optimistic rancher to expect yet further price increases, $\dot{m}_t$ will be positive, and subtracting this from the right-hand side of equation (90) results in a condition that says that the rancher should expand his herd. Thus one gets a negative short-run supply response, in that the effect of a price rise will be to reduce the cattle currently offered for sale.

Cattlemen know these perverse short-run effects occur, but until one looks at the dynamic theory, common practical behavior is hard to explain in static micro theory. For a deep and general theoretical explanation of dynamic supply phenomena see Caputo (1990). Antle and Howitt (1988) develop an example in international markets.

Constraints and Complications

Second-order conditions for dynamic problems can be complicated if stated in a rigorous manner (Kamien and Schwartz, 1981). For the interpretation, it is sufficient to use intuition on the Hamiltonian function. The Hamiltonian was shown above to characterize all the current and future effects on value; thus the second-order conditions will ensure a unique maximization of the Hamiltonian at all points in time. The first-order conditions for maximizing the unconstrained Hamiltonian simply equated the first partial derivatives to zero (67) and (73a). The second-order conditions for this case that are not general but usually suffice are that the Hamiltonian function is concave in states s_t and controls u_t at all time periods. Since state variables (s_t) can only be altered via controls, the simple second-order condition can be stated as

$$H_{uu} \leq 0 \qquad (91)$$

Constraints on the control variables have also been carefully avoided so far, but are critical to many empirical applications of firm comparative resource allocation. Constraints on control variables, and hence state variables, are easily incorporated in the discrete time Lagrangian approach. Dynamic inequality constraints are specified as time-independent Lagrangian constraints that are appended to the Hamiltonian. Where a control constraint is binding the constraint modifies the current control and state level, and thus also modifies the costate values for all time periods prior to the binding constraint. This counterintuitive result can be seen from the structure of equation (70). The costate value is *backwards recursive* in time with the recursive sequence starting at T and ending at t_0. Thus, the current value of the costate is dependent on the optimal actions to be taken in the future. The unconstrained dynamic optimization calculates the present costate variables and hence policy actions, on the assumption that the decision maker will be able to act optimally in future decisions. If unforeseen binding constraints prevent optimal action in the future, the supposedly optimal decisions in the past are now suboptimal. Unconstrained dynamic optimization subject to future constraints can be summarized by the phrase "It seemed a good idea at the time."

The interdependence of time periods significantly complicates the optimal constrained trajectory. Pontryagin's main contribution was in incorporating the constraint structure into the optimization conditions. For many empirical optimal control applications that use the backwards recursive solution suggested by Bellman (1957), constraints are a major problem. This does not apply to Bellman's proposal of using dynamic programming.

One common special case of constrained controls in microeconomic resource applications is termed "Bang Bang" controls. The bang bang control may occur when the control variable is linear in the Hamiltonian. In this case the first-order condition in (67) $\partial H(\cdot)/\partial u_t = 0$ results in the control action being on or off. If on, the control is set to the maximum upper bound; if off, the control is set to the lower bound constraint.

Reverting to the earlier example of polluting firm and the present valued

Hamiltonian specified in (65), the first-order condition for investment is

$$\frac{\partial H(\cdot)}{\partial I_t} = \beta_t \frac{\partial \pi(\cdot)}{\partial I_t} + \lambda_{t+1} = 0 \tag{92}$$

Equation (92) is termed the singular value function. In time periods when the future marginal value of capital λ_{t+1} exceeds the current reduction in profit from investment, investment should be maximized to its upper limit. If the opposite holds, investment is zero since it is usually considered irreversible. If the condition (92) holds exactly over time, the resulting trajectory of states and controls is termed the singular path.

Why is so much notation needed? In this chapter an attempt is made to take the reader from the familiar terminology of calculus and Lagrangians to perceptions of Pontryagin. This requires the development of the concepts of Hamiltonians, costates, terminal conditions, and their associated conclusions. In the analysis of resource use behavior and policy where "time is of the essence." one must have an analytical basis for realistic models and testable hypotheses. Just as it now seems hard to imagine understanding static microtheory without using Lagrange and calculus, so we believe future resource and production analysis will be incomprehensible without an elementary understanding of the maximum principle and Hamiltonians. Even if resource economists were convinced that statics were an adequate approximation for economic decisions, the dominance of the physical and biological dynamics of resource use and pollution accumulation forces economists to acknowledge the stock and flow properties of the problem. Given this essential characteristic, formal incorporation of the physical relationships with the microeconomics and institutions follows. The richness and reality of the dynamic behavioral conditions make the effort worthwhile.

REFERENCES

Anderson, J.R., J.L. Dillon, and J.B. Hardaker. *Agricultural Decision Analysis.* Ames, IA: Iowa State University Press, 1977.

Antle, J.M. and R.E. Howitt. "Economic Analysis of Agricultural Resources in an Open Economy: A Hybrid Model." In J.D. Sutton (ed.); *Agricultural Trade and Natural Resources.* Boulder, CO: Lynne Rienner, 1988.

Beattie, B.R. and C.R. Taylor. *The Economies of Production.* New York: John Wiley and Sons, 1985.

Bellman, R. *Dynamic Programming.* Princeton, NJ: Princeton University Press, 1957.

Caputo, M.R. "How to do Comparative Dynamics on the Back of an Envelope in Optimal Control Theory." *Journal of Economic Dynamics and Control* 14:655–683, 1990.

Chiang, A.C. *Fundamental Methods of Mathematical Economics.* New York: McGraw-Hill, 1974.

Dorfman, R. "An Economic Interpretation of Optimal Control Theory." *American Economics Review* 57:817–825, 1969.

Howe, C.W. *Benefit–Cost Analysis for Water System Planning.* Washington, D.C.: American Geophysical Union, 1971.

Just, R.E. and R. Pope. "Production Function Estimation and Related Risk Considerations." *American Journal of Agricultural Economics* 61(2):276–284, 1979.

Kamien, M.J. and N.L. Schwartz. *Dynamic Optimization.* New York: Elsevier, 1981.

Lambert, P.J. *Advanced Mathematics for Economists.* New York: Basil Blackwell, 1985.

Magnusson, G. *Production Under Risk: A Theoretical Study.* Uppsala, Sweden: Almquist and Wiksells, 1969.

McInerney, J. "The Simple Analytics of Natural Resource Economics." *Journal of Agricultural Economics* 27:31–52, 1976.

Paris, Q. *An Economic Interpretation of Linear Programming.* Ames, IA: Iowa State University Press, 1991.

Pontryagin, L.S.V.G. Boltyanskii, R.V. Gamkrelidze, and E.F. Mischenko. *The Mathematical Theory of Optimal Processes.* New York: John Wiley, 1962.

Ricardo, D. *Principles of Political Economy and Taxation.* London: G. Bell and Sons, 1903.

Roumasset, J.A., J.M. Boussard, and I. Sing (eds). *Risk, Uncertainty and Agricultural Development.* New York: Agricultural Development Council, 1979.

Rucker, R. and P.V. Fishback. "The Federal Reclamation Program: An Analysis of Rent-Seeking Behavior." In T.L. Anderson (ed.): *Water Rights: Scarce Resource Allocation, Bureaucracy and the Environment.* San Francisco: Pacific Institute for Public Policy Studies, 1983.

Sandmo, A. "On the Theory of the Competitive Firm Under Price Uncertainty." *American Economic Review* 61(2):65–73, 1971.

Turnovsky, S.J. "The Behaviour of a Competitive Firm with Uncertainty in Factor Markets." *New Zealand Economic Papers* 3(1):52–58, 1969.

Whitcomb, D. *Externalities and Welfare.* New York: Columbia University Press, 1972.

APPENDIX 2.1

The impact of uncertain input costs on production decisions can be found following the logic used in Sandmo (1971) for uncertain output prices.

Define the production function for a single output y using a single resource input x

$$y = f(x) \qquad f'(x) > 0 \qquad f''(x) < 0 \tag{a1}$$

The output price P is known, but the cost of the resource whose scarcity varies has a known distribution

$$c \sim N(\bar{c}, \sigma_c^2) \tag{a2}$$

If FC are fixed production costs, the profit function is

$$\pi(x) = Pf(x) - cx - FC \tag{a3}$$

Using the utility function

$$u(\pi) \qquad u'(\pi) > 0 \qquad u''(\pi) < 0 \tag{a4}$$

the expected utility of profit is

$$E\{u(Pf(x) - cx - FC)\} \tag{a5}$$

The first- and second-order conditions for the optimal resource allocation are

$$E\{u'(\pi)(Pf'(x) - c)\} = 0 \tag{a6}$$

$$E\{u''(\pi)(Pf'(x) - c)^2 - u'(\pi)(Pf''(x))\} < 0 \tag{a7}$$

Factoring condition (a6) and subtracting $E(u'(\pi)\bar{c})$ from both sides, we obtain

$$E\{u'(\pi)(Pf'(x) - \bar{c})\} = E\{u'(\pi)(c - \bar{c})\} \tag{a8}$$

Since $E(\pi) = Pf(x) - \bar{c} - FC$, then

$$E(\pi) + (\bar{c} - c)x = Pf(x) - \bar{c}x - FC + \bar{c}x - cx = \pi \tag{a9}$$

therefore

$$\pi = E(\pi) + (\bar{c} - c)x \tag{a10}$$

If $\bar{c} > c$ then $\pi > E(\pi)$ and from the properties of the utility function

$$u'(\pi) < u'(E(\pi)) \qquad \text{if} \qquad \bar{c} > c \tag{a11}$$

and therefore

$$u'(\pi)(\bar{c} - c) < u'(E(\pi))(\bar{c} - c) \tag{a12}$$

The relationship (a12) also holds if $\bar{c} < c$ because $u'(\pi) > u'(E(\pi))$ but the sign of $(\bar{c} - c)$ is changed, thus, reversing this effect. Therefore, (a12) holds for all $\bar{c}$ and c. Taking expectations of both sides of (a12)

$$E[u'(\pi)(\bar{c} - c)] < u'(E(\pi))E(\bar{c} - c) \tag{a13}$$

Since $E(\bar{c} - c) = 0$ (a13) implies that

$$E[u'(\pi)(\bar{c} - c)] < 0 \tag{a14}$$

Since

$$u'(\pi) > 0 \qquad \therefore (\bar{c} - c) < 0 \qquad \therefore (c - \bar{c}) > 0$$

Therefore substituting $E[u'(\pi)(c - \bar{c})$ into equation (a8)

$$E[u'(\pi)(Pf'(x) - \bar{c}] > 0 \tag{a15}$$

which implies that $Pf'(x) > \bar{c}$ at the optimum. In other words, expected utility is maximized when the value marginal product exceeds the expected factor cost.

3

The Economics of Nonrenewable and Renewable Resources

DAVID ZILBERMAN, MICHAEL WETZSTEIN, AND
MICHELE MARRA

When considering optimal resource use, a long-run perspective of resource management is required. A decision today may result in alteration of the resource base for years into the future. Individuals derive utility from both present and future resource use, where future resource use is composed of not only the individual's but also future generations' consumption. Thus, it is appropriate to consider long-run consequences in resource analyses and policies.

Economic modeling and analysis of the dynamics of natural resource use depend upon whether a resource is categorized as nonrenewable or renewable. Such categorization is not always an either-or proposition but is a continuum along which a resource can be placed. Placement depends upon several factors, including whether the resource can be returned to its preuse state (at a reasonable cost) within some relevant time frame.

Occasionally, the existence of available substitutes is relevant. Consider the case of a crop pest's genetic stock that responds to a certain pesticide. Over time, this genetic resource may be depleted as the pest develops resistance to the pesticide. However, other genetic characteristics of the pest may substitute for the depleted resource. Specifically, there might exist other cost-effective methods of control, either chemical or biological, which will substitute for the loss. If alternative methods do exist, then this resource is, in a sense, renewable. If they do not exist, the resource is best categorized as nonrenewable.

Another factor categorizing nonrenewable or renewable resources is the viewpoint of final resource users. For example, consider a stand of virgin forest. If society considers this forest to have value because virgin forests are becoming quite scarce, then it is at the nonrenewable end of the continuum. On the other hand, forest regrowth generally occurs within an economically relevant time frame at a reasonable cost, and thus, one stand of trees has many substitutes for the production of forest products. If society places little value on the forest being virgin, the resource is nearer the renewable end of the continuum.

Technological advances, including new exploration and mining techniques or chemical water treatments, have changed the nonrenewable and renewable categorization of certain resources over time. Given continued technological advances, some resources currently categorized as nonrenewable may be considered renewable in the future.

Renewability of a resource does not depend on the absolute length of time it takes to return to some preuse state but rather on whether that length of time is acceptable to resource users. Many natural systems are regenerated so slowly that a preuse state is achieved too far in the future to be relevant for making current decisions. The relevance of future resources and depletion rates depends upon how much future use is discounted relative to the present.

DISCOUNTING THE FUTURE

Discounting is a technique for calculating the present value of a future stream of benefits minus costs, net returns. The generally accepted method of comparing costs and benefits occurring at different points in time is to reflect their value in the same time period. Discounting assumes that individuals place a lower value on events, including resource use, occurring in future time periods relative to present or current events. Specifically, they discount the value associated with future resource use.

Interest Rate Determination

An interest rate is similar to a market-determined price for an exchange of goods or services at a point in time. It is the price in a market where trades are made across time. Suppliers are individuals who are willing to forego some consumption possibilities today, by saving, in exchange for greater consumption possibilities in the future. These savers generally must be compensated for waiting because they would prefer to consume today, given the choice of consumption today versus the same level of consumption in some future period. Specifically, they exhibit a certain impatience or time preference. Curve S in Figure 3.1. represents an indifference curve showing this rate of time preference between consumption now (C_t) and consumption later (C_{t+1}) for a homogeneous group of savers in an intertemporal market. It is assumed that indifference curves exhibit the property of diminishing marginal rate of substitution. The steeper, more negatively sloped, is S, the more these individuals prefer current consumption to future consumption, and thus the higher the rate of compensation required to entice them to forego a marginal unit of C_t.

Demanders of this foregone current consumption are individuals who are willing and able to pay suppliers a rate of compensation for current consumption. In Figure 3.1, curve IPP represents demanders' intertemporal production possibilities curve. The slope of IPP represents the rate at which present production can be transformed into future production, given the current state of technology and a fixed resource base.

If all resources are devoted to present production, OY_t can be produced and consumed. If all resources are saved for the future period, OY_{t+1} could be produced

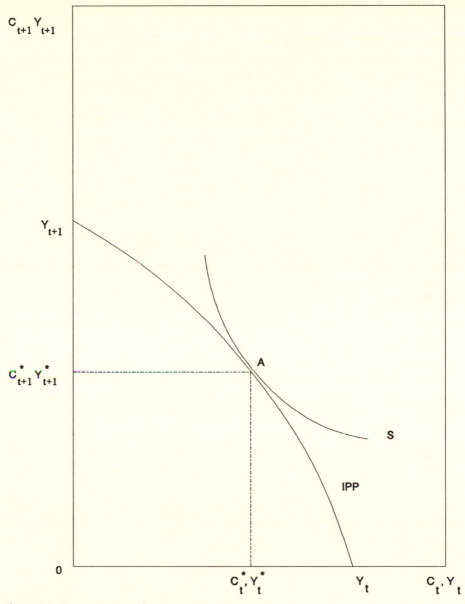

Figure 3.1. Determination of an interest rate.

and consumed. The optimal amount of present and future consumption and
production is found at the point of tangency of the curves S and IPP. At this
point, consumers are as well off as they can be, given the intertemporal production
possibilities. The absolute value of the slope of the curves at this tangency point
is $(1 + r)$ where r is the interest rate in this market. The equilibrium level of
foregone present consumption is measured by $OY_t - OC_t^*$.

There are a number of factors that affect the magnitude of r. First, the ability to use some resources today to produce a higher level of possible consumption in the future could be enhanced through technological progress. This would result in an outward rotation of IPP around the point Y_t. A higher indifference curve could be reached, and the equilibrium interest rate would be higher. This is because producers would be willing and able to pay a higher rate of compensation for the use of the foregone current consumption.

Another important factor is risk. With uncertainty about the future period, individuals may be more reluctant, and require higher compensation, to forego consumption today. Specifically, in the future period they may not be sure that they will receive the promised higher level of consumption possibilities. The more unsure they are, the more they have to be compensated. This would be reflected in a steeper indifference curve in Figure 3.1, resulting in a higher equilibrium interest rate.

The third factor is the underlying rate of time preference. For example, consider a group that places more value on future consumption possibilities. Their preferences will reflect consideration for the possibilities available for future generations. This group's intertemporal indifference curve, S, would become less negatively sloped and the equilibrium interest rate would fall.

Discounting Future Values

Discount rate and interest rate are synonymous terms normally applied when future net returns are discounted or when present returns are compounded. In equilibrium, the consumption value a saver can expect in the future if he or she foregoes \$1 worth of consumption today is

$$FV = \$1(1 + r)$$

or

$$FV = PV(1 + r)$$

where FV and PV denote the future and present values, respectively, and r is the periodic discount rate. This discount rate is the equilibrium rate of compensation derived previously.

If the future is divided into several periods, say, years, then the future value is given by

$$FV = PV(1 + r_p)^t$$

where r_p is the annual discount rate in year p, and t is the number of periods between the present and the relevant future period. This annual discount rate is the rate of compensation per period. To place some future value in terms of the present for comparison, solve for PV

$$PV = FV/(1 + r)^t$$

where the rate of compensation for period, r_p, is assumed constant. Specifically, a future value is discounted by the discount factor, $1/(1 + r)^t$.

The total present value, TPV, of a sequence of net returns from time period 0 to T, $R_0, R_1, \ldots, R_T$ is

$$TPV = \sum_{t=0}^{T} R_t/(1 + r)^t$$

In determining the optimal allocation of resource use through time, an objective function represented by total present value is often employed.

In continuous time the total present value of a sequence of net returns is

$$TPV = \int_0^T R_t \, e^{-rt} \, dt$$

The term e^{-rt} is the continuous or instantaneous discount factor, and r, in the continuous case, is the instantaneous discount rate. If the time units are the same in the discrete and continuous TPV, then

$$e^{-r_c} = 1/(1 + r)$$

where r_c is the instantaneous discount rate, and

$$r_c = \ln(1 + r)$$

For example, a 5 percent annual discount rate is equivalent to a continuous rate of 4.88 percent.

Real Versus Nominal Rate of Interest

Individuals are faced with considerable variation in interest rates. The degree of uncertainty associated with investments is a major cause of this variation. However, this variation also is highly correlated with the expected rate of inflation. Calculating the TPV in terms of purchasing power, the discount rate is generally not equal to the nominal or monetary rate. Instead the real discount rate is the difference between the nominal rate and the expected rate of inflation. The nominal interest rate may vary over a wide range. Countries experiencing high inflation rates may have nominal interest rates over 500 percent. However, real interest rates will generally remain within a narrow range of 2 to 8 percent.

In this and subsequent chapters the discount rate will refer to the real rate. It will generally be assumed that this discount rate is known and constant. However, as will be discussed later, this assumption may be the most heroic of all assumptions underlying the theoretical modeling of resource use.

Chapter Outline

First, the conditions for socially optimal resource allocation and the shadow price for resources are found for both nonrenewable and renewable resources. Second, policies are identified that allow an economy to attain this optimal resource allocation. Third, a two-period model of nonrenewable resource allocation is presented. Fourth, the two-period model is used as a framework to analyze a number of potential real world situations. Fifth, multiperiod analysis of non-renewable resources is presented, followed by a discussion of the appropriate modeling techniques for renewable resources. Sixth, discussion of the problem of irreversibility is followed by a section on the economics of resource replacement. Finally, two sections dealing with applications: range management, and the problem of an appropriate discount rate conclude this chapter.

NONRENEWABLE RESOURCES

The Two-Period Model of Resource Allocation

Let Y denote output from a resource consumed by consumers and $B(Y)$ denote the consumers' benefit from this consumption. $B(Y)$ can be interpreted as the area under the compensated demand curve or utility from consumption measured in monetary terms. To distinguish between consumption at different periods, let Y_t be the amount of output consumed at period t. In a two-period model t assumes two values, 0 for the first period (present) and 1 for the second period (future). Let us assume first that the benefit function does not vary over time; however, consumers have a positive time preference and the discount rate is denoted by r. Thus, the objective of resource allocation is to maximize the present value of net benefits

$$B(Y_0) + B(Y_1)/(1 + r)$$

Assume that a *nonrenewable resource*, for example a ground water pool, is being mined and consumed at zero cost. (See Chapters 1 and 8.) Let S_t denote the stock of the resource at the start of period t and S_0 denote the initial stock level. The *equation of motion* denoting the change in the *resource stock* is

$$S_{t+1} = S_t - Y_t$$

The equation implies that the resource stock is declining from one period to another by the amount mined.

In the two-period optimization model, optimal consumption or mining levels for each period, Y_0 and Y_1, have to be determined given the initial stock, S_0, and the equation of motion

$$S_1 = S_0 - Y_0$$

Furthermore, mining at any period cannot exceed the available stock or be negative, $S_t \geq Y_t \geq 0$. Thus, the optimization problem for the two-period model is

$$\underset{Y_0, Y_1}{\text{Max}} \ B(Y_0) + \frac{1}{1 + r} B(Y_1) \tag{1}$$

subject to $S_1 = S_0 - Y_0$, $S_1 \geq Y_1 \geq 0$, $S_0 \geq Y_0 \geq 0$. This problem is solved by first considering the case when the resource is exhausted at the end of the second period and there is no extraction cost. This outcome will always occur if it is assumed that consumers cannot be satiated with the resource, which implies nonnegative marginal benefits. In this case, $Y_1 + Y_0 = S_0$.

Using the Lagrangian approach introduced in Chapter 2, the constrained optimization problem becomes

$$L = \underset{Y_0, Y_1}{\text{Max}}\, B(Y_0) + \frac{1}{1+r}\, B(Y_1) + q(S_0 + Y_1 - Y_0) \tag{2}$$

where q is the *shadow price* of the resource in the first period. This shadow price is the price society is willing to pay for an extra unit, the marginal value, of the resource at time 0. The *optimal resource allocation rules* are derived by taking derivatives of (2) for each control variable, Y_1 and Y_0, and the shadow price q

$$L_q = S_0 - Y_1 - Y_0 = 0 \tag{3a}$$

$$L_{Y_0} = B_Y(Y_0) - q = 0 \tag{3b}$$

and

$$L_{Y_1} = B_Y(Y_1)\frac{1}{(1+r)} - q = 0 \tag{3c}$$

where $B_Y(Y_0)$ and $B_Y(Y_1)$ are the marginal benefits of consumption at the first and second time periods, respectively.

Optimal allocation rules (3b) and (3c) suggest that the marginal benefits of consumption at the first period and discounted marginal benefits of consumption in the second period are equal to the shadow price of the resource at time 0. The total benefit function $B(Y_t)$ denotes the area under the compensated demand curve, which implies $B_Y(Y_t)$ is the consumer's price of the resource, P_t, when Y_t units are consumed

$$P_t = B_Y(Y_t)$$

Conditions (3b) and (3c) then imply

$$P_1 = P_0(1 + r) \tag{4}$$

Solving for the discount rate, r, yields

$$r = \frac{P_1 - P_0}{P_0}$$

Thus, under optimal management, a resource is extracted so that the price increases at the rate of interest (Hotelling, 1931). Consumers are indifferent to paying P_0 in the first period for an additional unit of Y versus paying $P_0/(1 + r)$ in the second period. Prices P_1 and P_0 correspond to the same demand curve under the optimal solution and from (4) $P_1 > P_0$; given a positive discount rate, output declines over time, $Y_1 < Y_0$.

Alternatively, the resource constraint may be directly substituted into objective function (1) by replacing Y_1 with $S_0 - Y_0$ in (1). The optimal resource allocation rule for Y_0 becomes

$$B_y(Y_0) = \frac{1}{1+r}\, B_y(S_0 - Y_0) \tag{5}$$

However, $B_Y(Y_0)$ and $B_Y(s_0 - Y_0)/(1 + r)$ must be nonnegative. If either are negative, then (5) becomes $B_Y(Y_0) = B_y(s_0 - Y_0)/(1 + r)$. Equation (5) can be solved for this two-period problem given various benefit functions. In particular, consider a Cobb-Douglas benefit function

$$B(Y_t) = a Y_t^{1/2}$$

The optimality condition (5) for this function is

$$\frac{a}{2Y_0^{1/2}} = \frac{a}{2(1 + r)(S_0 - Y_0)^{1/2}}$$

Solving this equation for Y_0 and Y_1

$$Y_0 = S_0 \frac{(1 + r)^2}{1 + (1 + r)^2} \tag{6a}$$

and

$$Y_1 = S_0 \frac{1}{1 + (1 + r)^2} \tag{6b}$$

The marginal benefit function or the inverse demand function is

$$B_Y = \frac{a}{2Y^{1/2}} = P$$

Thus, given (6), resource prices are

$$P_0 = \frac{a}{2}\left(\frac{1 + (1 + r)^2}{S_0(1 + r)^2}\right)^{1/2} \tag{7a}$$

and

$$P_1 = \frac{a}{2}\left(\frac{1 + (1 + r)^2}{S_0}\right)^{1/2} \tag{7b}$$

The outcomes in (6) and (7) suggest that, as the initial resource stock, S_0, increases, consumption levels, Y_0 and Y_1, increase and output prices decrease in both periods. Furthermore, an increase in the discount rate increases Y_0 and reduces Y_1. To illustrate this last result, let $S_0 = 100$, $a = 10$, and $r = 0.5$, and assume that each period lasts 5 years. Substituting these values into (6) and (7) yields

$$Y_0 = 69.2, \quad Y_1 = 30.8, \quad P_0 = 0.6, \quad \text{and} \quad P_1 = 0.9$$

Now consider increasing the interest rate to $r = 1$. The solutions then become

$$Y_0 = 80, \quad Y_1 = 20, \quad P_0 = 0.56, \quad \text{and} \quad P_1 = 1.12$$

This numerical example demonstrates the critical role that discount rates play in determining resource allocation over time.

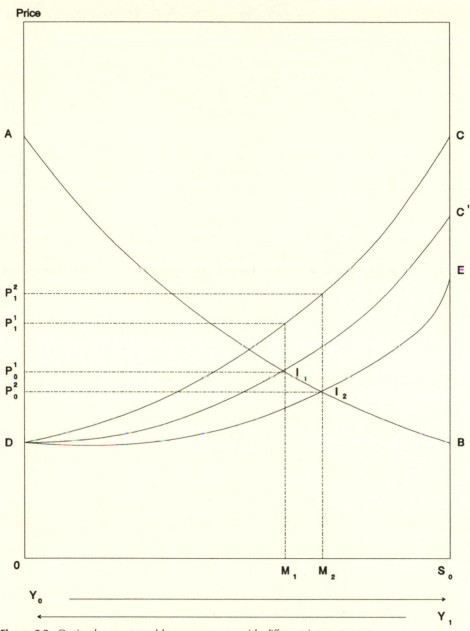

Figure 3.2. Optimal nonrenewable resource use with different interest rates.

Figure 3.2 illustrates graphically the two-period resource allocation problem. The horizontal axis in Figure 3.2 represents quantities, and the vertical axes represent monetary values. The segment between the origin and S_0 represents resource availability. Resource use in the first period, Y_0, starts at the origin and moves toward S_0 along the horizontal axis. Resource use in the second period,

Y_1, starts at S_0 and moves toward the origin. The curves AB and CD are marginal benefits of resource use in the first and second periods, respectively—$B_Y(Y_0)$ and $B_Y(Y_1)$. The curve $C'D$ is $B_Y(Y_1)/(1 + r_1)$—marginal benefits of consumption in the second period discounted at rate r_1 to time 0. Optimal resource allocation occurs at I_1, where AB and $C'D$ intersect. The segment OM_1 denotes resource use in the first period, and $S_0 - M_1$ denotes resource use in the second period. Associated prices of the resource in the first and second periods are P_0^1 and P_1^1, respectively.

The effect of an increase in the discount rate is illustrated in Figure 3.2, where $r_2 \geq r_1$. The curve representing the discounted marginal benefit of resource use in the second period, $B_Y(Y_1)/(1 + r^2)$, is ED, which is below $C'D$. The optimal outcome is I_2, where AB and ED intersect. Resource use in the first period is OM_2, in the second period it is $S_0 - M_2$, and resource prices are $P_0^2 < P_0^1$ and $P_1^2 > P_1^1$.

This graphical analysis is also useful in situations in which the assumption that demand is unsatiated is relaxed and the marginal benefit curve intersects the horizontal axis (Fig. 3.3). This case is especially relevant during the first period, when the resource stock is large relative to resource extraction. The curves KL and VR denote the marginal benefit of resource use in the two periods. Optimal resource use in the first period is OL and in the second period is $S_0 - R$. In both periods, marginal benefits of resource use and resource price are zero, and the resource is not depleted.

Institutional Setup for Optimality and the "Open Access" Problem

Optimal resource allocation is obtained only under certain market circumstances. For example, optimality occurs if the resource is privately owned by many price-taking and profit-maximizing firms with equality between the private and social discount rates. Optimality is demonstrated for unsatiated demand by noting that market-clearing equilibrium is possible only given (4). If

$$P_1 > (1 + r)P_0$$

sellers sell all the resource stock, S_0, in the second period, $Y_0 = 0$, $Y_1 = S_0$, and if

$$P_1 < (1 + r)P_0$$

sellers sell all S_0 in the first period, $Y_0 = S_0$, $Y_1 = 0$. Both corner solutions are inconsistent with well-behaved inverse demand functions, $P_Y = B_Y(Y_t)$ for $t = 0, 1$. Under the feasible, internal market-clearing solutions

$$P_1 = (1 + r)P_0$$

$$Y_1 = Y_0 = S_0$$

and thus, $(1 + r)B_Y(Y_0) = B_Y(S_0 - Y_0)$, which is exactly the optimality condition (5). Optimal resource allocation is also obtained when the resource is controlled by a government, and it sells Y_0 units in the first period and Y_1 units in the second period.

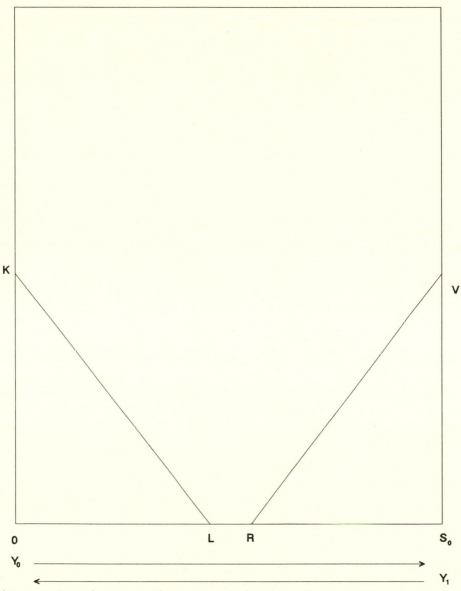

Figure 3.3. Optimal nonrenewable resource use when demand is unsatiated.

Resource allocation is suboptimal if the competitive users have *open access* to the resource. Examples include when many farmers pump water from the same aquifer, many fishermen fish one lake, or several herds of cattle graze a common pasture. In these cases, the resources belong to everyone and no one. None of the users has an incentive to conserve the resource because they cannot keep what they save. In the literature this is often referred to as "the tragedy of the commons."

The resource is consumed as long as the marginal benefit is greater than the marginal cost, which in this case is assumed to be zero. Thus, for a commonly held resource, the suboptimal solution is $Y_0 = S_0$ and $Y_1 = 0$. Policy intervention is required to attain optimality. Possible forms of intervention include a resource use tax of P_0 in the first period, or takeover of the resource by the government followed by either the sale of ownership to individual parties or the sales of licenses to extract Y_0 units of resource in the first period and Y_1 units in the second period.

If demand is satiated, a different set of outcomes is feasible. The curve AB in Figure 3.4 represents $B_Y(Y_0)$ and $C'D$ represents $B_Y(Y_1)/(1 + r)$. Under optimal resource allocation, resource use in the first period is OM_1, and in the second period is $S_0 - M_1$, with associated prices P_0^0 and P_1^0. Under open access, OB is consumed in the first period and $S_0 - B$ is consumed in the second period. Note that $OB > OM_1$, implying $S_0 - B < S_0 - M_1$, so the price in the second period is P_1^c, which is larger than the optimal price, P_1^0. Thus, when demand is not satiated, the resource is not necessarily exhausted in the first period when it is commonly held. However, relative to the optimal levels, it is overused in early periods and underused in later periods.

Monopoly Ownership of a Nonrenewable Resource

Consider a situation in which a nonrenewable resource is owned by a monopoly, for example, a case when the sole owner of an exhaustible aquifer is the only provider of water to a region. Given $P_t = B_Y(Y_t)$ for period t, the monopoly's profit at period t is $Y_t B_Y(Y_t)$ and, if the monopoly maximizes its discounted profits, the monopoly's decision-making problem is

$$\underset{Y_0, Y_1}{\text{Max}}\ Y_0 B_Y(Y_0) + \frac{1}{1 + r}\ Y_1 B_Y(Y_1) \tag{8}$$

subject to $Y_0 + Y_1 \leq S_0$.

Following the procedure used in solving the optimization problem (2), the Lagrangian problem for the monopolist case is

$$L = \underset{Y_0, Y_1}{\text{Max}}\ Y_0 B_Y(Y_0) + \frac{1}{1 + r}\ Y_1 B_Y(Y_1) + q(S_0 - Y_1 - Y_0) \tag{9}$$

The shadow price of the resource in the initial period, q, is the price the monopolist resource owner is willing to pay for an extra unit of resource in the first period. Assuming the constraint is binding, the optimal resource allocation rules are condition (3a) and

$$L_{Y_0} = B_Y(Y_0) + Y_0 B_{YY}(Y_0) - q = 0 \tag{10a}$$

and

$$L_{Y_1} = [B_Y(Y_1) + Y_1 B_{YY}(Y_1)]\frac{1}{(1 + r)} - q = 0 \tag{10b}$$

Price

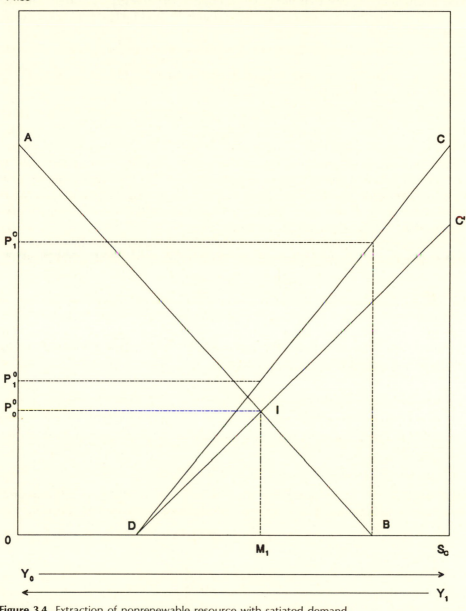

Figure 3.4. Extraction of nonrenewable resource with satiated demand.

To interpret conditions (10a) and (10b), define the *revenue* associated with output Y_t as

$$R(Y_t) = P_t Y_t = B_Y(Y_t) Y_t$$

and denote the associated *marginal revenue* function as

$$MR(Y_t) = B_Y(Y_t) + Y_t B_{YY}(Y_t)$$

These conditions suggest that marginal revenue in the first period and discounted marginal revenue in the second period are equal to the shadow price of the resource in the first period

$$MR(Y_0) = MR(Y_1)/(1 + r) = q \tag{11}$$

In addition, marginal revenue in each period must be nonnegative. Solving for the discount rate, r, yields

$$r = \frac{MR(Y_1) - MR(Y_0)}{MR(Y_0)}$$

When the resource is controlled by the monopoly, marginal revenue increases by the interest rate over time. Comparing condition (4) to (11), under the optimal resource allocation, the resource price rather than its original revenue increases by the interest rate over time. Thus, a resource controlled by a monopoly may suboptimally allocate resources over time.

As a further comparison of monopolistic and optimal outcomes, note that marginal revenue may be expressed as a function of price and demand elasticity

$$MR = P[1 + 1/\eta(Y)]$$

where

$$\eta(Y) \equiv Y_P(P/Y)$$

is the *price elasticity* of demand. Using this relation, (11) can be modified resulting in the monopoly price change over time

$$P_1 = P_0(1 + r) \frac{[1 + 1/\eta(Y_0)]}{[1 + 1/\eta(Y_1)]} \tag{12}$$

Note that in the special case when resource demand has constant price elasticity, (12) becomes

$$P_1 = P_0(1 + r)$$

and, from (4), the monopolistic price over time corresponds to optimal price behavior and outcomes. As an example, consider again the benefit function

$$B(Y) = aY^{1/2}$$

In this case,

$$P = B_Y = \frac{a}{2Y^{1/2}}$$

Solving for Y

$$Y = a^2/(4P^2)$$

which results in a constant price elasticity $\eta(Y)$ equal to minus two.

When the elasticity of demand for a resource is not constant, the monopoly solution will be suboptimal. For example, consider the case with linear resource demand

$$P = B_Y = a - bY$$

This demand function is derived from benefit function

$$B(Y) = aY - \tfrac{1}{2}bY^2 + c$$

where c is any constant. Solving (3a) and (3b) for this benefit function yields the optimality rules

$$Y_0^0 = \frac{1}{(2+r)} [S_0 + (ra)/b] \tag{13a}$$

and

$$Y_1^0 = \frac{1}{(2+r)} [S_0(1+r) - (ra)/b] \tag{13b}$$

Solving (10a) and (10b) for this benefit function yields resource allocation under monopoly

$$Y_0^M = \frac{1}{(2+r)} [S_0 + (ra)/(2b)] \tag{14a}$$

and

$$Y_1^M = \frac{2}{(2+r)} [S_0(1+r) - (ra)/(2b)] \tag{14b}$$

From (13) and (14)

$$Y_0^0 - Y_0^M = \frac{ra}{2b(2+r)} = Y_1^M - Y_1^0 > 0$$

Thus, when a resource is owned by a monopoly, it sells less and charges more in the early period than is socially optimal. In other words, while open access to a resource leads to excessive depletion, monopolistic ownership may lead to excessive conservation. A monopolist may act like a conservationist. However, if the costs of extraction are considered, the relationship between monopoly and social extraction policies becomes ambiguous.

Extraction Cost

Resource extraction, similar to any productive activity, is a costly process. Pumping ground water is costly, as is mining minerals, or any other extraction activity. Assume that extraction costs depend on output, and denote the extraction cost function by $C(Y_t)$. Net benefits at period t are $B(Y_t) - C(Y_t)$, and in a two-period model the Lagrangian problem is

$$L = \underset{Y_0, Y_1}{\text{Max}} \, B(Y_0) - C(Y_0) + \frac{1}{1+r} [B(Y_1) - C(Y_1)] + q(S_0 - Y_1 - Y_0) \tag{15}$$

Consider the case where the resource is exhausted at the end of the second period. The first-order conditions imply

$$L_q = S_0 - Y_1 - Y_0 = 0 \tag{16a}$$

$$L_{Y_0} = B_Y(Y_0) - C_Y(Y_0) - q = 0 \tag{16b}$$

and

$$L_{Y_1} = [B_Y(Y_1) - C_Y(Y_1)] \frac{1}{(1+r)} - q = 0 \tag{16c}$$

If $C(Y_t)$ is convex and $B(Y)$ is concave, then these conditions are necessary and sufficient.

The conditions in (16) state that the optimal solution occurs where the shadow price of the resource stock, q, is equal to the difference between marginal benefits and marginal costs of the resource in the first period. Replacing $B_Y(Y_t)$ with P_t in (16) and substituting for q yields

$$P_1 - C_Y(Y_1) = [P_0 - C_Y(Y_0)](1+r) \tag{17}$$

Solving for the discount rate, r,

$$r = \frac{[P_1 - C_Y(Y_1)] - [P_0 - C_Y(Y_0)]}{P_0 - C_Y(Y_0)}$$

When extraction costs exist, the difference between price and marginal extraction costs grows over time at a rate equal to the discount rate. With a slightly different interpretation, the same graphical analysis used to explain the determination of prices and quantities in the zero-cost case, Figure 3.2, can be used for this extraction-cost case. With extraction costs, AB and CD are now net marginal benefits, marginal benefits minus marginal costs, of resource use in the first and second periods, respectively. The curve $C'D$ represents second period discounted net marginal benefits. Thus, the optimal solution occurs at point I_1, the intersection between the curves AB and $C'D$. The optimal resource use of the initial period is segment OM_1 and in the second period is $S_0 - M_1$. The prices P_0^1 and P_1^1 are derived from the $B_Y(Y_t)$ curves.

From (17) the rate of change in the price of the resource between the two periods is

$$\frac{P_1 - P_0}{P_0} = r - \frac{(1+r)C_Y(Y_0) - C_Y(Y_1)}{P_0} \tag{18}$$

Consider the case where extraction costs per unit of output are constant and equal to c. In this case, (18) becomes

$$\frac{P_1 - P_0}{P_0} = r[1 - (c/P_0)]$$

When extraction costs exist, the rate of change in the resource price is smaller than the discount rate. This suggests that higher extraction costs lead to lower price changes, and thus, lower changes in extraction over time.

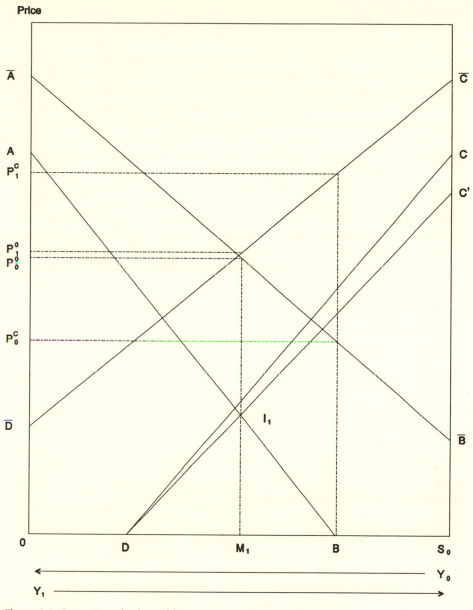

Figure 3.5. Extraction of exhaustible resources under extraction costs.

Figure 3.5 shows that in the case of open access, extraction costs may serve to prevent total exhaustion of the resource in the early period. The curves $\overline{AB}$ and $\overline{CD}$ denote $B_Y(Y_0)$ and $B_Y(Y_1)$, marginal benefit from resource use, demand, in the first and second periods, respectively. The difference between marginal benefits and marginal extraction costs in each period is depicted by the curves AB and CD.

When there is open access to the resource and it is extracted without regard for future availability, resource allocation occurs at point B. This is where, in the first period, marginal benefit of the resource is equal to marginal extraction cost, $B_Y(Y_0) - C_Y(Y_0) = 0$. The use in the first period is OB and in the second period is $S_0 - B$. This is in contrast to optimal resource allocation associated with point I_1, where curve $C'D$ denotes marginal benefits of consumption in the second period discounted at time 0. Optimal resource allocation use in the first period is OM_1 and in the second period is $S_0 - M_1$, with prices P_0^0 and P_1^0, respectively. Under open access, the price in the first period is $P_0^c < P_0^0$, and the second period price is $P_1^c > P_0^0$. There is excessive extraction in the first period and underextraction in the second period. One mechanism to obtain an optimal solution when resource ownership is not privatized is by taxing its use in the first period at a level $B_Y(Y_0) - C_Y(Y_0)$ associated with optimal resource allocation OM_1. In practice, a tax, called a severance tax, is generally proportional to the amount of resource extracted rather than the value of the resource, $B_Y(Y_0) - C_Y(Y_0)$. A severance tax has the effect of spreading resource use over time, and thus, lengthening the period of extraction. In contrast, a depletion allowance, which is a tax reduction that is proportional to resource use, accelerates use and shortens the period of extraction.

Example of Competitive and Monopoly Ownership with Extraction Costs

Table 3.1 presents results of four numerical examples to illustrate the impact of extraction costs on resource allocation under alternative scenarios. For all the examples, it is assumed that $r = 0.2$ and that inverse demand in each period is $B_y(Y_t) = 20 - 0.5Y_t$. Outcomes are obtained for situations with zero extraction costs, and when extraction costs per unit of output are equal to five, $C_Y(Y_t) = 5$. The analysis is conducted for cases with relatively large, $S_0 = 50$, and small, $S_0 = 24$, initial resource stocks. For each of the four scenarios, Table 3.1 presents resource use in the two periods, resource prices and discounted sums of producers, consumers, and total surpluses under three arrangements. (See Chapter 4.) The first is when the resource is separately owned by many competitive producers and there is no open access to the resource stock. This arrangement leads to optimal resource allocation, the sum of the discounted surpluses is maximized, and its output serves as a benchmark to assess performances under other arrangements. The second arrangement considered is when the resource is extracted by competitive producers, but there is open access. The third arrangement is when the resource stock is owned by a monopoly.

The socially optimal outcomes for $S_0 = 50$ and $C_Y(Y_t) = 5$ are obtained by solving equations (16a) to (16c) to obtain $Y_0 = 25.45$, $q^* = 2.275$, and $Y_1 = 24.55$. Introducing Y_0 and Y_1 into $P_t = 20 - 0.5Y_t$ yields $P_0 = 7.275$ and $P_1 = 7.725$. With these outputs and prices, discounted profit (producers' surplus) equals

$$113.65 = (25.45)(2.275) + (24.55)(2.725)/1.2$$

and discounted consumers' surplus equals

$$287.48 = (20 - 7.275)(25.45)/2 + [(20 - 7.725)(24.55)/2]/1.2$$

and thus, discounted social welfare equals 401.12.

Table 3.1. Numerical Example of the Impact of Extraction Costs on Management of Nonrenewable Resource

Variable	Optimal outcome	Open access	Monopoly
Scenario $S = 50$, $C_y(Y_t) = 0$			
Y_0	26.36	40	20
Y_1	23.64	10	20
P_0	6.82	0	10
P_1	8.18	15	10
Discounted profits	340.92	125	366.66
Discounted consumer surplus	290.14	420.83	183.33
Discounted welfare	631.06	545.83	549.99
Scenario $S = 50$, $C_Y(Y_t) = 5$			
Y_0	25.45	30	15
Y_1	24.55	20	15
P_0	7.275	5	12.5
P_1	7.725	10	12.5
Discounted profits	113.65	83.33	206.25
Discounted consumer surplus	287.48	308.33	103.125
Discounted welfare	401.12	391.66	309.375
Scenario $S = 24$, $C_Y(Y_t) = 0$			
Y_0	14.55	24	12.72
Y_1	9.45	0	11.20
P_0	12.725	8	13.64
P_1	15.275	NA	14.37
Discounted profits	305.4	192	308.59
Discounted consumer surplus	71.53	144	66.92
Discounted welfare	376.93	336	375.50
Scenario $S = 24$, $C_Y(Y_t) = 5$			
Y_0	13.64	24	12.27
Y_1	10.36	0	11.63
P_0	13.18	8	13.865
P_1	14.82	NA	14.185
Discounted profits	196.35	72	197.79
Discounted consumer surplus	68.87	144	65.82
Discounted welfare	265.22	216	263.61

When there is open access to the resource, in the case with $S_0 = 50$ and $C_Y(Y_t) = 5$, the extraction in the first period is obtained by equating marginal benefits, $B_Y(Y_0)$, with marginal extraction costs, $C_Y(Y_0)$

$$20 - 0.5 Y_0 = 5$$

resulting in $Y_0 = 30$ and $Y_1 = 20$. To analyze the outcomes when the resource is owned by a monopolist, notice that the marginal revenue at each period becomes $MR(Y_t) = 20 - Y_t$ and revenue at each period is maximized when $Y_t = 20$. When $C_Y(Y_t) = 5$, the monopolist's profit at each period is maximized where

$20 - Y_t - 5 = 0$ and $Y_t = 15$. When $S_0 = 50$, the resource availability constraints are not binding for the monopolist, and optimal output in each period is 20 when there are no extraction costs and 15 when extraction costs are $5.00 per unit of output.

When the initial resource stock is small, $S_0 = 24$, under competition and open access, all the resources will be utilized in the first period and the price will be $8.00 per unit of output, which is above the extraction cost. All of the resource stock will be exhausted under a monopoly, and optimal output in the first period, when $C_Y(Y_t) = 5$, is determined solving

$$20 - Y_0 - 5 = [20 - (24 - Y_0) - 5]/1.2$$

resulting in $Y_0 = 12.27$.

Comparison of the outcomes presented in Table 3.1 suggests that extraction costs reduce substantially the differences in resource use and prices between the two periods under the optimal solution. When the initial resource stock is relatively large, the performance of the open access solution, relative to the monopolistic outcome, will improve substantially when extraction costs are introduced and reduce tendencies to overextract in the first period. When the initial resource stock is relatively small, $S_0 = 24$, note that, while monopolistic ownership of the resource leads to extra conservation and a smaller efficiency loss than the optimal solution, it biases income distribution drastically in favor of producers. The efficiency losses between the competition and open access solutions are relatively larger when the initial resource stock is small.

Scarcity

In economics *scarcity* is a value concept. This is in contrast to a physical concept of scarcity used in biological and physical sciences. As indicated in (16), the discounted difference between resource price and the marginal cost of extraction is the shadow price of a resource. In perfect competition, this is the difference in what society would be willing to pay for an additional unit of a resource and what it costs society to extract the resource. If this difference is positive and large, then the resource is scarce. If this difference increases from one period to the next, then the resource is more scarce in the second period.

An example of increased scarcity is public rangeland in the western United States. Rangelands represent approximately 34 percent of the area of the United States and 43 percent of this area is under Federal management (Quigley and Bartlett, 1990). In 1986 the Bureau of Land Management (BLM) reported 18 percent of its rangeland was in poor condition, while the U.S. Forest Service reported 20 percent of its rangelands in an unsatisfactory management situation. As addressed in Torell and Doll (1991), the Federal Land Policy and Management Act and heightened interest in public land use by nonranchers have increased the scarcity of these public rangelands.

Ranchers who own grazing permits are allowed to use public rangeland to graze their livestock for a set grazing fee. The original grazing permits issued by state and federal land agencies, including BLM and the U.S. Forest Service, were freely given to ranchers and grazing fees were set low to encourage use and private investment on public lands. These permits acquired a market value through their incorporation into the land value of the ranch. It is estimated that 85 to 90 percent of ranchers owning grazing permits paid some amount for these permits in the form of a higher purchase price for their ranch.

Currently grazing fees are on the rise, especially on New Mexico State trust lands. Prior to 1982 grazing fees from New Mexico State trust lands were relatively low with expectation that low fees would continue. After 1982 significant increases in grazing fees were proposed with actual increases occurring from 1986 to 1990. Grazing fees increased from \$1.60/AUM in 1986 to \$3.16/AUM in 1990, where AUM denotes animal unit month. Also, in New Mexico, protection of endangered species habitat and recreational use, including off-road vehicles, have resulted in over 12 BLM Environmental Impact Statements and U.S. Forest Service planning documents since 1977. These reports emphasize resource conflicts with livestock grazing and propose major reductions in grazing (Torell and Doll, 1991). Starting in the early 1980s, 944,000 acres of BLM land in New Mexico were studied for possible designation as wilderness areas, and eventually 560,000 acres of BLM land were recommended for conversion to wilderness areas. Grazing is allowed on these lands; however, management problems would exist given increased difficulty of access and restrictions on vehicle use (Torell and Doll, 1991).

Increased grazing fees and environmental restrictions imply that what society would be willing to pay for an additional unit of the resource, rangeland, $B_Y(Y_t)$ in (16), is increasing. This indicates that rangeland is increasing in scarcity. Torell and Doll (1991) investigated this change in rangeland scarcity and determined that as a direct result of society's willingness to pay more for additional units of rangeland, the value of grazing permits is declining.

Changes in Demand Over Time

Population and economic growth may lead to increased demand over time requiring a relaxation of the assumption that demand is identical for the two periods. Let the rate of growth in benefits of resource use be denoted by ψ. The Lagrangian equation in a two-period model without extraction cost then becomes

$$L = \operatorname*{Max}_{Y_0, Y_1} B(Y_0) + \frac{1 + \psi}{1 + r} B(Y_1) + q(S_0 - Y_1 - Y_0) \tag{19}$$

The optimal resource allocations rules are

$$L_q = S^0 - Y_1 - Y_0 = 0 \tag{20a}$$

$$L_{Y_0} = B_Y(Y_0) - q = 0 \tag{20b}$$

and

$$L_{Y_1} = B_Y(Y_1) \frac{1 + \psi}{1 + r} - q = 0 \tag{20c}$$

Comparison of these conditions with equations (3a), (3b), and (3c) reveals that the optimal allocation rule, when demand grows at a rate of ψ, is equivalent to the optimal allocation rule in the base case where the interest rate is $(r - \psi)/(1 + \psi)$.

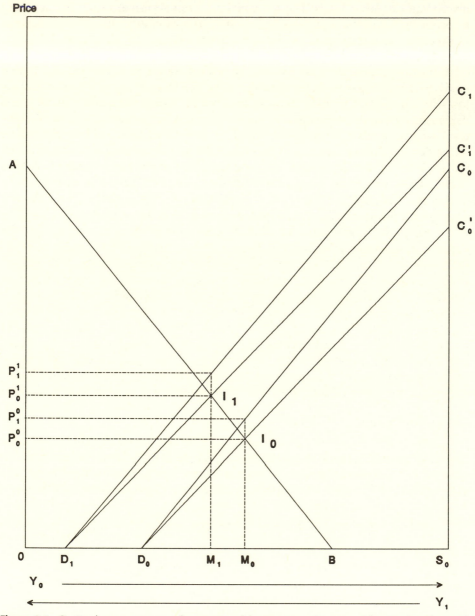

Figure 3.6. Optimal management of nonrenewable resources in case with growing demand.

Thus, compared with constant demand, growth in demand serves to reduce the effective interest rate, which results in a reduction in resource use in the first period and an increase in resource use in the second period.

Figure 3.6 illustrates the impact of growth in demand on resource use and prices. Again, AB denotes demand for the resource in the first period; $C_0 D_0$ is demand in the second period of the benchmark case with constant demand; and $C_0^1 D_0$ is the associated discounted second period demand curve. The optimal outcome for this case occurs at I_0 with P_0^0 and P_0^1 as resource prices OM_0 and $S_0 - M_0$ units of resource used in each of the periods. The curves $C_1 D_1$ and $C_1^1 D_1$ denote demand and discounted demand for the resource in the second period when demand grows over time. Optimal resource allocation is then I_1, where $C_1^1 D_1$ and AB intersect. The graphical analysis suggests that compared to constant demand, an increase in demand in the second period will cause the resource price to increase in both periods, $P_0^1 > P_0^0$ and $P_1^1 > P_0^1$. The increase in resource price in the first period corresponds to the reduction in the resource use in that period. Note that when demand grows between periods, the marginal benefit and price at the second period is

$$P_1 = (1 + \psi) B_Y(Y_1)$$

and that price grows at the rate of interest rate over time

$$P_1 = (1 + \psi) B_Y(Y_1) = (1 + r) P_0$$

Condition (20) suggests that in extreme cases when demand grows faster than the interest rate, optimal resource use should actually grow over time, $Y_1 > Y_0$ where $\psi > r$. Thus, more conservation must be exercised under conditions that lead to growth in demand for the resource over time. Furthermore, the misallocations associated with the open access problem are larger the more demand grows over time.

Backstop Technology and Exploration

Many exhaustible resource problems are alleviated by the introduction of alternative extraction methods, frequently in a renewable manner, or through exploration and discovery. A new alternative is referred to as *backstop technology*. This notion was popularized during the energy crisis of the 1970s when various alternatives to fossil fuels were advanced and a significant effort was directed toward exploration and discovery. In semiarid zones such as the California San Joaquin Valley, agriculture was established using exhaustible ground water resources. Over time, these nonrenewable resources were augmented by the importation of water from primarily renewable sources, for example, in California, the renewable snowmelt of the Sierra Nevada Mountains.

To incorporate situations with backstop technology in the two-period model, assume that the technology is available in the second period, and let Y_1^B denote output produced by this technology. The cost function of the alternative technology in $h(Y^B)$, and marginal costs are assumed to be increasing. Total consumption in the second period is denoted by Y_1, and the amount mined in the second period is $Y_1 - Y_1^B$. The new feature of this optimization problem is determining the optimal use of the backstop technology, Y_1^B. With this notation, the Lagrangian equation of the social optimization problem for the case with extraction costs and backstop technology becomes

$$L = \max_{Y_0, Y_1, Y_1^B} B(Y_0) - C(Y_0) + \frac{1}{1+r} [B(Y_1) - C(Y_1 - Y_1^B) - h(Y_1^B)]$$

$$+ q(S_0 - Y_1 + Y_1^B - Y_0) \tag{21}$$

The first-order conditions imply

$$L_q = S_0 - Y_1 + Y_1^B - Y_0 = 0 \tag{22a}$$

$$L_{Y_0} = B_Y(Y_0) - C_Y(Y_0) - q = 0 \tag{22b}$$

$$L_{Y_1} = [B_Y(Y_1) - C_Y(Y_1 - Y_1^B)]\frac{1}{(1+r)} - q = 0 \tag{22c}$$

and

$$L_{Y_1^B} = [C_Y(Y_1 - Y_1^B) - h_{Y^B}(Y_1^B)]\frac{1}{(1+r)} + q = 0 \tag{22d}$$

Conditions (22b) and (22c) state that resources will be extracted in each of the periods at the level where the discounted marginal benefits of resource use are equal to the discounted marginal extraction costs plus the shadow price of the resource stock. Condition (22d) states that the optimal level of resource extraction and alternative technology is where the discounted marginal costs of extraction are equal to the discounted marginal costs of the alternative technology minus the shadow price. Equations (22c) and (22d) suggest that production with backstop technology in the second period will be where marginal benefit from consumption $B_Y(Y_1)$ is equal to the marginal costs of the backstop technology $h_{Y^B}(Y_1^B)$. Thus

$$B_Y(Y_1) = P_1 = h_{Y^B}(Y_1^B) \tag{23a}$$

and from (22d)

$$P_0 = C_Y(Y_0) + \frac{1}{(1+r)} [h_{Y^B}(Y_1^B) - C_Y(Y_1 - Y_1^B)] \tag{23b}$$

Equation (23a) states that the resource price in the second period is equal to marginal cost of the backstop technology, and (23b) links the resource price in the first period with marginal extraction costs in the second period. This relationship between price and marginal extraction costs may be further investigated by assuming a constant marginal cost equal to h. In this case, $P_1 = h$ and

$$P_0 = C_Y(Y_0) + \frac{1}{(1+r)} [h - C_Y(Y_1 - Y_1^B)]$$

Thus, as h declines, extraction in the second period, $Y_1 - Y_1^B$, declines, while extraction in the first period, Y_0, increases. Also, price in the first period declines. If costs of production with backstop technology are sufficiently low, resource extraction may occur only in the first period. In this case, some of the resource may be left unused. These results suggest that construction of a canal using cheaper surface water may increase ground water pumping in the present, and that technological innovations promising to reduce the cost of solar energy will result in a reduction of the current price of fossil fuels.

Lessons From the Two-Period Model

It was demonstrated that when a competitive industry shares a nonrenewable resource, it is likely to overextract. Government intervention by taxation or assignment of property rights may lead to optimal resource allocation. For example, excessive pumping of ground water is likely to occur when many farmers pump independently the same aquifer. Government intervention may help remedy this situation, although intervention comes with no assurance of optimality. Private ownership of an exhaustible resource does not assure optimal utilization over time either. When owners, private or government, are myopic by not being aware of the effect of current decisions on future generations, resources may be overextracted in early periods. Education and taxation may remedy this situation.

It was also concluded that under optimal resource allocation, price tends to increase over time. The gap between price and marginal extraction costs grows at a rate equal to the interest rate minus the rate of growth in demand. When an exhaustible resource is managed optimally, its current price is affected by several factors. Price increases as the available stock decreases, the interest rate decreases, demand grows over time, and extraction costs rise. Availability of backstop technology is likely to reduce the current price of an optimally managed exhaustible resource. When resource owners form a monopoly, price is likely to rise, and they may underextract if the private and social rates of discount are equal.

Multiperiod Analysis

The two-period analysis presented some of the major findings of conceptual research on nonrenewable resources, but addressing some of the other issues requires more powerful tools of analysis. The optimal control methodology introduced in Chapter 2 is used here to analyze exhaustible resource problems with time, t, treated as a continuous variable. Resource use at time t is denoted by Y_t, and resource stock is denoted by S_t. The initial resource level is S_0 and the equation of motion is given by

$$\dot{S}_t = dS_t/dt = -Y_t \tag{24}$$

Consider the case where per unit extraction costs are constant at each moment but increase over time as the resource stock declines. Extraction costs at time t are denoted by $Y_t c(S_t)$, where $c(S_t)$ is per unit extraction cost and $c_s < 0$. For ground water, this indicates that average pumping costs are constant at each period but increase over time as the water in the aquifer declines. To consider resource management problems with an infinite time horizon, assume that marginal benefits from use become infinite as resource use approaches zero

$$\lim_{Y \to 0} B_Y(Y) = \infty$$

This assumption results in positive resource use throughout the time horizon. The social optimization problem is

$$
\left.\begin{array}{c}
\underset{Y_t, S_t, q_t}{\text{Max}} \int_0^\infty e^{-rt} [B(Y_t) - Y_t c(S_t)] \, dt, \\[2mm]
\text{subject to } \dot{S}_t = -Y_t, \ S_t \geq 0, \text{ and given } S_0
\end{array}\right\}
\tag{25}
$$

where q_t is the dynamic shadow price of the resource stock at time t. This shadow price is also referred to as the *user cost* of the resource. It is the marginal benefit of conserving the resource, and it measures the benefit from increasing the resource stock at time t by one unit. In the case of ground water, user cost, q_t, measures the value at time t of leaving one extra unit in the aquifer when the resource is optimally managed.

Optimal decision rules over time are derived from the temporal Hamiltonian function, following rules presented in Chapter 2. The temporal or current value Hamiltonian is

$$
H(t) = B(Y_t) - Y_t c(S_t) - q_t Y_t
$$

Optimal resource allocation rules that solve the resource allocation problem (25) are

$$
H_Y = B_Y(Y_t) - c(S_t) - q_t = 0
\tag{26a}
$$

$$
H_S = -Y_t c_S(S_t) = -\dot{q}_t + r q_t
\tag{26b}
$$

and

$$
H_q = \dot{S}_t = -Y_t
\tag{26c}
$$

for every t. The first optimality condition states that the marginal benefit of consumptive use of a resource at time t has to be equal to the sum of the marginal extraction costs and its user cost. This first-order condition can be rewritten as

$$
B_Y(Y_t) = c(S_t) + q_t = P_t
\tag{27}
$$

Equation (27) is analogous to (17) in the two-period model, and it states that optimal extraction cost at time t is where optimal resource price, P_t, which is equal to marginal benefit of consumption, is also equal to the sum of per unit extraction cost and user cost. Note that P_t denotes the prices of the extracted resources, and q_t is the price prior to extraction while it is in stock.

Conditions (26b) and (26c) are the equation of motion of the resource user cost (dynamic shadow price of the stock) and resource stock. The rate of change over time in the user cost is obtained from (26b) to be

$$
\frac{\dot{q}_t}{q_t} = r + \frac{Y_t c_S(S_t)}{q_t}
\tag{28}
$$

Condition (28) states that, when extraction costs are independent of the resource stock, $c_S = 0$, the user cost grows at the discount rate. However, when $c_S < 0$, the rate of growth in the price of the stock is less than the discount rate. As an explanation of this result, when $c_S < 0$, future savings of extraction costs serve as an incentive to conserve the resource and add to its value in earlier periods relative to later ones.

To obtain the use rate of the resource over time, take the total differential of (26a)

$$B_{YY}(Y_t)\dot{Y}_t - c_S(S_t)\dot{S}_t - \dot{q}_t = 0 \tag{29}$$

Using (26b) and (26c), $\dot{q}$ and $\dot{S}$ in (29) are replaced, and the change in resource use over time is

$$\dot{Y}_t = \frac{rq_t}{B_{YY}(Y_t)} \tag{30}$$

Recall that the elasticity of demand is defined by

$$\eta(Y_t) = \frac{P_t}{Y_t B_{tt}(Y_t)} < 0$$

Use it to replace $B_{YY}(Y_t)$ in (30) to express the dynamics of resource use as

$$\frac{\dot{Y}_t}{Y_t} = r\eta(Y_t)\frac{q_t}{P_t} \tag{31}$$

Given (27), equation (31) may be expressed as

$$\frac{\dot{Y}_t}{Y_t} = r\eta(Y_t)\left(1 - \frac{c(S_t)}{P_t}\right) \tag{31}$$

Optimal resource use declines faster over time as the interest rate increases, demand is more elastic, and the share of extraction cost to price is smaller. Given initial resource stock, S_0, the faster the rate of decline in resource use over time, the greater resource use in the first period. Thus, initial resource use and rate of decline in use are larger when the interest rate is high, and elasticity of demand is relatively larger than when the interest rate is low and demand is more inelastic.

Finally, to obtain an expression for the dynamics of output price, differentiate $P_t = B_Y(Y_t)$ with respect to time and, using the definition of demand elasticity

$$\frac{\eta(Y_t)\dot{P}_t}{P_t} = \frac{\dot{Y}_t}{Y_t}$$

Given (31)

$$\frac{\dot{P}_t}{P_t} = r\left(1 - \frac{c(S_t)}{P_t}\right) \tag{32}$$

This result is an extension of (18) for continuous time problems.

Outcomes Under Open Access

An open access resource used by profit maximizing producers results in a level of use for each period where resource price is equal to per unit extraction cost. Formally

$$P_t = c(S_t) = B_Y(Y_t) \tag{33}$$

Owing to the decline in the resource stock over time, extraction cost and the resource price under open access increase over time, while output declines. Total differentiation of (33) yield the equations of motion for prices and output under open access

$$\dot{P}_t = c_S(S_t)\dot{S}_t \tag{34a}$$

and

$$\dot{Y}_t = \frac{c_S(S_t)\dot{S}_t}{B_{YY}(Y_t)}$$

$$= \frac{\eta(Y_t)Y_t c_S(S_t)\dot{S}_t}{P_t} \tag{34b}$$

The increase in output price over time is equal to the decline in the resource stock times the marginal effect of this decline on extraction costs. The magnitude of the resulting effect on output depends on the marginal effect of this change in output price on demand.

To compare open access with optimal outcomes, let P_t^c, Y_t^c, and S_t^c denote competitive price, output, and stock under the open access case, and P_t^o, Y_t^o, and S_t^o denote these variables under the optimal outcome. Given (27) and (33), prices under the two systems can be compared

$$P_0^c = c(S_0) < P_0^o = c(S_0) + q_0 \tag{35}$$

From (35), $Y_0^c < Y_0^o$, which indicates, compared to the socially optimal outcome, that there is excessive use of the resource in the open access case. Figure 3.7a, b, and c depicts a general pattern of prices, output, and resource stock under the open access and optimal outcome. During the first period, from 0 to some point in time, t_a, more output is produced under open access. The extensive extraction up to that point in time depletes the resource stock and, from t_a on, less output is used under open access than under the optimal solution.

Nonrenewable Resources as Inputs

Nonrenewable resources serve as inputs in agricultural and other production processes. As an illustration of the relationship of nonrenewable resources, other inputs, and output, consider a case where output is produced by two inputs, one of which is a nonrenewable resource. Let Y_t denote output at time t, X_t the use at time t of an input that is a nonrenewable resource, and Z_t the other input. The production function is then

$$Y_t = f(X_t, Z_t)$$

and the equation of motion of the resource stock is

$$\dot{S}_t = -X_t$$

The price of the other input at time t is V_t, and per unit extraction cost is $c(S_t)$.

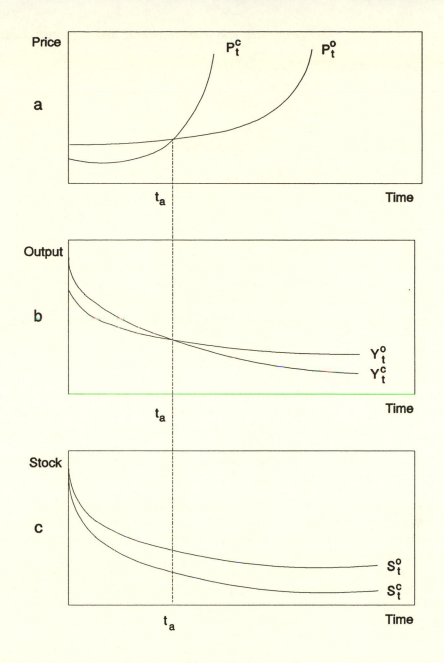

Figure 3.7. Management of nonrenewable resources optimal vs. competitive outcomes: the continuous case.

The optimization problem in this case becomes

$$\underset{X_t, Y_t, S_t, Z_t}{\text{Max}} \int_0^\infty e^{-rt}[B(Y_t) - X_t c(S_t) - V_t Z_t] \, dt \tag{36}$$

subject to $Y_t = f(X_t, Z_t)$, $\dot{S}_t = -X_t$, $X_t \geq 0$, and given S_0.

The *current value* Hamiltonian for this problem is

$$H = B(Y_t) - X_t c(S_t) - V_t Z_t - q_t X_t + P_t[f(X_t, Z_t) - Y_t]$$

The production function is introduced into the Hamiltonian as a constraint on output, and P_t is the optimal shadow price of output. Some of the first-order conditions in this case are

$$H_Y = B_Y(Y_t) - P_t = 0 \tag{37a}$$

$$H_Z = P_t f_Z(X_t, Z_t) - V_t = 0 \tag{37b}$$

$$H_X = P_t f_X(X_t, Z_t) - q_t - c(S_t) = 0 \tag{37c}$$

$$H_q = -X_t = \dot{S}_t \tag{37d}$$

$$-H_S = X_t c_S(S_t) = \dot{q}_t - r q_t \tag{37e}$$

This model extends the results of the simpler model presented previously. A detailed analysis of this type of model is in Dasgupta and Heal (1979). Equation (37a) states that the optimal output price should be equal to its marginal benefit. Equation (37c) states that the nonrenewable resource is used at a level where the value of its marginal product is equal to the sum of extraction and user costs. Equation (37b) states that the other input should be used where the value of its marginal product equals its price. Equation (37d) is the equation of motion of the resource, and (37e) is the equation of motion of the user cost.

Dasgupta and Heal (1979) demonstrate that when the price of the other input is constant over time, $V_t = V$, its use is increased over time owing to the reduction in resource stock and the increase in output price. The rate of increase in output price is smaller as the elasticity of substitution between the resource and the other input is larger. Thus, when capital serves as a substitute for ground water in production of agricultural crops, capital intensity of production should increase over time alleviating some of the impacts of increased water scarcity.

When there is open access to resources profit-maximizing input-use levels of firms are

$$P_t f_X(X_t, Z_t) = c(S_t) \tag{38a}$$

and

$$P_t f_Z(X_t, Z_t) = V_t \tag{38b}$$

Equation (38a) states that the resource is used at a level where the value of its marginal product is equal to extraction costs, and the other input is used at a level where the value of its marginal product is equal to its price. Comparison of these outcomes to the optimal conditions indicates that, under open access, there is overuse of the nonrenewable resource and underuse of alternative inputs in early periods, which leads to excessive resource depletion. This market failure may call for policy intervention in the form of either privatization of the resource, a tax of q_t dollars per unit of resource, or sale of extraction licenses by a management agency.

Backstop Technology and Uncertainty

In the continuous time framework, the timing of the introduction of the backstop technology is crucial in determining resource utilization. Consider the case where output is produced only with the resource. In the first period from time 0 to T, before the backstop technology is available, the production function is $Y_t = f^1(X_t)$. From time T on, the production function becomes $Y_t = f^2(X_t)$ with $f^2(X) > f^1(X)$ for every level of output.

Dasgupta and Heal (1979) show that under optimal allocation, more output and resources are used in the first period in cases where a backstop technology is available than when it is not available. It is very likely that, the earlier backstop technology is discovered, the more likely resource use is to decline while output increases.

Dasgupta and Heal (1979) also consider the case in which the timing of introduction of the backstop technology is uncertain. In their model, T is a random variable and the probability that a backstop technology is available at time t is equal to the probability that $T \leq t$. The criterion for social welfare maximization in the Dasgupta-Heal paper is maximization of expected net discounted benefits. They derive conditions under which the backstop technology considerations can be incorporated in a simpler (certainty) model of resource utilization by modifying (increasing) the discount rate. This risk premium added to the interest rate results in increased resource use in early periods as the introduction of backstop technology becomes more probable.

RENEWABLE RESOURCES

From a long-run perspective, dependence of agricultural systems on nonrenewable resources is infeasible. Agricultural systems based on resources that can regenerate themselves within an acceptable time period, *renewable resources*, are required for long-run *sustainability*. However, for optimal allocation of renewable resources, consideration of the limitations on growth of renewable resources are required. The research results summarized in this section represent some of the general principles of the economics and management of renewable resources. Most of these principles were developed in the economic literature on fisheries and forestry and are presented in detail in Clark (1976).

Some of the most important resources in agriculture are renewable. Rain is a renewable resource that is crucial for nonirrigated agriculture. Water resources that are replenished by snowmelt and rainfall are renewable resources for irrigated agriculture. Soils can be viewed as renewable resources when they have the capacity to regenerate themselves. Trees and livestock are also other prime examples of renewable resources in agriculture.

An important issue in the economics of renewable resources is the identification of efficient and sustainable resource allocation. A related issue is the development of policy interventions associated with inefficient markets.

The equation of motion of the resource inventory is the key relationship in the analysis of renewable resource systems. Its general form in cases when time is a discrete variable and when output, Y_t, is extracted is

$$S_{t+1} - S_t = g(\cdot) - Y_t$$

where $g(\cdot)$ is the growth function denoting the increase in the resource stock, S_t, during the period. The change in stock is the difference between the resource growth, $g(\cdot)$, and the amount extracted or harvested, Y_t. When the resource is a population of some livestock species, the growth function may be $g(S_t, L_t)$, reflecting that population growth depends on the initial population size and some input (labor) whose level is denoted by L_t. In the case in which the resource is a surface water storage facility receiving a fixed annual amount of water, M, through a canal, the equation of motion is

$$S_{t+1} - S_t = M - Y_t$$

A feature that distinguishes renewable resources from nonrenewable resources is the capacity of renewable resources to reach sustainability. A renewable resource system is at a sustainable state when the resource inventory does not change over time. In such situations the system results in constant yield, and extraction is equal to resource growth. There may be many possible sustainable states, and resource management policies entail choosing among them. Economists are interested in outcomes in which the whole system is in steady state. In such situations, both physical variables and their economic counterparts stay constant over time. In particular, resource-use levels and their prices do not change with time when they are at steady state. Economic research investigates whether resource management systems have steady-state outcomes, whether they will converge to these outcomes from their initial conditions, and whether these outcomes are stable. If a system returns to a steady state after an adjustment to a short-term shock, then the outcome is stable. Stable steady-state outcomes may be viewed as the dynamic equivalent of long-run equilibria, which are the subject of investigation of static economic analysis.

Economists have investigated the conditions under which optimal management of renewable resources result in steady-state outcomes and the stability of these outcomes. Much attention is given to the comparison of optimal and open-access outcomes and identification of policy intervention to correct market failures whenever they exist.

Consider first a situation where resource growth depends on the resource stock following the function $g(S)$ depicted in Figure 3.8. This growth function is especially appropriate when the resource is a biomass or group of livestock occupying a given environment. In this case the growth function is concave and assumes a positive value between 0 and S^* where S^* is the maximum sustainable stock. Figure 3.8 suggests that the resource growth is relatively small when the initial population is either too low, near $S = 0$, or too crowded, near $S = S^*$.

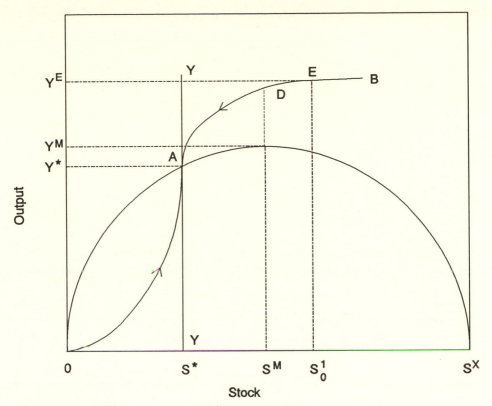

Figure 3.8. Renewable resources-case with zero extraction cost.

Extensive growth is likely to occur at a middle range of resource inventory, and growth reaches its peak when $S = S^m$. Resources growth in this case, $Y^m = g(S^m)$, is referred to as maximum sustainable yield and is the maximum output that can be extracted at steady state.

Does Y^m represent the optimal sustainable extraction rate? The answer to this question largely depends on extraction costs and interest rates.

The Continuous Time Optimization Problem

The social optimization conditions for a renewable resource problem are similar to conditions (26) for the nonrenewable resource problem. The equation of motion

$$\dot{S}_t = g(S_t) - Y_t$$

which is depicted in Figure 3.8, presents the only difference. Thus, the social optimization problem becomes

$$\left. \begin{array}{c} \underset{Y_t, S_t, q_t}{\text{Max}} \displaystyle\int_0^\infty e^{-rt}[B(Y_t) - Y_t c(S_t)]\, dt \\[2mm] \text{subject to } \dot{S}_t = g(S_t) - Y_t,\ S_t \geq 0,\ \text{and given } S_0 \end{array} \right\} \qquad (39)$$

The temporal Hamiltonian for this optimization problem is

$$H(t) = B(Y_t) - Y_t c(S_t) + q_t [g(S_t) - Y_t]$$

where q_t is user cost, or shadow price of the resource stock. Optimal resource allocation rules are

$$H_Y = B_Y(Y_t) - c(S_t) - q_t = 0 \qquad (40a)$$

$$H_S = -Y_t c_S(S_t) + q_t g_S(S_t) = -\dot{q}_t + r q_t \qquad (40b)$$

and

$$H_q = \dot{S}_t = g(S_t) - Y_t = 0 \qquad (40c)$$

for every t. The first optimal condition, (40a), which is identical with the condition for nonrenewable resources, (26a), states that resource use at time t is at the level where the sum of extraction costs and user costs are equal to the marginal benefit of consumption. Marginal benefit of consumption is equal also to the optimal price

$$B_Y(Y_t) = c(S_t) + q_t = P_t \qquad (41)$$

Conditions (40b) and (40c) are equations of motion for the resource stock and its shadow price. The rate of change over time in user cost can be obtained from (40b)

$$\frac{\dot{q}_t}{q_t} = r + \frac{c_S(S_t)}{q_t} Y_t - g_S(S_t) \qquad (42)$$

Equation (42) suggests that, under the optimal policy, the returns from extracting a marginal unit of the resource at time t are equal to the returns from keeping it in stock. In particular, the rate of change in the resource value associated with delayed extraction by one period, $\dot{q}_t/q_t$, is equal to the sum of three effects: 1) the discount rate, r, which is positive and serves as a compensation for delayed benefits; 2) the extraction-cost effect, $Y_t c_S(S_t)/q_t$, which is negative because larger stocks reduce extraction cost and thus serve to reduce the cost of maintaining stocks; and 3) the resource-growth effect $-g_S(S_t)$, where maintaining stocks tends to increase resource growth and is positive for larger stocks, $S_t > S^m$. Thus, condition (42) suggests that the user cost may decline during periods with relatively small resource stock when the extraction-cost and resource-growth effects may be stronger than the discount-rate effect. For periods with relatively large stocks, both discount-rate and resource-growth effects are positive, and this causes an increase in cost over time. There might be a middle range of resource stock levels where the three effects nullify one another, $\dot{q}_t/q_t = 0$, and user cost does not change with time.

Equation (42) provides the dynamics of the user cost, the shadow price of the resource before extraction. Total differentiation of (41) with respect to time obtains the equation of motion of resource price

$$\dot{P}_t = c_S(S_t)\dot{S}_t + \dot{q}_t \qquad (43)$$

Using equation (42) and (40c) to replace $\dot{q}_t$ and $\dot{S}_t$, respectively, in (43) results in

$$\dot{P}_t = rq_t + c_S(S_t)g(S_t) - g_S(S_t)q_t \tag{44}$$

Replacing q_t in (44) with $P_t - c(S_t)$ and dividing by P_t obtains the rate of change in resource price over time

$$\frac{\dot{P}_t}{P_t} = r\left(1 - \frac{c(S_t)}{P_t}\right) + \frac{c_S(S_t)g(S_t)}{P_t} - g_S(S_t)\left(1 - \frac{c(S_t)}{P_t}\right) \tag{45}$$

Equation (45) indicates how the rate of change in resource price can be decomposed into the discount rate, extraction-cost, and resource-growth effects. The larger the share of extraction cost in resource price, the more important is the extraction-cost effect relative to the other two effects.

The output equation of motion is derived from (45) given

$$\left.\begin{aligned}
\frac{\dot{Y}_t}{Y_t} &= \frac{\dot{P}_t}{P_t}\eta(Y_t), \\[2mm]
\frac{\dot{Y}_t}{Y_t} &= \left\{r\left(1 - \frac{c(S_t)}{P_t}\right) + \frac{c_S(S_t)g(S_t)}{P_t} - g_S(S_t)\left(1 - \frac{c(S_t)}{P_t}\right)\right\}\eta(Y_t)
\end{aligned}\right\} \tag{46}$$

Similar to the case of a nonrenewable resource, an increase in the discount rate will reduce output over time. However, because of the growth of the renewable resources, an increase in the extraction cost will increase resource use over time. Also, the impact of the growth effect, when $S_t < S^m$, corresponds to the extraction-cost effect. Thus, there may be a stock level when the output level does not change over time. Furthermore, output may increase over time for relatively small resource stock levels when the extraction-cost and resource-growth effects overcome the discount-rate effect. For large resource stock levels, optimal output is likely to decline over time. To investigate dynamic behavior under optimal outcomes further, consider two special cases, zero extraction cost and zero discount rate.

Renewable Resources With Zero Extraction Cost

Extraction cost of renewable resources may be negligible in the management of range for livestock within a relatively small enclosed area or in cases where soil is the renewable resource. When extraction costs are zero, the price of the resource is equal to the user cost

$$P_t = q_t = B_Y(Y_t)$$

as is indicated in (40a). This results in simpler equations of motion for all variables. In particular, the equations of motion of output, output price, and the resource stock become

$$\frac{\dot{Y}_t}{Y_t} = [r - g_S(S_t)]\eta(Y_t) \tag{47a}$$

$$\frac{\dot{P}_t}{P_t} = r - g_S(S_t) \tag{47b}$$

$$\frac{\dot{S}_t}{S_t} = g(S_t) - Y_t \tag{47c}$$

Optimal policy results in *steady-state* outcomes when the equations of motion in (47) are equal to zero. The line YY in Figure 3.8 depicts all the output and resource stock combinations that correspond to steady states of output and price, $\dot{Y}_t = 0$, $\dot{P}_t = 0$. From (47a) and (47c), at these points the marginal growth of the resource stock is equal to the discount rate. Because of the properties of the growth function depicted in Figure 3.8, all these points share the same resource stock level, S^*, where $r = g_S(S^*)$. Note S^* is smaller than S^M, because $g_S(S) \leq 0$ for $S \geq S_M$. The function $Y = g(S)$ presents the Y, S combinations when the resource stock is at steady state, $\dot{S}_0 = 0$. Point A, where $Y = g(S)$ intersects with YY, presents the output and resource-stock levels that will be attained when social optimization results in steady-state outcomes Y^* and S^*.

Unless the initial resource stock S_0 is equal to S^*, optimal resource management includes an adjustment period prior to arriving at a steady state. Changes in output and resource stock will follow (47a) and (47c), and the curve OAB in Figure 3.8 depicts the behavior of optimal output as a function of the resource stock along the path leading to the optimal steady state. Thus, if the initial stock is S_0^1, the corresponding initial output will be Y^E. In this case, both output and resource stock will decline over time, along the curve from E to A, until the optimal steady state is reached. Similarly, if the initial stock S_0 is smaller than S^*, there will be a stock buildup and an increased output period, following points along the segment OA, until the optimal steady state is attained.

Thus, if extraction costs are zero, the optimal sustainable output Y^* is smaller than maximum sustainable output Y^M. The reason is that time preference, represented by the discount rate r, makes it worthwhile to give up output in future periods in order to increase output in earlier periods. Even if the initial resource stock is S^M, output and resource stocks move along the segment DA until reaching the optimal steady state. It seems that it is more worthwhile to have a short initial period when output is greater than Y^M and have lower outputs thereafter than to extract Y^M at all times.

The optimal steady state gets further away from the maximum sustainable yield outcome as the discount rate increases. The analysis further suggests that the resource will be completely exhausted if the maximum marginal growth of the resource is smaller than the discount rate, max $g_S(S) < r$. Thus, when extraction-cost and resource-renewability rates are relatively lower than the discount rate, it may be socially optimal to exhaust the renewable resources. In other words, the fact that a resource is renewable does not guarantee that it is optimal to sustain it. This discussion indicates and the following example illustrates further the crucial role of the discount rate in establishing a resource management strategy.

A Numerical Example

Assume a quadratic resource-growth function

$$g(S) = \alpha S - \beta S^2/2$$

where α and β are parameters. This function is consistent with Figure 3.8. Maximum sustainable output occurs when $g_S(S) = 0$, which implies $S^M = \alpha/\beta$, and this yields $Y^M = \alpha^2/(2\beta)$. The maximum sustainable resource stock associated with $g(S^*) = 0$ is $S^* = 2\alpha/\beta$. The marginal growth of the resource is $\alpha - \beta S$ so that α is the maximum marginal growth associated with $S = 0$. Assume an infinitely elastic demand for the resource resulting in a constant price P. From (47a) and (47c), the resource reaches a steady state when

$$Y = \alpha S - \beta S^2/2$$

Thus, optimal behavior will lead to steady state outcomes with

$$S^* = \frac{\alpha - r}{\beta}$$

and

$$Y^* = \frac{\alpha - r}{\beta}\left(\frac{\alpha + r}{2}\right)$$

A steady state exists if $\alpha > r$, and if $\alpha < r$, the resource stock will be exhausted.

To illustrate the importance of the discount rate, suppose $\alpha = 0.2$ and $\beta = 0.05$ with a zero discount rate. Maximum sustainable yield is then $Y^M = 0.4$ resource units, occurring when $S^M = 4$ units of resource. If the discount rate is 0.1, then sustainable stock declines by 50 percent to two resource units, and steady-state output becomes 0.3. This 50 percent reduction in steady-state stock associated with a move from S^M to S^* results in a 25 percent reduction in steady-state output. If initial stock is $S_0 = 4$, it will be optimal to consume 50 percent of this stock, two units, on the way to the optimal steady state.

Renewable Resources With a Zero Discount Rate

The discount rate equals zero when decision makers value benefits in all periods equally.[1] The equations of motion associated with price, output, and resource stock are

$$\dot{P}_t = c_S(S_t)g(S_t) - g_S(S_t)[P_t - c(S_t)] \tag{48a}$$

$$\dot{Y}_t = \frac{-\eta(Y_t)Y_t\dot{P}_t}{P_t} \tag{48b}$$

and

$$\dot{S}_t = g(S_t) - Y_t \tag{48c}$$

Optimal policy results in steady-state outcomes when the equations of motion in (48) are equal to zero. Conditions (48) also provide the solution for the long-run equilibrium problem, which aims to find the welfare-maximizing sustainable outcome. This problem is formulated as

$$\left.\begin{array}{c} \underset{Y,S}{\text{Max }} B(Y) - Yc(S), \\[2mm] \text{subject to } g(S) - Y = 0 \end{array}\right\} \tag{49}$$

---

[1] To have a finite solution to the social optimization problem with a zero discount rate, the objective function in (39) has to be modified to maximize benefits over a finite time horizon. However, this time horizon can be very long, and the modification will not significantly affect the outcomes.

Note this is a static optimization problem so variables are not assigned a time index. This is less realistic but simpler than the dynamic optimization problem (39) because it does not provide a path leading to equilibrium and does not allow consideration of time preferences. The simplicity of the static analysis is a major cause for formulating a problem as (49). In our case, the Lagrangian form of the optimization problem in (49) is

$$L = \underset{Y,S,q}{\text{Max}}\, B(Y) - c(S)Y + q[g(S) - Y] \tag{50}$$

where q is the shadow price of the resource sustainability constraint. The optimality conditions are

$$L_Y = B_Y(Y) - c(S) - q = 0 \tag{51a}$$

$$L_S = -c_S(S)Y + qg_S(S) = 0 \tag{51b}$$

and

$$L_q = g(S) - Y = 0 \tag{51c}$$

Condition (51a), equating marginal benefits of consumption to the sum of the extraction cost and user cost, is identified as the dynamic optimality condition (41). Conditions (51b) and (51c) are equivalent to conditions (48a), (48b), and (48c) in steady state with $\dot{P} = \dot{S} = \dot{Y} = 0$. Thus, condition (51b) states that the optimal resource stock at steady state, is at a level where

$$c_S(S)Y = g_S(S)[P - c(S)] \tag{52}$$

Given $c_S < 0$, g_S at this optimal steady state is also negative. Thus, according to (52) at the optimal steady state with $r = 0$, the marginal extraction-cost saving of increased stock [left-hand side of (52)], is equal to the value of marginal reduction in resource growth. The relation $g_s < 0$ occurs when $S > S^M$, which indicates that extraction costs increase the optimal steady-state resource stock beyond the level that maximizes sustainable yield.

This point can be illustrated for a quadratic case. Again, let

$$g(S) = \alpha S - \beta S^2/2$$

and assume that extraction cost is inversely related to stock $c(S) = b/S$. The steady-state rule (52) becomes

$$-\frac{b}{S^2}\, Y = \left(P - \frac{b}{S}\right)(\alpha - \beta S) \tag{53}$$

Replacing Y with

$$Y = \alpha S - \beta S^2/2$$

in (53) yields

$$-\frac{b}{S}\left(\alpha - \frac{\beta S}{2}\right) = \left(P - \frac{b}{S}\right)(\alpha - \beta S)$$

Simplifying

$$-\frac{b\beta}{2} = P(\alpha - \beta S) \tag{54}$$

which results in the optimal steady-state outcomes

$$S = \frac{\alpha}{\beta} + \frac{b}{2P}$$

and

$$Y = \frac{\alpha 2}{2\beta} - \frac{\beta b^2}{8P^2}$$

The deviation of these optimal steady-state outcomes from the maximum sustainable-yield outcomes, $S = \alpha/\beta$ and $Y = \alpha^2/2\beta$, depends on the magnitude of extraction cost coefficient b relative to the price as well as on the rate of decline of marginal growth, β.

Social Optimality in Renewable Resource Allocation

The analysis of the previous section suggests that optimal renewable resource management over time and, in particular, the steady-state outcomes, depend on the discount rate, extraction costs, and the resource-growth function. Stronger preferences for present consumption, expressed in the form of higher discount rates, tend to result in smaller steady-state resource stocks. On the other hand, larger marginal costs of extraction, with respect to resource stock, tend to increase the steady-state resource stock.

Three major resource-use scenarios can be illustrated using Figure 3.9. The curve $Y = g(S)$ in Figure 3.9 denotes all the Y and S combinations where resource stock is in steady state. The YY curves denote alternative loci of points where the price and output are at a steady state. These curves are likely to be positively sloped under the assumptions introduced earlier, $\dot{P}$ as defined in (45) and $\dot{Y}$ in (46). The renewable resource systems attain steady states, $\dot{P} = \dot{Y} = \dot{S} = 0$, at points where YY and $Y = g(S)$ intersect.

The curve YY^1 in Figure 3.9 presents a situation where the extraction cost effect dominates the discount-rate effect, and the steady state resource stock, S^1, is greater than the stock associated with maximum sustainable yield, S^M. The curve YY^2 represents a situation where the discount-rate effect is stronger than the extraction-cost effect. The steady state in resource stock in this case is S^2, which is smaller than S^M. In the third case, the conditions that lead to steady-state prices are represented by YY^3, the discount rate is relatively large, and the optimal policy will not lead to a steady state. In this case the resource stock is likely to be exhausted.

The steady-state outputs in the cases with YY^1 and YY^2 are, by design, the same; thus, steady-state output prices are the same. However, the steady-state user cost, $q = P - c(S)$, is greater in the case with YY^1 when the extraction-cost effect is relatively smaller because $c(S^1) < c(S^2)$.

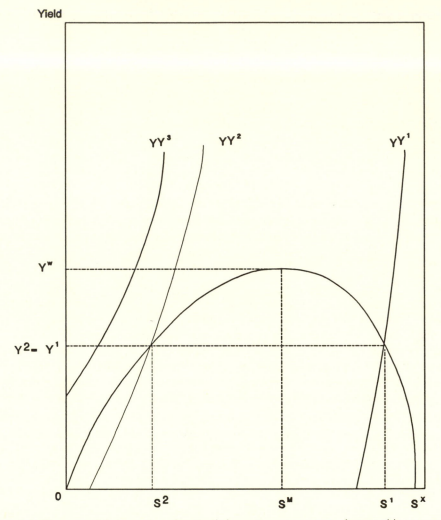

Figure 3.9. Three possible scenarios of optimal dynamic management of renewable resources.

This analysis suggests that if r is high, technological innovations that reduce extraction cost may lead to a lower steady-state resource stock and may make exhaustion of the resource optimal. Thus, considering soil as a renewable resource, the introduction of tractors caused optimal steady-state soil stocks to decline. Similarly, increases in demand over time, say by population growth, which effectively reduces the discount rate, may lead to larger optimal steady-state resource stocks.

Thus far, the discussion has centered on social optimization, but renewable resources, say pasturelands, may be utilized by competitive firms with open access. In these cases, output will be determined where price equals extraction costs

$$B_Y(Y_t) = c(S_t) = P_t$$

At each point, the resource stock adjusts according to the growth function, and the system reaches open-access steady state if, for some S and Y combination, Y^c, S^c

$$B_Y(Y^c) = c(S^c)$$

and

$$g(S^c) = Y^c$$

The disregard for user cost by producers under open access will lead to overextraction of renewable resources similar to the case of extraction costs. Under open access, there is no reason to look ahead, and the discount rate approaches infinity; complete extinction of the resource stock increases. Therefore, policies that may correct the misallocation associated with open access include the following: taxing the resource by the amount equal to optimal user cost, privatizing the resource stock, or issuing licences to harvest.

Use of Effort to Augment Resource Growth

Thus far, it was assumed that resource growth was not modified by human activities except for extraction. However, in many cases, effort can affect resource growth. For example, the growth of pasture can be enhanced by irrigation and the application of fertilizers, and fish populations can grow faster by providing food. Therefore, let us define L_t as the effort to *augment* the resource at time t. The equation of motion then becomes

$$\dot{S}_t = g(S_t, L_t) - Y_t \tag{55}$$

It is reasonable to assume that the marginal effect of effort is positive and decreasing, $g_L > 0$ and $g_{LL} < 0$, and that marginal growth increases with effort $g_{SL} > 0$.

Let W_t be the price unit of effort at time t. In this case the social cost has to include the effort cost so the social optimization problem becomes

$$\left. \begin{array}{l} \underset{Y_t, S_t, L_t}{\text{Max}} \int_0^\infty e^{-rt}[B(Y_t) - Y_t c(S_t) - W_t L_t]\, dt, \\[2mm] \text{subject to } \dot{S}_t = g(S_t, L_t) - Y_t, \, S_t \geq 0, \text{ and given } S_0 \end{array} \right\} \tag{56}$$

The temporal Hamiltonian for this optimization problem is

$$H(t) = B(Y_t) - Y_t c(S_t) - W_t L_t + q_t[g(S_t, L_t) - Y_t] \tag{57}$$

where q_t is again user cost, shadow price of the resource stock. Optimal resource allocation rules are

$$H_Y = B_Y(Y_t) - c(S_t) - q_t = 0 \tag{58a}$$

$$H_S = -Y_t c_S(S_t) + q_t g_S(S_t, L_t) = -\dot{q}_t + r q_t \tag{58b}$$

$$H_q = \dot{S}_t = g(S_t, L_t) - Y_t = 0 \tag{58c}$$

and

$$H_L = q_t g_L(S_t, L_t) - W_t = 0 \qquad (58d)$$

Comparing these optimality conditions to (40) indicates that inclusion of effort in the analysis results in an additional condition (58d). This condition states that at the optimal effort level, the price of effort, W_t, is equal to its value of marginal product. This value is the product of the resource-stock price, q_t, and the marginal contribution of effort to growth, $g_L(S_t, L_t)$. Conditions (58a) through (58c) are very similar to conditions (40a) through (40c) and have the same interpretation and implications except that effort affects these growth and marginal growth functions.

Differentiation of (58d) adds another dynamic equation depicting changes in effort over time

$$\dot{L}_t = \frac{\dot{W}_t}{q_t g_{LL}(S_t, L_t)} - \frac{g_L(S_t, L_t)}{g_{LL}(S_t, L_t)} \frac{\dot{q}_t}{q_t} - \frac{g_{LS}(S_t, L_t)\dot{S}_t}{g_{LL}(S_t, L_t)} \qquad (59)$$

Given $g_{LL}(S_t, L_t) < 0$, (59) suggests that the direct effect of an increase in the price of effort over time, $\dot{W}_t > 0$, is the reduction of effort. Considering cases with constant effort prices, $\dot{W}_t = 0$, (59) also suggests that effort is in steady state, $\dot{L}_t = 0$, when the natural resource stock and the price of stock are at steady state.

The steady-state levels of resource use and resource stock in cases with and without effort can be compared assuming a constant effort price. The resource use and stock combinations that result in steady state with and without effort are depicted by the growth functions $Y = g(S, 0)$ and $Y = g(S, L)$ in Figure 3.10. Effort increases the maximum sustainable yield from Y_0^M to Y_L^M and maximum sustainable stock from S_0^M and S_L^M. The S and Y combinations that result in steady state of both resource use and price and represented in Figure 3.10 by the curves YY_L^i for cases with effort and YY_0^i for cases without effort. The curves YY_0^1 and YY_L^1 correspond to lower discount rates than Y_0^2 and Y_L^2. To demonstrate that the YY_L^i curves are below and to the right of the YY_0^i curves, the same procedure that was used to derive equations (45) and (46) is used to obtain the dynamic equations of resource use and price for the case with effort

$$\dot{P}_t = [r - g_S(S_t, L_t)][P_t - c(S_t)] + c_S(S_t)g(S_t, L_t) \qquad (60a)$$

and

$$\dot{Y}_t = \frac{\dot{P}_t}{P_t}\eta(Y_t)Y_t \qquad (60b)$$

Equation (60a) suggests that the change in the resource price over time can be decomposed into the discount rate, $r[P_t - c(S_t)]$; extraction cost, $c_S(S_t)g(S_t, L_t)$; and resource growth effects, $-g_S(S_t, L_t)(P_t - c(S_t))$. The introduction of effort tends to increase the extraction-cost and the resource-growth effects. Because of these changes, the introduction of effort has a negative effect over time on $\dot{P}_t$ and a positive effect on $\dot{Y}_t$. Points on the YY_0^i curves in Figure 3.10, which correspond to $\dot{Y}_t = \dot{P}_t = 0$ in cases without effort, correspond to $\dot{P}_t < 0$ and $\dot{Y}_t > 0$ in cases

Yield

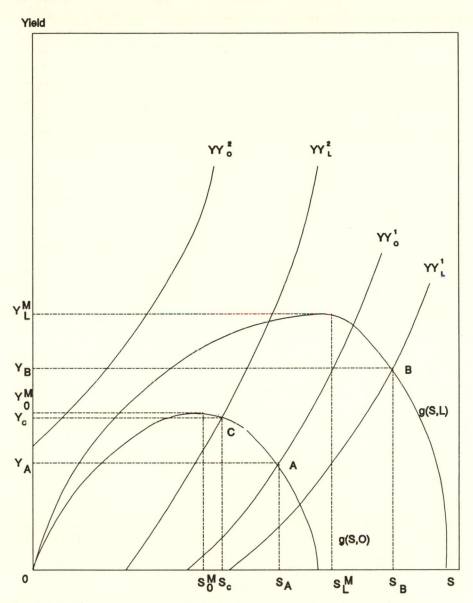

Figure 3.10. Optimal management of renewable resources with application of an input.

with effort. For any given S, the corresponding Y, which leads to $\dot{Y_t} = \dot{P_t} = 0$ in cases with effort, has to be smaller than the corresponding Y on the YY_0^i curve. Hence, in Figure 3.10, the YY_L^i curves are below the Y_0^i curves.

In Figure 3.10 two situations are considered for comparing steady-state outcomes with and without effort. For a low discount rate the steady-state outcome, when there is no effort to augment resource growth, is at point A. With optimal effort, the steady-state outcome is at B, where YY_L^1 and $g(S, L)$ intersect.

Thus, the introduction of effort increases both resource use and stock at steady state. It will also lead to a reduction in resource price and the price of resource stock at steady state. When the discount rate is high and equilibrium in resource use and price without effort are represented by YY_0^2, the system will not reach steady state. The curve YY_0^2 does not intersect with $g(S, 0)$, indicating the resource will be depleted in the long run. With optimal effort, the system will reach steady state at C, where $g(S, L)$ and YY_L^2 intersect. This extension of the renewable-resource model suggests that activities to increase and promote range growth or to increase soil fertility can result in long-run increases in resource use and stocks and may prevent resource depletion.

The inefficiency associated with open access to the resource, say open access to rangeland, is greater when resource augmentation is feasible than when it is infeasible. Given open access, none of the resource users has the incentive to put effort into improving the resource. Policy intervention in such cases could consist of a tax, q_t, to deter entry and effort, L_t^*, to improve the resource stock. The tax proceeds may be used to pay for the resource improvement.

Resources as an Input: Resource Stocks Provide Utility

Consider two extensions of the model. First, the renewable resource is used as an input with another input for producing an output. For example, pasture, a renewable resource, is used with grain to produce livestock; and in general, the renewable resource water is used with land to produce agricultural commodities. The output at time t is

$$Y_t = f(X_t, Z_t)$$

where X_t and Z_t are the resources and the other input at time t. The price of the second input is V_t, and the equation of motion for the resource stock is

$$\dot{S}_t = g(S_t) - X_t$$

with extraction cost of $X_t c(S_t)$.

The second extension is considering the resource as a direct consumption value. Benefits from the resource stock are given by the function, $R(S_t)$. The marginal benefit from the resource stock is assumed positive but decreasing, $R_S > 0$ and $R_{SS} \leq 0$. For example, the stock of water in a lake provides both a productive input, irrigation water, and direct consumption in the form of recreational benefits.

Adding the consumption benefits to the production benefits results in the following

$$\left. \begin{aligned} & \underset{Y_t, X_t, Z_t}{\text{Max}} \int_0^\infty e^{-rt}[B(Y_t) - X_t c(S_t) - V_t Z_t + R(S_t)]\, dt \\ \\ \text{subject to} & \\ \\ & Y_t = f(X_t, Z_t), \\ & \dot{S}_t = g(S_t) - X_t, \, S_t \geq 0, \text{ and given } S_0 \end{aligned} \right\} \tag{61}$$

The temporal Hamiltonian for this optimization problem is

$$H(t) = B(Y_t) - X_t c(S_t) - V_t Z_t + R(S_t) + P_t[f(X_t, Z_t) - Y_t] + q_t[g(S_t) - X_t] \tag{62}$$

where q_t is the optimal dynamic shadow price of the resource stock, and P_t is the optimal price of the output. Optimal resource allocation rules are

$$H_Y = B_Y(Y_t) - P_t = 0 \tag{63a}$$

$$H_Z = P_t f_Z(X_t, Z_t) - V_t = 0 \tag{63b}$$

$$H_X = P_t f_X(X_t, Z_t) - q_t - c(S_t) = 0 \tag{63c}$$

$$H_q = \dot{S}_t = g(S_t) - X_t = 0 \tag{63d}$$

and

$$H_S = -X_t c_S(S_t) + R_S(S_t) + q_t g_S(S_t) = -\dot{q}_t + r q_t \tag{63e}$$

Many of the results are similar to the ones introduced in the nonrenewable resource case. Equation (63a) states that the optimal output price should be equal to marginal benefits. Equation (63b) states that the value of marginal product of the other input should be equal to its price, and equation (63c) states that the value of the marginal product of the resource is equal to the sum of extraction cost and the shadow price of the resource stock. Equation (63d) is the equation of motion of the resource, and (63e) is the equation of motion of the price of the resource stock, q_t. Equation (63e) suggests that the rate of change in the shadow price of the resource stock is

$$\frac{\dot{q}_t}{q_t} = r + \frac{c_S(S_t)}{q_t} X_t - g_S(S_t) - \frac{R_S(S_t)}{q_t} \tag{64}$$

Equation (64) suggests that the rate of return from delayed extraction of a resource unit, $\dot{q}_t/q_t$, has to compensate for four effects: first the discount-rate effect, $r > 0$; second the extraction-cost effect, $c_S(S_t)X_t/q_t < 0$; and third, the resource growth effect, $-g_S(S_t)$, (which is greater than zero for larger stock) appeared earlier in (42). The fourth and new effect is the resource stock-value effect, $-R_S(S_t)/q_t$, which is negative because larger stocks increase consumption benefits from the resource, which reduces the cost of maintaining stocks.

The addition of this new effect shifts the YY^i curves in Figure 3.10 to the right. For example, it may lead to a move from steady state YY^2 to YY^1 or from YY^3 to YY^2. Thus, when direct-consumption benefits are accounted for, the likelihood of exhaustion of the resource is reduced. The inclusion of this effect also tends to increase the steady-state prices of the resource stock. Thus, if open-access inefficiencies are corrected by user fees equal to q, optimality can be achieved. Although users of the resource in production are subjected to higher direct costs, those benefiting from direct consumption of the resource are better off. In addition, indirect costs of the difference between the two groups should fall.

IRREVERSIBILITY

The management of resources in agriculture may have irreversible outcomes, and this has to be taken into account for modeling and analysis. For example, the clearing of forests and the drying out of wetlands to create agricultural lands may involve elimination of species and destruction of unique ecosystems that cannot be recovered. The damming of rivers and diversion of water sources may destroy fish and wildlife resources that cannot be replaced.

This section provides a basic discussion of modeling and implications of irreversibility for the management of agricultural resources. An insightful and extensive methodological and empirical overview of the incorporation of irreversibility in environmental management problems appears in Fisher (1981). In addition, Pindyck (1991) provides a useful survey of literature on irreversible investments, which discusses the tools for analyzing irreversibility problems in resource management.

Irreversibility occurs when activities in the present limit options in the future. Therefore, optimal policies are derived using recursive techniques. These techniques first derive optimal choices and rewards for future periods resulting from all possible present activities and only then select the optimal policies for the present.

Natural resource management choices as outlined in previous sections may be inefficient in situations when the resource in its natural state is a source of utility and its alteration is irreversible. If future changes in technology or preferences that will make the unspoiled resource valuable are ignored when present resource-use decisions are made, excessive amounts of the resource may be extracted in the present. This may lead to future volumes of the resource being irreversibly too low.

The Basic Model

Consider a resource that can be used as an input of agricultural production but that also can provide benefits in its natural form, say recreation. To be used in agricultural production, the resource has to be transformed or diverted in some way. Any amount can be diverted at any moment of time and can contribute to production from that moment on. However, once the resource is transformed, it cannot provide recreational or environmental benefits. This framework is appropriate to model land resources. Land use in agriculture may require clearing of vegetation, drying up of wetlands, and destruction of species.

Let E_t denote the amount of the resource providing recreational benefits at time t, K_t be the quantity of the resource that was transformed to agricultural activities before time t, and S_t be the resource available at the beginning of time t. These definitions suggest that $E_t = S_t - K_t$. Let the environmental and recreational benefits from the unspoiled resource at period t be denoted by $V(E_t)$. It is assumed that the marginal environmental benefits are a positive and decreasing function of the unspoiled resource, $V_E(E_t) > 0$ and $V_{EE}(E_t) < 0$.

Assume that the transformed resource is an input of an agricultural production activity with constant returns-to-scale technology. Let Y_t be output at time t, γ be output per resource unit, and c be production cost per resource unit. When all the transferred resource is utilized, $Y_t = \gamma K_t$ and consumption benefits are $B(Y_t) = B(\gamma K_t)$. If the resource is land, let S_0 denote the total land in a region. In the first period, K_0 of this land is cleared and converted to agricultural production, and $S_0 - K_0$ is left in its natural state. The coefficients γ and c are yield and cost per acre, and net benefits from land use at $t = 0$ are

$$B(\gamma K_0) - cK_0 + V(S_0 - K_0)$$

A nonnegative amount of land $K_1 - K_0 > 0$ may be transformed to agricultural production at $t = 1$, and the cleared land available for agricultural production in the second period is K_1. When all this land is utilized, net benefit from land use in the second period is

$$B(\gamma K_1) - cK_1 + V(S_0 - K_1)$$

Suppose that the cost of transforming the resource to agricultural use is zero and that both technology and preferences do not change over time. In this case, the amount of resource allocated to agricultural production will be constant in all periods and equal to K_0. This amount maximizes resource use in the first period as well as later periods, and is solved from[2]

$$\underset{K_0}{\text{Max}}\ B(\gamma K_0) - cK_0 + V(S_0 - K_0) \qquad (65)$$

The first-order condition for this optimization problem is

$$\gamma B_Y(\gamma K_0) - c - V_E(S_0 - K_0) = 0 \qquad (66)$$

Condition (66) indicates for an optimal allocation, the net marginal benefits from resource diversion to agricultural production, output per unit of resource times marginal benefit per unit of output minus production cost per resource unit, $\gamma B_Y(\gamma K_0) - c$, should be equal to marginal benefits from environmental and recreational benefits, $V_E(S_0 - K_0)$. Thus, $V_E(S_0 - K_0)$ is the marginal opportunity cost of using the resource in agricultural production. This condition further suggests that the optimal price should equal the sum of the marginal production costs and environmental opportunity costs of output

$$P_0 = B_Y(\gamma K_0) = c + \frac{V_E(S_0 - K_0)}{\gamma}$$

[2] The general optimization problem for $T + 1$ periods is

$$\underset{K_0, K_1 \ldots K_T}{\text{Max}} \sum_{t=0}^{T} \left(\frac{1}{1+r}\right)^t [B(\gamma K_t) - cK_t + V(S_0 - K_t)]$$

subject to $K_{t+1} \geq K_t$. However, $K_t = K_0$ when K_0 is solved from (65) provides an optimal solution to the general problem.

Outcomes Under Traditional vs. Modern Technology

Suppose that output can be produced with two technologies, traditional and modern. The modern technology may be a high-yield crop variety or a modern irrigation technology—drip or sprinkler irrigation. Typically, new technologies have higher operation costs but increase yields. Let γ^T and c^T be yield and cost per resource unit under the traditional technology and γ^M and c^M be yield and cost per resource unit under the modern one. The modern technology is assumed to increase yield, $\gamma^M > \gamma^T$, but requires higher per resource unit cost, $c^M > c^T$.

Consider first the case where only the traditional technology is available compared to the case where both technologies are available. Assume that the modern technology is superior, fully adopted, and for the relevant range of agricultural resource use levels

$$B(\gamma^M K) - c^M K > B(\gamma^T K) - c^T K$$

Also, assume demand elasticity for the final product is very inelastic, which is quite common for many agricultural markets.

Figure 3.11 depicts the determination of optimal resource diversion for agricultural use in cases where only one technology is used. The curve AB denotes the marginal benefit of land use in agriculture under the traditional technology, $\gamma^T B_Y(\gamma^T K_0)$, and curve CD denotes the marginal benefit of agricultural resource use with the modern technology, $\gamma^M B_Y(\gamma^M K_0)$. Because the elasticity of demand of the final product becomes more inelastic as output increases, there is a resource threshold level, K_0^B, where the marginal benefits of agricultural resource use under both technologies are the same, $\gamma^T B_Y(\gamma^T K_0^B) = \gamma^M B_Y(\gamma^M K_0^M)$. When $K_0 > K_0^B$ the marginal benefits of agricultural resource use with the modern technology are smaller than with the traditional technology. Note that, under $K_0 > K_0^B$

$$\frac{P_0^T}{P_0^M} = \frac{B_Y(\gamma^T K_0)}{B_Y(\gamma^M K_0)} > \frac{\gamma^M}{\gamma^T} = \frac{\gamma^M K_0}{\gamma^T K_0} = \frac{Y^M}{Y^T}$$

The relative reduction in price associated with the use of the modern technology is greater than the relative increase in output, which suggests that the elasticity of demand for the final product is larger than -1.

The curves EF and GH denote the sum of marginal production costs and environmental costs of agricultural resource use and diversion under traditional technology, $c^T + V_E(S_0 - K_0)$, and modern technology, $c^M + V_E(S_0 - K_0)$, respectively. Note the GH curve is above EF given $c^M > c^T$. When only the traditional technology is available, K_0^T units of resources will be diverted to agricultural use and $S_0 - K_0^T$ will be left in their natural state. By construction, $K_0^T > K_0^B$. When the modern technology is used in all periods, the resource use equilibrium in Figure 3.11 occurs where K_0^M resource units are diverted to agricultural use. In the example considered here, the availability of the modern technology tends to reduce resource use and increase conservation.

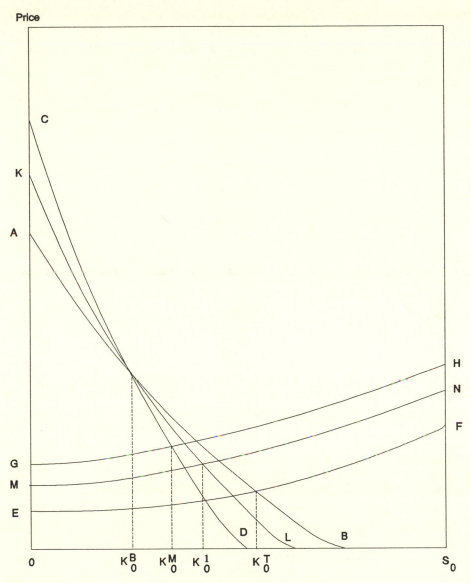

Figure 3.11. Transformation of irreversible resource to agricultural use.

Modern Technology Available in the Second Period

Suppose the modern technology is not available at the start of the planning horizon and is introduced in a later period. For analysis consider a two-period optimization problem, where the traditional technology is used in the first period and the modern technology in the second period. Without the constraint imposed by irreversibility, optimal resource allocation would have led to the use of $K_0 = K_0^T$ resource units in the first period and $K_1 = K_0^M$ resource units in the second period.

This solution becomes infeasible considering irreversibility, because irreversibility implies $K_1 \geq K_0$, but $K_0^T > K_0^M$. Irreversibility and the higher marginal benefit of agricultural resource use at the assumed range of outcomes, $K \geq K_0^B$, suggest that all the resource diversion occurs in the initial period and $K_1 = K_0 = K_0^1$. Thus, the social optimization problem becomes

$$\underset{K_0}{\text{Max }} B(\gamma^T K_0^1) - c^T K_0^1 + V(S_0 - K_0^1) + \frac{1}{1+r} [B(\gamma^M K_0^1) - c^M K_0^1 + V(S_0 - K_0^1)] \tag{67}$$

The first-order optimality condition of (67) solving for K_0^1 is

$$\gamma^T B_Y(\gamma^T K_0^1) - c^T - V_E(S_0 - K_0^1)$$

$$+ \frac{1}{1+r} [\gamma^M B_Y(\gamma^M K_0^1) - c^M - V_E(S_0 - K_0^1)] = 0 \tag{68}$$

By multiplying (68) by $(1 + r)/(2 + r)$ and rearranging terms, the optimality condition becomes

$$\frac{1+r}{2+r} \gamma^T B_Y(\gamma^T K_0^1) + \frac{1}{2+r} \gamma^M B_Y(\gamma^M K_0^1) = \frac{1+r}{2+r} c^T + \frac{1}{2+r} c^M + V_E(S_0 - K_0^1) \tag{69}$$

The left-hand-side of (69) is the discounted marginal agricultural benefit from resource diversion per period. Equation (69) suggests that it is equal to the discounted sum of marginal agricultural and environmental costs of the resource use and diversion per period. The determination of this optimal outcome is depicted graphically in Figure 3.11. The LHS of (69) is represented by the curve KL. This curve is constructed by a weighted sum of the curves AB and CD. Curve KL results when the curve AB is given a weight of $(1 + r)/(2 + r)$ and CD a weight of $1/(2 + r)$.

The right-hand-side (RHS) of (69) is represented by the curve MN. It is similarly constructed as a weighted sum of curves EF and GH. The intersection of the KL and MN curves yields K_0^1, the optimal diversion when a modern technology is available in the second period. Comparison of K_0^T with K_0^1 suggests that the availability of a new technology in the future can serve to reduce resource diversions when the demand for the product is inelastic and the diversion is irreversible. The resource conservation induced by the modern technology is $K_0^T - K_0^1$, and it becomes larger as the discount rate decreases, giving more weight to the future period.

Uncertainty About Future Technology

It is unlikely that decision makers will be completely certain about the availability of future technology. A more reasonable view assumes new technology availability as a probabilistic event that may or may not occur. Let δ denote this probabilistic event with the property that $\delta = 1$ in cases where the new technology is available at $t = 1$ and 0 otherwise. Denote the probability of having the modern technology, the probabilistic event, in the second period as β. Using these definitions, the distribution of δ is $\delta = 1$ with probability β and $\delta = 0$ with probability $1 - \beta$.

To analyze optimal choices, note first that optimal choices at $t = 1$ depend on resource diversion at $t = 0$. The analysis of choices under certainty suggests that diversion in the first period will not exceed K_0^T and will not be below K_0^M. It further suggests that, if the new technology is not available in the second period and initial diversion is smaller than K_0^T, resource diversion to agricultural use in the second period will increase to K_0^T. If the new technology is available in the second period, resource diversion is not likely to increase if $K_0 \geq K_0^M$. Thus, optimal resource diversion in the second period is

$$K_1^* = \begin{cases} K_0^T & \text{if } \delta = 0 \\ K_0 & \text{if } \delta = 1 \end{cases}$$

Thus, for $K_0^M \leq K_0 \leq K_0^T$, discounted social benefits for the two periods are random variables assuming two values

$$B(\gamma^T K_0) - c^T K_0 + V(S_0 - K_0) + \frac{1}{1 + r} [B(\gamma^M K_0) - c^M K_0 + V(S_0 - K_0)]$$

with probability β, and

$$B(\gamma^T K_0) - c^T K_0 + V(S_0 - K_0) + \frac{1}{1 + r} [B(\gamma^T K_0^T) - c^T K_0^T + V(S_0 - K_0^T)]$$

with probability $1 - \beta$.

Using expected net benefits as the welfare criteria, the social optimization problem aiming to find optimal initial diversion, K_0^*, becomes

$$\underset{K_0}{\text{Max}}\ B(\gamma^T K_0) - c^T K_0 + V(S_0 - K_0) + \frac{\beta}{1 + r} [B(\gamma^M K_0) - c^M K_0 + V(S_0 - K_0)]$$

$$+ \frac{1 - \beta}{1 + r} [B(\gamma^T K_0^T) - c^T K_0^T + V(S_0 - K_0^T)] \quad (70)$$

The first-order condition for this maximization problem is

$$\gamma^T B_Y(\gamma^T K_0^*) - c^T - V_E(S_0 - K_0^*)$$

$$+ \frac{\beta}{1 + r} [\gamma^M B_Y(\gamma^M K_0^*) - c^M - V_E(S_0 - K_0^*)] = 0 \quad (71)$$

Multiplying this expression by $(1 + r)/(1 + r + \beta)$ and rearranging the terms, the optimality condition becomes

$$\frac{1 + r}{1 + r + \beta} \gamma^T B_Y(\gamma^T K_0^*) + \frac{\beta}{1 + r + \beta} \gamma^M B_Y(\gamma^M K_0^*)$$

$$= \frac{1 + r}{1 + r + \beta} c^T + \frac{\beta}{1 + r + \beta} [c^M + V_E(S_0 - K_0^*)] \quad (72)$$

Condition (72) is similar to (69); it equates expected marginal net benefits and costs of resource diversion to agricultural use per period. In computing these per period marginal benefits and costs, a weight of $(1 + r)/(1 + r + \beta)$ is used in period 0 when traditional technology is used, and a weight of $\beta/(1 + r + \beta)$ is used in period 1 when modern technology is used with probability β. Condition (69) is a special case of (72) with $\beta = 1$, and condition (66), given $c = c^T$ and $\gamma = \gamma^T$, is a special case of (72) with $\beta = 0$. Thus, the optimal diversion of resources to agriculture with $0 \le \beta \le 1$ is between K_0^T and K_0^1 (Fig. 3.11). When the likelihood of the availability of the new technology is high ($\beta \to 1$), the initial diversion gets close to K_0^1. When the prospects for the new technology are low, ($\beta \to 0$), initial diversion gets closer to K_0^T. This suggests that the option of technological change occurring implies a reduction in resource diversion, and thus, greater resource conservation. The more likely this change is to materialize, the greater is $K_0^T - K_0^*$.

The welfare from following the optimal policy $K_0 = K_0^1$ and $K_1 = K_0^1$ when $\delta = 1$, and $K_1 = K_0^T$ when $\delta = 0$ is the sum of

$$B(\gamma^T K_0^1) - c^T K_0^1 + V(S_0 - K_0^1) + \frac{1}{1 + r}[B(\gamma^M K_0^1) - c^M K_0^1 + V(S_0 - K_0^1)]$$

with probability β, and

$$B(\gamma^T K_0^1) - c^T K_0^1 + V(S_0 - K_0^1) + \frac{1}{1 + r}[B(\gamma^T K_0^T) - c^T K_0^T + V(S_0 - K_0^T)]$$

with probability $1 - \beta$, whereas, welfare from diverting K_0^T at time $t = 0$ and adopting the modern technology if and when it is available is determined by replacing K_0^1 with K_0^T. Thus, the welfare gain from following the optimal policy is

$$\Delta W = \frac{1 + r + \beta}{1 + r}[V(S_0 - K_0^1) - V(S_0 - K_0^T)]$$

$$+ \frac{\beta}{1 + r}[B(\gamma^M K_0^1) - c^M K_0^1 - B(\gamma^M K_0^T) + c^M K_0^T]$$

$$- [B(\gamma^T K_0^T) - c^T K_0^T - B(\gamma^T K_0^1) + c^T K_0^1] \tag{73}$$

This welfare gain can be referred to as the option value of preserving $K_0^T - K_0^1$ extra units of the resource. It consists of extra recreational and environmental benefits, the first term on the RHS of (73), plus the extra expected net production benefits in the second period when the new technology is available, the second term, minus net production losses at the first period, the third term.

Using the example of land and given the inelastic nature of demand for agricultural products, this analysis suggests that ignoring the possibility of yield-increasing innovations in future periods may lead to overcultivation of land and excessive clearing of resources including wilderness areas and wetlands.

Changes in Environmental Preferences

The previous sections demonstrated that ignoring two features of agricultural industries, technological change and inelastic demand, in making irreversible resource management choices may lead to inefficient resource allocation. Fisher (1981) has emphasized another cause for wrong irreversible choices. Public preferences regarding environmental amenities are changing as a result of more knowledge, education, and higher incomes. Ignoring the possibility of such changes may lead to excessive transformation of resources from their natural state. This argument can be demonstrated by modifying the model presented earlier. Suppose there is one technology but the resource valuation function in the second period may be changed. This change in public preference is indicated by δ. The environmental benefit from the resource in the first period is $V(S_0 - K_0)$, and in the second period is equal to $(1 + \delta)V(S_0 - K_0)$, where δ is a random variable assuming two values of 0 or $\lambda > 0$. The distribution of δ is given by $\delta = \lambda > 0$ with probability β and $\delta = 0$ with probability $1 - \beta$.

Let K_0^0 be the optimal resource diversion of agriculture in the basic model (65), where environmental preferences do not change over time, $\beta = 0$. It is likely that diversion will not exceed K_0^0, $K_0 \leq K_0^0$, when $\delta = 0$. It is also unreasonable that resource diversion will increase in the second period when $\delta = \lambda > 0$ and it is realized that environmental preferences intensify over time. Thus, the optimal behavior in the second period is a random variable with distribution

$$K_1 = \begin{cases} K_0 & \text{with probability } \beta \\ K_0^0 & \text{with probability } 1 - \beta \end{cases} \tag{74}$$

Using expected net discounted benefits as criteria for the optimization, the social maximization problem becomes

$$\underset{K_0}{\text{Max}}\ B(\gamma K_0) - cK_0 + V(S_0 - K_0) + \frac{\beta}{1 + r}\left[B(\gamma K_0) - cK_0 + (1 + \lambda)V(S_0 - K_0)\right]$$

$$+ \frac{1 - \beta}{1 + r}\left[B(\gamma K_0^0) - cK_0^0 + V(S_0 - K_0)\right]$$

The first-order condition for determining the optimal diversion at period 0, K_0^* is

$$\gamma B_y(\gamma K_0^*) - c - V_E(S_0 - K_0^*) + \frac{\beta}{1 + r}\left[\gamma \beta_y(\gamma K_0^*) - c - (1 + \lambda)V_E(S_0 - K_0^*)\right] = 0$$

Multiplying by $(1 + r)/(1 + r + \beta)$ and rearranging terms yields

$$\gamma B_y(\gamma K_0^*) = c + \frac{1 + r + (1 + \lambda)\beta}{1 + r + \beta} V_E(S_0 - K_0^*) \tag{75}$$

Equation (75) equates marginal benefit from agricultural diversion to expected marginal production and environmental cost per period. Expected marginal costs increase resulting in K_0^* declining as β, the likelihood of increases in preferences for environmental preservation, or δ, the percent increase in preservation prefer-ences, increases. Thus, there will be a $K_0^0 - K_0^*$ reduction in optimal diversion in the first period when considering the possibility of increases in preferences for resource preservation.

Discussion and Extensions

The above analysis indicates that the planning of resource utilization activities that lead to irreversible changes must take into account probable future changes in the relative value of the environmental benefits provided by these resources. A higher likelihood of technological improvement or changes in preferences that increase the relative future value of the resources in their natural state reduces the optimal conversion of these resources to commercial use. Failing to incorporate these probabilities in the planning process may lead to overutilization of natural resources and excessive environmental degradation. Thus, there may have been excessive development of water projects if the likelihood of future development of efficient irrigation technologies or future increases in the value of recreational fishing were not considered when these projects were designed.

The model results further indicate that the option of maintaining resources and ecosystems in their natural states has economic value. They also point to the fact that better knowledge about future preferences and technologies is very valuable and may affect the design of a project in which irreversible resources play a role. The analysis in Pindyck (1991) suggests that obtaining such knowledge may justify delay in construction of new projects and affect their time schedules.

RANGELAND MANAGEMENT EXAMPLE

Range forage is a renewable natural resource that has the capability of contributing to the production of livestock and wildlife. This results in tensions between livestock producers and conservationists that directly impact the management of government-owned rangelands in the western United States. On government-managed rangelands livestock were traditionally permitted to graze for only a nominal grazing fee. Conservationists argue that this fee is too low, resulting in livestock degrading the range resources and contributing to a decrease in wildlife. For an analysis of this problem consider a growth function of forage that generally depends on the resource stock, $g(S)$ as depicted in Figure 3.8. S denotes the range biomass and Y the number of animals on the range. The choice of Y is the stocking decision. Every point on this growth curve represents a sustainable number of animals. Sustainability is the equality between the amount of forage consumed by the animals and net reproductive capacity of the biomass. The problem is to determine the optimal sustainable number of animals, Y^*, and range biomass, S^*, and how to maintain this optimal steady-state. Specifically, are unregulated market forces capable of achieving this optimal sustainable level or are governmental regulations required?

In general, the level of range biomass may be treated as a surrogate for rangeland condition. Maximum sustainable yield, Y^m, represents the upper bound of rangeland condition, so rangeland with a level of biomass in the neighborhood of S^m would be considered to be in excellent condition. Stocking of animals that reduces biomass below S^m could be considered degradation; however, this would imply that rangeland should never be exploited. Alternatively, degradation, as defined by Lindner (1990) and used for this discussion, is a reduction in biomass from S^*. Given some level of degradation, policies that generate an optimal path to the steady-state S^* require delineation. What types of governmental regulations, if any, are required, and what is the optimal length of time to achieve S^*? Unfortunately, S^* is a moving target. Biomass, S, is determined by both biological and economic forces that are by no means deterministic. The stochastic influences of these forces can result in unexpected levels of degradation, for example, a prolonged drought.

Existing degradation results from the short-run planning horizons of range managers who do not consider the long-run impacts of overstocking the range with animals (Lindner, 1990). This short-run horizon may result in a level of biomass below the socially optimal level indicating a misallocation of resources. Market failure resulting from this misallocation of resources is only a necessary condition for possible governmental regulation. It is a sufficient condition if the benefits exceed the cost from regulation.

As outlined by Lindner (1990), the following arguments support rangeland market failure:

1. Range managers have imperfect knowledge,
2. Range managers have incomplete property rights,
3. Social discount rate is less than the private discount rate, and
4. There exists option or existence value from rangeland improvement.

Lindner (1990) discounts the first argument by stating that managers have access to increasing amounts of literature addressing the subject of rangeland management. In contrast, incomplete property rights is becoming a major issue on publicly owned rangelands. Although grazing permits are generally not limited at some finite term, which suggest shorter planning horizons, possible future restrictions associated with permits may result in market failure. The increased scarcity of rangeland is enhancing the probability of future limits on the property rights of permit holders.

Many arguments exist justifying why the social discount rate should be less than the private rate. The dominant argument is that a lower or zero social discount rate is appropriate to allow for intergenerational considerations. A comparison of future generations' utility with the current generation's utility suggests a very low or zero discount rate. A detailed discussion on the social discount rate is provided in "The Search for the Social Rate of Discount" section.

Option and existence values are the amount current individuals other than the users of rangeland are willing to pay to improve or maintain rangeland conditions. As rangeland increases in scarcity, these values will take on more importance in the arguments for market failure.

Empirical investigation of range degradation resulting from range managers not considering the impact of current stocking decisions on future range conditions is addressed in Torell et al. (1991). They develop a dynamic model that considers the future impacts of current stocking-rate decisions. Optimal stocking rates, Y_t^*, determined by the dynamic model, are compared to decisions based on single-period (myopic) stocking-rate models.

In the single-period models GP denotes animal days of grazing per unit of forage. This standardization adjusts for grazing intensity differences as forage production varies owing to environmental factors. Stocking rate, Y, is the number of stockers, animals, grazing per hectare over a grazing period of length, v, and SD is the number of stocker days grazing per hectare, $SD = vY$. Current period grazing pressure, GP, is measured in stocker days of grazing per unit of biomass, S, $GP = SD/S$.

The relationship between average daily gain, ADG, and Y is a concave function

$$ADG = f[GP(Y)]$$

with $f_Y < 0$ and $f_{YY} \leq 0$. Average sale weight, W_s, depends on purchase weight, W_p, the length of the grazing period, v, and average daily gain, ADG

$$W_s = [W_p + vADG]$$

Increased stocking rates will decrease ADG and average sale weight.

Sale prices are determined by market forces, and a range manager determines which market price to accept by the size and quality of cattle produced. Heavier feeder cattle generally sell for less per unit of weight. Sale price P_s is then represented as

$$P_s = P_s(W_s, X)$$

where X is a vector of exogenous variables that identify relevant characteristics of the stocker cattle at time of sale. Breed, frame size, health, fill, sex, and muscling are examples of such characteristics.

A range manager selling in a competitive market determines a level of stocking rate, Y, that maximizes net returns

$$\pi(Y) = B(Y) - c(S)Y \tag{76}$$

where $B(Y) = P_s W_s(Y)$ and purchase price and weight, also influencing average extraction cost, are assumed fixed. First-order condition for profit maximization results in the value of marginal product equal to marginal resource cost. This solution to the myopic stocking-rate model might not be optimal when the impacts of current stocking rates on future forage production are considered.

In a dynamic setting, a range manager must determine the stocking rate that maximizes the present discounted value of economic returns. The impact of current stocking rates on future forage production may be modeled with an index of rangeland productivity, I_t, at time t, $0 \leq I_t \leq 1$. This index is a measure of average rangeland productivity relative to average production sustainable through time under light or no grazing, S^*. Average biomass production at time t is

$$S_t = I_t S^* \tag{77}$$

The impacts of grazing are capture through I_t. If relatively heavy stocking occurred in the previous year, the biomass production index for the current year may be reduced. The index is assumed to be a function of previous period's grazing pressure, index value, and other productivity declines not related to grazing-use rates. Other productivity declines might include naturally occurring brush invasion. Differentiating (77) with respect to t, the equation of motion for the state variable S_t is

$$\dot{S}_t = (\dot{I}_t S^*) = \Phi(Y_t, S_t, t) \tag{78}$$

Initial condition at the start of the planning period is $I_{t_0} = 1$, which implies $S_{t_0} = S^*$. Equation (78) defines the path of annual average biomass production, S_t, depending on the control path of stocking rates, Y_t. Average biomass production is expected to decline through time as brush invades a pasture, and heavier stocking rates are expected to accelerate the rate of brush invasion.

A profit-maximizing range manager will maximize the discounted net present value of grazing over an infinite planning horizon

$$PV = \int_{t_0}^{\infty} e^{-rt}[B(Y) - c(S)Y]\, dt$$

where $t_0 \geq 0$ reflects a grazing deferment policy for $S_{t_0} = \dot{S}$.

In both the single-period and dynamic model, grazing pressure directly impacts current period beef production through grazing pressure impacts to ADG. However, in the dynamic model, the effect of stocking intensity in previous years is captured through its impact on biomass production during the current period. To evaluate the differences in optimal stocking-rate time paths between the single-period and dynamic models, the single-period model can be iteratively solved for similar price and cost conditions. The myopic optimal stocking rate for the first year is determined, and then the equation of motion is used to define average biomass production that would result in year 2. The myopic stocking rate for year 2 is then calculated, and the procedure is repeated over the planning horizon. A similar procedure with dynamic interactions considered in the optimization is employed for the dynamic model.

As an application Torell et al. (1991) employ data from a long-term grazing study, years 1955 through 1969, conducted in eastern Colorado. The production function and equation of motion were estimated using ordinary least squares. A 10-year price cycle model by Schroeder et al. (1988) is used to estimate purchase and sale prices for feeder cattle. As indicated in this price model, heavier feeder steers generally sell for less per kilogram, and thus an increased stocking rate will increase sale price.

Torell et al. (1991) determined 40 year optimal biomass time paths associated with both the single-period and dynamic model. Figure 3.12 illustrates these paths. Biomass production varies optimally through time in a 10-year cycle defined by the price cycle. After an initial deferment in grazing, a time path indicates a reduction in biomass production for convergence to the 10-year cycle. Thus,

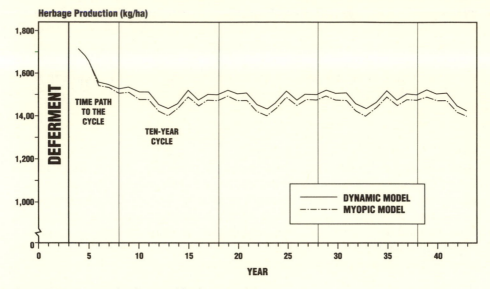

Figure 3.12. Time path of optimal herbage production.

producing at a maximum sustainable yield would not be optimal. Peak biomass production is not maintained under profit-maximizing stocking rates with either the myopic or dynamic models. Rangeland productivity is not devastated either. Within the 10-year cycle, optimal rangeland production is around 1,500 kilograms per hectare under the dynamic model and 1,450 kilograms per hectare for the myopic model. Toward the end of the planning horizon, biomass production declines because there is no additional future value to remaining forage. The opportunity cost of increased grazing is zero. This is represented by a decline in the time path at the end of the planning horizon.

The results of Torell et al. (1991) indicate little differences from using short-run planning horizons as opposed to considering the long-run impacts of overstocking. However, different biological and economic conditions can result in alternative conclusions. For example, Pope and McBryde (1984) developed a dynamic stocking-rate model for cow/calf operations. Their results indicate that planning horizons of 1 and 10 years result in little difference in stocking rates and biomass levels. At the end of 10 years a steady state had not been reached, and biomass was on the decline. However, considering an infinite planning horizon resulted in a steady-state solution within the 10-year period, with biomass significantly higher compared to the 1- and 10-year planning horizon at year 10. Thus, degradation of the rangeland may occur given short-run planning horizons. These results only consider the first two arguments for rangeland market failure. Further research considering the social discount rate and option and existence values is required. Limited evidence is provided by Pope and McBryde on changes in the discount rate. Changing the discount rate from 5 to 10 percent considering an infinite planning horizon resulted in only minor changes in the results.

REPLACEMENT AND RECYCLING OF NATURAL RESOURCES

A common characteristic of some renewable resources is that at a point in time they will regenerate to the extent that the original resource is replaced by a new resource. The resource has a growth function $g(\cdot)$ denoting the increase in the resource stock during the life of the resource. However, at some point the resource will be naturally replaced. However, at some point the resource will be naturally replaced. Forest trees are the classic example of resource replacement. At some point in time, an old stand of trees will be replaced by a new stand of trees. In agriculture, pomology and livestock are also characterized by resource replacement. These resources may provide a flow of output through time. For example, trees may yield fruits, nuts, or bark on an annual basis, cows produce a daily supply of milk, and laying hens supply eggs. The resources may also yield a final output at the time of replacement, called salvage value. For example, salvage value is the value of lumber from forest trees or meat from slaughtered livestock. It is the value of the harvest associated with the resource use. Thus, a resource can provide both a flow of output through time and a final salvage value when it is replaced. The relative value of a flow of output versus the salvage value depends on the nature of the resource. In the case of laying hens and fruit trees, the salvage values of the hens or trees are small relative to the flow of outputs, eggs, or fruit. Alternatively, for forest trees the salvage value may be the only output. The ability to control both the flow of output and salvage value depends on the nature of the renewable resource. For domesticated resources, including orchards or livestock, the flow of output and salvage value may be controlled by the inputs applied to the resource. For example, the level of pesticides or irrigation applications on fruit trees affects the quantity and quality of annual fruit harvest. For other renewable resources, limited ability for control exists. Generally, for forest trees, little if any input is used other than for fire control.

In general, the natural replacement of the resource does result in a sustainable resource allocation. However, this natural replacement may not result in an optimal sustainable allocation. Optimization criteria, including internal rate of return, maximum sustainable yield, or maximum net present value, may result in replacement decisions prior to natural replacement. As the resource ages, its flow of output and salvage value might at first increase; however, a point may be reached where one or both decline. This suggests replacement decisions prior to natural replacement.

A Simple Replacement Model

Faustmann (1968), Samuelson (1937), Prienreich (1938), Hirschleifer (1958), Jorgenson (1974), and Bellman (1957) provide a basic structure for the examination of replacement decisions. Consider first a resource that will not be replaced; the benefits derived from the resource are a function of time, $R(t) = B(t) - c(t)$, rather than output and stock of the resource, $B(Y) - c(S)$. The present value of the stream of returns associated with this resource is

$$PV = \int_0^T R(t)\, e^{-rt}\, dt + M(T)\, e^{-rt} \qquad (79)$$

where the resource is initiated at time 0 and removed in time T, and $M(T)$ is a salvage value for the resource. For forest trees the flow of benefits $R(t)$ may be zero or negative and only the salvage value, lumber, yields a positive return, whereas, in fruit or nut trees $R(t)$ may at first be negative as the tree stand initially matures, but at some point $R(t)$ will be positive. The salvage value, $M(T)$, may be negative for these trees, representing the cost to remove the old trees if the wood itself has no value. Equation (79) is the general form of the replacement problem considering both the flow of net returns through time and final salvage value. To determine the replacement age that maximizes the present value of the returns from one resource, T^*, the derivative of (79) with respect to replacement age T is set equal to zero

$$R(T^*) + M_T(T^*) = rM(T^*)$$

The *optimal replacement age*, T^*, occurs where marginal revenue equals marginal opportunity cost. Marginal revenue is residual returns, $R(T^*)$, plus changes in resource value, $M_T(T^*)$. Marginal opportunity cost is the interest that could be earned by selling the resource, $rM(T^*)$. Figure 3.13 illustrates paths for marginal revenue and opportunity cost and the optimal replacement age, T^*. As indicated in Figure 3.13, in the early stages of a resource's life, marginal revenue may be negative. The cost of maintaining the resource exceeds the returns and changes in resource value. For example, a laying hen may initially not produce sufficient egg volume to cover weekly maintenance and the change in resource value, measured as the increase in hen weight, is small. In pomology, it generally takes several years before fruit production is at a level where harvest returns cover costs. However, during this period, the value of the trees is increasing, measured as increases in resource value, $M_T(T^*)$. Marginal revenue may then be positive even in these early years. As a resource ages, marginal revenue will at some point start to decline. For example, egg production will be less for old hens. Also the change in resource value may decline. In the case of forest trees, disease and trunk damage will result in a point where the value of a tree in terms of lumber declines.

Risk and uncertainty also affect the timing of resource replacement. If there is uncertainty concerning the future value of a resource, future returns may be discounted more heavily. Such an increase in the discount rate, r, would result in an upward shift in the marginal opportunity-cost curve, Figure 3.13, reducing the optimal replacement age. Potential for some new technology may result in this uncertainty. For example, possible development of a new early-maturing pecan, which results in capturing the high early price, will decrease the value of existing pecan trees. This possible development results in uncertainty associated with future returns, and thus these returns may be discounted more heavily. A new technology may also increase the value of a resource. New freeze protection techniques in pomology would reduce the freeze damage to trees and prolong their productive life.

In general the resource will be replaced with another resource once it is considered exhausted. If the resource is replaced with an identical resource, called pure replacement, the resource problem is then to maximize the present value of the entire stream of returns, TPV, rather than just the stream associated with one

Returns

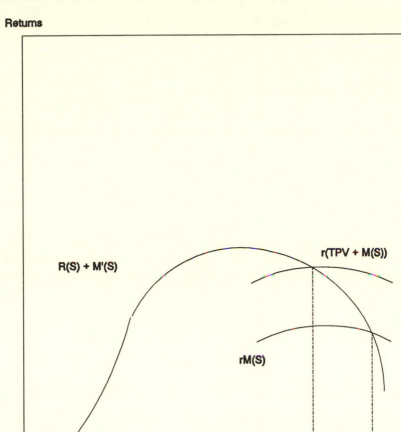

Figure 3.13. Optimal replacement age.

resource. This income stream is represented by

$$TPV = PV + PV\,e^{-rt} + PV\,e^{-2rt} + \cdots \tag{80}$$

Given the geometric series

$$1 + e^{-rT} + e^{-r2T} + \cdots$$

(80) reduces to

$$TPV = \frac{1}{1 - e^{-rT}}\,PV \tag{81}$$

If time is measured in years, this is an expression for the present value of a perpetual annuity received every T years. The optimal replacement age, $\hat{T}$, is derived from the first-order condition associated with (81)

$$[R(\hat{T}) + M_T(\hat{T})] \, e^{-r\hat{T}} = \left[\int_0^{\hat{T}} R(t) \, e^{-rt} \, dt + M(\hat{T}) \right] \frac{r}{e^{-r\hat{T}} - 1} \qquad (82a)$$

Equation (82a) states that the discounted marginal revenue must equal the annuity formed from the discounted total flow of returns from the resource plus the salvage value. The annuity

$$A(t) = \left[\int_0^{\hat{T}} R(t) \, e^{-rt} \, dt + M(\hat{T}) \right] \frac{r}{e^{-r\hat{T}} - 1}$$

is the flow of returns that would be realized if the resource is replaced at time T. This general principle of replacement is equivalent to stating that replacement age $\hat{T}$ is determined then average annual returns are maximized, which corresponds to where marginal and average returns are equal. Alternatively (82a) may be rearranged resulting in

$$R(\hat{T}) + M_T(\hat{T}) = r[TPV + M(\hat{T})] \qquad (82b)$$

Marginal revenue is equal to the marginal opportunity cost of not replacing the resource at age $\hat{T}$. Marginal opportunity cost is the interest earned by selling the resource, rM, plus the opportunity cost of postponing the earnings realized from the next and subsequent assets, $r(TPV)$. Figure 3.13 illustrates this optimal replacement age $\hat{T}$. This results in an earlier replacement age compared to considering only one resource, $\hat{T} < T^*$.

An increase in the salvage value, say an increase in the price of lumber, will shift the marginal opportunity cost curve in Figure 3.13 upward and reduce the optimal replacement age $\hat{T}$. In contrast to increase in the value of the flow of output through time, such as a price increase for fruit (P_1 to P_2) will not only shift the marginal opportunity cost curve upward (A) but will also cause a corresponding upward shift in the marginal revenue curve (R) (Fig. 3.14). As illustrated in Figure 3.14, when both the curves shift upward the influence on the optimal replacement age is small. A price change associated with the resource flow of output has little influence on the optimal replacement age.

As demonstrated by Perrin (1972), the effect of a change in the discount rate associated with replacement for a resource replaced with another resource is indeterminable. An increase in the discount rate might result in earlier or later replacement depending on the value of r, $M(T)$, and the path of $R(t)$. When the salvage value dominates returns, as is the case for forest trees, then an increase in the discount rate will unambiguously result in an earlier replacement age.

The optimal replacement age varies considerably by the types of resources. Laying hens are generally replaced within 1 to 2 years of starting their productive lives. Peach trees in the Southeastern U.S. generally are replaced approximately every 7 years. In contrast, rubber trees, as indicated in the example below are not

Returns

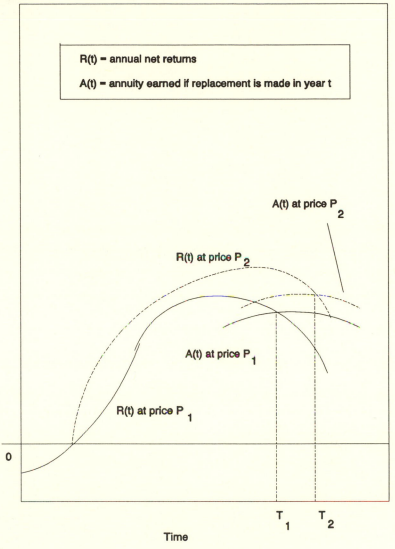

Figure 3.14. Effects of price changes on optimal replacement dates (T).

replaced until around year 32, and forest trees may not be replaced for 50 to 100 years or more. The opportunity cost of selecting a nonoptimal replacement age, T', and not T^*, is generally significantly greater for short-lived resources, poultry or peach trees, than for longer-lived resources (Fig. 3.15). As indicated in Figure 3.15, the foregone revenue associated with T' occurs at each time of replacement. For short-lived resources, this foregone revenue occurs more frequently through time. If laying hens are replaced yearly then in the space of 32 years the total loss of a wrong decision is the discounted value of 32 times the

Returns

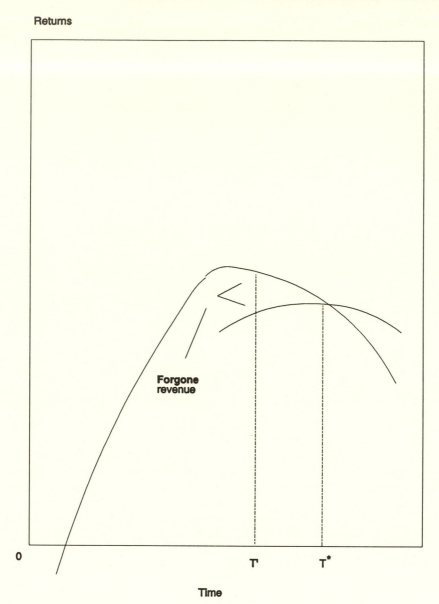

Figure 3.15. Foregone revenue from a nonoptimal replacement.

foregone revenue. This can be compared to only one loss for a nonoptimal rubber tree replacement.

Investigating the optimal replacement of rubber trees for the Peninsular Malaysian estate, Etherington (1977) developed a stochastic model for net returns based on rubber yield and price distributions. Results, illustrated in Figure 3.16, indicate very little variation about the mean optimal replacement time of 32 years. These results suggest that extension advice can be confidently given regarding the

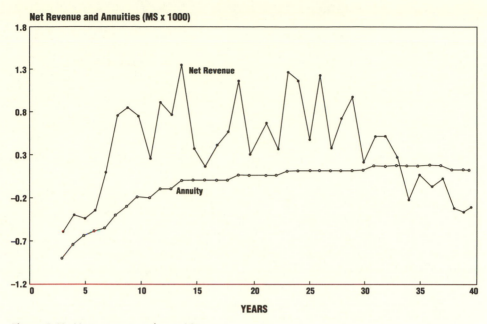

Figure 3.16. Net revenue and annuities.

optimal replacement data for this type of tree, and there is negligible cost to making a wrong decision. In contrast, short-lived resources, including poultry, may have substantially higher costs associated with a wrong replacement decision.

Etherington's results assume that the replacement is followed by a sequence of identical trees. If forecasts indicate lower prices or poor future yields, then the wrong decision is made by assuming a perpetual sequence of identical net-revenue cycles. This suggests that during "good times," estates should be encouraged to delay replanting, while during "bad times," earlier replanting should be encouraged. In terms of the model, this suggests using mean maximum annuity rather than the annuity derived from a perpetuation of the particular experience of the present tree. Figure 3.17 illustrates the reasoning for this conclusion. Low and high revenue streams, $R(t)_L$ and $R(t)_H$, respectively, and their associated annuities, $A(t)_L$ and $A(t)_H$, with a frequency distribution of maximum annuities is shown in Figure 3.17. The small divergence of optimal dates for perpetual sequences of identical net revenue streams is $T_L - T_H$, whereas, there is quite a difference between the optimal dates, $T_2 - T_1$, that should be adopted on the basis of the mean maximum annuity.

A General Replacement Model

In general, the flow of returns is a function of resource use, Y, and stock of the resource, S, which results in the equation of motion

$$\dot{S}_t = g(S_t) - Y_t$$

For example, in pomology, energy is generated and used in the production of fruit.

Net returns $

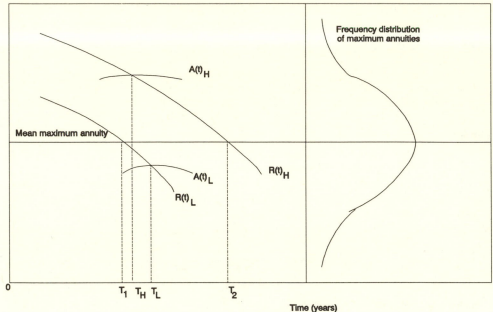

Figure 3.17. Alternative annual net revenues, annuities, and frequency distribution of maximum annuities.

Initially, in the early years, a tree matures and adds to its stock of resources S. However, in the declining output years, the resource stock declines. The benefits, $B(Y_t)$, are the value of the fruit harvested, and the extraction or harvest costs are $Y_t c(S_t)$. The present value of returns for a particular resource at the time of its introduction, $t = 0$, is

$$PV = \int_0^T [B(Y_t) - Y_t c(S_t)]\, e^{-rt}\, dt + M(T)\, e^{-rT} - F$$

where F is the initial fixed cost of the resource. In the case of fruit trees, F is the cost of planting. The objective function, defined over an infinite planning horizon, is

$$\text{Max } TPV = \sum_{i=0}^{\infty} PV\, e^{-riT} \tag{83}$$

subject to

$$\dot{S} = g(S_t) - Y_t,\ S_t \geq 0,\ \text{and given } S_0$$

where i denotes the ith resource. Equation (83) includes single resource injection, F, a flow of output associated with resource use, Y_t, and a single salvage value, $M(T)$. The decision variables are resource use, Y_t, and replacement time, T. Given the geometric series, the objective function (83) can be written

$$\text{Max } TPV = \frac{1}{1 - e^{-rT}} PV \qquad (84)$$

subject to

$$\dot{S} = g(S_t) - Y_t, \ S_t \geq 0, \text{ and given } S_0$$

The first-order conditions for this constrained maximization problem are equations (40) and (82) where $R(t)$ in (82) equals $B(Y_t) - Y_t c(S_t)$. These first-order conditions are necessary and sufficient given the strict concavity of the Hamiltonian in resource use, Y_t, and marginal revenue in (82) must be decreasing faster than the marginal opportunity cost.

Jarvis (1974) employs a modification of this model to explain why the slaughter of Argentine cattle responds negatively to a price increase in the short run. This behavior contrasts with the supply response of other agricultural products, including field crops, for which outputs are expected to rise immediately in response to price increases. For cattle, production can be increased only by increasing the size of the breeding herd or withholding animals for further fattening. Producers must then bid cattle away from consumers to increase the stock of the resource, S_t, which is the source of higher future beef production. Jarvis (1974) introduces a variable x denoting a fixed bundle of inputs to a steer at each time period, daily. Steer weight, Y^t, and costs are then a function of these inputs, x. Of interest is how the optimal age of a steer T^* and optimal input bundle x^* are influenced by changes in the model parameters. These parameters are price of beef, cost of inputs, and the discount rate. To determine the direction of T^* and x^* as a result of parameter changes, rough estimates of the price data and the growth functions pertaining to Argentine steers were used. This resulted in the following three conclusions: 1) A rise in beef price increases the marginal value product of each input, increasing the optimal feed ration and the optimal slaughter age. 2) A rise in the cost of inputs reduces both the daily input and the optimal slaughter age. Animals are fed not only less per day, but for a shorter period of time because they grow more slowly at any given age. 3) A rise in the discount rate reduces the daily feed inputs, because higher feed investment implies higher interest costs. The increase in the discount rate also reduces the optimal slaughter age, as it increases the interest foregone at every age. Specifically, these results indicate that a negative slaughter response for steers is expected in the short run.

Recyclable Resources

Decisions to *recycle* versus replace a resource frequently occur in agricultural production. The decision in layer flocks is whether to force molt (recycle) or replace a flock, and farm equipment may be either refurbished or replaced. Recycling is a major consideration in the decision-making calculus of resource use. There exists a tradeoff in efforts toward recycling currently used renewable resources or replacing these resources. This is particularly true in the presence of varying prices. In layer flocks, an annual egg price cycle directly influences replacement decisions.

Theoretically, let $R(t)$ and $V(t)$ be concave functions denoting the net returns in time t when a resource is first used and after it is recycled, respectively. The present value of the stream of returns for a resource that may be recycled is represented by

$$PV = -F + \int_0^Z R(t)\, e^{-rt}\, dt - C\, e^{-rZ} + \int_Z^{Z+T} V(t)\, e^{-rt}\, dt + M(Z+T)\, e^{-r(Z+T)}$$

$$(85)$$

where C denotes the fixed cost of recycling. The resource is initially used in time 0 and recycled in time Z and finally replaced in time $Z + T$, where T is the length of the recycled production period. The income stream for this resource is

$$TPV = PV + PV\, e^{-r(Z+T)} + PV\, e^{-r2(Z+T)} + \cdots + \qquad (86)$$

Given the geometric series, (86) reduces to

$$TPV = \frac{PV}{1 - e^{-r(Z+T)}} \qquad (87)$$

The first-order conditions from maximizing (85) with respect to recycle age Z and recycled production length T are

$$R(Z) + V(Z+T)\, e^{-rT} - V(Z) + (\partial M/\partial Z)\, e^{-rT} = r[(TPV + M)\, e^{-rT} - C] \qquad (88a)$$

and

$$V(Z+T) + \partial M/\partial T - r(TPV + M) \qquad (88b)$$

Condition (88b) is the classical Faustmann-Samuelson replacement criterion, which corresponds to (82b). Equation (88a) is a modification of the Faustmann-Samuelson criterion where at recycle time Z, marginal revenue equals marginal opportunity costs. Marginal revenue is defined as residual earnings $R(Z)$ plus the value $V(Z+T)\, e^{-rT} - V(Z)$ that is realized (or lost) from the recycling of the resource and the changes in resource value. Marginal opportunity cost is the discounted interest earned by selling the resource, $rM\, e^{-rT}$, minus the cost of recycling, C, plus the opportunity cost of postponing the earnings realized from the next and subsequent assets, $r(TPV)$. If the marginal revenue from recycling is less than the associated marginal opportunity cost for all time periods from 0 to $Z + T$, then the resource would not be recycled.

McClelland et al. (1989) provide an empirical example of optimal recycle and replacement policies for laying hens. Laying hens are recycled by force molting, which requires their removal from production, allowed a resting period, and then returned to production. The McClelland et al. (1989) analysis incorporates cyclical yearly prices, which results in possible varying recycle and replacement times, Z and T, respectively. The first-order conditions given cyclical prices are provided by McClelland et al. (1989). Investigating the optimal recycle and replacement of laying hens for egg-producing firms in northeast Georgia, McClelland et al. (1989) estimate the steady-state cycle and time paths to this steady-state. A steady-state cycle is an infinitely repeating set of optimal recycle and replacement times. Results

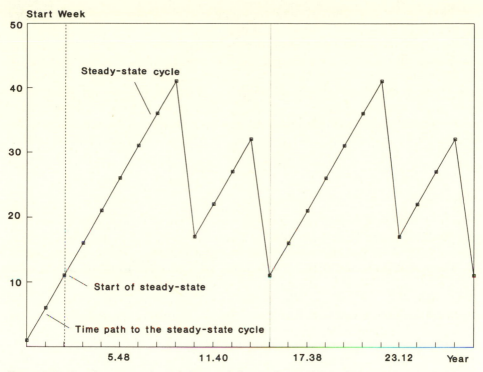

Figure 3.18. Steady-state cycle and time path for week 1 to this cycle.

illustrated in Figure 3.18 indicate the steady-state cycle and time path for weeek 1 to this cycle. The start weeks, 52 for the yearly price cycle, indicate when a new flock is placed in production. For the unique and stable steady-state cycle these weeks are 11, 16, 21, 26, 31, 36, 41, 17, 22, 27, 32, and then back to start week 11. Weeks 11, 16, 21, 26, 31, 36, 17, 22, and 27 are associated with a no-molt flock, and 41 and 32 are molted weeks. The time path to this cycle is 1, 6, and 11 start weeks. No-molting is associated with each of these start weeks. The time path to the steady-state cycle results from the general U-shaped nature of the egg price cycle, with relatively low prices between weeks 20 and 30, end of May to end of July, and high prices toward the end of the cycle, December. The maximum net revenues for this problem are associated with the juxtaposition of peak production with peak prices. Forced molting maintains the steady-state cycle within a neighborhood of maximum net revenues. The steady-state cycle indicates a forced molt at starting weeks 41 and 32 in the cycle, which will allow continuance of relatively high production levels through the peak price interval.

THE SEARCH FOR THE SOCIAL RATE OF DISCOUNT

Many of the results presented in this chapter have been found to be sensitive to the discount rate. In some cases, whether or not a resource is depleted depends on the size of the discount rate. Thus, it is important for decision-makers to choose an appropriate range for the social discount rate.

As described in the first section of this chapter, the private discount rate is determined by the behavior of individual consumers and producers operating in an intertemporal market. Of interest is whether or not these same factors are important in determining the appropriate social rate of discount for government investment decisions or resource policies. The arguments about the determinants of the social discount rate have come from both economists and conservationists. The literature on this issue is rich and interesting, for example refer to Lind (1986), Page (1977), or Pearce and Turner (1990).

Adjusting the Private Discount Rate

The questions surrounding the social discount rate can be divided into two, essentially separate, classes. Should the social rate equal or be derived from the private rate, or instead should the social rate equal zero.

The main points supporting a social rate being derived from the private rate are based upon economic efficiency and, given efficiency, the relevance of the factors affecting the private rate to the social rate of discount. Returning to Figure 3.1, economic efficiency is achieved and social welfare is maximized at point A. This suggests that market determination of the discount rate should apply to social decisions as well. A problem with this argument is the existence of market distortions, which result in several rates from which to choose. One distortion is the existence of corporate and personal income taxes. This drives a wedge between the amount of compensation savers must have in order to save and the rate of return borrowers must achieve in order to pay the savers what they require. In other words, the rate of return on capital in the economy, the marginal efficiency of capital, must be higher than the savers' pure rate of time preference. A second distortion is the influence of government monetary and fiscal activity on interest rates, which have little to do with the appropriate social discount rate (Page, 1977). Therefore, it is difficult to expect any particular market rate to reflect only those factors indicated in Figure 3.1.

Another complication in choosing from among market-determined rates is that the varying riskiness of various investment options leads to a large range of rates. It is argued that the discount rate applied to each particular public investment opportunity should be adjusted for risk in the same way. This would entail adding the risk premium associated with private projects having similar risk characteristics to some riskless social discount rate. Alternatively, it can be argued that discount rates associated with public investment projects should not be adjusted for risk at all, because the risk is spread over such a large number of people that the risk to any one individual is quite small (Arrow and Lind, 1970).

A Zero Social Discount Rate

Perhaps a more fundamental argument is: Should future benefits and costs resulting from public investment today be discounted at all? One logical answer is that interest rates exist, and thus, private individuals seem to discount the future. Because society is merely a collection of individuals, then to reflect the will of society, the social rate of discount should be positive.

Another argument for a positive social discount rate is based upon the assumption of diminishing marginal utility of consumption (Pearce and Turner, 1990). In general, historical growth rates suggest that societies will be richer in the future, so additional future benefits would result in lower additional utility compared to the same additional benefits today. Therefore, discount future benefits. A logical implication of this argument is that, as society becomes richer, it tends to place less value on additional units of consumption today. This would tend to result in willingness to pass more consumption opportunities on to future generations.

A third reason for a positive social discount rate is the illogical implications associated with a zero discount rate. If society values future benefits and present benefits equally, then, given an infinite future horizon, all benefits would be postponed indefinitely, or at least until the marginal utility of consumption in some future period has fallen to zero (Olson and Bailey, 1981).

Arguments for a zero or very low social discount rate are also put forward on ethical grounds. Conservationists argue that it is morally wrong to use up resources today in response to the preferences of today's society. They argue that intertemporal fairness dictates that society should value the preferences of future generations on equal terms with the wants and desires of the current generation. There is a problem with this view of lowering the social rate of discount to take account of environmental or resource considerations. Sometimes a lower discount rate can result in a faster depletion of resources than would a higher rate. For example, consider a public investment project such as a hydroelectric dam. A lower discount rate would make many more of these projects appear profitable and would also result in the accelerated loss of natural habitats. This is not consistent with the goals of conservation.

Two solutions to the above dilemma have been proposed. One is that public investment projects should be evaluated with a constraint of sustainability (Page, 1977). Some implications of this sustainability constraint were presented earlier in his chapter. However, this solution still does not answer the question about which discount rate to use. Alternatively it is suggested that one discount rate be chosen, based on the current best judgement, and used to evaluate all projects and policy options (Lind, 1986). Economists and government decision-makers have not adopted either of these suggestions. Instead, for policy analysis, a range of discount rates is generally applied to a particular problem. This range of discount rates both determines the sensitivity of results to changes in the discount rate and provides a set of results consistent with alternative underlying factors associated with the social rate.

CONCLUSION

Proper modeling and analysis of problems dealing with natural resource impacts on agriculture require taking a longer view than is generally assumed in other types of agricultural economic analysis. This chapter has presented the tools required to account for the different characteristics of resource problems.

Maximum economic efficient resource use will occur if the resource is privately owned by a price-taking, profit-maximizing firm that discounts the future at the same rate as does society. This does not occur very often in the real world, and thus, resource use tends to be suboptimal. The models developed in this chapter are used to describe a range of cases in which optimal resource use is not expected to be achieved in the absence of intervention and to explore which policy options might lead toward optimality. These cases include the shared resource, open-access problem, a monopoly owner of a nonrenewable resource, changes in demand for the product over time, the effect of backstop technology, nonrenewable resources as inputs in a multiperiod framework, the effect of extraction costs on renewable resource use, the effect of the discount rate on resource use, traditional vs. modern technology, the effects of uncertain future product demand and uncertain technological progress, and replaceable and recyclable resource use.

The chapter demonstrated that a simple two-period model can yield some useful implications, but the continuous time dynamic models, introduced in Chapter 2 and extended in this chapter, are very worthwhile for many types of analysis.

It is worth repeating three important points made in this chapter. First, there are many cases described above where unregulated resource use can lead to suboptimality and where intervention can, at least in theory, lead to optimal resource use. Such optimality generally relies on a regulatory authority that can determine the functional relationships associated with the problem, such as user cost or demand, with precision and with little or no cost. If this is not the case, then it may be better not to intervene. Second, when intervention is not feasible or is too costly, resource allocation under free competition is not necessarily more efficient than under a monopoly. Third, uncertainty about future resource availability, technologies, or preferences may justify resource conservation in the present.

REFERENCES

Arrow, K.J. and R.C. Lind. "Uncertainty and the Economic Evaluation of Public Investment Decisions." *American Economic Review* 60:364–378, 1970.

Bellman, R. *Dynamic Programming*. Princeton, NJ: Princeton University Press, 1957.

Clark, C.W. *Mathematical Bioeconomics: The Optimal Management of Renewable Resources*. New York: John Wiley and Sons, 1976.

Dasgupta, P. and G.H. Heal. *Economic Theory and Exhaustible Resources*. Cambridge: Cambridge University Press, 1979.

Etherington, D.M. "A Stochastic Model for the Optimal Replacement of Rubber Trees." *Australian Journal of Agricultural Economics* 21:40–58, 1977.

Fisher, A.C. *Resource and Environmental Economics*. Cambridge: Cambridge University Press, 1981.

Faustmann, M. "On the Determination of the Value Which Forest Land and Immature Stands Possess for Forestry." In M. Gane (ed.): *Oxford Inst. Pap. 42*, Oxford, UK, 1968.

Hotelling, H. "The Economics of Exhaustible Resources." *Journal of Political Economy* 39:137–175, 1931.

Hirschleifer, J. "On the Theory of Optimal Investment Decision." *Journal of Political Economy* 66:198–209, 1958.

Jarvis, L.S. "Cattle as Capital Goods and Ranchers as Portfolio Managers: An Application to the Argentine Cattle Sector." *Journal of Political Economy* 82:489–520, 1974.

Jorgenson, D. "The Economic Theory of Replacement and Depreciation." In W. Sellekaerts (ed.): *Econometrics and Economic Theory*. London: Macmillan & Co., 1974.

Lind, R.C. (ed.) *Discounting for Time and Risk in Energy Policy*. Baltimore: Johns Hopkins University Press, 1986.

Lindner, R.K. "Should Rangeland Rehabilitation be Paid for from the Public Purse?" *Australian Rangeland Journal* 12:61–66, 1990.

McClelland, J., M. Wetzstein, and R. Noles. "Optimal Replacement Policies for Rejuvenated Assets." *American Journal of Agricultural Economics* 71:147–156, 1989.

Olson, M. and M. Bailey. "Positive Time Preference." *Journal of Political Economy* 89:1–25, 1981.

Page, T. *Conservation and Economic Efficiency*. Baltimore: Johns Hopkins University Press, 1977.

Pearce, D.W. and R.K. Turner. *Economics of Natural Resources and the Environment*. Baltimore: Johns Hopkins University Press, 1990.

Perrin, R.K. "Asset Replacement Principles." *American Journal of Agricultural Economics* 54:60–67, 1972.

Pindyck, R.S. "Irreversibility, Uncertainty, and Investment." *Journal of Economic Literature* XXIX:1110–1148, September 1991.

Pope, C.A. and B.L. McBryde. "Optimal Stocking of Rangeland for Livestock Production within a Dynamic Framework." *Western Journal of Agricultural Economics* 9:160–169, 1984.

Prienreich, G.A. "Annual Survey of Economic Theory: The Theory of Depreciation." *Econometrics* 6:219–241, 1938.

Quigley, T.M. and E.T. Barlett. "Livestock on Public Lands: Yes!" In F.W. Obermiller and D. Reesman (eds.): Special Report 852, Oregon State University Extension Service, 1990, pp. 1–5.

Samuelson, P.A. "Some Aspects of the Pure Theory of Capital." *Quarterly Journal of Economics* 51:469–496, 1937.

Schroeder, T., J. Mintert, F. Brazle, and O. Grunewald. "Factors Affecting Feeder Cattle Price Differentials." *Western Journal of Agricultural Economics* 13:71–81, 1988.

Torell, A. and J.P. Doll. "Public Land Policy and the Value of Grazing Permits." *Western Journal of Agricultural Economics* 16:174–184, 1991.

Torell, A., K.S. Lyon, and E.B. Godfrey. "Long-Run versus Short-Run Planning Horizons and the Rangeland Stocking Rate Decision." *American Journal of Agricultural Economics* 73:795–807, 1991.

4

Aggregate Evaluation Concepts and Models

C. ROBERT TAYLOR AND RICHARD HOWITT

Economic impacts of resource policies fall into three broad categories. The first category includes all impacts that are manifested in the marketplace. Included in this category are, for example, impacts on agricultural producers, consumers (resulting from price changes caused by policy-induced production changes), processors, and input suppliers. A second category includes all public (i.e., governmental) costs or benefits associated with implementing and enforcing a policy. The third category includes all other nonmarket impacts. These impacts are referred to as external impacts or third-party effects.

Aggregate, as opposed to firm level, economic evaluations are called for when the resource policy in question will significantly shift aggregate supply and demand and thus significantly affect market prices and quantities. Furthermore, aggregate analyses of many agricultural resource issues must be done in a multicommodity framework because many commodities are related on both the demand and supply sides of the market. Many agricultural resource policies of contemporary interest have a differential impact on commodities and regions, thus calling for distributional analyses. Hence, aggregate analyses of resource policy needs to address impacts on producers, consumers, and taxpayers in a multiregional and multicommodity context.

Most agricultural chemical regulations, water use policies, and land use restrictions under consideration by States and by Federal agencies would impact enough agricultural producers to affect market prices. In such cases, firm level (i.e., partial-equilibrium) analyses can be quite misleading as to magnitude and direction of economic impact, unless such evaluations account for the aggregate price impacts. For example, consider a hypothetical pesticide regulation that would lower crop yield and increase production costs for users of the pesticide. Assuming that output prices did not change would lead to the conclusion that the users would be negatively impacted; farm income would decrease owing to the regulation. However, the lower profitability would lead to supply adjustments that would lead to a price increase for the crop on which the pesticide was used, and perhaps lead to a price decrease for other crops the affected producers might grow.

In general, income to producers as a group might be higher, rather than lower, with the pesticide regulation.

What economic concepts to use for measurement of aggregate effects manifested in the marketplace and what type of empirically based model to use for different types of resource policies are the subjects of this chapter. With many resource policies, such as possible pesticide regulations, there are some effects, such as changes in human health risks, that are largely nonquantifiable. While it is obviously important to address such nonquantifiable effects, it is equally important to address and estimate the quantifiable market effects so that informed policy decisions can be made. After introducing concepts for measuring aggregate market effects, a graphical and quantitative explanation of the aggregate paradoxes alluded to above will be provided.

No single quantitative model is in any sense "best" for evaluating every conceivable type of resource policy. There are special features of some resource policies that call for special types of models or at least models that emphasize factors such as input substitution, regional location of production, crop mixes, and output and input prices that are not central to other types of aggregate economic impact analysis. Thus, in this chapter we review the major types of quantitative models that could be used for resource policy evaluation and discuss relative strengths and weakness of each type for several classes of resource policies.

We begin with operational welfare evaluation concepts appropriate for measuring market effects of resource policies and then turn to illustration of the paradoxical aggregate effects usually encountered in aggregate evaluations. Finally, quantitative models and their use for resource policy evaluation are discussed.

AGGREGATE EVALUATION CONCEPTS

Analysis of the economic impact of resource policy on each individual impacted is not practical. Thus, it is common to identify impacts on segments of society, such as consumers of agricultural commodities, producers directly affected by the policy (e.g., users of a pesticide whose use may be restricted), producers that may be indirectly impacted by the policy (e.g., nonusers of the pesticide impacted by induced output or input price changes), taxpayer expense directly affected by the policy (e.g., publicly funded training of pesticide users), taxpayer expense indirectly affected by the policy (e.g., price support payment changes attributable to the price effect of the pesticide regulation), impacts on farm input suppliers, and impacts on foreign producers and consumers of affected commodities.

Although most economists would like to use some ideal measure of economic impacts, such as "utility," practical considerations dictate use of a more measurable and more operational concept. For effects manifested in the marketplace, such a concept is that of "economic surplus" accruing to producers or consumers of a commodity. In a market without price discrimination (i.e., where consumers pay the same price per unit for all units purchased), consumers are said to enjoy a surplus because they do not pay as much for intramarginal units consumed as

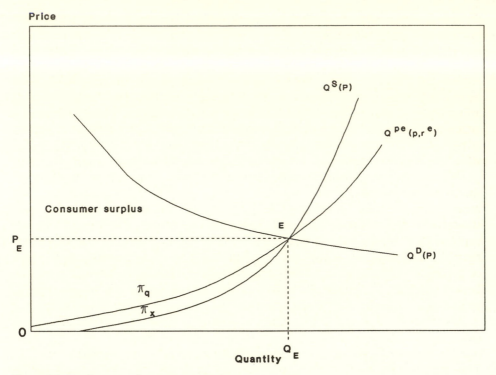

Figure 4.1. Producers and consumers surplus.

they are "willing to pay." A naive definition of consumers surplus is the area below the demand curve, $Q^D(P)$, above the equilibrium price, as shown in Figure 4.1.

Consumers surplus can be defined relative to ordinary (money income constant) demand curves, or defined relative to compensated (real income or utility constant) demand curves. Defined relative to ordinary demand curves, "surplus" as an area below the demand curve is an elusive concept to grasp, especially for decision makers not well trained in economics. However, surplus defined relative to compensated demand curves is a concept somewhat easier to grasp when it is viewed as the change in expenditures necessary to achieve a given level of satisfaction (utility). Note that this is not the change in *direct* expenditures (which is the rectangle OP^eEQ^e in Fig. 4.1), but the change in *indirect* expenditures associated with a given level of real income, which is the area under the compensated demand curve above the price line in Figure 4.1. Although selection of either of these definitions of surplus involves a value judgment (i.e., neither measure is sacred), we must, in empirical analyses, settle for surplus changes based on ordinary demand curves since compensated demand curves are not empirically observable, except in rare circumstances.

A useful concept related to consumers surplus is that of *producers surplus*, which is defined to be the area above supply (which is marginal cost in a competitive market) and below price (Fig. 4.1). Just and Hueth (1979) define producers surplus relative to *general equilibrium* supply curves, which differ from the common concept of (partial equilibrium) supply curves in that all other markets are allowed to make equilibrium adjustments. For example, in the simplified case of a single product market and a single factor market, the partial equilibrium supply curve in the product market would depend on both product and factor price. However, the general equilibrium supply curve in the product market has product price as its only argument since it accounts for equilibrium adjustments in the factor market (in response to changes in product price). A general equilibrium curve is given in Figure 4.1 as $Q^s(p)$, and one of the family of partial equilibrium curves (the one for a factor price of r^e) is shown as $Q^{pe}(p, r^e)$, which shows an expanded area of profit in factor markets.

With competitive markets and profit maximization, the area between price and the partial equilibrium product supply curve to the left of equilibrium quantity measures *profit in the product market*, π_q. However, as Just and Hueth (1979) showed, producers surplus defined relative to the general equilibrium product supply curve captures the net effect on profits in both the product and factor markets. That is, producers surplus measured in a particular market is the sum of profits in that market and all (lower) markets that supply inputs; the area between the partial and general equilibrium supply curves in Figure 4.1 measures profits in all lower markets, π_x.

Consumers surplus, measured from a general equilibrium demand curve (allowing all markets to adjust), is final consumers surplus plus profits in all markets between that market and the final consumer (Just and Hueth, 1979). Therefore, given general equilibrium demand and supply curves for the market(s) where the initial distortion (e.g., price) occurs, we can measure the net social welfare impacts of the policy that causes the initial distortion. Of course, in empirical studies identification of general equilibrium supply and demand curves as distinct from partial equilibrium curves is challenging, to say the least.

Theoretical and empirical measurement of the economic or welfare impacts of policies using surplus and other concepts of welfare have been the subject of considerable literature for several decades. Although many objections to the use of this concept for welfare evaluation have been raised, the following conclusion of Currie et al. (1971) appears to represent the consensus of economists:

> While it is easy to raise objections to the concept of economic surplus for providing answers for policy formulation, it is difficult to find any workable alternative.

For this reason, the concept of consumers and producers surplus is suggested as an operational measure of the effects on producers and consumers of resource policies that result in relatively small market changes. (See discussion and Figures 7.11, 7.12, 7.13, 8.8 and 10.8.)

A Note on Jargon

Much of the jargon (such as surplus) that is associated with aggregate economic evaluation has, unfortunately, little or no meaning to many key people involved in the policy process. When presenting results of an aggregate welfare evaluation to people that are not well trained in economics, it is imperative that the analyst translate concepts into more understandable terms. For example, the change in producers surplus can be termed net income changes, and the change in consumers surplus can be termed the change in expenditures necessary to maintain the initial level of consumer satisfaction. Without translation of jargon into terms and concepts which people without professional training in economics can understand, the efforts to estimate aggregate effects likely will be wasted. Throughout this book, we will use the jargon of welfare analysis, but we cannot overemphasize the need for translation in discussing specific resource policy impacts with most audiences.

Paradoxical Aggregate Effects

It is instructive to use the simple surplus concepts to illustrate several paradoxical market effects of certain resource policies that may not be apparent from micro analyses. Such effects are also referred to under the heading of the *fallacy of composition*. A fallacy of composition is said to exist when what is true of a part (i.e., a farm) is, on that account alone, alleged to be also true for the whole (i.e., the agricultural economy). Economists must be careful to avoid the fallacy of composition trap when evaluating and discussing proposed resource policy legislation.

In aggegate economic analyses of resource policies, we often encounter cases where a resource restriction would appear to lower income to the producer who is directly impacted, but which may indeed increase aggregate income to producers because of the resulting market adjustments. It is important to recognize that such a farm income paradox cannot be explained fully by the classical textbook inelastic demand argument, because this argument pertains only to gross revenue and not net revenue. Another way of viewing this caveat is that virtually all resource policies affect production costs and thus supply as well as the quantity supplied. That is, the inelastic demand argument implicitly takes an ex post view of supply (i.e., a perfectly inelastic supply curve), but for most policy assessments it would be appropriate to take an ex ante view of supply (e.g., an upward sloping marginal cost curve that may be shifted by the resource policy).

To measure aggregate effects of most policies on producers surplus, it is critical to take an a priori view of the supply curve rather than viewing supply a posteriori, as is the case with the classical inelasticity argument. With an a priori view, it can be seen that inelastic demand is not necessarily a condition for producers surplus to increase as a result of, for example, decreases in crop yield attributable to a pesticide regulation. These points are illustrated with Figures 4.2 and 4.3. In Figure 4.2 it can be seen that a shift in supply resulting from, say a pesticide regulation, will decrease producers surplus. However, the supply shift illustrated in Figure 4.3 shows a case where aggregate farm income will increase, even with elastic demand. This example illustrates the "paradoxical" effects that aggregate analyses seek to identify and quantify.

To simplify presentation of welfare concepts and paradoxes, we will often consider only a single market, although most aggregate assessment models discussed estimate general equilibrium effects. We caution once again that welfare

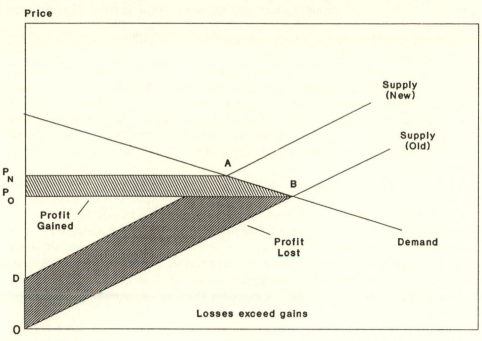

Figure 4.2. Situation where aggregate profits decrease.

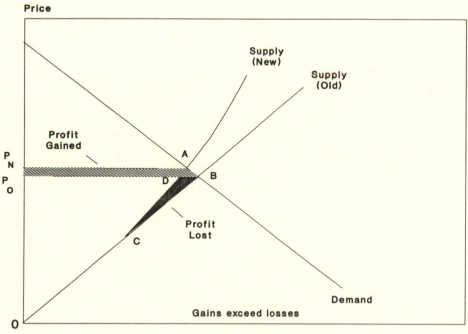

Figure 4.3. Situation where aggregate profits increase.

evaluation should be done in a general (multimarket) equilibrium context rather than a partial-equilibrium context.

Just as comparative static analysis can give valuable insight into behavior of an individual firm or consumer, such analysis can also give valuable insight into aggregate consequences of different resource policies. And, relationships derived from *aggregate comparative static analysis* can be used as an aid in explaining aggregate paradoxes, such as how aggregate farm income could go down from widespread adoption of a technology that would initially increase the income of any single adopter of the technology.

Efforts to derive general comparative static relationships that would cover a broad set of resource policies (such as a conservation reserve, adoption of integrated pest management, a pesticide ban, introduction of new technology, an input tax imposed for environmental quality reasons, or a pollutant tax) end up with so much mathematical notation that insights are difficult to obtain. Thus, derivations tailored for the particular type of resource policy being considered are recommended. To illustrate the comparative static analysis framework applied to aggregate relationships we therefore consider the case of adoption of integrated pest management (IPM). (Also, see Chapter 7.)

Most resource policies represent a distinct and discrete change from conventional pest control. Nevertheless, it is perhaps instructive for our IPM example to consider an infinitesimal change in the mix of pest control technologies and information systems. Letting M be a proxy variable denoting the technology–information mix, the change in net social benefits for an infinitesimal change in M will be

$$\frac{\partial W}{\partial M} = \frac{\partial \pi_0}{\partial M} + \frac{\partial CS_0}{\partial M} + \frac{\partial PS_x}{\partial M} + \frac{\partial E}{\partial M} + \frac{\partial G}{\partial M} \tag{1}$$

where W is net social welfare, CS is consumers surplus, π is producers profit, PS is producers surplus in factor markets, E is external benefit (or cost if negative), and G is government benefit (or cost if negative).

Let us now examine each of the terms on the right-hand side of equation (1) for a multiproduct, multi-input case. Mathematical treatment of profit effects of changes in a factor such as M commonly begins with an assumption about optimizing behavior on the part of producers. Here, however, it is not essential to make any restrictive assumption about optimizing behavior; rather, the analysis can be based on an assumed behavioral relationship. Then the analysis can focus on the profit incentive to adopt and the aggregate impacts of adoption. Consequently, consider a behavioral relationship for a multiproduct producer, postulating that acreage of the jth crop depends on per acre net returns of that crop and competing crops:

$$A_{ij} = A_{ij}(R_{i1}, \ldots, R_{in}) \qquad (j = 1, 2, 3, \ldots, n) \tag{2}$$

where A_{ij} is acreage of the jth crop for the ith producer; and R_{ij} is per acre net returns, defined to be

$$R_{ij} = P_j Y_{ij} - \Sigma_k r_k X_{ijk} \tag{3}$$

where P is the per unit price of the jth product, Y_{ij} is per acre yield, r_k is price of the kth input, and X_{ijk} is per acre input usage. The set of X's can be defined to include application rates for each pesticide, different methods of scouting for insects, and all nonpest control inputs. An implicit production function relates Y_{ij} to all X_{ijk}. Production of the jth crop by the ith producer will be $Q_{ij} = A_{ij}Y_{ij}$, and total production of the jth crop will be $Q._j = \Sigma_i A_{ij}Y_{ij}$.

Profit impacts

Profit to the ith producer can be represented by the *direct profit function*,

$$\pi_i = \Sigma_j A_{ij}R_{ij} \tag{4}$$

which can also be expressed as

$$\pi_i = \Sigma_j(P_j Y_{ij} - \Sigma_k r_k X_{ijk})A_{ij} \tag{5}$$

Since individuals view product demand and factor supply as perfectly elastic, the incentive for an individual to adjust the *IPM* technology-information mix, M_i, is

$$\frac{\partial \pi_i}{\partial M_i} = \Sigma_j(P_j Y_{ij} - \Sigma_k r_k X_{ijk})\frac{\partial A_{ij}}{\partial M_i} + \Sigma_j\left[P_j\frac{\partial Y_{ij}}{\partial M_i} - \Sigma_k r_k\frac{\partial X_{ijk}}{\partial M_i}\right]A_{ij} \tag{6}$$

Equation (6) will be positive, zero, or negative, depending on whether the producer is underutilizing M_i, using the profit-maximizing M_i, or overutilizing M_i. The remaining analysis in this chapter will focus on the case where (6) is positive, since this is the case commonly encountered in pest control.

Consider now the impacts of increased adoption of *IPM*, or increased use of M_i, on industry profits. Summing over producers, industry profits can be represented by using (3) and (4)

$$\pi_Q = \Sigma_i\pi_i = \Sigma_i\Sigma_j(P_j Y_{ij} - X_{ijk})A_{ij} \tag{7}$$

Because it is usually not appropriate to assume perfectly elastic product demand and factor supply at the industry level, the change in industry profits will be

$$\frac{\partial \pi_Q}{\partial M} = \Sigma_i\frac{\partial \pi_i}{\partial M_i} = \Sigma_i\Sigma_j(P_j Y_{ij} - \Sigma_k r_k X_{ijk})\frac{\partial A_{ij}}{\partial M_i}$$

$$+ \Sigma_i\Sigma_j\left(P_j\frac{\partial Y_{ij}}{\partial M_i} + Y_{ij}\frac{\partial P_j}{\partial M_i} - \Sigma_k r_k\frac{\partial X_{ijk}}{\partial M_i} - \Sigma_k X_{ijk}\frac{\partial r_k}{\partial M_i}\right)A_{ij} \tag{8}$$

Rearranging terms, equation (8) can be expressed as

$$\frac{\partial \pi_Q}{\partial M} = \Sigma_i\left[\Sigma_j(P_j Y_{ij} - \Sigma_k r_k X_{ijk})\frac{\partial A_{ij}}{\partial M_i} + \Sigma_j\left(P_j\frac{\partial Y_{ij}}{\partial M_i} - \Sigma_k r_k\frac{\partial X_{ijk}}{\partial M_i}\right)A_{ij}\right]$$

$$+ \Sigma_i\Sigma_j A_{ij}Y_{ij}\frac{\partial P_j}{\partial M_i} - \Sigma_i\Sigma_j\Sigma_k A_{ij}X_{ijk}\frac{\partial r_k}{\partial M_i} \tag{9}$$

The term in brackets on the right-hand side of (9) can be related to equation (6), which shows the individual incentive to adopt M. As noted previously, we are interested in the case where individuals are underutilizing M_i; hence, the term in brackets in (9) will be positive. Note, however, that the last two terms in (9) can be positive, negative, or zero, depending on industry adjustments as translated into price changes. The direction of impact is easier to see in the case of a single product. If adoption of IPM results in an acreage and output increase and thus a product price decrease, the second term on the right-hand side of (9) will be negative, depending on whether the weighted value impact on input usage increases or decreases. Hence, equation (9) can be either positive or negative, depending on changes in production, input usage, and the slopes of general equilibrium product demand and factor supply curves.

Effects of Input Use

Industry use of the kth input will be

$$X_{..k} = \Sigma_i \Sigma_j X_{ijk} A_{ij} \tag{10}$$

The change in total use of the kth inputs used in agricultural production, resulting from adoption of IPM, will be

$$\frac{\partial X_{..k}}{\partial M} = \Sigma_i \Sigma_j X_{ijk} \frac{\partial A_{ij}}{\partial M_i} + \Sigma_i \Sigma_j A_{ij} \frac{\partial X_{ijk}}{\partial M_i} \tag{11}$$

An interesting paradox relating to total pesticide use can be examined with equation (11). If an increase in M involves reduced per acre use of pesticides, the last term in (11) for a pesticide input will be negative. However, the first term in the right-hand side of (11) will be positive if acreage expands as a result of adoption of M. Thus, total pesticide use can increase, even though the intensity of pesticide use decreases.

Impact on Surpluses and Net Social Welfare

Consider now the impacts on net social welfare, equation (1), of a change in M. Close inspection of equation (9), which shows the impacts on industry profits, will reveal that the next to last term is the negative of the change in consumer surplus:

$$\frac{\partial CS_Q}{\partial M} = -\Sigma_i \Sigma_j A_{ij} Y_{ij} \frac{\partial P_j}{\partial M_i}$$

$$= -\Sigma_i \Sigma_j Q_{ij} \frac{\partial P_j}{\partial M_i} \tag{12}$$

Similarly, the last term in (9) is the negative of the change in surplus for producers of X:

$$\frac{\partial PS_x}{\partial M} = \Sigma_i \Sigma_j \Sigma_k A_{ij} X_{ijk} \frac{\partial r_k}{\partial M_i} \tag{13}$$

Substitution of (9), (12), and (13) into (1) gives:

$$\frac{\partial W}{\partial M} = \Sigma_i \left[\Sigma_j (P_j Y_{ij} - \Sigma_k r_k X_{ijk}) \frac{\partial A_{ij}}{\partial M_i} + \Sigma_j \left(P_j \frac{\partial Y_{ij}}{\partial M_i} - \Sigma_k r_k \frac{\partial X_{ijk}}{\partial M_i} \right) A_{ij} \right] + \frac{\partial E}{\partial M} + \frac{\partial G}{\partial M}$$

$$(14)$$

In the absence of externalities, E, and social overhead, G, equation (14) will be non-negative for any adjustment in the set M_i. Thus, we have the familiar result that if one or more producers are not using the profit-maximizing level of M, social welfare can be increased by an adjustment in the set M_i that moves it to, or closer to, the privately optimal level. However, whether these benefits accrue to producers, consumers, or both depends on the specific case considered.

With externalities and social overhead costs, equation (14) can be of either sign. In one case, the social overhead cost changes, $\partial G/\partial M$, could outweigh any benefits manifested in the marketplace. In another case, the changes in external costs could be negative because total pesticide use would increase with adoption of IPM, as was illustrated with equation (11).

Refined Welfare Evaluation

For refined welfare analysis it is useful to view markets as being horizontally and vertically related. Horizontally, we consider the many commodities produced at the farm level, or consider the many processed commodities sold to final consumers. Vertically, we can go from the markets for raw materials through the farm level, to the processing and distribution levels, to the final consumer level. As clarified by Just and Hueth (1979), a complete welfare evaluation can occur at any market level, *given* appropriate demand and supply relationships. That is, we can evaluate the net welfare impact of a chemical regulation or land-use regulation by considering supply and demand measures *only* at the farm gate, although we cannot necessarily establish the full distributional effects with such assessment. This is of considerable importance for applied agricultural resource policy evaluation since we rarely have the data to consider all market levels, particularly at the retail level where there are so many commodities, and since we rarely have adequate modeling or research resources to assess effects at all market levels.

AGGREGATE EVALUATION MODELS

A wide variety of empirically based aggregate models have been used to evaluate the market and welfare consequences of resource policies. Types of models that have been used range from, for example, the quick and simple "back-of-the-envelope" approach as manifested in the simple demand, supply, and surplus concepts illustrated in Figure 4.1, to large-scale econometric-simulation models, to interregional linear programming models, and to computable general equilibrium models. Because of compromises necessitated by data, time, and other resource constraints facing analysts, no single model is "best" suited for all of the many types of aggregate evaluations called for in the field of resource policy. In the remainder of this chapter, we will discuss many aspects of aggregate models, model development, and use. Specifically addressed are the following aspects of aggregate models: 1) a top-down versus a bottom-up approach to model development; 2) ex post versus ex ante policy evaluation; 3) specificity of the model in terms of inputs and outputs modeled; 4) linkages of the model to the rest of the economy; 5) regional specificity; 6) stochastic versus deterministic models; and 7) model types and major quantitative techniques used for analyzing resource policy issues. After each of these aspects is discussed, the perceived advantages and disadvantages of each of several commonly used models for specific types of resource policy evaluation are discussed and shown in Tables 4.1 and 4.2.

Modeling Approaches

Let us consider two possible conceptual approaches to aggregate model development (Taylor, 1983). One approach is from the top down, whereby two equations are used to estimate the value of an aggregate price index that will equate indices of aggregate supply and demand (Tweeten and Quance, 1969). While this approach may be acceptable for making highly aggregative projections of policy effects, it has at least four serious deficiencies for making detailed distributional and efficiency estimates. First, the *aggregation bias* inherent in the two-equation approach is likely to be quite large (see Theil, 1971, for exact conditions for aggregation). Second, there are econometric estimation biases that are difficult to circumvent in empirical application of this approach (Burt, 1971). Third, there are almost insurmountable problems in determining behavioral, production function, and interregional competition relationships that are necessary for a meaningful disaggregation of the aggregate estimates. Fourth, with the top-down approach, we lose sight of microeconomic theory that provides considerable guidance for aggregate (as well as firm level) model specification.

A second conceptual approach to aggregate development is from the bottom up. Ideally, an aggregate model comprises submodels for each firm and consumer in the sector or even economy. While this is an ideal approach, it is obviously not empirically or computationally feasible. Practical compromises must be made, either by constructing the aggregate model with specialized representative firm and consumer submodels or by aggregating these and other firm and consumer submodels.

With both the top-down and the bottom-up approaches, potential aggregation bias is pervasive owing to empirical and computational compromises. However, these biases are expected to be much less severe with the bottom-up approach because aggregation problems are apparent at each step of the aggregation process and can thus be minimized, while with the top-down approach, aggregation bias cannot be determined. To use a metaphor to compare the two approaches, you do not build a barn from the roof down; rather, you build it from the foundation up even if the foundation is not as strong as would be ideal. Since the bottom-up approach to aggregate model development is clearly preferred, it will be the focus of the remainder of this chapter.

Table 4.1. Comparing Features of Aggregate Models

Features	Conventional Partial Budgeting	Aggregate Partial Budgeting	Ex Post Econometric	Small Econometric Simulation	Large-Scale Econometric Simulation	Computable General Equilibrium	Linear Elasticity Based	Interregional Programming
Economic impacts estimated								
Aggregate efficiency	No	Yes	Not directly	Yes, usually for a single commodity	Yes	Can be, but focus is usually on prices, quantities	Yes	No
Distributional—groups	No	Yes	Not directly	Yes	Yes	Yes	Yes	No
Distributional—regions	No	No	Can be	No	Some	Can be	No	Yes
Differential risk	No	No	Possible, but has not been done	No	Some	No	No	No
International	No	Can be	Can be	Can be	Yes	Yes	Yes	Can be
Representative firm	Rarely	No	Can be used with firm level or aggregate data	No	Often informally link to rep. firm models	No	No	Implicit
Market clearing prices	No	Yes	Usually not done	Yes	Yes	Yes	Yes	Rarely
Multi-commodity	Rarely	Extremely difficult	Usually focuses on a single commodity	Rarely	Yes	Yes	Rarely	Yes
Linkages to factor markets	No	Rarely	Can be	Rarely	Usually	Can be	Can be	Can be
Linkages to rest of economy	No	No	Can be	No	Some	Can be	No	No
Commodity program interactions	No	No	Can be	Can be	Some endogenized program participation	No	No	Can be
Resource constraints								
Rate	Can be	Can be	Can be	Can be	Yes	Difficult	Difficult	Yes
Total	No	No	Can be	No	Difficult	Difficult	Difficult	Yes
Risk aversion by producers	No	Possible	Possible	Possible	Possible, but rarely done	No	No	Can be
Dynamics	No	No	Usually	Usually	Yes	No	No	No
Incorporation of Theoretical Concepts (sym, homo, etc.)	No	No	Can be	Can be	A few do	Yes	No	No
Data requirements	Few	Few	Moderate	Moderate	Immense	Moderate	Moderate	Immense
Ex post or ex ante	Ex ante	Ex ante	Ex post	Ex ante	Either, but normally used for ex ante	Ex ante	Ex ante	Ex ante
Normative or positive	Intended to be positive	Intended to be positive	Positive	Positive	Positive, but often subjectively modified	Spec. is from normative, but calibration is positive	Not clear	Normative

Table 4.2. Model Approaches to Resource Policies

Resource Policy	Aggregate Partial Budgeting	Ex Post Econometric	Small Econometric Simulation	Large-Scale Econometric Simulation	Computable General Equilibrium	Linear Elasticity Based	Interregional Programming
Pesticide bans and regulations	Yes	Yes	Yes	Yes	Not with price specification	Not with price specification	Yes
Chemical/energy tax	Yes	Yes	Yes	Yes	Yes	Yes	Yes
Fertilizer restriction Rate	Yes	Yes	Yes, with net return specification	Yes, with net return specification	No	No	Yes
Total	No	Yes	Difficult	Difficult	No	No	Yes
Erosion restriction	No	No	No	No	No	No	Best model option since soils can be constraints and cropping systems can be activities
CRP/removals of land from production	Yes	Yes	Yes	Yes	Yes	Yes	Yes
Restriction of production practices	Limited	Limited	Yes, as reflect in yield and cost	Yes, as reflected in yield and cost	No	No	Yes
Ethanol production	Yes	Yes	Yes	Yes	Yes	Yes	Changes fixed demands
Irrigation							
Water quantity	Difficult	Difficult	Difficult	Difficult	No	No	Yes
Water quality	No	No	No	No	No	No	Yes
Water price	Yes	Yes	Yes	Yes	Yes, if irrigation is explicit in model	No	Yes
Climate changes	No	Difficult	Difficult	Yes, if regionalized	Limited	Limited	Yes
Acid rain	No	Difficult	Difficult	Yes, if regionalized	Limited	Limited	Yes
Ozone depletion	No	Difficult	Difficult	Yes, if regionalized	Limited	Limited	Yes
LISA	No	Yes	Yes	Yes, if regionalized	Limited	Limited	Yes
General	Not suitable for resource policy evaluation unless the policy has an infinitesimal effect on aggregate output and input	Suitable if there has been adequate variation in the resource policy in question	Suitable for policies that result in small changes in variables if cross-commodity impacts and differential regional effects are very small	Good alternative for most non-erosion related policies, especially if the supply component of the model is regionalized and policy changes are within range of observed variation of key variables	Of limited value for resource policy because they do not incorporate dynamics, commodity programs, and regional supply	Value is limited because they do not incorporate dynamics, and regional supply	Best option for aggregate evaluation of erosion policies and water quality policies. However the models are typically not used to get market clearing prices, and some models are so constrained by arbitrary "flexibility" coefficients that they are not much more than accounting models

Ex Post Versus Ex Ante Evaluation

Resource policy analysts are typically involved in *ex ante* evaluations of proposed policies; that is, they are asked to provide estimates of effects of policies before they have been implemented. Compared to this is *ex post* evaluation of policies, or evaluating their effects at some point in time after they were implemented. Carefully note that the emphasis in this distinction is on evaluation and not models, per se; *models* parameterized with historical data (i.e., ex post) are usually required for ex ante policy *evaluation.*

To compare ex ante and ex post evaluation, consider the case of using econometrically estimated acreage response and demand functions to evaluate the effects of placing 45 million acres of land in a conservation reserve program (CRP) before the program was in place. Since the program had not been in effect when the analysis was done, CRP acreage could not be an explicit explanatory variable in an acreage response and thus the supply function (see Chapter 10).

In an ex ante evaluation, we must somehow synthetically modify acreage response functions to account for the CRP. A natural way of doing this would be to shift the acreage response function by an amount equal to the CRP acreage. The shifted acreage function could then be used to estimate market clearing prices with the CRP, and, compared to a baseline, changes in surpluses could be computed.

In an ex post evaluation, CRP acreage would be an explanatory variable (with associated statistics) in the acreage response function. The evaluation compared to the absence of a CRP could therefore be based solely on the econometric model. Differences in the evaluations could arise if the ex post econometric study showed, for example, that there was slippage in the program. Slippage occurs if, for each acre of land in the CRP, acreage planted is reduced by less than one acre, other things being equal. In the ex ante evaluation we assumed no slippage (alternatively we could have subjectively specified slippage), while in the ex post evaluation slippage was econometrically estimated. Similar subjective modification of models is typically required in ex ante evaluation of resource policies; such unavoidable subjective model modification of models influence the validity of model results and places a premium on the analyst's judgement.

Appropriateness of a specific type of model for a particular analysis depends to a critical extent on whether the analysis is to be ex post or ex ante. For example, a traditional econometric model specified to have a particular resource policy as an explanatory variable might be used for ex post evaluation of the effects of that policy on price, production, surplus, and so forth. On the other hand, ex ante evaluation of the same policy cannot be done in the same manner if there are no historical observations on that resource policy variable, or if the policy variable is outside the observed range. This being the case, a synthetically modified econometric-simulation model, or even a completely different modeling approach such as linear programming, might be required to perform the ex ante analysis.

To measure the accuracy of ex ante analyses, ex post analysis of policies should ideally be conducted after implementation of the policy. Unfortunately, such ex post assessments of ex ante evaluations are rare in the field of resource economics.

Model Specificity, Linkages, and Regional Detail

Specificity in terms of outputs and inputs needed for a particular resource policy analysis depends on the specificity of results needed and on available data for model development and verification. Economy-wide surplus effects can be estimated with appropriate general equilibrium demand and supply functions for the markets directly impacted (Just and Hueth, 1979), but estimates of distributional effects will usually require supply and demand equations for markets that are indirectly impacted. Net welfare effects of introducing a new technology that can be used only in corn production, for example, can be based on general equilibrium supply and demand equations for corn. However, the distributional effects in terms of effects on input suppliers, or on other agricultural products such as soybeans, requires a larger and more complex set of economic relationships.

The level of regional detail required for an analysis depends not only on the specificity of results needed, but also on the usually unknown aggregation biases resulting from more aggregative analyses. To minimize aggregation bias, it is generally desirable to incorporate as much regional detail into the model and associated analysis that time, resources, and data allow. It should be cautioned, however, that more detail comes at the expense of model complexity; more complexity reduces the chances that outsiders will critically evaluate the model but increases the chances of modeling errors.

Types of Aggregate Models

Types of models that can be used to analyze resource policy issues range from simple, subjective back-of-the-envelope analyses to highly sophisticated and quite expensive quantitative models of the agricultural economy. Major types of models that are often used for resource policy analysis are discussed below.

A technique often used for cursory analyses of proposed analyses is partial budgeting, which is also commonly referred to as a back-of-the-envelope approach to reflect that it can be done quickly, often subjectively. *Partial budgeting* used for aggregate analyses must be distinguished from the same approach that is commonly used for firm level analyses. With aggregate analyses, the partial budgeting approach must recognize that output and input prices may be affected by the policy in question. To implement such an aggregate partial budgeting analysis, relevant elasticities are typically specified from a literature search or simply the analyst's judgment. Then, effects of the policy on prices and perhaps surpluses are computed or "penciled out" without the aid of any quantitative model other than basic concepts of demand and supply. Often only the market directly affected is considered in such an analysis.

Although aggregate partial budgeting done with "pencil and paper" is very useful for obtaining first-approximation estimates of the impacts of a policy, it leaves much to be desired because it is virtually impossible to subjectively capture the complex cross-price interrelationships in demand and supply, or to capture the dynamics of supply and demand. Another criticism of such evaluation is that subjective estimates are rarely subjected to any rigorous type of "verification." Furthermore, estimates cannot be reproduced unless the analyst has saved all of the "envelopes" used for the calculations.

Development of large quantitative models for policy analysis is sometimes seen as an end in itself as well as a mechanism for providing "objective" economic impact estimates. Owing to data inadequacies and statistical considerations, however, results from quantitative models are rarely as objective as they might seem. Perhaps a more appropriate role for large quantitative models is to sharpen the judgment of modelers and analysts using the models. Not only can models sharpen judgment about the direction and magnitude of effects, they can assist in thinking through the logic of complex cross-price and dynamic linkages in the agricultural sector.

With this perspective on the proper role of quantitative models in mind, we turn to a discussion of the structure of major types of quantitative models used to empirically estimate the market impacts of resource policies. After presentation of the models, their usefulness for different types of policy analyses will be compared.

Econometric Models for Ex Post Analyses

As noted previously, a distinction must be made between econometric models used for ex ante evaluation and econometric models used for ex post evaluation. With ex post evaluation, a variable or set of explanatory variables pertaining to the policy in question is included in the model along with other explanatory variables.

A simplified example of such an ex post econometric assessment would be the single acreage equation (or a per-acre yield equation, or demand equation, or whatever variable is of interest),

$$A_t = f(P_t, X_t, A_{t-1}) \tag{15}$$

where A_t is acreage, P_t is price, and X_t is a resource policy or set of resource policies. With an appropriate set of data that reflects changes in X_t during the observation period, statistical estimates of the parameters characterizing (15) can be obtained. Ex post evaluation would focus on the significance and magnitude of the coefficient on the resource policy variable, X_t.

Economic assessment of the policy based on the empirically estimated econometric model can range from simple to complex. For example, the analyst can simply examine whether the policy variable in question is statistically significant. Or, based on estimated supply and demand equations, one or more of which are influenced by the policy variable, the analyst can conduct a full economic surplus evaluation. Given estimated econometric relationships, confidence intervals on the surplus estimates can, in principle, be derived.

To date, ex post econometric analyses usually concentrate on how a policy affects a particular behavioral relationship, such as demand or supply. Occasionally, ex post econometric analyses seek to determine impacts of the policy on commodity prices. Rarely are these models used for a full welfare evaluation, even though such an evaluation is quite possible. For the full surplus evaluation, appropriate supply and demand equations would have to be estimated. These, along with market clearing identities could be used to estimate market clearing prices and quantities with and without the policy in question. Integration of the demand and supply curves would permit estimation of surpluses and changes in surpluses associated with the policy. If the demand or supply equations were dynamic, which is often the case, the time paths of prices, quantities, and surpluses could also be traced out with and without the policy.

Econometric-Simulation Models for Ex Ante Analyses

Ex post or ex ante policy analyses typically focus on *changes* in key economic variables such as prices, income, surpluses, acreages, and resource use. With ex post evaluation, effects of the policy in question are manifested in the empirical data set used for the evaluation. Uncertainty about changes in economic variables therefore arises not from levels of the variables under the policy, but from levels of the variables that would have occurred *without* the policy. With ex ante evaluation, however, there is uncertainty about levels of important economic variables with *and* without the policy. Moreover, with an ex ante approach to policy evaluation based on an econometric model, we cannot rely completely on statistically estimated relationships. Thus, there is more uncertainty in ex ante than in ex post evaluation of policy.

Ex ante evaluation of resource policy with an econometric model is typically based on estimated values of economic variables with the policy compared to a baseline simulation. Numerical simulation of the econometric model is the standard practice largely because most sophisticated models are too complicated with respect to functional form and dynamics for them to be analytically manipulated: thus the term econometric-simulation model.

An example of a simple econometric-simulation model for ex ante policy evaluation of impacts on the market for a single commodity would be the system

$$A_t = f(R_t^*, A_{t-1}, Z_t) \tag{16}$$

$$QD_t = h(P_t, I_t) \tag{17}$$

where A_t is the acreage harvested of the crop, QD_t is quantity demanded, P_t is price, Z_t is a set of exogenous variables, I_t is consumer income, and R_t^* is expected per-acre net returns resulting from production. Return expectations might be defined as

$$R_t^* = P_{t-1}\hat{Y}_t - VC_t \tag{18}$$

where $\hat{Y}_t$ is expected per-acre yield, VC_t is per-acre variable production costs, and P_{t-1} is lagged prices, such as with a naive price expectations model. Such a net-return specification makes sense for agricultural crops since land is the major fixed factor of production (thus crops should compete on the basis of per-acre returns), and because it allows changes in supply to be explicitly derived for changes in yield and production costs associated with resources policies that have not been implemented to data. (Note that just using input and output prices in the supply equation will not allow explicit derivation of ex ante changes). In addition the return specification is parsimonious in parameters.

To complete the system for econometric estimation, we need a yield equation,

$$\hat{Y}_t = g(P_t, W_t) \tag{19}$$

where W_t is a vector of input prices, and a variable cost equation,

$$VC_t = \sum w_j x_j \tag{20}$$

where w_j is the price, and x_j is the quantity of factor j. To solve for market clearing prices, we neeed the market clearing identity that the quantity supplied ($= Y \cdot A$) to equal the quantity demanded,

$$Y_t A_t = QD_t \tag{21}$$

Typically, equations (16), (17), and (19) would be econometrically estimated, while equations (18) and perhaps (20) would be definitional relationships. The set of equations (16) through (21) can comprise a simulation model that would show the time path of price (and other endogenous variables) that would clear the market. With such a simulation model, it is common to compare a benchmark simulation with a policy simulation.

A simulation model based on the above system could be used for ex post evaluation of a policy for which data were available if the policy variable was included as an explanatory variable in appropriate equation(s). However, the most common use of an econometric-simulation model of this type is for ex ante evaluation. Ex ante evaluation is done by changing parameters or levels of variables in the econometric equation using estimates (not from the econometric model) of how the proposed policy would affect them. For example, a pesticide ban would change yield, Y, and per acre production costs, VC_t. Using estimates of the changes in these variables (from subjective models, pest-population, and plant-growth simulation models, expert panels, or other sources), the supply shift could be derived, the model simulated, and results compared to the baseline simulation.

An input tax provides another example of how an econometric-simulation model could be used for resource policy evaluation. In this case, the higher input prices would directly impact variable costs, (20), and yield (19), and thus indirectly impact prices and surpluses. Additional equations could be specified to model how input use changed with the tax. With input demand equations, tax revenue could also be computed from the model.

With the estimated supply and demand equations from a system such as (16) through (21), aggregate economic impacts in terms of consumers surplus and producers surplus (or returns computed from (18) and equilibrium values of endogenous variables) could be computed and compared to the baseline results. Dynamic models can trace out the time paths of the economic variables and surpluses of interest.

Econometric-simulation models for aggregate evaluation range from small two-equation demand and supply models such as the one outlined above to highly complex models based on hundreds of econometrically estimated behavioral relationships. The large-scale models require substantial capital investments, and thus are used for a wide variety of analyses. For detailed description and discussion of the structure of many of the large models used for agricultural and resource policy evaluation, the reader is referred to Taylor et al. (1993). Large-scale econometric-simulation models for policy evaluation differ in several critical ways. First, the level of detail provided by the model varies considerably. Types of detail for models currently operational emphasize detailed linkages to the macro-economy (Penson et al., 1992), emphasize detailed supply and demand in other major agricultural countries (Frohberg et al., 1993), or emphasize the regional dimension of agricultural production and resource use (Taylor, 1993).

A second way in which models differ or their use differs is in how econometrically estimated relationships are modified for ex ante evaluation. Ways in which models are modified include 1) extrapolation of estimated relationships, such as for the effect of target prices for agricultural commodities on supply; 2) externally computing the changes in production costs or yields that are used to explicitly shift a supply curve that has such variables as arguments in the estimated supply equation (Taylor et al., 1979); 3) synthetically shifting supply or demand curves based on pencil-and-paper calculations such as changing the intercept of a supply curve to reflect land taken out of production under a land-use policy; and 4) synthetic shifts in demand curves to reflect assumed new uses for commodities. Econometric-simulation models also differ considerably in their basic structure, functional forms used, appeal to economic theory concepts such as symmetry and homogeneity, and econometric estimation technique.

Although the exact conditions for aggregation in an econometric model are well known (Lau, 1978; Theil, 1971), the extent to which such biases distort ex ante or ex post evaluation of specific resource policies is largely uncharted territory. Aggregation bias is so dependent on a complex set of assumptions that it is difficult to draw meaningful conclusions for empirical work.

Insight into the aggregation problem and insight into difficulties in basing models on aggregate data can be gained with the aid of the following simple examples. First, suppose that we want to estimate the production function (or a supply or factor demand equation) given only time-series data for averages of individual firm data. Further, assume that for whatever *unobservable or unmeasurable* reason individual firms do not employ the same amount of the input even though they face the same technology (i.e., production function). By Jensen's inequality, the average data points will lie below the true production if it is strictly concave. Fitting a curve to a time-series of such points will thus result in a curve that lies below the true production function and, except in a special case, the marginal physical productivity based on the fitted curve will differ from the true production function. In this example, aggregate resource policy analyses requiring the true production function will suffer from aggregation bias if the fitted relationship is used. However, if the aggregate analyses require a *behavioral* relationship between input and output, then the fitted curve may suffice.

Aggregation bias in econometric models can arise from a variety of sources, including firms not having the same expectations of prices (Pope, 1981), firms facing different production functions, firms having different objective functions, firms using different input rates, and heterogeneous outputs or inputs. Additional discussion of the aggregation problem in terms of inputs and outputs is provided in Chapter 5 of this book.

Even if aggregation bias is important, however, there is often little that can be done about it for large-scale aggregate evaluation because 1) computational and other research resource constraints limit the size of the model; and 2) firm level time-series or cross-sectional data are not available to parameterize an aggregate model based on micro unit econometric relationships. Of course, one can hope that estimating economic impacts as the difference between a simulated baseline and a simulated policy scenario will cancel out any aggregation bias that may be in the aggregate model. If representative firm micro models are available, some insight into aggregation bias can be obtained by, for example, comparing input use and output from the micro model, using prices obtained from the aggregate model.

It should be noted that aggregation biases may also translate into biases in welfare evaluation based on surpluses measured from the (biased) aggregate relationships. The student is referred to Jorgenson et al. (1980) and to Muellbauer (1975) for a discussion of aggregation of consumers surplus.

Stochastic Analyses

Although most models are used for deterministic evaluation of policies, recent gains in numerical computational power and affordability permit use of these models for stochastic evaluation of resource policies (e.g., Bigman, 1988; Taylor, 1989). Empirically specified probability distributions for factors such as weather or crop yields, exchange rates, or even error terms in econometric equations can now be used to obtain numerically probability distributions for variables such as price, income, or resource use both with and without the policy in question.

Model Selection

Selection of the "best" way of specifying and developing an econometric model or selecting the best way of modifying an econometric-simulation model for ex ante policy evaluation involves considerable judgment, but more importantly, a thorough and deep understanding of the model and an even deeper understanding of the empirical problem. Such understanding can only be gained by extensive background research and "hands-on" experience with development of the model; however, some understanding and insight can be gained by careful review of alternative models. The book edited by Taylor et al. (1993) documents several of the major nonproprietary models and compares model results for a few agricultural and resource policies.

Computable General Equilibrium Models

Functional forms for demand and supply equations are often restricted to "convenient" forms such as Cobb-Douglas or linear to allow for ease of obtaining the vector of prices that simultaneously clear all markets modeled (see, e.g., Shoven and Whalley, 1989). Models based on such convenient forms are usually referred to as "computable general equilibrium models." Models based on less convenient functional forms, which is the case with most large-scale econometric-simulation models, use iterative numerical procedures to find the market clearing set of prices.

Computable general equilibrium (CGE) models have evolved over the past 25 years as researchers have attempted to make the general equilibrium models operational and empirically tractable. Most of the development and use of CGE models has occurred in the economic development literature owing to the perceived need for a more complete analysis than that available from a sectoral approach. Agricultural economists have more recently acknowledged the growing importance of the linkages with other sectors. The importance of monetary and fiscal policies on the agricultural sector has been recognized by Schuh (1979) and others; direct linkages between agricultural resources and international trade parameters is shown explicitly in the collection of papers edited by Sutton (1988) and is manifested in models such as *AG + GEM* that link a macro model (COMGEM by Penson et al., 1993) with a detailed agricultural supply and demand model (AGSIM by Taylor, 1993; Penson and Taylor, 1992).

This section provides a brief overview of how CGE models differ from econometric or programming models, and some of the advantages and disadvantages of their use in modeling agricultural resources.

The Social Accounting Matrix

The *social accounting matrix*, or SAM as it is universally referred to, is the basis of a simple linear approach to CGE models. The matrix of production coefficients in a SAM is similar to the intersectoral matrix in input/output models, in that it accounts for all the interdependent flows of economic activity between the participants in the economy. While the input/output matrix accounts for the flows of inputs and outputs between sectoral production activities, the SAM has to account for *all* economic flows.

An exact equality accounting between economic agents is needed to satisfy Walras' law that there exists a price vector in equilibrium such that the excess demands in all sectors equal zero. The SAM can be thought of as an extended input/output matrix that accounts for the flows of input and output between sectors, the value added by the institutions of labor, ownership, and management, the linkages between institutions and households, and finally those accounts that are specified as being exogenous, such as government, capital market, and exports and imports to the rest of the world. (See Aldeman and Robinson, 1986, for a mathematical specification of the structure of a SAM.).

SAM coefficients can be used in two ways. A simple impact analysis of the linear system can be made by specifying the exogenous accounts that are appropriate to the structure and the policies involved. Multipliers are then derived that show the effect on all parts of the economy of a unit change in an exogenous variable. An example of this approach is found in Aldeman and Robinson (1986) and Aldeman and Taylor (1988).

An alternative use of the empirical data in a SAM is to use it to calibrate a more general nonlinear set of production, consumption, and transfer equations, which show the same interlinked impacts, but with endogenous prices. This type of model is called a CGE. At the extreme, the model can be closed by including capital formation from savings.

CGE Model Calibration

A full CGE model is usually developed by specifying the functional form of the set of equations in the model, and then using the data in the base year SAM to derive a deterministic calibration of the parameters in the functions that satisfy the base period (i.e., baseline) data set. Usually, exogenous estimates of key parameters are used in the calibration. Elasticity of substitution and demand are normally specified to complete the calibration of parameters with the more flexible functional forms, such as constant elasticity or substitution (CES) production functions.

The partial or complete use of econometric estimates for the production or expenditure function parameters is possible (Lau, 1978), but rare in practice. Functional forms for these production and expenditure relations range over the simpler forms that show some degree of flexibility. Cobb-Douglas, CES, and linear forms are widely used.

As would be expected with general models, there are several different methods and viewpoints on calibration methods, trade specification, and model closure. The deterministic calibration is usually done by an optimization method; GAMS/MINOS (Brooke et al., 1988) is widely used for reasons of ease and consistency. An alternative approach is to use an iterative fixed point algorithm (Scarf and Shoven, 1989) to solve for the set of prices that satisfies the set of nonlinear production and expenditure functions and identities. A problem with calibrating a model against a single data set and elasticity estimates is that the resulting parameters have no measure of statistical robustness. The model results are consequently estimates of single realizations, rather than statistics. The realizations may be very close to an accepted statistic such as a maximum likelihood estimator, but the model maker has no formal method of testing this.

Choice of a calibration method, as in most empirical modeling, evolves into a tradeoff between model complexity, aggregation, and the precision of the available data base.

This brief overview of the application of CGE models to agricultural and resource problems hopefully leaves the reader with the impression that CGE models have, like the other empirical methodologies reviewed in this chapter, areas of superiority as well as drawbacks. As with the other methods reviewed, their suitability to a problem should be judged on an assessment of the important policy characteristics of the problem and on the data and empirical limitations of the analysis (Clarete and Raumasset, 1986; Dervis et al., 1982).

The CGE model approach allows the analyst to use more judgment in developing the model. However, it should be noted that development of an econometric model is not as objective as it sometimes may seem, as in developing the model the analyst must often make many largely subjective judgments in deciding on estimation technique, functional form, and the final set of included explanatory variables (Hertel, 1986; Howitt, 1986).

Use of subjectively specified demand and supply equations can be viewed as a strength of the model if the analyst's judgment is better than what econometric analysis can extract from time-series data that is often characterized by a high degree of multicollinearity. On the other hand, subjective development of a model can be viewed as a weakness because of its nebulous tie to empirical data generated by a functioning agricultural economy.

Interregional Programming Models

Programming models have a long history of use in the quantitative analysis of agricultural resources. In terms of the number of applications to regional and national resource problems, programming models are probably the dominant method of analysis. Reasons for this tenacity despite more sophisticated methodological advances in other areas have to be stronger than just tradition. Programming models are often better suited to the available data on resource problems, and their ability to incorporate a wealth of physical structural detail is often appealing where the physical structure dominates or strongly influences the behavioral response. (See Box. 2.1 for the solution of a simple programming model.)

A critical advantage of the econometric approach discussed previously is that it is positive in nature and based on actual behavior. The ability to test the statistical validity of parameters in econometric models is highly desirable, but is conditional on having the correct specification. Often, econometric specifications have to be simplified to enable valid tests with the restricted data available.

In contrast, programming models had their origin in normative farm management models, where the modeler assumed correct knowledge of technological parameters, and derived the behavioral response by imposing normative optimizing behavior on a detailed structure of constraints. With regional and national models of production and resource use, programming modelers have used a variety of methods, with varying success, to move away from the normative origins of the method and incorporate more positive behavior in the models, while retaining the structural detail that gives them much of their explanatory power.

Like the ex ante econometric-simulation model, programming models of resource allocation are typically oriented around crop acreage and other fixed resource allocations. Invariably, the production technology is specified as a *constant proportional* (Leontief) production function. This enables model construction from a minimal data base, but causes severe problems if production cost functions are also linear. The ability to define empirical inequality constraints on regional resource use and model the intraregional heterogeneity of land are major advantages of programming models for resource policy. In addition, many resource policies for production agriculture are defined in terms of physical inequality constraints rather than prices.

Most of the proposed environmental regulations that are pending for U.S. agriculture are formulated as physical constraints on the type or method of input (including land) use. While an ex ante simulation can incorporate any of these constraints, the important question is whether the constraints were incorporated as information in estimating the model parameters. Except on a macro scale, unconstrained estimates of agricultural resource technology are bound to contain some degree of misspecification.

The dilemma facing a modeler of regional agricultural resources can be summarized by stating that traditional econometric models which are specified on the basis of an optimization model (e.g., profit maximization) are characterized by interior solutions (no inequality constraints), whereas a traditional programming model is dominated by inequality constraints and corner solutions. Some combination of these extremes is probably more accurate for most regional resource problems.

The main properties of programming models can be summarized under the headings of the objective function, the technology specification, constraint structure, heterogeneity of the fixed resource base, calibration methods, and dynamics.

Objective Function Specification

Objective functions can be grouped as profit maximizing or cost minimizing, and linear or quadratic in production and resource allocation. The use of a linear profit-maximizing objective for resource analysis is constrained to small regional projects where the output prices and input costs can be assumed exogenous.

Large interregional programming models are typically specified with either a cost minimization objective function or a surplus maximization objective function. As Takayama and Judge (1971) showed, maximization of surplus gives a set of quantities and prices that are consistent with a competitive market solution. Note that unless the model incorporates equilibrium in factor markets, the meaning of "producers surplus" in the context of a programming model is really the return to fixed factors of production (i.e., profit).

The advantage of the surplus model relative to the cost model becomes apparent when evaluating a policy that shifts the supply curve. Suppose that S' in Figure 4.4 is the new supply curve and S the old curve. Note that the supply curve is implicit in the resource allocation component of the programming model; the supply curve has a stair-step look because of the linearity inherent in specification of a linear programming model. The surplus model provides a market equilibrium solution of P^e, Q^e with the old supply curve and an equilibrium solution of P^s, Q^s with the new supply curve (Fig. 4.4). However, the cost model, while perhaps providing the same baseline shadow price of P^e for a fixed demand quantity of Q^e, estimates the price effect of the policy that shifts supply to S' as P^c, which is lower than the market equilibrium price of P^s.

The surplus model is desirable because it directly gives a market equilibrium solution. Of course, a cost model can be manipulated (by parametrically changing the fixed demands) to discover the equilibrium solution. However, most applications of interregional programming models involve interrelated demands for multiple "consuming" regions, which greatly complicates use by interatively changing the fixed demands to approximate a market equilibrium solution with

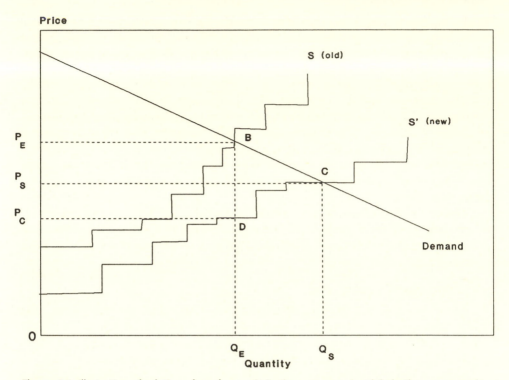

Figure 4.4. Illustration of solution of surplus maximization versus costs minimization programming models.

the cost model. Because of this difficulty, the cost model is rarely used to obtain an equilibrium solution; the shadow price of the fixed demand constraint is taken as an approximation of the price effect of the policy that causes the supply shift.

With linear demand functions, a quadratic objective function maximizes the sum of producer and consumer surplus, given resource constraints and technology. Thus, quadratic programming can be used to obtain market equilibrium solutions. An alternative method to the quadratic surplus function is to approximate the quadratic function by a stair-stepped approximation of the demand curves. This approach preserves linearity at the cost of substantially increased model dimensions (Duloy and Norton, 1973; Taylor and Frohberg, 1977).

Some models of resource use have added explicit risk terms in the objective function to improve the reality of the responses and the diversity of commodities produced. Specialization of production owing to the linear production technology, and consequently costs, has been a major problem for programming model construction and calibration. The most common risk specification uses the mean/variance approach, maximizing expected utility.

Interregional Dimension of Models

Aside from the objective function, formulation of the cost model and the surplus model for a particular application can be identical. To reflect the regional heterogeneity of production and the distribution of production, the region, country, or world being analyzed is typically divided up into many (sometimes a few hundred) producing regions. Consuming regions, which are often aggregations of producing regions, are also defined to permit specification of regional commodity demands and to make the interregional transportation of commodities endogenous to the model.

Homogeneity of production within a region is used as a criterion in defining producing regions. Data limitations and computational considerations dictate the number of producing regions used for a particular model. Additional production distinctions, such as farm size, irrigated versus dryland production, or soil type, can be made to provide detail and accuracy for the model (e.g., Devadoss et al., 1992; Taylor and Frohberg, 1977). Agricultural production activities (such as corn or corn/soybean rotations) using specific tillage systems (such as chisel plow or moldboard plow) and even using different input rates (such as fertilizer or pesticides) are defined for each producing region–resource situation combination. It should be carefully noted that the amount of producing region and resource situation detail has a critical influence on the accuracy (in a normative sense) of the model's solution.

Technology Specification

With very few exceptions, the fundamental technology in programming models is a constant returns to scale Leontief technology. This specification conveniently enables the input/output relations to be expressed in the familiar form of a matrix of linear input requirement coefficients, the $a(ij)$ values, which are then multiplied by the vector of output levels $x(j)$. The resulting vector of input requirements is constrained to be less than or equal to the available fixed inputs $b(i)$.

$$Ax < b \qquad (23)$$

If the cost of inputs is also linear, as in most models, the optimal solution to a cost-minimizing or profit-maximizing objective function is a corner solution. Linear algebra dictates that the number of nonzero activities in the optimal solution is equal to the number of binding constraints, giving rise to the previously mentioned problem of overspecialization in outputs.

Risk is introduced into the technological constraints using the chance constrained method (Hazell and Norton, 1986). The two sources of stochasticity in the production constraints are uncertainty in the available resources and uncertainty in the technical coefficients. If both the distributions are normally distributed, and the modeler is able to specify a critical probability with which the constraint must hold, the constraints can be reformulated to hold with the specified probability. Uncertainty in the $b(i)$ vector results in a linear modification of the $b(i)$ values used in the model right-hand side; stochastic $a(i \cdot j)$ values are accommodated in a similar way, but result in a quadratic constraint in x.

In the past decade, there have been some methodological developments that allow the model technology to be calibrated against a data base in a positive rather than normative manner. This approach is termed positive mathematical programming (PMP) (Howitt, 1990), and like computable general equilibrium models it calibrates to a specified data base and can incorporate non-Leontief technologies and prior elasticities on supplies and demands (Howitt, 1990). Currently, technologies that are quadratic in land, and Leontief in other inputs are one alternative, while Cobb-Douglas is the other. A CES production function is also possible. Details of the PMP approach are discussed under the calibration procedure.

Constraint Specification

Many agricultural resources have the property of quasifixed or allocatable inputs. They are defined as inputs that are fixed in total quantity, but allocatable among alternative production activities. Since the marginal allocation of these resources depends on their shadow value rather than their nominal price, econometric estimation of cost or production functions with allocatable inputs has proved difficult. Only recently has an acceptable method been proposed (Chambers and Just, 1988). The programming constraint structure optimizes with resources allocated so that their shadow values are equal in all production processes.

The set of constraints in programming models enables the model builder to impose physical relationships on the production processes. The most common type of constraint is a rotation between activities. While many agricultural systems have some crops with identifiable rotations, too often they are used to impose arbitrary constraints on the model that help it calibrate to the base year.

Constraints are very convenient for embedding physical relationships within an economic model. Concepts of water use, salinization, erosion, and forest rotations are a few examples. This greatly helps when resource economists have to work in interdisciplinary projects. Another widespread use of constraints is to model the institutional structure of agricultural resources. Policy institutions that use input constraints are mentioned above. Other constraints on property rights or access can be modeled explicitly in the constraint structure.

Calibration Procedures in Programming Models

One of the principle problems that has plagued programming models of agricultural resources is the difficulty of getting models that are linear in the profit (objective) function to calibrate to the base data set, without excessively constraining them. In most cases, the number of production activities that are observed in the base year for a given region exceed the number of binding constraints that can be empirically justified. Since the number of activities in a linear system cannot exceed the binding constraints, the model builder is faced with the dilemma of adding dubious constraints, or having a model that does not represent the base year data.

There are several methods to overcome the calibration problem. One method that begs the problem is to divide the model into many subregions, each of which can be considered homogeneous with respect to production. Resource constraints are also subdivided into these regions. The individual subregions will have the same problems of overspecialization, but if reported in larger aggregate regions, the results will show more heterogeneity of production.

A more transparent method of regional calibration is to use *flexibility constraints* to control the deviation of the model results from some base average value (Day, 1963). The constraints are ironically named, since the one thing that they prevent is flexibility of the solution. If used extensively, flexibility constraints can control the set of policy responses that are obtainable from the model. At an extreme, flexibility constraints that are tightly binding can reduce a resource model to an accounting model that scarcely adds up resource use. In short, flexibility constraints blur the extent to which these models can represent competitive behavior.

McCarl (1982) advocates a data based approach to model constraint specification. The linear models should be replete with as much detail on operational constraints as possible. Rotations are not defined as simple alternatives, but as a set of historical alternative rotations that have been observed. This is a substantial advance over flexibility constraints, but has the drawback that it restricts the model outcomes to linear combinations of past cropping patterns. In the case of a new production technology or an innovative policy design, the model may be unduly restricted by the past to reflect the new competitive solution.

Although the necessary and sufficient conditions for exact aggregation in LP models have been widely discussed (Day, 1963), we do not have sufficient data to determine the extent of aggregation bias in national LP models. However, regional analyses indicate that the bias can be serious.

It is not uncommon for modelers to add "flexibility" constraints to production activities to take into account model deficiencies arising from insufficient detail in the production or consumption component of the model. Often these flexibility coefficients are arbitrary (say restricting a cropping activity to plus or minus 50 percent of the acreage of that crop over a historical period) and may critically influence the solution to the model and thus critically influence the aggregate economic analysis based on such solutions.

Arbitrary flexibility constraints can be tightened to produce realistic model results. However, in this case the validity of the solution and resulting analysis is in doubt. Also, tight flexibility constraints make a normative or *behavioral* model (that is consistent with profit maximization or cost minimization and thus consistent with a competitive market) nothing more that an *accounting* model that largely adds up resource use. Most LP models of the United States agricultural economy have contained arbitrary flexibility constraints; thus the extent to which the models represent competitive behavior is blurred.

The positive programming approach overcomes the calibration problem by taking a more econometric view of model building and by hypothesizing that resource allocations that are not constrained by resources or empirical constraints result from first-order conditions. The simplest cost function that would result in these conditions is one that is quadratic in land allocated to a given activity. PMP uses the dual results from an initially constrained run to derive the quadratic cost coefficients that calibrate the model to the base data. The resulting model has a quadratic cost function calibrated for each nonzero regional activity in the base data. With modern algorithms, large models of up to 600 nonlinear functions have been solved on small workstations. PMP models have been calibrated with and without the use of priors on supply elasticities. The resulting models calibrate precisely, but are free to respond to changes in competitive equilibrium induced by policy or resource changes.

Dynamic Specifications

Programming models are essentially static in nature since they are calibrated and based on a single year or representative set of data. Resource models often assume dynamic properties based on the dynamics of the underlying resource in the model. A static model in a time period is linked by physical equations of motion to changes in water quantity or quality, or by changes in soil productivity from erosion. This approximation omits dynamic economic behavior such as changes in capital stock or expectations, or the cost of adjusting from the short run toward a long run equilibrium. Thus these dynamic resource models are not dynamic in the economic sense, but may be adequate if the equations of motion are dominated by physical systems, and the regional complexities are significant. Models such as these are common in the water resources literature. True nonlinear control and dynamic programming models of agricultural resources are restricted to more aggregate or micro applications at the present. The dimensionality of regional models usually swamps the current numerical ability to solve these true dynamic problems.

Day (1963) proposed an approximation to large-scale dynamic models which he terms recursive programming. Essentially, the approach is to constrain the static model by time varying flexibility constraints. The concept is the same as a myopic cost of adjustment model. Apart from the static calibration problem with the constraints, a difficulty with recursive programming is that of specifying the change in the flexibility constraints over time. Most constraints were set at an ad hoc level, which allowed a given percentage change each year. There have been some attempts to estimate the rate of change of the constraints econometrically or as an endogenous variable in the model. Neither of these approaches has been widely used.

The future of programming models for agricultural resource analysis depends on how one defines a programming model. If it is defined as a model that explicitly optimizes, but is not an econometric or CGE model, then there appears to be a long future for models that are applicable to physical resources and part way between an econometric and a CGE model.

There does not seem to be much development potential for the traditional LP approach in agricultural resource analysis. However, a model that can be calibrated with a minimal data set, incorporates econometric priors, and uses a flexible technology that is consistent with more macro models has a role to play in resource analysis in an era when the physical and institutional realities have to be represented by constraints.

ADVANTAGES AND DISADVANTAGES OF ALTERNATIVE TYPES OF MODELS

An important question pertaining to aggregate modeling for empirical analysis of resource policies is, "What is the most appropriate type of model to use?" The answer to this question is conditional on the type of policy to be analyzed, and even then the answer is not clear, in part because ex post assessment of the accuracy of ex ante evaluations is rare. Until such comparisons are made for a wide range of policies, the modeling recommendations can only be discussed in terms of intuition and modeling experience.

Table 4.1 compares the various modeling approaches in terms of various features of the models, while Table 4.2 assesses suitability of the models for different types of resource policies. The assessment given in Tables 4.1 and 4.2 refers to how the models are most commonly used and not to what is conceptually possible; although the assessments in Tables 4.1 and 4.2 are undoubtedly contentious, they should give the nonmodeler or beginning modeler some feel for the strengths and weaknesses of the alternative approaches. Overall assessments are at the bottom of Table 4.2.

For ex post policy evaluation, various econometric modeling approaches are the mainstay of the profession because they use traditional statistical techniques to try to attain objectivity. If, however, data are inadequate for econometric analysis, there is no well-defined modeling approach to use; rather, the analyst must rely on intuition and judgment using whatever sparse data may be available.

For policies that result in changes in variables within the range of historical observations, it appears that (positive) econometric-simulation or computable general equilibrium models based on literature elasticities would give the most accurate results for ex ante analysis. Despite many objections to interregional programming models, they remain the most realistic framework for investigation of policies outside the range of historical data. In addition, such models are the only practical alternative we have for analyzing a broad range of resource policies that focus on erosion-sedimentation issues because data are not available to parameterize a soil-specific econometric model.

With very complex and elaborate policy evaluation, which is increasingly common, the particular set of baseline and policy assumptions selected may have as much to do with estimated impacts as the type of model selected for the evaluation. In a comparison of results from seven large-scale models for specific policies with baseline assumptions dictated to the extent possible, it was found that different assumptions explained many differences in model results (Taylor et al., 1993).

In conclusion, development of accurate models for evaluation of economic impacts of resource policies requires feedback based on ex post evaluation of ex ante estimates, irrespective of the policies analyzed. Until such comparisons become a part of the model development process, definitive recommendations on which type to use are not possible. Modeling and model selection for resource policy analysis remains more art than science.

REFERENCES

Adelman, I. and S. Robinson. "U.S. Agriculture in a General Equilibrium Framework: Analysis with a Social Accounting Matrix." *American Journal of Agricultural Economics* 68(5):1196–1207, 1986.

Adelman, I. and J.E. Taylor. "Is Structural Adjustment with a Human Face Possible? The Case of Mexico." AAEA Meetings, New York, December 1988.

Bigman, D. *Food Policies and Food Security Under Instability: Modeling and Analysis*. Lexington, MA: Lexington Books, 1988.

Burt, O.R. "Positivistic Measures of Aggregate Supply Elasticities: Comment." *American Journal of Agricultural Economics* 53:674–675, 1971.

Brooke, A., D. Kendrick, and A. Meenaus. *GAMS, A User's Guide*. Redwood City, CA: The Scientific Press, 1988.

Chambers, R.G. and R.E. Just. "Estimating Multioutput Technologies." Working Paper 88-19. Department of Agriculture and Rural Economics, University of Maryland, 1988.

Clarete, R.L. and J.A. Raumasset. "CGE Models and Development Policy Analysis: Problems, Pitfalls, and Challenges." *American Journal of Agricultural Economics* 68(5):1212–1216, 1986.

Currie, J.M., J.A. Murphy, and A. Schmitz. "The Concept of Economic Surplus and Its Use in Economic Analysis." *Economic Journal* 81:741–799, 1971.

Day, R.H. *Recursive Programming and Production Response*. Amsterdam: North-Holland, 1963.

Decalauwe, B. and A. Movlins. "CGE Modelling and Developing Economics: An Empirical Survey of 56 Applications to 24 Countries." Centre de Recherche en Economique, Cabien No. 1686, Université de Montreal, Quebec, Canada, 1986.

Dervis, K., J. deMela, and S. Robinson. *General Equilibrium Models for Development Policy*. Cambridge: Cambridge University Press, 1982.

Devadoss, S., P. Westhoff, M. Helmar, E. Grundmeier, K. Skold, W.H. Meyers, and S.R. Johnson. "The FAPRI Modeling System: A Documentation Summary." In C.R. Taylor, S.R. Johnson, and K.H. Reichelderfer (eds.): *Agricultural Sector Models for the United States: Description and Selected Policy Applications*. Ames, IA: Iowa State University Press, 1993.

Duloy, J.H. and R.D. Norton. "CHAC: A Programming Model of Mexican Agriculture." In A.S. Manne and L.M. Gouveaux (eds.): *Multilevel Planning: Case Studies in Mexico*. Amsterdam: North Holland, 1973.

Frohberg, K., D. Maxwell, S. Aradhyula, S. R. Johnson, and G. E. Oamek. "The BLS Model Operated at CARD: A Documentation Summary." *Agricultural Sector Models for the United States: Description and Selected Policy Applications*. In C. R. Taylor, S. R. Johnson, and K. H. Reichelderfer (eds.): Ames, IA: Iowa State University, 1993.

Hazell, P.B.R. and R.D. Norton. *Mathematical Programming for Economic Analysis in Agriculture*. New York: Macmillan, 1986.

Hertel, T.W. "Double General Equilibrium Models: Discussion." *American Journal of Agricultural Economics* 68(5):1222–1224, 1986.

Howitt, R.E. "Positive Mathematical Programming Models." Working Paper, Department of Agricultural Economics, University of California-Davis, 1990.

Howitt, R.E. "Optimal Control of General Equilibrium Models: Discussion." *American Journal of Agricultural Economics* 68(5):1217–1221, 1986.

Jorgenson, D.W., L.J. Lau, and T.M. Stoker. "Welfare Comparisons Under Exact Aggregation." *American Economic Review* 70:268–272, 1980.

Just, R.E. and D.L. Hueth. "Welfare Measures in a Multimarket Framework." *American Economic Review* 69:947–954, 1979.

Lau, L. "Applications of Profit Functions." In M. Fuss and D. McFadden (eds.): *Production Economics: A Dual Approach to Theory and Applications*, Vol. 1. Amsterdam: North Holland, 1978.

McCarl, B. "Should Quadratic Programming Problems be Approximated." *American Journal of Agricultural Economics* 64:585–589, 1982.

Muelbauer, J. "Aggregation, Income Distribution and Consumer Demand." *Review of Economic Studies* 42:525–543, 1975.

Penson, J.B., Jr., D.W. Hughes, and Dean T. Chen. "General Design of COMGEM: A Macroeconomic Model Emphasizing Agriculture." In C.R. Taylor, S.R. Johnson, and K.H. Reichelderfer (eds.): *Agricultural Sector Models for the United States: Description and Selected Policy Applications.* Ames, IA: Iowa State University, 1993.

Penson, J.B., Jr. and C.R. Taylor. "United States Agriculture and the General Economy: Modeling their Interface." *Agricultural Systems* 39:33–66, 1992.

Pope, R.D. "Supply Response and the Dispersion of Price Expectations." *American Journal of Agricultural Economics* 63:161–163, 1981.

Scarf, H.E. and J.B. Shoven. *Applied General Equilibrium Analysis.* Cambridge and New York: Cambridge University Press, 1989.

Schuh, G.E. "The Exchange Rate and U.S. Agriculture." *American Journal of Agricultural Economics* 56:1–13, 1979.

Shoven, J. and J. Whalley. "Applied General Equilibrium Models of Taxation and International Trade." *Journal of Economic Literature* 22:1007–1015, 1989.

Sutton, J.D. *Agricultural Trade and Natural Resources: Discovering the Critical Linkages.* Boulder, CO: Lynne Review, 1988.

Takayama, T. and G. Judge. *Spatial and Temporal Price and Allocation Models.* Amsterdam: North Holland, 1971.

Taylor, C.R. "A Description of AGSIM, an Econometric-Simulation Model of Regional Crop and National Livestock Production in the United States." In C.R. Taylor, S.R. Johnson, and K.H. Reichelderfer (eds.): *Agricultural Sector Models for the United States: Description and Selected Policy Applications.* Ames, IA: Iowa State University, 1993.

Taylor, C.R. "Complementarities Between Micro- and Macro-Systems Simulation and Analysis." In K.H. Baum and C.P. Schertz (eds.): *Modeling Farm Decisions for Policy Analysis.* Boulder, CO: Westview Press, 1983.

Taylor, C.R. "The Nature of Benefits and Costs of Use of Pest Control Methods." *American Journal of Agricultural Economics* 62(5):1007–1011, 1980.

Taylor, C.R. *Stochastic Simulation of the Aggregate Impacts of Agricultural Policy and Technological Change.* Auburn University, Department of Agricultural Economics and Rural Sociology Series, ES89-7, April 1989.

Taylor, C.R. and K. Frohberg. "The Welfare Effects of Erosion Controls, Banning Pesticides and Limiting Fertilizer Application in the Corn Belt." *American Journal of Agricultural Economics* 59:25–36, 1977.

Taylor, C.R., S.R. Johnson, and K.H. Reichelderfer. *Agricultural Sector Models for the United States: Description and Selected Policy Applications.* 1993.

Taylor, C.R., R.D. Lacewell, and H. Talpaz. "Use of Extraneous Information with an Econometric Model to Evaluate Impacts of Pesticide Withdrawals." *Western Journal of Agricultural Economics* 4:785:792, 1979.

Theil, H. *Principles of Econometrics.* New York: John Wiley and Sons, Inc., 1971.

Tweeten, L.G. and L. Quance. "Positivistic Measures of Aggregate Supply Elasticities: Some New Approaches." *American Journal of Agricultural Economics* 51:342–353, 1969.

5

Technological Innovation, Agricultural Productivity, and Environmental Quality

JOHN M. ANTLE AND TOM McGUCKIN

The high rates of agricultural growth in the United States in the latter half of the 20th century were achieved with a science-based system of technological innovation in agriculture. These technologies were developed through a system of public and private research and were disseminated through agricultural education and extension and private marketing of agricultural inputs. Within this agricultural system, progress has long been considered synonymous with productivity growth and is typically measured as increases in output per unit of input.

The increasing public concern with the impacts of agricultural production on farmland, water resources, human health, and the larger natural environment has motivated the agricultural community to broaden its basis for the assessment of agricultural progress beyond conventional measures of agricultural productivity. This more comprehensive view of the innovation process is illustrated in Figure 5.1. The solid lines in the figure illustrate the conventional view, beginning with technological innovation and ending with productivity change. These relationships are well understood both theoretically and empirically. The dotted lines indicate the ways that public policies, such as commodity production subsidies or environmental regulations, may affect both agricultural productivity and environmental quality by changing the short-term and long-term production decisions made by farmers. Much research needs to be done before the impacts of policy on innovation and the impacts of production on the environment are fully understood.

In the short-run farmers must respond to policy changes with existing technology and capital investments. When most farmers are producing efficiently, policy changes that enhance environmental quality often come at the expense of productivity. For example, restrictions on pesticide use force farmers to use less economical pest management practices while reducing environmental contamination. Changes in commodity policies, such as set aside requirements and price support levels, also are likely to alter pesticide use and may thus affect both productivity and environmental quality. In this case, however, it is less clear what kinds of effects commodity policies will have. An increase in price supports may

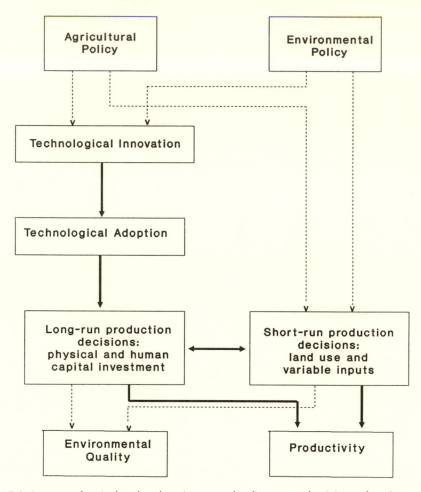

Figure 5.1. Impacts of agricultural and environmental policy on productivity and environmental quality.

increase the incentive to farm high-quality land intensively and may thus raise productivity but lower environmental quality. But an increase in set aside requirements may lead farmers to idle more environmentally sensitive land and thus raise environmental quality. Policy changes also may cause farmers to substitute among other inputs, such as labor and chemicals.

The long-term impacts occur through the types of innovations that are developed by researchers and adopted by farmers. If certain classes of chemicals are banned from use, such as the highly persistent organochlorines, researchers in both the public and private sector research institutions perceive a need and an incentive to develop alternative methods of pest control. These alternatives may take the form of less persistent chemicals, such as the organophosphates and carbamates, or they may take the form of nonchemical control methods such as development of resistant plant varieties. Over the longer term, technological innovation enhances the opportunity to improve both agricultural productivity and environmental quality.

It is thus clear that technological innovation, agricultural productivity, and environmental quality are inextricably linked in the process of agricultural growth. While there is a need to understand the process of technological change that is the driving force behind modern agricultural growth, there is also a need to understand the broader impacts of agricultural growth. This chapter introduces the reader to basic concepts of productivity measurement and technological innovation, and discusses some ways those concepts can be broadened to account for environmental impacts of agricultural production.

TECHNOLOGICAL CHANGE AND PRODUCTIVITY MEASUREMENT[1]

Modern agricultural production utilizes several important categories of inputs into the production process: the natural environment, including the quantity and quality of sunlight, air, and water resources; land of various qualities; human labor, including field labor and management decision making; mechanical power; chemical inputs, especially fertilizers and organic synthetic compounds used as pesticides; and biological inputs, which can be thought of as the genetic material embodied in types of plants and animals. As will be discussed in greater detail below, the specific way these inputs are utilized in agricultural technology will depend on the resource endowment that farmers and agricultural researchers have to work with, and the resulting resource scarcities these groups perceive. The United States has one the greatest endowments of arable land in the temperate zone and a relative abundance of physical capital, but has historically faced a relative scarcity of labor. Technological innovation in the United States has been *biased* toward the development of technology that has exploited this abundance of land and capital. In the jargon to be introduced below, the technology developed in the United States has typically been *land using, capital using, and labor saving.*

These patterns are revealed in the U.S. data for the 19th and 20th centuries. Table 5.1 shows yields for wheat, corn, and cotton from 1870 to 1985. From 1870 to 1950, the average yield increases per year were less than 1 percent for each of these crops, whereas from 1950 to 1970 the yield increases averaged between 3 and 6 percent per year. These pre-1950 and post-1950 differences in yield growth rates can be explained by innovations in biological and mechanical technology, and the increased use of complementary inputs, such as agricultural chemicals that complement modern crop varieties, fuels to power the machinery driven by internal combustion engines, and the skills and knowledge necessary for the use of the new technology. Table 5.2 illustrates the ongoing substitution of capital for labor in U.S. agriculture that was accelerated in the 1950s as modern crop varieties were rapidly adopted.

---

[1] This section draws upon material in Chapter 2 of Antle and Capalbo (1988), which may be consulted for a more in-depth discussion of productivity measurement and extensive references to the literature.

Table 5.1. Yields per Acre of Four Important Crops for Selected Years,[a] 1880–1985

Year	Wheat	Corn	Potatoes	Cotton
1880	12.7	26.1	52.6	174.2
1900	13.2	24.8	49.9	182.6
1930	14.5	23.6	65.9	177.6
1935	12.3	20.5	66.3	185.4
1940	15.4	30.0	77.4	240.8
1945	17.3	34.4	97.7	263.1
1950	15.7	37.8	145.0	273.4
1955	19.4	42.9	165.6	389.0
1960	24.0	56.5	188.2	448.3
1965	26.2	69.7	203.3	580.0
1970	31.8	80.8	226.3	436.7
1975	31.5	96.5	256.0	454.5
1980	34.4	101.6	265.0	401.0
1985	38.5	131.9	299.0	632.8

[a] Three-year average centered on the year; bu./acre for wheat and corn, cwt./acre for potatoes, lbs. for cotton.

Source: *Century of Agriculture in Chart and Tables*, Agricultural Handbook No. 318, U.S. Department of Agriculture, Statistical Reporting Service, 1966; and *Agricultural Statistics*, various issues.

A major force driving the post-1950 agricultural revolution was the acceleration in the growth of publicly funded agricultural research in the early to mid-20th century, combined with a growing level of private research. Combined with scientific advances in physics and chemistry during the 1940s, agricultural researchers in the years following World War II were able to make dramatic advances in both mechanical and biological technology. A rapid growth in the funding of extension work provided the means to communicate these technological advances to farmers and speed their successful adoption.

In the neoclassical theory of production, productivity is a function of the state of technology, the quantities and types of resources used as inputs into the production process, and the efficiency with which those resources are used.

Table 5.2. Percentage Composition of Agricultural Inputs, United States, Selected Years 1870–1976

Year	Labor	Real estate	Capital[a]	Total
1870	65	18	17	100
1900	57	19	24	100
1920	50	18	32	100
1940	41	18	41	100
1960[b]	27	19	54	100
1970	19	23	58	100
1976	16	22	58	100

[a] Includes all kinds of capital items: operating capital and physical capital other than land and buildings.

[b] The series for 1960 forward employs different, and more modern, weights than for the period 1870–1940.

Source: 1870–1940, *Productivity of Agriculture, 1870–1958*, U.S. Department of Agriculture Bulletin No. 1238, April 1961, p. 11; 1960–1976 unpublished estimates provided by Donald Durost of the Economic Research Service of U.S.D.A.

Output

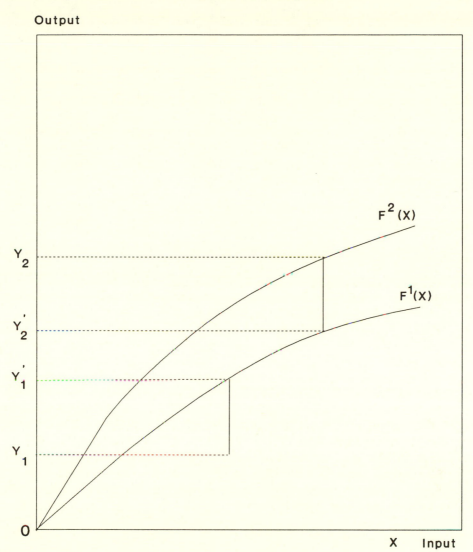

Figure 5.2. Changes in technology, scale, and technical efficiency.

The effects of these three factors on the measurement of average productivity are illustrated in Fig. 5.2. This figure shows two neoclassical production functions, $F^1(x)$ and $F^2(x)$, that represent technically efficient combinations of inputs and outputs for two production processes. We can think of y_1 and y_2 as outputs observed in two time periods with process F^1 used in period 1 and process F^2 used in period 2. A change in productivity from period 1 to 2 can be decomposed into three parts. First, since Y_1 is not on the first period production function, there is production inefficiency equal to the difference $(y_1' - y_1)$. Second, y_2 is produced with a higher level of input than y_1. Thus, there is a difference $(y_2' - y_1')$

attributable to an increase in the scale of production. Third, process F^2 represents a shift in the production function caused by technological change, which explains the difference $(y_2 - y_2')$.

The figure illustrates that changes in productivity can be due to changes in technical efficiency of resource use, scale of production, and the state of technology. There is overwhelming evidence that there have been significant changes in the scale of agricultural production and in the type of technology in use. Because technological change is the most important factor in science-based agricultural productivity growth since the 1950s, it is important for us to define carefully what we mean by technological change, and to understand its implications for productivity and resource utilization.

Technological Change

Technological change refers to the changes in a production process that result from the application of scientific knowledge. At the first level, these changes are realized in several ways. First, technological change can be *embodied* in inputs when there are changes in input quality. Second, *disembodied technological change* takes the form of knowledge about improved methods of production that is not embodied in physical inputs (although when knowledge is embodied in people it represents a component of human capital). Third, technological change can occur because of the invention of entirely new processes and new inputs. Many innovations involve a combination of these three phenomena. The development of hybrid corn varieties represented the embodiment of scientific knowledge in corn seed. Management knowledge was also needed for their successful use, and a set of new inputs in the form of pesticides were developed over time for use with the hybrids. A new input such as hybrid seed could be interpreted as an entirely new kind of input, or as a higher quality input of a type that already existed.

Disembodied technological change in an existing production process can be modeled as a shift in the production surface. For example, consider the simple Cobb-Douglas model in logarithmic form:

$$\ln y_t = \alpha \cdot t + \beta_1 \ln x_{1t} + \cdots + \beta_n \ln x_{nt} \tag{1}$$

Let the quantity $\ln X_t \equiv \beta_1 \ln x_{1t} + \cdots + \beta_n \ln x_{nt}$ be an "aggregate input." The rate of growth of output per unit of aggregate input is then $d \ln(y_t/X_t)/dt = \alpha$. More generally, however, technical change may result in nonneutral shifts in the production surface. This can be represented in the Cobbs-Douglas model by changes in the production elasticities, the β_i.

Embodied technological changes introduces the problems of measuring input and output quality changes. Economists have addressed these issues in discussions of the measurement of physical capital (Diewert, 1980). In agriculture, input quality measurement problems arise with changes in chemical inputs, management input, and the introduction of new plant and animal varieties through conventional breeding and newer biogenetic techniques, as well as in the measurement of physical capital such as machinery.

Consider the measurement of technological change in a production process with a single output (used here as an aggregate output index y) and multiple inputs. The aggregate production function is $y = F(x, t)$, where t denotes the state of the technology and $x = (x_1, \ldots, x_n)$ is a vector of the total amounts of each type of input used. Assume that F satisfies neoclassical regularity conditions: F is a positive, increasing, concave function of x and is increasing and differentiable in t.

Define the rate of growth in output measured with the production function, $\partial \ln F / \partial t$, as the *primal rate of technological change*. Totally differentiating $y = F(x, t)$ with respect to t, and rearranging, gives

$$\partial \ln F / \partial t = d \ln y / dt - (1/F) \Sigma_i F_i \, dx_i / dt \tag{2}$$

where F_i is the marginal product of x_i. In a competitive industry equilibrium in which price equals marginal cost and inputs are paid the value of their marginal products, the above equation can be rewritten as

$$\partial \ln F / \partial t = d \ln y / dt - (\partial \ln C / \partial \ln y)^{-1} \Sigma_i S_i \, d \ln x_i / dt \tag{3}$$

where r_i is the price of the ith input, $S_i = r_i x_i / \Sigma_i r_i x_i$ is the factor cost share, and C is total cost. The term $\partial \ln C / \partial \ln y$ is the elasticity of cost with respect to output, and can be used to measure returns to scale (note constant returns to scale implies $\partial \ln C / \partial \ln y = 1$). The term $\Sigma_i S_i \, d \ln x_i / dt$ can be interpreted as an index of the rate of growth of the inputs. Equation (3) shows that the primal rate of technological change equals the rate of growth in output minus a scale-adjusted index of the rate of growth of inputs.

As the production function shifts upward because of technological change, the firm's cost, revenue, and profit relationships also change. Indeed, it can be said that the cost, revenue, and profit functions embody the same economically relevant information about the technology as the production function $F(x, t)$.[2] Thus it should be true that these dual functions can also be used to define and measure rates of technological change.[3] Consider the cost function $C = C(y, r, t)$, where r is the vector of input prices corresponding to x. It is known from intermediate microeconomic theory that as the production function $F(x, t)$ shifts upward because of technological change, the corresponding cost function shifts downward. That is, since more output is obtained for a given input x, the total cost of producing any given output rate is lower. To represent this effect of technological change on the cost function, define the *dual cost rate of technological change* as $-\partial \ln C(y, w, t) / \partial t$. It can be shown that the primal and dual cost rates of technological change are related as follows:

$$-\partial \ln C / \partial t = (\partial \ln C / \partial \ln y)(\partial \ln F / \partial t) \tag{4}$$

This equation says that the dual cost rate of technological change is equal to the primal rate of technological change times a measure of returns to scale. Thus, the primal and dual rates are equal if and only if the elasticity of cost with respect to

[2] For definitions of cost, revenue, and profit function, see Varian (1978).
[3] The reader may wonder why a cost function would be used to estimate the production technology instead of a production function. For a discussion of this issue, see Pope (1982).

output, $\partial \ln C / \partial \ln y$, is unity, i.e., if and only if the technology exhibits constant returns to scale. Generally, primal and dual measures of technological change will differ because of scale effects. This happens because the primal rate is computed with input levels that are held constant, whereas the dual rate is computed with input levels adjusting optimally to technological change.

As noted above, technological change can affect input productivities and factor utilization differentially; it can also affect the optimal levels and proportions of outputs produced. Table 5.2 shows the remarkable trends observed in factor utilization in U.S. agriculture over the past century. Moreover, technological change may affect the outputs produced as well as the factor proportions used. As both transportation and production technology advanced in the United States during the 20th century, many regions of the country such as the "corn belt" in the Midwest and the "wheat belt" in the Great Plains increased their degree of specialization in production. Thus, both input requirement sets and production possibilities frontiers may not shift neutrally in response to technological change. This type of observation about the effects of technological change on input use led Hicks (1963) to distinguish between *factor-neutral* and *factor-biased* technological change; somewhat analogously, we can think of *output-neutral* and *output-biased* technological change. Hicks (1963, p. 121) originally defined factor-neutral and biased technological change using the marginal rate of technical substitution (MRTS or F_i/F_j). Neutrality was defined as a shift in the production function leaving the MRTS unchanged; factor bias occurred when the MRTS was changed by technological change. This definition can be ambiguous when applied to nonhomothetic technologies, i.e., production functions that do not have linear expansion paths, because the MRTS then also changes with the rate of output.

To interpret the Hicksian bias concept, define the *primal pair-wise measure of input bias* as

$$B_{ij}(X, t) \equiv \partial \ln(F_i/F_j)/\partial t, \qquad i \neq j \qquad (5)$$

Hicks neutrality implies $B_{ij} = 0$ for all i and j. If B_{ij} is positive, technological change uses input i and saves input j. This comes from the fact that at constant prices $B_{ij} > 0$ implies that the cost-minimizing firm would change its input mix employing relatively more of factor i and less of factor j. Noting that B_{ij} is defined at a point in input space, we can interpret the input bias as measuring the rotation of the isoquant at this point in response to technological change, as illustrated in Figure 5.3. The initial expansion path is $e(t_1)$ and the firm is producing at point A with isoquant Y_i. With the new technology t_2, the expansion path is $e(t_2)$. Isoquant Y_2 of the new technology also passes through point A. B_{ij} measures the change in the slope of the isoquant Y_1 to the slope of the isoquant Y_2. Clearly, if the expansion path is unchanged by the technological change, isoquant Y_2 lies on top of Y_1 and $B_{ij} = 0$.

How is the bias in technological change interpreted when there are more than two inputs? Pair-wise comparisons of all inputs can be made, but then if technological change saved factor i relative to factor j, but was using i relative to k, it would be unclear whether it was saving or using factor i overall. To address this problem, define the *overall primal measure of input bias* as

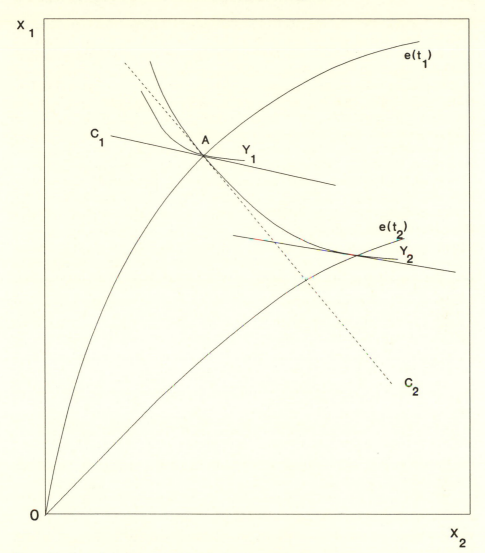

Figure 5.3. The primal measure of the bias in technological change.

$$B_i(x, t) \equiv \Sigma_j S_j B_{ij} \tag{6}$$

where S_j is the factor cost share. To interpret B_i, observe that if $dr_i/dt = dF_i/dt$ at the point x in input space, then prices would have changed so that the point x was on the firm's expansion path with the new technology. This condition allows the following derivation:

$$B_i = \Sigma_j S_j B_{ij} = \partial \ln F_i \, \partial t - \Sigma_j \, \partial \ln F_j/\partial t$$
$$= d \ln r_i/dt - \Sigma_j \, S_j \, d \ln r_j/dt$$
$$= \partial \ln S_i/\partial t|_x \tag{7}$$

Thus the overall bias is a cost-share weighted sum of the pair-wise biases and can be interpreted as the change in the factor cost share that would be caused by a change in factor prices needed to maintain point x on the firm's expansion path. Thus, if on average the marginal product of factor i is increasing relative to all others, then $B_i > 0$ and technological change is overall factor i using. It follows that if technological change is neutral so that all B_{ij} are zero, then all $B_i = 0$. This condition is necessary for Hicks neutral technical change and can be used to construct statistical tests of the hypothesis of neutrality.[4]

Various studies have estimated the bias in technological change in agriculture. Binswanger (1974) provided one of the first studies of U.S. agriculture, and found technology to be labor saving and capital using. Subsequent studies have supported this finding (see Capalbo and Antle, 1988). Hayami and Ruttan (1985) provide evidence of biases in the United States and Japan that are consistent with the induced innovation hypothesis.

Productivity Measurement

A simple measure of productivity, such as average productivity of land (yield), does not account for all the factors that contribute to productivity growth. For this reason, productivity research uses generalizations of the simple average productivity concept, such as *total factor productivity* (TFP), that are based on comprehensive aggregates of outputs and inputs. Defining Y as an aggregate output index and X as an aggregate input index, TFP $\equiv Y/X$, and the rate of growth in TFP is $d \ln(\text{TFP})/dt = d \ln Y/dt - d \ln X/dt$. Figure 5.4 illustrates a total factor productivity index for U.S. agriculture from 1948 to 1983 and indexes of land and labor productivity. Clearly, when the more comprehensive approach is taken, a different picture of growth is obtained. This section explores some of the theoretical and methodological issues involved in measuring total factor productivity.

The Growth Accounting Approach to TFP Measurement

The growth accounting approach utilizes detailed accounts of inputs and outputs. These data are aggregated into input and output indexes, which are, in turn, used to compute a TFP index. The advances in the theory of index numbers has shown that there is a direct correspondence between the technology's properties and the properties of index numbers. For example, the Lasperyes index used in most of the productivity studies done by the USDA has been shown to be exact for, or to imply, either a linear production function or a Leontief production function. A geometric index is exact for a Cobb-Douglas function, and a Tornquist-Theil index (discussed below) is exact for a homogeneous translog function. Thus, index number theory provides the link between the growth accounting approach to TFP measurement and production theory.

---

[4] Bias measures also can be based on the cost, revenue, or profit functions and have been used extensively in the empirical literature on the measurement of biased technological change.

INDEX VALUE

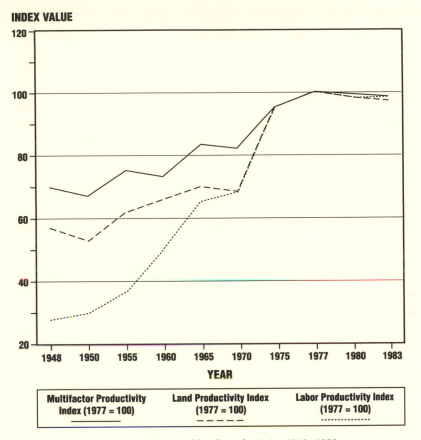

Figure 5.4. Indexes of multifactor, labor and land productivity 1948–1983.

Production economics has made much use of functional forms that are *flexible* in the sense that they do not impose a priori assumptions about economic behavior. Functions that are second-order approximations have this property (Fuss *et al.*, 1978). An index that is exact for a linear homogeneous flexible functional form is called a *superlative* index (Diewert, 1976). A superlative index that has received much attention is the Tornquist-Theil index YI, which in logarithmic form is

$$\ln(\text{YI}) \equiv \Sigma_i \tfrac{1}{2}(s_i^0 + s_i^1) \ln(x_i^1 I x_i^0) \tag{8}$$

where s_i^j is the share of the ith input in total factor payments for period j. The corresponding price index can be defined with input prices replacing the input quantities. Note that this index is a weighted average of the logarithmic differences $\ln(x_i^1/x_i^0) = \ln(x_i^1) - \ln(x_i^0)$, with the weights equal to the average factor share $\tfrac{1}{2}(s_i^0 + s_i^1)$.

The Tornquist-Theil index is often used for TFP measurement because it can be interpreted as a discrete-time approximation to the continuous-time Divisia index. The Divisia indexes for output and input are obtained by differentiating the value of aggregate output $Y = \Sigma_i\, p_i y_i$ and aggregate input $X = \Sigma_i r_i x_i$ with respect to time, holding prices constant, to obtain

$$d \ln Y/dt = \Sigma_j (p_j y_j / \Sigma_i p_i y_j)\, d \ln y_j/dt \tag{9}$$

$$d \ln X/dt = \Sigma_j (r_j x_j / \Sigma_i r_i x_i)\, d \ln x_j/dt \tag{10}$$

These formulas can be applied to measure TFP growth by using the corresponding Tornquist-Theil indexes to compute the change in TFP from one period to another as

$$\ln(\text{TFP}_t / \text{TFP}_{t-1}) = \ln(Y_t / Y_{t-1}) - \ln(X_t / X_{t-1}) \tag{11}$$

An index of TFP is obtained by choosing a base year for the index with a value, say, of 100 and then accumulating year-to-year changes using equation 11.

The Econometric Approach to Productivity Measurement

The econometric approach to productivity measurement utilizes econometric estimates of the production technology. This can be accomplished by direct estimation of the production function. For example, in the case of a Cobb-Douglas production function such as the one in equation (1), an econometric estimate of the rate of technological change is equal to rate of total factor productivity growth. To see this, note that equations (10) and (3) show that $\partial \ln F/\partial t = d \ln y/dt -$ $(\partial \ln C/\partial\, d \ln y)\, d \ln x$. When the production process exhibits constant returns to scale, $\partial \ln c/\partial \ln y = 1$ and thus $\partial \ln F/\partial t = d \ln \text{TFP}/dt$.

    To further illustrate the econometric approach, consider the translog production function:

$$\ln y_t = \alpha_0 + \Sigma_i \alpha_i \ln x_{it} + .5\Sigma_i \Sigma_j \alpha_{ij} x_i x_j + \beta_0 t + .5\beta_1 t^2 + t\Sigma_i \gamma_i x_i \tag{12}$$

Since $\text{TFP} \equiv Y/X$, to measure TFP it must be possible to express the production function in the separable form $Y = F(X, t) = A(t)F^*(X)$. In other words, technological change must be expressible in this form (note that this function implies that technological change is Hicks neutral). The above translog model satisfies this condition if $\gamma_i = 0$ for all i. But more generally, when $\gamma_i \neq 0$, it is not possible to measure TFP as conventionally defined. However, it is possible to define an alternative measure of TFP growth, which allows for nonneutral technological change.

    From the above translog function, we can derive a more general measure of TFP growth as

$$d \ln \text{TFP}^*/dt = d \ln y/dt - d \ln X/dt$$

$$= [(\partial \ln C/\partial \ln y) - 1](d \ln X/dt) + \beta_0 + \beta_1 t + \Sigma\gamma_i \ln x_i \tag{13}$$

With constant returns to scale, $\partial \ln C/\partial \ln y = 1$, and equation 13 becomes

$$d \ln \text{TFP}^* dt = \beta_0 + \beta_1 t + \Sigma\gamma_i \ln x_i \tag{14}$$

If extended Hicks neutrality is assumed ($\gamma_i = 0$ for all i) then $d \ln \text{TFP}^*/dt = \beta_0 + B_i t$.

    Duality theory ensures that productivity change also can be measured in terms of the cost, revenue, or profit function. As in the measurement of technological change, a dual measure of productivity growth generally will differ from a primal measure derived from the production function unless there are constant returns to scale.

Production Theory and Externalities

Externalities generated by industrial processes are typically emitted at a point source such as a smokestack. The quantity of pollution often can be determined in relation to the inputs into the process and the other outputs created. The principal problem in environmental economics is to measure the economic value of the externality. Agricultural externalities are complicated by the fact that they are not usually associated with a point source such as a smokestack. Agricultural externalities such as air or water pollution caused by soil erosion, or surface or ground water contamination caused by chemicals, are called nonpoint source pollution because they are associated with production over a large area with no one point, such as a specific farm field, to which the externality can be attributed. Modeling and analysis of agricultural externalities therefore must contend with the problems of measuring both the quantity of agricultural pollution and the economic costs of the pollution.

The production of externalities and other outputs can be represented in general as a joint production process $F(Y, Z, X) = 0$, where Y is ordinary output, Z is externality output, and X is input (note that Z can represent either an output with a negative social value or a common property resource that is used in production). Agricultural production processes typically generate ordinary outputs and externalities through the use of inputs such as mechanical cultivation, water, and chemicals. For example, suppose agriculture produces an externality such as water pollution that reduces production of recreation. Let recreation be generated by the function $H(R, Z, W) = 0$, where R is the quantity of recreation and W is other inputs into recreation production. If Z causes an externality it follows that H is a decreasing function of Z (Whitcomb, 1972; Archibald, 1988).

When the transformation function $F(Y, Z, X)$ is separable in inputs and outputs it can be written as two functions, the usual production function $Q = q(X)$ and a function $Z = z(X)$ relating input use to the production of the externality-causing quantities of Z. Owing to the location-specific character of agricultural production and the production of environmental damage, it may be important to model both processes at a disaggregate level, e.g., for a homogeneous unit of land. Then outputs can be statistically aggregated to a level useful for economic or policy analysis. Antle and Just (1991) construct a model in which each unit of land has a distinct production function and externality function according to the location-specific environmental attributes of the land that affect both land productivity and the generation of externalities. The last part of this chapter utilizes this approach.

One of the basic assumptions of Neoclassical production theory is that production possibilities sets are convex in outputs so that the production possibilities frontier has the usual shape (concave to the origin). The *convexity* of the production possibilities set is important to economic theory because it implies that a competitive equilibrium yields an efficient point on the production possibilities frontier.

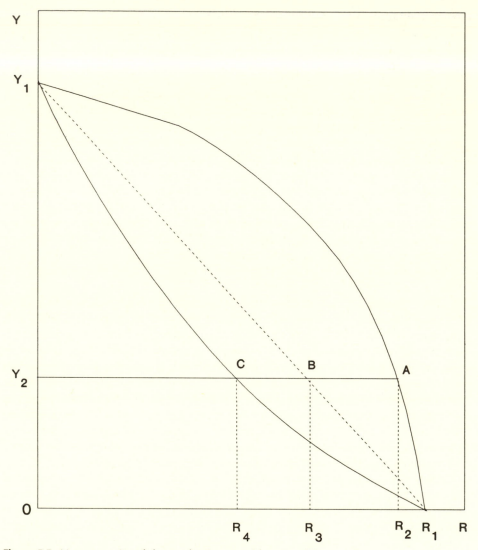

Figure 5.5. Non-convexity of the production set with externalities.

When production processes result in externalities, the convexity of the production set may be violated. Consider, for example, the production of two goods, agricultural output Y and recreation R. Figure 5.5 shows a convex production possibilities set $Y_1 AR$. Now suppose that agricultural production produces an externality, say it pollutes the water used for recreation, so that less recreation can be produced with the same set of inputs and technology. The production possibilities set is unchanged at the two corners Y_1 and R_1. At Y_1 there is no recreation so pollution does not reduce production of recreation, and at R_1 there is no agricultural output and thus no pollution. But at an interior point on the frontier, such as at A, as pollution increases there is a reduction in the amount of recreation that can be produced for a given level of agricultural output. For example starting at point A, as pollution increases R is reduced from R_2. If the externality reduces recreation below R_3 to a value like R_4, the production possibilities frontier becomes convex to the origin and the production possibilities set becomes nonconvex like curve $Y_1 C R_1$.

This heuristic argument can be developed formally (see Baumol and Oates, 1988). The importance of nonconvex production sets for economic theory is that competitive equilibrium no longer necessarily maximizes the value of output at market clearing prices. For example, in Figure 5.5, if the production possibilities set is $Y_1 C R$, an interior tangency of a price line with the production possibilities frontier could represent the point on the frontier with the lowest value instead of the highest. Thus, prices can no longer be relied upon to generate the desirable output allocation even if these prices reflect marginal social values. Some other means of selecting the efficient output set must be relied upon if there are nonconvexities in the production set.

Externalities, Nonmarket Goods, and Productivity Measurement

As discussed in the preceding section, most production processes result in marketed outputs as well as nonmarketed outputs (byproducts or residuals) that may be "goods" or "bads"; goods should receive a positive social value and bads should receive a negative value in the economy's social accounts. In the growth accounting approach to productivity measurement, these externality and nonmarket outputs can be included in the numerator of the TFP index with a positive value if they are goods or a negative value if they are bads. In an econometric approach to productivity measurement, externalities can be modeled as jointly producing conventional outputs and externalities. That is, define the externality and non-market outputs as $Y_j, j = M + 1, \ldots, Q$. The general form of the joint production process for conventional outputs $(Y_1, \ldots, Y_M)$, conventional inputs $(X_1, \ldots, X_N)$, and externality and nonmarketed outputs can be written

$$F[Y_1, \ldots, Y_M, Y_{M+1}, \ldots, Y_Q, X_1, \ldots, X_N] = 0 \qquad (15)$$

With observations of the conventional outputs and inputs and the nonmarket goods, this model can be implemented by adapting the index number approach or the econometric approach to productivity measurement as discussed above. But because the external effects are nonmarket goods and are not readily measured or valued, it will not usually be possible to include all of the external effects in productivity estimates. The reader may refer to the chapter on externalities for discussion of the measurement and valuation of nonmarket goods. In the remainder of this discussion it is assumed that the nonmarket goods all have been measured and valued.

Consider the problem of using the growth accounting approach to include externalities in total factor productivity measurement. Following the discussion of TFP, if estimates of the marginal social values of the external effects (i.e., their shadow prices) are known then the value of total social product as $\Sigma_j P_j Y_j$ and the corresponding generalized "revenue" shares can be computed as

$$R_j^* \equiv P_j Y_j \bigg/ \sum_{j=1}^{Q} P_j Y_j \tag{16}$$

where for $j = M + 1, \ldots, Q$, the P_j are the values of the nonmarket quantities Y_j (note that $R_j^* > 0$ if Y_j is a "good" and $R_j^* < 0$ if Y_j is a "bad"). Now applying the definition of TFP, the generalized measure of total factor productivity growth is

$$d \ln(\text{TFP}^*)/dt \equiv d \ln(Y^*)/dt - d \ln X/dt \tag{17}$$

where

$$d \ln (Y^*)/dt = \sum_{j=1}^{Q} R_j^* \, d \ln Y_j/dt \tag{18}$$

We can also define the shares

$$R_j^p \equiv P_j Y_j \bigg/ \sum_{j=1}^{M} P_j Y_j \tag{19}$$

$$R_j^s \equiv P_j Y_j \bigg/ \sum_{j=M+1}^{Q} P_j Y_j \tag{20}$$

$$R^p \equiv \sum_{j=1}^{M} R_j^* \quad \text{and} \quad R^s \equiv \sum_{j=M+1}^{Q} R_j^* \tag{21}$$

Using these shares, we can define Divisia indexes of conventional output and nonmarket effects as

$$d \ln Y^p/dt \equiv \sum_{j=1}^{M} R_j^p \, d \ln Y_j/dt \tag{22}$$

$$d \ln Y^s/dt \equiv \sum_{j=M+1}^{Q} R_j^s \, d \ln Y_j/dt \tag{23}$$

It follows that

$$d \ln Y^*/dt = R^p(d \ln Y^p/dt) + R^s(d \ln Y^s/dt) \tag{24}$$

and since $R^p + R^s = 1$, we have

$$d \ln \text{TFP}^*/dt = R^p(d \ln \text{TFP}^p/dt) + R^s(d \ln \text{TFP}^s/dt) \tag{25}$$

where

$$d \ln \text{TFP}^p/dt \equiv d \ln Y^p/dt - d \ln X/dt \tag{26}$$

$$d \ln \text{TFP}^s/dt \equiv d \ln Y^s/dt - d \ln X/dt \tag{27}$$

In words, in addition to the conventional measure of total factor productivity growth, $d \ln \text{TFP}^p/dt$, which includes only market goods as outputs, it is possible to define a measure of the rate of production of externalities and nonmarket goods, $d \ln \text{TFP}^s/dt$. The overall rate of total factor productivity growth, $d \ln \text{TFP}^*/dt$, including both market goods, externalities, and nonmarket goods, can be expressed as a weighted average of the conventional measure of productivity growth and the rate of production of externalities and nonmarket goods, with the weights given by the shares of market and nonmarket goods in total social product.

To illustrate how this kind of general productivity index might be utilized, consider the problem of defining and quantifying the concept of *sustainable technology*. The approach taken by Lynam and Herdt (1988) was to define sustainability as a characteristic of a system's productivity performance over time. Specifically, they define sustainability as the capacity of a system to maintain productivity at a level approximately equal to or greater than its historical average. Thus, a sustainable system is one characterized by a nonnegative trend in productivity. Lynam and Herdt (1988) suggest that total factor productivity is the appropriate measure of the system's performance, where the indexes of output and input capture all of the effects of the production system, both market and nonmarket. Thus, the Lynam and Herdt definition of a sustainable technology would be one that is characterized by $d \ln \text{TFP}^*/dt \geq 0$.

Environmental Policy, Productivity, and Technological Change

The induced innovation theory suggests that technological change is influenced by relative factor and product prices. It can be expected that relative factor prices induce research to save the more scarce resources, and relative product prices direct research toward the more valuable commodities. Consider now the implications of this theory when both "goods" and environmental "bads" are produced. If technological change is influenced by relative prices, environmental regulations that increase the cost (price) to firms of using common property resources or producing pollution will bias technology away from those activities. Environmental policy therefore has two important dimensions to it, a static one associated with the impact at a point in time on externalities produced with existing technology, and a dynamic one associated with the longer-run impacts of technological change and capital investment (McCain, 1978).

Environmental regulations may also have an impact on total productivity (Hazilla and Kopp, 1990). Input-use restrictions, such as pesticide restrictions in agriculture, reduce the number of cost-reducing technological options and thus can be expected to reduce productivity unless there are very close substitutes available. Other regulations may require firms to change the organization, location, or scale of operation to mitigate externalities and thus reduce productivity. For example, a size and location restriction on a feed lot operation to control water pollution would likely reduce its productive efficiency. There also may be dynamic effects of environmental regulations on productivity. If regulations force firms to allocate some of their capital investment to controlling environmental impacts, their profitability may be reduced and investors will shift toward alternatives with higher rates of return. The end result could be less capital investment and lower rates of productivity growth.

In the context of discussing the impact of environmental regulations and other policies on productivity it is important to define the type of productivity measure being used. If the conventional productivity measure TFP^p (equation 26) is used, which takes only market goods into account, then environmental policies generally can be expected to reduce productivity because of constraints placed on production activities. But if a broader measure of productivity such as TFP* (equation 17) is utilized, which includes the beneficial effects of environmental policies on nonmarket goods, and environmental policies that pass a benefit–cost analysis are implemented, the gains from the environmental policies should outweigh the losses in production and there should be a net improvement in productivity.

Measuring Resource Substitution and Resource Scarcity

Many economic policy questions involve the degree of substitution between inputs in the production process. When the government restricts pesticide use, for example, the impact of the restriction on output depends on the degree to which other inputs can be substituted for pesticides. The higher the degree of substitution, the more readily other inputs can be utilized in place of the pesticide, and the less is the impact on output, costs, and profits. Insecticides are substitutes for labor and management input; herbicides are substitutes for mechanical cultivation. Even in cases where fixed proportions must be utilized on a specific crop or in a certain location, input substitution is possible indirectly through substitutions across crops and by producing at different times and locations. One of the key factors determining how scarce a resource may be is the degree of input substitution. When substitutes are readily available, a small change in relative prices induces firms to use more of the relatively cheap resource. This section first discusses how input substitution in production can be measured, and then these concepts are used to discuss the meaning of resource scarcity.

A commonly used measure of substitution between inputs, the *elasticity of substitution*, was originally defined by Hicks (1963) and generalized by Allen (1938). In the two-input case considered by Hicks, the elasticity of substitution is defined as $d \ln(X_i/X_j)/d \ln(\mathrm{MRTS}_{ij})$, where MRTS_{ij} is the marginal rate of technical substitution between X_i and X_j. The elasticity of substitution measures the rate of change in the factor ratio as the MRTS changes along an isoquant while output is held constant. It can be thought of as a measure of the curvature of an isoquant; as the elasticity approaches zero, the isoquant becomes a right angle, and as the elasticity approaches infinity, the isoquant becomes a straight line.

In the more general case of multiple inputs, there are a variety of possible measures of input substitution, depending on what is held constant (Mundlak, 1968). The "partial" elasticity of substitution for the multiple input case developed by Allen can be defined as $\sigma_{ij} = \varepsilon_{ij}/S_j$, where ε_{ij} is the cross-elasticity of factor demand with output held constant, and S_j is the cost share of input X_j.

Although the Allen elasticity of substitution has been widely used in applied production economics research, it is not necessarily the most useful measure of input substitution. For example, Blackorby and Russell (1989) argue that the Morishima elasticity of substitution (MES) is a more appropriate generalization of Hicks' original concept of the elasticity of substitution than the Allen elasticity. The MES is defined as the proportionate change in cost-minimizing factor proportions with respect to a proportionate change in the factor price ratio, and can be shown to equal $M_{ij} = \varepsilon_{ji} - \varepsilon_{ii}$. Note that in contrast to the Allen elasticity, the Morishima elasticity is asymmetric (M_{ij} is not equal to M_{ji} in general). Blackorby and Russell show by way of example that the Morishima elasticity can be a better measure of curvature than the Allen elasticity.

The Allen and Morishima elasticities of substitution hold output constant and measure the changes in factor proportions in response to changes in factor prices. If the analyst does not wish to hold output constant while measuring input substitution, then the obvious measure of input substitution is the uncompensated cross-price input demand elasticity. Uncompensated demand elasticities may be more useful than compensated elasticities in policy analysis.

Once the analyst has chosen the type of measure of input substitution to be used, a production model can be formulated for estimation. For this purpose, either a primal representation of the technology (production function) or a dual representation (cost, revenue, or profit function) can be used. A variety of factors can influence the choice of estimation approach, including the type of substitution measure that is to be used and the type of data that are available. Generally, if a complete set of output and input quantity and price data are available, it may be preferable to estimate dual cost or profit function models because substitution elasticity estimates can be obtained more directly from them than from estimates of the production function.

Consider, for example, the use of the translog cost function to estimate the Allen elasticity of substitution. In general, the cost function is defined as the minimum cost required to produce a given level of output at given factor prices, and can be written as $C(y, r)$. The translog cost function is

$$\ln C = \beta_0 + \Sigma_i \beta_i \ln r_i + \tfrac{1}{2}\Sigma_i\Sigma_j\beta_{ij} \ln r_i \ln r_j + \gamma_1 \ln y + \tfrac{1}{2}\gamma_2(\ln y)^2 + \Sigma_i\gamma_{ri} \ln r_i \ln y \tag{28}$$

"Shephard's lemma" (see Varian, 1978) states that the compensated (output constant) input demand function is obtained by differentiating the cost function with respect to factor price. Thus the compensated factor demand function is $X_i(y, r) = \partial C(y, r)/\partial r_i$. It follows that the compensated cross-price demand elasticity is $\varepsilon_{ij} = \partial \ln X_i/\partial \ln r_j = \beta_{ij}/S_i - S_j$. Using this equation, it follows that for the translog cost function, $\sigma_{ij} = \beta_{ij}/S_iS_j + 1$ and $M_{ij} = (\beta_{ij} - \beta_{ii})/S_i$. Thus the translog cost function is an attractive tool for estimation of the elasticities of substitution because they are simple functions of the model's parameters and the factor cost shares.

The elasticity of substitution can be used to analyze the factors determining resource scarcity. Most economists would argue that relative price is the fundamental economic measure of scarcity. Clearly, the firm's ability to substitute among inputs, as measured by the elasticity of substitution, plays a role in input demand behavior and the resulting market price of a resource. Yet, this is not the only approach to resource scarcity taken in the literature. An influential study by Barnett and Morse (1963) concluded that natural resources were not becoming increasingly scarce. This conclusion was based on the "unit cost of extractive output" as a measure of scarcity, defined as L/Q where L is a composite labor–

capital input (excluding natural resources), and Q is the output of extractive industries. Barnett and Morse argued that if natural resources are growing more scarce, it will take increasing amounts of labor and capital to produce a unit of output with a given technology. Of course, technology is not constant over time, so the effect of technological change in the industry should be taken into account in the analysis of resource scarcity.

Brown and Field (1978) use the elasticity of substitution to show that the unit cost concept is not a meaningful measure of resource scarcity. They use the following example based on a constant-elasticity-of-substitution production function: $Q = (aL^{-\beta} + bR^{-\beta})^{-1/\beta}$, where $1/(1 + \beta) = \sigma$ is the elasticity of substitution, L is the composite labor–capital input, and R is a natural resource input. Utilizing the condition that input price equals value of marginal product in competitive factor markets, Brown and Field use the CES production function to obtain the following relationship: $L/Q = [a + b(aq/bw)^{\beta o}]/\beta$, where w is the price of L and q is the price of R. Now suppose we use this relationship to compare resource scarcity across industries. Observe that as the price of R rises relative to the price of L, the unit cost of producing the resource increases more rapidly the higher is σ. Brown and Field (1978, p. 232) conclude, "This is perverse. The unit cost of extractive output alarms us with signs of dramatically increasing scarcity when, in fact, technology has made it easy to decrease the use of natural resources. As steamships become better substitutes for sailing craft, followers of the unit–cost measure of scarcity would have grown even more strident in their demand to preserve the tall pole timber for masts."

THEORY OF INDUCED INNOVATION AND TECHNOLOGICAL ADOPTION

Hicks first proposed that innovations are induced by changes in the economic environment. Technological innovations "are the result of a change in the relative price of factors" (Hicks, 1963, p. 125). A change in the economic environment creates a market for new technologies. As with all markets, the market for new technology consists of two components: the supply of innovations and the adoption of technology by firms (demand). This section describes the Hicksian model of induced innovation that drives productivity change and input adjustment.

The Supply of Innovations Through Research and Development

There are several difficulties with modeling the supply of innovations; the most obvious is that innovations are not produced with a conventional production process. Inputs such as labor, capital, and human capital do not necessarily result in innovations; rather the process is more likely the result of trial and error and patient long-term research insulated from pressures of a competitive market. Schultz explains this as necessary because of economies of scale in research, the difficulty in capturing economic rents from innovations, the time horizon for research, and risks of untried products. Several authors have used such arguments when comparing the rate of technical change in oligopolistic versus more competitive industries.

Often, however, the major suppliers of agricultural innovations have been public education and research institutions. Development economists have long focused on the role of scientific and educational research institutions as mechanisms for technological change and increased agricultural productivity. Binswanger et al. (1978) describe a three-tiered technological frontier set. The first level is *scientific frontier*, the state of knowledge. Because increases in agricultural productivity (such as changes in yield per hectare) slowed down in the United States during the 1970s and 1980s, it is often assumed that the scientific frontier has been relatively static. It is likely, however, that the scientific boundary has extended outward because of rapid advances in molecular biology during the 1980s.

The second level is the technological frontier. Hayami and Ruttan (1985) describe this as the *metaproduction function*, which is an envelope of the short-run production functions achieved by the most technologically advanced countries. Each of these technologically advanced countries has adapted the available scientific knowledge to its particular resource endowment. This envelope thus represents the array of technologies that is potentially available to the low-productivity countries but can only be achieved by investment in the agricultural research that adopts the technologies to their particular resource endowments.

The third level is the *achievement distribution*, the actual level of technological productivity achieved by agriculture in different countries. This distribution is characterized by considerable diversity. It is here that the Hicksian induced theory of innovations has the most explanatory and predictive difficulty. On the supply side, advanced technology must be translated into workable technology within the existing infrastructure (often called technological transfer). The next section describes the Hayami-Ruttan model for public agricultural research institutions that localize technology to individual economic environments. Even if innovative technology is readily available, there is diversity in firms' willingness to adopt the new technologies. The implications of this diversity in achievement has major implications for resource policy.

Hayami and Ruttan (1985) argue that Hicks' theory can be applied to public supplied innovations in that these institutions respond to potentially profitable research. These authors follow the tradition of the Hicksian induced innovation theory in hypothesizing that each country adapts technology to its resource endowment in such a way that technological change uses the relatively abundant resources and saves the relatively scarce resources. But the authors go beyond the conventional induced innovation theory, which explains technological change in the private sector, and hypothesize that resource scarcity also affects innovation in the public sector. Public institutions such as land grant universities are sensitive to economic needs expressed through political processes. One factor in the success of the U.S. land grant system is that agricultural experiment stations are decentralized and have local objectives in research. Well-organized farm associations are often very successful in influencing the direction of this research. However, there are some indications that the close relationship between agricultural groups and land grant universities is changing: 1) Farm and rural groups are losing political clout generally and have less ability to influence agricultural research budgets, and 2) urban consumers and other interested parties such as environmental groups have discovered that the university research agenda can be redirected toward their goals. This leads to Binswanger's focus on induced institutional change.

Binswanger (1978) also suggests that research funding decisions are influenced by the expected present value of factor costs in the industry that would use the prospective innovations. However, a public institution and private adopting firms may have different perspectives on the immediacy of a new innovation. Public research administrators are more likely to be guided by underlying trends in relative resource endowments that are expected to prevail over a long-term horizon and may take a more social perspective toward trends that affect the common good. Competitive firms may have a shorter time horizon and are, of course, self-oriented. Antle and Crissman (1988) recently developed a model in which differing expectations are resolved through a dynamic learning process. Because suppliers of new agricultural technologies are generally public institutions, there is not a direct price link to users and the market for new technologies performs at a rudimentary level at best, characterized by disequilibrium of different expectations and information.

Adoption

The other component of the market for innovation is demand, the adoption of new technologies by firms. Feder et al. (1985) have commented that conventional microeconomic models applied to innovations have not adequately explained the variation in adoption across firms and countries and over time. Numerous theoretical and empirical studies have attempted to explain the observed patterns of technological change, especially in agriculture of less developed countries (LDCs), yet there is no consistent explanation why seemingly profitable technologies are sometimes not adopted by LDCs or by specific classes of farms, such as small farms. Possibly, the problem is that economic models have difficulty with the concept of heterogeneity. There is considerable heterogeneity of farms with regard to demand for new technologies, but it has been difficult to develop robust models that describe the source or consequences of this heterogeneity. The literature has separated this heterogeneity into three categories; entrepreneurial ability, risk preferences and the availability of complementary inputs.

Entrepreneurial Ability

Schultz (1964) provided one of the first explanations of the heterogeneity in demand for new technologies. New technologies disturb the equilibrium conditions of a competitive industry in that the relative prices of factors no longer equal the ratios of marginal products (the definition of allocative inefficiency). With changes in the technological environment, a farmer's entrepreneurial and in particular the allocative ability becomes increasingly valuable. It would be expected that such skills are not evenly distributed. Entrepreneurs who adjust their production decisions to reflect these new productivities, are in an advantageous competitive position, and their skill is highly valued in labor and management markets. Over time, other individuals realize the competitive advantages of new technologies and incorporate the innovations into production. The achievement distribution defined by Binswanger et al. (1978) (the distribution of the use of a technology among different production units) results in part from the distribution of allocative and technical skills among farmers.

Kislev and Schori-Bachrach (1973) expanded Schultz's propositions (1964) to a dynamic framework that will be developed in a following section. These authors hypothesized that the differentials in managerial capability separates early and late adopters. As general levels of managerial capability increases, late adopters catch up with early adopters.

Risk Preferences

Another source of heterogeneity among adopting firms is risk preferences. This subject has received considerable attention in the literature. The adoption of new or untried technologies always involves a degree of risk and uncertainty concerning the performance of the input. The introduction of seed varieties (such as hybrid corn) may have the potential to increase yields, but the variety may also entail more risks: 1) Yields may be more variable, and 2) the variety may be input intensive (farmers in developing economies often face increased economic risks in securing inputs at competitive prices). This example illustrates that the riskiness of adoption is multifaceted. Just and Zilberman (1983) constructed a model of a firm in which adoption of new technology was endogenous, embodied in new inputs that had risky elements. The model has testable implications: 1) Large firms are more likely to adopt new technologies because of diversification, and 2) the willingness to adopt new technologies depends on the statistical crosscorrelation among inputs. The Just and Zilberman model can be used to empirically explain the variations in adoption, but because of its general nature, the model does not specify factors that may limit adoption in a particular LDC.

Complementary Inputs

New technologies also must be integrated into existing production processes. Most innovations involve a package of complementary inputs. If these inputs are subject to constraints or other limitations, adoption of new technologies would be restricted. The most basic complementary input for new technologies is human capital. The literature has developed three different perspectives on human capital: 1) Human capital increases allocative efficiency (Schultz, 1975); 2) human capital is similar to other forms of capital and therefore has a positive impact on adoption of new technologies except that changes in the level of this capital require the time to learn (Huffman, 1977; Lindner, 1981); and 3) human capital increases technical efficiency (Kislev and Schori-Bachrach, 1973; Welch, 1970), which in turn increases the adoption of new technologies.

Other research has investigated the complementarity of credit and labor with adoption. Feder et al. (1985) in reviewing this literature conclude that constraints on labor influence the adoption of differing labor intensive technologies, but it is difficult to argue that such constraints restrict adoption per se. Empirical research is mixed. Lee and Chambers (1986) argue that credit is different from other inputs in that a credit constraint restricts the expenditure function. Other authors have argued that credit constraints do not restrict the adoption of scale neutral technologies (Schulter, 1971).

Dynamics of Technological Adoption

The rate of adoption (diffusion) of new technologies determines the rate of technological change. Griliches (1957) first developed an econometric model of *diffusion* with a logistic function to model the adoption of hybrid corn by U.S. farmers. Early empirical work of technological adoption estimated parameters associated with S-shaped cumulative adoption curves illustrated in Figure 5.6. This work generally lacked a rigorous theoretical structure that accounted for the dynamics of adoption behavior, until Kislev and Schori-Bachrach (1973) described a theoretical model of the innovation (adoption) cycle. The cycle starts with efficient producers first introducing a new technology that requires a threshold level of technical skill to profitable use. As skill levels of other producers increase through experience, the new technology is more widely adopted. The time path of adoption of the new technology can be analytically derived as a function of the distribution of technical ability among producers and the rate of change in technical skill.

Kislev and Schori-Bachrach (1973) used the concept of technical efficiency to neutrally shift the production function. They defined the function, $g(w, H)$, to represent efficiency with $0 \leq g \leq 1$ and used the function to shift the production function. The function has as arguments the opportunity cost of the entrepreneur's own labor, w, and the accumulated knowledge of the production process, H, obtained over time by the use of the new technology. The worker effect increases with both w and H.

At the start of an innovation cycle, producers are characterized by a distribution of efficiency. Figure 5.7 illustrates a hypothetical distribution of the efficiency among firms in the industry measured by the opportunity cost of entrepreneurs' wages (the assumption being that an efficient entrepreneur would have a high opportunity cost for his wages). In the figure, w_0 is the lowest level of wages (technical efficiency) in the industry, and w_h is the highest. The level $n(w)$ is the cumulative number of producers with wage w or lower and $n(w_h)$ is all firms in the industry. A new technology is first adopted by firms with the ability to make the technology profitable. Figure 5.8 illustrates the revenues and costs of firms that may potentially adopt the technology plotted against the wage or efficiency of the producer. The revenues of firms are concave in w because of the assumptions concerning $g(w, H)$. For simplicity, costs are assumed to linearly increase with w. The intercept, v, represents other nonlabor costs. In Figure 5.8, $\underline{u}$ is the lowest level of efficiency for which the technology is profitable, and producers with an efficiency greater than or equal to $\underline{u}$ adopt the new technology. With increasing experience with the new technology, the revenue function shifts upward and $\underline{u}$ shifts toward w_0. The greater output of the industry also has a price effect, which causes exit from the industry. Efficient early adopters exit from the industry to take

Number of producers: n

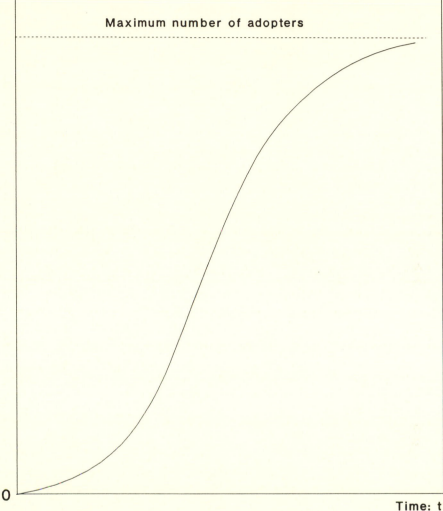

Figure 5.6. Accumulated distribution of adopters as a function of time.

advantage of other opportunities if $\bar{u}$ shifts below w_h, and very inefficient producers may no longer be viable. Kislev and Schori-Bachrach (1973) note that this is consistent with observations of a mature technology in which early adopters have left the industry.

Let N represent the number of producers that have adopted the new technology at time t. N is by definition

$$N = n(\bar{u}) - n(\underline{u}) \tag{29}$$

The rate of adoption over time, $\dot{N}$, is

Number of producers: n

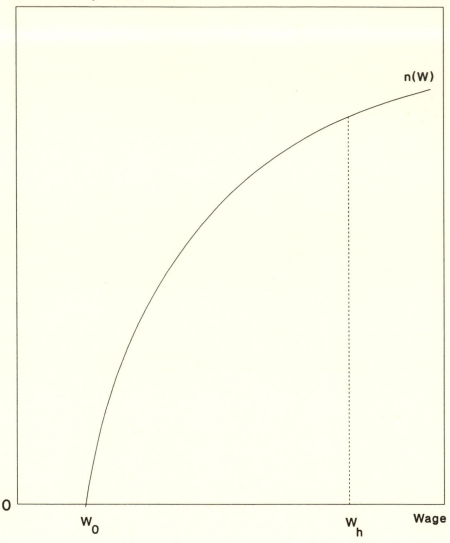

Figure 5.7. Accumulated distribution of producers as a function of opportunity wage.

$$\dot{N} = n'(\bar{u}) \, \partial\bar{u}/\partial t - n'(\underline{u}) \, \partial\underline{u}/\partial t \tag{30}$$

where n' is frequency distribution of producer efficiency. If efficient producers remain in the industry, $\bar{u} \geq w_h$ and $\partial\bar{u}/\partial t = 0$, then the lower bound determines the overall distribution rate,

$$\dot{N} = -n'(\underline{u}) \, \partial\underline{u}/\partial t \tag{31}$$

which has the following dynamics:

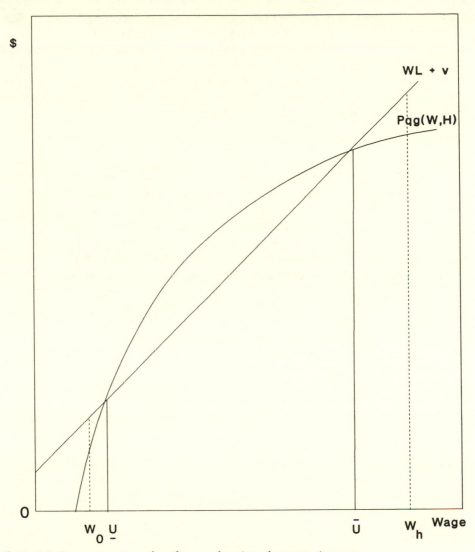

Figure 5.8. Revenue, costs and profits as a function of opportunity wage.

$$\dot{u} = \frac{P'\dot{Q}qg(u, H) + Pq\dfrac{\partial g}{\partial H}Q}{L - Pq\dfrac{\partial g}{\partial u}} \tag{32}$$

or

$$\dot{u} = \frac{\text{price effect} + \text{worker effect}}{-\dfrac{\partial \pi}{\partial u}} \tag{33}$$

Equation (32) consists of two separate effects: the worker effect and a price effect. At first, the new technology can only be profitably adopted by efficient producers. With time and the change in H, the typical producers become more efficient and the level of adoption increases (worker effect). With increasing productivity, however, output prices fall, and a number of producers exit the industry (price effect). The contrasting dynamics of the worker and price effects simulate the traditional logistic function of earlier empirical work.

Estimation of Inefficiency

Central to the adoption issue is the issue of heterogeneity: why firms differ in the willingness to adopt new technologies. The explanation as proposed by Schultz and operationalized by Kislev and Schori-Bachrach (1973) is managerial ability, more formally described as economic efficiency. With a distribution of inefficiency and estimates of how the distribution changes with increases in human capital, the model outlined in the previous section can be parameterized to predict the rate of adoption. The stochastic production frontier of Aigner et al. (1979) is a methodology that results in such a distribution.

Economic efficiency consists of three components: technical, allocative, and scale (Farrel, 1957). A firm is technically efficient if its observed production plan (Y^0, X^0) exactly satisfies $Y^0 = f(X^0)$ where f is the production frontier, Y^0 is output, and X^0 is input of firm 0. The firm is technically inefficient if $Y^0 < f(X^0)$, i.e., the firm operates inside the production frontier. The firm is allocatively efficient if the ratio of the marginal products of inputs equals the ratio of the input prices, $f_i(X)/f_j(X) = w_i/w_j$. Scale efficiency is achieved if the firm produces at a marginal cost that is the same as the price of the output. Allocative and scale efficiency jointly are the conditions for profit maximization and are labeled price efficiency.

Figure 5.9 illustrates *price and technical inefficiency* for a single input/output production function. The production frontier represents the most technically advanced method of producing Y using the input X. A specific firm is characterized by an individual production function with current production (input and output) shown at point A. This function lies below the production frontier. The firm is technically inefficient in that output could be increased to B with the same level of input.

For a single input production function, the necessary condition for price efficiency is $P_y MP_x = P_x$ because allocative and scale efficiency cannot be separated. At point B, the firm is price inefficient as maximum profit occurs at the tangency point between the production frontier and the input/output price ratio. The firm is both price and technically efficient (economically efficient) when production is adjusted to point C.

Measurement of price and technical inefficiency is also shown in Figure 5.9. Technical inefficiency is the percentage difference in output between the frontier and the individual's production function, $(Y_B - Y_A)/Y_A$, where Y_B and Y_A are output at points B and A, respectively. Price inefficiency is measured as the percentage loss in profit from producing at B instead of C. Using the intercept of the price line (a) as a measure of profit, ($a = \pi P_y$), relative price inefficiency is measured as $(a' - a)/a'$.

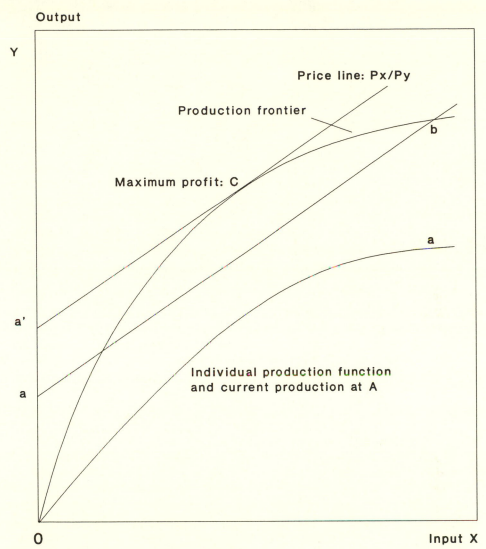

Figure 5.9. Measurement of economic efficiency.

To statistically estimate inefficiency, Aigner et al. (1979) and Meeusen and van den Broeck (1977) simultaneously developed the stochastic production frontier (SPF) model. The SPF model incorporates technical and allocative inefficiency as random variables within a model of profit maximization. In addition, the SPF contains a random variable for factors that are beyond the control of economic agents (such as weather). The stochastic variables of the SPF are 1) v, a normally distributed variable across firms that captures stochastic factors such as weather; 2) τ, a truncated normal variable ($\tau \leq 0$) that captures the effects of technical inefficiency; and 3) μ, a normal distributed variable that represents deviations from

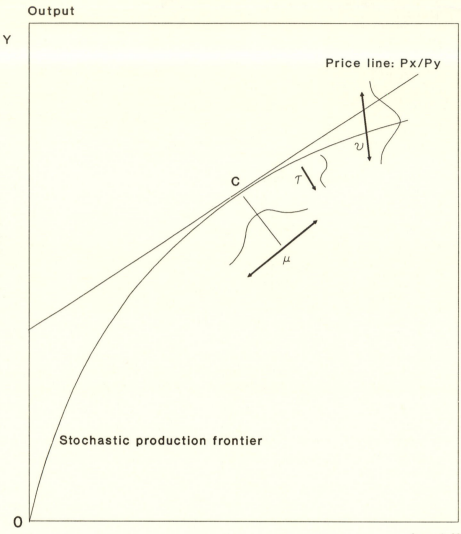

Figure 5.10. Components of economic inefficiency and stochastic variation.

first-order conditions of price efficiency. These stochastic terms are illustrated in Figure 5.10.

Technological adoption can be quite consistently explained by the literature of the SPF approach of Aigner et al. (1979) and Meeusen and van den Broeck (1977). Technical inefficiency has been shown to result in suboptimal input selections and reduced profitability (Lovell et al., 1987; Kumbhakar, 1987). If a new technology is viewed as an additional input in the production process, it follows that technical inefficiency provides a plausible explanation for a slow rate of technology adoption.

Table 5.3. Technical Inefficiency, Farm Size, and Adoption of New Technology

Technical inefficiency interval	Farm size[a]	Milk production per cow (lbs.)	Technological index
0.00–0.15	63	14,548	2,688
0.15–0.30	65	13,436	2,195
0.30–0.45	56	11,140	1,572
0.45–0.60	51	10,911	283

[a] Farm size is measured by number of milking cows.

Empirical results of an adoption model by McGuckin et al. (1991) confirm the influence of technical inefficiency on farm size and adoption. The results presented in Table 5.3 support the Kislev and Schori-Bachrach approach. This table indicates the distribution of farms according to technical inefficiency intervals and associated average size and level of expenditures on a new technological input. Notice the close correlation between technical efficiency and the production measure of output per cow. Generally, as technical inefficiency increases, both farm size and technological adoption decline. These findings indicate that 1) technical inefficiency can be in terms of observable production measures that are farm specific and 2) adoption of new technologies can be explained in terms of technical inefficiency. It was found that larger dairy farms are more technically efficient and therefore more likely adopters of new technology than smaller farms, a finding also consistent with Just and Zilberman (1983).

The Adoption of bST: A Policy Dilemma

A major objective of federal price support programs is to stabilize agricultural markets from short run price fluctuations (Gardner, 1986; Just and Hallam, 1982). A difficulty however is that price support programs often create instability in fiscal budgeting, especially if rapid technological change is occurring in the supported industry. The U.S. dairy industry is an excellent example of this problem. Steady increases in productivity resulted in large surpluses during the 1980s that were absorbed by a federal government through Commodity Credit Corporation (CCC) purchases.

Kalter et al. (1984), Kaiser and Tauer (1989), and Fallert et al. (1989), have examined the potential of synthetic bST (bovine somatotropin) to increase milk supplies. This technology will most likely be introduced in the 1990s. These authors all note the potential for large federal expenditures *if bST is rapidly adopted.* The rate of adoption and the relative rate among geographical regions will have significant implications for resource and agricultural policies. A high rate of adoption of this genetically engineered product would increase the cost of the dairy price support program. Sellschopp and Kalter (1989) indicate that the new technology may also accelerate regional shifts in production, though their results are extremely sensitive to different national policy assumptions. Such shifts would have implications for federal order programs, manufactured milk processing, land

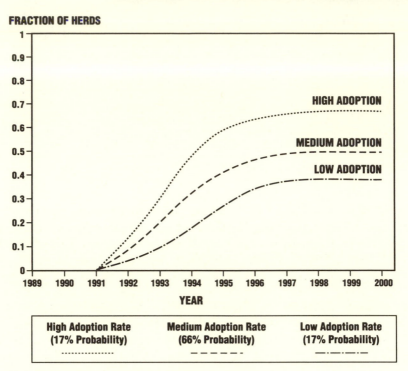

FRACTION OF HERDS

Figure 5.11. Percent of dairy herds adopting bST over time.

and water resources, and nonpoint pollution (dairy is a major nonpoint source of nitrate contamination in water supplies).

The key to the available government policy options is predicting the rate of adoption of bST. Using the Kislev and Schori-Bachrach model and the estimated distribution of technical inefficiency in the dairy industry, three alternative adoption rates are shown in Figure 5.11. The relevant question from a federal perspective is what support price will maintain CCC outlays at target levels that are mandated by current fiscal budget constraints. Pindyck (1973), Burt et al. (1982), Rausser et al. (1982), Gardner (1986), and Just and Hallam (1987) have all advocated using control models to achieve government targets. This methodology endogenizes government behavior as an economic agent in the market. The control model anticipates the structural changes from new technologies and adjusts the industry to new equilibrium levels that satisfy government targets.

An example of government control policy would be to achieve stability in CCC purchases of milk by minimizing deviations from a set goal, with the expectation that bST will further increase dairy production. Current U.S. policy indicates that the government is willing to buy between 2.5 and 5 billion pounds of milk products to stabilize the dairy market. The mechanism for achieving this objective is milk price supports. Other supply control programs could include the Dairy Termination program, elimination of federal marketing orders, and a national quota (see Kaiser and Tauer, 1989). The control model requires 1) empirical estimates of the structure of an economic system or industry, 2) linkages between policy variables and the structural model, and 3) an assumption of optimizing behavior by the government with respect to a criterion function. The control model would be represented as follows:

$$\text{Min} \sum_{t=1}^{N} (G_t - \bar{C})^2 \tag{34}$$

subject to

$$X_{t+1} = AX_t + BU_t + CZ_t \tag{35}$$

$$G_t = f(X_t) \tag{36}$$

$$U_t^1 \geq U_t \geq U_t^0; \tag{37}$$

and

$$X(0) = X_0 \quad \text{and} \quad U(0) = U_0 \tag{38}$$

where X is a vector of state variables representing the structural equations of an industry, U is milk support price, Z is other exogenous variables, G is CCC net milk purchases, and the parameter $\bar{C}$ is the targeted amount of milk purchases.

The results of using the control model in conjunction with the predicted adoption rates are illustrated in Figure 5.12. The figure outlines the path of support prices the government must implement if it wishes to maintain stable CCC purchases. The results indicate that in the face of continuing productivity changes and adoption of bST, U.S. dairy support policies must quickly evolve to a level that approximates market clearing prices. These conclusions give credence to the concerns expressed by Hueth and Just (1987). Emerging new and potent technologies such as bST will require significant readjustment of U.S. government farm policies. These results indicate that a transition to a market clearing support prices may be necessary to control a surge in government expenditures.

INTEGRATION OF PRODUCTION AND ENVIRONMENTAL MODELS FOR POLICY ANALYSIS

The public perception that agricultural policies are linked to environmental problems associated with agriculture has stimulated the desire within the agricultural community to broaden the realm of agricultural productivity analysis to include environmental impacts. As Figure 5.1 illustrates, policy changes can have productivity and environmental impacts through both short-run and long-run responses to them by farmers and the agricultural research system. This section presents a framework that can be used to analyze impacts of policy changes at a highly disaggregate level. These impacts can then be aggregated to evaluate the impacts at the regional or national level (Antle and Just, 1991, Fig. 5.13).

A fundamental characteristic of the natural environment is its heterogeneity. For example, a field on bottom land may be very fertile and the depth to ground water may be shallow, whereas an adjacent field on a hillside may have less fertile

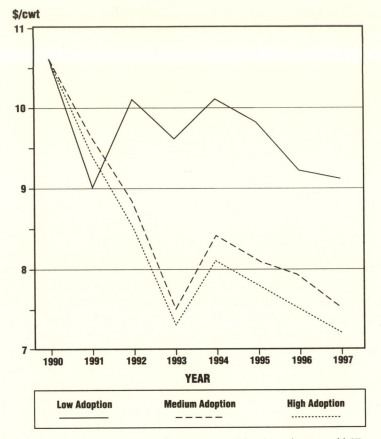

Figure 5.12. Time path of government milk supports anticipating adoption of bST.

land and depth to ground water may be much greater. Typically those two units of land would be farmed differently. Different amounts of fertilizers and pesticides would be applied, and the consequences of those chemical applications for ground water quality would differ between the two fields. Policies that affect farmers' incentives to use agricultural chemicals would also be likely to have different effects on each of the two fields. These interactions between production practices and the physical characteristics of the land may thus play a key role in determining the impacts of policy on both productivity and environmental quality.

To fix ideas and clarify some terminology, a water quality example can serve to illustrate the issues that arise in attempts to integrate production and environmental models for environmental policy analysis. Consider a hypothetical fertilizer run-off problem in a region characterized by four economically and environmentally different areas of equal size that each contribute to contamination of a body of water. Table 5.4 defines the productivity and physical characteristics of these four areas in terms of high and low yields and high and low levels of potential to cause water contamination (e.g., slope or proximity to the body of

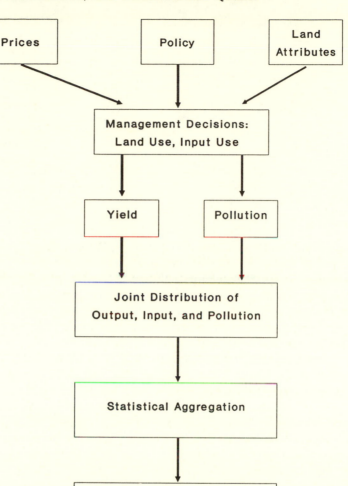

Figure 5.13. A conceptual framework for policy analysis.

water). Each cell shows the relationship between nitrogen use (N), yield (Y), and water contamination (C). Suppose the policy objectives set by the regulatory authority are 1) to achieve a water quality standard for the region by regulating fertilizer use, and 2) to achieve this standard at the lowest cost in terms of lost agricultural production (more general policy objectives would also account for changes in production cost). Now consider two scenarios for data availability to the regulatory authority and the associated types of regulation that could be used.

In the first scenario, yield and contamination data are collected independently without sufficient location-specific identifying factors so that characteristics affecting yield and contamination can be correlated. This is typical of much of the data

Table 5.4. An Example of Fertilizer Run-off Contamination of Water[a]

Area characteristic	High contamination	Low contamination
	Area 1	*Area 2*
High yield	$Y = 2\alpha N$	$Y = 2\alpha N$
	$C = 2\beta N$	$C = \beta N$
	Area 3	*Area 4*
Low yield	$Y = \alpha N$	$Y = \alpha N$
	$C = 2\beta N$	$C = \beta N$

[a] Y = yield, C = contamination, and N = fertilizer rate.
Source: Antle and Just (1991).

collected by the U.S. Department of Agriculture. With such data, the regulatory authority has no way to differentiate high and low contamination areas according to productivity. A typical regulatory solution is to impose a uniform maximum fertilizer application rate on the region sufficient to achieve the water quality objective. Another possibility is to require that a certain percentage of land be taken out of production. For example, commercial agricultural policies help accomplish environmental goals through acreage reduction programs. According to Table 5.4, the resulting cost of either standard in terms of lost production is $Y/C = \alpha/\beta$ in areas 1 and 4 but is higher, $Y/C = 2\alpha/\beta$, in area 2 and lower, $Y/C = .5\alpha/\beta$, in area 3 for an average cost of $1.125\alpha/\beta$.

In the second data scenario, yield and contamination data are collected jointly or on a location-specific basis so that they can be correlated. With these data, the regulatory authority can order the areas according to the production foregone to obtain a given contamination reduction. To achieve the water quality target at least cost, the regulatory authority would first restrict fertilizer use in area 3, obtaining a reduction in contamination at less than half the cost per acre of a uniform standard. If further reduction in contamination were needed, then areas 1 and 4 would be regulated.

This example illustrates several aspects of agricultural–environmental problems that need to be incorporated into a general representation. First, two important dimensions of production behavior interact with environmental considerations— the extent of acreage employed in production and the intensity of input use on the acreage employed in production. Economists refer to these two dimensions as the *intensive margin* and the *extensive margin*. Decisions at the intensive margin are management decisions regarding chemical application rates, water use, tillage practices, etc., made with respect to a given unit of land. Decisions at the extensive margin determine which land is used for production and thus determine the environmental characteristics of land in production. In the simple example of Table 5.4, the cost in terms of lost production of reducing contamination is the same at both the intensive and extensive margins. This, however, is not generally the case because marginal productivity is not equal to average productivity when the functional forms are not proportional. Second, the example also illustrates the central role played by the joint distribution of economic and physical characteristics of the population in the region. Table 5.4 defines this joint distribution for the example. The following sections discuss how this joint distribution can be defined in general and the role it plays in the analysis of agricultural–environmental interactions according to the effects that policies have on producer behavior at the intensive and extensive margins.

Interactions Between Production Agriculture and the Environment: A Conceptual Framework[5]

Corresponding to the above discussion of producer behavior, we can classify policies into two basic types: 1) those that affect management decisions at the intensive margin, such as a price support that increases chemical use per unit of land; and 2) those that affect management decisions at the extensive margin, such as diversion requirements for participation in a program that affects total land use. Some policies affect incentives at both margins, as might be the case with a price support that encourages chemical use on existing cropland and also encourages farmers to bring new land into production.

Based on the farm-level decision model, each unit of land that is in production has management and environmental characteristics that are functions of prices, policies, and technological and other farm-specific characteristics. The distribution of farm and environmental characteristics in the region induces a distribution of management practices and environmental attributes for land units in production. This joint distribution provides the basis for aggregation of outputs, inputs, and pollution to the regional level. Based on the properties of the policy criterion or welfare function chosen, one can then proceed to analyze the tradeoffs between production and pollution that are associated with alternative policies.

Various issues arise in translating this very general conceptual framework into a useful analytical model. At the disaggregated level, both the physical model and the economic model must be specified so they can be integrated into a tractable model of crop output and pollution. Numerous modeling issues arise, including the models' dynamics and the level of aggregation of inputs and outputs. Decisions at the intensive margin generally are short-run input decisions and are related to the intraseasonal dynamics of the production process. Decisions at the extensive margin involve placing a unit of land in production. These decisions may involve long-run considerations such as the interseasonal dynamics of crop rotations and capital investment.

Quantitative applications will require addressing the full range of issues that arise in applied production economics research including the dynamic aspects of the economic and physical models, as discussed in a subsequent section. For example, the physical models of soil erosion and chemical transport and fate generally involve dynamic processes that relate the farmers' intraseasonal and interseasonal management decisions to environmental impacts. Since the 1970s, a variety of models has been developed and is being developed to quantify soil

[5] This section is based on Antle and Just (1991).

erosion, chemical run-off into surface water, and chemical transport through soils to ground water (Wagenet and Rao, 1990). Most of these models comprise systems of differential equations that express changes in environmental quality as functions of management actions and environmental parameters, and require detailed information regarding the timing of input decisions and location-specific environmental attributes (Donigian and Dean, 1985). Users of quantitative applications must address a variety of methodological issues in the integration of these physical models with economic models, including level of aggregation across space and time, analytical tractability, and use of experimental and nonexperimental data (Capalbo and Antle, 1989).

Another set of general issues arises in aggregating and conducting welfare analyses. A number of approaches can be taken to address the problem of analyzing the tradeoffs between crop production and pollution. First is the question of the appropriate level of aggregation. Should policy be addressed to a region associated with a particular agroecosystem, or is national policy at issue? The second major issue is the choice of a welfare criterion. How are social costs associated with agricultural pollution or resource depletion valued in welfare and policy analyses? In an absolute physical standard (e.g., parts per billion of contaminant in drinking water) to be met, or can crop production and pollution literally be "traded off" in the policy calculus? Economists are wont to analyze environmental policy using tradeoffs between pollution and output and to regard economic efficiency as an important aspect of policy design. The public and policy makers, however, tend not to consider tradeoffs in assessing environmental issues and most environmental policies are based on standards that usually are not considered by economists to be economically efficient.

In actual policy decision making, one can view the tradeoffs illuminated by a detailed analytical framework as leading to more informed decisions—decision makers weigh, either explicitly or implicitly, the social benefits of agricultural production against the social costs it generates.

A Disaggregate Production Model

Consider a region defined in relation to an environmentally meaningful geographical unit, such as a watershed or aquifer. The jth acre in the region has a set of environmental characteristics ω_j, such as soil type, slope, and depth to ground water, that affect both its agricultural productivity and the production of pollution. A variety of complex physical models is being developed to measure pollution caused by agricultural production, such as surface and ground water contamination. The stylized physical model here is represented by the function $z_j = z(x_j, \omega_j)$, where x_j is the level of input use on the jth acre and z_j is pollution generated by production on the jth acre.

The economic model is based on the optimal allocation of land and other inputs in production as functions of prices, policies, and the environmental characteristics of the land managed by the farmer. To focus on the role of land quality all farmers are assumed to be risk neutral and to produce with identical technology. Farms are differentiated only by the *environmental characteristics* of their land (a more general model would include a vector of farm-specific characteristics). In the production period, the ith farmer manages n^i acres with environmental characteristics $\omega^i = (\omega^i_1, \omega^i_2, \ldots)$. Define the indicator function δ^i_j such that $\delta^i_j = 1$ if acre j is in production and 0 otherwise, and let $\delta_i = \{\delta^i_j\}$. The vector of attributes of land in production on farm i is then $\omega(\delta_i) = (\omega^i_1 \delta^i_1, \omega^i_2 \delta^i_2, \ldots)$, and total acreage in production on the ith farm is $\Sigma_j \delta^i_j$.

All farms in the region face the same vectors p and ψ of prices and policy parameters. Define x^i_j as the input allocation of farmer i to acre j and x^i as the vector of x^i_j. The ith farmer's decision problem can then be cast as

$$\max_{x^i, \delta^i} \pi[x^i, \omega(\delta^i) \mid p, \psi, \omega^i]$$

where π is the farmer's objective function embedding the production technology and ψ is a vector of policy parameters.

The solution to this maximization problem generates the demand functions $x^i_j = x(p, \psi, \omega^i_j)$ and $\delta^i_j = \delta(p, \psi, \omega^i_j)$. The environmental characteristic of each unit of farm land in the region is fixed at a point in time and can be viewed as being distributed across the acres in the region with a distribution defined by the parameter vector θ. The distribution of environmental attributes induces a joint distribution for input use x^i and land use δ^i in the region. The environmental attributes of the land in production, $\omega(\delta^i)$, are determined by land use decisions. Yield and pollution are functions of input use and the environmental attributes of land in production. Thus, farmers' production decisions generate a joint distribution of output, input, environmental attributes, and pollution in the region.

Policy may impose restrictions on the distributions of x and ω that must be taken into account in analysis and estimation. When land-use restrictions limit the range of environmental attributes available for production, the distribution will be truncated in the ω dimension. The distribution of x and ω also may be censored, as when there is a positive probability that input use occurs at zero. Similarly, the distribution may be censored at a positive limit, as when policy limits water or chemical use. When truncation or censoring are not important, it is possible to greatly simplify the modeling by assuming a common continuous distribution such as a joint lognormal distribution.

The implementation of an environmental policy such as a restriction on input use per acre may alter farmer behavior and induce other changes in the distribution of x and ω in addition to its censoring. According to the optimization problem defined above, farmers jointly choose which acres to place in production and the input levels used on those acres, each as functions of environmental attributes of the land. If the jth acre is profitable at $x_j > x_0$, but not at $x_j = x_0$, then that acre would not be put into production under a restriction at x_0. Hence, the resulting joint distribution of x and ω for acres in production would also be different. Suppose, for example, that ω and x are positively correlated, and all acres with $\omega > \omega^*$ were unprofitable with $x = x_0$. The policy would thus result in the truncation of the distribution at ω^* for values of $x > x_0$. As a result, the distribution would shift toward the origin in the ω dimension and would also be truncated at x_0. It can be concluded, therefore, that policies can have complex effects on the joint distribution of x and ω. Similar conclusions can be drawn for the joint distribution of inputs and pollution. The challenge facing researchers is to achieve a better understanding of the effects policies may have on both farmer behavior and the environment.

Statistical Aggregation and Policy Analysis

The heterogeneity of the producer population and the natural environment is the basis for the statistical approach used in the preceding section to describe the producer population in a study region. Once the region under study has been represented statistically, the next step is to statistically aggregate to the level desired for policy analysis. Statistical aggregation provides the link from the individual, heterogeneous production units where production and environment interact to the regional level where policy analysis is conducted.

Productivity analysis typically involves data that are aggregated in a number of ways. At the firm level, it is necessary to aggregate across time because production takes place over time and inputs are applied over time. It is also necessary to aggregate across firms to the industry level. In all cases, the basic aggregation problem is to "add up" the attributes of the individuals in the group (the population) and to determine the relationship of the individual attributes of the group (the aggregate). One approach to the aggregation problem is to investigate conditions under which individual functional relationships are preserved in aggregation (e.g., Theil, 1954). Exact aggregation generally holds only for linear relationships and is of limited usefulness. An alternative and more powerful approach is to formulate the aggregation problem in a statistical framework. The aggregation problem then is defined as the adding up of individual characteristics to obtain summary statistics for the group (Stoker, 1982). In this section, the statistical approach to aggregation is used to develop a prototypical policy analysis.

In the disaggregate model of production presented in the previous section, farmers' fields are differentiated according to the parameter vector ω, which represents the physical characteristics of the field. More generally, this vector could represent any attributes specific to the farm or the field, such as technology, characteristics of the farm manager, histories of inputs and outputs, expectations, and so forth. As discussed in the previous section, this vector is a random variable distributed in the population of firms. Define the joint distribution of input use and other attributes associated with a specific field as $\phi(x, \omega \mid p, \psi, \theta)$ where θ is the parameter characterizing the population. Letting the firm's input demand function be $x(p, \omega)$ for price vector p, the population mean input is

$$\mu(p, \psi, \theta) \equiv E(x \mid p, \psi, \theta) = \iint x(p, \psi, \omega)\phi(x, \omega \mid p, \psi, \theta)\, dx\, d\omega$$

Under some reasonable assumptions (see Antle, 1986), it follows that aggregate output Y and aggregate pollution Z can be interpreted as conditional expectations of output and pollution in the population, given prices, policy parameters, and population parameters:

$$Y(p, \psi, \theta) = \int y[x(p, \psi, \omega), \omega]\phi(x, \omega \mid p, \psi, \theta)\, dx\, d\omega$$

$$Z(p, \psi, \theta) = \int z[x(p, \psi, \omega), \omega]\phi(x, \omega \mid p, \psi, \theta)\, dx\, d\omega$$

By inverting the function $\mu(p, \psi, \theta)$ to get $p = h(\mu, \psi, \theta)$, substitution into the above equations shows that aggregate output and pollution can be expressed as functions $Y(\mu, \psi, \theta)$ and $Z(\mu, \psi, \theta)$. When the number of units is large, aggregate input X can be interpreted as approximately equal to μ, so aggregate output and pollution in the population can be expressed as $Y(X, \psi, \theta)$ and $Z(X, \psi, \theta)$.

Two important conclusions emerge from this analysis. First, it is possible to define aggregate production functions $Y(X, \psi, \theta)$ and $Z(X, \psi, \theta)$ and aggregate input demand function $X(p, \psi, \theta)$, which can be interpreted as population means. These functions can be used for policy analysis. Second, the aggregate functions for output, input, and pollution depend on the vector θ defining the distribution of individual firm characteristics in the population. A change in θ causes a shift in the aggregate production function. Therefore, analysts must take care to recognize that policy analysis should account for structural shifts caused by changes in the distribution of individual firm characteristics in the population. For example, the models of innovation discussed earlier in this chapter imply that as technology advances certain kinds of farm operators, such as those with relatively low educational levels, may leave the industry. This change in the producer population would in turn cause a change in the distribution of manager characteristics and technology in the industry, implying there would also be a different relationship between aggregate output and input. Similarly, if changes in industry structure lead to a change in the environmental characteristics of the land in production, the aggregate pollution production function Z would change.

To illustrate aggregation and policy analysis using this approach, consider the following example. Let yield on a unit of land be given by the function

$$y = x^{\eta}\omega^{\nu}, \qquad 0 < \eta < 1$$

and let pollution z on a unit of land be a simple function

$$z = x^{\alpha}\omega^{\beta}, \qquad \alpha, \beta > 0$$

where x and ω are scalars measuring variable input per unit of land and a physical attribute of the land, such as soil quality, that affects both productivity and pollution. Note that α, β, and η are assumed to be positive, but the sign of ν is unrestricted. This latter parameter is positive if the environmental attribute that is positively associated with pollution is also positively associated with productivity. This could be the case, for example, when the environmental attribute ω measures soil quality and high-quality soils are located in proximity to surface water or shallow ground water so that high yields are positively correlated with water pollution. The parameter ν is negative when an environmentally sensitive condition, such as a highly erodible soil, is associated with high levels of pollution and low productivity.

Assume further that x and ω are characterized by a lognormal distribution, i.e.,

$$\begin{bmatrix} \ln x \\ \ln \omega \end{bmatrix} = N[\mu, \Sigma \mid p, \psi, \theta]$$

where μ is a (2×1) vector of means and Σ is a (2×2) covariance matrix. Further define $e' = (1, 0)$, $\gamma = (\alpha, \beta)$, and $\tau = (\eta, v)$. It then follows that

$$X = E(x) = \exp(e'\mu + e'\Sigma e/2)$$

$$Z = E(z) = \exp(\gamma'\mu + \gamma'\Sigma\gamma/2)$$

$$Y = E(y) = \exp(\tau'\mu + \tau'\Sigma\tau/2)$$

Using these results, it is possible to evaluate the effects that changes in policy have on production and pollution. For example, an analyst may specify a policy objective function $W(Y, X, Z)$ to represent society's preferences for trading off productivity against pollution. Using the fact that μ and Σ are functions of the policy parameters, the analyst can compare the effects of alternative settings of the policy parameters on the policy objective function.

To illustrate, let the policy parameter ψ represent the level of a price support for a program crop. The analyst could examine the effects on the policy function of varying the level of the price support:

$$\partial W/\partial \psi = W_X(\partial X/\partial \psi) + W_Z(\partial Z/\partial \psi) + W_Y(\partial Y/\partial \psi)$$

If society values output positively and pollution negatively, it should be true that $W_X < 0$, $W_Z < 0$, and $W_Y > 0$. It would also be reasonable to expect that the effects of a price support on input use and output would be positive, so that $\partial X/\partial \psi > 0$ and $\partial Y/\partial \psi > 0$. It is often argued that price supports should also result in higher pollution because they encourage input use, so that $\partial Z/\partial \psi > 0$. This latter result does not necessarily follow, however. In this model, if only the mean vector μ is a function of ψ, then

$$\partial Z/\partial \psi = \alpha(\partial \mu_x/\partial \psi) + \beta(\partial \mu_\omega/\partial \psi)$$

The first term on the right-hand side of this equation should be positive, but the second term could be either positive or negative. This outcome is possible when an increase in the price support causes the mean value of the environmental attribute to decline enough to more than offset the positive effect on input use.

This example illustrates why an accurate evaluation of a policy change may need to take both productivity and environmental effects into account. Ignoring the environmental effects of a change in the price support would be equivalent to assuming that $W_Z = 0$ or $\partial Z/\partial \psi = 0$. If these terms are in fact nonzero, then the result of ignoring them would be to bias the estimated impacts on the price support.[6]

---

[6] For further examples of this modeling approach and its implications for policy analysis, see Antle and Capalbo (1991) and Opaluch and Segerson (1991).

CONCLUSION

This chapter began with the proposition that technological innovation, agricultural productivity, and environmental quality are inextricably linked in the process of agricultural growth. This chapter has explored some of the basic concepts in production analysis and productivity measurement and how they may be generalized to investigate these links between agricultural production and the broader environmental impacts of agricultural growth. The following chapters in this book explore in greater detail specific classes of resources, such as water and land, and the use of inputs such as pesticides, and the agricultural and environmental policies that have been discussed in general terms in this chapter. Perhaps the greatest challenge facing agricultural economists is to understand how all of these parts of the puzzle fit together into the larger picture of agriculture and the environment.

REFERENCES

Aigner, D.J., C.A.K. Lovell, and P. Schmidt. "Formulation and Estimation of Stochastic Frontier Production Function Models." *Journal of Econometrics* 6:21–37, 1979.

Allen, R.G.D. *Mathematical Analysis for Economics.* London: Macmillan and Co., 1938.

Antle, J.M. "Aggregation, Expectations, and the Explanation of Technological Change." *Journal of Econometrics* 13:213–236, 1986.

Antle, J.M. and S.M. Capalbo. "An Introduction to Recent Developments in Production Theory and Productivity Measurement." In S.M. Capalbo and J.M. Antle (eds.): *Agricultural Productivity: Theory and Measurement.* Washington, D.C.: Resources for the Future, 1988.

Antle, J.M. and S.M. Capalbo. "Physical and Economic Model Integration for Measurement of the Environmental Impacts of Agricultural Chemical Use." *Northeastern Journal of Agricultural and Resource Economics* 20:68–82, 1991.

Antle, J.M. and C.C. Crissman. "The Market for Innovations and Short-Run Technological Change: Evidence From Egypt." *Economic Development and Cultural Change* 37:669–690, 1988.

Antle, J.M. and R.E. Just. "Effects of Commodity Program Structure on Resources and the Environment." In N. Bockstael and R. Just (eds.): *Commodity Policy and Resource Use in Agricultural Systems.* New York: Springer-Verlag Publ. Co., 1991.

Archibald, S.O. "Incorporating Externalities Into Agricultural Productivity Analysis." In S.M. Capalbo and J.M. Antle (eds.): *Agricultural Productivity: Theory and Measurement.* Washington, D.C.: Resources for the Future, 1988.

Barnett, H.J. and C. Morse. *Scarcity and Growth: The Economics of Natural Resource Availability.* Baltimore: Johns Hopkins Press [for Resources for the Future], 1963.

Baumol, W. and W.E. Oates. *The Theory of Environmental Policy*, 2nd Edition. New York: Cambridge University Press, 1988.

Binswanger, H.P. "The Measurement of Technical Change Biases With Many Factors of Production." *American Economic Review* 64:964–976, 1974.

Binswanger, H.P. "Induced Technical Change: Evolution of Thought." In H.P. Binswanger, V. Ruttan, et al. (eds.): *Induced Innovation: Technology, Institutions and Development*. Baltimore: The Johns Hopkins University Press, 1978.

Binswanger, H.P., V. Ruttan, et al. (eds.): *Induced Innovation: Technology, Institutions and Development*. Baltimore: The Johns Hopkins University Press, 1978.

Blackorby, C. and R.R. Russell. "Will the Real Elasticity of Substitution Please Stand Up?" *American Economic Review* 79:882–888, 1989.

Brown, G.M. and B.C. Field. "Implications of Alternative Measures of Natural Resource Scarcity." *Journal of Political Economy* 86:229–244, 1978.

Burt, O.R., W.W. Koo, and N.J. Dudley. "Optimal Stochastic Control of United States Wheat Stocks." In G.C. Rausser (ed.): *New Directions in Econometric Modeling and Forecasting in U.S. Agriculture*. New York: North-Holland, 1982.

Capalbo, S.M. and J.M. Antle, (eds.). *Agricultural Productivity: Measurement and Explanation*. Washington, D.C.: Resources for the Future, 1988.

Capalbo, S.M. and J.M. Antle. "Incorporating Social Costs in the Returns to Agricultural Research." *American Journal of Agricultural Economics* 71:458–463, 1989.

Diewert, W.E. "Exact and Superlative Index Numbers." *Journal of Econometrics* 4:115–145, 1976.

Diewert, W.E. "Aggregation Problems in the Measurement of Capital." In D. Usher (ed.): *The Measure of Capital, Studies in Income in Wealth*, Vol. 45. Chicago: University of Chicago Press, 1980, pp. 433–528.

Donigian, A.S. and J.D. Dean. "Nonpoint Source Pollution Models for Chemicals." In W.B. Neely and G.E. Blau (eds.): *Environmental Exposure From Chemicals*. Boca Raton, FL: CRC Press, Inc., 1985.

Fallert, R., T. McGuckin, C. Betts, and G. Brunner. *bST and The Dairy Industry: A National, Regional, and Farm-Level Analysis*. USDA Agricultural Report 579, 1989.

Farell, M.J. "The Measurement of Productive Efficiency." *Journal of Royal Statistical Society* Series A, 120:253–290, 1957.

Feder, G.R., E. Just, and D. Zilberman. "Adoption of Agricultural Innovations in Developing Countries: A Survey." *Economic Development and Cultural Change* 34:255–296, 1985.

Fuss, M., D. McFadden, and Y. Mundlak. "A Survey of Functional Forms in the Economic Analysis of Production." In M. Fuss and D. McFadden (eds.): *Production Economics: A Dual Approach to Theory and Applications*. Amsterdam: North-Holland, 1978, pp. 219–268.

Gardner, B.L. "Price Discrimination or Price Stabilization: Debating with Models of U.S. Dairy Policy." *American Journal of Agricultural Economics* 66:763–768, 1986.

Griliches, Z. "Hybrid Corn: An Exploration in the Economics of Technical Change." *Econometrica* 25:501–522, 1957.

Hayami, Y. and V.W. Ruttan. *Agricultural Development: An International Perspective*. Baltimore: The Johns Hopkins University Press, 1985.

Hazilla, M. and R.J. Kopp. "Social Cost of Environmental Quality Regulations:

A General Equilibrium Analysis." *Journal of Political Economy* 98:853–873, 1990.

Hicks, J.R. *The Theory of Wages.* New York: St. Martins Press, 1963.

Hueth, D. and R.E. Just. "Policy Implications of Agricultural Biotechnology." *American Journal of Agricultural Economics* 69:427–431, 1987.

Huffman, W.E. "Allocative Efficiency: The Role of Human Capital." *Quarterly Journal of Economics* 91:59–80, 1977.

Just, R.E. and J.A. Hallam. "New Developments in Econometric Valuations of Price Stabilizing Policies." In G.C. Rausser (ed.): *New Directions in Econometric Modeling and Forecasting in U.S. Agriculture.* New York: North-Holland, 1982.

Just, R.E. and D. Zilberman. "Stochastic Structure, Farm Size and Technology Adoption in Developing Agriculture." *Oxford Economic Papers* 35:307–328, 1983.

Kaiser, H. and L. Tauer. "Impact of the Bovine Somatotropin on U.S. Dairy Markets Under Alternative Policy Options." *North Central Journal of Agricultural Economics* 11:89–116, 1989.

Kalter, R.J., R. Milligan, W. Lesser, W. McGrath, and D. Bauman. "Biotechnology and the Dairy Industry: Production Costs and Commercial Potential of the Bovine Growth Hormone." A.E. Research Report No. 82-22, 1984. Department of Agricultural Economics, Cornell University.

Kislev, Y. and N. Schori-Bachrach. "The Process of an Innovation Cycle." *American Journal of Agricultural Economics* 55:28–37, 1973.

Kumbhakar, S.C. "The Specification of Technical and Allocative Inefficiency in Stochastic Production and Profit Frontiers." *Journal of Econometrics* 34:335–348, 1987.

Lee, H. and R. Chambers. "Expenditure Constraints and Profit Maximization in U.S. Agriculture." *American Journal of Agricultural Economics* 68:856–865, 1986.

Lindner, R.K. "Farm Size and Time Lag to Adoption of a Scale Neutral Innovation." Mimeographed. Adelaide: University of Adelaide, 1981.

Lovell, C., A. Knox, and R.C. Sickle. "Testing Efficiency Hypothesis in Joint Production: A Parametric Approach." *Review of Economics and Statistics* 65:51–58, 1987.

Lynam, J.K. and R.W. Herdt. "Sense and Sustainability." *Agricultural Economics* 3:381–398, 1988.

McCain, R.A. "Endogenous Bias in Technical Progress and Environmental Policy." *American Economic Review* 68:538–546, 1978.

McGuckin, J.T., S. Gosh, and S. Kumbhakar. "A Generalized Production Function Approach for Estimating Determinants of Inefficiency in U.S. Dairy Farms." *Journal of Business and Economic Statistics* 9:279–286, 1991.

Meeusen, W. and J. van den Broeck. "Efficiency Estimation from Cobb Douglas Production Functions with Composed Error." *International Economic Review* 18:435–1977.

Mundlak, Y. "Elasticities of Substitution and the Theory of Derived Demand." *Review of Economic Studies* 35:225–236, 1968.

Opaluch, J.J. and K. Segerson. "Aggregate Analysis of Site-Specific Pollution Problems: The Case of Groundwater Contamination from Agriculture." *Northeastern Journal of Agricultural and Resource Economics* 20:83–97, 1991.

Pindyck, R.S. *Optimal Planning for Economic Stabilization.* New York: North-Holland, 1973.

Pope, R.D. "To Dual or Not to Dual?" *Western Journal of Agricultural Economics* 7:337–352, 1982.

Rausser, G.C., E. Lichtenberg, and R. Lattimore. "Developments in Theory and Empirical Applications of Endogenous Governmental Behavior" In G.C. Rausser (ed.): *New Directions in Econometric Modeling and Forecasting in U.S. Agriculture.* New York: North-Holland, 1982.

Schulter, M. *Differential Rates of Adoption of New Seed Varieties in India: The Problem of the Small Farm.* United States Agency for International Development, Occasional Paper No. 47, Ithaca, New York, 1971.

Schultz, T.W. *Transforming Traditional Agriculture.* New Haven: Yale University Press, 1964.

Schultz, T.W. "The Value of the Ability to Deal With Disequilibria." *Journal of Econometric Literature* 13:827–846, 1975.

Sellschopp, J. and R.J. Kalter. *Bovine Somatotropin: Its Impact on the Spatial Institution of the U.S. Dairy Industry.* Cornell Univ. Agr. Exp. Station, A.E. Research 89-14, September 1989.

Stoker, T.M. "The Use of Cross-Section Data to Characterize Macro Functions." *Journal of the American Statistical Association* 77:369–380, 1982.

Theil, H. *Linear Aggregation of Economic Relations.* Amsterdam: North-Holland, 1954.

U.S. Department of Agriculture. *Agricultural Handbook.* No. 318. Statistical Reporting Service, Washington D.C., 1966.

U.S. Department of Agriculture. *Agricultural Statistics.* Washington D.C., Various years.

U.S. Department of Agriculture. *Productivity of Agriculture.* Bulletin No. 1238, Washington D.C., 1961.

Varian H.R. *Microeconomic Analysis.* New York: W.W. Norton & Co., 1978.

Wagenet, R.J. and P.S.C. Rao. "Modelling Pesticide Fate in Soils." H.H. Cheng (ed.): *Pesticides in the Soil Environment: Processes, Impacts, and Modeling.* Madison: Soil Science Society of America, 1990.

Welch, F. "Education in Production." *Journal of Political Economy* 78:35–57, 1970.

Whitcomb, D. *Externalities and Welfare.* New York: Columbia University Press, 1972.

The second part of the chapter addresses empirical problems in externality analysis. They include measurement of economic impacts of externalities, assessment of society's preferences for environmental quality, and the modeling of pollution generation processes. Finally, the chapter addresses two specific topics not discussed elsewhere in the book: the management and perception of environmental and human health risks related to agriculture and agricultural waste management.

Economists are interested in addressing externality problems for a number of reasons. They are situations where *laissez faire* may not result in an efficient allocation of resources and some sort of outside intervention may be justified. Many potential remedies exist for these problems including assignment of property rights by courts or legislation, direct bargaining between the parties involved, a ban, a tax, an emission standard or license, or a tradeable permit. If the number of individual economic agents involved is large, then chances are that an externality problem will not be solved by the agents themselves because of the high *transaction costs* involved. It is important to emphasize again, however, that failure to resolve an externality problem without intervention does not mean that intervention will result in an efficient solution. There is no guarantee that government can solve the problem in an efficient manner. In many cases, the resource cost of government intervention is greater than the cost of the externality.

EVOLUTION OF THE THEORY OF EXTERNALITIES

Early thinking about the problem of externalities and potential solutions to it centered around three basic ideas. The first of these was Pigou's (1932) exposition of potential *market failure* when an externality is present. Second was the notion of the suboptimal overuse of a commonly shared resource. Third was Ronald Coase's argument that competition and bargaining can solve externality problems regardless of the initial assignment of property rights if bargaining (transaction) costs are low. We present and discuss briefly these three ideas in this section.

Externality as a Source of Market Failure

Pigou (1932) was the first to identify the potential market failure associated with externalities. The essence of his argument is depicted in Figure 6.1, Panel A, which uses a partial equilibrium model. Figure 6.1, Panel A represents the situation where the supplier of a good does not bear all of the costs of producing the good, or where the marginal private cost (MPC) is less than the marginal social cost (MSC) of the good. This can happen when property rights are not assigned or transaction costs inhibit negotiation between the supplier and demander. The difference between the two at each level of output is the marginal cost of the externality (MEC), assumed constant in this example. If this type of externality occurs, then the producer of the good produces more than is socially optimal ($Y_0 > Y^*$). This misallocation of resources (market failure) results in a loss of welfare measured by area abc in Figure 6.1A. A solution to this problem is to induce the producer

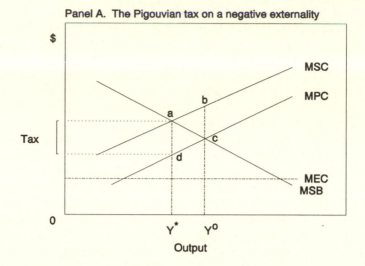

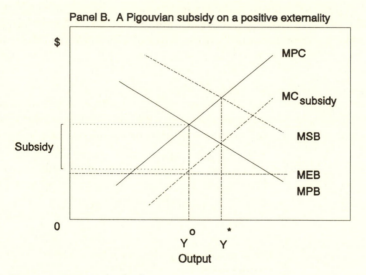

Figure 6.1. Pigouvian taxes and subsidies.

to supply the socially optimal amount of the good by imposing a *Pigouvian tax* on each unit of production such that the private marginal cost is increased to the point where it equals the marginal social cost of the production of the good. Meade (1952) generalized the Pigouvian model for situations where private production results in additional social benefits, as well. As represented in Panel B of Figure 6.1, the solution to the market failure (supplying less of the good than is socially desirable) is to subsidize the producer so that his private marginal cost is reduced to the point where he is willing to supply the socially optimal amount of the good (in an amount equal to MEB).

The Problem of the Shared Resource

The market failure identified by Pigou (1932) involved two separate agents with two separate resources. Another important class of externality problem is the market failure that results from socially inefficient use by two or more agents of a commonly owned, or common property, resource. The classic example of this type of externality is the *Tragedy of the Commons,* first popularized by G. Hardin (1968). A group of peasant herdsmen would use a common pasture for grazing their animals. Each peasant would ignore the impact of grazing his animals on the available supply of grass to others, thus, the commons were overgrazed. That each peasant would ignore the negative impact of grazing his animals on others is a result of rational behavior. Put yourself in his place. What is the utility to you of grazing one more animal on the common pasture? It is the proceeds from the sale of the additional animal. The negative component of the additional animal's grazing certainly affects you, too, because it leaves less grass for your other animals. But the effects of overgrazing are borne not only by you, but by all the other users of the pasture, so that your individual portion of the negative component is just a fraction of the additional utility you receive. The benefits outweigh the costs to you, so you add another animal and another .... This rational action on your part (and on the parts of all the other herdsmen) result in lower aggregate productivity than in the sole owner case where herdsmen would have to pay a user fee to account for (or internalize) the externality they cause others.

More formally, when the problem is a commonly shared resource, the cost of production for each individual user becomes a function of the output of all users of the resource. Therefore, the objective of each profit maximizing producer is

$$\text{Max Profit} = (PY^0 - C(Y^0, Y^1, \ldots, Y^n))$$
$$\text{w.r.t. } Y^0$$

where P is output price, Y^0 is the user's output, C is total cost, and $Y^1, \ldots, Y^n$ are the outputs of the other producers using the resource.

To see this point more clearly, consider the two panels of Figure 6.2 (Scott, 1955). The top panel depicts how a user of the commonly shared resource will choose the optimal amount of the resource to use if no one is given property rights to the resource and no regulations exist on its use. The total private benefit from using the resource is derived from the profit or utility that use of the resource generates. The total private cost of using the resource can take many forms. The classical cost curve illustrated here is just one. If the user is a profit maximizer, he/she will use the resource, say irrigation water from a commonly shared aquifer, until the additional benefit from doing so equals the additional cost at X^0. But the total cost of using different amounts of the resource is not captured in the top panel. The additional cost of using the resource is the net present value of the loss in future productivity for each additional unit of the resource used by the user today (the social or *user cost*). This is the true opportunity cost of each unit of resource used today. This additional cost is depicted in the bottom panel of Figure 6.2 as the user cost curve. When the lost future productivity is taken into account,

[margin note: WIDELY USED EXAMPLE]

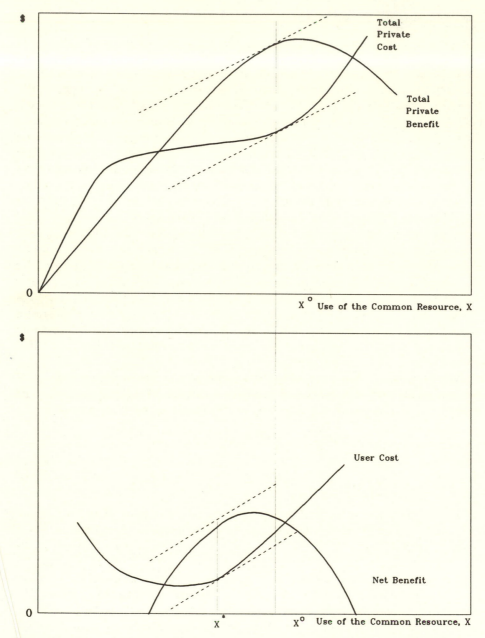

Figure 6.2. Effect on common property resource use of internalizing future reductions in productivity.

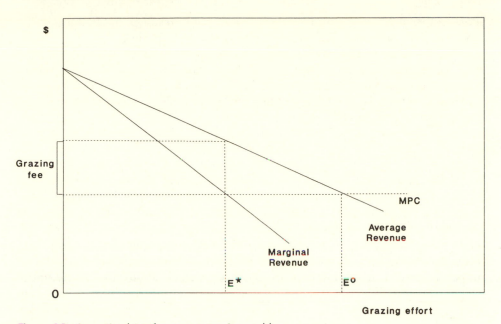

Figure 6.3. An optimal tax for an overgrazing problem.

the user of the resource will want to maximize current net returns while keeping future returns from the resource as high as possible. This is accomplished by equating the additional (marginal) net revenue today with the additional (marginal) opportunity loss in present value terms, at X^*. The question is, then, how do we get the individual user of this commonly shared resource to take account of all of the costs of his actions? One way is to assign or sell the resource to one owner. The rational owner would take account of future profits when deciding how much of the resource to use today. This solution still may not ensure optimal use of the resource from society's point of view because the private owner's rate of discounting the future profits may not coincide with society's. It would, however, result in resource allocation equivalent to the private property case. The other solution is to assign ownership of the resource to society as a whole and let society's agent (government) regulate its use by any of the methods available to it: a *tax* equal to the user cost at each level of resource use, a *quota system* for users of the resource, etc. This solution, as well, may not result in an optimal outcome, since there is no guarantee that government will discover the true user cost or optimal resource use, either.

Figure 6.3 illustrates the common property problem from the standpoint of an individual user of the resource, say a rancher, who shares common grazing lands with other ranchers (Gordon, 1954). The individual user will equate average revenue (AR) to marginal private cost (MPC) and put forth E^0 grazing effort. The marginal revenue (MR), or additional benefit accruing to each animal, is affected by all other users of the resource. As cattle begin to interfere with each other, the marginal benefit to each declines faster for each animal. The optimal amount of effort will be at E^*. An appropriate grazing fee could result in optimal use of the resource, but again, its exact determination is not an easy task.

Whether there will be overgrazing depends upon the regeneration rate of the resource: in this case, the growth rate of the grass relative to E^0 or E^* levels of grazing effort. Overgrazing can occur at both points, at either, or at neither point. This static scenario is analogous to Figure 6.2 if the MPC includes the discounted future costs of overgrazing.

The Coase Theorem

While the initial literature on externalities advocated a direct interventionist solution to the problem, Ronald Coase (1960), 1991 Nobel Laureate in economics, began the argument that market failure would not occur in the first place if property rights were properly defined. He argued that in a world with full information, low transaction costs, and strict enforcement of contracts, the distortion resulting from an externality can be resolved by the clear definition of property rights. He argued further that the socially efficient allocation of resources will be obtained *regardless of the allocation of the property rights* among the agents. Figure 6.4 illustrates the argument. Suppose a farmer were applying chemicals to his crops, and these chemicals were polluting a nearby lake through soil run-off. The owner of the only other property abutting the lake is an avid fisherman and swimmer. Assume there are no laws against polluting lakes and

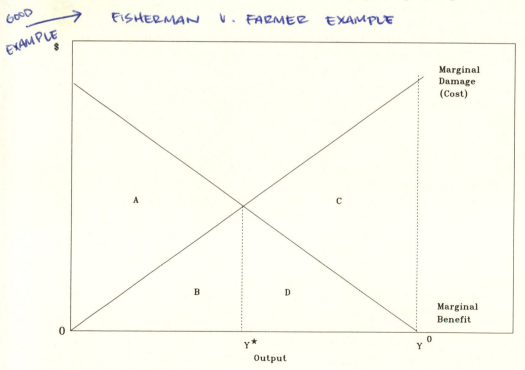

Figure 6.4. The Coase theorem.

Table 6.1. Comparing the Pigouvian Tax to the Coase Theorem—The Case of the Externality of Pesticide Drift[a]

(1) Sprays per year	(2) Cotton farm profit	(3) Cotton Farm marginal profit (2')	(4) Dairy farm damage	(5) Cotton profit − damage (2) − (4)	(6) Dairy farm profit $35 − (4)	(7) Dairy farm marginal profit (6')	(8) Cotton + dairy farm profit (2) + (6)
0	40	60	0	40	35		75
						−10	
1	100	50	10	90	25		125
						−5	
2	150	25	15	135	20		170
						−15	
3	175	10	30	145	5		180
						−15	
4	185	−5	45	140	−10		175
						−15	
5	180		60	120	−25		155

[a] Values are in dollars/acre/year.

that the fisherman has no protected rights to the lake water. How will this dilemma be resolved? If the farmer's marginal net benefit from the pollution is the downward sloping line in Figure 6.4, and the fisherman's marginal damage is the upward sloping line, then it is clear that the farmer would like to produce pollution corresponding to Y^0 level of output, and the fisherman would like zero pollution. Let us first assume that the farmer is given the right to pollute the lake. The fisherman would be willing to pay the farmer up to areas C + D to entice the farmer to reduce pollution to that level associated with Y^*; the farmer will be willing to reduce polluting to Y^* for any payment over an amount equal to area D. If the fisherman is given the right to clean water in the lake, then the farmer is willing to pay up to areas A + B to produce Y^* pollution, and the fisherman would be willing to accept Y^* for any payment over area B. The gains from trade will result in an equilibrium amount of pollution, Y^*, regardless of who has the right to the lake water if the transactions costs of trading are less than the gains.

The different outcomes that can be achieved through use of a Pigouvian tax and bargaining as prescribed by the *Coase Theorem* can be illustrated through a simple, numerical example as in Table 6.1. Suppose that a cotton farm and a dairy farm exist on adjoining land. To control pests, the cotton farmer wants to use an insecticide to spray his crop every year. The relationship between the number of sprays per year and the cotton farmer's profits is depicted in columns 1 and 2 of the table. The highest profit the cotton farmer can achieve is with 4 sprays per year. But each additional spray causes additional external damage to the dairy farmer in terms of additional lost milk production from his cows when they ingest the pesticide that blows over onto his pastures. The relationship between spray numbers and the dollar value of the damage to the dairy farm is depicted in columns 1 and 4 of the table. Column 4 is, then, a measure of the externality caused by the insecticide sprays. If the cotton farmer were to be assessed the external damage caused by the sprays through a Pigouvian tax, his resulting profit is shown in column 5 of the table. The new highest profit number of sprays is three, resulting in a profit of $145. Optimal pesticide use is reduced from 4 to 3 sprays in this case.

Now, suppose that the only government intervention is to assign property rights (spray or nonspray) to one of the farmers and that it is costless for the two farmers to bargain with each other. First, let the government assign property rights to the cotton farmer. He would initially choose to spray four times per year. However, if it is costless for the dairy farmer to bargain, he will be willing to pay the cotton farmer to reduce the number of sprays to three per year. To see this, compare columns 3 and 7. In moving from four to three sprays, the cotton farmer will lose $10 in profit, while the dairy farmer will gain $15. Therefore, the dairy farmer will be willing to pay at least as much as the cotton farmer would have to be compensated for reducing the number of sprays from four to three. Would there be any further reduction in sprays?

Now, let us see what the solution would be if the property rights were assigned to the dairy farmer. He would prefer zero sprays, since his profit is highest then. The cotton farmer would gain $60, $50, and $25 for the first, second and third sprays, respectively. The dairy farmer would lose only $10, $5, and $15, respectively. The cotton farmer would be willing to pay more than the dairy farmer would have to be compensated for the first three sprays. The solution (three sprays per year) would result, then, no matter who is assigned the rights to use the air above the dairy farm.

In the real world, there are few situations when the assumption of costless bargaining would apply. Simply the act of two people getting together and spending the time to work out a solution has an opportunity cost, so the question is this: How high do transaction costs have to be before Coase's conclusions do not apply? First, assume that the cost of bargaining equals $2. Will this change things? Since the differential gains and required compensation are greater than $2, no matter who is assigned the property rights, then the Coase Theorem still holds. What if transaction costs were $8? In this case, if the cotton farmer were assigned the rights and the dairy farmer were assigned the burden of compensation, then the marginal gain to the dairy farmer from reducing sprays from four to three, coupled with the transaction costs of $8, would make the dairy farmer better off from three rather than four sprays. If the dairy farmer were assigned the rights, the cotton farmer would still bargain for and prefer three sprays to four. The assignment of property rights begins to make a difference in the outcome if transaction costs are $5 or greater in our example.

Another interesting result can be illustrated by the example in Table 6.1. Suppose, again, that the Pigouvian tax equal to the dairy farm damage has been imposed, resulting in three sprays per year and total profit (total social product, assuming no administrative costs of the tax, in our two-person world) of $180. Consider the marginal gain to the dairy farmer of reducing sprays from three to two per year. He would be willing to pay up to $15 for this reduction, while the cotton farmer would be willing to accept any amount above $10 for the same reduction. Therefore, if bargaining costs are less than $5, then the bargaining would take place, and total social product would be reduced to $170 per year! This illustrates what could happen with the imposition of a tax, where incentives to bargain still remain.

EXPLAIN HOW t- COSTS EFFECT BARGAINING?

It should be clear by now that the imposition of taxes to deal with externalities can be fraught with peril and should not be considered lightly. Wherever possible, allowing the affected parties to work out a solution is preferable on efficiency grounds (but not necessarily on equity grounds) to government intervention because the solution achieved in this way will ensure that all incentives to change the outcome are exhausted. Even when transaction costs are high, direct government intervention may not be the best solution. It might be that, in some cases, government resources would be better spent on attempting to lower transaction costs, rather than on regulation and enforcement.

The Coase Theorem is much richer than these simple examples depict, but they do serve to illustrate the basic point of his argument. The three lines of thought discussed in this section spawned literature that tried to amplify and implement, as well as challenge, some of the models' basic ideas.

THE RESOLUTION OF EXTERNALITIES WITHOUT DIRECT INTERVENTION

Many externality problems are solved every day and do not come to the attention of economists or government officials. This is because the problem is worked out between the affected parties before it reaches a public forum. This is usually the case when there are a small number of agents involved and the costs of negotiation between them are relatively low. This is not always the case, however. Collective action by a large number of people has been accomplished in many cases to solve externality problems without government intervention. An example is the recent growth of private organizations, such as the Nature Conservancy and the American Farmland Trust, which purchase wilderness areas, wetlands, or agricultural lands to preserve them or the species within them in their current state for future generations. The externality, in these cases, has characteristics of the commonly shared resource—that of "overuse" of the land from society's (or a segment of society's) point of view. These organizations, in effect, internalize the externality by acquiring the property rights to the land. These organizations are made up of many individuals with a common goal who have overcome the high transaction costs of their large numbers by joining and purchasing common bargaining agents and lobbyists.

There are many situations, however, when a solution is not found easily by the affected parties. This is generally when the costs of negotiation (transaction costs) are high. This is usually because of large numbers of people involved but could be for other reasons. Potential reasons for high transaction costs include any nonexclusion and nonrivalry aspects of the problem, as well as the cost of acquiring additional information or the cost of negotiation when many agents are involved.

An example of an externality problem having the nonexclusion property is the overuse of a ground water aquifer by multiple interests for municipal, industrial, and agricultural uses. Anyone in the area, for the cost of drilling a well, can tap into the water resource and cannot be excluded (at a reasonable cost) from using the resource. This nonexclusion property makes it difficult to solve the problem through private negotiation or assignment of property rights because of the large number of agents involved.

The concept of nonrivalry generally is associated with the provision of public goods, such as national defense. In this context, nonrivalry means that one person's consumption of a good does not affect the consumption possibilities of another. In the case of negative externalities, the term means that the use of a resource by one person does not affect the physical ability of another to use the resource. For example, the use of the air by one farmer as a reservoir for pesticide drift does not hinder another farmer's use of the air in the same way. Therefore, the problem of pesticide drift has some nonrivalry aspects to it. It does, however, hinder the nearby public's use of the air for breathing—hence, the externality.

These two properties described above apply to political groups, as well. They can result in *free rider* problems where those who share a common concern are, nevertheless, reluctant to pay for membership, since the benefits of the group's activity will accrue to them anyway.

Coase's work has spawned a large body of literature aimed at understanding when and how externality situations can be resolved by voluntary negotiation between private parties within a well-specified legal system (Demsetz, 1967). This literature investigates the economic implications of legal concepts and compares the outcomes of alternate legal rules to control externalities. Calabresi and Melamed (1972) were the first to address the sharp distinction between *property rights rules* and *liability rules* as legal institutions.

Property rules establish an initial entitlement and stipulate that the holder of a property right under this entitlement cannot be forced to give it up. For example, the fabled Pigouvian smokestack factory might be given a property right to emit smoke. The factory cannot be required to produce less smoke no matter how great the gains to the nearby laundries. Reciprocally, if the laundries have the property right to prohibit smoke then they cannot be required to allow smoke emissions no matter how great the value to the factory. Coase argued that the factory and the laundries will reach some kind of Pareto-improving bargain when gains from trade exist, regardless of who holds the property right. However, there is scope for *strategic behavior* on the part of firms wishing to buy off the holder of the property right—a free rider problem can be expected to exist where each of the laundries figures that the other laundries will pay to prevent most of the damage even if it does not pay anything. Further, because there is no economic principle that delineates how the laundries should divide the gains, the parties may not move all the way to the efficient solution because of strategic bargaining behavior. Indeed, they may be unable to agree at all, and an inefficient level of the externality will continue to be generated. In cases where large numbers of actors are involved, bargaining costs will likely be so high that Pareto-improving trades will not take place.

Liability rules also begin with an initial entitlement. Now, however, the party not holding the entitlement can violate the property right as long as it compensates the holder; the amount of compensation is established by a third party. The third party will ordinarily be a government agency or a court. Liability rules have the advantage that they render strategic behavior by the property rights holders ineffective. They have the disadvantage of requiring *full information* about the costs and benefits of the externality to all parties in order to achieve an efficient level of externality generation.

In a sense all Pigouvian taxation solutions to externality problems are liability rule institutions. It was this liability rule institutions that Coase challenged by showing the efficiency of property rules (under a very particular set of assumptions). Calabresi and Melamed (1972) outline the situations in which each of four institutions can be expected to work well—property rules with the entitlement going to the generator of the externality (polluter) and to the recipient (pollutee), and the same two entitlement schemes for liability rules. A property rule with rights to the recipient of the damage (e.g., a right to clean water) would be chosen when the generator could avoid the damage more cheaply (with lower marginal social cost) than the recipient. A property rule with rights to the generator would be preferred when the recipient was in a better position to balance the costs and benefits of avoiding the externality. If transaction costs were low, and there was no strategic behavior, then we would expect that bargaining would result in the same outcome regardless of which of these two rules was in force. If transaction costs are significant, as they most frequently are in pollution externalities involving large numbers of actors, then a liability rule appears more attractive. The normal rule in law is to give the recipient of the externality the entitlement against the generator—polluters must pay in order to continue their polluting activities. Calabresi and Melamed (1972) point out that when the recipients can more easily avoid damage or when transaction costs for collective action are higher for the generators than the recipients of an externality, then a liability rule with the entitlement given to the generator (the polluter has the right to pollute but may be paid to reduce or discontinue polluting) may be the best option. They also identify the key tradeoff in selecting a rule as that between overall economic efficiency and the desirability of the resulting distribution of income.

Calabresi and Melamed (1972) also identify a fifth institution—*alienability*. This occurs when a property right may not be sold or transferred even if both parties agree to the transaction. An extreme example is the illegality in the United States of selling one's self into slavery. Another example is a class of occupational health regulations where individuals, such as farm workers, are not allowed to work under extremely hazardous conditions even if they voluntarily contract to do so with full knowledge of the risks involved. They cannot transfer their right to public protection of their health and welfare.

Polinsky (1980a) examined the choice between property and liability rules in a formal economic model. He usefully focused on the fact that the initial entitlement is not an all-or-nothing affair, but in fact a particular point on a continuum. For example, a dairy might be given an entitlement for generating X tons of waste per acre per year. Polinsky's (1980a) comparison of liability and property rules assumes that government has two criteria for evaluation of policy outcomes—efficiency and income distribution. Circumstances where liability rules are likely to result in more efficient outcomes than property rules are when government has full information, parties behave strategically, and transaction costs are high. Liability rules may also result in much less desirable income distribution effects and there policy makers may prefer property rules.

With Polinsky's (1980b) interpretation of initial entitlements, direct controls of producer behavior can be viewed as enactments of property rules, and the efficiency vs. equity considerations affecting choices between liability and property rules apply also to choices between the use of a tax and direct control in the social management of externalities.

The selection of the best policy (which includes the option of laissez faire) under the circumstances requires careful analysis and understanding of key features of the externality problem.

THE SELECTION OF POLICY TOOLS

Coase's work (1960) and the literature it spawned analyzed the circumstances under which externality problems can be resolved by the working of a competitive economy and a well-defined and enforceable legal system. Parallel research approaches have been developed to investigate situations where direct government intervention is needed to remedy externality problems. Selection of policy tools is discussed in this section.

Least Cost, Second Best Taxation

The seminal work, *The Theory of Environmental Policy*, by Baumol and Oates (1975) was the driving force behind using a general equilibrium framework to generalize externality analysis and to crystallize some of the problems associated with implementation of Pigouvian taxes to address externality problems. The first point they raise is the difficulty associated with measuring marginal externality cost (the health and environmental costs of externalities) so that an optimal tax can be imposed. The optimal tax is often referred to as the *first best* correction of an externality problem. They suggested instead a *second best* solution that the policy maker set some aggregate environmental targets and that the least-cost policy be implemented to reach those targets. For example, in the case of an agricultural run-off pollutant such as nitrogen, which can eventually cause human health damage, the Pigouvian view of the world would support an optimal tax based on the marginal social cost of the nitrogen pollution. Since such measurements as the value of human life are involved in such an optimal tax, Baumol and Oates argue for setting an aggregate regional target level (standard) for nitrogen disposal and then finding the cost-minimizing policy to attain this target. Such a policy generally will be a tax, but this tax would not necessarily result in the optimal output in the Pigouvian sense, but, rather, a second best solution. By measuring the costs associated with different potential target levels, economists can provide policy makers with the tradeoff relationship between aggregate pollution levels and economic costs. The policy makers, then, can choose the target level given this tradeoff curve and their preferences.

Baumol and Oates (1975) attempted to develop a more realistic decision framework for environmental policy, but even their framework called for the use of taxes as policy instruments for pollution control while, in reality, policy makers still use *standards* as the preferred policy tool. This set the agenda for another series of works dealing with the comparison of alternative policy tools for addressing environmental problems.

Political Economy of the Regulatory Process

Buchanan and Tullock (1975) argued that, although taxes and standards theoretically can reach the same optimal resource allocation, standards are imposed much more often than taxes because producers of the externalities can earn rents with standards. They analyzed a situation where an industry is producing output that is polluting. The standard, which limits total output, acts as a cartel-producing mechanism. Figure 6.5 illustrates their point. If firm A is producing Y^0 amount of output before the regulation and Y^* is the socially optimal output, the reduction in output can be achieved by the imposition of a tax in the amount of $P'' - P'$ or by simply limiting output to Y^* by the regulatory body. If output is limited then the producer is earning rents, depicted by the shaded area in Figure 6.5. If a tax is imposed, then the shaded area is the tax revenue to the regulatory body, and the rents to the producers disappear. Not only do producers have an incentive

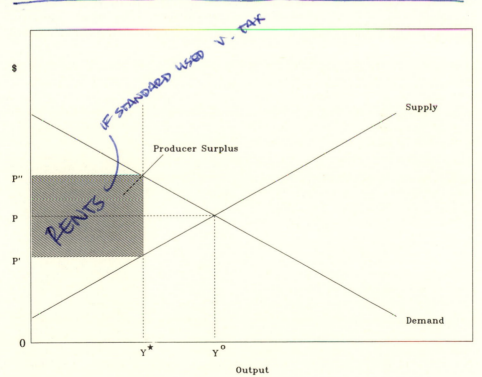

Figure 6.5. Effects on producers of taxes and standards.

to lobby for regulation as opposed to taxes, but, in doing so, they find some support from the environmentalists (Maloney and McCormick, 1982).

Since producers are usually smaller in number and can organize more easily to lobby the regulatory body than the affected consumers can, the producers will have both the incentive and the means by which to argue for the standard, as opposed to a tax, i.e., they will tend to *capture* the regulatory body.

Another important observation in the political economy of the regulatory process is that regulatory bodies tend to be made up of people very familiar with the industry to be regulated, i.e., they usually are dominated by a subset of the producers of the externality. This is a reasonable course of action from the standpoint that these individuals will have the best knowledge of the marginal cost to the industry of various regulatory schemes and could, theoretically at least, devise the most efficient regulations. These individuals, however, may be biased inherently toward more careful consideration of industry concerns than society's as a whole! This, too, may bias regulations toward standards rather than taxes.

Information Availability and Policy Tool Choice—Taxes vs. Direct Control

Weitzman (1974) argues that policy makers are uncertain about the exact shape of the response function of the regulated industries, and, thus, they are uncertain about the outcome of their regulation. The selection of a tax vs. direct regulation to combat a pollution externality depends on the shape of these functions and takes into account the desire of policy makers to reduce their prediction error when imposing a policy. Thus let *MC* in Figure 6.6 be the marginal social cost

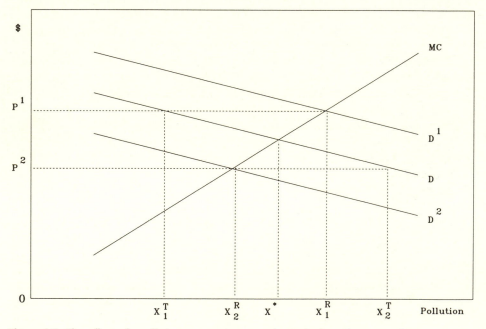

Figure 6.6. The effect of prediction error on taxes and standards under uncertainty.

of pollution and D be the private demand for pollution derived from the industry's production choices, which is uncertain from the policy maker's point of view. The optimal pollution level is X^*. The policy makers may overestimate demand with 50 percent probability and use D^1 or underestimate it with 50 percent probability and use D^2. Assume that this set of demand curves corresponds to rather high demand elasticities. If the policy makers use a tax to control pollution, the tax levels will be P_1 and P_2 (with 50% probability, respectively), and the resulting pollution level will be X_1^T or X_2^T. If they use direct regulation, the resulting pollution level will be X_1^R and X_2^R. Obviously from the figure the errors under direct regulation are smaller and the policy maker is likely to prefer standards rather than taxes to regulate pollution. Using the same reasoning, one can argue that taxes are preferred when demand is inelastic or when MC is less well known than demand.

On Carrots, Sticks, and Permits

The determination of appropriate policies to control externalities was not limited to the comparison of taxes and standards. The externalities literature compared alternate monetary incentive schemes, such as taxes and subsidies, aimed to regulate pollution. While early studies considered the Pigouvian tax and subsidy *symmetric* policies, which have similar effects on social welfare but vary only in their distributional implications, later studies argue for sources of asymmetry. Baumol and Oates (1975) agree that under certainty Pigouvian taxes and subsidies have the same short-run allocational impacts, but their long-run impacts may be different. The use of subsidies as a mechanism for pollution reduction may induce the introduction of new sources of pollution as individuals see the gain associated with pollution reduction. Another reason for asymmetry between taxes and subsidies may be risk and risk aversion. Just and Zilberman (1979) argue that when a pollution event is uncertain (an oil spill or accidental run-off, for example) and polluters are risk averse, subsidies are likely to result in higher likelihood of pollution than taxes but a lower likelihood than a subsidy under risk neutrality (or when perfect insurance against pollution losses are available).

Under certainty, at least in the short run, taxes, subsidies, and direct controls can attain the efficient resource allocation for an externality problem, but with differing equity outcomes. Political economic considerations suggest that producers will pursue subsidies as their preferred policy over either taxes or controls, while government may prefer pollution taxes, because they can be used as a source of government revenue. Direct regulation (a standard restricting the pollution of the industry) can be a reasonable compromise. Implementation of such a standard may be costly, especially when the polluting industry is competitive with many firms. A solution for such problems may be issuing *transferable pollution permits* up to the level that is socially optimal. Initial distribution of the permits may be proportional to production (or pollution) before regulation, and trade in the permits will assure efficiency in production. At equilibrium the permit price will be equal to the optimal pollution tax. When the industry's output is the source of the externality (as in the case of tobacco), implementation of the permit system is especially appealing, since it can be done through transferable production quotas.

THE MULTIDIMENSIONALITY OF EXTERNALITY PROBLEMS

There are two types of features that must be specified in modeling a problem where an externality exists. First are the physical features: the actors in the system (the pollutors, the pollutees, and, possibly, the regulatory agent) and the nature of the externality (what the pollutor does and how it affects the pollutees). Second are the transaction costs features: How much information do the pollutors, the pollutees, and the regulatory agents have regarding the source of and the extent of the effect of the externality and what are the costs to each of additional information? What are other costs associated with bargaining between the parties? All of these features unique to each case, can have a bearing on which type of policy is preferable.

Policies that address externalities problems can be categorized into two groups: regulatory and legal interventions. Regulatory interventions include such policies as taxes, standards, and bans and can affect directly relative prices and resource allocation. Legal intervention is through the assignment or reassignment of liability rules and property rights. Although this type of intervention can result in changes in resource allocation, the spirit of *laissez faire* remains because the government is implicated less directly in the solution. Persuasion, coupled with the threat of intervention, sometimes can be an effective policy, as well, to achieve a voluntary agreement between the parties.

Some of the basic issues of externality control can be addressed with simple models that consider small numbers of policy issues and assume homogeneity among agents and rather simple technological relationships. Development of more operational models requires explicit introduction of some of the complexities that make externality problems difficult to address in real life.

Almost all the studies cited so far that refer to pollution standards assume that standards take the form of a restriction on emissions that is uniform across all firms. However, a number of different forms of standards are used by different pollution control agencies. While some examples exist of *uniform emissions controls*, much more common are restrictions on emissions per unit of output or input; other forms of standards include specifications of control technologies, or even restrictions on use of polluting inputs. Use of different standards changes the incentives provided to firms: For instance, a standard expressed as pollution per unit of an input might lead to higher use of the input used for scaling, since its increased use can lead to increased levels of emissions.

Helfand (1989) found that, if these different pollution standards are all normalized to achieve the same level of emissions for a firm, then a pollution standard gives the firm the highest profits. However, a standard expressed as pollution per unit of output or input, or a requirement for a pollution-abating technology, produce higher levels of output; restricting output or a polluting input reduce output as well as profits below the levels for a pollution standard.

If firms vary (for instance, in how pollution-intensive they are), Helfand (1989) also showed that a standard that permits more individual-firm flexibility, such as the pollution-per-unit-of-input or -output standard, can be more efficient than the rigid uniform emissions standard. Thus, if firms in an industry are likely to be very similar, an emissions standard may be more efficient for firms; but if firms in an industry show a large amount of variation, then a pollution-per-unit-of-output standard is both more efficient and produces more output.

The Impacts of Production and Pollution Technologies on Pollution Control Policies

Selection of antipollution strategies depends substantially on technological relationships between production and pollution activities and technological options polluters and pollutees have in addressing pollution problems. For example, availability of pollution abatement activities or pollution damage-reducing actions may alter policy tools and levels chosen. This section presents a static model highlighting some of the key technical relationships affecting pollution and pollution damage and their effect on policy tool selection.

Consider an agricultural industry with $i = 1, \ldots, N$ farms. The output of the ith farm is y_i, and total industry output is

$$Y = \sum_{i=1}^{N} y_i \tag{1}$$

The output of the ith farm is produced according to the production function

$$y_i = f(x_i, k_i, e_i) \tag{2}$$

where x_i is a variable input used by farm i, such as water, pesticides, or fertilizer; k_i denotes the level of services of a fixed asset (such as land) used by farm i; and e_i is an indicator of environmental condition (it can denote weather, soil quality, etc.). The *pollution generation function* of the ith farm is denoted by

$$z_i = h(x_i, k_i, a_i, e_i) \tag{3}$$

where z_i denotes the ith farm pollution and a_i denotes the level of its pollution abatement activity. Pollution is assumed, therefore, to be a function of regular inputs, pollution abatement, and environmental conditions. Theoretically, one can aggregate over farms to obtain the industry's variable input use, X, asset use K, pollution abatement, A, and pollution Z.[2]

$$X = \sum_{i=1}^{N} x_i; \qquad K = \sum_{i=1}^{N} k_i; \qquad A = \sum_{i=1}^{N} a_i; \qquad Z = \sum_{i=1}^{N} z_i \tag{4}$$

[2] Although theoretically straightforward, aggregation in empirical studies has a significant array of problems, familiar to anyone who has attempted a study of this type.

The industry's output is a source of utility. Let $U(Y)$ denote a monetary measure of utility derived from consumption of aggregate level Y. It may be thought of as the area under a compensated demand curve. The industry's pollution is a source of social cost. Let $C(Z, B)$ be a measure of this cost, which is a function of pollution level Z and damage reduction activity (*averting behavior*) B. If, for example, the farmer we are analyzing contaminates ground water using agricultural chemicals, the consumer of the water can reduce health damages by using filters to purify the water. In this case B is a measure of the extent (or cost) of the use of filters and C is a monetary measure of the negative welfare effects of pollution.

Pollution abatement (A) in the agricultural context may be related to land allocation (crop rotations), conventional input use methods (e.g., banding rather than broadcast applications of chemicals), or the choice of output levels or mixes. Its cost is usually internal to the firm. Averting behavior costs (B) can be borne by the firm in the form of additional labor or capital costs to avoid exposure and/or by individuals external to the firm (e.g., neighbors or food consumers).

Let us assume that input prices are fixed to the industry where w_a, w_b, w_k, and w_x denote prices of abatement, damage reduction (averting) behavior, fixed asset service, and variable input prices, respectively. Summing all benefits and costs from production, consumption, and the externality and assuming this welfare sum to be the objective for social maximization, optimal choices are derived solving

$$\max_{\substack{X, Y_i^1, a_i, x_i, \\ k_i, Z, B}} \left[U(Y) - C(Z, B) - w_b B - w_a \sum_{i=1}^N a_i - w_k \sum_{i=1}^N k_i - w_x \sum_{i=1}^N x_i \right] \quad (5)$$

Subject to:

$$Z = \sum_{i=1}^N h(x_i, k_i, a_i, e_i)$$

$$Y = \sum_{i=1}^N f(x_i, k_i, e_i)$$

Let P denote the shadow price of output and λ denote the shadow price of pollution. Using this notation the social optimization problem becomes

$$\max U(Y) - C(Z, B) - w_b B - w_a \sum_{i=1}^N a_i - w_k \sum_{i=1}^N k_i - w_x \sum_{i=1}^N x_i$$

$$- P \left[\sum_{i=1}^N f(x_i, k_i, e_i) - Y \right] - \lambda \left[\sum_{i=1}^N h(x_i, k_i, a_i, e_i) - Z \right] \quad (6)$$

Assuming all the regulatory conditions to obtain internal solutions, the necessary conditions that hold at the optimal outcome include

$$\partial U / \partial Y = P \quad (7)$$

Condition (7) suggests that the shadow price of output is equal to the marginal utility of consumption. Moreover, since $U(Y)$ can be interpreted as the area under the demand curve to the left of Y, $\partial U/\partial Y$ denotes the inverse (price-dependent) demand curve, and condition (7) suggests that optimal price and quantity of output are related by the demand function. Another first-order condition

$$\partial C/\partial Z = \lambda \tag{8}$$

suggests that at the optimal solution, marginal social cost of pollution is equal to the pollution's shadow price. Another optimality condition

$$-\partial C/\partial B = w_b \tag{9}$$

suggests that the optimal level of damage reduction activity is where marginal benefit from damage reduction is equal to marginal cost of damage-reducing activity.

The optimal decision rules at the farm level are

$$P \, \partial f/\partial x_i - w_x - \lambda \, \partial h/\partial x_i = 0 \qquad \text{for all } i \tag{10}$$

$$P \, \partial f/\partial k_i - w_k - \lambda \, \partial h/\partial k_i = 0 \qquad \text{for all } i \tag{11}$$

$$\lambda \, \partial h/\partial a_i - w_a = 0 \qquad \text{for all } i \tag{12}$$

Conditions (10) and (11) show that for every farm, when inputs are used optimally, the input's value of marginal product is equal to the sum of its price and the value of the marginal pollution (i.e., $\lambda \, \partial h_i/\partial x_i$) it produces. Thus, the greater the shadow price of pollution and/or the marginal impact of the input on pollution, the larger will be the gap between the value of its marginal product ($P \, \partial f/\partial x_i$) and its price. Thus, producers will use less of the inputs that pollute, relative to the optimal use of them if they were not polluting inputs. Condition (12) suggests that the optimal level of pollution abatement is when the value of damage reduction from abatement ($\lambda \, \partial h/\partial a_i$) is equal to the marginal cost of abatement.

Situations Leading to First Best Performance

The optimality conditions (8)–(12) set a standard for first best performances. It is instructive to identify situations and institutional arrangements that may lead to such outcomes.

Consider a situation where both polluters and pollutees are price taking producers. In this case the utility function $U(Y) = PY$, and $C(Z, B)$ represents loss of profit to pollutees. The externality problem is solved when all the production is by one regional firm. For example, if polluters operate a fish processing plant at a river basin and pollutees are fishermen who fished the river, the externalities problems are internalized and addressed when they are combined with a basin-wide firm (Whitcomb, 1972). (Refer to the example of the dairy farmer and the cotton farmer above and see what would happen if the two were combined into one firm.)

The fact that polluters and pollutees are not part of one firm, but constitute many different firms is the source of the inefficiency here, an inefficiency that requires intervention. In essence, the externality problem in this case is a horizontal integration problem. There are many small producers rather than one big one, and this can be corrected by a structural change.

If the combined firm controls a significant share of the market, then welfare losses can occur with this solution. The assumption of price taking behavior on behalf of producers is needed, therefore, to prevent loss of welfare as a result of monopolistic practices. At the same time, if pollution is directly related to output, monopolistic behavior can reduce the external costs of pollution relative to the competitive case through lower output levels.

In cases where polluters are many farms who together face a negatively sloping demand curve, and/or pollution damage does not reduce business profit but reduces health of individuals or environmental quality or amenities, direct intervention can result in efficient resource allocation. There are many policy options, but they must have two components—a mechanism to reduce pollution and another to reduce pollution damage. Such a combination may be a pollution tax of λ and direct provision of damage preventing activities at the level dictated by condition (9) ($\partial C/\partial B = w_b$). For example, if agricultural chemical residues on food are the source of the externality problem, a tax on residues may reduce chemical crop treatment and/or induce reduction of residue on food by pre-marketing treatment at the farm level. Education activity by government may affect consumption activities to reduce health damage. If agricultural drainage is a source of environmental degradation, a policy combining taxation of drainage by farmers and treatment of drainage generated to reduce health and environmental damage can yield optimal resource allocation. The two components of the policy must be established simultaneously to make the solution optimal. The optimal tax λ is suboptimal if B is lower than its optimal level. If, for example, the damage reduction activities are restricted to be at a level $B = B_1$, which is lower than the optimal B dictated by (9), a different optimal tax must be established. This tax is theoretically derived by solving the optimization problem in (6) with an added constraint, $B_1 \leq B$. Under reasonable assumptions it can be proved that higher pollution taxes are required to reach optimality as the level (or choice) of damage prevention activities becomes more restricted. Thus, the optimal drainage tax is higher, the fewer options (or facilities) for drainage treatment are available. Therefore, in situations where optimal pollution taxes are being established to address agricultural problems, allowing a wider range of damage reduction activities by the government (education, drainage treatment facilities, etc.) serves well the interests of farmers.

Monitoring of externalities is not an easy task. It is technically difficult to measure, for example, seepage of chemicals into ground water or smoke generated by burning rice or blueberry fields. Thus taxation or direct regulation of pollution by itself may be difficult. Instead, regulation or taxation of inputs or output sometimes are considered as a way of controlling pollution. To illustrate this issue, we will use the model introduced earlier but simplify it somewhat by concentrating on the pollution reduction choices and not allowing damage reduction activity choices (B is predetermined).

Consider first a case where pollution is a function of variable inputs and abatement only. This may occur, for example, when the polluting variable input is a chemical (pesticides, fertilizer) and abatement activities are reflected by extra care and equipment use in application that reduce the contamination of the environment. In this case, the pollution generation function becomes

$$z_i = h(x_i, a_i) \tag{13}$$

The first-order conditions for social optimum presented in equations (7), (9), (10)–(13) are modified in this case (equation 8 no longer applies since B is given). They suggest that one mechanism to achieve social optimum is to tax the variable input of each farm at a level equal to $\lambda \, \partial h / \partial x_i$ and to set a standard requiring that abatement will be at the level where $\lambda \, \partial h / \partial a_i = w_a$. The abatement standard and variable input tax have to be instituted and enforced simultaneously to obtain the optimal solution.

If for some farmers actual abatement levels cannot meet the optimal standard (because of, say, a credit constraint), a new, higher variable input tax must be instituted taking into account actual abatement levels in computing the tax. The tax and abatement standard may drain the polluting farmers financially. The policy of full or partial subsidy of abatement efforts using the tax proceeds can partially alleviate this problem.

While this analysis has treated abatement as a continuous choice variable, in many cases it involves a choice between a small number of distinct alternatives. A standard in this case is easier to enforce, and use of pollution abatement standards (such as lining of drainage and disposal facilities) is widespread.

The general specification used here resulted in a variable input tax of $\lambda \, \partial h / \partial x_i$ that varies across producers. Such discriminating policy may be difficult to institute politically and to enforce. On the other hand, a uniform variable input tax would be optimal only when $\lambda \, \partial h / \partial x_i$ does not vary among farmers. For a continuous a_i, $\lambda \, \partial h / \partial x_i = \gamma$ (when γ is constant) only when $h_i(x_i, a_i) = \gamma x + \tau(a_i)$ (where τ is a decreasing function of a_i). Such an additive specification is very restrictive. It implies a fixed coefficient relating input use to gross pollution and implies that some of this pollution is eliminated by the abatement activities. The amount eliminated by abatement is assumed to be independent of gross pollution, which is rather unlikely.

If there are only a small number of distinct abatement technologies, the circumstances leading to a uniform input tax may be more likely. For example, suppose a fixed proportion generation process of gross pollution from the variable input and removal of a fixed fraction of gross pollution by each distinct abatement technology. In this case

$$z_i = h_i(x_i, a_i) = \gamma x_i [1 - \theta(a_i)] \tag{14}$$

where γ is the gross pollution-variable input ratio and $\theta(a_i)$ is the gross pollution elimination fraction of abatement technology a_i. In this case the variable input tax is uniform when abatement choice is uniform, i.e., all farmers are using the same distinct abatement strategy.

While input taxes, output taxes, and regulatory standards have been discussed as generally separate options above, they need not be considered as mutually exclusive. As the last section illustrates, they may be complementary in some cases.

Firm Heterogeneity

As we have illustrated above, the assumption of identical firms may be very misleading, especially in externality problems. Certain technologies and certain localities are much more likely to pollute, for example, than others. Hochman and Zilberman (1978) introduced a framework to illustrate the implications of heterogeneity. They considered an industry with many production units, and each unit produces output and generates pollution with a fixed coefficient technology, with the technology coefficients allowed to vary across firms. This technological setup is especially appropriate for short-run analysis when the fixity of farmers' capital equipment results in production rigidities. (This utilizes the *putty-clay* approach for the case where output is produced by one input (labor) and generates pollution. Let x denote the labor output ratio and z the pollution output ratio. Output price is denoted by P, labor price by w, and the impacts of the two policy tools are analyzed—a pollution tax of $\$V$ per unit of pollution and a standard setting an upper bound of z^m on the pollution/output ratio.

The vertical axis of Figure 6.7 measures the labor/output ratio. The technological coefficients of production units of the industry are inside the rectangle OGHJ. Assuming profit maximization, when pollution is not regulated, production units with labor/output coefficients smaller than P/w (the ones with coefficients in OAFJ) operate at full capacity while less efficient production units (with coefficients in AFGH) do not operate. A pollution tax reduces the range of production units that operate to all those with $wx + Vz \leq P$ (the ones in triangle OAE) while the relatively less efficient and/or more pollution intensive units in AFJE stop operating. A pollution standard that restricts the pollution/output ratio to below z^m reduces the region of operating units to OABD. Figure 6.7 demonstrates that environmental policies vary in their impact on the industry's structure. An antipollution tax may force relatively inefficient but low polluting units (the ones in ABC) to stop operating while allowing very efficient but polluting-intensive units to continue to operate (units in CDE). On the other hand, direct regulation setting an upper limit on the pollution/output ratio may cause efficient but pollution-intensive facilities to stop operating while allowing relatively inefficient and low pollution units to stay in business. This problem could be mitigated by allowing units of pollution to be traded among firms in the form of tradeable emission permits.

To compare the overall effects of the two policies, consider the case where the tax and standard are designed to attain a target level of aggregate pollution, Z. Bajmol and Oates (1971) proved that the tax is an efficient policy and thus attains the aggregate target with least cost. Using Figure 6.7 it can be demonstrated, however, that when the standard is used, aggregate output is greater than under taxes. When both policies attain the same pollution level, the production units in ABC (which operate only under a standard) generate the same pollution as the production units in CDE, which operate only under the tax. But the pollution/output ratio of the units in ABC is smaller than that of the units in CDE; therefore the units in ABC produce more output than the units in CDE, and, hence output under the standard (produced by units in OACD and ABC) is greater than output

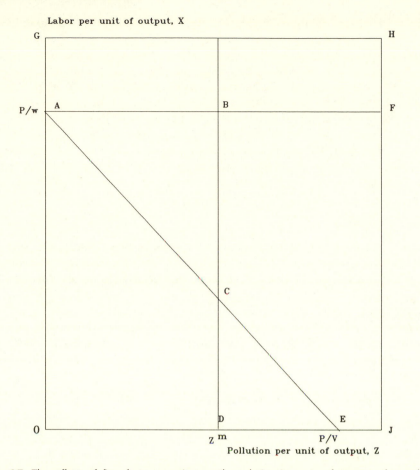

Labor per unit of output, X

Figure 6.7. The effect of firm heterogeneity on the relative impacts of taxes and standards.

under the tax (produced by units in OACD and CDE). This argument can be expanded to cases when demand is not perfectly elastic and suggests that while a pollution tax obtains an aggregate pollution target with least cost, it may attain it with greater (and more negative) impact on the industry's output and output price than a standard restricting pollution/output ratios. Policy makers who may be interested not only in efficiency, but also in maintaining price and output levels, may, therefore, prefer a direct regulation to a tax.

The assumption of fixed proportion technology associated with putty clay models may be quite restrictive even for short-run analysis. Just and Antle (1990) expanded the framework for analysis of impacts of environmental policies on heterogeneous industries to allow two types of responses to pollution taxation. Some production units may find operation under pollution taxes impossible and stop operating while others may modify their operation, reducing the generation of pollution by substituting pollution with other inputs or using pollution abatement strategies.

In cases where pollution abatement is capital intensive, credit availability and wealth are sources of heterogeneity that substantially affect the impacts of environmental regulations. Funding of investments in agriculture requires some self finance and the use of existing assets as collateral. Environmental regulations are likely to reduce the value of agricultural assets (which reflects the profitability of these assets) and farmers' ability to borrow. Thus highly leveraged farmers may not be able to introduce pollution abatement equipment in response to environmental regulation even when they present the most efficient response. In such situations governmental credit guarantees or even credit subsidies may be required to accompany environmental regulations in order to reduce their negative impacts on output and prevent bankruptcies (Hochman and Zilberman, 1978).

Spatial Externalities

Several dimensions may be the source of *heterogeneity* among producers including wealth, location, asset mix, human capital and other life-cycle characteristics, and risk preferences. Locational heterogeneity is especially important in externality problems, and its treatment and implications are analyzed explicitly below.

Two types of externality problems with spatial variability have been analyzed conceptually. The first includes those where the externality, say pollution, affects economic agents outside the polluting industry. The second type is that where the externality generated by a subset of producers in an industry affects others within the industry.

Externalities Affecting Agents Outside the Industry

Hochman et al. (1977) considered pollution problems where producers are distributed at different distances from a center of business activities and generate pollution that affects negatively agents in this center. This may be the case when wastes of farms located along a river contaminate the estuary at the mouth of the river or when smoke, dust, and noxious residues generated by farms spread to a nearby urban center or suburban neighborhood.

Two types of spatial considerations are introduced in the analysis of this problem. 1) Pollution is assumed to dissipate in its journey from its source to the affected areas. Thus, the farther a farm is from the affected center, the smaller is the fraction of its pollution that is actually causing damage. 2) Transportation costs reduce the actual price received by producers located farther away from the business center. When pollution is not regulated, transportation costs are the dominant factor in determining spatial patterns of resource allocation, and the Von-Thunen model holds, namely, that profit maximization will lead to more intensive production closer to the business center and land rents decline with distance from the center. Because of the dissipation, the penalty for pollution (pollution fee) should decline as farmers are located farther from the business center. That provides an incentive to intensify production farther from the business center. Thus, transportation costs and pollution penalties operate in opposite directions in determining farm location. When the pollution penalties effect dominates the transportation costs effect, introduction of pollution penalties may significantly alter agricultural land use and land rents patterns. Agricultural activities with high production (and pollution) intensities will move away from the center, and production intensities near the center will become relatively low. Similarly, pollution penalties may make land rents near the center become lower than rents at locations farther from the center. When pollution penalties do not dominate transportation costs, introduction of a pollution penalty may modify spatial patterns of agricultural production and rent but to a lesser extent. In these cases, pollution taxation will reduce the value of location and the premium paid for operating lands closer to the center. In all cases, introduction of pollution taxation tends to reduce agricultural land rents and may lead to more urban development as pollution taxation may make agricultural activities less lucrative than urban development (see Chapter 9).

There are often external costs from industrial and urban development on agriculture. Ozone and acid damage to agricultural crops are areas that Adams et al. (1982, 1986) have examined. They found extensive damage, and have evaluated corrective measures. Damage over wide areas can affect crop prices, and welfare effects must be traced through several markets (see Chapter 4).

Externalities Affecting Agents Inside the Industry

Hochman et al. (1977) considered a situation where an industry is located at a basin and the pollution of uphill farms reduces the profitability of the downhill farms. In their model pollution accumulates as one moves downhill, and exposure to pollution is greater the further downhill the location of a farm. This assumption is in contrast to the dissipation assumption made in the previous section. A situation such as this results in a suboptimal resource allocation in the absence of a negotiated solution or intervention, namely, excessive production by some uphill farms and substantial underutilization of resources by downhill farms. The accumulation of pollution causes the pollution of uphill farms to affect more farms and cause more damage than does the pollution of the downhill farms. One possible remedy to the suboptimality is a pollution fee that is declining the farther downhill a farm is. Uphill farms will pay a higher price for their pollution because of the accumulation of pollution over space.

In the long term, with stable pollution fees, uphill farmland will become cheaper relative to downhill land. The downhill farmers may, therefore, receive some compensation in the form of land value appreciation.

There also may be situations with positive externalities within industries. In some water districts where downstream farms use run-off water from upstream farms. This run-off water may include sufficient fertilizers for it to reduce the fertilizer costs of the downstream farms.

Dynamic Aspects of Externalities

Many agricultural resource problems, such as waterlogging, pesticide resistance, and ground water depletion and contamination are *dynamic* in nature. In all of these problems the externality results from accumulation of past activities by the affected industry. Understanding of the dynamic accumulation processes is essential in addressing such problems, and the solutions may require policies that vary substantially over time.

To view this problem more formally, let Y_{it} denote output of the ith farm at time t and let its production function be $Y_{it} = f(X_{it}, S_t)$ where X_{it} is input use by the ith farm at time t and S_t is a stock of externality. Obviously marginal productivity of the input is nonnegative and marginal productivity of the externality stock is nonpositive ($\partial f/\partial S_t \leq 0$).

It is assumed that input use by the farms is the source of the externality and the externality generation function of the ith farm at time t is $g(X_{it})$ with $\partial g/\partial X_{it} \geq 0$). There are I farms in the industry, where I is assumed to be large, and the externality *stock accumulation function* is

$$S_t = S_{t-1} + \sum_{i=1}^{I} g(X_{it-1}) \qquad (15)$$

To prevent the necessary conditions for efficient resource allocation, let P_t and W_t denote output and input prices, respectively, at time t and V_t denote the shadow price of the externality at time t. Input use of the ith farm at time t when resources are allocated efficiently is determined according to

$$P_t \, \partial f/\partial X_{it} = W_t + V_t \, \partial g/\partial X_{it} \qquad (16)$$

When resources are allocated efficiently, the value of marginal product of input use is equal to the sum of the input price and the cost of the marginal externality generated by the input ($V_t \, \partial g/\partial X_{it}$). The shadow price of the externality generated at time t, V_t, represents the discounted marginal damage it will generate as it becomes part of the externality stock, S.

The analysis in Dasgupta and Heal (1974) and Wienstein and Zeckhauser (1975) is useful for the cases with a positive discount rate and constant input price and consumer demand over time. In these cases, the efficient solution requires that input use and output decline over time while the price of the externality and output price (if demand is not perfectly elastic) increases.

The reduction in input use and output over time and the increase in the cost of pollution reflect both time preference (there is a positive premium for earlier consumption) and reduction in the marginal productivity of input associated with the higher stock.

The efficient resource allocation is not likely to be obtained by the competitive markets without intervention. The profit-maximizing farmers are likely to ignore the externality and dynamic considerations and determine their input use at time t according to $P \, \partial f/\partial X_{it} = W_t$, namely, by selecting input at a level where its price equals its value of marginal product.

Ignoring the externality cost tends to result in overuse of the input and accelerated build-up of the externality stock in the early periods. The growth of the stock of externality will cause a reduction in output and input use over time also in the competitive case. A comparison of resource allocation under the efficient and competitive solution suggests that in early periods the competition results in more output while there is a critical point in time when this relationship is reversed. The excessive accumulation of externality in the early periods tends to result in a substantial reduction in productivity in the long run with output levels declining much below what is required by the efficient solution.

Thus, to attain an efficient resource allocation to a dynamic externality problem, interventions such as a tax on input use or output or direct control of the input are needed. The intervention levels are likely to become more restrictive over time. In the case of our example the tax on input use is ($V_t \, \partial g / \partial X_{it}$) and it is increasing since V_t is increasing over time.

Another element that determines the level of intervention is the initial stock of the externality, S_0. Thus, in regions with waterlogging problems, the higher the initial level of ground water, the stricter the optimal policy regulations. Again, while appealing theoretically, measurement of V_t and even S_0 can be difficult.

Gradual tightening of environmental policies over time is quite common. Fuel efficiency standards for cars are becoming stricter as time goes up, removal and cancellation of pesticides is a gradual process, and in many cases the pollution fees are introduced gradually and become more severe with time. These changes in policy over time do not necessarily reflect dynamic externality considerations. There are other dynamic processes (besides externality accumulation) that result in changes in environmental regulation over time.

Processes of technological change, research and development, innovation, and diffusion are time consuming. Policy makers realize that these processes are likely to lead to improved technology and reduction of costs of pollution control and abatement. Direct regulations (or pollution tax) schemes may take that into account and may increase the severity of the requirements over time.

In both cases discussed above the development of new technology (directly by the government or indirectly) is a part of the aim of the environmental policies, and regulations are developed to take into account improved technology over time.

Learning is another factor affecting policy dynamics. Rausser and Howitt argued that part of the regulatory procedure is aimed at gaining information regarding pollution generation and damage. Policies may be modified as more information is gathered. In many situations pollution control strategies should include research and extension activities leading to technological changes especially regarding pollution management. Moreover, Hayami and Ruttan (1985) have demonstrated empirically that many agricultural innovations have been induced by market conditions. Pollution taxation and regulations that make pollution generation more costly are likely to induce new pollution abatement innovations.

APPLIED EXTERNALITY ANALYSIS

The literature also is taking another direction in addition to theoretical development—toward applications. Several key problems arise here. Regardless of which policy instrument (or combination) is under consideration in a particular situation, the successful implementation of the policy hinges on the accurate assessment of the costs and benefits of removing the externality. An efficient solution to the problem is to control the negative externality to the point where the additional cost of control just equals the additional benefits of control—an appealing concept, but to quantify these benefits and costs is a difficult, if not impossible, task in many cases. It may be, in fact, that the cost of measuring the externality exceeds any efficiency gains of eliminating it.

The additional benefits of control are usually in the form of damage avoided. The important concept underlying all forms of evaluation of the benefits of externality control is that utility is derived from characteristics of goods. When these characteristics change, then the value of the goods to individuals changes, as well. Economic value is measured in terms of consumers' and producers' net willingness to pay. Net willingness to pay is the maximum price a person would be willing to pay for a good or service minus current costs (Cooper and Loomis, 1990). Thus, one can infer value using market data, programming techniques, or questionnaires to assess the characteristic content of goods of interest and, combining characteristic values and content, evaluate the goods.

Measurement of the value of the damage avoided sometimes requires measurement of values of goods not traded directly in markets, such as aesthetic values, the value of wildlife, or even the value of human health. The goods to be valued can be thought of as being along a continuum from directly valued in markets to no (or very little) relationship to existing markets. The methods of valuation form a continuum along the same lines from direct use of readily available market prices to the survey methods of nonmarket valuation used in situations where the least amount of behavioral information exists.

Evaluation of the Benefits of Control

Methods Based on Market Prices

One way to determine the benefits of externality control is to measure a direct relationship between externality levels (intensities) and the value of market-traded goods. For example, expenditures on insurance can be related to the value placed on various types of losses by different groups of individuals. Housing or land values have also been used to derive the value placed by individuals on avoiding certain types of pollution damage. Another application has been to estimate the value of time lost owing to accidents by examining the relationship between expenditures by different groups of individuals on accident prevention and changes in the likelihood of an accident causing a certain amount of lost time.

Crocker (1971) provides an interesting attempt to relate pollution levels to land values. After World War II several superphosphate fertilizer plants coexisted with nearby citrus and beef cattle producers in Polk County, Florida. Emissions from the phosphate plants in the form of atmospheric fluorides were found to cause damage to both the citrus and beef cattle industries. To attempt to place an economic value on the damage in each industry, prices per acre for sales of agricultural land for continued agricultural use were regressed on various hedonic site characteristics plus the frequency with which a particular site was exposed to fluoride pollutant dosages above 40 parts per million. The regression results with respect to the pollution variable on citrus land prices appear in Table 6.2. They are interpreted as follows. Potential damage to citrus by fluoride pollution first

Table 6.2. Regression Results for Fluoride Damage to Citrus Land Prices in Polk County, Florida[a]

	Years							
	1947 to 1950	1951 to 1953	1954 to 1956	1957 to 1958	1959 to 1960	1961 to 1962	1963 to 1964	1965 to 1966
Coefficient for the pollution variable (std. error)	.00 (.101)	.043 (.091)	−.069 (.042)	0.086* (.039)	−.113* (.040)	−.174* (.057)	−.106* (.044)	−.078 (.040)

[a] These coefficients are the result of estimation of the log-linear form and, therefore, can be interpreted as the elasticity of land prices with respect to additional fluoride pollution doses.
* Statistical significance.

became known about 1952. This damage was sufficiently documented to appear in a technical journal in 1955. Dissemination of this knowledge occurred in the next few years, causing the damage coefficient to become significantly negative for a time. Then, as public pressure mounted, the phosphate industry began to institute control measures. The industry spent more than twice as much on the capital costs of pollution control from 1959 to 1965 than in all previous years combined. The result was that expected pollution damage to citrus declined, causing no further capitalization of the damages in the selling price of citrus land.

This study provides evidence that the value of damage caused by a negative externality can be derived by measuring the changes in asset values. The informational requirements are formidable, however. For example, how many times would we have access to detailed information on the frequency with which a particular site was exposed to an amount of pollutant?

Programming Methods

Implied shadow proces of pollutants can also be obtained from normative programming models. The values derived from this method will be the shadow prices of quality or characteristic constraints. In other words, a value derived from a programming model is the marginal value of one more available "unit" of the characteristic. Assessing the value of nutrients in different animal rations is one example of a valuation problem that lends itself to the programming approach.

Programming models require a great deal of information if they are to approach sufficient realism, but generally not as much information as is required by economic techniques. Generally, they do not provide value estimates implied by actual behavior, so, in this case, can be considered a nonmarket method. Also, the restrictions required to make the models manageable pose the danger of biasing the shadow values considerably.

Nonmarket Valuation Methods

Nonmarket valuation methods are all attempts to estimate what the market clearing price would be if a good or amenity were traded in a market. The techniques used include the hedonic pricing approach, the travel cost method, and the contingent valuation method.

Hedonic Pricing. Hedonic pricing, which is mostly due to Lancaster (1966) and Rosen (1974), distinguishes between *characteristics* that are sources of utility (these characteristics may be nutrients and taste elements in food, sensual and aesthetic values in open space, etc.) and traded commodities that embody these characteristics. Smith (1991) reviews the household production models that form the basic optimization framework in many environmental evaluation studies. Goods are basically packages of characteristics, and the value of goods is a function of the value of the characteristics they embody. This concept has a wide range of uses. Cropper et al. (1988) assess econometric techniques to infer hedonic prices from observed market prices. Beach and Carlson (1993) apply the method to farmers' choice of herbicides and find that they are willing to pay more for less persistent, less mobile (safer) herbicides that will not leach into the ground water. The more well defined the characteristic of interest is, the easier hedonic pricing methods are to use (Palmquist, 1991).

Travel Cost Method. The travel cost method of valuation of some types of environmental amenities has been used successfully in some cases (Bockstael et al., 1991). Particularly in the area of recreational amenities, such as national parks, this method attempts to attribute a value to the amenity based upon how much individuals paid in terms of travel and equipment costs to enjoy the amenity.

This method does not account, however, for the value of the amenity to people who have not actually traveled there. This aggregate, off-site value can be substantial. For example, suppose you have never been to the Grand Canyon. Would it mean nothing to you if the Grand Canyon suddenly did not exist? You may plan to travel there some day or you may even attach some value to it even if you never plan to travel there. These two components of value are *option values* (an insurance premium you might be willing to pay to insure the availability of the Grand Canyon to you in the future) and *existence values* (you place a value on simply knowing it exists). Option values represent the value preserving an environment because of irreversibility or uncertainty considerations (Fisher, 1981; Krutilla and Fisher, 1975). Another component of value is that which is placed on a good or amenity's availability for the enjoyment of future generations. This is its *bequest value.*

It may be possible to measure some off-site values of goods using hedonic techniques, but they may be relatively unimportant for market-traded goods (Randall and Stoll, 1983). In the case of valuation of environmental amenities, such as clean water or open space, they can be important components of value. The only nonmarket valuation technique able to account for these off-site values in these cases is the contingent valuation method discussed in the next section.

Contingent Valuation Method. For environmental amenities, such as wildlife, recreational areas, or open space, estimates of the benefits derived from them have been elicited using the relatively new survey method of contingent valuation

(Bishop and Hiberlein, 1979; Boyle and Bishop, 1988; Loehman et al., 1984). This approach to the valuation problem is based on construction of an artificial market for the externality to ascertain its value for different groups. A group of potentially affected individuals is surveyed to ascertain how much they would be willing to pay to keep the resource or how much they would have to be compensated if the resource were to be lost to them. These measures are aggregated to construct the value to society of the nonmarket goods. The recent book by Mitchell and Carson (1989) presents a thorough review of the methodological foundations and basic techniques of this approach.

Research has shown that the economic value derived by this method is sensitive to the framing of the survey questions (Gregory and McDaniels, 1987). Willingness to accept compensation is not limited by budget constraints and is likely to be much higher than willingness to pay. Further, people are likely to ask more to prevent adding stress or unpleasant environmental factors to their life than they will be ready to pay to remove these negative elements once they exist. This method is subject to the potential distortion of value because respondents are not required to make the payments they state they are willing to make. The value is based on what people say, rather than what they do, as in values derived from actual transactions of some type. An interesting evaluation of the performance of the contingent valuation method can be found in Welsh (1986). Simultaneous markets were established for deer hunting permits, one where hunters could actually buy permits and one identical with the first except hunters were surveyed to assess their willingness to pay for the permits with no cash changing hands. Comparison of the values implied by the two markets revealed a value 25 percent higher in the contingent valuation market.

Primary data collection of this type is also an expensive undertaking. Contingent valuation is, however, a way to allow us to place values on important environmental amenities where market data are sparse or nonexistent and where off-site values are important components of total economic value. As it is refined, this technique should prove to be very useful in future work.

Issue: Environmental Health Risk

Many times, the issue in damage valuation is changes in human health as a result of an externality. This requires the input and effort of many disciplines. Changes in health can result in increased medical costs and lost work days that could be a measure of value, but they do not capture any disutility of illness. To assess the health risk impact of ground water contamination by pesticide use, one needs hydrological knowledge and soil science expertise to track the movement of the chemicals from the field to the ground water reservoir and behavioral, epidemiological and toxicological knowledge to translate ground water contamination into health risk terms.

In modeling health risk generation processes (this type of analysis is also referred to as *risk assessment*) Spear (1978) distinguishes among three processes—contamination, exposure, and dose response. The final product of these processes is health risk. It is measured either by the expected number of individuals who will suffer from a certain negative health condition or by the probability of suffering from a negative health condition resulting from a pollution activity. Here we will use the second definition and denote health risk by r. Certain activities may result in several health risks—risks of mortality, risk of loss of a limb, etc. Spear (1978) argues that a particular health risk can be represented as the product of three functions

$$r = f_3(B_3)f_2(B_2)f_1(B_1, Z)$$

where $f_1(B_1, Z)$ is a function relating contamination to pollution by farmers and damage control activity (B_1) at the affected site. The exposure of an individual to the toxic material is determined by $f_2(B_2) \cdot f_1(B_1, Z)$, where $f_2(B_2)$ is the exposure coefficient and is dependent on activities (education, use of protective clothing, etc.) to reduce exposure. The function $f_3(B_3)$ is a dose-response function relating health risk to exposure levels. Again, it depends on damage control activities—preventive vaccinations, medical treatment, etc.

Schematically, this health (or environmental) risk generating process can be thought of as

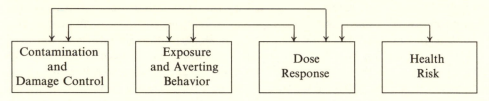

Note the interdependencies this construct reveals. The first two of these functions can be affected by technologies to reduce the health risk involved. The third is the driving force.

Estimates of these functions are fraught with uncertainties because of the randomness of nature, the variability of the environment and affected populations, and substantive gaps in scientific knowledge. In response to these uncertainties, environmental health legislation and regulatory procedures correspond to a *disaster avoidance* to decision making (Beavis and Walker, 1983). Lichtenberg and Zilberman (1988) took a safety rule approach to incorporate these uncertainties into an economic decision-making framework. Their model can be expanded to analyze choices that maximize market welfare subject to a probabilistic constraint that limits health risk below a threshold level $\Re$ with significance level α. Specifically, using the notation we presented earlier their model can be presented as

$$\text{Max } U(Y) - \sum_{i=1}^{3} w_{bi}B_i - w_x X - w_k K - w_a A \qquad (17)$$

$$\text{s.t. prob } [r \le \Re \ge 1 - \alpha]$$

$$\text{and } r = f_3(B_3)f_2(B_2)f_1(B_1, Z)$$

with X, Z, r, and A defined by (11) and (4).

In this case α is the significance level and "prob" denotes probability. Higher α corresponds to greater aversion to uncertainty by the policy makers. With uncertainty aversion, each policy is assessed by its contribution to the reduction of risk and the reduction of uncertainty about risk. Lichtenberg and Zilberman's (1988a–c) analysis demonstrated the value of research that reduces uncertainties and generates better information regarding health benefits and called for expanded research on contamination and exposure processes.

Valuing Life and Limb

Solving the Lichtenberg-Zilberman model for different $\Re$s can generate a tradeoff curve between market welfare (U) and the threshold of health safety not to be exceeded with significance level α. For each point of the curve the slope ($\partial U / \partial \Re$) represents the marginal cost of risk reduction with a margin of safety α. When the risk involved is loss of life, the slope of the tradeoff curve at a point corresponding to an actual policy choice implies an uncertainty adjusted marginal value of saving of life.

The notion of *value of life* plays a prominent role in assessing policies affecting health choices. Mishan (1971) argued that health safety regulations, pesticide policies, and expenditure and designs of road and freeways and similar choices are results of choices based on tradeoffs between cost and risk to life and each implies "statistical value of life" ("value of life," in short). The "value of life" can be thought of as the willingness to pay for risk reduction. Most of these choices involve situations where the risk of life loss for each individual is very small, the affected population is very large, and the value of statistical life is determined by the tradeoff between cost and expected life saved at the margin. For example, suppose a $100,000 increase in annual water treatment cost reduces the risk of death by 10^{-6} for a population of 10,000 people. This cost increase resulted in a saving of .1 statistical lives and implies a value of life of $1,000,000.

Mishan (1971) argued that from an efficiency perspective the discussions that involve small risk events will be based on the same value of statistical life. Zeckhauser (1969, 1970) followed by suggesting that the value of life tends to increase as the risk of the individuals exposed is increasing and their identity becomes known. He called for consistency in value of life choices in decision making involving small risks to unidentified individuals. Reviews of empirical studies (Zeckhauser, 1970; Cropper and Freeman, 1991) show vast variation in values of life implied by both public and private choices. Zeckhauser (1969) attributes this variation to peoples' preferences regarding controllability in risks. Values of life associated with choices controlled by the individual affected (flying a private plane) were much smaller than that from choices controlled by others (flying in an airplane). Lichtenberg and Zilberman (1988) argued that some of the variation in value of life estimates result from the uncertainty associated with estimated parameters of the health risk generation function and suggested that estimates of values of life will be uncertainty adjusted (based on a consensus significance level). They also argued that the differences in estimated values of life from market or nonmarket studies tend to decline as they are adjusted for uncertainty.

Environmental Health Regulation: Empirical Evidence

Some recent studies have analyzed agriculture-related environmental health problems using the framework presented above. Lichtenberg et al. (1989) estimated the tradeoffs associated with water quality regulation (in this case, standards for DBCP contamination of drinking water) in Fresno County, California. More stringent standards reduce the risks of cancer at an increasing cost (owing to the need to install filters or drill new wells in more areas). The risk estimates are uncertain because of randomness associated with exposure and uncertainty of dose response and contamination estimates. Figure 6.8 depicts three tradeoff curves. The one closest to the origin depicts tradeoff between costs and mean level of risk, the second curve between costs and a risk level that will not be exceeded at a 95 percent probability, and the third between costs and risk levels that will not be exceeded at a 99 percent probability. It is obvious that uncertainty and risk aversion matter. Also, abatement costs to assure safety often increase at an increasing rate. It costs about $80 million to assure that for a resident of Fresno County, the cancer risk of drinking water is below 10^{-6} with a 95 percent probability; and it will cost $100 million to assure that cancer risk will not exceed the same upper level with a 99 percent probability.

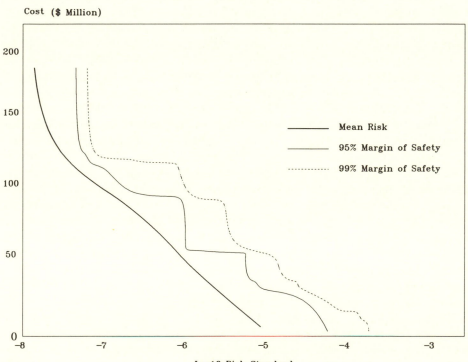

Figure 6.8. Risk cost tradeoffs in DBCP contamination and drinking water quality: the least cost approach.

In developing the tradeoff curve, the model presented least cost policies that restrict risk below various threshold levels at the 95 and 99 percent probability levels. These policies recognized the heterogeneity of the population in the region. For agricultural sections of Fresno County, the policies set water quality standards (upper bound DBCP concentrations) that, if violated, led to installment of filters. For urban sections, the policy set water quality standards that, if violated, led to drilling new wells. The reason for the policy differences is that in the urban sections a large number of people consume water pumped from each well, and the cost of drilling a new well is shared by many individuals. In the rural sections each well may supply one or two families, and the cost of drilling per user is much larger than the cost of filter installment. Here the heterogeneity of the population affected requires a site-specific policy as well as monitoring of DBCP contamination at each site. This is feasible in the Fresno situation, but cost of monitoring and design of site-specific regulation may be quite high and may hinder the overall cost effectiveness of policies that require these efforts. This was pointed out in the following study of pesticides contamination in ground water.

Anderson et al. (1985) examine the relationship between Aldicarb (a highly toxic pesticide at low dosages) applications on potato fields in Rhode Island and Aldicarb concentrations in nearby wells with the goal of establishing "optimal" application rates. They hypothesized that the contamination of a particular well is a function of the Aldicarb application rate on nearby potato fields, the timing of applications, soil characteristics, and well depth and distance. Assuming the objective is to assure that all wells in the area of influence conform to the EPA maximum contaminant level of 10 ppb at minimum farmer cost, they found that the safe applied rate for a 40 foot well is approximately 1.3 pounds a.i. of Aldicarb per acre in their study area. Instead of a complete ban on the use of Aldicarb on potatoes, their results suggest a combination of lower application rates and relocation of shallow wells to a site farther removed from the potato fields. Their concluding comments include, ". . . it may be necessary to set on-site standards on a regional basis. . . . Clearly, the data requirements for setting on-site standards are staggering."

Issue: Agricultural Waste Management

The management of waste has become one of America's biggest problems in the latter part of the 20th century. The externalities associated with agricultural waste, concentrated by larger production units and intensified by proximity to population centers, are a major source of concern for the safety of ground and surface water in some areas.

Waste is an economic term. That which is defined as "waste" very often can change with changing economic conditions. It is important, therefore, in determining strategies for waste management to have knowledge not only of the technical aspects of the generation function, but also of the important economic factors affecting waste generation. One important economic factor in the generation of some types of agricultural waste is the value of output. Consider, for example, graded agricultural products such as tablestock potatoes. Off-grade, or rejected, potatoes often end up in "cull piles" that pose a threat to local ground water supplies as well as act as a vector for disease for neighboring potato fields. The size of these cull piles is inversely related to the price of tablestock potatoes in a particular season, however. As the value of the crop increases, the opportunity cost of culling increases, as well.

Tolley et al. (1985) examined the economics of solid waste generation and the supply of waste disposal services for municipal waste. Their analytical framework and empirical techniques should prove useful for analysis of the demand for and supply of agricultural waste. They examine the demand for waste disposal services (the waste generation function) and find that it is a function of the economic determinants of demand similar to any other demand function. The demand for agricultural waste disposal services should also be a function of the usual determinants of demand, although there has been no empirical analysis of this problem that we know of to date. The supply of waste disposal services in the case of agricultural waste would be a function of the relative costs of disposal options such as recycling, holding facilities, etc.

Potential remedies to the agricultural waste externality problem include waste reduction, recycling, and improved disposal methods. Each situation should be analyzed carefully in the context of the market for waste disposal services and keeping in mind the major points emphasized in this chapter to determine the optimal remedy or combination thereof for the efficient solution to the problem.

There have been several recent empirical studies of agricultural waste management regulation. Moffitt et al. (1978) examined the problem of water pollution from large dairy herds in California. They used a putty-clay production function approach to examine the relative efficiency of taxes on dairy waste disposal versus dairy waste control standards. Using an empirical estimate of the relationship between dairy waste and added water salinity, they derived the cost and pollution tradeoff curves under a pollution tax, least-cost standards, and proposed standards for the Santa Ana region. Figure 6.9 illustrates their results.

The proposed standard did not distinguish between different types of waste (solid and liquid), and its enforcement to meet the regional standard would have eliminated 66 percent of the economic surplus generated by the industry forcing 40 percent of the dairies out of production. A least cost waste management regulation that regulates differently solid and liquid waste attains regional pollution targets (3,600 tons of salt contribution) while reducing surplus generated by the industry by only 10 percent. This policy was less efficient than a tax, but only by 15 percent. On the other hand, it serves to demonstrate what was argued in the conceptual discussion. Net income of producers under the least cost standard was much higher than under the tax, and that may serve as a reason for the dairymen to support such a policy.

In another study Lichtenberg and Zilberman (1987) examined alternate policies (taxes and standards) to regulate dairy run-off contamination of shellfish in San Francisco Bay. The analysis explicitly recognized the heterogeneity among dairymen and the uncertainty that was due to rainfall and weather variability. They derived a tradeoff curve between the cost of building run-off containment facilities and the risks of food poisoning. Their analysis applied the model presented in (17). Their results show that the marginal costs of safety are

Annual Cost (Million Dollars)

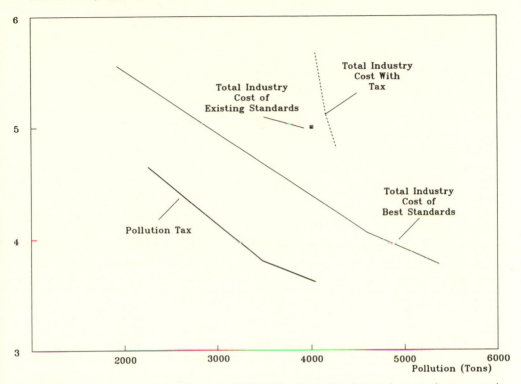

Figure 6.9. Abatement cost, pollution tradeoff in the Santa Ana dairy industry under taxes and standards.

increasing (the costs of marginal reduction in risk are greater for smaller risks). Moreover, the cost induced by higher reliability (higher probability that risk will not exceed threshold levels) increases as risk becomes smaller. The analysis in this case was made possible by a survey of all of the dairies (300) that required much time and effort. The survey, however, allowed establishment of individual standards for each dairy—a more theoretically efficient solution that may be difficult to monitor and enforce.

A major difficulty with deciding upon the optimal tax or *surcharge* to achieve the desired level of control of an externality is knowing how producers will respond to different tax levels. Several studies have approached this problem by estimating the derived demand elasticities from a theory of the firm framework. McLamb and Seagraves (1979) estimate the percent change in the derived quantity demanded of waste water, biological oxygen demand (BOD) and suspended solids (SS) with respect to the percent changes in the prices of each for poultry processing firms generating waste water into municipal water systems. Their results indicate that processors are responsive to a surcharge both on additional BOD and SS. An example of the derived demand for waste water treatment from this study appears in Figure 6.10.

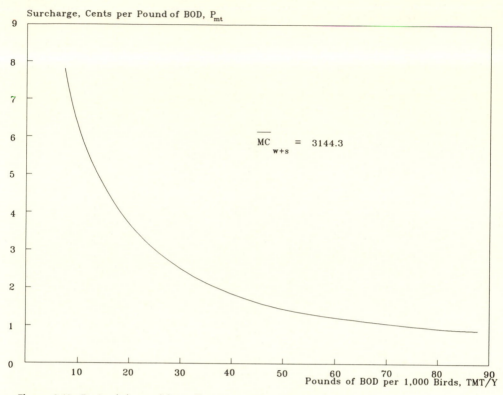

Figure 6.10. Derived demand for pollution control of poultry processors.

Monitoring and Accountability

Given that an appropriate combination of emissions standards and averting behavior, such as the solution above, can be found, the problem remains of monitoring the behavior of the affected particles. In some cases, this can be accomplished at a reasonable cost. In others, it cannot. The problem becomes more complex when the source of the pollution cannot be traced to identifiable economic units. This is the case with nonpoint source pollution. Acid precipitation is an example of a *nonpoint source externality problem.* The cost of determining each polluter's degree of accountability and of monitoring compliance with a policy option easily could become prohibitive in these cases.

Another problem is what to monitor. For example, past thinking by the experts was that monitoring average exposure levels to air pollution was correct, while the current thinking is that peak exposure levels are more important in estimating the health consequences.

Issue: Risk Perceptions

One issue drawing the recent attention of economists, other social scientists, and policy makers is the public's reaction to various types of environmental and health risks. The reaction, in many cases, has been much stronger than the statistical

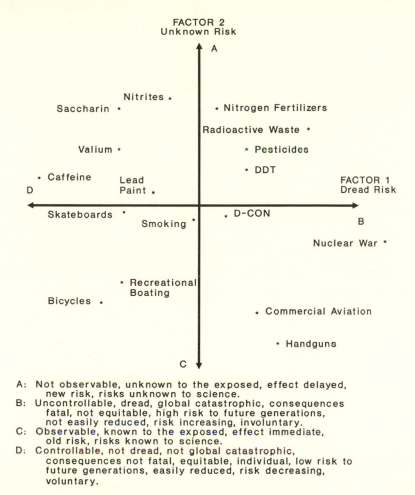

FACTOR 2
Unknown Risk

A: Not observable, unknown to the exposed, effect delayed,
   new risk, risks unknown to science.
B: Uncontrollable, dread, global catastrophic, consequences
   fatal, not equitable, high risk to future generations,
   not easily reduced, risk increasing, involuntary.
C: Observable, known to the exposed, effect immediate,
   old risk, risks known to science.
D: Controllable, not dread, not global catastrophic,
   consequences not fatal, equitable, individual, low risk to
   future generations, easily reduced, risk decreasing,
   voluntary.

Figure 6.11. Classification of risks by two factors.

probability of loss of life or health would predict. This has led to serious investigation of the perception of risk and to recent attempts to account for this phenomenon in economic models of individual behavior.

Some examples of this type of reaction include the substantial decrease in demand and loss of farm or processor income from the discovery and announcement of the presence of cyanide in two Chilean grapes, the detection of Alar in apples, the detection of small amounts of a toxic substance in the Hawaii milk supply, or the discovery of benzene in a few lots of Perrier bottles. Social scientists have found that these types of reactions may not be wholly explained by the public's ignorance of the risks (in terms of statistical probabilities) but more by the nature of the risks themselves. This implies that improved communication of the statistical probabilities may not be the solution.

One method to attempt to quantify the components of risk perceptions is illustrated in Figure 6.11. This figure provides a representation of survey respondents' rankings of various risks according to the characteristics embodied in the risks (Slovic, 1989). Points to the northeast in Figure 6.11 have higher levels of both sets of undesirable characteristics of risk. Further, this study also provides from the same set of respondents the intensity of their attitudes in favor of regulation of the causes of each of the risks in Figure 6.11. The respondents showed a stronger desire for regulation of the risks to the right of the vertical line in Figure 6.11, with those in the northeast quadrant receiving the stongest response. Notice the relative position of the risks associated with agriculture!

This line of inquiry shows promise in improving our ability to describe and quantify the characteristics of risk and to incorporate them in our behavioral models. A parallel line of inquiry is the development of extensions of the standard economic models of behavior under risk to accommodate these risk characteristics. The result of this effort so far is a set of multicomponent extensions of expected utility theory such as regret, rejoice models (Loomes and Sudgen, 1982; Bell, 1982), the multiattribute utility model (Finkelstein and Chalfant, 1989), and the status model (Buschena and Zilberman, 1990). These approaches allow the incorporation of risk characteristics other than statistical probabilities, such as anxiety or fear, proximity to bankruptcy, or multiperiod risks, into the analysis.

The current consensus seems to be that we may be moving away from a unified model useful for all risky situations and the characteristics of the risk and/or the decision maker may dictate different analytic approaches. Further, formally taking account of risk perceptions in policy formulation models, such as those described previously, is important. Much work is left to be done in this area before we are able to make useful predictions or recommendations in areas where externalities involve environmental or health risks.

CONCLUDING REMARKS

As we discussed at the beginning of this chapter, there are many types of externalities associated with the agricultural industry in the United States. The externalities that, perhaps, cause the most concern are the ones stemming from the production and processing of agricultural products that affect segments of society outside of agriculture. In particular, they stem from agriculture's use of natural resources including soil, water, air, and genetic diversity. Some of these externalities are embodied in agricultural products and some are not. Some create external effects in the present period and others create intertemporal problems.

Most of the remainder of this book is about the relationship between agricultural production and our stock of natural resources. Whole chapters are devoted to agricultural use of land, water, pesticides, and new technology as it relates to resource use. Before proceeding with these chapters, it is important to keep in mind that the isolation of the issues implied by these chapter divisions is, in large part, artificial. There are important spillover effects and distortions to be considered both within the externality generation process itself and across resource issues.

Some agricultural externality problems and solutions are notably interdependent across resources. Soil erosion and ground and surface water contamination are two salient examples, but there are others. For both of these problems, fairly sophisticated production technologies and allocation schemes to solve each externality problem have evolved through public and private efforts. Some interesting interdependencies in those solutions also have become apparent.

Consider the example of soil erosion. One of the soil-saving techniques that has been developed to deal with this problem is generally referred to as conservation (or minimum) tillage. This technique, which leaves as much of the soil undisturbed and as much of the previous crop residue on the field as practicable, may be responsible, in some cases, for substituting an intertemporal externality associated with the loss of soil productivity for a more immediate health risk associated with ground water contamination. Conservation tillage restricts weed and insect control to methods other than cultivation and, therefore, may be responsible for increased pesticides in the ground water in some areas. The increased crop residue may harbor more insects and plant pathogens as well, creating additional potential ground water problems when these pests are treated with pesticides.

Moreover, farmers may be uncertain about the effect conservation tillage will have on potential crop damage from pests. They may tend to increase their use of pesticides in response. Marra and Carlson (1986) found, however, that, with increased familiarity with conservation tillage over time through learning or educational efforts, soybean farmers tended to reduce the initial increase in pesticide use. More certainty about the technology may, therefore, reduce the tradeoff between one externality and another.

Identification of the interdependencies and the resulting tradeoffs is a valuable contribution we can make as economists. Both farmers and the affected parties are subject to uncertainties about agricultural externalities and the technologies that evolve to deal with them. More information about the uncertain relationships involved in the externality generation and pollution abatement processes will likely have net social benefits. We likely are still at the stage of extremely high marginal gains from additional information about these relationships and their inter dependencies. We, as those most concerned with the economic relationships involved, should combine our expertise with those in other disciplines to provide producers, consumers, and policy makers with the information they need to make informed decisions.

There are other externalities associated with the agricultural industry in the United States that are not a direct result of agricultural production. One is the positive externality of open, rural lands discussed previously. Another is the set of externalities generated primarily by other segments of society that affect agricultural production firms. Among these are the problems of acid rain, ozone depletion, and global climate change. These issues will be discussed in more detail in the final chapter in this book.

REFERENCES

Adams, R.M. et al. "An Economic Assessment of Air Pollution to Selected Crops in Southern California." *Journal of Environmental Economics and Management* 9:42–58, 1982.

Adams, R.M. et al. "Pollution, Agriculture and Social Welfare: the Case of Acid Deposition." *Canadian Journal of Agricultural Economics* 34:3–19, 1986.

Anderson, G.D., J.J. Opaluch, and W. Sullivan. "Nonpoint Agricultural Pollution: Pesticide Contamination of Groundwater Supplies." *American Journal of Agricultural Economics* 67(5):1238–1243, 1985.

Babcock, B.A., E. Lichtenberg, and D. Zilberman. "Estimating the Productivity of Pesticides in Controlling Yield and Quality Damage." *American Journal of Agricultural Economics* 74:163–172, 1992.

Baumol, W.J. and W.E. Oates. *The Theory of Environmental Policy.* Englewood Cliffs, NJ: Prentice-Hall, 1975.

Baumol, W.J. and W.E. Oates. "The Use of Standards and Prices for Protection of the Environment." *Swedish Journal of Economics* 73:42–54, 1971.

Beach, D. and G. Carlson. "A Hedonic Analysis of Herbicides: Does Safety Matter?" *American Journal of Agricultural Economics* 75:(forthcoming), 1993.

Beavis, B. and M. Walker. "Achieving Environmental Standards with Stochastic Discharges." *Journal of Environmental Economics and Management* 10:103–111, 1983.

Bell, D.E. "Regret Theory in Decision Making Under Uncertainty." *Operations Research* 30:961–981, 1982.

Bishop, R. and T. Hieberlein. "Measuring values of Extramarket Goods: Are Indirect Measures Biased?" *American Journal of Agricultural Economics* 61:926–930, 1979.

Bockstael, N. et al. "Recreation." In J.B. Braden and C.D. Kolstad (eds.): *Measuring the Demand for Environmental Quality.* Amsterdam: North-Holland Publishing Company, 1991.

Boyle, K.J. and R.C. Bishop. "Welfare Measurements Using Contingent Valuation: A Comparison of Techniques." *American Journal of Agricultural Economics* 70:20–28, 1988.

Buchanan, J. and Stubblebine. "Externality." *Economica* 371–384, 1962.

Buchanan, J.M. and G. Tullock. "Polluters' Profits and Political Response: Direct Controls Versus Taxes." *American Economic Review* 65(1):139–147, 1975.

Buschena, D. and D. Zilberman, "What We Know About Decisionmaking Under Uncertainty and Why Do We Not Use What We Know." In *Quantifying Long Run Risks in Agriculture*, proc. S-232 conf. Gainesville, FL. Univ. of Florida, 1990.

Calabresi, G. and A. Douglas Melamed. "Property Rules, Liability Rules and Inalienability: One View of the Cathedral." *Harvard Law Review* 85(6):1089–1128, 1972.

Coase R.H. "The Problem of Social Cost." *Journal of Law and Economics* 3:1–44, 1960.

Cooper, J. and J. Loomis. "Economic Value of Wildlife Resources in San Joaquin Valley: Hunting and Viewing Values." Unpublished manuscript, U.C. Davis, Davis, CA.

Crocker, T.D. "Externalities, Property Rights, and Transactions Costs: An Empirical Study." *Journal of Law and Economics* 14:451–464, 1971.

Cropper, M.L., L.B. Deck, and K.E. McConnell. "On the Choice of Functional Form for Hedonic Price Functions." *Review of Economics and Statistics* LXX/4:668–675, 1988.

Cropper, M.L. and A.M. Freeman III "Environmental Health Effects." In J.B.

Braden and C.D. Kolstad (eds.): *Measuring the Demand for Environmental Quality*. Amsterdam: North-Holland Pubishing Company, 1991.

Dasgupta, P. and G. Heal. "The Optimal Depletion of Exhaustible Resources." *Review of Economic Studies, Symposium on the Economics of Exhaustible Resources* 41:3–28, 1974.

Demsetz, H. "Toward a Theory of Property Rights." *American Economic Review* 57(2):347–359, 1967.

Finkelstein, I. and J.A. Chalfant. Portfolio Choices in the Presence of Other Risks. Dept. of Agricultural and Resource Economics Working Paper No. 505, University of California at Berkeley, Berkeley, CA, 1989.

Fisher, AC. *Resource and Environmental Economics*. Cambridge: Cambridge University Press, 1981.

Gordon, H.S. "The Economic Theory of a Common-Property Resource: The Fishery." *Journal of Political Economy* 62:124–42, 1954.

Gregory, R. and T. McDaniels. Valuing Environmental Losses: What Promise Does the Right Measure Hold? *Policy Sciences* 20:11–26, 1987.

Hardin, G. "The Tragedy of the Commons." *Science* 162(2):1243–1248, 1968.

Harper, C.R. and D. Zilberman. "Regulating Pesticides Under Uncertainty: Application to Cotton Pest Control Workers." Dept. of Agric. and Res. Econ., Univ. of MA, Res. Paper Series #88-1.

Hayami, Y. and V. Ruttan. *Agricultural Development: An International Respective*. Baltimore: Johns Hopkins University Press, 1985.

Helfand, G.E. *The Effects on Production and Profits of Different Pollution Control Standards*. Unpublished PhD. dissertation. Dept. of Agricultural Economics, University of California-Davis, Davis, CA, 1989.

Hitzhusen, F., R. Macgregor, and D. Southgate. "Private and Social Cost-Benefit Perspectives and a Case Application on Reservoir Sedimentation Management." *Water International* 9:181–184, 1984.

Hochman, E., D. Pines, and D. Zilberman. "The Effects of Pollution Taxation on the Pattern of Resource Allocation: The Downstream Diffusion Case *Quarterly Journal of Economics* XCI(4):625–638, 1977.

Hochman, E. and D. Zilberman. "Examination of Environmental Policies Using Production and Pollution Microparameter Distributions." *Econometrica* 46(4)739–760, 1978.

Hochman, E. and D. Zilberman. "Two-Goal Environmental Policy: An Integration of Micro and Macro Ad Hoc decision Rules." *Journal of Environmental Economics and Management* 6:152–174, 1979.

Just, R. and J. Antle. "Interactions between Agricultural and Environmental Policies." *American Economic Review* 80:197–202, 1990.

Just, R.E. and D. Zilberman. "Asymmetry of Taxes and Subsidies in Regulating Stochastic Mishap" *Quarterly Journal of Economics* XCIII(1):139–148, 1979.

Krutilla, J.V. and A.C. Fisher. *The Economics of Natural Environments*. Baltimore: Johns Hopkins Press, 1975, pp. 84–121, 122–146.

Lancaster, K. "A New Approach to Consumer Theory." *Journal of Political Economy* 74:132–157, 1966.

Lichtenberg, E. and D. Zilberman. "Efficient Regulation of Environmental Health Risks." *Quarterly Journal of Economics* CIII/1:167–178, 1988.

Lichtenberg, E. and D. Zilberman. "Regulation of Marine Contamination under Environmental Uncertainty: Shellfish Contamination in California." *Marine Resource Economics* 4:211–225, 1987.

Lichtenberg, E., D. Zilberman, and K.T. Bogen. "Regulating Environmental Health Risks Under Uncertainty: Groundwater Contamination in California." *Journal of Environmental Economics and Management* 17:22–34, 1989.

Loehman, E., D. Boldt, and K. Chaikin. "Measuring the Benefits of Air Quality in the San Francisco Bay Area." Report to the U.S. Environmental Protection Agency, Office of Policy Analysis, 1984.

Loomes, G. and R. Sudgen. "Regret Theory: An Alternative Theory of Rational Choices Under Uncertainty." *Economic Journal* 92:805–824, 1982.

Maloney, M.T. and R.E. McCormick. "A Positive Theory of Environmental Quality Regulation." *Journal of Law and Economics* 25:99–123, 1982.

Marra, M.C. and G.A. Carlson. *Double-Cropping Wheat and Soybeans in the Southeast: Input Use and Patterns of Adoption*, USDA Ag. Econ. Rpt. 552, U.S.G.P.O., Washington, DC, 1986.

McLamb, D.W. and J.A. Seagraves. "Industrial Demand for City-Supplied Water and Waste Treatment." *Journal of Environmental Economics and Management* 17:22–34, 1979.

Meade, J.E. "External Economies and Diseconomies in Competitive Situation." *Economic Journal* 62:54–67, 1952.

Mishan, E.J. "The Postwar Literature on Externalities: An Interpretative Essay." *Journal of Economic Literature* 9:1–28, 1971.

Mishan, E.J. "What is the Optimal Level of Pollution?" *Journal of Political Economy* 82(6):1287–1299, 1974.

Mitchell, R.C. and R.T. Carson. *Using Surveys to Value Public Goods: An Assessment of the Contingent Valuation Method*. Washington: Resources for the Future, 1989.

Moffitt, L. J., D. Zilberman, and R. Just. "A 'Putty-Clay' Approach to Aggregation of Production/Pollution Possibilities: An Application in Dairy Waste Control." *American Journal of Agricultural Economics* 60(3):452–459, 1978.

Palmquist, R.B. "Hedonic Methods." In J.B. Braden and C.D. Kolstad (eds.): *Measuring the Demand for Environmental Quality*. Amsterdam: North-Holland, 1991.

Pigou, A.C. *The Economics of Welfare*, 4th Ed., Section II. London: Macmillan & Co., Ltd., 1932.

Polinsky, A.M. "On the Choice Between Property Rules and Liability Rules." *Economic Inquiry* XVIII:233–246, 1980a.

Polinsky, A.M. "The Efficiency of Paying Compensation in the Pigouvian Solution to Externality Problems." *Journal of Environmental Economics and Management* 7(2):142–148, 1980b.

Randall, A. and J. Stoll. "Existence Value in a Total Valuation Framework." In R. Rowe and L. Chestnut (eds.): *Managing Air Quality and Scenic Resources at National Parks*. Boulder, Co.: Westview Press, 1983.

Rausser, G. and R. Howitt. "Stochastic Control of Environmental Externalities." *Annals of Economics and Social Measurement* 4:271–292, 1975.

Rosen, S. "Hedonic Prices and Implicit Markets: Product Differentiation in Pure Competition." *Journal of Political Economy* 82:34–55, 1974.

Ruttan, V.W. "Technology and the Environment." *American Journal of Agricultural Economics* 53:707–717, 1971.

Scott, A. "The Fishery: The Objectives of Sole Ownership." *Journal of Political Economy* 63:116–124, 1955.

Smith, V.K. "Household Production Functions and Environmental Benefit Measurement." In J.B. Braden and C.D. Kolstad (eds.): *Measuring the Demand for Environmental Quality.* Amsterdam: North-Holland Publishing Company, 1991.

Spear, R.C. *Organophosphate Residue Poisoning Among Agricultural Workers in the U.S.: Towards a Strategy for a Long Term Solution.* CRES Report AS-R-18. Australian National Univ., Sidney, 1978.

Tolley, G. et al. (eds.). *Environmental Policy: Solid Wastes*, Vol. 4. Cambridge, Mass.: Ballinger Publishing Company, 1985.

Weinstein, M.C. and R.J. Zeckhauser. "The Optimal Consumption of Depletable Natural Resources." *Quarterly Journal of Economics* 89:371–392, 1975.

Weitzman, M.L. "Prices vs. Quantities." *Review of Economic Studies* 41:477–491, 1974.

Welsh, M. *Exploring the Accuracy of the Contingent Valuation Method.* Unpublished PhD. dissertation, Department of Agricultural Economics, Univ. of Wisconsin, Madison, WI, 1986.

Witcomb, D. *Externalities and Welfare.* New York: Columbia University Press, 1972.

Zeckhauser, R.J. "Resource Allocation with Probabilistic Individual Preferences." *American Economic Review* 59:546–552, 1969.

Zeckhauser, R.J. "Uncertainty and the Need for Collective Action." In R. Haveman and J. Margolis (eds.): *Public Expenditure and Policy Analysis.* Chicago: Markham Publishing, 1970.

7

Pesticides and Pest Management

GERALD A. CARLSON AND MICHAEL E. WETZSTEIN

The publication of the book *Silent Spring* by Rachael Carons in 1962 marked the beginning of an era of widespread public concern over the environmental effects of pesticides. Over the past 30 years, improvements in the chemistry of detection of minute quantities of pesticides in food and water has heightened public concern about food and water safety. Legal suits to force the Environmental Protection Agency (EPA) to ban or severely restrict use of particular pesticides have frequently occurred. Over this same period, there have been increases in public research and extension activities to develop improved management of agricultural and other pests. Integrated pest management (IPM) to reduce pesticide use and improve farmer profits and pesticide regulations for human and environmental safety have become a two-pronged public program to provide both safe, low-cost food and a high quality environment.

After a brief discussion of trends in pesticide use and special features of pesticide resources, we begin our examination of pesticide and pest management by reviewing models of individual producers. Pest management decision models are one of the primary inputs in developing recommendations to farmers on the quantities and types of pesticides and other resources to use. Several prescriptive models that have been used to assist farmers in substituting management for pesticides are reviewed. Next, we present several empirical models that have been used to understand and evaluate pesticide and other pest management choices of farmers. In the last section aggregate models are examined. Because pests and pesticides often have external effects on consumers and producers, aggregate models for analysis of group pest management, pesticide externalities, and pesticide regulations are needed by economists and local and national policy makers.

Pests, like adverse weather, are important sources of crop damage. Agricultural pests include insects, diseases, nematodes, mites, and weeds that reduce crop or livestock yield or quality. A pest problem exists when insects or some other species competes with man. *Pesticides* include a wide range of chemical compounds used to reduce pest levels or reduce pest damage. Other pest management resources are resistant crop varieties, pest predators, and all types of cultural practices. Many new and innovative pest management strategies are currently in the developing stages. The process of combining multiple methods for managing pest populations with other components of a crop management system is commonly referred to as *integrated pest management*. The emphasis in IPM systems is on including all efficient forms of resource management to control pest numbers and damage rather than, necessarily, killing all pests. In some cases individual farmers or groups of farmers can completely eradicate pest species from certain areas, but usually pest management involves suppressing pest populations in an economically efficient manner to enhance long-term profitability.

Pest management inputs include a wide range of labor, chemical, mechanical, and genetic, as well as land resources, but pesticides remain a major pest management resource. Units of pesticide use can be measured in pounds of active ingredients, acres of treatment with standard dose, or expenditures per season. Because of the wide range of pesticide efficacy (kill rate, longevity, spectrum of pests controlled) and different chemical combinations, caution is needed in assuming that simple quantity units such as pounds or acres treated are equivalent and can be easily aggregated to measure the amount of resource use.

Most actions to manage pests are taken by individual farmers to maximize profits and obtain acceptably low levels of income variability. However, there are special features of both pests and pest management resources that create unique resource management problems. Because some pest types are mobile, severe open access or common property problems may arise. That is, property rights to pests are not assigned and individual farmers may not consider the effects of their pest management actions or inactions on nearby farmers or others. Similarly, pesticides can move with wind currents, water, or other media to cause damage to nontarget species including adjacent crops, livestock, wildlife, and domestic animals. Pesticides may also affect the human health of farmers, farm workers, and other people who come into contact with farming or farm products. Because of the potential external effects of both pests and pesticides to producers, consumers, and laborers, independent choices by these economic agents may not provide the level of pest control and safety that people desire.

A vast array of federal and state regulations affects pest movement and pesticide use. Methods of pesticide application, maximum dosages, preharvest intervals, and restrictions on use near water are specified on legally binding pesticide labels. Labor protection is provided by field reentry limits, loader-mixer handling rules, and required warning signs. The effects of regulatory constraints on production costs and human safety are frequent areas of scientific and economic research. Since some pesticides persist for long periods with accumulation of residues, models involving time and stock externalities described in Chapters 2 and 3 are relevant for pest management and policy analysis.

Pest control activities are also affected by public and private research to find substitutes for pesticides. Genetic resources (crop varieties, biotechnology products), new trapping systems (pheromones), and improved pest monitoring and forecast systems are major recent developments. Public investments in pest management systems are primarily justified by reduction in pesticide externalities and size

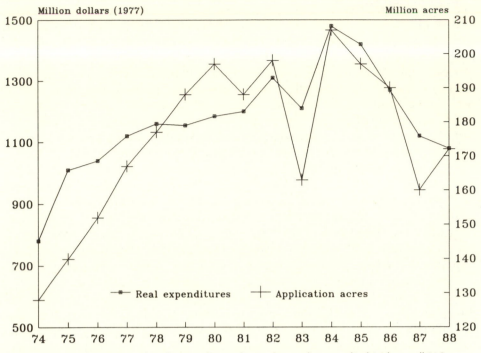

Figure 7.1. Applications and real expenditures for soybean plus corn herbicides – all U.S.

economies in the development and use of more efficient pest control methods that are not easily patented.

Total pesticide use in the United States has steadily increased over the period 1950 to 1984 (see Chapter 1). However, for all pesticides used in the United States, the upward trend in total use that has occurred over the past 30 and 40 years began to reverse itself in the 1980s. For example, total expenditures and acre applications of herbicides used on corn and soybeans are shown in Figure 7.1. The upward trend in the past was partly due to falling prices of pesticides relative to both pest management resources and other agricultural inputs (Dabrakow and Reichelderfer, 1988). At the same time, herbicides and some other pesticides have improved in quality. For example, many insecticide treatments were formerly applied at dosages of about one pound of active ingredient per acre, while today many products require about one-tenth to one-fourth that amount. In addition, herbicides have been developed that are less damaging to the primary crop and nearby crops. One of the current research areas in the application of biotechnology in agriculture is to develop crop varieties that are more tolerant to existing herbicides. This may allow lower dosages to be used, which will result in lower external costs.

Public and private research funds are incurred in an effort to discover new pesticides. The search process is complex because both efficacy and safety characteristics are needed. In recent years large sums have been expended for

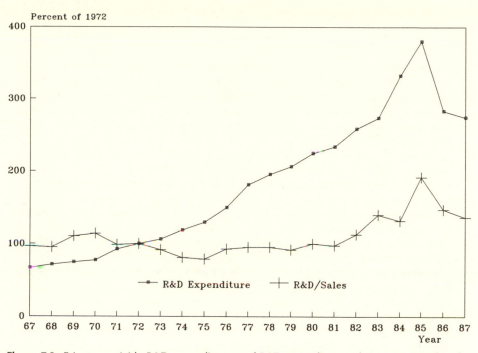

Figure 7.2. Private pesticide R&D expenditures and R&D expenditures relative to pesticide sales.

herbicide discovery because this has been a rapidly expanding market. At the same time development of resistance to pesticides, particularly by insects and mites, has offered new opportunities for replacement insecticides. The effect of increased stringency in pesticide safety regulations on research discovery effort is uncertain because it offers both new opportunities when compounds are canceled, but stiffer regulations also lower the chance that any given compound will meet safety and environmental standards. Private R & D expenditures for pesticides are highly dependent on level of pesticide sales. However, the upward trend in R & D expenditures per dollar of sales has reversed itself in the last few years. (See Figure 7.2.) The vignette (Box 7.1) describes the links between insecticide resistance, regulations, and insecticide research efforts.

A final feature of pest management is the important role played by information. Pest characteristics (species, age, density) are often highly variable across fields and over time. Pesticide efficacy is affected by changing weather, pest characteristics, and crop status. The possibilities of substituting management, pest control advice, and pest density information for scheduled treatments of pesticides are more viable for cases in which pesticide efficacy and potential pest damage are more variable. Information itself can have public good characteristics that may lead to its underproduction and underuse by individual farmers. Both the private decision-making process and regional approaches to pest management information are developed in the following sections.

Box 7.1. Technical Change, Insecticide Resistance, Externalities, and Induced Pesticide Regulations

When the external plus private costs of particular pesticides increase relative to those for substitute pest controls, there are economic and political incentives for changes in pesticide regulations and private research efforts. Incentives to speed the discovery and approval of new pesticides (and banning of others) under federal legislation is well illustrated by the use pattern of major insecticide classes during the 1960s through the 1980s.

During the 1960s most insecticides used on cotton, fruit, vegetables, and other crops were organochlorines such as DDT. The high level of use of these relatively inexpensive and persistent compounds led to rapid development of resistance by major species of insect pests. This made the compounds less effective relative to available organophosphate insecticides. Private costs of using the organochlorides per unit of output were rising relative to substitute materials as well as nonchemical controls (crop rotation, pest monitoring). At the same time there was increased scientific evidence on the link between use of organochlorides and environmental degradation such as the thinning of the eggshells of birds and the build-up of the long-lasting chlorine compounds in food chains. The external costs of organochlorine use loomed even higher when tests on laboratory animals indicated that, at high dosages, some of the compounds were carcinogenic or teratogenic to mammals. Beginning in 1972 with DDT, over the course of 8 years EPA banned or tightly restricted the use of all organochlorine insecticides.

The organochlorides were rapidly replaced with organophosphate and carbamate insecticides, which had been developed during the 1950s and 1960s. These materials were less persistent, but they were much more toxic to farmers and field workers. Field reentry regulations and extension education programs were instituted to help prevent direct intoxications. There was private development of new loading equipment and of materials to encapsulate pesticides to help reduce human and wildlife exposure. There was also technical change in the form of discovery and development of synthetic sex attractants, called pheromones, for many insect species during the 1970s. These, along with computers and advances in insect management and monitoring practices, helped farmers and pest control advisors more closely tie insecticide applications to pest densities.

However, insecticide resistance and potential health effects of the organophosphate materials gave rise to a new class of insecticides beginning in the late 1970s. Synthetic pyrethroid insecticides were rapidly introduced. They could be applied at much lower rates (about 1/10 to 1/20) and they were very effective against most foliar insect species. The lower rates and relatively low acute toxicity of these materials to mammals made them safer to farm workers, wildlife, and food consumers. But during the late 1980s insect resistance to the synthetic pyrethroids began to appear. Also, development of pyrethroid compounds, which move readily in soils or are taken up by crop roots, has eluded scientist and left important groups of insects to be controlled by crop rotation and soil insecticides. Residues of some of the latter compounds can be found in food, ground water, or surface water. There are renewed political pressures to ban more pesticides.

The cycles of increased external costs, and reduced private benefits (from resistance), leading to increased pesticide regulations and increased incentives for new pesticide discoveries represent a complex example of induced institutional change and induced technical change, respectively. The biological dynamics of pesticide resistance development together with the expanding demand for safe food, water, and working conditions give rise to investments in new technologies and more stringent pesticide regulations. Pesticide restrictions in turn affect the speed of development of resistance to the remaining insecticides. Profitability of research investments are changed by both pesticide bans and resistance development. New discoveries in biotechnology are allowing genetic manipulations of crops so that they will develop and express "naturally occurring" insecticides. Models, data and methodologies for estimating and understanding these innovations, and regulatory processes are needed if we are to have a steady supply of safe pest management tools available (Carlson, 1977, 1989).

FIRM DECISIONS AND BEHAVIOR IN PEST MANAGEMENT

To understand how farmers make pest management choices, and to assist biological researchers in developing specific *pest control recommendations* it is helpful to develop decision models. These models begin with the standard static optimization framework searching for marginal conditions (see Chapter 2). However, there are features of the pest damage abatement process that can make input demand and optimal pest control conditions different from conventional optimal input use patterns. First, pests affect plant growth and yield in specific ways. Second, pesticides and other pest management inputs are less costly to use jointly with other inputs or in fixed dosages regardless of crop stage or pest density. Frequently, they directly affect crop growth and product quality. Pesticides are sometimes rendered less effective by the presence of beneficial organisms, which when disrupted lead to higher levels of pests in later periods. In addition, inputs such as fertilizer, water, and cultural practices can alter starting pest population levels or pest growth rates. Finally, farmers often have more limited information on pest levels than they do on the levels of other inputs such as labor, machinery, and soil fertility. Each of these features is examined to determine how it can influence optimal farmer behavior.

Economic Threshold Models

One frequently used decision model is the *economic threshold*. This concept recognizes the importance of pest density or potential crop loss in the decision to use a pesticide or other pest management resources. The idea of keying the timing of pesticide use to pest density is an old one, used formally in insect control recommendations since the 1930s. Later, Stern and associates (1959) noted that detectable crop yield reductions did not occur in many crop–pest situations until a minimum "threshold" level of pest density was observed. The importance of marginal pest control costs, marginal pest damage, and timing of the pest damage was introduced by Headley (1972). Hall and Norgaard (1974) further divided the threshold problem into determining both the *optimal time to treat* as well as *what type (dosage)* of treatment to make.

The simplest version of the threshold model, known as an *action threshold*, occurs when a treat or not treat decision is to be made. The problem is to determine what minimum pest density must be present before the marginal value of the crop saved will equal the marginal cost of treatment. The cost (r) of using a standard treatment or several alternative pesticides with different dosages can be compared with the extra benefits of treatment at various pest densities (N). Potential crop value depends upon expected yield with no crop damage (A) and expected crop price (p).

Experimental or other data on crop damage per pest unit (a) and average percent reduction in pest numbers with a pesticide treatment (b) are needed for a representative farm in a region. Ignoring other costs because they remain constant, profits (π) without treatment can be written as

$$\pi = p(A - aN) \tag{1}$$

where N is the pretreatment pest density.

Profits with treatment are

$$\pi = p[A - a(1 - b)N] - r \tag{2}$$

in which r is the material and application cost of a pesticide application. The threshold pest population (N^*) for the region is found by equating equations (1) and (2) and solving for (N^*)

$$N^* = r/pab \tag{3}$$

We can see that N^* is the pest population to initiate treatment so that the marginal cost of taking an action (r) is just equal to the marginal value of crop saved ($pabN^*$).

Sometimes pesticides can directly increase or decrease crop growth or change product quality. If there is a direct negative or positive effect of the pesticide on the potential output (A) equal to T units, then the threshold population is derived in the same manner as above and gives

$$N^* = [(A \pm T)p + r]/pab \tag{4}$$

Damage per pest (a) usually differs by crop stage and may not remain constant over pest densities. *Pesticide efficacy* (b) can change with the stage of development of the pest or under various weather conditions. Also, potential yield and future pest densities for the season may not be known at the time the pesticide use decision must be made. These complications may make threshold estimates such as (3) using mean levels of these parameters imprecise and in some cases impractical. However, slight elaborations of (3) with sensitivity analysis for changes in economic and biological parameters may provide useful starting points for recommendations, especially for weeds and some insects (Marra and Carlson, 1983; Talpaz and Frisbie, 1975).

An economic threshold model that is biologically more realistic, but requires a simultaneous determination of pest control intensity and pest density, incorporates profit, yield, and abatement functions (Moffitt et al., 1984b):

$$\pi = py - rz - F \tag{5}$$

$$y = A - an \tag{6}$$

$$n = N e^{-bz} \tag{7}$$

Here π denotes returns net of pest management costs; p and r denote output price and variable per unit pest management costs, respectively; y and z are output and pest management (or pesticide) input, respectively; n denotes postapplication pest densities; F is the total fixed cost of pest management; and A, a, N, and b represent positive parameters measuring potential yield with no pest damage, damage per pest, pretreatment pest density, and percent pest reduction from pest management, respectively. Equation (5) defines profit, π, as gross returns, py, minus the total cost of pest management ($rz + F$). The yield equation (6) subtracts yield loss or pest damage (an) from potential yield (A). The abatement or kill function is represented by a negative exponential function where pest numbers decline with pest management intensity, $dn/dz = -nN e^{-bz} < 0$ and $d^2n/dz^2 - b^2N e^{-bz} > 0$. (Various functional forms can be used for the *abatement function*, see Lichtenberg and Zilberman, 1986b.) Increasing the level of pest management decreases pest density at a decreasing rate.

The economic threshold concept assumes that producers attempt to maximize profits when managing pests. Substituting (6) and (7) into (5), and recognizing that pest management or pesticide use levels must be nonnegative, results in the following maximization problem

$$\text{Max } \pi(z) = p(A - aN e^{-bz}) - rz - F, \tag{8}$$

subject to $a \geq 0$

Assuming constant prices in the input, r, and output, p, markets, the first-order condition for (8) is

$$\partial\pi/\partial z = paNb e^{-bz} - r = 0 \tag{9}$$

The first and second terms on the right-hand side of (9) are the marginal value product (MVP) and marginal resource cost (MRC) of pest management inputs, respectively. Solving (9) for z gives the optimal use rate

$$z^* = \ln(paNb/r)/b \tag{10}$$

Substituting (10) into (7) provides an estimate of the economic threshold, that is the level of pest density, n^*, where the MVP of pest management is equal to the MRC

$$n^* = r/pab \tag{11}$$

In (10) and (11) pest management use level z^* and optimal pest density n^* must be simultaneously determined. There is a different optimal pretreatment pest level N for each possible level of pesticide use. Alternatively, you can think of a different optimal pesticide dosage for each possible pretreatment pest level, N. Only if all pesticide use levels give similar abatement levels is there a unique N^*.

The action threshold (3) simplifies pest management decisions by reducing the choice set to a discrete decision of either not changing the current strategy, $z = 0$, or applying a fixed dosage, $z = \hat{z}$. In the case of $z = 0$ the fixed application costs, F, will also be zero, and postapplication pest densities, n, will equal starting pest density, N. Specifically, the constraint in (8) is modified so that the threshold problem is

$$\text{Max } \pi(z) = p(A - aN e^{-bz}) - rz - F, \tag{12}$$

subject to $z = \hat{z}$ or $z = 0$

Profits are maximized by comparing the level of returns at $z = 0$ with those at $z = \hat{z}$. The optimal pest management level is $\hat{z}$ if

$$p(A - aN e^{-bz}) - rz - F > p(A - aN) \tag{13}$$

and zero otherwise. Solving for preapplication pest density, N, in (13), the optimal action threshold pest management strategy is

$$N^a = \begin{cases} \hat{z} & \text{if } N > (rz + F)/[pa(1 - e^{-bz})], \\ 0 & \text{otherwise} \end{cases} \tag{14}$$

In summary, there are two major threshold cases: 1) an action threshold with fixed pesticide dosages (equation 3), and 2) economic thresholds where both dosage and pretreatment pest density N varies (equations 10 and 11). Action thresholds require only a determination of preapplication pest density, and if this density exceeds a specified threshold density a predetermined pest management strategy is implemented.

Figure 7.3 illustrates how an action threshold is determined based on the

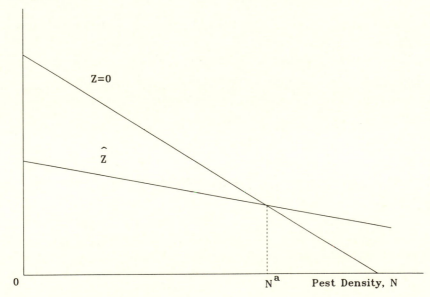

Figure 7.3. Action threshold determination.

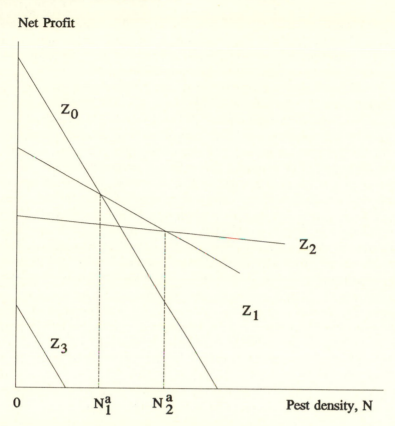

Figure 7.4. Action threshold for various management costs (Z_i).

functions (5) through (7). The curve $\hat{z}$ represents the level of profits applying a fixed dosage for various pest population levels

$$\pi(\hat{z}) = p(A - aN\, e^{-bz}) - r\hat{z} - F$$

and $z = 0$ represents the profit levels without an application

$$\pi(0) = p(A - aN)$$

As illustrated by (13) and (14) if $N < N^a$, $z = 0$ results in a higher level of profits, whereas, if $N > N^a$, $z = \hat{z}$ is the profit-maximizing action. Equation (14) indicates that the action threshold, N^a, will increase with costs, $rz + F$, and decline with output price, p, damage per pest, a, and the kill parameter b.

Flexibility in use of the action threshold can be obtained by computing the break-even pest density, N^a, for several actions, z, input costs, r or F, output price, p, or biological parameters (A, a, b). Prices may vary between years, whereas biological parameters may differ by crop variety, crop stage, or location. Figure 7.4 illustrates three curves z_1, z_2, and z_3 associated with three levels of input costs $r_1 < r_2 < r_3$. In this case the optimum strategy is $z = 0$ for $N < N_1^a$, z_1 for populations between N_1^a and N_2^a, and z_2 for $N > N_2^a$. The input price r_3 results in no break-even action threshold, because no pest control action results in a higher profit than no treatment at any level of pest density, N. The case with $r = r_3$ is a common one in which no pesticide is the optimal treatment.

Action thresholds are typically developed on a regional basis and implemented by pest monitoring in individual fields by producers. The biological parameters (A, a, b) are estimated from experimental data for typical growing conditions in a region, often by time of the season. Software programs for rapidly comparing net returns for various pest complexes, pest densities, input costs, and output prices are being developed. For example, the software program HERB will rapidly compare net profits for approximately 30 common soybean weed species and approximately 15 major herbicides under several different field conditions (moisture levels) and weed stages, changing parameters A, a, b (Wilkerson et al., 1988). One limitation to the regional action threshold concept is that the damage parameter (a) is estimated based on a typical potential yield (A), which will differ by producer. This can be corrected by estimating damage parameters (a) for various yield potential situations.

These threshold models are static and deterministic, and for some rapidly changing pest types they abstract greatly from reality. Pest populations especially for foliar insects and diseases naturally fluctuate through time, which motivates development of stochastic threshold models incorporating information updating and producer risk preferences. An example of the type of daily updating needed for leafspot control in peanuts is described in Box 7.2. Consequences of pest management actions are not always instantaneous as assumed in the above models. A pest management action at one point in time may change the pest density over a number of future periods. Thus, the stochastic nature of pest populations and the dynamic characteristics of the problem may justify more detailed threshold models (Regev et al., 1976). When external costs of pesticides are known these costs can be added to private costs to obtain socially optimal pest threshold recommendations (Moffitt, 1986). Moffitt et al. (1984a,b) have also shown how thresholds can be modified to include farmers' risk aversion.

In practice, complex decision rules based on these more detailed threshold models have generally not replaced simpler rules including action thresholds (Musser et al., 1986). One possible explanation suggested by Hall and Moffitt (1985) is the relatively small amount of net revenue lost by using simpler decision rules. However, this use of simpler rules should not be recommended in all cases. For example, Smith et al. (1987) indicate cases where adjustment to action thresholds may be warranted. Further research is required for a definitive statement on this issue. Specifically, research such as that by Szmedra et al. (1990), which models action thresholds in a dynamic stochastic framework, is required.

Pest Interaction Models

Interactions may exist from pesticide applications directed at a primary pest population resulting in an increase in a secondary pest species through a predator–prey chain. The pesticide not only reduces the primary pest population but also

Box 7.2. Pest Management for Peanut Disease Control

Leafspot, a fungus that attacks peanuts in the southeastern United States, is a major agricultural pest. Conventional control of leafspot involves a preventive approach in which routine fungicide applications are made to suppress leafspot below the economic threshold level prior to knowing if the disease will develop. This will result in fungicide applications even if weather conditions are not favorable to the spread of leafspot. These potentially unnecessary applications result in higher pesticide costs with associated lower returns and possible health and environmental damage. These control actions are justified by the belief that the expected prevention cost is smaller than the expected reduction in total revenue for peanuts if the fungus went untreated. However, the potential existed for the development of a pest management program that would eliminate or reduce some of the fungicide applications.

The North Carolina Agricultural Extension Service has developed such a program. The program is designed to aid growers in determining when to apply fungicides. It employs a relationship between minimum daily temperature, hours of high (94%) relative humidity, and leafspot development. This model can be used to accurately estimate when peanut leafspot will occur. Based on this model and timely measurements of moisture and temperature, warnings of disease-conducive weather, called leafspot advisories, are developed.

Introduced in 1983, this program relies on farmer volunteers who monitor temperature and humidity and phone in this information to county offices. County staff use these data to calculate spray advisories and make the information available to all growers in the county on a telephone recorder. Beginning in 1988, forecasts of weather conditions for 3 days were made available to the county offices so that advisories could be provided 3 days in advance. University agricultural meteorologists distribute forecasts for minimum daily temperature and hours of leaf wetness through electronic mail to counties. This gives growers some advance warning of leafspot development, and also allows continuity over weekends and holidays when the system was previously not operational.

A survey was conducted in Northampton county, North Carolina to determine the extent to which the leafspot advisories were being used as a method of making management decisions. Results indicated that 71 percent of the growers had heard of peanut leafspot advisories and 51 percent of the growers were using this service. Growers surveyed estimated that they saved 2.4 applications per year (about 40%) using the advisory system. These reduced applications result in increased returns to growers and may enhance environmental quality.

reduces the population of a predator species associated with the secondary pest. Thus, while decreasing crop losses from one pest species, pesticide applications may increase crop damage from a second pest type. Additionally, and probably more frequently, yield-increasing inputs such as water or fertilizer may also increase starting pest density even if secondary pests are not present. Modifications of the single pest, single pesticide model can improve pest control recommendations when pest–pesticide interactions are important (Harper and Zilberman, 1989).

The biological relationship for an interaction model begins with a production or yield function

$$y = A(x)[1 - D(n_1, n_2)] \tag{15}$$

where y denotes output, and x denotes quantity of a nonpesticide input that influences both potential output and the primary pest with density, n_1. $A(x)$ represents potential output in the absence of pest damage, n_1 and n_2 denote the primary and secondary postapplication pest densities, respectively, and $D(n_1, n_2)$ is the crop damage function. It is assumed that x has the usual properties of increasing yield at a decreasing rate: $dA/dx > 0$, $d^2A/dx^2 < 0$. Both pests increase damage; $\partial D/\partial n_1 > 0$, and $\partial D/\partial n_2 > 0$.

The pest abatement and predator kill functions may be represented as

$$\left. \begin{array}{l} n_1 = N_1(x)[1 - k_1(z_1)] \\ n_2 = N_2(n_3)[1 - k_2(z_2)] \\ n_3 = N_3[1 - k_3(z_1)] \end{array} \right\} \tag{16}$$

where n_3 denotes postapplication predator density, N_1, N_2, and N_3 are preapplication levels of the two pest types and a predator, z_1 and z_2 denote quantity of pesticide used to control the primary pest and the secondary pest, respectively, and k_1, k_2, and k_3 represent the kill functions or percent reduction in pests and predators. The primary pest's density is a function of the nonpesticide input, x, and the secondary pest density is influenced by z_2 and the posttreatment predator density, n_3. The reduction in the predator population from controlling the primary pest density with pesticide z_1 results in an increase in the secondary best population. This is a common interaction sometimes referred to as *secondary pest outbreak* (Harper and Zilberman, 1989).

The pest management problem is to determine the profit-maximizing levels of pesticides, z_1 and z_2, and nonpesticide input, x. Let p denote output price, r_1 and r_2 denote unit price on pesticides z_1 and z_2, respectively, and w be the unit cost of x. The optimization model is

$$\text{Max } pA(x)[1 - D(n_1, n_2)] - r_1 z_1 - r_2 z_2 - wx \tag{17}$$

while maintaining the three abatement functions in (16).

For analysis purposes, the problem can be divided into two submodels, Submodel 1 and Submodel 2. Submodel 1 considers only one pest (n_1) and one pesticide (z_1) and an input x that affects both output y and pest density. The Lagrangian expression for Submodel 1 is

$$L = pA(x)[1 - D(n_1)] - r_1 z_1 - wx + \lambda_1\{n_1 - N_1(x)[1 - k_1(z_1)]\} \tag{18}$$

where λ_1 denotes the Lagrange multiplier associated with the primary pest population. First-order conditions for optimality are

$$\left. \begin{array}{l} \partial L/\partial n_1 = \lambda_1 - \partial D/\partial n_1[pA(x)] = 0 \\ \partial L/\partial x = p(\partial A/\partial x)[1 - D(n_1)] - w - \lambda_1(\partial N_1/\partial x)[1 - k_1(z_1)] = 0 \\ \partial L/\partial z_1 = \lambda_1 N_1(x)(dk_1/dz_1) - r_1 = 0 \\ \partial L/\partial \lambda_1 = n_1 - N_1(x)[1 - k_1(z_1)] = 0 \end{array} \right\} \tag{19}$$

The first condition defines the Lagrange multiplier. The shadow price of pest density, λ_1, is the value of the marginal yield damage caused by the unit change in the pest, $\partial D/\partial n_1[pA(x)]$. The second optimality condition states that the optimal level of the related input is where its marginal value product is equal to its price w plus the marginal cost of x in increasing the pest density, n_1. By influencing potential output and the growth rate of pests (N) the use of related inputs can influence optimal pesticide use. A common result of this type of model is that it may be profitable to reduce an input such as fertilizer to a level below its optimal level in the absence of pests. This model is also handy for examining multiple pest controls such as a herbicide and cultivation. The marginal condition for the pesticide, z_1, is to equate its MVP in reducing the pest with the cost of the pesticide, r_1. In a slight modification of this model one can include the positive effects of pesticides on the marginal product of other inputs or output quality. An example is when a pesticide controls pests and enhances product storability.

Submodel 2 considers two pests and two pesticides, and pesticide z_1 induces secondary pest outbreaks by destroying beneficial predators, N_3. Also, in this model no pest stimulating input x is present. The Lagrangian expression is then

$$L = pA(x)[1 - D(n_1, n_2)] - r_1 z_1 - r_2 z_2$$
$$+ \lambda_1\{n_1 - N_1(x)[1 - k_1(z_1)]\}$$
$$+ \lambda_2\{n_2 - N_2(n_3)[1 - k_2(z_2)]\}$$
$$+ \lambda_3\{n_3 - N_3[1 - k_3(z_1)]\} \tag{20}$$

First-order conditions for optimality involve derivatives of (20) for each of the pest types (n_1, n_2, n_3), pesticides (z_1, z_2), and three pest constraints ($\lambda_1, \lambda_2, \lambda_3$). The unique feature of this submodel is that part of the marginal cost of using z_1 is that the crop loss function increases the secondary pest, and this leads to the following:

$$\lambda_1 N_1(x)(\partial k_1/\partial z_1) = r_1 + \lambda_3 N_3(\partial k_3/\partial z_1) \tag{21}$$

Failure to consider these possible interactions associated with pesticides and other inputs or between pests and predators is myopic and may lead to suboptimal profits. Harper and Zilberman (1989) illustrate this by comparing the benefits and costs of two ways of controlling pest populations on cotton in California's Imperial Valley. Regular season cotton together with pesticide use induced two secondary pest species, and thus, a shorter growing season with less water was found to dominate. Other practical examples include thresholds with and without predators (Gutierrez and Daxl, 1984; Reichelderfer and Bender, 1979), and use of inputs that decrease pest populations such as crop rotation (Lazarus and Swanson, 1983) or resistant crop varieties (Herdt et al., 1984).

Analysis of Pest Management Resources

Estimation of pest thresholds for optimal timing and selection of the best pesticide dosages and types is only part of the economic analysis of pest management. Other major resources in IPM are labor, information, land, and management. To implement thresholds, labor and information are needed. Sometimes IPM will be combinations of chemicals, land use changes, and crop varieties which are technology bundles or packages. Over the past two decades there have been publicly supported IPM programs that have attempted to reduce farmer costs of pest control. Economists have evaluated pest monitoring, adoption of recommended thresholds, and control of some major pests when there is uncertainty about pest densities. Both normative and positive studies of the use of scouting, pesticides, and thresholds can help us see the complexities of the use of these resources at the individual farm level.

Monitoring Resources

A conventional pest management decision involves the optimal application of pesticides. Information on pest density is a prerequisite to determining when an application is required. Techniques and instruments developed for *monitoring* pests continue to improve. Light traps were one of the first instruments employed for sampling agricultural insects. Bayesian and classical sampling statistics are used to estimate pest densities. Pest pheromones and assay methods that lower the cost of monitoring and identifying pest species are currently available. Adaptation of communication instruments including computers and satellites will give further aid in monitoring pest densities.

In addition to instruments monitoring pest densities, labor is employed to scout pest conditions in fields and determine pest densities. Although the practice of field scouting began in the 1930s, it did not expand rapidly until the 1950s. Field scouts provide pest information to determine the appropriate timing, type, and quantity of pesticide applications. This increased information may cause a reduction in scheduled applications, which could diminish the negative external effects. However, better pest monitoring can also lead to the discovery of unknown damage leading to more pesticide use per unit area, but higher returns to all resources.

Pest monitoring and demand for pest information can be examined by investigating labor markets such as private *pest management consultants* and public extension service (Carlson, 1980). Currently, such markets exist throughout the United States, and both public and private consultants supply information to producers. However, research by Regev et al. (1976) and Musser et al. (1986) indicates that these unregulated markets may not yield an optimal allocation of resources because of the public good nature of pest information. Information provided to one producer may be easily copied by another producer at zero or low marginal resource cost. In an unrelated market, this positive external effect is not readily incorporated in the selling price of the information; thus, this type of information may be underproduced in a private setting from a societal point of view unless it is subsidized (see Chapter 6).

Pest information is currently being provided in a number of forms. Producers may pay private or public consultants for pest information, or they may receive it as a service from a governmental agency, for example, the Cooperative Extension Service. Wetzstein (1981) in considering the public good characteristics of pest management information found that some producers may utilize the information obtained from another producer who acquired the information (the participant) without reducing the participant's utility. A nonparticipant may obtain the participant's information from a county extension agent, by attending extension or other local meetings, or by talking directly to the participant. Thus, participation by a producer increases the information available to nonparticipating producers and increases regional output. Provided there is relatively elastic product demand this will yield benefits in excess of the sum of the direct benefits to participants.

Pest information may also be characterized by asymmetry. Participants in public information programs can affect the utility of nonparticipants, but non-participants' actions may not affect the utility of participants. This asymmetry usually holds if intraseasonal migration of pests among farmers is negligible. However, in terms of a multiperiod perspective, a pesticide management program by one producer may affect pest population levels or pesticide resistance for an entire region. Information in this case may exhibit a symmetrical, joint effect.

Pest information obtained by nonparticipants from participants may not directly relate to a nonparticipants' production situation. The pest density or species information may not be a perfect substitute for field-specific data that nonparticipants would have obtained if they were participants. Nonparticipants would tend to discount the available information from participants the more distant the participant and the more spatially variable the pest. Thus, resembling participants, nonparticipants have the option of using all or a portion of participants' information, provided that participants do not attempt to suppress it.

Adoption of Thresholds and Use of IPM Services by Farmers

Technologies, including pest management information, are generally composed of several *characteristics*. Smith et al. (1987) noted that evaluating pest information in terms of a joint technology package provides the flexibility to consider adoption of parts of pest management recommendations by farmers. The ordering and clustering of characteristics within a package can help farmers choose components. This approach is not to suggest abandoning the package approach in carrying recommendations to producers. In general, a pest management package may still be recommended; however, suggestions on how this package may be modified based on a particular producer's pest, soil, and management conditions can be provided by local advisors.

As an example of a pest management package composed of characteristics, Georgia extension entomologists established three pest management character-istics for insect field scouting (Smith et al., 1987 and Wetzstein et al., 1985). These characteristics dealt primarily with producer response to scouting reports on cotton, peanuts, and soybean. The first characteristic measured the proportion of "proper" pesticide applications to the total number of pesticide applications. A pesticide application was considered "proper" if both the type of pesticide and the timing of application was consistent with Extension Service recommendations. The second characteristic measured the number of treatments by farmers relative to the total number of action thresholds found by expert pest monitoring. The third characteristic measured the number of chemical sprays made after an action threshold was reached minus sprays made before a threshold relative to total number of sprays. Spraying after a threshold is reached allows producers to maximize the effects of beneficial insects for pest control. Spraying before a threshold increases the probability of destroying beneficial insects.

In a partial equilibrium framework, the influence of pest management characteristics on profits may be evaluated (Smith et al., 1987). The relation between the total pest management package, z, and three pest management characteristics may be denoted by $g_i(z)$, $i = 1, 2, 3$. An individual producer's profit, π, resulting from the application of pest management may then be defined as

$$\pi = pf[X, v, g_1(z), g_2(z), g_3(z)] - rz - wX \tag{22}$$

where p denotes the competitive output price, $f[\cdot]$ is the producer's production function, X denotes a vector of production inputs other than pest management characteristics, v represents a vector of environmental conditions including pest density, and r and w are the price of pest management and the price vector associated with X, respectively. The first-order conditions for maximizing π in terms of z are

$$\partial\pi/\partial z = MVP_1 + MVP_2 + MVP_3 - r \leq 0 \quad \text{and} \quad z(\partial\pi/\partial z) = 0, \tag{23}$$

where $MVP_i = p(\partial f/\partial g_i)(\partial g_i/\partial z)$ is the value of marginal product associated with pest management characteristic i. If the sum of the MVPs is less than the cost of pest management, r, according to (23) a producer will not participate in the pest management program. Furthermore, even if MVP is zero or negative for some pest management characteristics a producer may still partially participate in pest management if the sum of the positive MVPs equals or exceeds the cost of pest management, r.

Pesticide use and pest levels are often positively correlated. This can complicate the evaluation of the productivity of pesticides and monitoring resources. As indicated by Burrows (1983) the possibility that pesticide use choices help determine use of private consultants may result in simultaneous equation bias when one tries to estimate the demand for pesticides with use of consultants as an explanatory variable. This bias will occur if there is some unmeasured variable that is correlated with both pest management and pesticides. Candidate variables are actual pest population level, pest resistance, or the producer's perception of pest level. The following model was proposed to account for this possible relation between pest management and pesticides when estimating pesticide demand

$$z = \delta PM + \beta x \tag{24}$$

$$PM = \gamma a \tag{25}$$

where z denotes pesticide usage, PM denotes level of pest management ranging from zero for nonparticipation to one for full participation, x denotes a vector of other variables affecting pesticide usage, and a denotes a vector of variables affecting adoption of the use of a consultant. In some cases the dependent variable in (25) is binary with only zero and one values, and a logit or probit econometric model would be appropriate for estimation. Consistent parameter estimates are obtained by making (25) a reduced-form equation through the exclusion of z from *a*. Equation (25) is then estimated to create an instrument, PMHAT, the predicted probability of adoption. Finally, the instrument, PMHAT, is used in the estimation of the demand for pesticide in (24).

As an application of the model (24, 25) Burrows employed data on 47 San Joaquin Valley cotton producers from 1970 to 1974. Results indicate a positive relationship between yield and pesticide use, and a negative relationship between farm size and pesticide demand. A reduction in pesticide demand can be associated with other pest management inputs, and thus, the aggregate effects of pest management or IPM adoption may result in a reduction in pesticide demand $(\delta < 0)$.

There have been other studies examining the introduction of various IPM resources. Carlson (1970) estimated the value of a regional forecast of peach disease control, Reichelderfer and Bender (1979) evaluated the economic effects of release of a predator insect for insect control in soybeans, Antle (1988) examined a monitoring and threshold recommendation program for insects of tomatoes, and Zacharias and Grube (1984) developed a dynamic programming model of crop rotation and chemical methods for control of corn root worm and soybean cyst nematode on corn–soybean farms. Introduction of pest-resistant crop varieties have been evaluated for alfalfa (Zavaleta and Ruesink, 1980) and rice (Herdt et al., 1984). Several studies have been conducted on the effects of tillage or planting systems on pests and pesticide use (Moffitt et al., 1984a; Marra and Carlson, 1986).

Risky Pest Management Decisions

There are many different models and techniques that are employed in finding efficient levels of pest management when pest damage or other components are highly variable (Cochran and Boggess, 1988; Antle, 1988). The models and methods for both normative and positive analysis follow those given in Chapter 2 and textbooks on uncertainty (Anderson et al., 1977). Assuming *risk averse* producers with the objective of maximizing expected utility by choosing the appropriate level of pesticides, *z*, Feder (1979) proposed the following model

$$\underset{z}{\text{Max }} EU\{(\pi) - aN[1 - k(z)] - rz\} \tag{26}$$

where E denotes the expectations operator, $U(\cdot)$ is a concave utility function from risk averse agents, π denotes profits realized if no pests were present, a represents the damage caused by a single pest, and $N[1 - k(z)]$ represents the damage function where $k(z)$ is the kill function. The critical assumption is that pesticides have to be applied prior to knowing random variables such as the pest level (N).

First-order conditions for an optimum are

$$\partial E(U)/\partial z = E[U'(aNk' - r)] \leq 0 \quad \text{and} \quad z[\partial E(U)/\partial z] = 0 \tag{27}$$

The cost term rz in (26) can be expanded to include random health and wildlife damage costs, which will result in reduced optimal amount of pesticides implied by the first-order conditions (27).

The impact on production decisions by a risk averse producer can also be assessed when the four elements, π, a, N, and $k(z)$ are assumed to be random. Variability can be measured as the spread about the mean level of a parameter. Feder (1979) demonstrated that the optimal economic threshold, N^*, determined from (27) will decline when the damage per pest, a, or pesticide efficacy, $k(z)$, increases, and when the variability of any of a, N, or $k(z)$ increases. Thus, for a risk averse producer, increased variability results in a lower economic threshold and increased use of pesticides. This general finding plus the widely fluctuating pest populations have led to the notion that providing better pest density information can lower pesticide use. This need not be the case when the pest-free profit becomes more variable. In this case higher variance of π can lead to higher thresholds and lower pesticide use than with more stable π levels (Pannell, 1991). Pingali and Carlson (1985) show that farmers' estimate of pest damage can be biased, and that there can be high returns to information programs and farmer education.

The Feder model can be made more realistic by incorporating the phytotoxic or growth-stimulating effects of pesticides on crops, multiple pests, interdependence of output price and crop damage, and inclusion of other sources of variability (Carlson, 1970, 1984). Pest management inputs such as *crop rotations* and variety selection can influence pest variability as well as mean profits. The variables $p(z)$ and $y(z)$ are expressed as functions of z to emphasize that variations in product quality (price) and yield are influenced by pesticide level and type. Specifically, profit, for a fixed farm size, resulting from land allocations A_i ($i = 1, \ldots, 4$), $NR(A)$, is

$$NR(A) = A_1[\pi_s(p_s, y_s)] + A_2\{\pi[p(z), y(z)] - \sum_{j=1}^{M} a_j N_j[1 - k_j(z)] - rz\}$$

$$+ A_3\left(\pi - \sum_{j=1}^{M} a_j N_j\right) + A_4\left(\pi - \sum_{j=1}^{M} a_j N_j\right) \tag{28}$$

Variables π_s, p_s, and y_s denote profit, price, and yield of the substitute or nonhost crop, respectively; A_1, A_2, A_3, and A_4 are acres allocated to the substitute crop, the major crop including a pesticide, the major crop without the pesticide, and the major crop following rotation from a substitute crop, respectively; n denotes pest density following rotation, a_j is damage from pest type j, and M is the number of pest species. Substitution of this multiproduct profit equation into (26) gives optimal input results similar to those of (27). It also extends the results by suggesting that the more uncertain the efficacy of the rotation is in reducing the pest density (variance of a_j) the longer the nonhost crop should be grown.

Lazarus and Swanson (1983) employ a mean-variance criterion to investigate insecticide use and crop rotation for rootworm control in corn using a less elaborate version of a model like (28). Simulation was employed to model sources of uncertainty including pest density, root damage, yield loss, and crop prices and yield. The two pest management resources considered were a single insecticide application and rotation to soybean, which is not affected by the pest. Producers are assumed to have 600 acres of cropland managed in 30 fields. Results are based on three levels of risk aversion: risk neutral, risk averse, and very risk averse. The optimal actions for the risk neutral producer are to rotate the four most heavily infested fields, apply insecticide to 13 fields, and plant three fields using no insecticide. The risk averse producer increases soybean fields to six and reduces untreated fields to two. Insecticide use continues to decline slightly for the very risk averse producer with one additional field rotated. Thus, increased risk aversion causes soybean production to enter the solution as a means of reducing risk. This effect reduced the rotation threshold more than the insecticide threshold, reducing insecticide use. This finding is important because it shows that farmers with higher risk aversion may actually use less pesticides because rotation can dominate insecticides in providing low pest damage levels.

Moffitt (1986) extends the Feder model by allowing the pesticide use rate to be variable:

$$E[U(\pi)] = E[U(\pi)|N > N^T] \cdot \Pr(N > N^T) + E[U(\pi)|N \leq N^T] \cdot \Pr(N \leq N^T)$$

$$= \int_{N^T}^{\infty} U[py(n(z, N)) - rz - F]h(N)\, dN$$

$$+ \int_{-\infty}^{N^T} U[py(n(0, N))]h(N)\, dN \tag{29}$$

where N^T and n denote a pest density threshold and pest density following pesticide treatment, respectively, and $h(N)$ denotes a probability density function for pests.

Expected utility (29) is a function of threshold, N^T, and application rate, z. Risk efficiency is obtained by finding the (N^T, z) pair that results in the maximum expected utility. The first-order conditions for this model are found by taking derivatives of (29) for z and N^T and solving them simultaneously to get optimal pesticide rate and pretreatment pest density (N^*). The risk efficient pesticide use rate(z^*) and pest threshold will only be the same as those in (27) if there is little chance to vary dosage per application as in (14).

The impact of risk aversion for average pesticide use may be investigated by considering the expected value of optimal pesticide use

$$E(\text{pesticide use}) = z^* \cdot \Pr(N > N^*) \tag{30}$$

Average pesticide use need not be larger owing to the presence of risk aversion relative to risk neutrality when producers manage pests according to a threshold. Profit variability can be reduced by treating with a larger dosage but treating less frequently. The frequency of application may in fact be reduced to the point of offsetting the increase in dosage, resulting in reducing average pesticide use. Specifically, from (30) risk aversion will result in a larger z^* than would be efficient under risk neutrality; however, treatment conditions, $\Pr(N > N^*)$, may be narrowed sufficiently to reduce average pesticide use. In terms of externality prevention policies, with risk averse producers, regulatory actions such as restricting the maximum pesticide dosage per treatment may result in larger pesticide load in the environment than would prevail without the restriction.

If data are available on utility functions and pest probabilities, then optimal pesticide and other pest controls can be estimated. Techniques such as stochastic dominance, $E - V$ analysis, and utility maximization have been applied for major crop–pest situations. For example Moffitt et al. (1984a), compared early and long season cotton pest management programs, in the same cotton production zone evaluated by Harper and Zilberman (1989). Most pest problems in the Imperial Valley of California tend to occur during the last weeks of summer, and thus, one possible pest management program would be to terminate production early. Although some yield loss would occur in early termination, reduced pest control and other variable costs including irrigation and fertilizer may offset this potential lost revenue. Field experiments were conducted covering two crop years to compare the two programs. Yield and variable input costs were monitored for 15 commercial cotton fields where all production practices were the same for each program. Certainty equivalents, CE, corresponding to early termination and long season cotton for various levels of constant absolute risk aversion, were calculated assuming a negative exponential utility function and a normal yield distribution. Early termination was found to be associated with a higher CE compared with long season production for risk neutral and farmers with weak risk aversion. For higher levels of risk aversion, long season cotton has a higher CE compared to early termination. Thus, depending on producers' risk preference, early termination may not be adopted even though its expected value of profit exceeds that of the long season program.

Musser et al. (1981) compare risk efficiency results of first and second degree stochastic dominance with the $E - V$ criterion. Their objective was to select the risk efficient set from four different management levels of pest control for a cropping system in the southeastern United States consisting of turnip greens, field corn, and southern peas. Data were collected from experimental plots with six replications in a randomized block design that were repeated for five years from 1975 through 1979. Employing EV analysis, two pest management systems were risk efficient, however, both stochastic dominance criteria indicated that only the most intensive use of pest management was risk efficient. Similarly, Zacharias and Grube (1984) were able to use stochastic dominance to rank a number of herbicide and crop rotation choices for weed control on Midwestern corn–soybean farms. The effects of many other pesticide and IPM programs on farm income risk have been summarized by McCarl (1981), Carlson (1984), and Pannell (1991).

There is a high level of heterogeneity in pest conditions across farms and over time. The spatial variability requires researchers to emphasize *key pests* in the development of thresholds, monitoring schemes, and recommendations for optimal responses to risky pest damage (Wetzstein et al., 1985). Over the past 20 years researchers and pest control advisors have developed threshold models and recommendations for many key insect, weed, and disease pests. Because of the diffuse nature of the information few economic evaluations of the costs and returns of these research efforts are available. This lack of economic evaluations plus the continuous changes in available pesticides owing to cancellations, new discoveries, resistance development, and new pests require continuous biological and economic research in pest management.

PEST MANAGEMENT ON A REGIONAL LEVEL

Pests, pesticides, and pest control information can lead to external effects when individual farmers manage pests. Group pest management (including pesticide resistance management), evaluation of pesticide externalities, and methods used in pesticide regulations are reviewed in this section.

Group Pest Management

In the presence of mobile pests, pesticide drift, and other biological interrelationships pest suppression on an area-wide basis can sometimes be more effective than that on a farm by farm basis. Size economies and geographical proximity have led to use of voluntary and compulsory organizational structures for pest suppression, pest monitoring, eradication, quarantine, and other joint activities. In addition, group pest control might be able to better internalize some of the adverse environmental effects of pest control inputs caused by drift off the farm. Much of the information used in pest management decisions has public good properties, that is, use by one individual does not necessarily diminish its value to others in a region. Groups may also internalize costs of pest movement and pesticide resistance spillovers.

Various types of organizations and financial arrangements are used in group pest management. Private community groups, cooperatives, as well as regional (districts, counties, state) organizations that have local government authority may be formed specifically for pest management. Abatement districts for mosquitoes, orchard insects, weeds in irrigation water, and community insect management groups are examples. An indirect form of coordinated pest control is a regional or state ordinance prescribing mandatory actions such as uniform planting dates or required pest habitat destruction.

Three major economic problems unique to regional pest management are 1) unequal pest control demand among current or potential members of a group, 2) determining optimal size of an organization, and 3) cost sharing arrangements. These economic problems together with biological and terrain characteristics can result in conflicts between individual and group pest management. In addition, direct costs of organization and free-rider problems may necessitate mandatory rather than voluntary organizations.

The incentives involved in the decision of farmers to join a *voluntary group* for pest suppression are illustrated in Figure 7.5 (Rook and Carlson, 1985). The cost of a unit of pest control (measured as amount of pest damage abated for a given period) is assumed to be provided at a lower cost by the group (P_g) than by independent farmers (P_i). An independently operating farmer, A, with demand curve D_A would choose pest abatement level I_A. Another farmer in the same production area may demand a higher level of pest control (D_M) because of higher expected pest levels, higher potential yield, or higher risk aversion. In addition to lower costs, groups often have the potential to provide a higher service quality as reflected by the curves D'_A and D'_M for the marginal value products or demand curves for the group pest control service by individuals A and M, respectively.

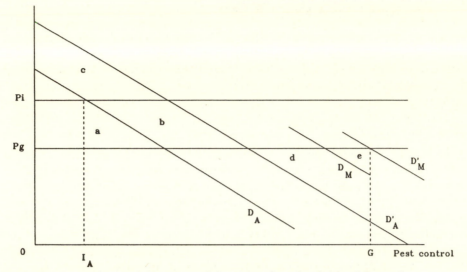

Figure 7.5. Regional control decisions with low (A) and median (M) level demand.

Assume that the current group of farmers is composed of members with both higher and lower demands, and for most groups with similar marginal products of pest control (single peaked preference) majority voting will tend to lead to the median level of pest control. For simplicity, suppose the median demand of the group was that of D'_M. The optimal level of abatement chosen when the cost is P_g would be G. This is the uniform level of service provided to all farmers who join the group. They are required to pay an equal share of the total abatement costs given by the rectangular area P_g times G. By joining the group, a farmer such as A would receive additional benefits of area $a + b + c$, but incur additional cost shown by the area $d + e$. If this difference is a positive value, then we would expect farmers such as A to join the group. If private pest control cost, P_i, increases or group cost, P_g, declines, this will raise benefits and lower costs of joining. Likewise, it is easy to see in Figure 7.5 that the more similar the demand of individual A is to the median level of demand, the smaller is cost area d; consequently A will join the group. In most cases (except where P_g is near P_i) farmers with demands higher than the median level can benefit by joining the group and supplementing with private pest control. Sometimes economies of size may allow some individual farmers to have costs lower than P_i, which reduce incentives to join. On the other hand, large farms are critical to the success of some groups so higher services or lower costs may be offered as an inducement to join.

The community pest management organizations for cotton insect control in the southern United States illustrate some of these organizational features. Mobile insects such as bollworms and boll weevil can be suppressed at lower cost on a regional than on an individual farm basis (Rook and Carlson, 1985; Cochran, 1986). Farmers voluntarily join groups to receive field scouting, record keeping, and pest control recommendations or decision making (choosing correct pesticides, dosages, timing, etc.). In return they pay fees per acre of cotton grown. Some of these organizations provide coordinated pest suppression service or implementation of IPM practices such as the release of natural enemies of pests (Reichelderfer and Bender, 1979). Rook and Carlson examined the decisions of individual North Carolina cotton farmers to join groups. In this area cotton pests were very mobile and larger farmers when acting individually did not have cost advantages over smaller farmers. This was confirmed when it was found that larger farms (more acres) were more frequent joiners. The study did not find that larger groups were more attractive to farmers than smaller ones. (This would be expected if larger group management areas can reduce pest infestation levels). However, they did find higher probabilities of joining if an individual farmer's demand as reflected by historical pesticide use was closer to that service level chosen by the group.

Bollworm Management Communities (BMC) have been in existence in Arkansas cotton production since 1976 (Cochran, 1986). Uniform insecticide treatments for control of bollworms over large areas are made to prevent spread and reproduction. In 1985 there were approximately 150,000 acres (out of about 400,000 acres in the state) in six regional groups. Comparison among three groups and four check areas (nonjoiners) for the 1978–1981 period showed an increase in net return from both higher yields and a slight reduction in insecticide expenditure per acre. In the BMCs many of the actions of farmers (pesticide type, dosage) are independent, but these farmers are more likely than nonparticipants to follow recommended IPM practices on scouting interval and pest density thresholds.

Pest Monitoring

Monitoring of pest densities, pest types, and crop status is frequently an important part of individual and group pest suppression efforts. This information is collected either by private sources (scouts, consultants, or farmers) or by regional, public agencies including the Federal Extension Service, Forest Service, APHIS, or state departments of agriculture.

Public pest density information can either be a complement or substitute for private pest control information. It is a complement when used to raise the marginal product of private information. An example is the use of Weather Bureau information together with Extension Service insect trap information to indicate when farmers might begin or terminate field scouting. Similarly, when the Extension Service identifies a new pest species and recommends that private consultants should search for it, this is a complementary relationship. Public pest information is a substitute for private pest information when it duplicates field pest density information to the extent that private monitoring is reduced or pest losses become higher. Carlson (1980) developed and estimated a regression model of private pest consultant demand and supply that indicated that public IPM employees may be more of a substitute than a complement for private consultants.

The effect of accuracy of regional pest information was evaluated by Moffitt (1986). A model of individual farmer choices was developed for monitoring insects and treating soybean fields under Illinois conditions. With known costs, crop prices, and farmer scouting accuracy, the net returns from a public pest density forecast received by farmers prior to when they conducted private field scouting was estimated. Farmers were assumed to choose insecticide use and private scouting to maximize expected returns based on pest density probabilities conditioned by both the private and public (regional) forecasts. It was found that midwestern farmers should not expect any effect from increased accuracy of the public forecasts until they became more accurate than the private scouting (90%). When public forecast accuracy was between 91 and 94 percent private scouting was reduced and pesticide use increased. Public forecasts had to be very accurate (>94%) before they would reduce pesticide use and private scouting in this case study. Other monitoring studies may find greater possibilities for joint efforts between public and private pest monitoring.

Mandatory Pest Control

When pests are both mobile across farms, and capable of reproducing rapidly it may not be possible for a voluntary organization to efficiently manage pests. Pests that develop on a nonparticipating farm and spread to other farms can reduce the effectiveness of area-wide control efforts. Groups can tolerate some nonparticipants (*free-riders*), but when the nonparticipants become a continuous source of new pests it will usually be advantageous for the group to institute mandatory pest control. Important examples are abatement districts, pest control ordinances, and eradication programs. Usually state or local legislation is needed for initiating these activities, and some form of government or quasigovernment entity is created.

Mosquito abatement districts have been modeled as cost minimizers to reach target levels of mosquito density (Lichtenberg, 1987), and as utility maximizers (Carlson and DeBord, 1976). For one large district in California, Lichtenberg (1987) found that increases in rice acreage in the district and use of predatory fish could reduce both insecticide treatments and monitoring per acre. By evaluating information from 30 districts on the southeastern U.S. coast, Carlson and Debord (1976) found excess permanent control activities (ditching and drainage) relative to insecticide expenditures and excess total expenditures relative to residents' willingness to tax themselves for control. Abatement districts were formed in geographical areas where pest densities and human populations per unit area were high. These studies explain short-term decisions such as pesticide use as well as long-term changes in infrastructure (drainage, equipment, predators), but they require long-term data collection to evaluate the latter.

Another example of mandatory regional pest management is the uniform planting date (UPD) of cotton for control of the boll weevil in the Rolling Plains of Texas (Masaud et al., 1984). Beginning in 1972 with two counties and expanding to 27 counties by 1981 the UPD program was adopted and expanded by farmer vote at the county level. By delaying planting and using short-season cotton varieties most of the boll weevils (90%) will emerge and die because the cotton squares (fruit) are the only food source for the weevil. Using a regression model with data from 1970 to 1981 for the 27 counties, Masaud et al. (1984) found that adoption of the UDP increased lint yield by an average of 11 percent and decreased insecticide use by 50 percent. This type of pest control requires that high percentages of the farmers in the area participate, thus, the need to make participation mandatory.

Pest Eradication

Complete removal of a pest species from a region is known as *eradication*. Some pest management efforts by individual farmers are devoted to pest eradication especially when farmers attempt to grow crops for seed. Removal of weeds or diseases to prevent contamination of the seed is required for certification. However, most eradication efforts, such as the fruit fly eradication programs in various parts of the world, are mandatory regional programs to prevent insects or weeds from being established (Mangel et al., 1986). There are also examples of successful eradication of some animal and a few crop pests from established habitats.

The U.S. boll weevil eradication program in cotton is an effort to remove a major agricultural pest from areas where it has been established for approximately 90 years. In North and South Carolina the success of this program has removed the necessity for individual farm insecticide treatments directed at the boll weevil since 1979 in one region and since 1983 in the remainder of North Carolina and most of South Carolina. Eradication efforts are in progress in Georgia, Florida, and parts of Alabama, Arizona, and California (Carlson et al., 1989).

The boll weevil eradication program illustrates the problems of unequal pest control demand, external benefits, and output price effects on other regions. The initial question is whether the optimal pest population for a region is eradication (zero population) or some positive pest population level. This question is similar to that in Figure 7.3 for an individual farm, but is now illustrated with the pest situation for two distinctly independent regions (I, II) as shown in Figure 7.6. Multiple year (discounted) net return in each region for various pest densities is shown as the No Treatment (NT) line. The break-even population for region II is at N^* where net returns are equal with suppression (NR_{II}) and without treatment. Eradication is not warranted in region II. Region I (NR_I), on the other hand, has higher net returns than the no treatment choice as the pest population approaches zero. This is an area favoring eradication.

The benefits of eradication of a pest can extend to an entire region and not just the area planted to the host crop. This follows from the common property

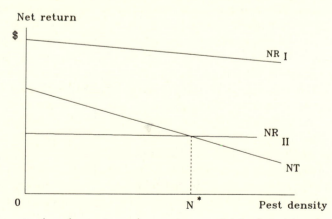

Figure 7.6. Present value of net return when pests are maintained at various levels.

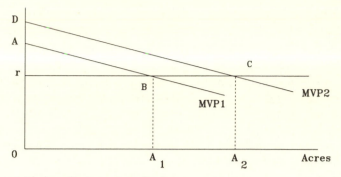

Figure 7.7. Area-wide benefits to pest eradication.

feature of mobile insects. In the boll weevil example, eradication has led to an expansion of the area planted to cotton in addition to yield increases and insecticide savings. The welfare gain to eradication due to crop expansion is shown in Figure 7.7. With eradication, land is switched from alternative crops to cotton. The initial marginal value of land for cotton (MVP_1) is a decreasing function of area planted, owing to the scarcity of land suitable for cotton production. The value of land for other uses is assumed to be constant at r. The equilibrium amount of land planted to cotton is at area A_1. Eradication leads to an increased marginal value of land for cotton to MVP_2, and the equilibrium acreage is A_2. The welfare gain is the area ABCD. This is a gain to all land owners who currently produce cotton and to those who have land that has potential for production of the crop protected by the eradication. In North and South Carolina there was about a 90% increase in cotton area planted after accounting for crop price and other factors in an acreage response model (Carlson et al., 1989). This area-wide acreage increase resulted in an additional gain to eradication (besides yield increase and insecticide savings) of about $14 per acre per year, or about 1 percent of the land value.

Another welfare effect of area-wide programs such as eradication is the change in income between groups of producers and consumers. A program that is large enough relative to the total market for the crop in question can increase total supply sufficiently to decrease crop prices. Producers in the eradication area will usually gain from the supply shift, but producers of the same crop not benefiting from eradication will suffer a welfare loss from the lower crop prices. This situation is depicted in Figure 7.8. Region I is the area of crop production where eradication is not undertaken and region II is the area eradicated. Following eradication, national supply is assumed to shift from S_{I+II} to S^*_{I-II} to give consumer gain equal to the area $a + b$ and producer welfare change of $d - a$. In the left diagram of the figure the supply curves of the two regions are shown. The eradication that increases yield and reduces costs will shift the supply curve in region II from S_{II} to S^*_{II}. The welfare gain of producers in region II is $i - (e + f)$. However, with the expansion of total supply, price declines to P^* and producers in region I will lose welfare equal to the area e. The magnitude of the supply and price changes will be determined by the percent reduction in marginal costs, the elasticities and

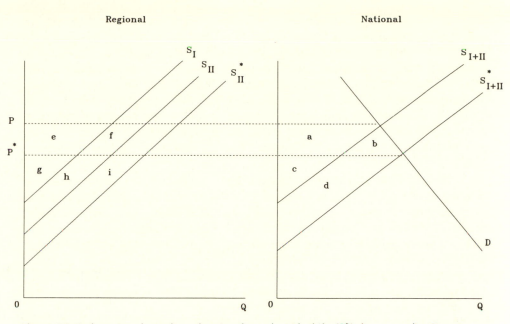

Figure 7.8. Industry total supply and regional supply with shifts (S_{II}^*) due to eradication.

supply and demand, and the relative shares of production in the eradicated and noneradicated areas. Analysis assuming constant elasticities and parallel supply shifts can employ the same model as was developed for evaluating the cancellation of pesticides that are only used on part of a crop (Lichtenberg et al., 1988). Taylor et al. (1983) utilized a multiple crop, econometric model including cotton and substitute crops to simulate six different options in a national boll weevil eradication program. They found that consumers benefited from all options, and because prices were suppressed some cotton farmers would have reduced benefits (Chapter 4).

Regional Pesticide Resistance Management

Although often measured on a micro level, pesticide resistance must often be managed on a regional level. Pests are difficult to manage because they are *mobile* and they often develop resistance to pesticides as less susceptible pests survive and reproduce. Resistance has been documented in several ways: by enumerating pest species found to be resistant at one or more locations for at least one crop season for various pesticides (Georghiou, 1986), by aggregating resistant pests for major crop areas at various points in time, and by measuring farmer pesticide use choices over time for various pesticide classes (Carlson, 1977). Regional rather than farmer management of pesticide resistance will be more profitable as pest mobility, spatial uniformity, and resistance severity increase.

The economically efficient level of resistance may change over time. We can think of pest susceptibility (absence of resistance) to a given pesticide or group of pesticides as a *stock resource* (see Chapter 2). The stock of susceptibility is renewable by altering pesticide use patterns or other activities, but these actions will usually reduce current output, increase current costs, and reduce profits. In addition, expansion of pest susceptibility is possible in the long run by introduction of new pesticides or regulatory decisions on pesticide cancellations. Major factors that decrease pest susceptibility are frequency and dosage of a given pesticide or related pesticides (called cross resistance). The more pests are shared across farms, the more actions that change resistance will affect the efficacy of pesticides on farms within a common region. Thus, the optimal pesticide use decisions for regions will differ from those of individual farmers within the region (Regev et al., 1976).

Individual farmers, groups of farmers, and other economic agents (pesticide companies or the extension service) can take actions that can affect the rate that pests develop resistance to pesticides. This process takes place over time and because there is a tradeoff between obtaining current versus future benefits it is an example of the dynamic optimization models given in Chapter 2. As long as current pesticide use rates will effect the biological efficacy of the pesticides in future periods, there is the possibility that efforts to conserve pest susceptibility may be profitable (Miranowski and Carlson, 1986). Conservation of susceptible pests has similarities to soil or water conservation processes.

However, because pests are sometimes shared across farmers there is an additional complication. This can be an example of the *open access*, or the common property resource management problem (Clark and Carlson, 1990). The more mobile various pests are the more likely it will be that common property management will be called for.

The major features of pesticide resistance development with and without the shared pest complications can be illustrated by a simple two-period production process. It will be assumed that the only way to reduce resistance is by reducing current pesticide use rates, that pesticides do not interact with other inputs in the production process, and that output and pesticide prices are known with certainty. Resistance can also be reduced by exogenous pesticide discoveries or fortuitous weather. For a model with exogenous resistance changes, pesticide–other input interactions, and long-term price forecasting see Clark and Carlson (1990). Regev et al. (1983) provide a continuous time version of the resistance problem with static price expectations and a *backstop technology*. The two-period Lagrangian model for a quadratic production function and a linear resistance build up process can be written as

$$L = \pi_t = b^{t-1}[f_1 X_t + f_2 R_t - .5(f_{11}X_t^2 + f_{22}R_t^2) + f_{12}R_t X_t - q_t X_t]$$
$$- \lambda(R_{t+1} - R_t = -\alpha X_t), \qquad 0 \leq \alpha < 1 \qquad t = 1, 2 \qquad (30)$$

where

π_t = profits or net returns to all inputs but pesticides
X_t = pesticide use rate
R_t = pest resistance to pesticide (stock)
q_t = price of pesticides relative to output price
α = depletion in resistance stock per unit of pesticide use

b^t = discount factor = $1/(1 + r)^t$
f_{ij} = production parameters, and
λ = Lagrangian multiplier reflecting the future value of pest susceptibility

In this problem resistance stock (R_t) changes between the two periods as pesticide use changes as shown in the Lagrangian constraint. The period 1 resistance stock (R_1) is given by actions in earlier periods. The optimal use levels (X_1^*, X_2^*) for the individual farmer with no pest spillovers from neighbors can be found by examining first-order conditions:

$$\partial L/\partial R_2 = b(f_2 - f_{22}R_2 + f_{12}X_2) + \lambda = 0 \tag{31}$$

$$\partial L/\partial X_1 = f_1 - f_{11}X_1 + f_{12}R_1 - q_1 + \lambda\alpha = 0 \tag{32}$$

$$\partial L/\partial X_2 = b(f_1 - f_{11}X_2 + f_{12}R_2 - q_2) + \lambda\alpha = 0 \tag{33}$$

$$\partial L/\partial \lambda = R_2 - R_1 + \alpha X_1 = 0 \tag{34}$$

The marginal revenue product of the second period resistance stock (MP_{R2}) is found to be equal to $-\lambda$ from equation (31). This can be used in equation (32) to show that optimum first period pesticide use is X_1^* such that $MP_{x1} - \alpha b MP_{R2} = q_1$. The optimal second period pesticide use X_2^* can be found from (33) and (34), given X_1^*. That is, X_2^* is chosen such that $MP_{x1} - \alpha f_{12}X_1^* = q_2$. In this case, $\alpha f_{12}X_1^*$ is the reduction in the marginal product of pesticides in period 2 from the use of pesticides in period 1, which changes resistance stock from R_1 to $R_2[\partial\Delta R/\partial X_1 \cdot \partial MP_{x1}/\partial R \cdot X]$. These relationships can be seen in Figure 7.9.

The first period optimum is at X_1^* for the no pest mobility or private property case. If there is a highly mobile pest population, then the farmers will act

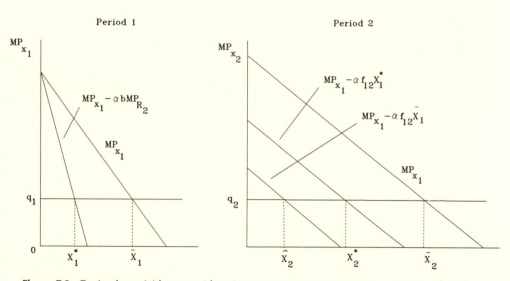

Figure 7.9. Optimal pesticide use with private property or open access pests, and with no resistance build up, two periods.

independently, ignore the cost of resistance build-up ($abMP_{R2}$), and choose the $\bar{X}_1$ level of pesticide. In the second period, the marginal value product of pesticides depends on first period use level unless there is no resistance build-up, $\alpha = 0$ and $MP_{x1} = MP_{x2}$. The major difference between private property and open access pests is that in the latter case farmers act as if they have a zero discount rate ($b = 0$) and completely ignore costs of resistance build-up. In a test of a more elaborate version of this model using insecticide, fungicide, and herbicide use data, Clark and Carlson (1990) found that: (1) insects in the United States were treated as common property (open access) with resistance build-up, (2) resistance was found for fungicides, and (3) weeds exhibited neither resistance build-up nor pure open access characteristics. This model does not require an estimate of R, which is often difficult to measure, but it must use a simple, linear resistance build-up process.

The optimal utilization level of resistance stock can sometimes be influenced by market structure. If there is a pest control market in which one pesticide producer has a pesticide with few substitutes, then we can expect underutilization of the resource in early years relative to later years (Dasgupta and Heal, 1979). The pesticide manufacturer will set prices to reduce pesticide use and slow resistance development relative to the competitive condition. In this setting the private firm may replace a regional organization in managing resistance, especially if the latter must contend with free-riders. The monopolistic firm management of resistance is similar to closed access management of common property. Whereas individual farmers will tend to overapply pesticides, a monopolistic firm will tend to operate where marginal benefits and costs are equated (Miranowski and Carlson, 1986). The clearest example of this are actions by private pesticide companies to limit use of their products by reformulating them as mixtures and recommending against high use rates. Management of the spread of pesticide resistance is like reduction of a negative externality of pesticide use.

Negative Pesticide Externalities

Wind, water, and movement of agricultural products carry pesticides from user sites to unintended locations sometimes causing *negative* effects on individuals inside and outside of agriculture. Aerial applications, irrigation, and certain weather conditions can add to the drift distances and severity. Both legal and illegal use procedures, together with accidental spills, can lead to unintended effects on food and water consumers and those working closely with pesticides.

Pesticide regulatory actions have changed the external effects over the past 20 years. Actions under federal and state regulations have entirely removed some of the most harmful pesticides from the marketplace. Other regulations limit worker reentry into treated fields, provide loader-mixer handling rules, and require warning signs that affect labor exposure. Pesticide label restrictions limit applications near water, residential, and other sensitive areas. Methods of application, maximum dosages, and timing of applications prior to harvest are sometimes specified on the label. However, even with these regulations external costs remain.

Information on health and environmental hazards of pesticides is constantly evolving. The technology for detecting minute quantities of residues has increased dramatically. Pesticides are some of the most studied chemicals in our environment. Economists may be able to assist in quantifying the negative externalities of pesticides, which can then be used in welfare evaluations of pesticide cancellation, registration, and other pesticide use decisions. It is useful to separate external health effects into short-term (*acute*) and long-term (*chronic*). Short-term human health effects include illnesses and even deaths from accidental or incidental exposure, whereas chronic effects are mutagenic, oncogenic (tumor), and neurological, and are discussed under long-term externalities.

Short-Term Externalities

Farmers, farm workers, and other laborers are exposed to pesticides in all stages from pesticide manufacturing, to distribution and application, to harvest and postharvest food handling. The risks of exposure and short-term ill effects influence occupational choices and may lead to wage differentials under different health risk situations. For the case in which there is knowledge about health risks in labor markets, models have been developed to attempt to measure the wage differentials from different risk exposures.

It is possible to conceptualize the external effects of pesticides on hired labor by application of a simple market model. Assume the market is made up of two types of firms: type 1 uses a hazardous pesticide and a second set of firms does not use the compound. Type 1 pays wage w_1 per month to workers, and type 2 pays wage w_2. Because of the differing susceptibility of workers to the pesticide, and random factors that affect exposure time and dosage, there is a probability m that any worker will be involved in an accidental exposure, and $(1 - m)$ that he will not. Assume that all probabilities and other factors are measured on a monthly basis. Further, assume that the average effect of an accident measured in medical cost, days lost from work, and suffering effects will total h percent of a months' wage. For risk neutral workers on type 1 farms the expected wage $E(w_1)$ after adjusting for health effects is

$$E(w_1) = w_1(1 - m) + w_1(1 - h)m = w_1(1 - mh) \tag{35}$$

In this market workers will compare working conditions, pesticide use levels, and wages, and relocate between the two types of firms. In the long run, expected wages in the two firm types will be equal

$$w_2 = w_1(1 - mh) \text{ or } w_1 = \frac{w_2}{(1 - mh)} \tag{36}$$

What equation (36) indicates is that the wage in type 1 firms will be bid up above those in type 2 firms by higher accident rates (m) and health costs per accident (hw_1) by the amount (mhw_1).

In most farming situations a variety of pesticides (z_i) with accident rates (m_i) and other factors affecting accident rates (f_i) occur. If wage rates (w_i) and other factors affecting earnings can be compiled, then earnings equations, which are

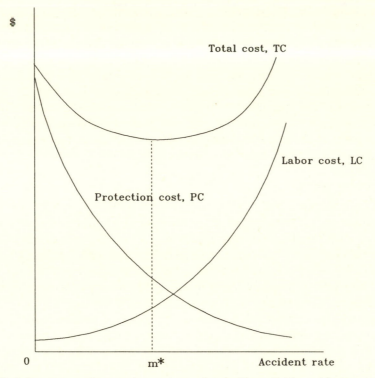

Figure 7.10. Labor costs and protection cost associated with pesticide accidents.

expanded versions of equation (36), can be developed and estimated. Although there are as yet few published estimates of wage differentials for pesticide exposure, such a model has been used by Crocker and Horst (1981) to find increased wages for farm workers owing to weather irritants and air pollutants.

From a farmer's point of view the labor cost (LC) of using hazardous pesticides is the difference in wage he must pay times the number of man months utilized (L_1)

$$LC = L_1(w_1 - w_2) \tag{37}$$

Using the w_1 value in (36) we find that this labor cost is

$$LC = L_1 w_2 \left[\frac{1}{(1 - mh)} - 1 \right] = \frac{L_1 w_2 mh}{1 - mh} \tag{38}$$

The general shape of a *labor cost equation* such as that in (38) associated with the use of hazardous chemicals is shown in Figure 7.10. It begins with a positive intercept with no accidents and increases with accident rate (m) at an increasing rate. (The second derivative of LC with respect to m is positive.) Labor cost will shift upward to the left as wages on nonchemical farms (w_2) rise, with the use of more labor (L_1), or with rising cost per accident (hw_1). Including risk aversion, increases in medical fees or new information on adverse health effects might increase the implicit values placed on health costs per accident.

Farmers using hazardous chemicals can reduce labor accidents by various methods. Use of protective clothing, altering pesticide loading procedures and equipment, using more supervisory labor, or switching to less dangerous but more expensive pesticides are possibilities. An indirect cost function for pesticide accident prevention (PC) might be represented as

$$PC = PC(w, g, r, x, m) \qquad (39)$$

Here w, g, r represent labor, pesticide, and other input prices, x is a vector of fixed factors, and m is the accident rate. This function is similar to the averting behavior model described in Chapter 6. This function could be estimated using individual farm or regional data for uniform crop mixes and labor use per unit area. The framework could also be broadened to include alterations in crop mix that will affect accident rates and labor requirements using aggregate models (see Chapter 4).

A pesticide protection function is shown as PC in Figure 7.10. It will decrease at a diminishing rate because it will be more and more expensive to drive the accident rate to zero with positive levels of use of hazardous pesticides. The total costs of pesticide accidents are given by the sum of protection (PC) and additional labor costs (LC). The *minimum total cost* is at accident rate m^* where the marginal cost due to labor plus prevention are equal to zero.

$$\partial TC/\partial m = \partial LC/\partial m + \partial PC/\partial m = 0 \qquad (40)$$

The market equilibrium accident rate for pesticides (m^*) may not be the social optimum under some circumstances. If workers do not know the accident probabilities from exposure to various pesticides they may tend to underestimate m. This is especially true when the scientific community cannot determine these effects because health symptoms do not occur until long periods after exposure. A more basic problem is that some pesticides may have such high accident and health effects relative to their benefits or private protective costs that zero exposure is the optimum. This would occur if PC was below LC as m approaches zero in Figure 7.10. In this case regulatory actions to remove the chemical from the market place or regulate worker exposure should be considered.

Labor market wage differentials, ($w_1 - w_2$), may not adequately reflect pesticide accident risks to farmers themselves. If farmers (and their family members) are primarily providing all labor and incurring all the exposure to pesticides in the production process, then farmer choices among pesticides and between pesticides and other inputs may reflect perceived pesticide risks (Capalbo and Antle, 1989). A farm household production model that includes farmer health was developed and used by Pitt and Rosenzweig (1986). In a utility maximization model in which farm income increases with chemical use, while farmer health decreases with chemical use, farmers would tend to choose chemicals and substitute inputs to maximize utility by finding the chemical use level where the marginal disutility of health is equal to the marginal utility of the income from the pesticide. As Capalbo and Antle (1989) suggest, if it were possible to obtain individual farmers' use of chemicals with different levels of health risk, then the value of the health effects could be inferred from the correlation between chemical use and health risk.

Another market in which health and other external costs of pesticides might be revealed is in the pesticide market itself. As indicated in the labor market and farmer household utility models there are likely to be *premiums* paid for pesticides (z_i) with less health costs (h), less environmental effects (e), and less potential for food (fc) and water contamination (wc). New pesticides come on the market and others have been canceled. These products have measurable characteristics that affect farm productivity (MVP) as well as safety. A price equation for a pesticide with price r_i might be expressed as a hedonic model that includes the above characteristics

$$r_i = r(h_i, e_i, fc_i, \text{NC}_i, \text{MVP}_i, z_i) \tag{41}$$

Utilizing a model similar to (41), Beach and Carlson (1993) found that farmers are paying higher prices for herbicides with lower leaching potential and lower toxicity to mammals. R and D investments of private firms, as well as cancellation and registration decisions of EPA can alter the mix of characteristics available. Objective market estimates of implicit weights given to particular safety characteristics of pesticides would be helpful in regulatory and marketing decisions. For example Reichelderfer (1990) found that there is a growing use of safety claims being made in pesticide advertisements in farm magazines. Pesticide recommendation manuals frequently include oral toxicity and water leaching ratings of pesticides.

Long-Term Pesticide Externalities

The primary long-term externality of pesticides is generally believed to be changes in human health related to direct occupational exposure or through food and water residues (National Research Council, 1987). Some risk models focusing on long-term, low-level contaminants (radon, pesticides, radiation) are available. They include those emphasizing estimation variability (Lichtenberg and Zilberman, 1986), learning rates (Viscusi and Magat, 1988), and risk perceptions (Smith and Johnson, 1988).

In *cancer risk assessments*, tumor-inducing dosages (potency factors or Q^*) of specific pesticides are determined by extrapolation of tumors per unit of body weight from animal feeding studies. Human exposure is estimated from lifetime consumption levels (CL) of foods multiplied by the residue levels per unit of food. Residues levels in food are highly variable, but maximum or legal tolerance levels (TL) are established when each pesticide is first registered for use on each of the major foods. In the NRC (1987) study the extra tumor risk (TR) from consuming all foods (J) over a lifetime related to a particular pesticide (z_i) was estimated as

$$\text{TR}_i = \sum_j^J \text{TL}_{ij} \cdot \text{CL}_j \cdot Q_i^* \tag{42}$$

In the absence of information on the actual residues of various pesticides present in food, the NRC study assumed that every unit of food had residues of every pesticide for which the pesticide was registered for use at the maximum permissible or tolerance level (TL_{ij}). The tolerance level residue levels were multiplied and summed over lifetime consumption levels (CL_j), and this product was multiplied by the tumor potency factor (Q_i^*). This computation was carried out to give a "worst case" exposure and tumor risk assessment for each pesticide and each major food group (NRC, 1987).

Since the NRC model is in a multiplicative form, estimation errors are compounded from each of the three variables. TL residues assume use of pesticides on every acre of many crops for which they are rarely if ever used. Tolerances are set at 10 to 1,000 times the highest levels of residues ever found in actual food samples (Archibald and Winter, 1989). Most pesticides have only been found in certain food parts (fruit and vegetable skins, or one meat organ) and not on the full weight of the food, and some residues are reduced by food preparation. Upper 95% confidence interval values rather than mean levels of per capita consumption and tumor probability per unit of pesticide are used in many risk assessments. In addition, many pesticides cannot be clearly classified as oncogenic from animal studies. For example, the high dosages (necessary to find positive effects) of plant pesticides (fungicides) used in animal feeding studies may be inducing side effects separate from tumor effects.

Cancer is a complex, three step process, and some compounds only induce one of the three necessary steps of mutation, promotion, and progression (Ames et al., 1987). Quite different results are obtained from different extrapolation models (linear, threshold, single or multiple hit). In addition there are tumors and cancers associated with many natural and other chemical sources that are much more prevalent than from pesticides (Ames et al., 1987). Overall, even if one accepts the pessimistic cancer risk assumptions made by the NRC, cancer risks from exposure to 28 major pesticides only change the base cancer risk from all causes from .25 to .2558; a 2.3 percent increase (Carlson, 1991).

Another type of cancer risk assessment is followed in epidemiological studies of long-term exposure of farmers to pesticides. Farmers live longer and have fewer cancers than people in most occupations. Also, certain leukemia rates are higher for residents of rural than urban counties. For example, Hoar (1986) found a sixfold increase in one cancer type (non-Hodgkins lymphoma, NHL) for farmers in the Plains States exposed to 20 or more days of herbicide use per year compared to those farmers who used no herbicides. But statistical problems abound with epidemiological studies of human health because of small sample sizes, lack of adjustment for age and other omitted variables, and lack of confirmation by other assessment methods. The Hoar study examined 297 men with NHL, but only five were using herbicides more than 20 days per year. Years of herbicide exposure was significant in the statistical model, but this independent variable is highly correlated with age, a highly significant variable in explaining all cancer rates. Finally, the phenoxy herbicide, 2, 4-D, used by most of the farmers in the Hoar study has not been shown to be carcinogenic in animal feeding studies. One encouraging factor in the Hoar study was that it showed that farmers who use protective clothing and equipment had significantly lower cancer rates than those who do not.

A final area of growing concern is exposure of people to pesticides in ground water used for drinking. Nielson and Lee (1987) used county level estimates of use of a group of soluble pesticides together with an index of soil and ground water characteristics to estimate the potential for ground water contamination from pesticides. There are many soil micoorganisms, soil pH, weather, and other environmental variables that influence pesticide movement and degradation in soils. Refinements to include these factors and better pesticide use estimates than those used by Nielson and Lee (1987) have been undertaken to improve regulatory decisions and private adjustments to water contamination (Danielson et al., 1993). However, the Nielson and Lee study did give general indications of where ground water threats are highest, and they did indicate how information on sales of water filtration systems could be used to infer demand for water safety.

Information from several Midwest states indicates that large shares (up to 70%) of measured contaminations of wells with pesticides are in close proximity to pesticide loading sites (Mueller, 1989). This may indicate that usual farm application rates of pesticides are not necessarily the main source of contamination of ground water. It also indicates that safer loading, equipment, storage facilities, and containers are probably needed by farmers and pesticide dealers. Ground water is an important natural resource in many rural areas that can sustain long-term damage if seriously contaminated. Studies are needed on the willingness of rural households to pay for reduced levels of pesticides in drinking water.

Understanding the human and environmental damages from pesticides is very difficult. The problem is more complex when one must assess long-term health effects and indirect effects of pesticide build-up in the environment. As indicated in the studies above, care is needed in interpreting use, movement, exposure, and dosage-response relationships. Many newer pesticides degrade rapidly, but metabolites, inert ingredients, and combinations of pesticides may also pose threats. The studies reviewed here indicate that economists may have a role to play in finding tradeoffs between productivity and safety of pesticides. Most of the studies examining these benefits and hazards follow from the federal regulatory statutes that require such analysis, and to which we now turn.

Pesticide Regulation Analysis

Federal and state pesticide regulations are primarily designed to reduce potential damage to human health and the environment. The original federal legislation is the Federal Insecticide, Fungicide, and Rodenticide Act (FIFRA) of 1947 with numerous, subsequent amendments (National Research Council, 1980; Reichel-derfer and Hinkle, 1989). This legislation explicitly calls for analysis of changes in social costs and benefits of pesticide introductions, cancellations, and other use regulations to avoid "any unreasonable risk to man or the environment taking into account the economic, social, and environmental costs and benefits of any pesticide."

The basic concepts of market supply and demand and consumer and producer surpluses can assist in determining the economic consequences of introducing or canceling a particular pesticide or group of similar pesticides for particular crops and locations. The simplest case of the *welfare effects* of a proposed cancellation of a pesticide is shown in Figure 7.11. For cases with several crops and prices being affected by a cancellation, the models in Chapter 4 are applicable. The initial

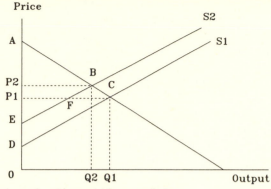

Figure 7.11. Reduced supply with pesticide cancellation.

industry marginal cost of production is represented by the supply curve S_1, with equilibrium price P_1 and output level Q_1. Suppose the cancellation of a pesticide will increase marginal costs of production of the single crop in question to S_2. In this case the shift is represented by a parallel shift in the linear supply function.[1] Following cancellation there would be a new equilibrium at point B. The cancellation is not assumed to change the demand for the good in question. That is, the external costs of the pesticides are not imposed on the consumers of the good, but on other individuals. The change in consumer surplus (CS) is the area $CS_1 - CS_2 = ACP_1 - ABP_2 = BCP_1P_2$. The change in producer surplus with the cancellation is the area $CDP_1 - BEP_2 = CDEF - BFP_1P_2$. The total welfare loss would be the combined producer plus consumer surplus changes or the area CDEB. The welfare gains from increased safety and environmental protection would need to be compared with this welfare loss.

In the case depicted in Figure 7.11, consumer surplus will always decline with the pesticide cancellation, but producer surplus can either be smaller or larger. The changes in producer surplus are more likely to be positive for products with more inelastic demand curves since the change in price will be more than offset by the smaller quantity that is produced. If the product in question has a very elastic demand curve such as for exported products or when the pesticide restriction only pertains to a small part of the market for a given commodity, then producers (users of the chemical) will necessarily lose while consumers will lose very little.

The welfare change from a pesticide introduction such as for a new pesticide or the expansion of a pesticide to a new crop is merely the reverse of that shown in Figure 7.11. S_2 is the initial marginal cost curve, and the new technology lowers cost to S_1. This would result in total welfare changes of BCDE. Consumers gain BCP_1P_2 while producers may either gain or lose; the change is the area $CDEF - BFP_1P_2$.

---

[1] Various types of supply shifts are possible from technology introductions or cancellations. See Lemieux and Wohlgenant (1989) for a justification of a parallel shift and Norton and Davis (1981) for a general discussion.

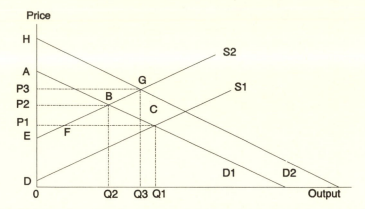

Figure 7.12. Welfare changes when pesticide cancellation reduces supply and expands demand.

A different welfare evaluation is necessary if consumers of products produced with pesticides can recognize potential safety changes and adjust consumption. The combined cost increase and demand increase of a pesticide cancellation are illustrated in Figure 7.12. The increase in marginal cost of production is from S_1 to S_2 as before, but this is accompanied by a shift in demand for the safer good from D_1 to D_2. Equilibrium price increases from P_1 to P_3 while equilibrium quantity shifts from Q_1 to Q_3. The change in consumer surplus is the area $CP_1A - GP_3H$, which can either be positive or negative. Producer surplus change is $CDP_1 - GEP_3$. Total welfare change in this market is the combined change in consumer and producer surplus, which can be represented by the area $GBAH - CDEB$. In Figure 7.12 this is the area between the two demand curves less the area between the two supply curves. The factors affecting the change in consumer and producer surplus are illustrated below. If the pesticide has externalities in other markets besides where it is used as an input, then these welfare gains of the cancellation should be added to the welfare change $GBAH - CDEB$.

Two of the most difficult tasks in evaluating welfare costs and benefits of pesticide regulations are estimating the shifts in supply and demand and determining new equilibrium prices and outputs. For small shifts in supply and demand, constant price elasticities can be assumed (Lichtenberg et al., 1988). With linear demand and supply curves one can use estimates of supply and demand elasticities to determine percent changes in price and quantity. Given these values it is possible to compute the changes in producer and consumer welfare as indicated by the areas in Figures 7.11 and 7.12.

As an example of how to compute new equilibrium prices and quantities, assume that estimates of final good supply (e) and demand (n) elasticities are available. The percentage shifts in the quantity demanded and supplied from the pesticide cancellation must be estimated; let these amounts be represented by the parameters b and a, respectively. The demand and supply equations with these parallel shifts can be written in differentiated form where $Ex = dx/x$, or percent change in x where x is P or Q:

$$\text{Demand:} \quad Q = f(P) + b = EQ = nEP + b \tag{43}$$

$$\text{Supply:} \quad Q = g(P) + a = EQ = eEP + a \tag{44}$$

These two equations can be solved for the two unknowns, percent change in price (EP) and percent change in quantity (EQ), by first equating percent change in supply and demand to obtain the percent change in price

$$\left. \begin{array}{l} nEP + b = eEP + a \\ EP = (a - b)/(n - e) \end{array} \right\} \tag{45}$$

The percent change in equilibrium quantity is

$$\left. \begin{array}{l} (EQ - b)/n = (EQ - a)/e \\ EQ = (eb - na)/(e - n) \end{array} \right\} \tag{46}$$

When price supports are present or strong multicommodity effects should be included, solutions to many equation models can be found by matrix inversion (Gardner, 1987).

As an example of the analysis of welfare changes consider the case of the cancellation of an insecticide used exclusively on apples for fresh consumption. Let demand elasticity, n, be $-.5$, and assume that the supply elasticity, e, is $+.3$, that cancellation reduces supply by 4 percent, and that demand expands 2 percent because of increases in perceived safety to apple consumers. Initial price and quantity are 20 cents per pound for 5 billion bushels of apples. Using the price change equation the percent change in price, $(P_3 - P_1)/P_1$ in Figure 7.12, would be $EP = (-6/-.8) = 7.5\%$ and $P_3 = 1.075P_1$ or \$.215. The change in output can be computed similarly using the quantity change expression:

$$EQ = [.3(2) + .5(-4)]/(.3 + .5) = -1.75\%$$

or $Q_3 = (1 - .0175)5 = 4.9125$. The other values needed to locate point B in Figure 7.12 can be computed using equation (45) and assuming that there is no demand shift $(b = 0)$ so that P_2 is \$.21 and Q_2 is 4.875. For linear, price-dependent demand and supply curves the points D, E, A, H in Figure 7.12 for this example are $-.466$, $-.44$, $.6$, and $.608$, respectively.[2] The net gain in consumer surplus (area GBAH) is \$63.3 million per year, but the loss to producers is \$130 million; therefore, the net loss from the cancellation is \$66.7 million. This net loss should be compared with the gain in increased safety (besides the apple demand shift) to assist in arriving at a cancellation decision.

Regulations With Price Supports and Pest Heterogeneity

Pest densities are highly variable across crops and locations in the United States. Because farmers observe pest levels and adjust dosages and type of pesticide used, there can be very heterogeneous pesticide use patterns in different regions. The introduction or cancellation of a pesticide will have quite different effects on users

---

[2] The supply curve intercepts are negative in this case.

versus nonusers of that pesticide. For a cancellation, users will experience both the increase in marginal cost and the increase in product price, whereas nonusers will only experience the increased product prices. Lichtenberger et al. (1988) show how a linear demand and supply model like (45) can be modified to estimate changes in producer surplus for the users and nonusers. The supply equation (44) is modified by computing a different shift parameter, $a' = ak$, where k is the share of total production accounted for by users of the pesticide in question, and a is the percent reduction in output for these producers. The change in producers surplus for nonusers is estimated by letting a equal zero. Other divisions of producer and consumer surplus can also be computed such as for foreign versus domestic consumers, or for producers in various regions. The data required are the shares of production and consumption in each area and the regional demand and supply elasticities.

Frequently, farmers in different regions will have very different opportunity costs of resources; hence, supply elasticities for the same crop will differ. The major finding that comes from models that include spatial variability in pests is that losses in producer surplus from pesticide cancellations vary greatly, and that the gains to nonusers of the pesticide in question relative to the losses of users will increase as either demand or supply becomes more elastic. Likewise, the share of welfare losses that consumers experience relative to producers will rise as demand and supply become more elastic. Lichtenberg et al. (1988) use the example of the cancellation of parathion on three tree crops to illustrate these points. Consumer surplus gains are usually larger if there are expansions in demand from banning a pesticide. However, as Osteen and Kuchler (1987) and other studies on pesticide restrictions have shown, it is possible to get an increase in aggregate health risks when banned pesticides are replaced by other pesticides used at high rates. Therefore, it is necessary to carefully estimate pesticide market shares following a cancellation to conduct risk–benefit analyses.

For several of the major field crops grown in the United States there are price support programs that operate to hold producer prices 15–40% above world equilibrium prices in some years (Gardner, 1987). This distortion in raw agricultural markets increases output and alters the changes in producer and consumer surplus from a pesticide cancellation. For a permanent government price support program with price support or target price P_T above equilibrium price P_1 the consumer and producer surpluses can be illustrated following Lichtenberg and Zilberman (1986) (see Fig. 7.13). S_1 and D are the supply and demand curves for an agricultural crop with equilibrium output at Q_1 before pesticide cancellation. With pesticide cancellation there is a supply shift to S_2 and quantity sold is Q_2. Loss in consumer surplus is equal to the area $g + h + i + j + k + l$, and losses to producers are equal to $a + b + c$. Government expenditures going to producers to maintain the price support are decreased because of the reduced output associated with the cancellation by the amount equal to the area $c + e + f + g + h + i + j + k + l$. The net change in welfare is $e + f - (a + b)$. This is also equal to the direct regulatory loss $(-a)$ and the reduction in dead weight loss from $d + e + f$ to $b + d$. The consumer and producer welfare changes can be positive or negative. The total welfare effect depends upon the relative size of demand and supply elasticities and

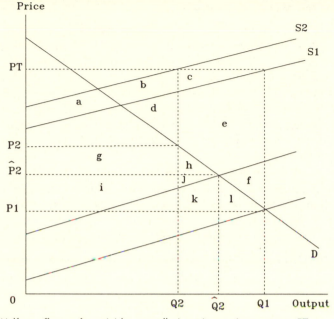

Figure 7.13. Welfare effects of pesticide cancellation given price support, PT.

the supply shift as discussed above. But in this case the welfare effect is also affected by the percent price distortion owing to the price support $(P_T - P_1)/P_1$. The larger the price distortion and the more elastic the supply, the larger is area e and, consequently, the larger will be the reduction in government payments from a given shift in supply.

In this model consumers as taxpayers usually *gain* from the cancellation while producers' welfare is reduced. This is in contrast to the simple model (Fig. 7.11) in which consumers always lose by a pesticide cancellation and producers can either lose or gain. A model that combines taxpayer savings and a demand expansion (such as in Fig. 7.12) would increase the welfare gains to consumers of a pesticide cancellation. The combination of price supports and benefits accruing primarily to consumers has tended to lead agricultural producers as a group to not favor pesticide cancellations while consumers favor them. Farmers are more likely to favor certain pesticide restrictions when some of the safety benefits accrue to them such as with local ground water residues or direct effects on on-farm labor.

Caution is needed in applying the models above, especially when choosing supply elasticities, which are frequently estimated when a variety of farm program requirements such as minimum diverted acreage is in effect. Also, all of the above models are sensitive to the estimated magnitudes of the marginal cost shifts from the regulations. Regional models that explicitly account for the multiple-product nature of supply and product demand substitution can help estimate welfare effects of new technology introduction and technology bans (see Chapter 4).

Yield and Cost Effects of Pesticide Regulations

Often complete information is not available to accurately compute changes in marginal cost from banning a pesticide. As discussed by the National Research Council team (NRC, 1980) analysts frequently try to represent the change in marginal cost from a cancellation by a change in pesticide cost to produce the same level of output. However, this does not include other factors of production that will change unless all other inputs are separable in production from pesticides. If there is a sizable shift in supply and fairly elastic demand, then output will decline and other costs of production may decline. Finally, yield per unit area may decline when a pesticide is banned.

Taylor et al. (1979) present a model for computing the effects of pesticide cancellations or introductions that combines information on yield and variable cost changes. This model allows estimation of the welfare changes for those farmers who produce substitute crops. Also, it can indicate how agricultural production along with producer and consumer surplus changes through time. Yield and acreage are represented by

$$Y_t = g(t) \tag{47}$$

$$A_t = f(A_{t-1}, NR_t^*, G_t) \tag{48}$$

where Y_t is yield, t is time measured in annual units, A_t is acreage planted in year t, NR_t^* is expected net revenue per acre, and G is a vector of agricultural policy variables. Together the acreage and yield equations give supply: $Q_t^s = A_t Y_t$. Demand and market equilibrium are represented as

$$Q_t^d = h(P_t, I_t) \tag{49}$$

$$A_t Y_t = Q_t^d \tag{50}$$

where Q_t^d is quantity demanded in year t, P_t is output price, and I_t is a vector of demand variables. When there is a cancellation of a pesticide there is a discrete change in supply, ΔQ_t, so that the new supply curve is

$$(Q_t^s + \Delta Q_t) = (A_t + \Delta A_t)(Y_t + \Delta Y_t) \tag{51}$$

where ΔX is a discrete change in any variable X.

Substituting values from equations (47) and (48), the supply equation following the cancellation can be written as

$$(Q_t^s + \Delta Q_t) = [f(A_{t-1}, NR_t^*, G_t) + \Delta f(A_{t-1}, NR_t^*, G_t)][g(t) + \Delta g(t)] \tag{52}$$

The change in per acre yield, $\Delta g(t)$, from the pesticide withdrawal depends on the change in use of alternative pesticides (postcancellation market shares) and acreage shifts. Let yield be the weighted average of expected yield obtained from each pesticide

$$Y_t = g(t) = \sum_i y_{it} F_{it} \tag{53}$$

where y_{it} is yield using pesticide i, and F_{it} is the fraction of the acreage treated with the ith pesticide. In a similar way, the change in yield is based on the change in the market share of pesticide treatments for pesticide i, including no treatment:

$$\Delta g(t) = \sum_i y_{it} \Delta F_{it} \tag{54}$$

The change in use of various pesticides when one pesticide is canceled (ΔF_{it}) can be estimated by expert opinion, a separate marketing model, or simply setting it equal to the historical market shares of the pesticides excluding the pesticide being evaluated.

Change in crop acreage patterns is another important response to a cancellation. One way to estimate change in acreage is to compute changes in costs and net revenue from exogenous information and then use NR^* as an independent variable in econometric estimation of acreage equations by region. Let expected net revenue be

$$NR_t^* = P_t^* Y_t^* - C_t \tag{55}$$

where P_t^* is expected per unit output price, Y_t^* is expected yield, and C_t is per acre variable costs. Using the change in net revenues from equation (55) in the acreage change part of equation (52) gives

$$\Delta f = \Delta f / \Delta NR_t^* \cdot \Delta NR_t^*$$
$$= \Delta f / \Delta NR_t^* \cdot (P^* \Delta Y_t^* - \Delta C_t) \tag{56}$$

The first term on the right-hand side of (56) is the econometric estimate of the effect of net revenue in the acreage response equation (48). To estimate the final term on the right side of (56), independent estimates of expected change in yield (ΔY_t^*) and change in variable costs (ΔC) are needed. The values from equation (54) should give farmers' estimates of yield change from the cancellation. Changes in variable cost ΔC_t can be obtained from

$$\Delta C_t = \sum_i c_{it} \Delta F_{it} \tag{57}$$

where c_{it} is level of variable cost using pesticide i, and ΔF_{it} is the change in the fraction of acreage treated with pesticide i.

What the above derivation shows is that if one has econometric estimates of yield [$g(t)$] and acreage response functions (f), these can be combined with estimates of c_{it}, Y_{it}, F_{it}, ΔF_{it}, and ΔY_t^* to determine the new supply function. Taylor et al. (1979) used this model to determine the effects of withdrawing all insecticides from cotton production in the United States for the 1977–1985 period. With estimated regional yield reductions of 5–28 percent and per acre variable costs increasing 1–20 dollars per acre, aggregate, annual producer plus consumer surplus loss was estimated to be $775 million dollars.

As the realism of multiproduct firms, nonseparable pest control functions, estimation errors, farm policies, farmer risk aversion, and consumer preferences for food safety are added to models to evaluate pesticide restrictions, the transparencies of changes in cost, changes in yield, and changes in consumer utility are sometimes lost. Differing assumptions and modeling approaches can give different estimates of welfare losses of pesticide regulations (Swanson and Grube, 1986; Taylor et al., 1992). Care is needed to see that a range of parameter values is evaluated to determine the tradeoffs brought about by pesticide regulations.

Other Pesticide Regulations

Considerable premarket safety data are required by law before pesticides are registered for use. Therefore, changes in data requirements may affect expected profits and pesticide R & D investments (CAST, 1980). Also, cancellation of pesticide products may both increase opportunities for new products and signal an overall higher cost of maintaining the registration of a pesticide. Economists have investigated the new product development process and have determined that regulations are slowing the investment level and discovery rate. Hatch (1983) found that delays in the time from discovery to first registration (about 6 years on average) increased the cost per new product registered with an elasticity of approximately .8. He did not find any quantifiable effects of the introduction of the 1972 FIFRA amendments. These amendments increased the pesticide review process. Because of the lengthy pesticide discovery process it is difficult to explain changes in pesticide R & D. However, the recent (1984–1989) decline in pesticide sales may be contributing to the first decline in pesticide R & D expenditures in the past two decades (see Fig. 7.2).

There are also economic dimensions to policy questions such as the appropriate level of patent and other market protection to stimulate pesticide and other research investments. Legislation has been proposed to restore the *patent life* of pesticides similar to that accomplished for drugs in 1984. With increased safety tests required, longer periods elapse between pesticide discovery and market introduction, which leads in turn to a shorter time of effective patent protection. The shorter effective patent lives may partly account for the reduced level of private R & D expenditures on pesticides in recent years (Carlson, 1989).

In addition, when a pesticide goes off patent there is a provision in FIFRA called "data compensation," which specifies that companies that seek follow-on registrations must cite all the safety data that the original registrant developed (since 1970 and within 15 years of the original date of submission) and offer compensation for use of this safety data. This provision was included to help eliminate duplicate testing, but at the same time compensate original developers of the safety information. A method for determining adequate compensation is not specified in the statute. Whether opportunity costs of regulatory delays, compensation for foregone interest or testing costs, or early entry benefits should be part of the compensation is not clear. An equitable sharing of costs should recognize business risks undertaken by the original registrant, but should also determine the extent to which restricting entry of new generic products will increase pesticide prices to farmers. Pesticide prices in various markets are influenced by product discoveries and introductions as well as presence of generic products of off-patient pesticides.

Many of the group pest control, health and environmental costs, and subsequent regulatory responses reflect the negative and positive externalities for pesticides and pests. Control of pests or pesticide resistance by one farmer can provide positive externalities to neighboring farms and reduce agricultural commodity prices. Pesticide movement to wildlife, food, and water will frequently result in negative externalities for consumers and others. Regulatory actions and subsidies to find safer pest management methods continue to evolve. Information on the relative net benefits of various public programs and regulations will continue to be a major area of research for economists and others. Efficient pest management is closely linked to water quality, technological developments, land, human capital, and other agricultural resources.

Pesticides and other resources to manage pests are an integral part of crop systems. Recommendations for treatment at efficient pest densities (economic thresholds) are needed. These recommendations must incorporate interactions between predators and pests, pesticides and other inputs, and pesticides and crop growth. Many pests are best managed by multifarm units since pests are often quite mobile. Pesticides and pests move across farms, and pesticides damage nontarget species. Human health effects can be measured by both simulated effects on test animals and by protective (averting) actions taken by consumers. Regulatory effects on producers and consumers must recognize commodity program effects as well as changes in pesticide use following pesticide cancellations. These evaluations have been increased over the past 20 years and economists have a key role to play in finding the correct balance between benefits and hazards of pesticides.

REFERENCES

Ames, B.N., R. Magawand, and L.S. Gold. "Ranking Possible Carcinogenic Hazards." *Science* 236:271–280, 1987.

Anderson, J. et al. *Agricultural Decision Analysis*. Ames, IA: Iowa State Univ. Press, 1977.

Antle, J.M. "Pesticide Policy, Production Risk, and Producer Welfare." Resources for the Future, Washington, D.C., 1988.

Archibald, S.O. and C.K. Winter. "Pesticide Residues and Cancer Risks." *California Agriculture* 43(6):6–9, 1989.

Beach, O.D. and G.A. Carlson. "A Hedonic Analysis of Herbicides: Does Safety Matter." *American Journal of Agricultural Economics* 75:(forthcoming), 1993.

Burrows, T.M. "Pesticide Demand and Integrated Pest Management: A Limited Dependent Variable Analysis." *American Journal of Agricultural Economics* 65:806–810, 1983.

Capalbo, S.M. and J.M. Antle. "Biological and Economic Models for the Measurement of Pollution Externalities." *American Journal of Agricultural Economics* 71:458–463, 1989.

Carlson, G.A. "Risk Assessment and Regulatory Priorities for Pesticide Residues in Food." In W. Furgeson and P. Szmedra (eds.): *Pesticide Residues and Food Safety*. ERS, USDA Research Report, Washington, D.C., 1991.

Carlson, G.A. "A Decision-Theoretic Approach to Crop Disease Prediction and Control." *American Journal of Agricultural Economics* 52:216–233, 1970.

Carlson, G.A. "Risk Reducing Inputs Related to Agricultural Pests." Risk Analysis for Agricultural Production Firms: Concepts, Information Requirements and Policy Issues. S180 Proceedings. Department of Agricultural Economics, University of Illinois, 1984.

Carlson, G.A. "Externalities and Research Priorities in Agricultural Pest Control." *American Journal of Agricultural Economics* 71:453–457, 1989.

Carlson, G.A. "Long-run Productivity of Insecticides." *American Journal of Agricultural Economics* 59:543–548, 1977.

Carlson, G.A. "Economic and Biological Variables Affecting Demand for Publicly and Privately Provided Pest Information." *American Journal of Agricultural Economics* 62(5):1001–1006, 1980.

Carlson, G.A. and D.V. DeBord. "Public Mosquito Abatement." *Journal of Environmental Economics and Management* 3:142–152, 1976.

Carlson, G.A., G. Sappie, and M. Hammig. Economic Returns to Boll Weevil Eradication. USDA, ERS Research Report, Washington, D.C., 1989.

Carson, R. *Silent Spring.* Boston: Houghton Mifflin Co., 1962.

CAST. Impact of Government Regulation on the Development of Chemical Pesticides for Agriculture and Forestry. Report No. 87. Council on Agricultural Science and Technology, Ames, Iowa, 1981.

Clark, J.S. and G.A. Carlson. "Econometrically Distinguishing Between Private and Common Property: The Case of Pesticide Resistance." *Journal of Environmental Economics and Management* 19:45–60, 1990.

Cochran, M.J. "Economic Methods and Implications of IPM Strategies for Cotton." In *Integrated Pest Management of Major Agricultural System.* R.E. Frisbie and P.L. Alkisson (eds.): College Station, TX: Texas Agricultural Station, 1986.

Cochran, M.J. and W. Boggess. "Integrated Pest Management: Risk Implications for Natural Resources Use." In *Incorporation of Risk in Analysis of Farm Management Decisions Affecting Natural Resource Use.* Corvallis, OR: Oregon State University, Agricultural Experiment Station Special Report 821, 1988.

Crocker, T.D. and R.L. Horst, Jr. "Hours of Work, Labor Productivity, and Environmental Conditions: A Case Study." *Review of Economics and Statistics* 63:361–385, 1981.

Cropper, M.L. et al. "Determinants of Pesticide Regulation: A Statistical Analysis of EPA Decision Making." *Journal of Political Economy* 100(1): 175–197, 1992.

Daberkow, S. and K.H. Reichelderfer. "Low-Input Agriculture: Trends, Goals and Prospects for Input Use." *American Journal of Agricultural Economics* 70:1159–1166, 1988.

Danielson, L.E. et al. *Ground Water Contamination and Costs of Pesticide Restrictions in the Southeastern Coastal Plain.* Water Resources Research Institute, North Carolina State University, Raleigh, North Carolina, 1993.

Dasgupta, P. and G.H. Heal. *Economic Theory and Exhaustible Resources.* New York: Cambridge University Press, 1979.

Feder, G. "Pesticides, Information and Pest Management Under Uncertainty." *American Journal of Agricultural Economics* 61:97–103, 1979.

Gardner, B.L. *The Economics of Agricultural Policies.* New York: Macmillan Pub. Co., 1987.

Georghiou, G.P. "The Magnitude of the Resistance Problem." *Pesticide Resistance:*

Strategies and Tactics for Management. Washington, DC: National Academy Press, 1986.

Gutierrez, A.P. and R. Daxl. "Modeling Predation." In G. Conway (ed.): *Pest Management.* New York: John Wiley and Sons, Inc., 1984.

Hall, D.C. and R.B. Norgaard, "On the Timing and Application of Pesticides." *American Journal of Agricultural Economics* 55:198–201, 1974.

Hall, D.C. and L.J. Moffitt. "Application of the Economic Threshold for Interseasonal Pest Control." *Western Journal of Agricultural Economics* 10:223–229, 1985.

Harper, C.R. and D. Zilberman. "Pest Externalities from Agricultural Inputs." *American Journal of Agricultural Economics* 71:692–702, 1989.

Hatch, U. The Impact of Regulatory Delay on R & D Productivity and Costs in the Pesticide Industry. Ph.D. Dissertation. University of Minnesota, St. Paul, Minnesota, 1983.

Headley, J.C. "Defining the Economic Threshold." *Pest Control Strategies for the Future.* Agricultural Board, Washington, DC: National Academy Press, 1972, pp. 100–108.

Herdt, R.W. et al. "The Economics of Insect Control on Rice in the Philippines." In *Judicious and Efficient Use of Insecticides in Rice.* Manila, Philippines: International Rice Research Institute, 1984.

Hoar, S.K., et al. "Agricultural Herbicide Use and Risk of Lymphoma and Soft Tissue Sarcoma." *Journal of the American Medical Association* 256:1141–1147, 1986.

Lazarus, W. and E.R. Swanson. "Insecticide Use and Crop Rotation Under Risk: Rootworm Control in Corn." *American Journal of Agricultural Economics* 65:738–747, 1983.

Lemieux, C.M. and M.K. Wohlgenant. "Ex Ante Evaluation of the Economic Impact of Agricultural Biotechnology: The Case of Porcine Somatotropin." *American Journal of Agricultural Economics* 71:903–914, 1989.

Lichtenberg, E. "Integrated Versus Chemical Pest Management: The Case of Rice Field Mosquito Control." *Journal of Environmental Economics and Management* 14:1–9, 1987.

Lichtenberg, E., D.D. Parker, and D. Zilberman. "Marginal Analysis of Welfare Effects of Environmental Policies: The Case of Pesticide Regulation." *American Journal of Agricultural Economics* 70:867–874, 1988.

Lichtenberg, E. and D. Zilberman. "The Welfare Economics of Regulation in Revenue-Supported Industries: The Case of Price Supports in U.S. Agriculture." *American Economic Review* 76(5):1135–1141, 1986a.

Lichtenberg, E. and D. Zilberman. "The Econometrics of Damage Control: Why Specification Matters." *American Journal of Agricultural Economics* 68:261–273, 1986b.

Mangle, M. et al. (eds.). *Pest Control: Operations and System Analysis in Fruit Fly Management.* New York: NATO ASI Series, Springer-Verlag, 1986.

Marra, M.C. and G.A. Carlson. "An Economic Threshold Model for Weeds in Soybeans (Glycine max)." *Weed Science* 31:604–609, 1983.

Marra, M. and G.A. Carlson. "Double Cropping Wheat and Soybeans in the Southeast." Agricultural Economics Report 552, ERS, U.S. Dept. of Agriculture, Washington, D.C., 1986.

Masaud, S.M. et al. "Economic Implications of a Delayed Uniform Planting Date for Cotton Production in the Texas Rolling Plains." Texas Agri. Experiment Station Bulletin 1489, College Station, Texas, 1984.

McCarl, B.A. "Economics of Pest Management: An Interpretive Review of the Literature." Oregon State University Special Report 636, Corvallis, Oregon, 1981.

Miranowski, J.A., and G.A. Carlson. "Economic Issues in Public and Private Approaches to Preserving Pest Susceptibility." *Pesticide Resistance: Strategies and Tactics for Management*. Washington, D.C: National Academy Press, pp. 436–448, 1986.

Moffitt, L.J. "Risk-Efficient Thresholds for Pest Control Decisions" *Journal of Agricultural Economics* 37: 69–75, 1986.

Moffitt, L.J., T. Burrows, J.L. Baritelle, and U. Sevacherian. "Risk Evaluation of Early Termination for Pest Control in Cotton." *Western Journal of Agricultural Economics* 9:145–151, 1984a.

Moffitt, L.J., D.C. Hall, and C.D. Osteen. "Economic Thresholds Under Uncertainty With Application to Corn Nematode Management." *Southern Journal of Agricultural Economics* 16:151–157, 1984b.

Mueller, W. "Dealers at the Source: A Source of Groundwater Contamination Could Be As Close as Your Own House Yard." *Agrichemical Age* February: 8–22, 1989.

Musser, W., M.E. Wetzstein, S.Y. Reece, P.E. Varca, D.M. Edwards, and G.K. Douce. "Beliefs of Farmers and Adoption of Integrated Pest Management." *Agricultural Economics Research* 38:34–44, 1986.

Musser, W., B.V. Tew, and J.E. Epperson. "An Economic Examination of an Integrated Pest Management Production System with a Contrast Between E-V and Stochastic Dominance Analysis." *South Journal of Agricultural Economics* 13:119–124, 1981.

National Research Council (NRC). *Pesticide Resistance: Strategies and Tactics for Management*. National Academy Press, Washington, D.C., 1986.

National Research Council (NRC). *Regulating Pesticides in Food: The Delaney Paradox*. Washington, D.C: National Academy Press, 1987.

Nielson, E.G. and L.K. Lee. *The Magnitude and Costs of Groundwater Contamination from Agricultural Chemicals: A National Perspective*. Washington, DC: U.S. Department of Agriculture, Agricultural Economic Report No. 576, 1987.

Norton, G.W. and J.S. Davis. Evaluating Returns to Agricultural Research: A Review? *American Journal of Agricultural Economics* 63:685–699, 1981.

Osteen, C. and F. Kuchler. "Pesticide Regulatory Decisions: Production Efficiency, Equity and Interdependence." *Agribusiness* 3(3):307–322, 1987.

Pannell, D.J. "Pests and Pesticides, Risk and Risk Aversion." *Agricultural Economics* 5:361–383, 1991.

Pingali, P.L. and G.A. Carlson. "Human Capital, Adjustments in Subjective Probabilities, and the Demand for Pest Controls." *American Journal of Agricultural Economics* 67:853–861, 1985.

Pitt, M.M. and M.R. Rosenzweig. "Agricultural Prices, Food Consumption and the Health and Productivity of Indonesian Farmers." In I. Singh, L. Squire, and J. Strauss (eds.): *Agricultural Household Models: Extensions Applications and Policy*. Baltimore, MD: The Johns Hopkins University Press, 1986.

Regev, U., A.P. Gutierrez, and G. Feder. "Pest as a Common Property Resource:

A Case Study in Alfalfa Weevil Control." *American Journal of Agricultural Economics* 58:186–197, 1976.

Regev, U. et al. "On the Optimal Allocation of Pesticides with Increasing Resistance: The Case of Alfalfa Weevil Control." *Journal of Environmental Economics and Management* 10:86–100, 1983.

Reichelderfer, K.H. "Environmental Protection and Agricultural Support: Are Trade-Offs Necessary?" In K. Allen (ed.): *Agricultural Policies in a New Decade.* Washington, D.C: Resources for the Future, pp. 201–230.

Reichelderfer, K.H. and F.E. Bender. "Application of a Simulative Approach to Evaluating Alternative Methods for the Control of Agricultural Pests." *American Journal of Agricultural Economics* 61:258–267, 1979.

Reichelderfer, K. and M.K. Hinkle. "The Evolution of Pesticide Policy." In C.S. Kramer (ed.): *The Political Economy of U.S. Agriculture: Challenges for the 1990's.* Washington, D.C: Resources for the Future, 1989.

Rook, S.P. and G.A. Carlson. "Participation in Pest Management Groups." *American Journal of Agricultural Economics* 67:563–566, 1985.

Smith, G.S., M.E. Wetzstein, and G.K. Douce. "Evaluation of Various Pest-Management Characteristics." *Southern Journal of Agricultural Economics* 19:93–101, 1987.

Smith, V.K. and F.F. Johnson. "How Do Risk Perceptions Respond to Information? The Case of Radon." *Review of Economics and Statistics* 70:1–8, 1988.

Stern, V.M., R.F. Smith, R. van den Bosch, and K.S. Hagen. "The Integration of Chemical and Biological Control of the Spotted Alfalfa Aphid, Part I: The Integrated Control Concept." *Hilgardia* 29:81–101, 1959.

Swanson, E.R. and A.H. Grube. "Economic Impact of Trifluralin on Soybeans: A Comparison of Selected Estimation Models." *North Central Journal of Agricultural Economics* 16(4):769–775, 1986.

Szmedra, P.I., M.E. Wetzstein, and R.W. McClendon. "Economic Threshold Under Risk: A Case Study of Soybean Production." *Journal of Economic Entomology* 83:641–646, 1990.

Talpaz, H. and R.E. Frisbie. "An Advanced Method for Economic Threshold Determination: A Positive Approach." *Southern Journal of Agricultural Economics* 7:19–25, 1975.

Taylor, C.R., R.D. Lacewell, and H. Talpaz. "Use of Extraneous Information with an Econometric Model to Evaluate Impacts of Pesticide Withdrawals." *Western Journal of Agricultural Economics* 4(1):1–8, 1979.

Taylor, C.R., G.A. Carlson, F.T. Cooke, Jr., K.H. Reichelderfer, and I.R. Starbird. "An Aggregate Economic Evaluation of Alternative Boll Weevil Management Strategies." *American Economics Research* 35:19–28, 1983.

Taylor, C.R. et al. *Agricultural Sector Models for the United States: Description and Selected Policy Applications.* Ames, IA: Iowa State University Press, 1992.

Viscusi, W.K. and W.A. Magat. *Learning About Risk.* Cambridge, MA: Harvard University Press.

Wetzstein, M.E. "Pest Information Markets and Integrated Pest Management." *Southern Journal of Agricultural Economics* 13:79–83, 1981.

Wetzstein, M.E., W.N. Musser, D.K., Linder, and G.K. Douce. "An Evaluation of Integrated Pest Management with Heterogeneous Participation." *Western Journal of Agricultural Economics* 10:344–353, 1985.

Wilkerson, G.G., et al. HERB V2.0 Herbicide Decision Model for Postemergence Weed Control in Soybeans. Users Manual, Bulletin 113, Department of Crop Science, North Carolina State University, Raleigh, N.C., 1988.

Zacharias, T.P. and H.H. Grube. "An Economic Evaluation of Weed Control Methods Used in Combination with Crop Rotation: A Stochastic Dominance Approach." *North Central Journal of Agricultural Economics* 6:113–120, 1984.

Zavaleta, L. and W. Ruesink. "Expected Benefits from Nonchemical Methods of Alfalfa Weevil Control." *American Journal of Agricultural Economics* 63:801–805, 1980.

8

Economics of Water Use in Agriculture

WILLIAM BOGGESS, RONALD LACEWELL, AND
DAVID ZILBERMAN

> Man is a complex being; he makes
> deserts bloom, and lakes die
>   Gil Stern

In the quotation cited above, Stern captures in a single sentence the impact and complexity of the issues associated with agricultural water use. While water is used for industrial, municipal, recreational, and aesthetic purposes in the United States, agricultural irrigation is by far the largest user of water. About one-sixth of the U.S. agricultural acreage is irrigated, and this land produces about one-third of the product value grown in the country. In the western United States, irrigated agriculture accounts for 86 percent of total water use (Office of Technology Assessment, 1983). The linkages among alternative sources of water, the fact that water sources cross geographical and political boundaries, the value of water in production and its potential for degradation, and the stiff competition for water among users all result in challenging economic issues.

This chapter addresses the economics of water use in the United States and the related issues of water quantity and quality. Particular attention is paid to demand for agricultural water and the economics of irrigation. The chapter also describes various irrigation technologies and outlines their adoption across regions in the United States. We will see that there are significant differences between the development of irrigated agriculture in the Southwest, the Midwest, and the West.

Water allocation and pricing policies must address a complex set of interrelated variables, including quantity, and temporal distribution of water. Water may be available from a variety of sources, e.g., rainfall, ground water, local surface storage, and interbasin transfers. Each source has differing quantity, quality, and spatial and temporal supply dimensions that jointly determine the availability and cost of water for various uses. Furthermore, different water uses require varying degrees of quality and generate varying levels of contamination. Particularly with regard to agriculture, the spatial and temporal dimensions of demand for water interact with the quantity and quality dimensions. For example, a relatively small amount of high-quality irrigation water, available during critical growth stages, is considerably more valuable than a large amount of low-quality (i.e., highly saline) water available when the crop cannot use it.

The multiplicity of sources and uses of water have led to a myriad of water right doctrines and resource allocation mechanisms. Resource allocation mechanisms distinguish among three types of water systems: ground water systems; surface water systems that rely on water from lakes, rivers, and projects; and conjunctive use systems that utilize both ground and surface water. Assessment of water allocation mechanisms has to address changes in technology and preferences and issues related to equity and balance between demand and supply forces.

The next section overviews the main finding on the economics of the most important agricultural water use; irrigation. The second section integrates irrigation with other water uses and surveys knowledge on water demand. That is followed by an overview of major findings on water supply. The details of major allocation mechanisms for surface and groundwater are presented, and then their economic implications.

While the first part of the chapter emphasizes water quantity management problems, the latter part discusses water quality problems. There is an overview of the economics of water pollution abatement and a discussion of the technical relationships between agricultural production processes and water quality. Economic models and empirical studies of water quality problems, together with water quality institutions, are presented in the last two sections.

THE ECONOMICS OF IRRIGATION

In most of the world, farmers rely on rainfall for water. However, since the introduction of irrigated agriculture in the Southwest during the 1890s, irrigated acreage in the United States has steadily increased. By 1980, irrigated land accounted for one-third of the total value of agricultural output (Day and Horner, 1987). In 1985, demand of water for agricultural irrigation was five times greater than for industry and utilities (U.S. Bureau of the Census, 1989).

Irrigation can be used to augment rainfall, to extend the growing season, or to make farming possible in dry seasons or regions. Factors that affect farmers' decisions related to irrigation include crop price, water cost, risk, expected yield effect, and water availability. Irrigation management requires an understanding of irrigation technologies and soil–plant–water processes.

Irrigation technology has changed substantially over the last 40 years. There have been significant improvements in water pumping and conveyance technologies as well as the introduction of sprinkler and drip irrigation. Adoption of these technologies has had dramatic impacts on water use, crop yields, crop production patterns, and the trade and market conditions of many crops.

Irrigation Patterns in the United States

Irrigation diverts ground and surface water for agricultural purposes. Pumping technology (on-farm wells) enables farmers to manage ground water independently. Surface water, diverted from rivers and lakes, frequently supplies a large number of farmers, and its utilization requires substantial investment in conveyance systems.

Traditional irrigation technologies rely upon gravity to deliver water to crops. Modern technologies use energy and equipment for water delivery. Traditional technologies include furrow and flood-and-border irrrigation, which require substantial volumes of water over a short period of time. Irrigation of fields utilizing these traditional technologies is quite infrequent (once every 2 to 3 weeks, or even less). During irrigation, large amounts of water are deposited on the fields for short periods of time.

Modern irrigation technologies such as LEPA (Low Energy Precise Application) sprinkler, center-pivot sprinkler, and drip irrigation use energy and equipment (rather than gravity) to deliver water to plants. This results in more frequent irrigation, improves irrigation distribution uniformity, and reduces water losses to deep percolation and run-off. In essence, the output produced with a given amount of water is increased with these modern technologies. Although modern technologies require higher capital costs and extra energy to maintain pressure, they generally save labor costs and water and, when used to apply chemicals (fertilizers, pesticides), may improve efficiency in the application of these chemicals.

Gravitational irrigation is still the most common form of irrigation in most states, particularly in the West. Sprinkler irrigation was introduced in the 1950s and is used for field crops, fruits, and vegetables. Drip irrigation was introduced in the 1970s and is most commonly used with high-value fruits and vegetables and in low-water-quality or high-water-cost regions.

Although traditional methods of irrigation began as early as the late 19th century in some western and southwestern states, for much of the United States, development of irrigated farming began in earnest after World War II. The introduction of sprinkler technology had a great impact on agricultural production in the West and the Midwest. For example, adoption of center-pivot technology in irrigate corn, soybeans, and sorghum in Nebraska and Kansas dramatically affected the markets for these products by greatly increasing their supply.

In contrast, lands on the Mississippi Delta continue to be irrigated with traditional technology. For example, in Mississippi where water is inexpensive, furrow irrigation is the principal system. In most eastern states, rainfall is generally adequate, and demand for irrigation water is low. The exceptions are Florida and Southeastern Coastal Plains, which are characterized by sandy soils and extensive use of irrigation, particularly for high value crops—tobacco, peanuts, ornamentals, fruits and vegetables.

Drip irrigation, which spread very quickly in Florida and California, was introduced in the United States in the early 1970s and is currently in use on 1.5 million acres. The technology tends to be adopted with high-value fruit crops and high-value vegetable crops (fresh market vegetables) in locations mainly with sandy soils, uneven lands, and high water costs.

Table 8.1 presents regional distributions of irrigated acreage by technology and crop for five periods from 1960 to 1985. In almost all states, increases in water scarcity have led to increases in the use of sprinkler irrigation. In some areas, sprinkler or drip irrigation replaces traditional irrigation systems, and in others the use of these water-conserving technologies allows extension of the irrigated land base. According to the table, the acreage using gravity irrigation reached

Table 8.1. Acreage Under Different Irrigation Technologies Over Time For Selected States in the United States[a]

Region	Gravity					Sprinkler					Drip	
	1960	1970	1975	1980	1985	1960	1970	1975	1980	1985	1980	1985
CA	7,100	7,200	7,200	7,999	7,500	900	1,450	1,559	2,025	2,589	305	350
HI	119	113	97	125	146	9	17	27	50	123	29	108
FL	520	1,040	1,097	1,452	1,058	228	545	821	816	837	36	298
GA	2	0	0	0	0	102	145	230	1,013	1,080	5	45
NB	2,415	3,563	3,973	4,509	4,404	250	866	1,642	3,128	3,793	0.1	0
TX	5,152	6,660	6,700	5,620	4,617	610	1,700	1,918	2,197	2,141	20	0
WA,OR	690	2,100	1,922	1,444	1,365	354	1,200	1,609	2,367	2,577	6	13
SW[b]	2,772	1,985	3,304	3,461	3,536	37	180	207	294	294	4	42
WEST[c]	8,472	12,076	11,535	10,517	9,913	392	1,600	3,076	3,733	4,030	1	2
KS, OK	920	1,971	2,306	2,802	2,539	100	560	953	1,754	1,677	0.7	3
MI	0.2	0.2	1	0	0	71	139	112	302	422	9	36
IA, IL	30	44	41	23	5	45	73	104	359	438	1	2
NE[d]	6	0.7	0.4	4	97	126	206	336	327	226	2	7
Total	28,197	36,693	38,177	37,956	35,181	3,223	8,680	12,594	18,365	20,225	419	906

Source: Casterline et al. (1989).
[a] Values are in thousands of acres.
[b] Arizona, Nevada, and New Mexico.
[c] Idaho, Montana, North Dakota, Wyoming, Utah, and Colorado.
[d] Maine, New Hampshire, Vermont, Massachusetts, Rhode Island, Connecticut, New York, Pennsylvania, New Jersey, Maryland, and West Virginia.

its peak in 1975, when agricultural commodity prices were relatively high. The slight decline in gravity-irrigated acreage since that time is the result of lower commodity prices and transition to sprinkler irrigation. Sprinkler-irrigated acreage (this acreage includes drip irrigation) increased by nearly 60 percent between 1960 and 1980 and continues to grow slowly. The 1970s saw vast diffusion of center-pivot irrigation. The spread of this technology accounts for much of the growth in sprinkler-irrigated acreage in this decade.

Figure 8.1 shows a more detailed view of the diffusion of center-pivot irrigation in field-crop production and depicts the dynamics of total-irrigated acreage and sprinkler irrigation (actually, center-pivot irrigated acreage) in Nebraska from 1955 to 1985 (Casterline et al., 1989). The diffusion of center-pivot in Nebraska is seen as an S-shaped function of time. Diffusion started off slowly (1957–1972), then soared (1973–1977), and finally tapered off (1978 to present). The takeoff period occurred when grain prices were relatively high and thus provided an incentive for adoption of the technology. Since prices stabilized in the 1980s, demand for irrigation has fallen.

There are broad regional differences in the patterns of irrigation over time. Modern technologies are most likely to be adopted in regions with high output revenues and water prices and with low water and land quality. At issue is the development of a theory to explain under what conditions farmers will adopt appropriate irrigation technology.

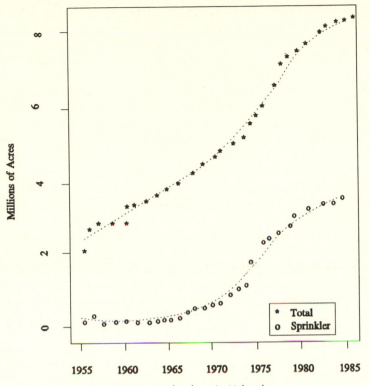

Figure 8.1. Diffusion of modern irrigation technology in Nebraska.

Modeling Irrigation Behavior

Understanding the basic concepts of irrigation is required for modeling irrigation choices. First, one has to distinguish between *effective water* (the amount of water actually utilized by plants) and *applied water*. Irrigation efficiency is defined as the ratio of effective water to applied water (Lynne et al., 1987). Traditional technologies that rely upon gravity to deliver water tend to have lower irrigation efficiencies than modern technologies that use energy and equipment for water delivery. Typical *irrigation efficiency* of gravitation methods is about .6, but drip or sprinkler irrigation may increase irrigation efficiency up to .95 (Hanemann et al., 1987).

The principle of hydrologic balance is also crucial for modeling irrigation. This principle states that water entering a given area must equal the water leaving that area. In the case of an irrigated field, the hydrologic balance statement will include all water sources (applied water and precipitation, run-on, dew fall, and capillary rise) as well as account for all water leaving the field, e.g., evapotranspiration (ET), run-off, and deep percolation. The change in stock of soil moisture is considered to be a water use. In essence, it can be viewed as effective water—water actually used by the crop. The difference between applied and effective water depends upon irrigation technology, environmental conditions, and land characteristics.

Areas with poor land quality (steep slopes and sandy soil) are likely to have greater gains in irrigation efficiency with transition from traditional to modern technologies. On the other hand, the irrigation efficiency of traditional technologies is likely to be quite high on flatlands and heavy soils, and not much can be gained by transition to modern technologies.

Recent literature shows increased attention to the effects of water use on crop yields and growth (see surveys by Vaux et al., 1981, and Hexem and Heady, 1978). Experimental studies in small homogeneous environments found that the Von Liebig production function explains the behavior of yield as a function of ET (Stewart et al., 1974) or applied water (Grim et al., 1987). The Von Liebig production functions assume that output grows as a linear function of the input until maximum output is reached (if x is the input, y is the output, and y^m the maximum output, the Von Liebig production function is $y = ax$ when $x < y^m/a$; $y = y^m$ if $x > y^m/a$).

The Von Liebig production function generalizes to a constrained, fixed-proportion production function when there are many inputs. The production coefficients of water crop production functions vary across environments. Berck and Helfend (1989) argue that environmental heterogeneity within commercially operated fields (differences in soil fertility and water-holding capacity) requires aggregation to obtain water-crop relationships for such crops. These functions are likely to be concave and have a production saturation level.

The most widely accepted model of yield response to irrigation expresses the ratio of actual yield to potential yield as a function of the ratio of actual to potential ET. Actual yield, Y_A, can be predicted by

$$Y_A = Y_M * \prod_{i=1}^{n} \left[\frac{ET_i^a}{ET_i^p} \right]^{\alpha_i} \tag{1}$$

where Y_M is a maximum yield estimate, n is the number of identified growth stages of the crop, ET_i^a is the total of actual evaporation and transpiration during period i, ET_i^p is the total potential evaporation and transpiration, and α_i is a sensitivity factor. The model has been well documented for corn (Stegman and Aflatouni, 1978; Stewart et al., 1975) and soybeans (Wilkerson et al., 1981). Similar relationships have been estimated for over 25 crops (FAO, 1979).

Caswell and Zilberman (1985, 1986) incorporate some of the physical features of irrigation systems into their irrigation choices model. Assuming constant returns to scale, let y denote the yield per acre, e the effective water per acre, and $y = f(e)$ be a concave production function relating the two. Consider a case with two irrigation technologies, one traditional (gravitational) and the other modern (sprinkler or drip irrigation), and let i be a technology indicator that equals 1 for the traditional technology and 2 for the modern technology. Land is assumed to vary in its contribution to irrigation, and q is a land quality measure where $0 < q \le 1$. For a_i, as applied water per acre with technology i, the resulting effective water is determined according to $e = h_i(q)a_i$ where $h_i(q)$ is the irrigation efficiency of technology i on land quality q. Irrigation efficiency can vary in value from zero to one, and the modern technology is likely to have higher irrigation efficiency than the traditional one ($h_2(q) \geq h_1(q)$). Moreover, the relative gain in irrigation effectiveness associated with transition from traditional to modern technology [i.e. $h_2(q) - h_1(q))/h_1(q)$] is smaller at higher land qualities. Each technology has a fixed cost per acre denoted by c_i, and it is assumed that $c_2 > c_1$. Finally, let p denote output price, $R(q)$, the rental rate of land of quality q, and W the price of applied water.

The maximum profit under technology i, π_i, can then be determined by solving equation (2)

$$\pi_i(q) = \text{Max } Pf[a_i h_i(q)] - Wa_i - c_i - R(q) \qquad i = 1, 2 \tag{2}$$

The strategy of profit-maximizing irrigation involves a *sequential process*. First, optimal water use levels for both technologies are determined. Then resulting profits are compared. The modern technology is selected if $\pi_2 \geq \pi_1$ and if $\pi_2 \geq 0$. The traditional technology is used when $\pi_1 > \pi_2$ and $\pi_1 \geq 0$.

Optimal water application with technology i [determined from the first-order condition for equation (2)] occurs at a level where the value of marginal product of applied water is equal to its price, that is,

$$Pf'h_i(q) = W \tag{3}$$

The value of marginal product of applied water is a product of output price, marginal product of effect water, and irrigation efficiency. Note that $W/h_i(q)$ is the price of effective water and equation (3) can be modified

$$Pf' = W/h_i(q) \tag{4}$$

Profit maximization under technology i occurs where the value of marginal product of effective water (Pf') is equal to its price. The two technologies have the same production function of effective water. The new technology increases the fixed costs but reduces the price of effective water. Having a lower effective water price, the new technology will use more effective water than the traditional technology, and thus the new technology will have a higher yield ($y_2 > y_1$). Although the new technology uses more effective water ($e_2 > e_1$), it also has a higher irrigation efficiency, which means that the required amount of applied water does not necessarily increase. Figure 8.2 helps to identify situations in which conversion to modern technology leads to decreased water usage. The curve EF is the value of marginal product of effective irrigation in the economic phase of the production function (when marginal productivity is positive and declining).

Consider a case where the irrigation efficiency of the modern technology is twice that of the traditional one, say, $h_2 = 0.8$ and $h_1 = 0.4$, and there are two water prices, one high (W^h) and one low (W^l). Points A and B denote the profit-maximizing choices for the modern technology and for the traditional technology, respectively, where water price is low. C and D denote the outcome from the modern and traditional technologies, respectively, where water price is high. With a low water price, the yield with both technologies is close to the maximum yield (i.e., point F). There is a small difference in effective water use between the two technologies (i.e., $W_a - W_b$). Thus, transition from traditional to

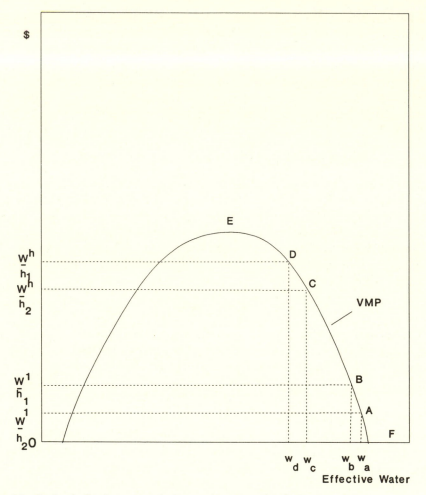

Figure 8.2. Optimal effective water choices under two technologies.

modern technology has only a small effect upon yield. However, when considering applied water, the amount of water saved by the transition is substantial. In the case of high water price, transition to the modern technology substantially increases the effective water use (i.e., $W_c - W_d$), and thus the yield effect is large. In general, the switch in technology produces a larger yield and a smaller water-saving effect as water price increases.

Empirical evidence and numerical simulations suggest that transition to modern technology generally tends to both save water and increase yields. It follows that increases in either output price or water price are likely to increase adoption of modern technologies. Obviously, reduction of the fixed cost of the new technology has the same effect. Adoption behavior is likely to vary substantially with land quality. With high land quality, the difference in irrigation efficiency between modern and traditional technologies is likely to be quite small,

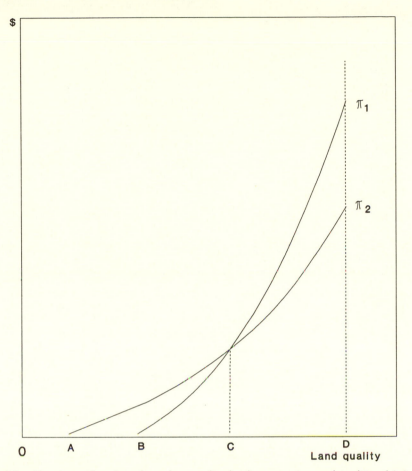

Figure 8.3a. Quasi-rent functions for a low quality land augmenting and traditional irrigation technologies.

making the extra fixed cost of the new technology an unwarranted expense. As land quality declines, the gain in irrigation efficiency associated with the use of the modern technology increases. Thus, there exists a particular land quality above which traditional technology is profit maximizing, and a land quality below which modern technology is more profitable. There may also be a range of low land qualities for which the traditional technology is preferable because the low productivity of land cannot cover the fixed cost of the modern technology.

Figure 8.3 presents two patterns of behavior of the *quasi-rent functions* of both technologies as land quality varies. Because crop values increase, quasi-rents increase with land quality and may be negative with low land qualities. Figure 8.3a presents a more likely scenario. Before the modern technology is introduced, the traditional technology is utilized only on land in the land quality segment *BD*, where quasi-rents are nonnegative (e.g., $\Pi_1 > 0$). The introduction of the modern technology increases the utilized land qualities to include those in the land quality

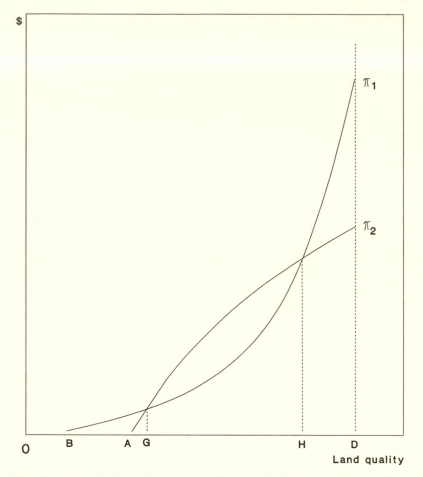

Figure 8.3b. Quasi-rent functions for an intermediate quality land augmenting and traditional irrigation technologies.

segment AB. Segment BC represents land qualities which profit from the introduction of the modern technology. Figure 8.3b represents the case where the introduction of the new technology results in a change of irrigation technology only for a middle range of land qualities (between G and H) while high and very low quality lands continue to use the traditional technology.

The framework presented here can be expanded to incorporate additional options and considerations associated with water use choices.

1. For example, the productivity of water declines as water quality declines (salinity increases). Letey et al. (1989) suggested that modern irrigation technologies are more likely to be adopted in locations with low water quality. Moreover, introduction of technologies like drip and sprinkler may increase the ranges of water quality used in agricultural production.

2. The impact of *chemigation* (application of chemicals with modern irrigation technologies) on the efficiency of use of chemicals is similar to the impact

of modern irrigation technologies on irrigation efficiency. Therefore, adopting modern technologies is likely to increase as chemical prices increase, chemical requirements are higher, or more precise application (management) of chemicals is required.

3. Crop choices can be treated in a similar way to technology choices, since some crops require less water, have more tolerance to salinity, and utilize water more effectively than other crops. Moreover, certain technologies are better matched to certain crops. The introduction and adoption of new irrigation technologies may be associated with a transition to crops that become more profitable with this technology. Lichtenberg (1989) found that the introduction of center pivots in western Nebraska coincided with the transition from wheat to corn.

4. In many cases, run-off or deep percolation caused by irrigation are the subject of environmental concern. Taxation of these waters is considered in some situations. For example, in locations with waterlogging problems, deep percolating water may be drained and assessed a drainage fee. Let z denote drainage per acre, and V the drainage fee. Factors that increase irrigation efficiency reduce drainage generation. Drainage generation per unit of applied water is denoted by $g_i(q)$. Modern technologies result in lower drainage $[g_2(q) < g_1(q)]$, and drainage will increase as land quality declines. With a drainage fee, the variable cost of applied water under technology i becomes $[W + Vg_i(q)]a_i$. Because $g_1(q) > g_2(q)$, introduction of a drainage fee is likely to make traditional technology less attractive, encourage adoption of modern technology, and reduce water application (Dinar et al., 1989).

5. Because modern irrigation technologies improve the uniformity of water distribution, the gains from transition to modern technologies do not depend on homogeneous land quality. Feinerman et al. (1983) demonstrate that the likelihood of adoption of modern irrigation technologies increases with increased variability of the water-holding capacity of the soil and with increased slope of the land. In effect, technology is adopted to offset a natural resource limitation.

6. Modern irrigation technologies, in particular, sprinkler irrigation, require extra pressure to deliver water to crops. Let pressurization cost be denoted by m_i. Adding this to the other components of water costs, variable water costs under technology i become $(m_i + W)a_i$. In certain situations (shallow ground water, cheap project water) pressurization costs may dominate water price, and the price of effective water under modern technologies may be higher. Increases in energy costs that raise pressurization costs relative to water costs may actually deter farmers from using modern technologies. Higher energy costs may also induce farmers to switch from high-pressure sprinkler systems to low-pressure systems.

7. Modern technologies, especially drip and trickle irrigation, are likely to have lower evaporation losses than gravitational and sprinkler irrigation. Adoption of these technologies is likely to increase in high temperature regions or in response to global warming resulting from the greenhouse effect.

8. Modern irrigation technologies have other advantages besides increased irrigation efficiency and irrigation uniformity. The increased frequency of irrigation associated with modern irrigation technology is likely to be another source of

increased productivity, for which economic impacts may be investigated. Similarly, sprinkler irrigation is used effectively for frost protection and is, therefore, more likely to be adopted in regions with frost problems.

Empirical Findings

Thus far, the emphasis has been on mostly normative findings that simulate profit-maximizing policies given economic and environmental conditions. Empirical studies of water use and irrigation technology choice have demonstrated that actual behavioral patterns are consistent with the normative model findings. Some of these studies (Caswell and Zilberman, 1985, on California; Lichtenberg, 1989, on Nebraska; and Schaible et al., 1991, on the Pacific Northwest) attempted to explain adoption of irrigation technologies by farmers through a statistical analysis of factors affecting changes in land shares of different technologies utilized on irrigated land in different regions. Other studies (Negri and Brooks, 1988, for the United States; Dinar and Yaron, 1990, for Israel) use cross-section data on technology choices by individual farmers and statistical analysis of discrete choice data (Amemiya, 1981) to identify factors that affect choice of drip, sprinkler, and center-pivot irrigation. Nieswiadomy (1988) used detailed farm level data from the Texas Plains to assess irrigation choices with emphasis on substitution between water and other inputs (capital, labor). He used expenditure on irrigation equipment as his major measure of intensity of adoption. His finding and the findings of most of the other empirical studies are consistent with the predictions of the conceptual and experimental studies mentioned earlier. They show that the likelihood of adoption of modern irrigation technologies is apt to increase as the prices of water, labor, and output increase; as soil slope increases and water-holding capacity declines; and in regions with higher temperatures. These studies suggest that introduction of modern technology tends to save water and increase yields, and both effects are stronger with lower land qualities.

Risk and Dynamic Considerations in Irrigation Choices

The static and deterministic models presented above are very useful for analyzing seasonal water demand and irrigation technology choices by risk-neutral individuals. However, agricultural activities are risky, and irrigation affects their risks. Thus, risk considerations may have important effects at least on irrigation choices of risk-averse individuals. Furthermore, crop production is the result of growth processes, and dynamic models are needed for analysis of water-use patterns during the season.

Just and Pope (1978) presented a simple form of a production function that represents the impacts of input use on expected output and production risk. In their model

$$Y = f(x) + g(x)\varepsilon$$

where Y is output, x is a vector of inputs, and ε is a random variable with $E(\varepsilon) = 0$.

When $g_x < 0$ for a certain input, it can be referred to as risk reducing. Similar formulations have been presented to separate impacts of inputs on the expected value and risks of revenues or profits.

Under reasonable assumptions, the impacts of an input on the standard deviation or variance of output (or profit) are the appropriate measure of the risk effect. A study by Lee (1987) for the Texas high plains indicates that irrigation is a risk-reducing input at both the per acre and the whole farm level in a semiarid environment. Thus, risk aversion is likely to lead farmers to irrigate more than is required for expected profit maximization (see Chapter 2). Furthermore, water application rates are likely to be higher in regions with more risky production conditions. This suggests that insurance policies (that will reduce risk) have the potential to reduce water application levels.

In humid regions (especially in the South and East), rainfall is the main source of water and irrigation is merely supplemental. In these regions irrigation may increase the expected values, but more often reduces output variability. Boggess et al. (1983) show that supplemental irrigation in the humid Southeast results in a reduction in the overall variance of net returns. However, investments in irrigation systems in humid regions have been shown to increase farmers' financial risk in some cases (Boggess and Amerling, 1983).

The VMP values presented for irrigation water in Equation (3) represent an average annual value, disregarding specific growth stages of the crop. Irrigation of a crop is a dynamic process during the growing season. The quantity of water applied and the timing of application during the year determine crop yield. Each crop has stages of growth when water is most critical to yield. For example, yield from sorghum for grain is dramatically affected by water availability in the "boot" and the "dough" stages of growth. However, some water stress early in the plant's cycle can be compensated by more water in later stages.

Crop response to timing and amount of irrigation water provides the foundation for addressing *irrigation scheduling* (Middle et al., 1990) to determine water application during the season. The application levels are outcomes of dynamic optimizations under uncertainty, subject to technological and institutional constraints.

Irrigation scheduling decisions are made under three types of uncertainties: biological relationships, states of nature, and prices. Crop growth models integrate component submodels of various processes in the soil-plant-atmosphere system to provide predictions of growth and yield of crops under alternative environmental and management regimes. Their predictions are subject to errors reflecting lack of complete knowledge about the natural processes governing agricultural production. Farmers also lack complete knowledge about present and future conditions of key variables affecting productivity (soil moisture, weather, pest population, etc.). Collecting information about the state of some of these variables (e.g., soil moisture) requires monitoring efforts or adoption of advanced monitoring technologies. Thus, technological constraints affect farmers' capacity to control timing and volume of water application over time. Growers' flexibility with respect to water application is also constrained by rules and regulation of water providers (water districts).

Antle (1988) provides a conceptual model for analyzing stochastic dynamic, sequential decision problems such as irrigation scheduling. This work derives decision rules for a risk-neutral firm choosing the optimal sequence of variable input use levels over time to maximize the present value of profit, given technology and information available at each moment. This framework suggests that optimal water application at each decision point *t* is determined by comparing the benefits of incremental irrigation against its cost. The benefits of irrigation at time *t* depend upon crop conditions (which is estimated given data provided by monitoring efforts and equipment), crop growth patterns, and expectations regarding future environmental and economic conditions. Costs of irrigation depend on input prices (water, energy, labor) and expectations regarding future water supplies.

Procedures for estimating economically optimal allocations of irrigation across a growing season that utilize crop-growth simulation models have been developed (Musser and Tew, 1984; Boggess and Ritchie, 1988; Bryant, 1991; Swaney et al., 1983). Several studies indicate that irrigation scheduling resulted in using less irrigation water than typically applied; yet, higher net returns to the producer resulted (Zavaleta et al., 1979; Harris and Mapp, 1980; Yaron and Dinar; McGuckin et al., 1987).

Only a fraction of the farmers in the United States use irrigation scheduling for water allocation. The current status of irrigation scheduling programs leaves room for much improvement. More research is needed to improve performance of crop growth models and to develop better hardware and software for monitoring environmental conditions and making irrigation choices. In some cases, water allocation policies of water districts have to be modified to allow more flexible water allocation schemes. Yet, existing evidence suggests that irrigation scheduling substantially improves water productivity in irrigation and that irrigation management-improving technologies are likely to grow in their use and importance in the future.

WATER DEMAND

There are several competing demands of water: irrigation, other agricultural (livestock production and aquaculture), industrial and residential, recreational, and hydroelectric. Irrigation is the major consumptive user of ground and surface water in the United States. The demand for irrigation water is a *derived demand* evolving from the value of agricultural products produced. Figure 8.4 demonstrates the relationship between irrigation water (in this case, applied water, not effective water, which was used earlier) and water price for an agricultural industry facing inelastic product demand.

In this case, VMP represents an initial value of marginal product curve. The marginal cost for successive units of water is defined as the marginal factor cost (MFC) of water. It is assumed that a single firm in a water supply industry has an MFC of water that is the same as the price of water because the single firm cannot influence price by its purchases alone. MFC′ in Figure 8.4 represents an initial water price that results in X' of irrigation water demanded for the

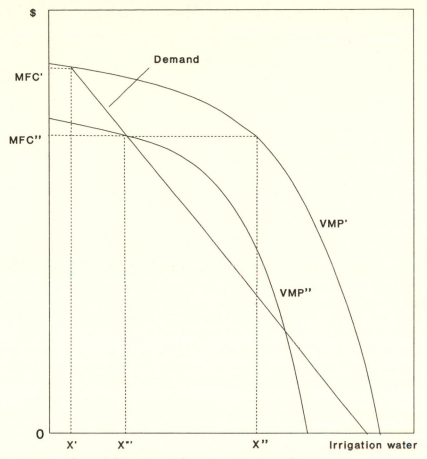

Figure 8.4. Factor demand for water used as an input in agriculture.

production of an irrigated crop. To the single firm, VMP′ represents its demand
for irrigation water. Thus, were the price of irrigation water to decline to MFC″,
the firm's demand, or use of water, would increase to X''. If there are only a few
firms affected by the change in the cost of irrigation water and the amount of
product produced is low enough that there is no change in the price of the product,
a new equilibrium is reached. But in the case where the lower price of irrigation
water is available to a sufficient number of farmers such that they all increase
water use, there can be an increase in output of irrigated crops. This increase in
supply can cause prices to decline, which, in turn, affects the VMP of water. With
a decline in product price, the VMP curve shifts to VMP″. With the new cost of
irrigation water, change in use of irrigation water, and resultant change in amount
of product produced (hence, change in product price), the new equilibrium amount
of irrigation water is X'''. After all the adjustments in prices, amount used, and
changes in amount of product produced, a derived demand for irrigation water
can be estimated and is given as "Demand" in Figure 8.4.

Since agricultural water use is a derived demand, the elasticity of demand for a factor is a convenient concept for exploring expected changes. Following Layard and Walters (1978), under constant returns to scale, the own price elasticity of demand for a factor can be shown to be a function of the elasticity of demand for the product being produced (output effect) and the elasticity of substitution between the various factors of production (substitution effect),

$$e_{ii} = v_i \eta^0 - (1 - v_i)s_{ij}$$

where e_{ii} is the price elasticity of demand for water in agriculture, v_i is the relative share of water in production costs, η^0 is the price elasticity of demand for agricultural products, and s_{ij} is the elasticity of substitution between water and other inputs.

Thus, one likely effect of the rising supply price of water is a reallocation of water within agriculture toward higher valued crops with inelastic demands. A second effect will be the substitution of other inputs for irrigation water within existing production systems. Finally, the increasing real price of water is also likely to drive the development and adoption of new technologies that facilitate the substitution of other inputs for water.

The value of irrigation water is partially a function of the price of the crop produced. Low value crops such as alfalfa and pasture typically are associated with relatively low VMPs for irrigation water. These types of crops are generally large users of water and in many regions the price elasticity of demand for irrigation water is relatively elastic. That is to say, a small percentage increase in the price of water results in a much larger percentage reduction in water used for irrigation. Howitt et al. (1980) estimate the price elasticity of demand for irrigation water in 1976 dollars to be -1.5 for a water price between \$51 and \$79 per acre foot, and -0.46 for a water price between \$79 and \$102 per acre foot. There are regions with dryland production alternatives where large acreages of crops such as pasture, corn, soybeans, and cotton are irrigated. Here increasing water price substantially reduces irrigation water use and, in some cases, as for example parts of the Texas High Plains, has resulted in conversion to dryland production altogether (Lacewell and Lee, 1988).

The value of water in agriculture (principally for irrigation) is often estimated by the VMP. Quantitative techniques for estimating the value of irrigation water have ranged from mathematical models (that identify the shadow price of irrigation water) to econometric models and application of calculus. The VMP of irrigation water provides a base of comparison to the value of water in other uses. The Office of Technology Assessment (1983) indicated that the value of a per acre foot of water used in irrigation ranges from \$9 to \$103 per acre foot. Pasture and alfalfa are typically associated with lower values of irrigation water, while vegetables have higher imputed values for the irrigation water. Some of the studies that address irrigation water values in the western United States include Ayer and Hoyt (1981), Hoyt (1982), Lacewell et al. (1974), Willit et al. (1985), Condra et al. (1975), Martin and Snyder (1979), Shumway (1973), Young and Gray (1972), Kelso et al. (1973), and Moore (1991).

The value of water in other uses varies greatly across the nation and the world. In municipal use, as the available water approaches zero, the marginal value approaches infinity (Gibbons, 1986). This suggests that a municipality facing a severe water supply constraint may bid relatively high values for marginal increments of water. Some recent prices for water rights in Colorado have exceeded $2,578 per acre foot (Office of Technology Assessment, 1983). Putting this on an average annual acre foot basis, the value is $387 or more. The Office of Technology Assessment (1983) gives a range from $19 to $322 per acre foot for water in domestic uses.

Values estimated in 1982 for water for hydroelectric power generation range from $4 to $39 per acre foot (Office of Technology Assessment, 1983). This suggests that agriculture is competitive with hydroelectric generation. Another issue relates to the extra cost to generate electricity by increasing irrigated acres in the Pacific Northwest. Hamilton and Whittlesey (1986) indicate that diverting and consumptively using water in Southeast Idaho would cost about $387 per year to generate the electricity used and hydropower lost to a typical acre of irrigation. The water diverted would potentially pass through 21 existing sets of turbines, and the area of land irrigated would require intensive energy for pumping.

Industrial use of water is estimated to have a value of $0 to $160 per acre foot compared to recreation, which is valued at $3 to $17 per acre foot (Office of Technology Assessment, 1983). Values for water in many uses are very difficult to estimate. Uses such as recreation, shipping, waste dilution, and beauty do not have a market to provide values. Issues related to placing a value on water for instream use include public good problems, multiple use problems, and a water policy at the national level that assumes that water used for hydropower and navigation should be free. Recently, much progress has been made in the development of contingent valuation methods for measuring nonmarket values. Mitchell and Carson (1989) provide a comprehensive discussion of contingent value methods and procedures, and Smith and Desvouges (1986) apply several nonmarket valuation techniques to the problem of measuring water quality benefits.

The MVP of water in agriculture is generally less than in industrial and municipal uses, and the price elasticity of demand for industrial and municipal water is more inelastic than that for agriculture. This means that, when the need for additional supply arises for municipal and industrial users, they can offer higher prices for water than can agriculture.

The difference between the VMP of water in agricultural and industrial and municipal uses is largely due to the limited use of markets for allocation of water among users. For example, water from reservoirs and transport facilities constructed by the Bureau of Reclamation is allocated according to water rights based on past use rather than willingness to pay, and trading has been constrained. Nevertheless, the vast amount of water used for irrigation cannot be fully explained by barriers to trade and inefficient allocation practices. In many regions, there is ample water available to satisfy both agricultural and nonagricultural users. Elsewhere, there is less nonagricultural demand of water, such as in much of the Great Plains. However, there are regions were additional water is in demand by nonagricultural users, and, although their willingness to pay is greater than that of agricultural users, massive amounts of water continue to be used for agricultural irrigation because of the existing systems of water rights.

WATER SUPPLY

Supply is typically defined as that quantity of a good or service that is produced at alternative prices. However, water does not fall neatly into this definition. For example, water may become available for use in agriculture in the form of precipitation. In this case, water is a natural resource that occurs in an average expected amount but with a stochastic element. Analysis of optimal use is based upon a recurring amount with an element of variability.

Firm Level Supply Considerations

Water supply based on pumping from an aquifer or developed surface sources may be viewed according to traditional supply analysis. For example, Figure 8.5 presents a hypothetical supply function for water. The supply curve represents the *marginal cost to develop and deliver* alternative quantities of water. In most regions, optimal reservoir locations have been developed. New sites present engineering challenges and are more costly. This means sharply increasing average and marginal costs associated with developing new surface supplies (El-Ashry and Gibbons, 1988).

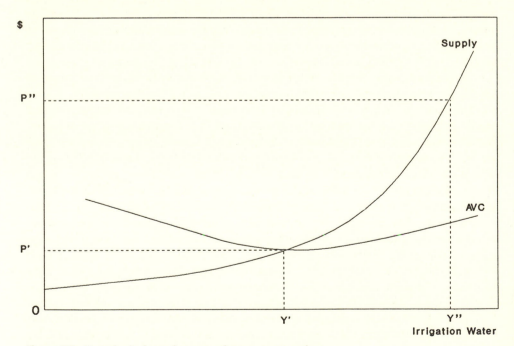

Figure 8.5. Hypothetical supply curve of water as a product.

A supply function for water is derived by considering water as a product to be sold. A production function for water is

$$y = f(x_i) \tag{5}$$

where x_i represents the inputs required to capture and transport the water.

The variable costs associated with water capture and transport are factor price times quantity used, which is a function of the level of water produced and the factor prices:

$$VC = f(y, r_i) \tag{6}$$

From the VC function, marginal cost (MC) is calculated by taking the first derivative with respect to water (y):

$$MC = \frac{dVC}{dy} = f'(y, r_i) \tag{7}$$

Marginal cost is the change in variable cost for a one-unit change in water supplied. For the profit-maximizing firm, water is produced at that level where its marginal cost is equal to the price received for the water. Thus, the supply function for water would be represented by the marginal cost curve for any quantity above minimum average variable cost (Beattie and Taylor, 1985). In Figure 8.5, the supply function begins at y' quantity of water that is produced at a price of p'. A price of p'' is needed before y'' quantity of water is supplied.

This discussion of water supply is most applicable to water districts or other entities that develop and transport water to users. Water is traded as a commodity, and it is assumed there is a competitive market for the water. The influence of water subsidies, governmental regulation, or property rights associated with the water have not yet been considered.

The allocation and cost of surface water to agriculture have been strongly influenced by both *water supply organizations*, which function primarily to benefit farmers, and the government, which underwrites the cost of providing water to these organizations (Frederick and Hanson, 1982). The organizations typically provide water at cost to members (irrigation farmers). Thus, the goal of the organizations has been to gain new cheaper water supplies for their customers. The government is typically involved because of the economies of scale entailed in the construction of dams, canals, ditches, and pumps, and because of its ability to finance large projects.

Frederick and Hanson (1982) reviewed surface water irrigation charges by alternative irrigation organizations. In 1977 dollars, the Bureau of Reclamation charged California irrigators only $5.87 per acre foot in 1980. This is compared to a charge of $60.88 by the California Department of Water Resources. In many cases, not all of the costs of construction, maintenance, and operation of surface water facilities are passed on to irrigators. There are cases where the Bureau of Reclamation has defrayed 95 percent or more of actual construction costs.

Huffaker and Gardner (1986) examine the distribution of benefits derived from subsidized water in California's Imperial Valley. They find that cash lease markets transfer nearly all economic rents anticipated by leasers to the landowners. Such distribution problems could exacerbate water conservation efforts and have direct implications for government policies in limiting access to subsidized water on the basis of owned and leased acreages.

Water districts that charge on a per unit of water basis are analogous to the pumping situation. Here the supply function for water is the cost per unit or MFC. As a profit maximizer, the producer has an incentive to produce where VMP = MFC. Referring back to Figure 8.4, on land with a water right and an annual charge on a per acre basis with no cost attached to each unit of water, the farmer demands that quantity of water where the VMP approaches zero. Alternatively, by attaching a cost to each unit of water, the procurer in his efforts to equate VMP with MFC, has an incentive to reduce the quantity of water demanded. This is reflected by MFC" and water use, x'', in Figure 8.4. Economic efficiency in water allocation suggests, therefore, that water be priced by quantity rather than land units, with the price reflecting the full cost of delivering each unit of water. This will reduce net returns to farmers owing to added water costs and reduction in use.

Water supply can also be seen from an individual user's viewpoint. In this case, cost of obtaining water is the focus and can be related to a production function for water. Ground water may best fit a production function dimension because there is a cost per unit for the water pumped from an aquifer. This is shown in Figure 8.5 where the horizontal axis now represents effective irrigation water. In this case, the farmer's water supply function is the MFC. The MFC is the cost for the next marginal unit of water. Supply of water withdrawn from an aquifer is, therefore, a function of the cost of pumping and distributing the water over fields. Lynne et al. (1984) examined the water supply process from ground water pumping by farmers. They demonstrate that the supply curve of effective water is positively sloped even when the marginal cost of pumped water is constant, since field losses (i.e., evaporation, run-off, and leaching) increase disproportionately. The firm has an economic incentive to use that amount of water where the MFC = VMP. Thus, the MFC is the supply function for one firm while the VMP curve is the demand function.

Regional Supply Considerations

Historically, water projects such as aqueducts and dams have provided water to whole regions and have served as anchors to growth and development of many regions. Total irrigated cropland in the United States was over 46 million acres in 1987, down from over 50 million acres in 1978 (U.S. Bureau of the Census, 1989). Approximately, one-half received surface water (Moore, 1991).

Costs have been an important feature in shaping the structure of regional surface water supplies. Bain et al. (1966) overview the implications of economies of scale in the construction of reservoirs and transport facilities. In addition to economies of scale, fixed costs are a large part of total surface water costs in large-scale water developments. These factors have strong implications as to the absence of private enterprises, evolutions of coalitions working together for development, high concentration of buyers and sellers, and rigidity in allocation arrangements.

To provide insight into economies of scale as related to surface water projects, data for Northern California presented by Bain et al. (1966) are used. They consider a large number of reservoirs and canals and develop comparative cost figures for alternative sizes. The construction costs per acre foot of storage are indexed with the smallest reservoirs (20,000 acre feet) represented by 100. The index of construction costs per acre foot of storage using Corps of Engineers data declined from 100 at 20,000 acre feet to an index of 22 for 5,000,000 acre feet. These data support the supposition of economies of scale in surface water projects. This is also important for understanding the organization and structure of many water systems.

Additional considerations, outlined below, affect the cost of providing water in regional water systems and affect system structure, design, and water supply parameters. First, there are the costs of construction of the internal delivery systems. These costs depend on characteristics of the buyers—mostly water districts. Water districts differ in size (requiring different size canals) and have different locations and elevations. Second, there are the costs of removing the water from its original use. Unlike construction costs, it is likely that the marginal cost of water removal will increase with size. Many of these costs are associated with nonmarket activities, since water captured by water projects is likely to be supporting an ecosystem that cannot otherwise be sustained. Third, there are water transportation costs (especially if interregional water transfer is used for regional water supply). These are variable costs and depend on the project's parameters (canal length, diameter, elevation, etc.). And, finally, the benefits from water flows must be considered. Existing water flows may provide hydroelectric power as well as recreation opportunities. These benefits are likely to be of substantial import-ance when decisions about water projects are made. They are also very important in determining water pricing schemes—especially when agricultural water prices are designed so that public investments repay themselves.

The costs of development of new regional water supply sources are likely to increase over time for two reasons. First, water sources that are near consumers are generally tapped first, and new projects have to harness more distant sources requiring more construction and transportation. Second, valuation of environ-mental amenities has increased over time, leading to more restrictive regulations of water projects' design specifications. Furthermore, environmental concerns have led the public to vote against construction of several water projects (including the peripheral canal in California). Thus, growth in regional water supply has slowed dramatically in recent years, and unless new technology is available (e.g., desalination), regional water supply will reach its limit in the near future.

Institutional Arrangements and Water Rights

In a broad sense, *institutions* can be thought of as the rules that govern behavior in society. Thus, markets, laws, and customs are parts of the institutional structure that guide human activities. The legal rights and responsibilities associated with the ownership and use of property (e.g., land and water) are particularly important components of the institutional structure governing water use.

Institutions relating to water development, distribution, and quality evolved from society's goals and objectives. In the 19th century, water supply was the major goal with the federal government assuming a predominant role, particularly in the West. With economic growth, increased population, and greater awareness, goals other than supply have become increasingly important (e.g., water quality).

Water laws, regulations, and institutions have direct impact on water use efficiency. Efficiency of water use depends upon the ease with which it can be transferred among users in response to changing conditions including water demand and social goals. Many laws and institutions, particularly in the western United States, restrict the transfer among users. Examples include irrigation water rights that are attached to specific lands, limitations on the diversion of surface water out of the basin of origin, beneficial-use provisions that support the philosophy of "use it or lose it," and rights of third parties (Frederick and Hanson, 1982).

The principal role of regulating water use is left to the states (Frederick and Hanson, 1982), and most of the state-level water laws are a product of court decisions, not legislation. Furthermore, water law has evolved separately for rivers and streams (watercourse), ground water, and diffused surface water. Diffused surface water refers to water standing or flowing across the land not in a definite bed or stream. Water law doctrines are markedly different in the western United States as compared to the eastern part of the nation. Following the format of Carriker (1985), state water doctrines are discussed for watercourse, ground water, and diffused water.

Watercourse Doctrines

The *riparian doctrine* holds that private water rights are tied to the ownership of land bordering a natural watercourse. This right to water in a stream or river represents the right to use water given the quality is not diminished or other riparians are not denied access to the water.

The Prior Appropriation Doctrine assigns user rights to water from a common source based upon the dates when use is initiated. This is commonly referred to as "first in time, first in right." The senior or prior (earlier) appropriator has a right that is superior to later appropriators (junior or subsequent rights). Under this doctrine, the right to use water is initiated when application of the water to a beneficial use is initiated. The water does not have to be applied to land that borders the source of the water and may be transported within and between watersheds. In most western states, this water right is transferable.

Administrative law involves a permitting system for appropriating water that is not based on the Prior Appropriation Doctrine. To obtain permits, new users must demonstrate that the water will be used for beneficial purposes, not conflict with existing legal water uses, and be in the public's best interest (Carriker, 1985).

Ground Water Doctrines

Ground water that is a part of an underground watercourse or is a tributary to surface water is typically subject to watercourse doctrine. This section covers state law related to ground water that is percolated and is not considered an underground stream.

Absolute Ownership Doctrine (English Doctrine) gives the surface landowner the right to extract an unlimited amount of water from beneath the surface, without regard to effect on adjacent landowners, for use at the site or to transport to another area for use. The only constraints to extraction of the ground water are that there is no waste and no negligence or malicious interference. In effect, this doctrine gives overlying land an easement for extraction of ground water where ownership is assigned as the water is removed. Absolute Ownership Doctrine has been rejected by most states. Box 8.1 describes the Edwards Aquifer and conflicts arising between several sectors.

Reasonable use Doctrine (American Doctrine) allows a landowner to extract as much ground water as needed. Sale or transfer of water to distant lands is considered unreasonable if it impairs the ground water supply of another landowner.

The Doctrine of Correlative Rights (California Rule) gives surface owners equal rights to reasonable uses of ground water from a common source. Water is prorated among all overlying owners, and uses are not allowed that cause injury to a surface user.

The Doctrine of Prior Appropriation as applied to ground water is basically the same as for surface water. One significant exception is for aquifers that are being mined. Here, the doctrine is applied by specifying a given lifetime for the aquifer. This protects senior water rights by restricting new users. Ground water permit systems are also used in some locations to allocate ground water. This method is not based on traditional allocation doctrines (Carriker, 1985).

Diffused Surface Water Doctrines

Generally, diffused water is considered as the property of the owner of the land on which it occurs. The Common Enemy Doctrine allows an upper watershed landowner to protect property from the destructive effects of diffused water by draining the water with no liability for injuries imposed on other landowners. Upper landowners may not, however, affect the flow of diffused water maliciously or negligently.

Civil Law Doctrine, however, makes the landowner liable for injuries imposed on others by their changing the natural flow of diffused water. Reasonable Use Doctrine is a compromise between Common Enemy Doctrine and Civil Law Doctrine. Liability for interference with natural flow is based on whether the action was reasonble and/or negligent, reckless, or ultrahazardous (Carriker, 1985).

Box 8.1. The Edwards Aquifer: A Fugitive Resource

The Edwards Aquifer underlies the region around San Antonio, Texas. Water from the Edwards Aquifer is used for irrigation, for municipal, industrial, and military uses, recreation, and stream flow. Much of the recharge zone is in the irrigated area. This is referred to as the Winter Garden and occurs on the western part of the region. The water flows east beneath the city of San Antonio and then north to New Braunfels and San Marcos. The springs are located in San Antonio, New Braunfels, and San Marcos. The aquifer is about 180 miles long and varies from 5 to 40 miles wide.

Recharge to the aquifer from 1934 to 1982 averaged over 600,000 acre feet (188 billion gallons) annually (CH2MHill, RPC Engineering). Spring flow ranged from 580,000 acre feet in 1977 to less than 70,000 acre feet in 1956. Stream flow has averaged 360,000 acre feet annually. Of the five major springs, all but San Marcos have ceased discharging at least once in the 1934–82 period.

The Edwards Aquifer is the primary source of water for 1) irrigation in the Winter Garden, 2) is essentially the sole source of water for San Antonio and rural communities, 3) military installations in the region, and 4) livestock. By the 1980s, water withdrawals had reached over 100,000 acre feet for irrigation and 244,000 acre feet for municipal, industrial, and military uses. The City of San Antonio boasts of having the largest water pump in the world: 16,000 gallons per minute.

The Edwards Aquifer represents a water supply where ownership to individual units of ground water is assigned as the water is removed. The water in the Edwards Aquifer flows rapidly from the recharge zones toward the east. The ground water is, therefore, an example of a fugitive resource where ownership is accomplished only by pumping the water to the surface.

Texas law currently gives ownership of ground water to the surface owner. This aquifer is characterized by lack of exclusion (all surface owners may drill wells and pump from the Edwards Aquifer) and high rates of lateral movement. The lack of exclusion or lack of a property right to a specific quantity of water makes the Edwards an open access resource. All surface owners have access to the water by simply drilling a well and pumping. As a common property resource, there is a strong incentive for exploitation of this aquifer.

Pumping from the Edwards Aquifer by agricultural, municipal, industrial, and military sectors is sufficient so that now one user group's pumping impacts all other users. Therefore, externalities are associated with the evolving high levels of pumping. The externalities include a declining static water level, which reduces well yields and increases pumping costs for water users. Beyond the externalities of one user impacting another user, the decline of the static water level represents a threat to the continuation of stream flow. With current Texas law, stream flow is projected to cease by 2015 (CH2MHill, RPC Engineering). The user of stream flow, beyond recreation, is the public interest as related to several endangered species. Under current institutions the Edwards Aquifer is an open access resource with the water a fugitive resource where extenalities are being imposed by users on one another and on the public trust. A driving force in changing the policy for allocation of water from the Edwards Aquifer is the public trust concept and protection of stream flow to ensure survival of threatened endangered species. Governmental (either state or federal) intervention is inevitable, the outcome is not. There is an opportunity to establish a viable water market by defining property rights to the ground water.

CH2MHill, RPC Engineering, "San Antonio Regional Water Resource, Study", One Ten Broadway, Suite 350, San Antonio, Texas, January, 1986.

RESOURCE ALLOCATION IN AGRICULTURAL SYSTEMS

Regions with irrigated agricultural systems differ according to the source of water used (ground water, surface water, or a combination) and water allocation arrangement. Economic research efforts have been devoted to identifying optimal (efficient) resource allocation for different environments, assessing the performance of existing institutional arrangements, and suggesting policy changes to improve resource allocation.

In the case of ground water systems, *common pool problems* may prevent competitive markets from attaining optimal resource use and justify government intervention as discussed in Chapters 3 and 6. In the case of surface water, water rights systems are essentially queuing systems that are inefficient relative to competitive markets. Some findings on the performance of different types of water systems are presented below.

Ground Water Systems

Ground water occurs in most areas of the United States and around the world. Ground water is heterogeneous in that it occurs in many formations and depths, quality varies dramatically, and the aquifer may or may not recharge. Ground water represents a critical source of water for agriculture in terms of households, animals, and irrigation.

In 1985, approximately 40 percent of irrigation water in the United States or 75/maf was from ground water (Guldin, 1988). Principal regions using ground water include the Mountain, Pacific, and Great Plains. Some 31 million acres are irrigated from ground water sources with 14 million of these acres irrigated from aquifers that are being mined (Day and Horner, 1987).

An aquifer with little or no recharge that is being mined represents a nonrenewable resource. The optimal rate of mining of a nonrenewable aquifer is that rate where the net marginal benefits of water used at the present is equal to the present value of net marginal benefits of water in the future (Randall, 1987). The *net marginal benefit* of water is the difference between marginal benefits (value of marginal product) of water and pumping costs. Chapter 3 indicates that, if water technology and demand stay constant over time, optimal mining of a ground water aquifer should decline over time and the price of ground water (which equals pumping cost plus user cost) should increase.

When aquifers are recharged substantially, they represent renewable resources. Chapter 3 [Equation (40a)] suggests that again optimal ground water pumping should be at a level where marginal benefit from water use equals the sum of pumping costs and user costs. When recharge levels are substantial, optimal use may reach a steady state where ground water pumping equals recharge.

Aquifers may be shared by many users, actually many aquifers such as the Ogallala, which underlies much of the Great Plains, cross state borders. This means residents of one state may be affected by ground water use in a neighboring state. Aquifers shared by many users are common property resources. As Chapter 3 argues, market failure is associated with open access to common pool resources.

The differences in outcomes between optimal (efficient) resource allocation and open access to a common ground water aquifer by many small competitive farmers are presented in Figure 3.7. In early periods, open access results in overuse of water relative to the controlled access outcome. Thus, overutilization results in a quick depletion of the water resources and, beyond a certain time period t_a in Figure 3.7, open access behavior results in underuse of water and underproduction relative to optimality. In both cases water use declines but, under open access, it declines faster. Note also that in both cases output declines over time; however for $t < t_a$, open access results in more output, while for $t > t_a$, it results in less output.

When several technologies or crops are available, the results of Shah *et al.* (1993) suggest that, under both open access and Pareto optimality, farmers will switch to more advanced technologies over time. The reason is that the decline in water stock increases pumping costs and, hence, marginal value of water over time also must increase in order to maintain economic efficiency. The changes of technology will result in decreases in water use but will also be accompanied by temporary *increases* in output. Figure 8.6a depicts the behavior of water use under the open access outcomes when two technologies are available. Technology switch will occur at t_2 and will be associated with a decrease in water use. Figure 8.6b denotes output under open access; at t_2 output will increase but then will decline again. The switch to the new technology under the optimal resource allocation is likely to occur earlier than under open access, and that will allow further saving of water in the early period, which will result in a much higher production under controlled access in later periods.

The suboptimal resource allocation under open access can be remedied by several means. One form of intervention is water taxation, with the tax being equal to the optimal user cost. Alternatively, optimality can be obtained by establishing and distributing tradable ground water rights (permits) with the aggregate volume of permitted pumping restricted to be equal to the optimal level.

Inability to monitor pumping levels may prevent attaining first-best solutions, but these outcomes can be approximated by taxation based on observables such as crop and irrigation technology. If, for example, the optimal user cost in a region is $10/AF, and alfalfa production with furrow irrigation is estimated to use 6 *AF* of water per acre, while production of tomatoes with drip irrigation is estimated to use 2.5 AF of water per acre, the alfalfa growers will be required to pay $60/acre while the grower of tomatoes with drip will be required to pay $25/acre. To increase the political acceptability of such policies, it may be useful to use some of the proceeds for subsidizing investments in water conservation practices.

Ground water exhibits many common property features. However, there are factors which may limit an aquifer being used in a common property mode. If the hydrologic conductivity of an aquifer is sufficiently low, there will be limited lateral movement in the aquifer and little impact of one farm's pumping on the pumping costs of neighboring farms (Beattie, 1981). More formally, the Gisser-Sanchez rule, as presented by Nieswiadomy (1985) states that

$$\psi^2 = [kC_1(\alpha - 1)/AS]^2 \tag{8}$$

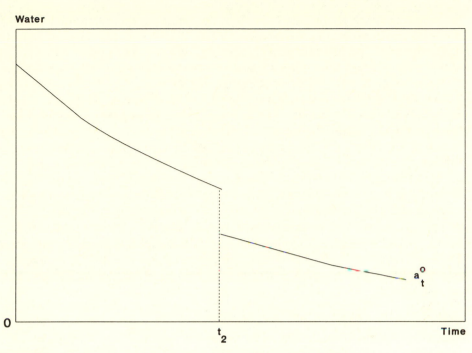

Figure 8.6a. Water use over time – open access with two technologies.

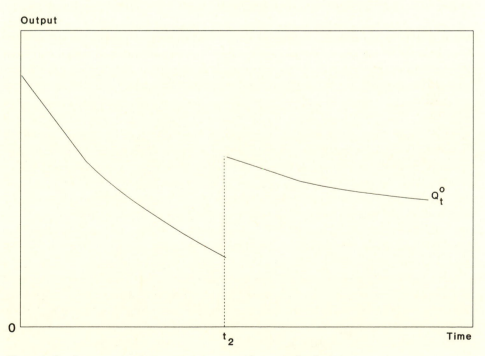

Figure 8.6b. Output over time – open access with two technologies.

must be approximately zero for there to be no significant intertemporal misallocation under open access to ground water. In Equation (8) k is the slope of the water
demand curve, C_1 is the pumping cost per unit of water per foot of lift, A is area
of the aquifer (acres), S is storability coefficient or specific yield, and α is the return
or recharge coefficient. The Gisser-Sanchez rule indicates that, if natural recharge
is slow, the slope of the demand curve for groundwater is small relative to the area
of the aquifer times storability, and if water rights are exclusively assigned, then
there is no significant intertemporal misallocation of the ground water. The
Nieswiadomy (1985) study considered parts of the Ogallala aquifer in Texas and
showed that the specific yield of the Ogallala is about 15 percent, or in 1 foot of
saturated sand, there is 0.15 foot of water. Further, there are no nonagricultural
competitors for most of the area. A specific yield of 15 percent suggests the aquifer
is composed of a tight (versus coarse) sand with little lateral movement and limited
pumping capacity. With pumps spaced at one-quarter mile or more, there is limited
annual withdrawal in the growing season and minimal influence between wells.
Thus, as suggested by Beattie (1981), the ground water in most of the Ogallala
aquifer is not subject to serious depletion by actions of neighboring irrigators.

Conjunctive Use of Surface and Ground Water

In considering management strategies for water, both surface and ground water
need to be evaluated *together*. Surface water and aquifers are commonly interlinked. Surface water may percolate to an aquifer or there may be a stream–aquifer
where there is direct movement in both directions. For the latter, use of one supply,
surface or aquifer, directly impacts the other; i.e., excessive pumping will lower
the water level of a stream. Typically, the hydrologic relationship between surface
water and an aquifer is very complex but essential to devising a management plan
(Buras and Nunn, 1989). The characteristics of the relationship between surface
water and an aquifer can be divided simplistically into three types. First, there is
the stream and directly linked aquifer where withdrawals from one source directly
affect the other. Second, there is the case of a confined aquifer with limited
recharge undergoing a mining situation where surface water is imported to meet
demand. Third, in many cases surface water supplies, though relatively inexpensive, are limited and subject to randomness. In these cases ground water is used
conjunctively to increase supply and mitigate undesirable fluctuation in rainfall
and water supply. The first represents management of complex stream–aquifer
interaction, the second relates to timing and amount of water import schemes,
and the third considers conjunctive use of ground water stocks to supplement
random surface water supplies and will be analyzed below.

Consider a case when a region obtains water from a stream, with cost of v
dollars per acre foot and a very large ground water aquifer where pumping cost
is c dollars per acre foot. It is assumed that the regional water use is small and
does not affect the ground water level and that ground water costs are larger than
surface water cost, $c > v$. It is also assumed that annual surface water availability,
R, is a random variable (this water may be snowmelt, and snowfall varies over
time), with density function $g(R)$.

Let annual water consumption be denoted by Y. The annual benefit from water is denoted by $B(Y)$, where $B(Y)$ represents the area under the derived demand curve. Water use is the sum of ground water use Z and surface water use X. At any period, surface water use cannot exceed surface water availability, $X \leq R$. Surface water availability is known when surface and ground water use levels are determined, so that for a given R, optimal choices are determined by solving the following constrained optimization:

$$L = \underset{X, Z, \lambda}{\text{Max}} \; B(X + Z) - vX - cZ + \lambda[R - X] \qquad X, Z \geq 0 \qquad (9)$$

where λ is the shadow price of the surface water availability constraint. Necessary optimality (Kuhn-Tucker) conditions for this problem are

$$L_Z = B_Z(X + Z) - c \leq 0; \qquad L_Z Z = [B_Z(X + Z) - c]Z = 0 \qquad (10a)$$

$$L_X = B_X(X + Z) - v - \lambda \leq 0; \qquad L_X X = [B_X(X + Z) - v - \lambda]X = 0 \quad (10b)$$

$$L_\lambda = R - X \geq 0; \qquad L_\lambda Z = [(R - X)\lambda]Z = 0 \qquad (10c)$$

Let Y_c denote the water use level where marginal benefit equals ground water pumping cost (i.e., $B_Y(Y_c) = c$) and Y_v denote the level when the marginal benefit of water equals surface water cost (i.e., $B_Y(Y_v) = v$).

These two water use levels are depicted in Figure 8.7. Using these definitions with conditions (10a)–(10c) suggest three types of outcomes (depicted in Fig. 8.7) that depend on surface water supply:

1. In dry years with $R < Y_c$, all the surface water will be used, some ground water will be pumped, water use will be at the level where demand is equal to pumping cost (i.e., Y_c), and water price will equal ground water pumping cost c. In this case $Y = Y_c$; $X = R$, and $Z = Y_c - R$. Surface water owners gain a premium of $c - v$.

2. In medium surface supply years, when $Y_c < R < Y_v$, all surface water will be used, no ground water will be pumped, and water price will be between surface and ground water cost. Such an outcome occurs when $R = X = Y_u$ in Figure 8.7. In this case, water price is equal to u and the premium for surface water will be $\lambda = u - v$.

3. In wet years when $R > Y_v$, not all surface water will be consumed, and water use will be at the level when marginal benefits equal surface water cost. In this case, $Y = X = Y_v$, $Z = 0$ and no quasi-rents accrue to surface water.

This analysis suggests that, for ground water aquifers nearer the surface (c is smaller), the frequency and volume of ground water pumping will be greater. In also suggests that the reliance and importance of conjunctive management of surface and ground water is likely to increase as the variability of surface water supply increases. To illustrate this point, compare situations when surface water is stable at $R = Y_u$ versus when the surface water supply is randomly distributed with $R < Y_c$ with probability of one-third. Obviously, there will not be any ground water pumping in the first case when surface supply is stable and equal to Y_u, but $Y_c - R$ units of water will be pumped one-third of the time if surface water supply is random.

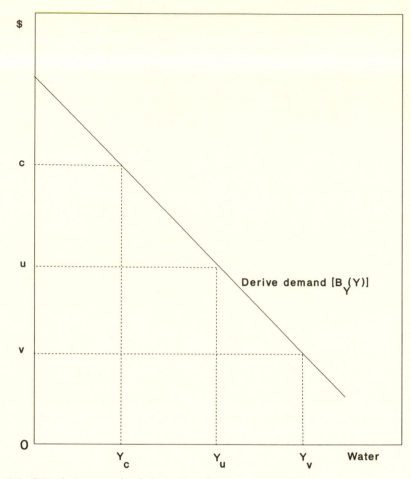

Figure 8.7. Critical water use levels in conjunctive use management.

In many cases ground water pumping, as well as irrigation activities, sub-stantially affect the water level in the aquifer. Taking this effect into account requires dynamic modeling. Indeed, the literature on conjunctive use of ground and surface water relies on a dynamic framework, (e.g., Tsur, 1990). The model presented in equation (9) is expanded below to incorporate water aquifer dynamics. Let S_t be the stock of water in ground water aquifers at time t. The equation of motion of this stock is $S_{t+1} - S_t = g(Y_t) - Z_t + U_t$ where $g(Y_t)$ denotes replenishment of ground water aquifers due to percolation of irrigation water* and U_t is a random variable denoting *replenishment* of ground water aquifers from other sources. Thus, the change in the stock of water is the result of pumping and replenishment. When ground water varies, pumping cost per acre foot is a

---

* Actual hydrological modeling of the percolation process is more complex, and there may be lags between irrigation and replenishment of ground water. The model here is simplified for instructional purposes.

function of the water stock, $c(S_t)$, and the unit pumping cost declines as the stock of water increases, $c_S < 0$.

Using these definitions, expected discounted net benefits from water use in the future can be presented as

$$V(S_1) = \underset{Z_t, Y_t, X_t}{\text{Max}} \sum_{t=1}^{\infty} E\left\{\left(\frac{1}{1+r}\right)^t B(Y_t) - c(S_t)Z_t - vX_t\right\} \tag{11}$$

s.t. $S_{t+1} - S_t = g(Y_t) - Z_t + U_t$; $\quad Y_t = X_t + Z_t$; $\quad 0 \le X_t, Z_t$; $\quad X_t \le R_t$; $\quad t = 1, \infty$

where E is the expectation operator and r is the discount rate. In making present water use decisions, future ground water effects have to be taken into account; therefore, the optimal conjunctive water use problem becomes

$$\text{Max } B(Y_0) - c(S_0)Z_0 - vX_0 + V(S_1) \tag{12}$$

$$\text{s.t. } Y_0 = X_0 + Z_0; \quad X_0 \le R_0; \quad 0 \le X_0, Z_0$$

By appropriate substitution, the Lagrangian form of the optimization problem becomes

$$L = \underset{X_0, Z_0, \lambda_0}{\text{Max}} \ B(X_0 + Z_0) - c(S_0)Z_0 - vX_0 + V$$

$$\times [(S_0 - Z_0) + g(X_0 + Z_0) + U_0 + \lambda(R_0 - X_0)] \quad X_0, Z_0 \ge 0 \tag{13}$$

The necessary (Kuhn-Tucker) optimality conditions of this optimization problem are (the operators of the functions are eliminated for convenience):

$$L_{x_0} = B_{Y_0} - v + g_{Y_0}V_{S_1} - \lambda \le 0 \qquad L_{X_0}X_0 = 0 \tag{13a}$$

$$L_{Z_0} = B_{Y_0} - c(S_0) - (1 - g_{Y_0})V_{S_1} \le 0 \qquad L_{Z_0}Z_0 = 0 \tag{13b}$$

$$L_{\lambda_0} = R_0 - X_0 \le 0 \qquad L_{\lambda_0}\lambda_0 = 0 \tag{13c}$$

Comparison of these conditions with (10a)–(10c) suggests that optimal behavior at time 0 depends on the initial stock of water in the aquifers, S_0, and the random replenishment of the aquifer, U_0, in addition to the surface water supply, R_0. In particular, the two critical water use levels, Y_v and Y_c become functions of S_0 and U_0.[2] Here again, one can identify three types of outcomes:

[2] Y_v is determined by solving (13b) for the case with $\lambda = 0$, $R_0 = X_0 = Y_v$. In particular, it is solved from

$$B_Y(Y_v) = V - g_{Y_0}V_{S_1}[S_0 + U_0 + g(Y_V)]$$

It denotes the maximum amount of surface water supply that is completely used. Y_c is determined solving (13b) for the case $R_0 = X_0 = Y_v$, $Z_0 = 0$ and $L_{Z_0} = 0$. In particular, at Y_c

$$B_{Y_0}(Y_c) = c_{S_0}(S_0) + [1 - g_{Y_0}(Y_c)]V_{S_1}[S_0 + U_0 + g(Y_c)]$$

It denotes the minimum amount of surface water supply that does not require augmentation by ground water.

a. In a dry year, with $R < Y_c(S_0, U_0)$ where ground water is pumped, $Z_0 > 0$, condition (13b) suggests that optimal pumping is determined at the level where

$$B_{Y_1} = c(S_0) - (1 - g_{s_1})V_{S_1} = P_0 \qquad (14)$$

where P_0 is the optimal price of water at time 0. The left-hand side of (14) is the marginal benefit of water, and the right-hand side is the sum of pumping costs and the marginal reduction in expected benefits of water in the future because of ground water pumping and use. Note that $V_{S_1} > 0$ beause a larger aquifer in the future is likely to increase future social benefits. Also, the net effect of pumping one unit of water on the aquifer will be to reduce it by the amount pumped and to increase it by the amount replenished. Condition (14) suggests that less ground water will be pumped as the aquifer is smaller since pumping costs and the value of water that remains in the aquifer are higher when it is smaller. Assuming $v < c(S_0)$, all the surface water will be used in dry seasons when ground water is pumped.

b. When $Y_c(S_0, U_0) < R_0 < Y_v(S_0, U_0)$, the ground water aquifer is sufficiently low and rainfall is in a middle range so that all surface water is used but no ground water is pumped.

c. In wet years when $Y_v(S_0, U_0) < R$, not all surface water will be used, and condition (13a) suggests that the optimal surface water use is determined where the marginal benefit from the use of the water is equal to the cost of surface water minus the expected benefit resulting from the replenishment of the aquifer, namely,

$$B_{Y_1} = v - g_{Y_0}V_{S_1} = P \qquad (15)$$

Equation (15) suggests that more surface water will be used when surface water is low because the value of ground water replenishment associated with irrigation is higher in such situations.

Further analysis can show that likelihood and volume of ground water pumping increases as the surface water supply gets smaller and the water stock in the aquifer is larger. The likelihood and extent of not completely using surface water supply increase as this supply becomes larger and the water stock in the aquifer is lower.

There are many other studies that address conjunctive use of ground and surface water. Burt's (1964) seminal paper introduces a framework to study conjunctive use. This dynamic optimization framework admits randomness, at least of surface water supply, and sets ground water demand relationships depending on the state of surface water, prices, and ground water depth. Gisser (1983) addresses the conjunctive use problem using a static, steady-state framework that allows approximation of the more general dynamic problem.

Models of *conjunctive use* differ in their specifications of the interrelationship between the two sources of water. In cases where surface water is stream flow emanating from aquifers, ground water and surface supply are highly correlated (Young and Bredehoeft, 1972). In other studies, surface water and ground water supply are independent (Cummings and Winkelman, 1970). The role of ground water as a buffer stock is likely to increase as the correlation between surface and ground water supply diminishes.

In many cases, conjunctive management of water resources may include simultaneous management of several water inventories, namely, the ground water aquifer and water inventories of one or several surface water reservoirs. It may also involve choices regarding construction of new facilities, such as dams, reservoirs, or water canals. According to Reisner's "Cadillac Desert," (1986) the construction of the big water projects in California was motivated by the overdraft of ground water aquifers in the San Joaquin Valley and concern for the future of agriculture in this valley as its ground water resources were being depleted.

Similar development occurred in other regions. The construction of water conveyance facilities that allow importation of source water transformed the water management problems of many regions from water-mining problems to conjunctive use problems.

Conjunctive management of complex hydrologic systems normally involves a maturing water economy characterized by 1) water scarcity with high and rising prices; 2) inelastic long-run supply of reservoir water; 3) growing demand for water; 4) deteriorating facilities for surface water supply; 5) competition among different users, such as agriculture, municipal, recreation, and industrial; 6) increasing costs associated with externalities; and 7) high and increasing social costs to subsidize development of alternative sources; (Buras and Nunn, 1989). One of the major sources of inefficiency in such situations is reliance on queuing mechanisms (water rights systems) rather than markets for allocation of water.

Water Allocation by Queues Versus Allocations by Market

Studies (Burness and Quirk, 1979; Wade, 1987; Wahl, 1989) have investigated the economic implications of alternative water allocation doctrines and compared their performance to water markets. This area of research is likely to grow in importance since the reform of water allocation mechanisms is becoming a major topic of public and political debate. The issue of transferring water among users is especially critical in times of drought.

In essence, both riparian and appropriative rights systems are *queuing systems* where water allocation is determined according to location or the order in which consumers first seek use of the water. Queuing is an essential feature of the following conceptual model that analyzes the impact of water rights doctrines and compares their outcomes to those of water markets. The analysis compares output, land use, producer welfare, and technology choice under the two allocation rules.

Suppose a water body (lake or river) supplies a region of L acres with A units of water annually. The production technology, with constant returns to scale, is the same as was introduced in Eq. 1. The per acre production function is $y = f(e)$, where e is effective water per acre. The region has homogeneous land quality, thus irrigation efficiency with the traditional technology is h_1 and with the modern one is h_2. Assume that there is a fixed cost of zero for the traditional technology ($c_1 = 0$), that output price is given and denoted by P, and that there are no pumping or water conveyance costs. Furthermore, assume that the water rights system ranks the land parcels in the region, that the land parcels receive their water in sequence, and that each unit of land gets as much water as it needs for production as long as water is available. The system disallows water trading but, once water is available, a farmer can apply any amount as long as its marginal productivity is nonnegative. Thus, profit-maximizing landowners who receive water use the traditional technology, and their per acre applied water has zero marginal productivity and is denoted by a^{max}. Let e^{max} be effective water per acre that maximizes yield (corresponding to point F in Fig. 8.2). Thus, $a^{max} = e^{max}/h_i$. Assume that the region is sufficiently large that not all land is irrigated under the water rights system. In this case, the irrigated area is $A/a^{max} < L$. Per acre profit on the irrigated land is $PF(e^{max})$ and zero on lands with junior rights that are not irrigated.

Consider now the case where there is a *water market* and only the traditional technology is available. Assume that all land is utilized. Applied water per acre becomes A/L, effective water per acre is $h_i A/L$, and water price is $Ph_i f'(h_i A/L)$. The transition from the water rights system to a water market increases utilized land from A/a^{max} to L. These added lands receive $(L - A/a^{max})L/A$ units of water and produce $(L - A/a^{max})f(h_i L/A)$ units of output. Because of the declining marginal productivity of water, overall output increases as a water market is introduced, with the gain in output $dQ = Lf(A/L) - (A/a^{max})f(e^{max})$. This increase in output results in a net efficiency gain (measured by gain in net social welfare, which, in this case, is equal to producer surplus gain) of

$$dW = PdQ = P[Lf(A/L) - A/a^{max}f(e^{max})] \qquad (16)$$

The inefficiency associated with the water rights system increases with the lower irrigation efficiency of the traditional technology (h_i) and with the larger area of the region, L. When acreage of the system is not a constraint, the introduction of a water market reduces effective water per acre to $e*$, where marginal productivity of effective water is equal to average productivity (point E in Fig. 8.2). In this case, applied water is $a_i^* = e*/h_i$ the area is A/a_i^*, and the price of effective water is $h_i Pf(e*)$.

When transition to a water market improves efficiency, the possible equity effects and impacts on noneconomic factors may make it objectionable. The equity effects depend on the assignment of property rights for the water. If the agency that controls the water receives the proceeds from its sale, the profit of all farmers is

$$Pf(h_i L/A - h_i f'(h_i L/A)L/A \qquad (17)$$

Under these property rights the profit declines as L increases, and when the area of the region is not a constraint, the introduction of a water market reduces farmers' profit per acre to zero. Obviously, landowners with *senior water rights* (which operate under the water rights system) lose from the transition to a water market when they have to pay for the water. Their loss per acre consists of a revenue loss of $P[f(e^{max}) - f(h_i A/L)]$ and the extra water cost of $Ph_i f'(h_i A/L)$. These landowners are likely to strongly oppose the introduction of a water market. If the water market operates with different water rights assignments and landowners with senior water rights receive the proceeds from water sales, their profit per acre consists of the sum of the revenue from sales of output and proceeds of sales of water to individuals with junior property rights and is equal to $P[f(h_iA/L) + f'(h_iA/L)h_ia^{max}(L - A/a^{max}/A^2]$.

In this case, the profit is greater than under the water rights system since the income from the sale of extra water in a water market is greater than the value of the output the water generates when it is not sold. Thus, landowners with senior water rights may support a water market when they retain the proceeds from water sales.

A transition from a water rights system to a water market system may induce technological change. Under a water rights system, landowners with senior water rights do not have much incentive to invest in the new technology. But under a water market, the modern technology is adopted if the added revenue it provides can cover the fixed cost, namely, if $Pf(h_2A/L) - Pf(h_1A/L) > C_2$. The lack of incentive to adopt the new technology under a water rights regime is another source of inefficiency. The adoption of the new technology is likely to result in lower water prices and thus reduce objections to the replacement of property rights by a market in cases where landowners with senior water rights have to pay for the water.

The analysis thus far considers the case of a small price-taking region. When the affected region faces a negative sloped demand for its output, transition from a water rights system to water market system increases supply, and that tends to reduce prices and benefit consumers, but may also reduce producer surplus. In such cases, landowners with senior water rights may object to the introduction of a water market even if they control the proceeds from water sales. The loss of revenues from output sales may be larger than the gains from water sales.

Water systems are subject to weather uncertainty, which affects water availability over time. The inefficiency of resource allocation with the water rights system under uncertainty is demonstrated by Burness and Quirk (1979). One source of inefficiency associated with water rights under uncertainty may be overinvestment in irrigation equipment by individuals with junior water rights and underinvestment in irrigation equipment by landowners with senior water rights. In most situations, individuals with senior rights are likely to secure large volumes of water, and thus they may use traditional irrigation technology or grow crops with high water requirements. Individuals with junior water rights are likely to adopt modern irrigation technologies with high irrigation efficiency or grow crops with low water requirements.

One tool for viewing movement toward a market system of water distribution is producer and consumer surplus. Figure 8.8 illustrates hypothetical supply and demand functions for water in both nonagricultural and agricultural uses and aggregate supply and demand where the two user groups are summed. Viewing agriculture first, it is assumed that quantity Q_a of surface water is supplied to agriculture at price f under existing institutions. Thus, the supply of surface water to agriculture is fixed and represented by S_a^* on Figure 8.8. However, there is a supply function or marginal cost curve to society associated with delivering this water to agriculture, given as S_a. To evaluate the surplus implications of this allocation, we begin with the consumers or the irrigation farmers. Consumers surplus is the area def in Figure 8.8. The producer in this case is the government

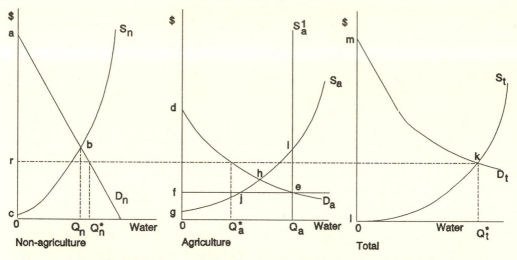

Figure 8.8. Hypothetical illustration of agricultural and non-agricultural water demand and supply.

entity (society) providing the water. Producer surplus is the area fjg less the area jie. The area jie is that amount of the cost to provide this water to agriculture above what the farmers pay; e.g., a subsidy to irrigated agriculture. Total producer plus consumer surplus is the sum of each. The area jhe is consumer surplus, but it is also a net cost to society or loss in producer surplus, so it may be ignored in estimating total surplus. Thus means total surplus is dhg less hie.

Nonagricultural users of water face separate demand and supply schedules when agriculture is provided with a fixed quantity of water. Figure 8.8 shows nonagricultural water supply as S_n and demand as D_n. In this case, total consumer (nonagricultural users) and producer (water supplier) surplus is abc for nonagriculture if agriculture receives a fixed quantity of water equal to Q_a. Thus, total surplus in this case is abc plus dhg minus hie.

The third graph of Figure 8.8 illustrates aggregate supply and demand for water. By shifting to a market system of water allocation, Q_t^* is demanded and an equilibrium price of water, r, established. This implies the price of water declines for nonagricultural users and quantity demanded increases from Q_n to Q_n^*. Conversely, the price of water is expected to increase in agriculture from f to r and, consequently, the quantity demanded declines from Q_a to Q_a^*.

The aggregate implication of movement to a market system of water allocation is total consumer surplus plus producer surplus of mkl. The area mkl is clearly larger than total agricultural and nonagricultural surpluses when a fixed quantity of water is supplied to agriculture at a price less than the cost of delivery. However, the consumer surplus to agriculture is significantly reduced.

Although a market system of water allocation increases total surplus conceptually, there are critical and controversial issues related to the redistribution of wealth, income, and utility. Further, this greatly exaggerated simplification ignores externalities (management of rivers as environmental and recreational assets) and effects on businesses serving the declining agricultural sector.

Institutions with impacts on water development and allocation schemes extend beyond governmental agencies and organizations. There is a new emphasis on improving the efficiency of existing water supplies by designing improved water allocation schemes. Alternatives range from accelerating the development of water markets, with the market system providing signals of highest and best use, to more restrictive laws legislating technical efficiency or reduced use by selected users.

Water Marketing Issues

Theoretically, improved allocation of water can be achieved through a market system. A market provides an organized way of trading rights to the resource and approximating the maximum net social value from its use. In the absence of a market, water allocation is the responsibility of government. Typically, government intervention does not provide efficient management; political and legislative forces tend to make allocation decisions without full consideration of the value of water in alternative uses. At present, there is strong incentive to give the market system greater opportunity to allocate water.

The scheme of a *water market* is simple. However, implementation may be extremely difficult. First and foremost, it is essential that there are enforceable property rights to the water (Saliba and Bush, 1987). This often requires court action and expensive and lengthy court hearings. Furthermore, it is expensive to transport and store water and, for many uses, the value of water at the margin is relatively low. In such cases, the benefits are not sufficient to provide an incentive to implement a market system (Saliba, 1987).

Several characteristics cause water to deviate from the competitive market model (Saliba and Bush, 1987). These include

1. External (third party) effects whereby buyers' and sellers' decisions affect others who are not directly involved in the decisions. Externalities occur when there are beneficiaries other than water users, such as agricultural processors of irrigated crops; the processors have a vested interest in seeing no change in water allocations to irrigated agriculture. In another example, instream flows are recognized as a beneficial use in most states, but nonconsumptive water users do not have access to markets as do farmers, municipalities, and industry (Saliba, 1987).

2. Public goods aspects of water resources whereby some benefits of water use are enjoyed by more than one individual. Benefits may accrue to users other than those paying for the water. This is called nonexcludability. A market excludes those who will not pay the going price. Thus, in many cases, market prices do not effectively consider the use of water for aesthetic and recreational purposes.

3. Imperfect competition whereby individual buyers and/or sellers influence price (such as very large users or suppliers).

4. Risks owing to lack of information regarding potential supply shortfalls. Efficiency of competitive markets assumes complete knowledge availability and quality.

5. Equity issues whereby government intervention is required to address water rights conflicts and the redistribution of benefits.

These characteristics and issues have great effect on the development of water markets to reallocate water. In addition, water is mobile; it changes form and moves from higher areas to lower areas. This makes it difficult to identify specific units of water and assign property rights. In addition, there may be many users of the same water, some of whom have no market rights, such as fishermen. The market system fails to properly allocate when the same water serves several users at different points along the waterway. Water with many uses is a public good. Simultaneous uses of water in a particular reservoir include boating, aesthetics, and flood control. Identifying value and property rights in these cases is difficult and complicates development of a balanced market system.

Although there are serious issues to be resolved in implementing a water marketing mechanism, there are many active water markets in the West. The relative effectiveness of several markets is reviewed by Saliba (1987). Water is moving to higher value uses, typically from agriculture to municipal and industrial users. This has resulted in a reduction in acreage of low-value crops and some increase in acreage of high-value crops, with a net flow of water out of agriculture.

Rights have been selling for a wide range of values, for example, from $706–1,294 per acre foot in the Tucson area; $941–1,529 per acre foot in the Phoenix region; around $1,700 per acre foot in New Mexico; $1,411–2,352 per acre foot in the Reno and Sparks, Nevada, area; near $1,000 per acre foot in Colorado; $150 per acre foot in Utah, and $400–500 per acre foot in the Texas Lower Rio Grande Valley. Water transactions are reported in the monthly *Water Market Update*. Values for water vary dramatically based on changes in supply and demand as well as on policies governing water transfer. Water rights have risen as high as $4,000 per acre foot in Colorado. This evidence suggests to Saliba (1987) that water markets are functioning in some parts of the West and work well to allocate water among agricultural, municipal, and industrial sectors.

Water Use Problems Over Time

The emergence of markets for water in the West may reflect an increase in the relative scarcity of water. That is to say, growth in water demand has outpaced water supply. Figure 8.9 depicts patterns of behavior for several categories of water use between 1960 and 1985. Both agricultural and urban water use levels rose rapidly between 1960 and 1985 (agricultural water use in 1979 was 60 percent higher than in 1960). Agricultural and urban water use levels declined slightly in the early 1980s owing to low commodity prices, a slumping economy, and much above average rainfall (strong El-niño effect), but industry and utility water use continued to grow, and water use levels stayed high. The graph does not reflect the amount of water used for maintaining environmental amenities (wetlands, fisheries), but no doubt, there has been growing demand for this water use category.

Institutional changes and transition to market-like mechanisms for water resource allocation have not been smooth, and in many cases have occurred when the water system was in a vulnerable situation. Box 8.2 describes changes occurring because of the 1987–1991 drought in California.

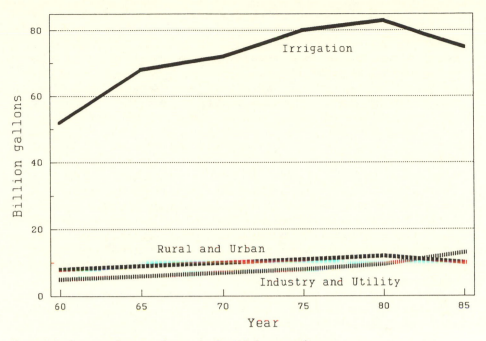

Figure 8.9. Consumptive use of water in the U.S. by type of use.

Box 8.2. How California Responded to the 1987–1991 Drought

The Central Valley of California is a semiarid zone that has become one of the most productive agricultural regions in the world. Agricultural production in the region relies heavily on surface water that originates in the Sierra Mountains to the east of the Valley. The east side of the Central Valley receives most of the surface water, which diverts water resources at the Sierra foothills. Two main water projects—the state water projects (S.W.P.) and the Central Valley projects (C.V.P.)—transfer water from Northern California to the west side of the Valley. These water projects also deliver water to cities and industries in the southern part of the state. In most cases, water rights of farmers in the east side of the Valley are senior to those of farmers in the west side of the Valley.

Between 1987 and 1991, California suffered a severe drought where annual rainfall and snow melt were between 50 and 80 percent of normal. The response of the state and its farmers to the drought is consistent with the predictions of the economics of water management as we will argue below.

Surface water resources are stored in many reservoirs, mostly in the Sierra foothills. The decisions about water deliveries from the reservoirs are dependent on the stock of water they contain and not necessarily on inflows from recent snowmelt. At the early stages of the drought, the reservoirs were relatively full and, therefore, normal amounts of water were delivered to the farmers in the first 2 years of the drought. Over time, as the reservoir declined, the deliveries to agriculture declined as well. As Table 1 shows, most of the decline was absorbed by farmers who received their water from the state and federal projects and who had relatively junior water rights.

Farmers' water use choices are dependent on water availability, and farmers' water use choices were not affected much during the first 2 years of the drought since surface water deliveries did not change. However, during the later period of the drought, farmers' water use choices changed drastically. The three types of changes are as follows: 1) Farmers drastically increased the use of ground water, and in many cases ground water replaced surface water. Again, Table 1 shows that ground water use increased substantially throughout the drought. The table shows that the volume of water pumped by water districts, which were surveyed in the drought response study, doubled in the last year of the drought relative to the first year. 2) Lack of water forced farmers to reduce their irrigated land base and increased the amount of fallowed land. This trend is clearly shown in Table 1. Note that in the last year of the drought, there was an increase in the fallowed land relative to the last 2 or 3 years of the drought. Farmers reduced their acreage of relatively low value crops (field crops), but their acreage of fruits and vegetables did not show significant changes. 3) Farmers improved their water use efficiency by switching to modern irrigation technologies or improving existing technologies. Vegetable growers greatly increased their use of drip irrigation, particularly in the production of vegetables for processing. Cotton growers began using sprinklers for preirrigation and shorter rows with gravitational irrigation.

The long drought also resulted in some very important institutional changes. Zusman and Rausser developed a political economic approach to explain the institutional changes in water resource management. They argued that interest groups are able to delay the introduction of efficiency-enhancing changes as long as crisis situations do not occur. The drastic reduction in surface water provision to some water districts, especially in the later years of the drought, led them to introduce *tiered water pricing*. Water use below a threshold level (about 80% of average consumption) is charged a relatively low price. The amounts above the threshold level are charged a much higher price. For example, a cotton grower may be charged $16/AF for the first 2.8 AF/acre and $40/AF for everything above it. Some districts use the extra revenues to finance subsidized loans for water conservation technologies.

A more drastic change occurred in the 5th year of the drought with the introduction of the *water bank*. It provided a means to transfer water from those districts with water surpluses to those with shortfalls. Last year the seller price was $124/AF and the buyer price was $175/AF at the Delta; 825,000 AF were purchased and 435,000 AF were sold. Metropolitan water districts (which provide water to Southern California) purchased 370,000 AF (85% of the total), and the remaining 82,000 (15%) went to agriculture.

Table 8.1. Water Deliveries and Fallowed Acres for Sample Districts[a]

	Project water	Nonproject water	Ground water pumped	Acreage fallowed[b]
1987	3,188	7,980	425	259
1988	3,163	7,730	532	264
1989	3,382	8,430	363	276
1990	2,641	8,238	592	258
1991	1,606	8,120	923	397

[a] Values are in thousands of acre-feet.
[b] Thousands of acres.

Changes in water regulation are not limited only to water quantity problems. The last 30 years have also seen a growing concern for water quality. Models and policies to address quality problems appear in the following sections.

ECONOMICS OF PREVENTION, MITIGATION, AND TREATMENT OF AGRICULTURAL WATER POLLUTION

In addition to agricultural commodities, the agricultural production processes generate residuals (i.e., manure, nutrients, pesticides, suspended solids, etc.) that can contaminate ground and surface water causing various health and environmental quality problems (see Box 8.3). Conceptually, it is useful to think of these damages as the basis of a demand function for cleaner water (i.e., pollution damage mitigation) (Fig. 8.10). This composite demand function includes derived demands arising from quality effects on intermediate uses of water (e.g., irrigation, industrial, commercial fishing), on final demands for water (e.g., drinking, recreation), and on option and existence values of water resources (Smith and Desvouges, 1986).

Derived demands for water quality arise from the productivity value of improved water quality in the production process. Thus, the demand for improved water quality is dependent upon the nature of the production process, the value of the product being produced, the prices of other inputs to the process, and the price of improved water quality. For example, the demand for less saline irrigation water is dependent upon the effect of salinity on crop growth, the price of the crop, the cost of substitute inputs such as land or increased quantities of water, and the price of higher quality irrigation water.

Final demands arise from the utility gains (preferences) associated with improved water quality. For example, a recreator's utility is increased if improved water quality reduces the potential health risks and improves aesthetic aspects of swimming, boating, or other recreational activities. Final demands for improved water quality are dependent upon population, preferences, income levels, and the prices of alternative goods. Thus, we would expect that the demand for recreation (improved water quality) would increase as population, income, and prices of substitute sources of entertainment increase or as preferences for clean water increase.

The other half of the conceptual equation is the supply of improved water quality (emissions reduction) (Fig. 8.10). Improved water quality, like any other good, costs money to produce. The supply curve reflects the marginal cost of additional improvements in water quality. Water quality can be improved by reducing loadings, delivery rates, or transport rates or by treating the water prior to reuse. Conceptually, the overall supply curve is a composite function of the marginal costs of these various processes for producing improved water quality.

The intersection of the demand and supply curves in Figure 8.10 reflects the socially optimal level of emissions (m^*). At this point the marginal value of improved water quality just equals the marginal cost of additional emissions reduction, maximizing the sum of producer and consumer surpluses (see Chapter 4). Obviously, the level of m^* will vary as the demand and/or the supply curves

Box 8.3. Man, Agriculture, and Water Ecosystems

One hundred years ago, south Florida fresh water circulated in a slow, rain-driven cycle (40–65 inches per year) of meandering rivers and streams, shallow lakes, and wetlands including unique saw grass marshes. Starting at a chain of lakes south of Orlando, water flowed into the Kissimmee River. The Kissimmee meandered 103 miles south into Lake Okeechobee. During wet seasons, water spilled over the Lake's low southern rim, and flowed south across the everglades saw grass in a 50-mile wide sheet moving at a rate of approximately one hundred feet per day toward Florida Bay.

Modification of the natural freshwater system in south Florida began in the late 1800s as investors began developing the area. Over the next 100 years, a series of development, drainage, floor protection, and water supply programs resulted in the construction of 1,400 miles of canals and levees. The most important project was the massive federally funded, flood-control and water supply project known as The Central and Southern Florida Flood Control Project authorized by Congress in 1948. Major modifications included 1) the channelization of the Kissimmee river into a 56 mile-long, 300 foot-wide, 60-foot deep canal known as C-38; 2) construction of the 25 foot-high, Herbert Hoover Dike encircling Lake Okeechobee; and 3) creation of three water conservation areas south of Lake Okeechobee to store excess flood waters and to provide supplemental water supply.

Agriculture first began to develop around Lake Okeechobee in the 1920s. Originally agriculture was limited by poor drainage and poor soils. Identification of micronutrient deficiencies in the Everglades Agricultural Area (EAA) led to a significant increase in production in the 1930s. Establishment of the sugar program in the 1960s led to a dramatic increase in sugarcane and winter vegetable acreage. During this period water quality problems first began to develop south of the Lake. Agriculture north of the Lake consists primarily of dairy and beef cow/calf operations with limited acreage of citrus and vegetable production. Dairying, the most important agricultural industry, first began to develop in Okeechobee County in the early 1950s. Originally the south Florida dairy industry had been concentrated around Miami, but urban development after World War II forced them to move. The south Florida dairy industry, centered in Okeechobee County just north of Lake Okeechobee, provides fresh milk for the large urban centers along Florida's lower east coast.

The combination of drainage and the resulting urban and agricultural development has had tremendous impacts on the natural system including loss of wetlands, accelerated eutrophication of lakes, and the potential loss of the unique Everglades biosphere. Current concerns over water quality in central and south Florida have manifested themselves as three separate efforts: 1) the Kissimmee River Restoration Project, which aims to "restore" the natural meandering flow of the river through oxbows and wetlands; 2) the Lake Okeechobee Surface Water Improvement and Management (SWIM) plan, which is designed to control agricultural run-off in order to protect the Lake's vital water supply, recreational, and ecological benefits; and 3) the Everglades SWIM plan designed to address concerns about the quantity, temporal distribution, and quality of water released from the Everglades Agricultural Area (EAA) south through the Water Conservation Areas (WCs) into the Everglades National Park.

For more information see Boggess et al. (1992). See Boxes 8.6 and 8.7 for related issues.

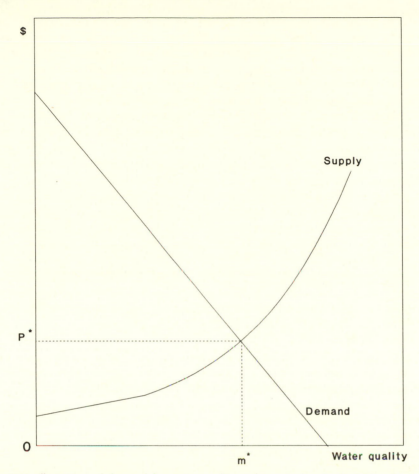

Figure 8.10. Illustration of demand for water quality and marginal cost of additional improvements in water quality.

shift in response to changes in the various underlying parameters. Chapter 6 discusses the welfare effects associated with alternative means (e.g., taxes, property rights, regulation) of correcting for the impacts of externalities.

AGRICULTURAL PRODUCTION PROCESSES AND WATER QUALITY

Residuals from agricultural production processes can be grouped into six major categories—soil sediments, nutrients, pesticides, mineral salts, heavy metals, and disease organisms. Water is a primary pollutant delivery and transport mechanism. Water transports pollutants via four processes—rainfall, surface run-off, percolation/leaching, and irrigation drainage. These joint effects of water use in agriculture lead to a number of important resource issues that complicate water allocation decisions.

Water pollutants are often classified as *point source* or *nonpoint source* pollutants. Point source pollutants are those that can be traced to a precise source, such as a pipe, ditch, well, or container. In agriculture there are relatively few point sources of pollution although concentrated confinement livestock facilities, chemical loading and mixing sites, confined irrigation return flows, and some greenhouse facilities, for example, would qualify as point sources.

Activities that encompass a large areal extent making it difficult to trace pollutants to a precise source are nonpoint or diffuse sources. The majority of pollution from agriculture is classified as nonpoint and arises from run-off leaching from manure disposal areas, and from land used for crop and livestock production.

The distinction between point and nonpoint sources has important implications for the design of pollution control practices, the assignment of liability for ultimate damages, and thus the choice of institutional framework for controlling point versus nonpoint sources. These issues will be discussed further later in the chapter.

Loading, Transport, and Fate of Agricultural Chemicals

Figure 8.11 illustrates the major factors affecting the loading, fate, and transport of agricultural chemicals with an emphasis on water transport and receipt of pollutants (Bailey and Swank, 1983). Although not the focus of this chapter, agricultural chemicals and soil particles are also moved by the wind and can create serious air pollution problems. Furthermore, these airborne particles can subsequently have raindrops form around them, resulting in "acid rain."

As indicated in Figure 8.11, management practices and weather factors combine to determine pollutant loads from agricultural land uses. Georgescu-Roegen (1972) provides a conceptual model of production processes that illustrates how the laws of thermodynamics dictate that all production processes generate residuals or waste flows; and for a system to be sustainable, total inflows over time must balance total outflows. The technology utilized in a production process determines the potential flows of outputs and wastes from the production process. This *materials balance framework* illustrates several important aspects of agriculture's role in water pollution. First, the generation of residuals is an unavoidable byproduct of production. Production processes that generate waste flows in excess of the environment's assimilative capacity are inherently nonsustainable.

Second, economic decisions including changing crop mixes, changing production practices (e.g., input substitution and timing of applications), or developing new technologies that alter the output/waste ratio affect the composition and timing of agricultural waste flows. The goals would be to reduce the amount of potential pollutants in the waste flows and to modify the timing of the outflows in order to reduce the likelihood that the potential pollutants are delivered to a watercourse or to mitigate the damages caused.

Third, the production process also affects the spatial and temporal dimensions of water outflows, which in turn affect the delivery and transport of the potential loadings. This is particularly important in irrigated agriculture, where irrigation return flows augment the natural water flows facilitating the transport of

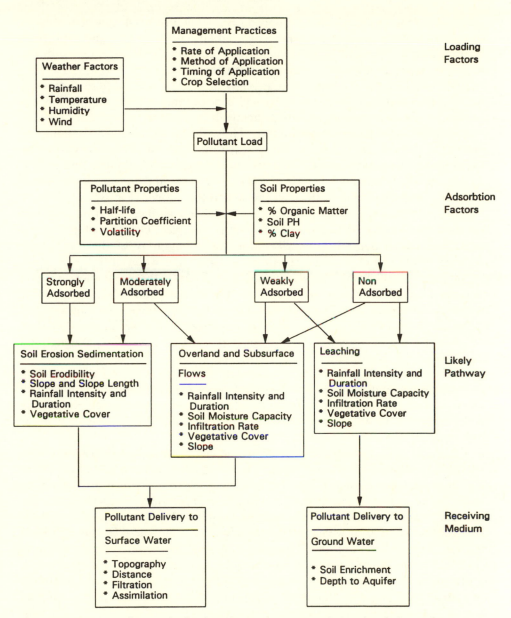

Figure 8.11. Factors affecting the loading, fate and transport of agricultural chemicals.

pollutants. This introduces important interactions and tradeoffs between potential loadings and ultimate delivery to ground or surface waters.

Pollutant transport and fate is determined by a set of complex processes including hydrologic, physical, chemical, biological, and hydrodynamic factors. Many of these processes are governed by the properties of the chemical and the properties of the soil to which it is applied (Fig. 8.11). Potential water contamination depends upon the pollutant transport and fate in the surface and subsurface environment. The central issue is whether the contaminants will move with the water phase phase or adsorb to the soil particles.

The movement of chemicals that strongly adsorb to the soil (e.g., potassium and DDT) is determined primarily by soil erosion and movement, whereas the movement of non or weakly adsorbed chemicals (e.g., nitrogen, salts, or aldicarb) is determined primarily by water fluxes. Thus, the more strongly a compound adsorbs to the soil, the less likely it is to leach into ground water and vice versa. The ultimate pollutant pathway depends upon a number of physical and hydrologic factors that determine the rate of soil erosion, overland and subsurface water flows, and water percolation through the soil to the aquifer (Fig. 8.11).

The ultimate delivery of pollutants to receiving surface or ground waters depends additionally on a number of *off-site* variables. Delivery of pollutants to surface waters depends primarily upon the topography of the region, the distance traveled, and the medium through which the water travels. Likewise, delivery to ground waters depends upon the distance to the aquifer and soil medium through which the water travels. The number and complexity of the processes governing the transport and fate of soil sediments and agricultural chemicals has spawned the development of a number models designed to simulate leaching and run-off processes (see, for example, Haan et al., 1982; Wagnet and Rao, 1990, for a description of some of these models).

The environment has a *natural assimilative capacity* that varies depending upon environmental, weather, and pollutant properties. For pollutants for which the environment has some assimilative capacity, the rate at which they accumulate in the environment is less than the loading rate and, if the absorptive capacity is high enough, they may not accumulate at all.

Chemicals that rapidly break down in the environment are degradable (e.g., organic compounds), those that are slow to break down are considered persistent (e.g., inorganic compounds), and those that do not break down are known as stock chemicals (e.g., heavy metals). Chemicals degrade via a number of processes including volatilization, photodegradation, chemical degradation, and biological degradation. The rate at which a chemical degrades is measured by the chemical's half-life, (i.e., the length of time required for one-half of the remaining amount of the chemical to degrade). It is important to recognize that in some cases, the intermediate degradation compounds or "daughter products" are equally as troubling as the original compound. In general, degradation rates differ greatly in soil, surface water, and ground water mediums.

Chemicals with long half-lives such as DDT (half-life of 3,837 days) tend to persist and accumulate in the environment. Persistent compounds, along with stock pollutants such as heavy metals, tend to bioaccumulate in the tissues of animals, at times reaching toxic levels. For example, bioaccumulation of DDT resulted in the rapid decline in the American bald eagle population in the 1960s, and accumulation of selenium in the Kesterson Reservoir in California reached levels toxic to waterfowl.

As an example of the environment's natural assimilative capacity consider what

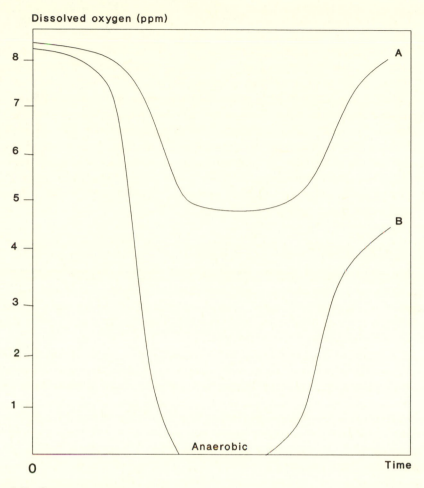

Figure 8.12. Oxygen-sag curves.

happens when an effluent bearing a substantial load of degradable organic residuals is discharged into an otherwise "clean" stream. Stream biota, primarily bacteria, feed on the wastes and decompose them into their inorganic constituents—nitrogen, phosphorus, and carbon. As part of this process, some of the oxygen naturally present in dissolved form is used up by the bacteria. But this depletion tends to be offset by the reoxygenation that occurs through the air–water interface and also as a consequence of photosynthesis by the plants in the water. If the biological oxygen demand (BOD) is not too great, the dissolved oxygen concentration in the stream will initially drop and then rise again. This relationship is illustrated by curve A in Figure 8.12 and is commonly known as the *oxygen-sag* curve (Freeman et al., 1973).

If the BOD load is too great, the process of degradation may exhaust the dissolved oxygen and the degradation process becomes anaerobic (i.e., curve B in

Fig. 8.12). Anaerobic conditions are highly undesirable since they result in fish kills and the water becomes foul, black, and gaseous.

Different environmental mediums vary greatly in their assimilative capacity. Wetlands, for example, have nutrient assimilative capacities that are an order of magnitude or more greater than normal stream flows. As a result of these assimilative capacities, wetlands are sometimes used to treat wasteflows from agriculture and municipalities. The "Water Conservation Areas" in South Florida for example, provide wetland buffers that filter agricultural run-off from the Everglades Agricultural Area before it enters the Everglades National Park (see Box 8.3). Wetlands can be very effective mechanisms for removing nutrients; Kadlec and Alvord (1989) report that a natural peatland in Michigan removed 96% of the phosphorus and 97% of the nitrogen from municipal wastewater discharged over an 11-year period.

Impacts of Agricultural Pollution

The generation of residuals and ultimate transport to receiving water bodies is of concern for two reasons. One concern revolves around the on-site effects on agricultural productivity. Erosion and loss of nutrients reduce soil productivity and increase costs of production. Likewise, pesticide losses reduce their effectiveness, lowering yields and increasing costs.

The primary *on-site costs* associated with erosion are borne by the land owner via reduced yields, increased costs, and lower land values. Thus, as discussed more fully in Chapter 9, it is expected that farmers will generally optimally invest in soil conservation practices with respect to the on-site effects of erosion. However, society as a whole may be concerned about the intergenerational implications of resource depletion if private and social discount rates differ or if lack of information or uncertainty about the future prevent individual land owners from optimally investing in soil conservation.

The second general area of concern about agricultural pollution arises from the externalities or off-site damages caused. These effects are external to agricultural production in that the damages are incurred by other users of surface waters (rivers, lakes, estuaries) or ground water aquifers.

It is extremely difficult and in some cases impossible to estimate the costs associated with all of the in-stream and off-stream impacts caused by agricultural nonpoint pollutants in surface waters. Clark et al. (1985) undertook the most complete and comprehensive attempt to date at quantifying the annual damages caused by nonpoint pollution. Their best estimate of total damages that can be quantified is $7.1 billion annually, $2.6 billion of which are attributed to agricultural cropland. However, they also note that the unquantified biological effects might well outweigh any of those that were quantified and that the ranges on their estimates are quite wide. Moreover, Clark and coauthors did not attempt to estimate the costs of damage to ground waters.

Agricultural pollution can also cause serious ground water contamination problems (Canter et al., 1987). Ground water contamination can arise from both point and nonpoint sources. Agricultural nonpoint source pollutants include:

nutrients (particularly nitrates), pesticides, mineral salts, heavy metals, and disease pathogens. Agricultural point sources include confinement livestock facilities, pesticide mixing and loading sites, and cropland that drains into a sink hole or abandoned well.

Ground water contamination effects are quite similar to off-stream impacts of nutrient, pesticide, and mineral salt contamination of surface waters. These contaminants can create serious health concerns in drinking water, cause corrosion and chemical reaction problems in domestic and industrial water uses, and can affect the productivity of irrigated lands.

There are no adequate data available on a national scale to quantify the extent of ground water contamination or to assess the economic impacts of this contamination. It is extremely difficult and expensive to test for contamination and even more difficult and expensive to ascertain the potential damages associated with various concentrations and mixtures of contaminants. The most comprehensive study of the extent of ground water contamination to date is the EPa's National Survey of Pesticides in Drinking Water Wells (US EPA, 1990). Between 1988 and 1990, EPA tested for 101 pesticides, 25 pesticide degradates, and nitrate in a nationwide sample of 1,350 drinking water wells. Of the 127 analytes, nitrate was the most frequently detected. EPA estimates that nitrate is present, at or above the analytical minimum reporting limit of 0.15 mg/l in over 50 percent of the wells nationwide. The Survey detected pesticides and pesticide degradates in drinking water wells much less frequently than nitrate. Twelve of the 126 pesticides and pesticide degradates included in the Survey were found in the sampled wells at levels above minimum reported limits. EPA estimates that 10 percent of community water system wells and 4 percent of rural domestic wells in the United States contain at least one pesticide or pesticide degradate. The two pesticide analytes most frequently detected were DCPA acid metabolites and atrazine. These contamination findings, along with the general level of uncertainty surrounding the extent and potential effects of contamination, have created a great deal of concern over the safety of ground water supplies and an increase in governmental activity aimed at ground water quality protection.

Source reduction is commonly emphasized in policy discussions as a means of mitigating against the risk of ground water contamination from agrichemicals. One such strategy is to base pesticide use decisions on their potential to leach into ground water. Chemicals that strongly adsorb to soil are less likely to leach but more likely to move with eroded soil particles into surface water. Thus, there may be important tradeoffs between ground and surface water pollution associated with substitutions between pesticides. Crutchfield and Brazee (1990) provide a useful framework for evaluating these tradeoffs.

ECONOMIC MODELS OF WATER QUALITY PROBLEMS

Economic models of water quality problems build on the dynamic resource use models presented in Chapter 2 and the pollution control model presented in Chapter 6. Equation (6) in Chapter 6 represents a static model of social welfare maximization where the production of output also generates pollution

$$\underset{a_i, x_i, k_i, B}{\text{Max}} \quad U(Y) - C(Z, B) - w_b B - w_a \sum_{i=1}^{n} a_i - w_k \sum_{i=1}^{n} k_i - w_x \sum_{i=1}^{n} x_i$$

$$- P\left[\sum_{i=1}^{n} f(x_i, k_i, e_i) - Y \right] - \lambda \left[\sum_{i=1}^{n} h(x_i, k_i, a_i, e_i) - Z \right] \quad (18)$$

where $U(Y)$ denotes a monetary measure of utility derived from consumption of output, Y; $C(Z, B)$ denotes the social cost of pollution, which depends upon the level of pollution (Z) and society's pollution damage averting behavior (B); $f(x_i, k_i, e_i)$ is the production function for the production of Y where x_i represents the variable input use by firm i, k_i denotes the level of services of fixed assets used by firm i, and e_i is an indicator of environmental condition; $h(x_i, a_i, e_i)$ denotes the ith firm's pollution generation function where a_i reflects the firm's pollution abatement activity; w_b, w_a, w_k, w_x are the respective input prices; and P and λ denote the shadow prices of output and pollution, respectively.

The optimality conditions (Equations (7)–(12) in Chapter 6) establish social welfare maximizing levels of input use and pollution abatement activities for each firm and the optimal level of pollution damage aversion by consumers.

This model provides a useful conceptual framework for exploring tradeoffs between pollution generation, abatement, and damage aversion activities. The difficulties lie in trying to empirically implement this framework. Pollution generation and abatement processes tend to be complex, dynamic, and poorly understood and the shadow price of pollution is generally unknown and nearly impossible to measure. Recognizing these problems, Baumol and Oates (1988) suggested that a second-best approach where policy makers set environmental targets and then least-cost methods of achieving the targets are implemented (i.e., cost effectiveness) provides a more functional approach.

Antle and Capalbo (1991) provide a theoretical model for analyzing the impacts of agricultural chemical use that incorporates some of the dynamics and complexities associated with pollution generation, transport, and fate. Their conceptual framework is based on an underlying benefit-cost approach to public policy analysis. The expected benefits associated with a policy that restricts the use of pesticide j is given by

$$E(B_i) = -dE(D_i)/dx_j = -d\{m(x_j)[qC_s + (1 - q)C_m)]\}/dx_j \quad (19)$$

where D_i are the damages associated with use of chemical j; x_j is the level of use of pesticide j; $m(x_j)$ is the damage function relating changes in surface application of x_j to changes in the amount reaching the ground water, $dm/dx > 0$; q is the probability that contamination would be detected; C_s is the cost of responding to known contamination (C_s is a function of m); and C_m is the health cost incurred if contaminated water is used (C_m is an increasing function of the level of pollution and population). The right-hand side of Equation (19) provides an estimate of the damages avoided (i.e., the expected per unit cost of pesticide pollution times the amount of pesticide that shows up in the ground water aquifer) as a result of a policy restricting the use of pesticide j.

The concentration of the chemical in the ground water is expressed as an equation of motion of a capital stock, $K_t = (1 - \delta)K_{t-1} + I_t$, where K_t is the stock, δ is the depreciation rate of the stock, and I_t is gross investment. Under this interpretation, the concentration of the chemical in the ground water is given by

$$C_t = \exp\{h^*(m + 1)\}c_{t-1} + x_{t-m}R_{t-m,t} \tag{20}$$

where

$$R_{kt} = r \exp\{h^*\{t - (m + k)]\} \quad \text{if } t - (m + k) > 0$$
$$= 0 \qquad\qquad\qquad\qquad \text{if } t - (m + k) < 0$$

where R_{kt} is the fraction of chemical remaining at time t from application at time k, including the effects of transport to ground water and decay in the ground water; x is the quantity of chemical applied; C is the concentration of chemical x in the ground water; z is the depth to ground water; m is the time for transport from the surface to the ground water; r is the fraction of chemical remaining after transport to ground water; t is the time period, $t = 0, 1, 2, \ldots$; h is the *half-life* of the chemical in the ground water; and h^* equals $0.693/h$.

In equation (20), $\exp\{h^*(m + 1)\}$ represents the depreciation of the "stock" of contamination that is due to the decay of the chemical already in the ground water, and $x_{t-m}R_{t-m,t}$ represents the gross investment or the additional chemical applied a time $t - m$ that leaches into the ground water at time t.

Antle and Capalbo link the physical model specified in Equation (20) with a simple economic model of farmer behavior. The simple economic model assumes production of a single crop Q with a single variable input, the chemical X, on a unit of land. The farmer is assumed to choose X to maximize profit subject to the production process $Q = a_0 X^{a_1}$.

Solving the profit-maximization problem,

$$\text{Max } \pi = PQ - WX$$
$$_{x}$$

gives

$$X = \left[\frac{1}{a_1}\frac{W}{P}\right]^{1/(a_1 - 1)} \tag{21}$$

The joint physical [i.e., Equation (20)] and economic model [i.e., Equation (21)] can be used to examine the impact of policy changes on chemical use and ground water quality. For example, consider a policy that sets $P_t = P^*$ for all $t > t^*$. The elasticity of C_t with respect to X_t is

$$\varepsilon_{tt'} = X_{t'}R_{t't}/C_t \tag{22}$$

The elasticity of X_t with respect to P_t is

$$\eta_t = 1/(a_1 - 1), \qquad \text{for all } t \tag{23}$$

Using (22) and (23), the point elasticity of the change in ground water quality as a result of a change in product price at time t^* is

$$\xi = \sum_{k=t^*}^{t} X_k R_{kt}/C_t(a_1 - 1) \tag{24}$$

Equation (23) indicates that an increase in output price stimulates an increased use of chemical X. Equation (22) indicates that an increase of X may or may not result in an increase in ground water contamination. If chemical use is sufficiently low, all of the chemical degrades in the soil prior to reaching the aquifer (i.e., $r = 0$). Hence, a policy that induced an increase in chemical use would not affect contamination until input use reached the critical level at which r becomes marginally positive.

Returning to the original policy example, in this simple model, a policy to increase output price will increase the amount of chemical applied. Groundwater contamination will in turn increase after a delay of m units of time (i.e., the time required for transport from surface to ground water), if r is positive.

The simple model illustrates several general results. First, the effect of a policy change on ground water quality is a function of all of the physical and economic parameters required to obtain $\varepsilon_{tt'}$ and η_t, whether these values are estimated from simple or complex models. Second, a policy that increases input use does not necessarily increase ground water contamination. Finally, the information needed to evaluate the impacts of policy changes are location specific and chemical specific. As noted in Figure 8.11 these information needs include the characteristics of the chemical that determine the probability of its leaching into ground water or run-off in surface water; the characteristics of the soil and aquifer that determine the likelihood and amounts of the chemical reaching the ground water or surface water; and farm level data on management practices and application rates.

Empirical Studies of Water Quality Control Policies

There is a growing body of empirical studies analyzing water quality control policies in agriculture; in this section we review a few representative studies. Difficulties involved in measuring marginal externality costs often prevent the use of a general equilibrium framework; thus much of this research has concentrated on comparing alternative regulations aiming to attain a regional quality standard or on estimating the cost of attaining alternative quality standards. Less attention has been given to determination of optimal quality (and quantity) of water incorporating both demand and supply considerations.

A large number of studies have used mathematical programming techniques to evaluate the impacts of alternative policies or standards. Kramer et al. (1984) use a mathematical programming model to analyze the effects of 12 alternative policy scenarios on farm income, production levels, soil loss, nitrogen run-off, and phosphorus run-off in two Virginia watersheds draining into the Chesapeake Bay. Their results indicated that regulatory programs can have differing environmental effects depending upon which pollutant is targeted. They also showed that regulatory and effluent tax approaches can create significant financial difficulties for farmers and are difficult to implement and enforce. Cost share approaches, on the other hand, increase farm income but require significant government expenditures. Ogg et al. (1983) used a similar framework to assess phosphorus loadings to the Greenlane Reservoir in Pennsylvania, as did Jenq et al. (1984) to study point and nonpoint source loadings of phosphorus to a eutrophic lake in New Jersey.

The majority of the water quality studies using mathematical programming models have been deterministic. Milon (1987) questioned the validity of the premise that long-term average loadings are appropriate control variables given the stochastic nature of these discharges. He proposed a more comprehensive stochastic optimization framework (chance constrained programming) that assigns probabilities to the loading constraint. His results show that increasing the probability that a given loading constraint is not violated can be more costly than making the average annual loading constraint more restrictive.

Many recent studies have used run-off or *leaching models* in combination with economic models to evaluate water quality policies. The run-off and leaching models have the advantage of incorporating more of the critical processes governing pollutant transport and fate, and many provide probabilistic estimates. Heatwole et al. (1990) use a combined economic and water quality framework to evaluate the impacts of alternative policies and management practices for reducing nitrate movement to ground water from dairy farms in Virginia. The CREAMS model was used to estimate nitrate leaching from the root zone for various management practices, and a mixed-integer programming model was used to analyze the effects of water quality, policy, and economic constraints on the profitability of alternative cropping and nutrient management systems. Results of some additional empirical studies of water management regulations aimed to control ground water and surface water contamination by animal waste are presented in Chapter 6.

A number of studies have used watershed models to analyze regional surface water pollution policies. Lovejoy et al. (1985) applied the ANSWERS model and economic analysis to evaluate the cost effectiveness of four programs aimed at reducing sediment yield from the Findley Creek watershed in Indiana. Similarly, Frevert and Crowder (1987) used the AGNPS model to estimate nutrient losses within the St. Albans Bay watershed in Vermont.

Irrigation water use has caused substantial water pollution problems that have been the subject of much regulation and research. Some of the water applied for irrigation ends up as run-off or percolates below the root zones. Percolating water may encounter impenetrable layers leading to accumulation over time which may eventually result in waterlogging problems. In this case, the presence of the saline water in or near the crop root zone will lead to reduced agricultural productivity. Installation of tile drainage is a solution for this problem, but the disposal of the drainage may cause a new problem.

For example, drainage water from the San Joaquin Valley in California was used to create wetlands to be used as wildlife preserves (the Kesterson Reservoir) (see Box 8.4). It was found, however, that this drainage water contained selenium that was severely harmful to the wildlife there. This finding initiated imposition

Box 8.4. The San Joaquin Valley Drainage Problem

Applied water that is not utilized by the crops they irrigate may percolate and, over time, accumulate, raise water level to the root zone, and make agricultural production impossible. This phenomenon is called waterlogging, and it is responsible for the demise of agriculture in old Mesopotamia and for the loss of agricultural land base in many other locations.

The west side of the San Joaquin Valley in California has a waterlogging problem, arising from the existence of an impenetrable layer of clay not far under the surface. The usual solution to waterlogging problems is the installment of tiles under the irrigated fields to carry percolating water to drainage canals. The drainage water is then disposed of somewhere, usually at sea or other bodies of water. Indeed, two drainage canals, parallel to the Nile, have allowed the Nile delta to sustain its agricultural production for thousands of years. In many cases, however, the water-logging problem is ignored when new water projects are designed. That may be done to exclude the costs of the drainage canals and tiles from the initial investment, when the project is assessed, and make the project look more attractive financially. Drainage costs were ignored when the Central Valley Project (which delivers water to the western San Joaquin Valley) was designed.

The earliest stages of construction of drainage canal projects, which were intended to divert the Westlands San Joaquin drainage water to San Francisco Bay, were begun in the 1960s. However, environmental considerations, in particular, objection to the transfer of drainage water to the San Francisco Bay and Delta, halted the drainage canal projects. Instead, the drainage water was diverted to a region in the Valley called the Kestersen Reserve. Plans were made to turn this area into a wetland. In the early stages, the results seemed quite impressive. The Kestersen Reserve was becoming a flourishing wetland, and the Bureau of Reclamation that designed this project was quite proud of its achievements. However, from 1983 on, it was found that some of the young water fowl in the reservoir were deformed, and the deformities were linked to high concentrations of selenium in the drainage water. The selenium was bioaccumulating in the vegetation of the wetlands, and high concentrations of selenium were harmful to the birds. These discoveries led to the disallowing of drainage water disposal in Kesterson and required finding alternative solutions to the San Joaquin Valley drainage problems.

Several studies (summarized in Dinar and Zilberman (1991)) present some of the technological and managerial options for solving this drainage problem. Some of the technical solutions include:

1. *Conservation* (*source reduction*). Adoption of modern irrigation technologies, such as sprinkler or drip irrigation to irrigate cotton and other crops in the regions, will increase irrigation efficiency and reduce drainage generation. By doing so, it will reduce the amount of water that has to be disposed of.

2. *Abatement.* There are several alternative mechanisms for getting rid of the drainage once it is generated. They include the use of evaporation ponds, alternative chemical processes, and biological processes (for example, the use of organisms like algae or bacteria that will consume the water and digest and separate the selenium).

3. *Conjunctive use.* This entails ground water pumping and reuse for irrigating crops.

4. *Disposal of the water in another site.* One possible solution is building a drainage canal that will dispose of the water in the Pacific Ocean instead of the San Francisco

Bay Delta. This canal will be much longer that the one envisioned earlier, but the objection to disposal of the drainage water deep into the ocean seems to be minimal.

Some of these technical solutions have obvious drawbacks. The use of evaporation ponds, while technically feasible and cheap, may result in many new "Kestersens." The evaporation ponds, which accumulate selenium and may also attract birds, may become an environmental hazard themselves. Many of the other abatement technologies are at early stages of experimentation and are not available yet for commercial use. Conjunctive use may be a reasonable solution in the short run, but reuse of the water in irrigation will increase their salinity over time and, after some time, will not be appropriate for irrigation of most crops.

Other studies that aim to solve the drainge problems have generated some new basic knowledge. In particular, it was found that the tolerance of crops to salinity increases as they become older. Therefore, Rhoades and Dinar (1991) suggest another type of solution, namely, developing reservoirs of water of different qualities and varying the quality of water at different stages of plant life. For example, fresh water will be used with young cotton plants but, as the plants get older, they will be exposed to drainage water or water of lower quality.

A similar technical solution is what we can refer to as "biological filtering." This solution (see Swain, 1991) envisions that fresh water will be used for salt-intolerant crops like tomatoes. The run-off and drainage water from this crop will be used with crops that are more tolerant of salt and chemicals, e.g., mature cotton. The drainage of this crop will be used for crops that are even more tolerant to drainage or crops that will benefit from extra amounts of selenium such as alfalfa (alfalfa containing high levels of selenium is desirable in the east side of the Valley where livestock suffer from selenium deficiency). The drainage from this process may be used to irrigate eucalyptus trees because they can serve as biological evaporators because of the high evapotranspiration. Drainage from the eucalyptus trees will be so concentrated that it may be of high value as a chemical.

Economists have to evaluate the costs and benefits of these technical solutions and develop incentives that will allow the introduction of an optimal policy mix. A tax on drainage or, if monitoring problems make measurement of drainage infeasible, a tax on water use that differs according to the irrigation technology (namely, smaller tax on drip than on furrow reflecting the fact that the percolation will drip much lower), can serve as an incentive for adoption of water conservation technologies that will reduce the amount of drainage. A tax on drainage may induce farmers to adopt some form of abatement. The proceeds from the tax may be used to subsidize adoption of conservation technologies or to support the research and development activities in the development of abatement technologies. A tax on the drainage may induce farmers to reuse drainage water. In some cases it may be worthwhile to subsidize reuse of drainage water. The computation of parameters for drainage policies may be derived from a dynamic optimization problem that will model the dynamics of drainage accumulation and take into account the production function of output and the cost and technical features of each of the technological options.

It is quite clear that the subsidization of water in the San Joaquin Valley and the prior appropriation rights systems used for allocation of this water have contributed to high percolation of water and accelerated the waterlogging problems in the Valley. Removal of the subsidies and a transition to water markets can alleviate a lot of the drainage problems. It will provide incentives to farmers to adopt modern irrigation technologies, and that will lead to drastic reduction in the percolation of water under the root zone and slow the waterlogging process. The new knowledge about the

> impacts of water quality on irrigation activities suggests that water should not be treated as one homogeneous good but, rather, water of different qualities should be treated as different commodities. As water markets are introduced, it may be that, instead of having one market for water, we may have several markets for water of different qualities. Having markets for inventories of water of different qualities will allow biological filtering and varying water quality during the seasons and between crops.

of standards on selenium and other heavy metals in the San Joaquin Valley. Hanemann et al. (1989) analyzed the economic impact of many of these standards. Since selenium concentration in the river varies (it is lower in wet seasons than in dry seasons, i.e., lower in the winter when it rains than in the summer), the standards are probabilistic. They impose an upper bound that should not be exceeded with a certain degree of statistical significance. Stricter policies have a lower upper bound and/or require higher statistical significance. Concentration can be reduced by treatment of the drainage water and/or by adoption of water conservation technologies (drip, sprinkler, irrigation) that will reduce deep percolation and, hence, drainage. Conservation and clean up can be combined—conservation will reduce clean-up costs by reducing drainage generation.

The analysis recognized that the farm population that generated the drainage was heterogeneous. Sources of heterogeneity were water price, land fertility, and debt/asset ratios. Differences among farms will lead to differences in responses to regulation. Farmers in locations with relatively less fertile lands and high water costs are not likely to operate under conditions that will allow the rest of the industry to continue to operate. The analysis considered several upper bounds on selenium concentration in water. It found that a slight modification in production practices (a reduction in the length of furrow runs) will lead to attaining loose selenium regulations. However, these modifications can be induced by a rather modest drainage fee. Compliance with strict selenium regulations will require adoption of drip or LEPA irrigation and extensive clean-up activities. These technological changes are likely to be induced by a rather high drainage fee or a substantial increase (200 percent) in water price.

The analysis found that assuring higher probabilities that the regional water quality goals are met tends to be more costly than making these standards more restrictive. Finally, the analysis evaluated the impacts of regulation on both resource use and farmer wealth situations. It found that only 5 to 10 percent of the land will go out of production with very strict selenium regulations. These regulations may cause bankruptcy for more than 30 percent of the farm population. Thus, the impact of quality regulations on farmers' wealth may be much more of a policy concern than their efficiency impacts. Water quality policies may need to include some transfer that will compensate farmers for some of their wealth losses.

As illustrated earlier, many of the key parameters that determine potential surface and ground water pollution loadings are site specific (Fig. 8.11). Recognition of the importance of this heterogeneity has recently stimulated studies linking site-specific spatial databases (e.g., land use, soil parameters, hydrology, hydrography), leaching or run-off simulation models, and economic policy models. For example, Braden et al. (1989) developed a model that explicitly considers both reduction and containment of emissions as means to control surface water pollution associated with soil erosion from agricultural lands. They use a simulation model (SEDEC) to simulate the profit, erosion, and transport consequences of specific management alternatives for each field in a watershed and dynamic programming algorithm to identify the least cost management regime for attaining all possible levels of gross sediment loads. The result is a full abatement cost frontier derived as the difference between maximum profit obtained by treating the whole watershed uniformly and the optimal profit taking spatial diversity into account.

GIS (Geographic Information Systems) have also begun to be used extensively to help model ground and surface water pollution problems (e.g. Prato et al., 1989; Halliday and Wolfe, 1991). GIS programs provide the capability for storing, manipulating, and displaying spatial databases, and for linking the databases to other computer models. GIS procedures are currently being used in conjunction with the CREAMS model, a phosphorus delivery model, and an economic policy model to examine the cost effectiveness of alternative combinations of best management practices and phosphorus treatment practices to control phosphorus loadings to Lake Okeechobee in Florida (see Box 8.5).

WATER QUALITY INSTITUTIONS, POLICIES, AND REGULATIONS

The market equilibrium framework of Figure 8.10 provides a useful concept for investigating underlying water quality demand and supply forces. However, there are a number of aspects of the demand and supply of improved water quality that complicate the application of a private market approach. First, the optimal or efficient solution is dependent upon a particular set of property rights. Bishop and Heberlein (1979) show that the payment a user would be willing to accept to part with clean water would likely be greater than he would be willing to pay to acquire a new supply of clean water. The initial allocation of property rights therefore, will influence estimates of the demand and supply of water quality improvement. An additional problem is that historically, property rights in water quality have not been clearly defined.

A second complication is that the causes and effects of water pollution are generally separated temporally and spatially. This makes is extremely difficult to calculate marginal costs and benefits and greatly complicates the matching of "buyers" and "sellers" in order to carry out the necessary transactions. Irreversibilities of damages are also an important temporal concern. Irreversible effects rule out treatment as an option and the focus normally shifts to prevention via highly reliable, safety-first mechanisms such as banning chemical use.

A third complicating factor is that many water quality based goods are *public goods* or what Randall (1987) would call rival, nonexclusive or nonrival, non-

---

Box 8.5. Lake Okeechobee Agricultural Decision Support System (LOADSS)

LOADSS is a GIS-based regional planning decision support system for developing and evaluating the cost effectiveness of alternative plans to achieve the phosphorus reduction goal for Lake Okeechobee (Lal et al., 1991). LOADSS was developed as a planning and evaluation tool for regional water quality managers.

LOADSS contains a number of spatial databases including soils, weather regions, land use, hydrography, dairy farm layouts, and political boundaries. Overlays of the spatial databases result in 7,000 unique combinations or polygons in the 1.5 million acre drainage basin. Attribute databases provide descriptions of soil types, historical weather data, details about input use and outputs from alternative land uses, information about the length and types of flowpaths, and descriptions and costs of alternative phosphorus control practices.

The field scale CREAMS-WT run-off and nutrient model is used to estimate nonpoint phosphorus run-off from unique combinations of land use, soil type, weather zone, and management practice. Other process analysis models are used to assess the impacts of alternative point source (e.g., recycling and treatment of dairy wastes) and basin scale (e.g., wetland filters) phosphorus control practices. A nutrient transport and assimilation algorithm is used to estimate the delivery of phosphorus from each individual polygon to the Lake based on the type and length of flowpath.

The GIS system manipulates the databases and generates phosphorus balance, material budget, and economic information for specified geographial extents ranging from individual polygons to the entire basin. This information can be displayed in a variety of map and report formats.

LOADSS allows the user to analyze the relative cost effectiveness of 1) nonpoint versus point source controls, 2) on-site phosphorus controls versus off-site treatment, 3) alternative nonpoint plans that treat individual land uses or soil types differently, and 4) alternative nonpoint plans that vary spatially depending upon the relative delivery rate of phosphorus to the Lake (see Boxes 8.3, 8.6, and 8.7).

---

exclusive goods. Because it is impossible to collect payments for the provision of nonexclusive goods, they cannot be offered in private markets. Nonexclusivity introduces a number of issues including how to determine the socially optimal level of the good to provide, how to provide it, and how to pay for it.

Finally, the overall lack of information about water quality damages and the cost of water quality improvement introduces tremendous uncertainty. This uncertainty limits the willingness of private individuals to participate in "market transactions" and introduces a safety-first perspective as the public strives to achieve an acceptable level of reliability (Milon and Boggess, 1988). Thus as uncertainty increases there is a tendency to focus on prevention rather than treatment and to employ more reliable control mechanisms.

The complexities of the demand for and the supply of improved water quality combine to suggest that a private market institution is inadequate for solving many water quality problems. As a result, a variety of institutional approaches have been and likely will continue to be used to deal with particular water quality problems.

Federal Programs Related to Water Quality and Agriculture

The federal government has been involved in soil conservation efforts since the 1930s. Historically, the primary focus has been on preventing on-site degradation of the nation's cropland resources. However, beginning in the late 1960s, the focus began to shift from a pure conservation orientation to a joint consideration of conservation and water quality. In the 1970s and 1980s, the federal government became a central force in water pollution control, protection of drinking water quality, and in the registration and regulation of pesticides. The Office of Technology Assessment (1990) provided an excellent summary of the major federal programs relating to water quality and agriculture (Table 8.2).

Table 8.2. Major Federal Programs Related to Water Quality and Agriculture

---

U.S. Department of Agriculture

1985 Food Security Act Provisions

Conservation Reserve Program (CRP) provides annual rental payments to land owners and operators who voluntarily retire highly erodible and other environmentally critical lands from production for 10 years. It also provides technical assistance and cost-sharing payments of up to 50% of the cost of establishing a soil-conserving cover on retired land. Over 30 million acres of cropland have been enrolled.

Conservation Compliance requires that farmers who produce agricultural commodities on highly erodible cropland have approved conservation plans by Jan. 1, 1990, and finish implementing them by Jan 1, 1995, or lose eligibility for USDA program benefits.

Sodbuster provisions require that farmers who convert highly erodible land to agricultural commodity production do so under an approved conservation system, or forfeit eligibility for USDA program benefits.

Swampbuster provisions bar farmers who convert wetlands to agricultural commodity production from eligibility for USDA program benefits, unless USDA determines that conversion would have only a minimal effect on wetland hydrology and biology.

Continuing Assistance Programs

Agricultural Conservation Program (ACP) provides financial assistance through the Agricultural Stabilization and Conservation Service (ASCS) to farmers for implementing approved soil and water conservation and pollution abatement practices. Except for Water Quality Special Projects, conservation priorities are set by States and counties based on local soil and water quality problems. Program initiated in 1936. ASCS also administers the Integrated Crop Management (ICM) program, a pilot ACP project to improve agrichemical management through cost-share assistance for crop advisory and soil testing services. Program initiated in 1990.

Conservation Technical Assistance (CTA) provides technical assistance by the Soil Conservation Service (SCS) through Conservation Districts to farmers for planning and implementing soil and water conservation and water quality improvement practices. Program initiated in 1936.

Great Plains Conservation Program (GPCP) provides technical and financial assistance in Great Plains States to farmers and ranchers who implement total conservation treatment of their entire operation. Program initiated in 1957.

Small Watershed Program provides Federal technical and financial help to local organizations for flood prevention, watershed protection, and water management. Program initiated in 1954.

Resource Conservation and Development Program assists multicounty areas to enhance conservation, water quality, wildlife habitat and recreation, and rural development. Program initiated in 1962.

(continued)

Table 8.2. (*Continued*)

Emergency Conservation Program provides financial assistance to farmers in rehabilitating cropland damaged by natural disasters. Program initiated in 1978.

Rural Clean Water Program is an experimental program implemented in 21 selected projects. It provides cost-sharing and technical assistance to farmers voluntarily implementing best management practices to improve water quality. Program initiated in 1980; ends in 1995.

Forestry Incentives Program provides cost-sharing of up to 65 percent for tree planting and timber stand improvement for private forest lands of 1,000 acres or less.

Water Bank Program provides annual payments for preserving wetlands in important migratory waterfowl nesting, breeding, or feeding areas. Program initiated in 1970.

Environmental Protection Agency

FIFRA Pesticide Programs

The Federal Insecticide, Fungicide, and Rodenticide Act (FIFRA) gives EPA responsibilities for registering new pesticides and for reviewing and re-registering existing pesticides to ensure that, when used according to label directions, they will not present unreasonable risks to human health or the environment. Under FIFRA provisions, EPA may restrict or cancel use of any pesticide determined to be a potential hazard to human health or the environment.

National Survey of Pesticides in Drinking Water Wells

The National Survey tested for the presence and concentration of 127 commonly used agricultural chemicals in 1,350 statistically selected wells in all States. Water samples were analyzed and questionnaires filled out by well owners, operators, and local area experts on well construction locale, and cropping and pesticide use patterns.

Safe Drinking Water Act Programs

The Safe Drinking Water Act (SDWA) requires EPA to publish maximum contaminant levels (MCLs) for any contaminants, including pesticides, which may have adverse health effects in public water systems (those serving over 25 persons or with 15 connections). Standards established by EPA under the SDWA are also being used as guidelines to assess contamination of groundwater in private wells. The EPA also sets nonregulatory health advisory levels on contaminants for which MCLs have not been established.

The SDWA also established a Wellhead Protection Program to protect wells and wellfields that contribute drinking water to public supply systems. Each State must prepare and submit to EPA a Wellhead Protection Program delineating the recharge areas around public water wells, identifying potential sources of groundwater contamination within these areas, and addressing options for protecting the public water supply.

1987 Water Quality Nonpoint Programs

Section 319 of the Act requires States and territories to file assessment reports with EPA identifying navigable waters where water quality standards cannot be attained or maintained without reducing nonpoint-source pollution. States must also file management programs with EPA identifying steps which must be taken to reduce nonpoint pollution in those waters identified in the State assessment reports. The Act authorizes up to $400 million total in Federal Funding for implementing the programs. To date, 43 States and territories have submitted nonpoint-source pollution assessments to EPA, and 36 have submitted final management programs.

1987 Water Quality Act Clean Lakes Programs

Section 314 of the Act requires States to submit assessment reports on the status and trends of lake water quality, including the nature and extent of pollution loading from point and nonpoint sources. Also, methods to control pollution and to protect/restore the quality of lakes impaired or threatened by pollution must be described.

Table 8.2. (*Continued*)

Financial assistance is given to States to prepare assessment reports and to implement watershed improvements, as well as to conduct in-lake restoration activities. Several USDA small watershed projects (PL-566) have been coordinated with Clean Lakes projects.

1987 Water Quality Act National Estuary Program

Section 320 of the Act provides for identification of nationally significant estuaries threatened by pollution, preparation of conservation and management plans, and Federal grants to prepare the plans. Twelve major estuaries have planning underway.

Near Coastal Waters Strategy

Through its Near Coastal Waters Strategy, EPA is integrating its water quality programs to target priority programs and prevent pollution in near coastal waters. This includes the implementation of nonpoint source management programs in coastal counties and will, in several cases, encompass accelerated implementation of agricultural conservation programs.

Regional Water Quality Programs

The EPA and other Federal agencies are cooperating on several regional programs to reduce nonpoint source pollution, including the Chesapeake Bay Program, the Colorado River Salinity Control Program, the Great Lakes Program, the Gulf of Mexico Program, and the Land and Water 201 Program in the Tennessee Valley Region.

U.S. Geological Survey

Coordination and Dissemination of Federal Information on Groundwater

The USGS releases a comprehensive report on water resources annually: the National Water Summary. This report includes comprehensive documentation on water resource quantity and quality for each State, and includes case studies of nonpoint source contamination. USGS also maintains a computerized National Water Storage and Retrieval System (WATSTORE) and a computer-based National Water Data Exchange (NAWDEX).

National Water Quality Assessment Program

Since 1986 the NAWQA program has conducted assessments of national and regional status of groundwater resources and monitors trends in factors that can affect groundwater quality. Agrichemical nonpoint source contamination problems are under study in seven pilot projects.

Regional Aquifer Systems Analysis Program

The RASA program was established in 1978 to gather data on the quantity of water resources available in the nation's aquifers. RASA's objectives for each aquifer system study are to determine the availability and chemical quality of stored water and discharge-recharge characteristics, and to develop computer simulation models that may assist in understanding the groundwater flow regime and changes brought about by human activities. Twenty-eight aquifer systems have been identified for study; fourteen of which have been completed.

Federal-State Cooperative Program

USGS supports local efforts to collect data on ground and surface waters through cost-sharing arrangements with State and local governments. For example, USGS has provided support for mapping State aquifers, for monitoring pesticide contamination problems, and has assisted in developing wellhead protection programs.

Toxic Substances Hydrology Program

Under the TSHP, USGS conducts research on transport and fate of groundwater contaminants to develop information on means to improve waste disposal practices and mitigate contamination problems.

(*continued*)

Table 8.2. (*Continued*)

Mid-Continent Initiative

USGS also is working in cooperation with the USDA's Midwest Initiative on a "Mid-Continent Initiative," a 5- to 10-years research program characterizing the environmental fate of the widely-used agricultural herbicide atrazine. The area under study, roughly bounded by the Upper Missouri and Ohio River Basins, was chosen largely because of the coincidence of hydrologic boundaries with a region of intensive agrichemical-use cropland.

Source: OTA (1990).

Institutional Mechanisms for Achieving Water Quality Goals

A wide variety of policy instruments have been used in water pollution control programs. The policy instruments can be classified as voluntary, cross-compliance, and regulatory, based on the nature of the incentives provided to decision makers to alter their behavior. Voluntary approaches include technical assistance and cost sharing (e.g., Agricultural Conservation and Conservation Technical Assistance Programs), long-term land retirement (e.g., Conservation Reserve Program), and purchases of property rights or conservation easements. An example of the latter is the dairy easement program implemented in south Florida to reduce phosphorus loadings to Lake Okeechobee. Dairy farmers in the basin were offered a payment of $602 per cow if they agreed to cease dairying at that site within 6 months and have a deed restriction placed on the land that prevented future owners from dairying or other confinement livestock operations at that location. Other agricultural uses of the land were not restricted by the easement (see Box 8.6).

Cross-compliance requires that the farmer complies with the restrictions of one program in order to be eligible for the benefits of a second program. This approach was first introduced in the 1985 Food Security Act. This Act specified that farmers had to comply with the conservation compliance, sodbuster, and swampbuster provisions in order to be eligible for commodity program, disaster assistance, and credit benefits (see Chapters 9 and 10).

Regulatory programs have a long history in point source water pollution control and are becoming more prevalent in nonpoint source pollution control. Regulatory approaches can be broken down into quantity regulating mechanisms and pricing mechanisms. Quantity regulating mechanisms include standards and market approaches.

Two types of regulatory standards are commonly used in water pollution control programs. Technology-based *standards* (i.e., command-and-control regulation) specify a *particular technology* a firm must use to comply with the law. Performance standards are more flexible than technology-based standards. Performance standards typically specify a performance measure, but allow firms to select the best technology for meeting the standard.

Market based quantity regulating approaches reflect the polar opposite of performance standards. Performance standards allow a firm to emit a specified amount, but do not allow the firm to trade this right to emit. *Marketable permit*

Box 8.6. Economic Impacts of Environmental Regulations

In 1987 the Florida legislature enacted the "Dairy Rule" (F.A.C. 17-6.330–17-6.337). The rule specified that dairies in the Lake Okeechobee drainage basin had to implement specified technologies to 1) collect all waste water and run-off from barns and high intensive use areas for a 25-year, 24-hour storm; 2) dispose of nutrients by approved methods, particularly land application by irrigation; 3) fence cattle from waterways; and 4) monitor water quality discharges to insure system adequacy. A total of 49 dairies (approximately 45,000 cows) came under the jurisdiction of the rule.

The dairy industry requested, and were granted, a dairy ceasing operations program for dairies that chose not to comply with the rule. Dairymen were offered a payment of $602 per cow in exchange for a deed restriction prohibiting the property from being used for a dairy or any other concentrated livestock operation. The dairymen retained ownership of the cows and the property. A total of 19 dairies signed ceasing agreements that eliminated approximately 15,000 cows from the basin. The remaining 30 dairies elected to comply with the rule.

The 19 dairies that accepted the easement tended to be smaller (i.e., average herd size 775 cows versus 1,050 cows for the dairies that complied) and closer to the Lake, or had particularly serious drainage problems. Mulkey and Clouser (1991) estimated that the closing of the 19 dairies reduced milk production by over 200 million pounds resulting in reduced milk sales in the range of $30–34 million. Annual losses to the local economy were estimated at between $47.6 and $54.3 million in sales, between 465 and 531 full-time jobs, and between $9.0 and $10.2 million in earnings. These losses amount to over 6 percent of the total economic activity in Okeechobee County.

For the 30 dairies that remain, Boggess et al. (1991) estimated that complying with the rule will cost an average of approximately $1,200 per cow or $1.2 million per dairy, net of cost share received. Amortized over the economic life of the systems, these estimates reflect an increased production cost of approximately $1.10 per hundredweight of milk.

See Boxes 8.3, 8.5, and 8.7 for related issues.

schemes, on the other hand, define an overall level of emissions rights for all firms and then allow firms to trade these rights freely (Hahn, 1989).

The idea of marketable permits is becoming increasingly popular in the United States as an economical way of addressing water pollution problems. The actual experience with marketable permits, however, is quite limited and the results are mixed (Hahn, 1989). Marketable permit schemes have been used to control water pollution in two cases. In 1981, Wisconsin implemented a program to allow for limited trading of marketable BOD discharge permits aimed at controlling BOD on a part of the Fox River. However, in the first 6 years the program was in operation, only one trade occurred. The second case is a Colorado program that allows limited trading between point and nonpoint sources for controlling phosphorus loadings to the Dillion Reservoir. In this case, no trades have occurred between point and nonpoint sources during the first 7 years of the program.

There are numerous reasons for the limited success of marketable permits as a means of solving water quality problems. Most cases of market failure in the water quality arena arise as a result of the physical inability to control or accurately measure emissions or are due to the lack of specified property rights to the waste assimilative capacity of the environment. In the case of nonpoint source water pollution both technical and political dimensions of market failure are germane. First, in most nonpoint pollution cases, it is generally either technically infeasible or prohibitively expensive to measure the emissions of individual producers. This is generally not the case for point sources such as manufacturing plants or power plants. Not surprisingly the only successful applications of marketable permits to date have dealt with point source emissions (primarily air pollution).

Second, even if individual emissions can be physically controlled and measured, selling the right to emit requires a legal property right. Many environmental groups oppose on purely ethical grounds any program that grants a legal right to pollute. The concern is that certain levels of pollution are legitimized. Hahn (1989), Dudek and Palmisano (1988), Atkinson and Tietenberg (1991), and Boggess (1992) review a number of explanations including transactions costs, political concerns, and technical constraints that limit the applicability and efficiency of marketable permit schemes (see Box 8.7).

Regulatory *tax schemes* (see Chapters 3 and 6) have received less frequent use in the United States than either standards or marketable permits. Two types of taxes have been employed in the environmental arena—emission fees assessed on the basis of actual or expected emissions (i.e., Pigouvian taxes) and input fees assessed on the content of a potential pollutant in a particular input (e.g., taxing fertilizer on the basis of the phosphorus content). Recently, fees have enjoyed increasing popularity in Europe primarily as a means of raising revenue, which is then used to promote environmental quality (Opschoor and Vos, 1989). In the majority of the cases, the charges have been set relatively low and thus have had only limited impact on firm behavior.

The Role of State Government

Although water quality issues have received increasing attention at the federal level, state governments have historically exercised primary authority over the use, management, and protection of ground water (Henderson et al., 1984). The states are likely to retain that primary role for several reasons. First, a well-developed system of laws and programs already exists in most states, with evidence that state governments have accepted responsibility for protecting the public health interest in ground water quality. Second, the nature of ground water and potential sources of contamination differ from state to state, making it impractical to establish a uniform or comprehensive federal program. Third, many of the proposals for ground water protection involve land use controls, a role historically reserved for state and local units of government pursuant to the "police power" for the protection of health and welfare. Finally, for these and other reasons, states have typically assumed responsibility for administering federally enacted pollution control laws.

Water pollution law by states is generally not based on water law but on tort law or the infringement against rights of persons and property. Some states have

---

Box 8.7. Marketable Permits and Everglades Preservation

The use of a marketable permits program has recently been proposed as means to help control phosphorus emissions in run-off from the Everglades Agricultural Area (EAA) to help preserve the Everglades biosphere. The driving force behind the proposal is the belief that the use of market incentives will create an environment where growers can reduce phosphorus emissions more cheaply than under the current plan which taxes growers in order to cover the cost of off-site biological treatment.

The potential applicability of a marketable permits scheme hinges on the grower's ability to accurately and economically measure individual phosphorus discharges. This appears to be feasible since all agricultural run-off from the EAA is controlled by a series of drainage canals and pumps. Thus, agricultural run-off in the EAA is in effect a quasi point source problem. The growers would also need the legal property right to buy and sell permits.

The essence of the proposed marketable permits program is as follows: 1) The South Florida Water Management District (SFWMD) and the land owners would establish a master permit covering all areas that drain through a well-defined discharge point; 2) The SFWMD would monitor total discharges through the discharge point and assign phosphorus credits to the master permit; 3) The landowners covered by a master permit could organize an Environmental Protection District (EPD), which would be responsible for allocating the phosphorus credits among the land owners and for governing trading of credits within the EPD; 4) The SFWMD would monitor emissions at the main discharge point to insure that they did not exceed the total credits owned by the EPD. The SFWMD would also be responsible for administering trading between EPDs. If emissions exceeded credits, the SFWMD could assess the EPD a fee of $X per ton to cover the costs of off-site treatment.

The proposed use of marketable permits has several attractive features. First it is consistent with the major provisions of the settlement agreement (i.e., the resolution of a federal lawsuit aimed at forcing the State to protect the Everglades National Park), reducing the likelihood of protracted legal challenges and renegotiation. Second, it exploits the flexibility and cost effectiveness of a market approach. Third, by allowing the growers to self-organize EPDs to allocate credits, monitor individual emissions, and govern trades, it keeps government out of the credits market. Finally, it allows the SFWMD to focus on overall monitoring and enforcement of emissions from the major discharge points, on maintaining appropriate hydroperiods in the Park, and on the operation of the off-site treatment areas rather than on micro-management of grower's operations.

See Boggess (1992) for more information. See Boxes 8.3, 8.5, and 8.6 for related issues.

---

extensive statutory programs. Others have very little statutory basis for ground water quality protection.

In a 1986 report, the National Research Council developed a set of six recommendations for state and local ground water protection programs, based on a composite of existing state programs. First, the Council urged all states and localities to develop detailed information about the geohydrology of the jurisdictions within which ground water quality is a concern. Second, the Council recommended a permanent inventory system for potential contaminants of ground water. Third, a comprehensive aquifer classification system was recommended. For example, the EPA ground water strategy would define aquifers used as drinking water supplies to be Class I. Waters for uses that are less sensitive to quality, such as irrigation (which can tolerate nutrients, but not salts) would have a II or perhaps a III designation. Fourth, standards of quality should be defined and established for each aquifer class. Fifth, the Council recommended that the states devise and implement programs to control known sources of contamination. Finally, the Council recommended that states assist local units of government in developing land use controls in designated sensitive areas. A detailed survey of existing state strategies for managing ground water pollution is provided by Batie et al. (1989).

CONCLUSIONS

Water plays a crucial role in a multitude of agricultural activities. Water conditions strongly affect agricultural production patterns and institutional structure. We are living through a period of great change in the water economy of the United States. In the past, water was viewed, to a large extent, as a free good, and major water policies were designed to harness water resources and induce producers to use them. Over time the water economy has matured, water demand has outpaced water supply, and water is becoming increasingly scarce with many competing bidders. Furthermore, past excesses led to water quality deterioration, and preservation and upgrading of water quality has become a major social objective.

These changes in the water economy are likely to lead to changes in water policies and institutions. In particular, public policies are likely to underemphasize new water supply projects and instead focus on changes leading to more efficient utilization and management of water resources. The use of markets and economic incentives as a means to help solve water allocation and quality problems has recently been gaining considerable currency. The current favorable climate for market approaches appears to be the result of several factors, including the general trend toward privatization and market economies throughout the world highlighted by recent events in the former Soviet Bloc, recent successes with water markets and with marketable permits to control air pollution, budget constraints at both state and federal levels, and increasing concern over the costs of regulations and their effects on competitiveness. Economists are playing and should play a crucial role in shaping new institutional arrangements. Increased reliance on market forces and economic incentives can be cornerstones of a transition to a more efficient and environmentally sound water sector. However, to be effective in the design of new water institutions, economic research and analysis must combine sound economic principles with knowledge of technological and institutional factors.

REFERENCES

Amemiya, T. "Qualitative Response Models: A Survey." *Journal of Economic Literature* 19:1483–1536, 1981.

Antle, J.M. and Susan M. Capalbo. "Physical and Economic Model Integration for Measurement of the Environmental Impacts of Agricultural Chemical Use." *Northeast J. of Agricultural and Resource Economics* 20(1):68–82, 1991.

Antle, J.M. *Pesticide Policy, Production Risk and Producer Welfare*. Washington, DC: Resources for the Future, 1988.

Atkinson, S. and T. Tietenberg. "Market Failure in Incentive-Based Regulation: The Case of Emissions Trading." *Journal of Environmental Economics and Management* 21:17–31, 1991.

Ayer, H.W. and P.G. Hoyt. "Crop-Water Production Functions: Economic Implications for Arizona." U.S. Department of Agriculture. Technical Bulletin 242. Agricultural Experiment Station. University of Arizona, 1981.

Bailey, G.W. and R.R. Swank, Jr. "Modeling Agricultural Nonpoint Source Pollution: A Research Perspective." In F.W. Schaller and G.W. Bailey (eds.): *Agricultural Management and Water Quality*. Ames, IA: I.S.U. Press. 1983, pp. 27–47.

Bain, J.S., R.E. Caves, and J. Margolis. *Northern California's Water Industry*. Baltimore, MA: Published for *Resources for the Future* by the Johns Hopkins Press, 1966.

Batie, S.S., W.E. Cox, and P.L. Diebel. *Managing Agricultural Contamination of Groundwater: State Strategies*. National Governors' Association. State Policy Report. Washington, D.C., 1989.

Baumol, W.J. and W.E. Oates. *The Theory of Environmental Policy*. Englewood Cliffs, NJ: Prentice-Hall, Second Edition, 1988.

Beattie, B.R. and C.R. Taylor. *The Economics of Production*. New York: John Wiley and Sons, Inc., 1985.

Beattie, B.R. "Irrigated Agricultural and the Great Plains: Problems and Policy Alternatives." *Western Journal of Agricultural Economics* 6(2):289–300, 1981.

Berck, P. and G. Helfend. "Reconciling the Von Liebig and Differentiable Crop Production Functions." Department of Agricultural and Resource Economics. University of California, Berkeley, 1989.

Bishop, R.C. and T.A. Heberlein. "Measuring the Values of Extra Market Goods: Are Indirect Measures Biased?" *American Journal of Agricultural Economics* 61(5):926–930, 1979.

Boggess, W.G. "On The Use of Marketable Emission Credits to Help Preserve the Everglades: Observations and Suggestions". Food and Resource Economics Department. Institute of Food and Agricultural Sciences, University of Florida, Gainesville. SP 92–13, 1992.

Boggess, W.G., J. Holt, and R.P. Smithwick. "The Economic Impact of the Dairy Rule on Dairies in the Lake Okeechobee Drainage Basin". Food and Resource Economics, Institute of Food and Agricultural Sciences, University of Florida, Gainesville. SP 91–39, 1991.

Boggess, W.G. and J.T. Ritchie. "Economic and Risk Analysis of Irrigation Decisions in Humid Regions." *Journal of Production Agriculture* 1(2):116–122, 1988.

Boggess, W.G., G.D. Lynne, J.W. Jones, and D.P. Swaney. "Risk Return Assessment of Irrigation Decisions in Humid Regions. *Southern Journal of Agricultural Economics* 15(1):135–143, 1983.

Boggess, W.G. and C.B. Amerling. "A Bioeconomic Simulation Analysis of Irrigation Decisions in Humid Regions." *Southern Journal of Agricultural Economics* 15(2):85–92, 1983.

Boggess, W.G., E.G. Flaig, and C.M. Fonyo. "Florida's Experience with Managing Nonpoint Source Phosphorus Runoff Into Lake Okeechobee." In C. Russell and J. Shogren (Eds.): *The Management of Nonpoint Source Pollution.* Kluwer Press. Forthcoming, 1992.

Braden, J.B., G.V. Johnson, A. Bouzaher, and D. Miltz. "Optimal Spatial Management of Agricultural Pollution." *American Journal of Agricultural Economics* 71(3):404–413, 1989.

Bryant, K.J. "An Intraseasonal Irrigation Decision Aid: Texas High Plain." Unpublished Ph.D. dissertation, Department of Agricultural Economics, Texas A & M University, 1991.

Buras, N. and S.C. Nunn. "Critical Issues in the Combined Management of Surface and Groundwaters." In E. Custodio and A. Gurgui (eds.): *Groundwater Economics.* Elsevier, New York.

Burness, H.S. and J.P. Quirk. "Appropriative Water Rights and the Efficient Allocation of Resources." *American Economic Review* 69:25–37, 1979.

Burt, O.R. "The Economics of Conjunctive Use of Ground and Surface Water." *Hilgardia* 36:31–111, 1964.

Canter, L.W., R.C. Know and D.M. Fairchild. *Groundwater Quality Protection.* Chelsea, MI: Lewis Publishers, Inc., 1987.

Carriker, R.R. *A Synthesis and Annotated Bibliography: Water Law and Water Rights in the South.* Southern Rural Development Center. SRDC Synthesis Bibliography Series No. 16. Mississippi State, Mississippi, 1985.

Casterline, G., A. Dinar, and D. Zilberman. "The Adoptions of Modern Irrigation Technologies in the United States". A. Schmitz (ed.): *Free Trade and Agricultural Diversification.* London, England: Westview Press, 1989.

Caswell, M. and D. Zilberman. "The Effects of Well Depth and Land Quality on the Choice of Irrigation Technology." *American Journal of Agricultural Economics* 68(4):798–811, 1986.

Caswell, M. and D. Zilberman. "The Choices of Irrigation Technologies in California." *American Journal of Agricultural Economics* 67(2):224–234, 1985.

Clark, E.H., II, J.H. Haverkamp, and W. Chapman. *Eroding Soils: The Off-Farm Impacts.* Washington, DC: The Conservation Foundation, 1985.

Condra, G.D., R.D. Lacewell, J.M. Sprott, and B.M. Adams. Texas Water Resources Institute Technical Report No. 68. College Station, 1975.

Crutchfield, S.R. and R.J. Brazee. "An Integrated Model of Surface and Groundwater Quality." Paper presented at AAEA Annual Meetings. Vancouver, B.C., 1990.

Cummings, R.G. and D.L. Winkelman. "Water Resource Management in Arid Environments." *Water Resources Research* 6:1559–1560, 1970.

Day, J.C. and G.L. Horner. "U.S. Irrigation Extent and Economic Importance." Agriculture Information Bulletin No. 523. Economic Research Service. USDA. Washington, D.C., 1987.

Dinar, A. and D. Zilberman. Editors. *The Economics and Management of Water and Drainage in Agriculture.* Norwell, MA: Kluwer Academic Publishers, 1991.

Dinar, A., K.C. Knapp, and J. Letey. "Irrigation Water Pricing Policies to Reduce and Finance Subsurface Drainage Disposal." *Agricultural Water Management* 16:155–171, 1989.

Dinar, A. and D. Yaron. "Influence of Quality and Scarcity of Inputs on the Adoption of Modern Irrigation Technologies." *Western Journal of Agricultural Economics* 15(21):224–235, 1990.

Dudek, D. and J. Palmisano. "Emissions Trading" Why is This Thoroughbred Hobbled?" *Columbia Journal of Environmental Law* 13:217–256, 1988.

El-Ashry, M.R. and D.C. Gibbons. "New Water Policies for the West." In M.T. El-Ashry and D.C. Gibbons (eds.): *Water and Arid Lands of the Western United States.* New Rochelle, NY. Cambridge University Press, 1988, pp. 377–395.

FAO. *Yield Response to Water.* FAO Irrigation and Drainage Paper. Food and Agricultural Organizaton of the United Nations. Rome, 1979.

Feinerman, E., J. Letey, and H. Vaux, Jr. "The Economics of Irrigation with Non-uniform Infiltration." *Water Resources Research* 19(6):1410–1414, 1983.

Frederick, K.D. and J.C. Hanson. *Water for Western Agriculture.* Washington, D.C.: Resources for the Future Inc., 1982.

Freeman, A.M., III, R.H. Haveman, and A.V. Kneese. *The Economics of Environmental Policy.* New York: John Wiley and Sons, Inc., 1973.

Frevert, K., and B.M. Crowder. *Analysis of Agricultural Nonpoint Pollution Control Options in the St. Albans Bay Watershed.* No. AGE870423. Washington D.C. U.S. Government Printing Office, 1987.

Georgescu-Roeger, N. "Process Analysis and the Neoclassical Theory of Production." *American Journal of Agricultural Economics* 54(2):279–294, 1972.

Gibbons, D.C. *The Economic Value of Water.* Washington, D.C. Resources for Future Inc., 1986.

Gisser, M. "Groundwater: Focusing on the Real Issue." *Journal of Political Economy* 91:1001–1027, 1983.

Grimm, S., Q. Paris, and A.W. Williams. "A von Liebig Model for Water and Nitrogen Crop Response." *Western Journal of Agricultural Economics* 12(2):182–192, 1987.

Guldin, R.W. *An Analysis of the Water Situation in the United States, 1989–2040: A Technical Document Supporting the 1989 RPA Assessment.* Washington, D.C.: Forest Service, USDA, 1988.

Haan, C.T., H.P. Johnson, and D.L. Brakensiek. (Editors). *Hydrologic Modeling of Small Watersheds.* St. Joseph, MI. American Society of Agricultural Engineers, 1982.

Hahn, R.W. "Economic Prescriptions for the Environmental Problems: How the Patient Followed the Doctor's Orders." *Journal of Economic Perspectives* 3:95–114, 1989.

Halliday, S.L., and M.L. Wolfe. "Assessing Groundwater Pollution Potential from Nitrogen Fertilizer Using a Geographic Information System." *Water Resources Bulletin* 27(2):237–245, 1991.

Hamilton, J.R. and N.K. Whittlesey. "Energy and the Limited Water Resource: Competition and Conservation." In N.K. Whittlesey (ed.) *Energy and Water Management in Western Irrigated Agriculture.* London: Westview Press, 1986, pp. 309–327.

Hanemann, W.M., E. Lichtenberg, D. Zilberman, D. Chapman, L. Dixon, G. Ellis, and J. Hukkinen. *Economic Implications of Regulation Agricultural Drainage to the San Joaquin River.* Technical Committee Report to the State Water Resources Control Board, Sacramento, California, 1987.

Hanemann, M., E. Lichtenberg, and D. Zilberman. *Conservation Versus Cleanup in Agricultural Drainage Control.* Department of Agricultural and Resource Economics. Working Paper #88-37. University of California, Berkeley, 1989.

Harris, T.R. and H.P. Mapp, Jr. "A Control Theory Approach to Optimal Irrigation Scheduling in the Oklahoma Panhandle." *Southern Journal of Agricultural Economics* 12(1):165–171, 1980.

Heatwole, C.D., P.L. Diebel, and J.M. Halstead. "Management and Policy Effects on Potential Groundwater Contamination from Dairy Waste." *Water Resources Bulletin* 26(1):25–34, 1990.

Henderson, T.R., J. Trauberman, and T. Gallagher. *Groundwater Strategies for State Action.* Washington D.C.: Environmental Law Institute, 1984.

Hexem, R. and E. Heady. *Water Production Functions and Irrigated Agriculture.* Ames, IA: Iowa State University Press, 1978.

Howitt, R.E., W.D. Watson, and R. Adams. "Crop Production and Water Supply Characteristics of Kern County." University of California Giannini Foundation Information Series 80–1. Berkeley, 1980.

Hoyt, P. "Crop-Water Production Functions: Economic Implications for New Mexico." Economic Research Service Staff Report No. AGEC-82101. USDA. Washington, D.C., 1982.

Huffaker, R.G. and D. Gardner, Jr. "The Distribution of Economic Rents Arising From Subsidized Water When Land Is Leased." *American Journal of Agricultural Economics* 68(2):306–312, 1986.

Jenq, T.R., M.L. Granstrom, S.F. Hsueh, and C.G. Uchrin. "A Phosphorus Management LP Model Case Study." *Water Resources Bulletin* 20(4):511–520, 1984.

Just, R.E., and R.D. Pope. "Stochastic Specification of Production Functions and Economic Implications." *Journal of Econometrics* 7:67–86, 1978.

Kadlec, R.H., and H.A. Alvord, Jr. "Mechanisms of Water Quality Improvement in Wetland Treatment Systems." In D.W. Fisk, (ed.): *Wetlands: Concerns and Success.* Bethesda, MD: American Water Resources Association, 1989.

Kelso, M.M., W.E. Martin, and L.E. Mack. *Water Supplies and Economic Growth in Arid Environments an Arizona Case Study.* Tucson, AZ: The University of Arizona Press, 1973.

Kramer, R.A., W.T. McSweeney, W.R. Kerns, and R.W. Stavros. "An Evaluation of Alternative Policies for Controlling Agricultural Nonpoint Source Pollution." *Water Resources Bulletin* 20(6):841–846, 1984.

Lacewell, R. D. and J.G. Lee. "Land and Water Management Issues: Texas High Plains." In M.T. El-Ashry and D.C. Gibbons (eds.): *Water and Arid Lands of the Western United States.* New Rochelle, NY. Cambridge University Press, pp. 127–168, 1988.

Lacewell, R.D., J.M. Sprott, and B.R. Beattie. "Value of Irrigation Water with Alternative Input Prices, Products and Yield Levels: Texas High Plains and Lower Rio Grande Valley." Texas Water Resources Institutes Technical Report No. 58, College Station, 1974.

Lal, H., C. Fonyo, B. Negahban, W.G. Boggess, G.A. Kiker. "Lake Okeechobee

Agricultural Decision Support System (LOADSS)." ASAE Paper No. 91-2623. St. Joseph, MI. Chicago, Illinois, 1991.

Layard, P.R.G. and A.A. Walters. *Microeconomic Theory.* New York: McGraw-Hill Book Company, 1978.

Lee, J.G. "Risk Implications of the Transition to Dryland Agricultural Production on the Texas High Plains." Unpublished Ph.D. dissertation, Department of Agricultural Economics, Texas A & M University, 1987.

Letey, J., A. Dinar, C. Woodring, and J.D. Oster. "An Economic Analysis of Irrigation Systems." *Irrigation Science* 11:37–43, 1989.

Lichtenberg, E. "Land Quality, Irrigation Development, and Cropping Patterns in the Northern High Plains." *American Journal of Agricultural Economics* 71(1):187–194, 1989.

Lovejoy, S.B., J.G. Lee, and D.B. Beasley. "Muddy Water and American Agriculture: How to Best Control Sedimentation from Agricultural Land." *Water Resources Research* 21(8):1065–1068, 1985.

Lynne, G.D., W.G. Boggess, and K. Portier. "Irrigation Water Supply as a Bioeconomic Process." *Southern Journal of Agricultural Economics* 16(2): 73–82, 1984.

Lynne, G.D., K. Anaman, and C.F. Kiker. "Irrigation Efficiency: Economic Interpretation." *Journal of Irrigation and Drainage Engineering* 113(3):317–333, 1987.

Martin, W.E. and G.B. Snyder. "Valuation of Water and Forage from the Salt-Verde Basin of Arizona." Report to the U.S. Forest Service, 1979.

McGuckin, J.T., C. Mapel, R.R. Lansford, and T.W. Sammis. "Optimal Control of Irrigation Using a Random Time Frame." *American Journal of Agricultural Economics* 69(1):123–133, 1987.

Middle, J.W., R.D. Lacewell, H. Talpaz, and C.R. Taylor. "Economics of Irrigation Management." In G.J. Hoffman, T.A. Howell, and K.W. Solomon (eds.): *Management of Irrigation Systems.* St. Joseph, MI: American Society of Agricultural Engineers, 1990, pp. 411–449.

Milon, W.J. and W.G. Boggess. "The Implications of Reliability Theory for Environmental Design and Decision Making." *American Journal of Agricultural Economics* 70(5):1107–1112, 1988.

Milon, J.W. "Optimizing Nonpoint Source Controls in Water Quality Regulation." *Water Resources Bulletin* 23(3):387–396, 1987.

Mitchell, R.C. and R.T. Carson. *Using Surveys to Value Public Goods: The Contingent Valuation Method.* Washington, D.C.: Resources for the Future, 1989.

Moore, M.R. "The Bureau of Reclamations New Mandate for Irrigation Water Conservation: Purposes and Policy Alternatives." *Water Resources Research* 27(2):145–155, 1991.

Mulkey, D. and R.L. Clouser. "The Economic Impact of the Dairy Industry in Okeechobee County, Florida." Food and Resource Economics Department, Institute of Food and Agricultural Sciences, University of Florida, Gainesville. SP 91–40, 1991.

Musser, V.N. and B.V. Tew. "Use of Biophysical Simulators in Production Economics." *South Journal of Agricultural Economics* 16(1):74–86, 1984.

National Research Council. *Groundwater Quality Protection: State and Local Strategies.* Washington, D.C.: National Academy Press, 1986.

Negri, D.M. and D.H. Brooks. "The Determinants of Irrigation Technology Choice." Economic Research Service. USDA, 1988.

Nieswiadomy, M. "The Demand for Irrigation Water in the High Plains of Texas." *American Journal of Agricultural Economics* 67(3):619–626, 1985.

Nieswiadomy, M.L. "Input Substitution in Irrigated Agriculture in the High Plains of Texas, 1979–1980." *Western Journal of Agricultural Economics* 13(1):63–70, 1988.

Office of Technology Assessment. *Water Related Technology for Sustainable Agriculture in U.S. Arid/Semiarid Lands.* U.S. Congress OTA-F212. Washington, D.C.: U.S. Government Printing Office, 1983.

Office of Technology Assessment. *Beneath the Bottom Line: Agricultural Approaches to Reduce Agrichemical Contamination of Groundwater.* Washington, D.C.: U.S. Government Printing Office, 1990, 79 pages.

Ogg, C.W., H.B. Poinke, and R.E. Heimlich. "A Linear Programming Economic Analysis of Lake Quality Improvements Using Phosphorus Buffer Curves." *Water Resources Research* 19(1):21–31, 1983.

Opschoor, J. and H. Vos. *Economic Instruments for Environmental Protection.* Paris, France: Organisation for Economic Cooperation and Development, 1989.

Prato, T., H.-Q. Shi, R. Rhew, and M. Brusven. "Soil Erosion and Nonpoint-source Pollution Control in an Idaho Watershed." *Journal of Soil and Water Conservation* 45:323–328, 1989.

Randall, A. *Resource Economics: An Economic Approach to Natural Resources and Environmental Policy.* New York: John Wiley & Sons, Inc., Second Edition, 1987.

Reisner, M. *Cadillac Desert: The American West and Its Disappearing Water.* New York: Viking, 1986.

Rhoades, J.D. and A. Dinar. "Reuse of Agricultural Drainage Water to Maximize the Beneficial Use of Multiple Water Supplies for Irrigation." In A. Dinar and D. Zilberman (eds.): *The Economics and Management of Water and Drainage in Agriculture.* Norwell, MA: Kluwer Academic Publishers, 1991.

Saliba, B.C. "Do Water Markets 'Work?' Market Transfer and Trade-Offs in the Southwestern States." *Water Resources Research* 23(7):1113–1122, 1987.

Saliba, B.C. and D.B. Bush. *Water Markets in Theory and Practice Market Transfers, Water Values, and Public Policy.* London: Westview Press, 1987.

Schaible, G.D., C.S. Kim, and N.K. Whittlesey. "Water Conservation Potential from Irrigation Technology Transitions in the Pacific Northwest." *Western Journal of Agricultural Economics* 16(2):194–206, 1991.

Shah, F., D. Zilberman, and U. Chakravorty. "Water Rights Doctrines and Technology Adoptions." In A. Braverman, K. Hoff, and J. Stiglitz, (eds.): *Agricultural Development Policies and the Theory of Rural Organization.* Oxford University Press, 1993.

Shumway, C.R. "Derived Demand for Irrigation Water: The California Aquaduct."*Southern Journal of Agricultural Economies* 5(1):195–200, 1973.

Smith, V.K. and W.H. Desvouges. *Measuring Water Quality Benefits.* (Boston: Kluwer Academic Publishers, 1986.

Stegman, W.C. and M. Aflatouni. "Corn Yield Responses to Water Stress Management." Selected Paper presented at ASEA winter meeting. Chicago, Illinois, 1978.

Stewart, J.I., R.M. Hagan, and W.O. Pruitt. "Functions to Predict Optimal Irrigation Programs." *Journal of Irrigation Drainage Division.* ASCE 100(2):179–199, 1974.

Stewart, J.I. et al. "Irrigating Corn and Grain Sorghum with a Deficient Water Supply." *Transactions of the ASEA* 18:270–280, 1975.

Swain, D.G. "A Conceptual Planning Process for Management of Subsurface Drainage." *The Economics and Management of Water and Drainage in Agriculture*. In A. Dinar and D. Zilberman (eds.): Norwell MA: Kluwer Academic Publishers, 1991.

Swaney, D.P., J.W. Jones, W.G. Boggess, G.G. Wilkerson, and J.W. Mishoe. 'Real-Time Irrigation Decision Analysis Using Simulation." *Transactions of the ASEA* 26(2):562–568, 1983.

Tsur, Y. "Managing Drainage Problems in Conjunctive Ground and Surface Water System." Unpublished paper. Department of Agricultural and Applied Economics. University of Minnesota. St. Paul, 1990.

United States Bureau of Census. *Statistical Abstract of the United States*. (109th Edition). Washington, D.C., 1989.

United States Environmental Protection Agency. "Summary Results of EPA's National Survey of Pesticides in Drinking Water Wells." Washington, D.C., 1990.

Vaux, H.J., Jr., W.O. Pruitt, S.A. Hatchett, and F. De Souza. *Optimization of Water Use With Respect to Crop Production*. University of California, Riverside, California, 1981.

Wade, R. "The Management of Common Property Resources: Collective Action as an Alternative to Privatization or State Regulation." *Cambridge Journal of Economics* 11:95–106, 1987.

Wagenet, R.J. and P.S.C. Rao. "Modeling Pesticide Fate in Soils." In H.H. Cheng (ed.), *Pesticides in the Soil Environment*, Madison: Soil Science Society of America, 1990. Soil Science Book Series No. 2.

Wahl, R.W. "Markets for Federal Water: Subsidies, Property Risks, and the Bureau of Reclamation." *Resources for the Future*, Washington, D.C., 1989.

Wilkerson, G.G., J.W. Jones, K.J. Boote, K.T. Ingram, and J.W. Mishoe. "Modeling Soybean Growth for Crop Management." *Transactions of the ASAE* 26(1):63–73, 1981.

Willitt, G.S., S. Hathorn, Jr., and C.E. Robertson. "The Economic Value of Water Used to Irrigate Field Crops in Central and Southern Arizona, 1975." Department of Agricultural Economics Report No. 9. University of Arizona. Tucson, Arizona, 1975.

Yaron, D. and A. Dinar. "Optimal Allocation of Farm Irrigation Water During Peak Seasons." *American Journal of Agricultural Economics* 64(4):681–689, 1982.

Young, R.A. and S.L. Gray. "Economic Value of Water: Concepts and Empirical Estimates." Technical Report to the National Water Commission NITS No. PB210356. National Technical Information Service. Springfield, Virginia. 1972, pp. 144–146.

Young, R.A. and J.D. Bredehoeft. "Digital Computer Simulation for Solving Management Problems of Conjunctive Groundwater and Surface Water Systems. *Water Resources Research* 8:533–555, 1972.

Zavaleta, L.R., R.D. Lacewell, and C.R. Taylor. "Economically Optimum Irrigation Patterns for Grain Sorghum Production." Texas High Plains. Texas Water Resources Institute, TR-100. College Station, Texas, 1979.

9

Economics of Land in Agriculture

JOHN MIRANOWSKI AND MARK COCHRAN

OVERVIEW

Land as an input into production has some unique characteristics. First, it is fixed in location and geoclimatic environment. Second, there is a relatively limited supply of land suitable for specific productions activities. Third, land is a heterogeneous resource, varying in soil type, topography, climate, and cultivated vegetation.

Ricardo was among the early economists to address land resource issues and implications. In the U.S., agricultural economics as a subdiscipline can be traced in part to the "land economics" school of thought. For a very thorough historical and institutional treatment of the subject, see Castle et al. (1981).

We begin with a general discussion of the broad intertemporal and interspatial dimensions of land as an agricultural resource including changes in U.S. land use, patterns of farmland ownership, and changes in land values. Next, the role of soil as land resource is developed, and the role of the market in efficiently allocating and using the soil resource is assessed. The conditions under which the market may fail are identified and evaluated. A dynamic model of optimal soil resource use is posited, and the role and impact of policies to alter the use of soil resources over time are evaluated. Then, land institution, property right, and tenure issues, including leasing, are discussed. This discussion is followed by consideration of analytical frameworks for addressing land use implications, especially spatial location concepts. Finally, land as a capital asset is considered, and interspatial, acquisition, intertemporal, and land improvement investment decisions are analyzed. An interspatial (hedonic) model of soil characteristics is presented and discussed. Then, a model of land acquisition is specified, and then the circumstances under which a farmer would choose to acquire land through purchase are evaluated. Also, the implications for soil resource use are assessed. The determination of agricultural land values which has received much attention in the recent agricultural economics literature is reviewed, alternative hypotheses are compared, and a possible structural model to assess changes in land values is discussed.

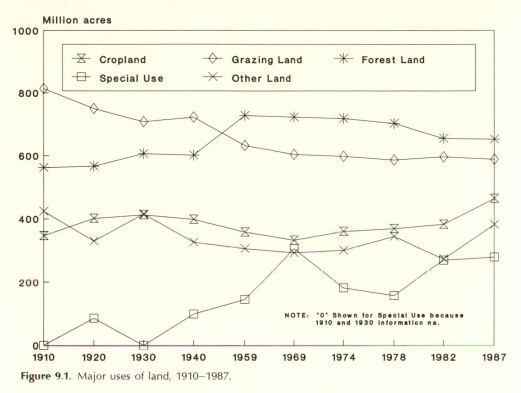

Figure 9.1. Major uses of land, 1910–1987.

Investment in land improvements and soil conservation are considered, first from the perspective of the individual firm or farm and then in the aggregate context of recent land improvement investment decisions.

Much of the land in the United States is cropland, pasture and range, or forestland (Fig. 9.1) (U.S. Department of Agriculture, 1991). In spite of the "Sagebrush Rebellion" concerns of the early 1980s, the split between Federal and non-Federal ownership of land has been relatively stable over the last 30 years (Fig. 9.2) (U.S. Department of Commerce, 1991). The remainder is in parks, farmsteads, roads, defense and industrial uses, urban, desert, marsh, and tundra. In recent years, significant amounts of land have been added to our national land preservation system (Fig. 9.3) (U.S. Executive Office of the President, 1991). The regional variations in land use patterns are important with cropland accounting for less than 10 percent of the land in the Mountain States and over 50 percent of the land in both the Corn Belt and Northern Plains.

Although concerns about rapid changes in land use patterns, e.g., urbanization, wetland drainage, are frequently expressed in the published media, the annual loss of agricultural land to other uses is small, i.e., less than 800,000 acres (Vesterby and Heimlich, 1989). Simultaneously, a similar amount of land is converted to new cropland each year. A more important concern may be the loss of environmentally sensitive lands such as open space and wetlands to more traditional production activities.

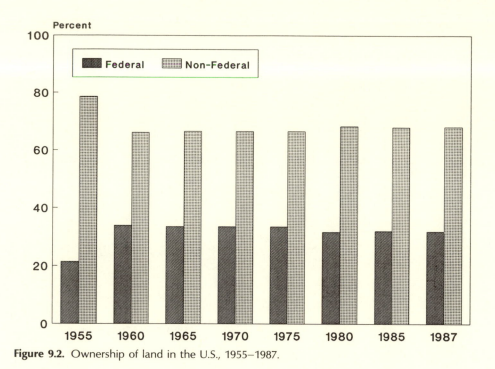

Figure 9.2. Ownership of land in the U.S., 1955–1987.

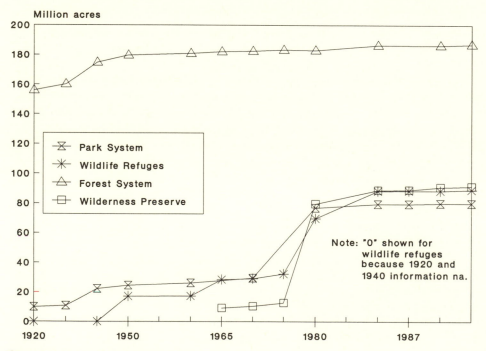

Figure 9.3. National land preservation.

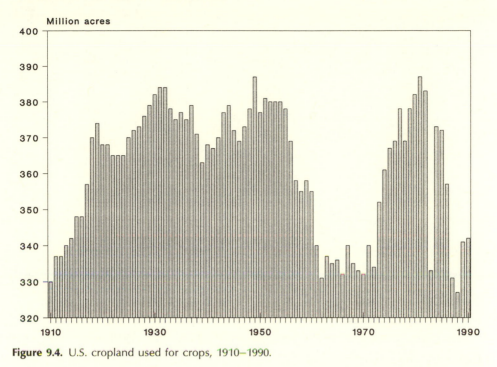

Figure 9.4. U.S. cropland used for crops, 1910–1990.

The nation's total cropland base, estimated at 464 million acres in 1987, has changed little since 1920. What does fluctuate more over time is cropland uses—for crops, idle cropland, and cropland pasture—but even these changes have been modest. Figure 9.4 (U.S. Department of Agriculture, 1992b; Daugherty, 1991) indicates fluctuations in cropland used for crops. Additionally, the productivity of this cropland base is enhanced by irrigation development. The increase in irrigated farmland (Fig. 9.5) (U.S. Department of Commerce, 1991) has been significant, not only in the western states, but also in the southern states. When we are concerned about environmental problems associated with agricultural production activities, the specific crops grown and the cropping practices employed are critical to the residuals generated by erosion, run-off, and percolation. Not only are such patterns of production driven by market forces but by commodity programs, which may distort the mix of crops produced as well as the choice of production practices.

If cropland adjustments over time have been modest, what has happened to control of the land resource? The proportion of nonfarm landlords and the portion of farmland they own has remained relatively constant over time, as has the amount of cropland operated under lease. The amount of farmland changing hands each year is small (2–5 percent), and Figure 9.6 (U.S. Department of Agriculture, 1992a) indicates the mix of buyers over time as well. Thus, it is easy to conclude that intertemporal patterns of ownership have changed slowly, if at all.

Unlike ownership and use, land values have demonstrated much greater variability, especially beginning in the 1960s. Prior to the latter period, both

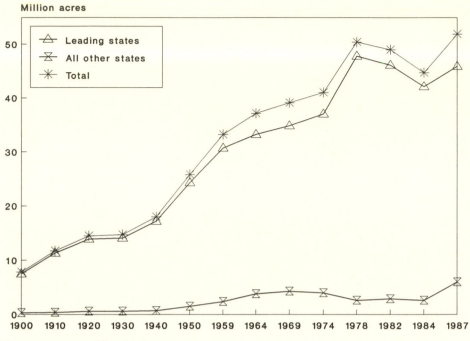

Figure 9.5. Irrigated farmland, 1990–1987.

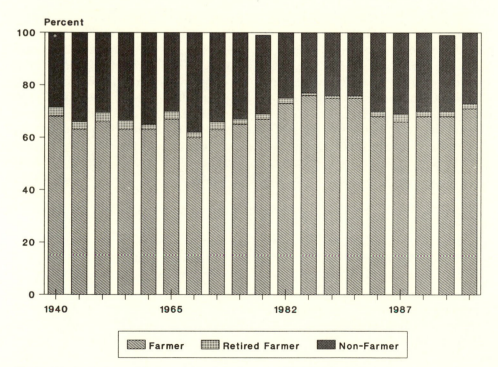

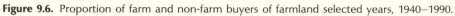

Figure 9.6. Proportion of farm and non-farm buyers of farmland selected years, 1940–1990.

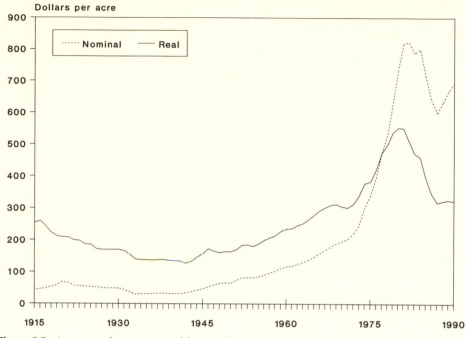

Figure 9.7. Average value per acre of farm real estate, 1915–1990.

nominal and real values exhibit modest temporal adjustments (Fig. 9.7) (U.S. Department of Agriculture, 1992a). State and regional patterns of land values do differ from the national average (Fig. 9.8) (U.S. Department of Agriculture, 1992b) but the movements have been similar except in the northeast states. These changes in land values are of special interest to the extent that they reflect the value of an important agricultural resource over time. Thus a better understanding of what is driving land values is needed to distinguish between the causal impacts of resource scarcity, macroeconomic and international events, and government programs.

SOIL AND THE LAND RESOURCE

Agriculture is an activity that modifies the natural environment for the purpose of enhancing the flow of goods and services from natural resources. Accompanying these environmental modifications may be consequences that impair the long-run potential of the land to sustain production of agricultural goods and services and that impair the flow of other goods and services from the land, air, and water.

A potential consequence of more intensive agricultural production is increased soil erosion from cropland. Soil loss rates that exceed the rates of generation of new top soil may reduce soil productivity, at least in the long run. Soil erosion also can result in air and water pollution. Another dimension of the erosion

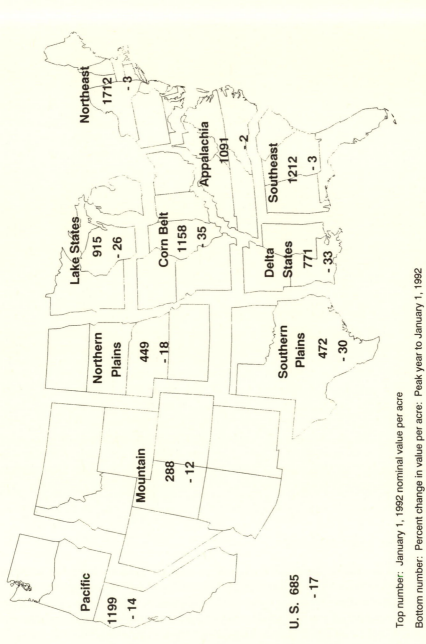

Top number: January 1, 1992 nominal value per acre

Bottom number: Percent change in value per acre: Peak year to January 1, 1992

Figure 9.8. Regional farmland values: Despite recent value increase, corn belt and lake states average 45 percent below 1981 peak.

problem is that agricultural practices that result in higher soil erosion rates may disrupt the productivity of the land resource for other uses such as upland wildlife habitat (Miranowski and Bender, 1982). Fish and wildlife, as well as recreational services, are other goods and services flowing from the land and water. Thus, optimal conjunctive management of the soil resource and environmental quality to maximize the net benefits to society has become a significant social goal.

The market for the services of land is functioning efficiently if it is not possible to increase the welfare of any individual without making someone else worse off. Of course, efficiency is not the only goal of resource policy; other goals, such as intertemporal equity and income distribution, also enter society's decision process. The primary focus of this section is on the efficiency with which the market allocates the services of land and where market failures may arise. One common justification for government intervention is based upon some form of market failure.

Sources of Market Failure

There are a number of reasons that the market for land services may not operate efficiently. Some of the reasons may lead to profligate use of land resources, while other reasons may lead to excessive conservation. These reasons will be evaluated in terms of their effects on land resource utilization and the efficacy of government intervention to improve land resource allocation. The government has historically intervened in the market for land resources, e.g., conservation, drainage, and irrigation programs, land use planning and zoning regulations, farm commodity and land retirement programs. These interventions may have introduced inefficiencies in the allocation of land resources.

A number of sources of market failure are noted in the natural resources literature (Stiglitz, 1979; Howe, 1979; Dasgupta and Heal, 1979). The more important sources of market failure include monopoly, absence of future markets, absence of risk markets, common resource problems, externalities, private interest rates diverging from the social discount rate, and tenancy arrangements. Stiglitz (1979) considers a number of sources of resource market failure that can be extended to the land resource.

Monopoly

Even though there is concern over increasing farm size and land ownership concentration, it is difficult to develop a convincing argument that a lack of competitive behavior occurs in the market for land resources. In general, inefficiencies in land markets are not created by monopolistic behavior except in isolated situations. Boxley (1985) noted that in 1979 roughly 30 percent of farmland was owned by nonfarmers, and these individuals made up 40 percent of farmland owners. This statistic changed little over the previous four decades.

Absence of Future Markets

Given the lack of long-run futures markets, investors must guess about future prices. Systematic errors in guessing about future demands (prices) may cause bias toward either underconservation or overconservation. Yet, there are strong incentives within the market for discovering systematic errors, incentives that do not necessarily exist within the government bureaucracy for managing private land resources.

The government may have a role in providing improved information if the information has a public good dimension. In the public good case, too little investment in information may occur because market participants cannot exclude others from the information that is generated. For example, lack of information may lead landowners to underestimate or overestimate the costs of erosion in terms of foregone soil productivity. Without such information, there is no reason to conclude that the government would make a more informed choice of soil management practices. Thus, public investment in information production and dissemination may be important, but managing land resources may best be left to landowners except when an externality, caused by sediments, nutrients, and pesticides in streams or the loss of wildlife habitat is created.

Absence of Risk Markets

Risk and uncertainty arise in land resource utilization decisions. Typical sources of uncertainty include technological innovations, development of substitutes for agricultural commodities, and future demands (and prices) for agricultural commodities. Analysis of risk and uncertainty and its effects on land resource use has proceeded under restrictive assumptions concerning the nature of risk and uncertainty and the nature of the farmer's risk preferences. Even if it is observed that risk and uncertainty cause a deviation from optimal land resource use, public decision makers do not necessarily have better knowledge regarding technology, substitutes, and future demands than private entrepreneurs, who have the incentive to acquire improved information and to gain from the errors of other individuals.

Externalities

An important source of market failure with respect to land resources is the presence of externalities (erosion and sedimentation) in production. A case in point is the offsite water and air quality damages from erosion. Because the market does not reflect these costs, the farmer lacks signals or incentives to adjust production. Clearly, a case for government intervention may be made in this situation.

However, the long history of concern for soil erosion and the relatively recent attention given to water and air quality damages suggests that external effects other than those associated with environmental quality may be present. The tone of public debate suggests that society may place an added value on the existence of productive agricultural lands. This phenomenon may be an expression of public desire for a stock of productive land to ensure adequate food production in the future. An argument can be made for conserving soil use in the short run until better information becomes available (e.g., quasioptions demand).

A related argument can be made for a "minimum safety standard" (Ciriacy-Wantrup, 1968) or level of soil productivity preservation to prevent highly unlikely but potential outcomes with socially disastrous consequences (e.g., starvation). An individual decision maker looks only at the expected future outcome but society may be concerned with the consequences of particular (episodic) outcomes even though they have low probability. Likewise, there may be amenity and aesthetic values associated with highly productive cropland as opposed to an eroded landscape that is unreflected in the market. Essentially, this factor is equivalent to a preservation, or existence, value.

Common Property Problems

The common property nature of a resource may lead to inefficiency in its use. For example, cropland can be used to produce both agricultural commodities and wildlife. Many crop and livestock management practices, which enhance agricultural productivity, reduce the quality of wildlife habitat, and ultimately wildlife populations. Given the common property nature of wildlife populations, especially with the smaller-scale agriculture that exists in many of the crop-producing areas of the nation, some form of government intervention may be justified. Such a decision to intervene must be weighed very carefully and is only justified if the potential net social benefits are positive.

There are sound reasons to believe that given the common property dimensions associated with wildlife, land management practices may be less than socially optimal.

Divergence of Time Preferences

Frequently the argument is made that the private rate of time preference is higher than the social discount rate. If the market rate is in excess of the social rate, the rate of resource use will be too rapid and soil productivity will decline at an excessive rate. Under such a situation, if the private market is allowed to function unimpeded, then future generations will be faced with an extremely limited resource situation. In other words, society's planning horizon exceeds the individual decision maker's time frame. The resource economics literature has devoted a considerable amount of space to this topic with little resolution of the issue (e.g., Lind, 1982). Suffice it to say that if such a divergence exists, then macroeconomic policy should be designed to equate the two rates. Any attempt to correct the situation only for soil resource use will bring about a weak "second best" solution.

A related argument is that society has an infinite planning horizon and the individual has a finite planning horizon. Theoretically at least, this should cause no market failure. Assuming that the individual disposes of the resource at the terminal date, then he will attempt to maximize

$$\int_0^T N(t)\, e^{-rt}\, dt + R(T)\, e^{-rT} \tag{1}$$

where $N(t)$ is the net return to the resource, and $R(t)$ is the terminal value (sale value) at time T. If the soil resource market functions efficiently, then

$$R(T) = \int_T^\infty N(t)\, e^{-rt}\, dt \tag{2}$$

Thus, the private individual is equivalently maximizing

$$\int_0^\infty N(t)\, e^{-rt}\, dt \tag{3}$$

The length of the individual's planning horizon should not distort the outcome.

Lease Arrangements

A potential source of market failure that does not appear in the literature on resource market efficiency but that has received consideration by the agricultural economics profession is tenure or lease arrangements. More specifically, the nature of the tenure arrangement may result in a suboptimal level of soil resource use.

If tenure arrangements do cause excessive soil loss, the loss in productivity should be reflected in land values. Thus landlords have an incentive to enter into lease arrangements that maximize the net present value of the land resource, including the impact on its terminal value. Adjustments in leases would be forthcoming if the gain from restricting the tenant's behavior exceeded the foregone rent from doing so.

Other Arguments

A number of other arguments for market failure have found their way into the media and sometimes the professional literature: for example, the cost-price squeeze in farming, land costs, reduced interest in stewardship of family property, and trend toward fewer owner-operators. The last two issues have been dealt with above. Although the cost-price squeeze may have short-run impacts, it should have little impact on long-term investment unless the landowner expects a decrease in net returns over the long run. If higher land prices are based on the present net value of the expected returns to the land resource, it should not affect the conservation decision.

Thus, the arguments for government intervention to protect soil resources can be limited to situations in which serious externalities exist or in which the nonmarket benefits of the land resource are important. Other forms of land resource allocation inefficiencies provide little rationale for intervention.

A Dynamic Soil Conservation Model

McConnell (1983) presents a theoretical foundation for examining the economics of soil conservation. In his model, the farmer maximizes the net value of the farm, which is divided into two components: the present value of the income stream and the present value of the terminal value of the farm. Soil erosion can impact the productivity of the land and hence the income stream. If markets work, soil erosion will also influence the terminal value as reflected in future income streams. This intertemporal linkage to the asset market will cause the rational farm manager to exhaust his soil resources only if he is compensated for the loss in resale value of the land at time T.

The McConnell model is expressed as

$$\int_0^T e^{-rt}[pg(t)f(s, x, z) - cz]\, dt + R[x(T)]\, e^{-rT} \tag{4}$$

subject to

$$\dot{x}(t) = k - s(t) \tag{5}$$

$$x(0) = x_0 \tag{6}$$

where $g(t)f(s, x, z) = $ output

$s(t) = $ soil loss
$x(t) = $ soil depth
$z(t) = $ index of variable inputs
$g(t) = $ neutral technical change
$c = $ variable input cost
$r = $ farmer's discount rate
$p = $ per unit output price
$R = $ resale value of farm
$k = $ exogenous addition to soil base

It is assumed that *soil loss*, $s(t)$, or farming more intensively in period t impacts positively on output but at a decreasing rate so $f_s \geq 0$ and $f_{ss} \leq 0$. The *depth of soil*, $x(t)$, also has a beneficial effect on output, but at some point additional depth adds nothing to productivity. Hence, $f_x \geq 0$ and $f_{xx} \leq 0$.

McConnell (1983) argues that soil loss does not necessarily imply that farmers do not consider the future, but that soil losses can occur through rational farm management decisions as farmers repond to market conditions, soil productivity, and finite resources.

Variable input z will be applied until the value of the marginal product (pgf_z) equals its cost (c). Soil loss will occur until the value of returns obtained from additional soil loss (pgf_s) equals the implicit cost of using the soil. Soil loss will increase when the returns increase or the implicit user's cost decreases. Likewise, it will increase with reductions in the impact that soil depth has on resale value. It should be noted that the discount rate plays a pivotal role in these calculatons. As the discount rate rises, the implicit cost of saving the soil increases, resulting in more soil loss. The discount rate determines the marginal cost of soil loss throught time.

The implicit *user cost* in such a model can be perceived as having two components: 1) the impact of soil loss on the income stream generated while land is still under current ownership; and 2) the impact of soil loss on the resale value of land at time T. To analyze the implications of resale values determined by nonagricultural demand as opposed to soil productivity, let the first component of the implicit cost of soil loss in time t be

$$V = \int_{t+1}^T e^{-rt}[pg(t)f(s, x, z) - cz]\, dt \tag{7}$$

and let the resale value be

$$R[x(T)] e^{-rT}$$

So the implicit user cost would be

$$UC = \frac{\partial V}{\partial s} + \frac{\partial R}{\partial x} \cdot \frac{\partial x}{\partial s} \tag{8}$$

So optimal conditions occur when

$$pgf_z = cz \tag{9}$$

$$pgf_s = \frac{\partial V}{\partial s} + \frac{\partial R}{\partial x} \cdot \frac{\partial x}{\partial s} \tag{10}$$

If the resale value is dominated by nonagricultural demand unrelated to soil depth, the implicit user cost will be smaller, and more soil loss will result. However, in agricultural land markets we would expect that $R_x > 0$ and the second component of the implicit user cost would be relevant and significant. McConnell's model does not incorporate any of the externalities that soil erosion imposes on water and air quality. But McConnell (1983) does argue that government intervention in soil conservation may be most appropriately justified by market failures associated with water quality. This contention finds empirical support in a study by Strohbehn (1986) which concludes that roughly two-thirds of the benefits of federal soil conservation programs could be attributed to water quality improvements.

By contrasting the results from his firm level model with a framework to determine the path of soil depletion that maximizes social welfare, he is then able to identify conditions of firm level profit maximization that generate socially optimal rates of soil loss through government intervention. With the latter framework, the value to society of a single farm is

$$V = \int_0^\infty e^{-\delta t}[pgf(s, x, z) - cz] \, dt \tag{11}$$

where δ = the social discount rate.

McConnell (1983) shows that if $r = \delta$ and asset markets work efficiently, the profit-maximizing soil loss for the firm will be identical with the socially optimal plan, regardless of the form of ownership (family or corporate). Soil loss equaling annual replenishment will be socially optimal when the marginal value of soil approximates infinity as depth goes to zero and the social discount rate is zero. This implies that the welfare of all future generations is treated identically and that no relevant technical changes and input substitutions are likely.

Using a multiple-period linear programming model with a penalty function in the terminal period, Miranowski (1984) illustrates the intertemporal productivity impacts of soil loss in crop production and management for an Iowa case. The results indicate the importance of relative price and potential yield loss impacts in determining dynamic crop production and management decisions, re-emphasizing McConnell's conclusion that efficiency is achieved when soil loss occurs at the level where the value of returns associated with additional soil loss equals the implicit cost of using the additional soil (i.e., marginal foregone future returns). First, higher levels of yield loss per unit of soil loss will significantly lower total soil loss during a given period. In other words, if the farmer places a higher value (i.e., greater foregone yield) on an inch or unit of topsoil, he will make a greater effort to reduce soil loss and save the topsoil. Second, if agricultural output prices are increasing over time, more soil-conserving practices are adopted, and these are frequently adopted in earlier periods. A review of agricultural prices indicates that the general trend of real output prices is downward over time. Thus, if these farmers expect output price patterns to continue in the future, the market incentives to prevent soil loss may be declining over time. Finally, lower discount rates increase the net present value of all solutions, especially those with greater benefits in the more distant future. Higher real private discount rates will encourage more profligate soil use or reduced efforts to prevent soil loss. Yet, examining the real rate of return to land investments in agriculture implies that the real private discount rate is relatively low, leading to hypothesized soil-conserving behavior on the part of farmers.

Finally, Shortle and Miranowski (1983) urge the use of dynamic models of soil conservation behavior when assessing producer response to erosion control policies, especially when the damages associated with soil erosion are high. Static models used to investigate the economics of erosion control policies fail to recognize the endogenous incentives for erosion control arising from the conservation benefits accruing to the farmer. The framework proposed by McConnell (1983) and illustrated by Miranowski (1984) confirms the importance of using a dynamic model when the costs of soil erosion are large. These results indicate the potential policy importance of using a dynamic framework when addressing a variety of intertemporal agricultural resource issues that involve significant user costs.

From society's perspective, the dynamic framework may be even more informative than for a farmer who compares the private gains from cropping practices with the foregone profits associated with decreases in soil productivity. Shortle and Miranowski (1987) find that the social planner's problem of weighing social gains of erosive cropping practices against foregoing future profits and water quality benefits is far more complicated. Under certain situations, moving to a more efficient erosion control path can actually involve increases in near term erosion, complicating the design of erosion control policies when significant productivity losses are involved.

INSTITUTIONS, PROPERTY RIGHTS, AND TENURE

Property rights and the institutions that govern the use of land are important concepts in understanding the functioning of land markets. There is a rich tradition of institutional economics that has influenced how land is studied. Part of the structure of the market economy that guides land use is the definition of property rights. Broadly defined *property rights* prescribe the means of access to and control over the assets of society. They establish the rules under which resources such as land can be used and traded and determine who receives the benefits generated by the resources. Only to the extent that the community abides by these rules do property rights exist (Shaffer and Schmid, 1985).

Property rights in land have developed that usually are not as absolute as rights in other commodities. Laws that allocate property rights can be complicated and involve a number of jurisdictional authorities. The tradition of fee simple rights further emphasizes the fact that land ownership can be considered as a bundle of rights rather than absolute control over the land resource. The presence of joint products and externalities involved in the use of land has fostered the evolution of these rights. The decision by society as to who will have access to the flow of benefits from land is an evolutionary process that necessitates a re-examination when changes in the flows of benefits occur or when the costs of exclusion are significantly altered.

One critical issue in this evolution is the definition of jurisdictional boundaries. The jurisdictional boundary refers not only to geographic and demographic delineations but also to the specification of authority within these delineations. During the Sagebrush Rebellion and the New Federalism of the Reagan Administration many of these jurisdictional boundary issues attracted national attention. Previously, much of the debate about land use planning and the administration of zoning ordinances reflected these issues as well. The definition of the jurisdictional boundary will determine who has a voice in deciding the definition of property right conflicts.

The resolution of the jurisdictional boundary issue will be greatly influenced by four factors: the sense of community, externalities, homogeneity of tastes and preferences within society, and economies of scale (Shaffer and Schmid, 1985). The sense of the community relates to the identification on the part of voters and government officials to the opposing parties in any conflict involving property rights. It encompasses both the question of who is considered a part of the community (with valid claims to property rights) and the intensity of the commitment to that party. The presence of externalities and the costs of excluding affected parties help define conflicts in property rights. The severity and extent of the externalities will impact on the appropriate jurisdictional boundary for the resolution. The homogeneity of tastes and preferences can clarify the appropriate boundaries for expressing the demand and hence value for goods, services, and externalities. Heterogeneity in tastes may force the political process to articulate whose preferences will count and the final distribution of benefits and costs. Economies of scale may affect the costs of producing and consuming goods and services to the extent that trade-offs in resolving property right conflicts can be greatly altered. Economies of scale may also play a role in evaluating the costs of exclusion in joint products. Finally, it must be recognized that equity concerns related to land and its uses cannot be completely separated from the definition of property rights.

The distribution questions arising from property right conflicts are in fact challenges to the definition of property rights and a recognition that their resolution is an evolutionary process. Furthermore, efficiency questions are also related to the definition of property rights since they are the rules of how resources can be employed in a production process. Separating efficiency from equity implies that the existing definition of property rights is acceptable and ignores the dynamics of their development.

Leasing Arrangements

It is often argued (Newberry, 1983) that rental arrangements result in more efficient allocations of land, equipment, and managerial expertise. Since equipment is frequently purchased in indivisible units, incentives exist for overcapitalized equipment owners to lease additional land to lower average fixed costs and realize an efficient level of production. Similarly, allocations of managerial expertise can be enhanced by lease arrangements. Managerial expertise of the landowner can supplement that of the tenant and vice versa. Hallagan (1978) proposes that initial endowments of managerial expertise where the tenant is a qualified manager and the landowner has limited expertise tend to favor cash rental arrangements. However, in reverse cases where a transfer of expertise from the landowner to the tenant will increase production efficiency, share leases are common. He further develops the argument to suggest that landowners can even use share leases, in the long run, to generate information on the responsibility, quality, and managerial expertise of tenants. Newberry (1983) extends this notion by introducing the idea that a significant factor in leasing arrangements is the cost of monitoring the use of the asset. As proximity and familiarity between landowner and tenant increase, less managerial time of the landowner is required for monitoring, and hence share leases should be more common than cash rental leases.

Robison and Barry (1987) examine the efficiency of *share leasing* from the perspective of the efficient levels of output. Comparisons are made between the optimal levels for owner operated farms and optimal levels for various share leases. Assume that owner-operator labor, L, and a tract of land, T, are combined with other inputs, z, in the following production function to produce an output, q:

$$q = f(L/T, z) \tag{13}$$

where $f' > 0$ and $f'' < 0$.

So, with w as the wage rate, profit per unit of land can be represented as

$$y = pf(L/T, z) - w*(L/T) \tag{14}$$

Optimal production occurs where the marginal value product of labor equals the wage rate or where

$$pf'(L*/T, z) = w \tag{15}$$

Now under a lease arrangement where the tenant exchanges his labor for α percent of the value of the output, the optimal level of production is obtained where

$$\alpha p f'(L^*/T, z) = w \tag{16}$$

Since $0 < \alpha < 1.0$, the optimal level of production with the share lease on the output but not on the inputs results in less efficient production from the tract of land than in the case of the owner-operator. An alternative share lease arrangement would be for the landowner to provide $(1 - \alpha)$ of the labor and receive $(1 - \alpha)$ of the value of production. In this case, the optimal level of production occurs when the landowner equates his marginal value product with the wage rate and the tenant does likewise. In both first-order conditions the following result is obtained:

$$p f'(L/T, z) = w \tag{17}$$

This identifies the identical level of production as determined in the case of the owner-operator. So with share leases where output but not inputs are shared, resulting production levels can be inefficient while sharing both the inputs and the outputs should generate more efficient levels of production.

A missing but critical component of the above model is the recognition that the land value can be influenced by the level of production and the quality of labor invested. Topsoil can be eroded by some production practices, while conservation can maintain or increase the land value. A more appropriate profit function for the landowner is

$$y_L = p f(L/T, z) - w^*(L/T) + \partial V(T/L)/\partial L \tag{18}$$

where the last term measures per unit loss in land value equal to the present value of the remaining stock of services. The optimal level of production for the landowner now occurs where

$$p f'(L/T, z) = w - \partial^2 V(T(L))/\partial L^2 \tag{19}$$

It is now uncertain how this level of production compares to the optimal level for the tenant because the sign of the last term is unknown. Hence, the efficiency of share leases cannot be unambiguously answered when the impact of production on the land value is considered.

The second motivation for share leases is the one that has received the most attention. The risk management implications of share lease arrangements have been examined by numerous authors (Chueng, 1969; Stiglitz, 1974; Sutinen, 1975; Hiebert, 1978; Robison and Barry, 1987). Sutinen reaches several interesting conclusions. In his model, it is assumed that the landowner determines all input levels and that both the tenant and the landlord are risk averse. He concludes that the optimal output share is dependent upon the risk attitudes of the two parties. Specificallly,

$$\alpha = R_L(x)/(R_T(x) + R_L(x)) \tag{20}$$

where $R_L(x)$ and $R_T(x)$ are the absolute risk aversion coefficients of the landowner and the tenant, respectively. The optimal level of production under the share lease will be greater than without a share lease if both agents are risk averse. Finally, Sutinen (1975) demonstrates that there may not be a fixed relationship between the amount of risk and the optimal share arrangement. This supports the notion that share leases are not always predominant in the production of the most risky commodities.

Hiebert (1978) extends the basic Sutinen (1975) model to allow the tenant to influence the input level. His results show that the share lease percentage, α, is unchanged by switching the control of the input decisions, but the output level can be different. However, the direction of the difference is indeterminant.

Robison and Barry (1987) combine the models of Sutinen and Hiebert and explore the consequences that changes in the *soil productivity* can have on the share lease arrangement. With perfect land markets that reflect changes in soil productivity through land values, it can be shown that the landowner's share of the output will increase with increases in soil productivity. This occurs because the value of land is one of the wealth components of the absolute risk aversion coefficient of the landowner and it is commonly assumed that decision makers show decreasing absolute aversion. So as $R_L(x)$ decreases with an increase in wealth from rising land values, α will decline. A converse result will be observed from a decline in soil productivity.

Unfortunately, there is little empirical evidence on the effects of share leasing, and the preceding discussion centers around a largely empirical question. However, Allen and Lueck (1992) provide some empirical observations from Nebraska and South Dakota. They examine the impact on lease arrangements emphasizing the importance of contracts that mitigate soil exploitation and crop underreporting. Cash rents predominate for crops that are not independently measured and graded, that are easy to store, that do not require heavy working of the soil, and that require significant field drying. In addition, factors such as irrigation (reducing need to manage soil–water balance), institutional land ownership (e.g. banks, Indian tribal lands, municipalities), and significant nonagricultural demand for land (reducing concerns for soil exploitation) all favor cash rents. Crops that are taken to an independent party for measurement, grading and storage, as well as those that require tillage and soil manipulation to enhance current profits at the expense of future crops are usually cropshared.

Allen and Lueck (1992) discuss the relationship between proportional shares of input expenses and proportional output (harvest) shares. Citing Heady's earlier work, they show that if it is rational to share input expenses, the share should be equal to the harvest share to insure optimal input use levels. The data from South Dakota and Nebraska indicate that in 96 percent of cropshare contracts the renter pays either all input costs or a share equal to his output share. Finally, Allen and Lueck address the operation of local land markets and the reputation of land renters. Gross violations of soil exploitation laws or misrepresentation of input usage and harvests are not usually addressed through law enforcement agencies or the courts, but rather, through the land market. The reputation of the renter is a key determinant of rental land availability and of land rental contracts. Farmers with poor reputations realize a reduced stream of benefits in future land rental agreements.

LAND USE

Spatial Location Concepts

Spatial characteristics influence the price of land. Location does not necessarily alter the productive capacity of land, but it is a factor in the proximity to markets for the products it is used to produce. Location characteristics of concern can be either natural or man-made. Natural characteristics include topographic features and proximity to rivers, waterways, or scenic wonders, while the more common man-made ones are related to the provision of infrastructure. Location can affect land values through three factors: distance, absence of nuisances, and presence of exceptional attractions (Dovring, 1987).

Distance is the location characteristic that attracted the most attention of classical economists (Brooks, 1987). The on-site demand for agricultural products is influenced by the transportation costs of the commodities to final markets. Given that distance and transportation costs are related, greater distance from the final markets increases the cost of supplying commodities and impacts negatively on the value of land, all other things being equal. One of the classical economists who examined this relationship in detail was Von Thunen (1966). He proposed that in the case of an isolated community or final market, agricultural production patterns would form a series of concentric rings. These rings would reflect the costs of transportation. Perishable and hard-to-transport commodities would be produced in the inner rings, while those that could be stored and transported more easily would be produced in the outer rings. The rings would be altered by waterways and other modes of transportation, presence of secondary markets, and interspatial land productivity differences.

In Von Thunen's (1966) model, at each location a *rent* per unit of land would be bid equal to the value of the crop less costs of production and transportation to market. Assuming that the costs of production (exclusive of land costs) are the same, the maximum bid rent offered for any location–crop combination will depend on distance to the market. Bid rent for any parcel decreases with distance from the market, reflecting the increasing transportation cost of the parcel's product.

The bid rent functions for each crop depend on crop prices, technological choices, and costs of transportation. The crop producing the highest net returns (rent) at a location will outbid other crops for land at that location. Because transportation costs and net returns vary for crops at the market, different crops tend to be produced at different distances from the market.

Von Thunen (1966) further demonstrates that rent per acre decreases with distance from market forming concentric rings of agricultural production with constant rents. Going out from the market, rent per acre decreases in each succeeding ring until bid rent goes to zero when the costs of production and transportation totally absorb market value for all crops. Thus we observe decreases in rent with distance from the market as well as local crop specialization even in regions with similar geoclimatic conditions.

Economic Model of Spatial Distribution

To illustrate the spatial location concepts, a model is developed for situations where agricultural activity creates an externality. Consider the case of agricultural producers located along a rectangular basin with length L and with a trade center located at 0, where all output is sold. Suppose output is produced with a constant return-to-scale technology using land, a variable input (say, labor), and a fixed land preparation effort. Let y denote output per acre, x equal labor per acre, and the production function per acre be $q = f(x)$. It is assumed that the production function is well behaved, namely marginal productivity of labor is positive and decreasing ($f' > 0$, $f'' < 0$).

Let l be a location indicator. In the analysis each variable will be identified by its location since we are interested in locational patterns. The indicator variable 1 assumes values from 0 (at the market) and L at the farthest end of the basin.

Let output price at the market be denoted by P. Output requires transport, and transportation cost per unit of output per unit of distance is v. Thus, producer output price at l is $P - vl$. Input price does not vary with distance and is denoted by w. The fixed cost per acre is denoted by u.

With profit-maximizing producers, the choice problem at location l is

$$\text{Max}_{x} \ (P - vl)f[x(l)] - wx(l) - u \tag{21}$$

The first-order condition for this problem is

$$(P - vl)f'[x(l)] = w \qquad x(l) > 0 \tag{22}$$

Condition (22) suggests that at each location labor will be used at a level which equates its price and value of marginal productivity as long as labor application is also the minimum required. The value of marginal product is the product of marginal productivity of labor and producer price. Since producer price declines with distance, condition (22) argues that labor and production per acre declines with distance.

The *quasi rent* denoted by $r(l)$ is the difference between revenue and cost per acre whenever it is positive, that is,

$$r(l) = (P - vl)f[x(l)] - wx(l) - u \geq 0 \tag{23}$$

The spatial pattern of optimal production suggests that quasi rent declines with distance. At l_c quasi rent is zero and the locations closest to market have positive quasi rents. If farming is the only operation, land rental rates are equal to the quasi rents. The behavior of rental rates with distance is denoted in Figure 9.9. The curve r_a denotes rental rate for a base case. Rents are positive and declining at locations closer than l_a^c; no production occurs beyond l_a^c. Comparative statics analysis can show that increases in output price tend to increase profitability of production, labor intensity, the land rents, and the utilized land base. The curve r_b denotes behavior of rent for a higher price than the base curves. A reduction in transportation cost tends to reduce locational differences in rents and increase the utilized land base. Both r_a and r_c are associated with the base output price, but the curve r_c corresponds to a situation with a lower transportation cost.

Rental rate

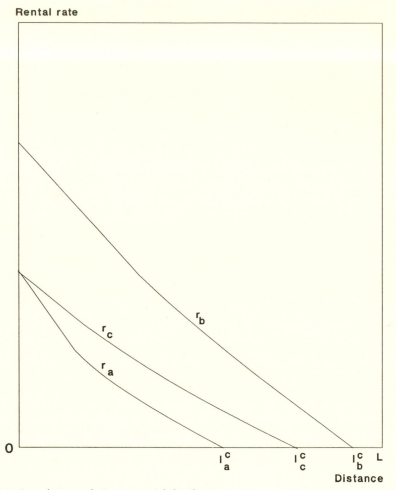

Figure 9.9. Rental rates relative to spatial distribution.

Externality Considerations

Now consider the case where agricultural production is a source of a negative externality affecting the welfare at the basin mouth. For example, run-off from the farms contaminate a fishery at the entry to the basin. Assume that pollution is related to output, and it is accumulated as one moves closer to the business center. It is also reasonable to assume that the pollution output ratio of faraway farms is much smaller than those of farms closer to the business center. Let $h(l)$ denote a pollution output ratio as a function of location; it is assumed that $h' < 0$. Let Z denote total pollution of the industry as is computed by aggregation over all farms. Since the width of the basin is one unit of distance,

$$Z = \int_0^L h(l)f[x(l)]\, dl \tag{24}$$

Let social cost of pollution at $l = 0$ be denoted by $g(Z)$ where the marginal costs of pollution are assumed to be positive and increasing. Socially optimal resource allocations maximize benefits from production minus cost of the externality. Thus, the social optimization problem is

$$\max_{(x_l, Z)} \int_0^L [(P - vl)f[x(l)] - wx(l) - u] \, dl - g(Z) \tag{25}$$

when

$$Z = \int_0^L h(l)f[x(l)] \, dl$$

Hochman et al. (1977) solved this problem using optimal control. They argued that, at the optimal solution, pollution is assigned a price that is denoted by λ. Conditions for optimality are

$$g'(Z) = \lambda \tag{26}$$

$$[P - vl - \lambda h(l)] f'[x(l)] = w \qquad \text{for } l \leq l^c \tag{27}$$

$$x > 0 \qquad \text{if } [P - vl - \lambda h(l)] f[x(l)] - wx(l) - u \geq 0 \tag{28}$$

Condition (26) suggests that the price of pollution is equal to its marginal costs. Condition (28) suggests that both transportation cost vl and externality cost $\lambda h(l)$ have to be subtracted from an output price to compute values of marginal products of labor. Finally, equation (27) suggests that no output will be produced at a location at all $l > l^c$ where quasi rent per acre is negative. When an externality exists, two contradictory forces affect resource intensity and quasi rents. Transportation cost effects an increase in production intensity as one approaches the business center. An externality cost effects a change in the other direction, namely, it causes increased production intensity and quasi rent as one goes farther away from the business center. An optimal land-use pattern depends on the relative magnitudes of these two effects.

Taxation of pollution may be required to obtain optimal resource allocation in a competitive economy. An introduction of such taxation is likely to reduce the utilized land base and producers' rents compared to the case with no intervention. The pollution tax effect equal to λ in (26) is illustrated in Figure 9.10. The transportation cost effect is assumed to be larger than λ, thus the rent curves slope downward to the right. r_a is the base agricultural land rent and it shifts to r_λ after the pollution tax is imposed. If r_0 is the rent curve for another non-polluting land use, then the tax changes the extensive margin for agricultural land from l_a^0 to l_λ^0.

Urban Demand Consideration

Now suppose that a city is located in the basin near the business center. Basic writings of urban economist (Alonso, 1964) suggest that urban land rent declines substantially with the distance to the business center. The curve r^u in Figure 9.11 denotes urban land rent, and r_a is the agricultural land rent under competition. Since land will be utilized in the activity when it is most valuable, the area between the business center and l_a^u will be urban and between l_a^u and l_a^c and will be

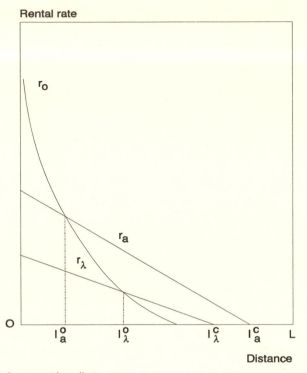

Figure 9.10. Rental rates with pollution tax.

agricultural. Population growth, or other reasons that increase the demand for urban land demand (shifting urban land rent for r_a^u to r_b^u), will result in an urban sprawl and a switch of the land between l_a^u to l_b^u from agricultural to urban activities.

When combining the externality and urban demand considerations, note that, when agricultural externalities are taxed, agricultural land rent declines and that may encourage urban sprawl.

Land Use With Multiple Activities

Land may be used for many agricultural activities, and each activity may use several inputs. The framework introduced previously can be generalized to accommodate this reality. Consider a case with no externality. Let i be output index, i assumes value from i to I; price of crop i is P_i; its transportation cost of ouput per unit of distance is v_i^0; and its fixed cost per acre is u_i. Assuming constant returns to scale, the per acre production function of the ith crop is

$$y_i = f_i(X_{il}, \ldots, X_{ij}) \tag{29}$$

where j is an input index, j assumes values from l to J, and x_{ij} is per acre quantity of input j in production of i. The price of input j is w_j and in transportation cost

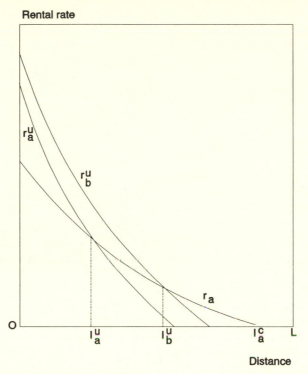

Figure 9.11. Rental rates with urban demand.

per unit of distance is v_j^x. Let the land share allocated to crop i be denoted by S_i,

$$l \geq \sum_{i=1}^{I} S_i \tag{30}$$

The optimal land use choices of location l are determined by

$$\underset{S_i x_{ij}}{\text{Max}} \sum_{i=1}^{I} (P_i - v_i^0 l f [x_{il}(l), x_{ij}(l)] - \lambda(w_j - v_j^x l) x_{ij}(l) - u_i) S_i \tag{31}$$

subject to

$$\sum_{i=1}^{I} S_i < l, S_i \geq 0 \tag{32}$$

This optimization problem can be solved in two stages. First, the optimal input mix for each crop is selected. The optimality conditions for this choice are

$$(P_i - v_i^0 l) \frac{\partial f}{\partial x_{ij}} - (w_j - v_j^x l) = 0 \qquad \text{for } j = l, J \tag{33}$$

Each input is selected at the level when its value of marginal product is equal to its producer price. The producer price for both inputs and output are adjusted to the location.

The selection of the optimal input mixes leads to the derivation of quasi rents for each of the crops. Let r_i be the quasi rent of the ith crop. Then the optimal shares are determined solving

$$\text{Max}_{S_i} \sum_{i=1}^{I} r_i S_i \tag{34}$$

$$\sum S_i \leq 1, \qquad S_i \geq 0 \tag{35}$$

This optimization problem is likely to have a corner solution; hence, each location is likely to have an optimal crop (or no crop at all). The quasi rent of the optimal crop will become the agricultural land rent.

The analysis suggests that, for each crop, production will be more intensive as one comes closer to the business center. Use of inputs with relatively high transportation cost is especially likely to increase as one nears the business center. Furthermore, high-valued crops with high transportation costs (or inputs or output) are likely to be produced closer to the city while low-valued products with less transportation costs are more likely to be produced farther away.

A complete and rigorous determination of spatial allocation of resources requires a general equilibrium framework where demand considerations are addressed explicitly and product prices are endogenously determined. Von Thunen (1966) was the first to raise the spatial resource allocation problem, and more general formal models appear in Takayama and Judge (1971) and are surveyed in Randall and Castle (1985).

The literature that followed the Von Thunen (1966) tradition and that emphasized the role of transportation cost in explaining land-use patterns argued that there will be several rings of activities around cities. The high transportation cost activities will be farther away. Thus, dairies will be the closest to the city, followed by poultry, vegetable farmers, fruit growers, and finally, field crops. Generally speaking, these types of predictions held quite well in years past.

Smoke, noise, and agricultural pollution considerations might have resulted in some modification of this predicted order. For example, dairies and poultry farmers moved farther away from the cities, and the urban fringe is more frequently encountering tree groves and vegetable patches.

It seems, however, that governmental policies and technological change have combined to reduce the importance of transportation cost and increased the importance of locational differences (in terms of weather, land quality, etc.) when explaining the distribution of agricultural activities.

The emergence of the American Midwest, and later the West, as major food baskets owes much to the establishment of a railroad network on the North American continent and to the development of engine-powered boats. The establishment of the intercontinental freeway networks and the improvement of refrigeration technologies are highly responsible for the concentration of production of vegetables and fruits in California and Florida in spite of their long distance from many important population centers. For example, according to U.S. agricultural statistics, only 22 percent of the U.S. fresh vegetable production in 1939 was in California and Arizona, while in 1988 52 percent of the vegetables came from these states. On the other hand, the share of fresh vegetables in the Atlantic states (except Florida) declined from 30 percent in 1937 to about 12 percent in 1989 (U.S. Department of Agriculture, 1991). Furthermore, improvements in air freight may affect the location of fresh food, fruit, and vegetable production even further.

Improved refrigeration, transportation, and large-scale production technologies, combined with the introduction of "boxed meat" technology, have contributed to the movement of slaughterhouses and livestock-finishing activities away from the cities (with high land and labor cost) to the hinterlands over the last 20 years. These factors have also contributed to a movement of egg production facilities away from urban centers and toward a concentration of much of the U.S. poultry production in southeastern states.

The big California water projects of the 1960s and 1970s and the introduction of the cotton harvester in the late 1950s were partly responsible for the growth of the California cotton industry and the decline of the South as a cotton-producing region. For example, about 22 percent of the 1954 U.S. cotton acreage was in southeastern states, and it declined to 7 percent in 1989. California and Arizona had less than 2 percent of the cotton acreage in 1938, about 6.5 percent in 1955, and 15 percent in 1988.

The Von Thunen model assumes a freely operating private land market that can be applied to explain the location of agricultural commodity production or urban development patterns. Yet, there have been few attempts to use the model to explain the interface between agricultural and urban development activities or to modify the model to specifically address externalities or nonmarket impacts associated with the patterns of land use explained by the model. Interesting illustrations of potential limitations of the Von Thunen model in a policy context are the prime agricultural land and open space issues.

As land rents and values increase nearer market or urban centers, agricultural production activities tend to shift to higher valued crops. But eventually, further increases in land values and rents, plus environmental and zoning regulations that increase the cost of farming in the city's shadow, will make most, if not all, agricultural activities unprofitable. The normal operation of land market forces has raised two public concerns. First, that the growth of urban centers is depleting the supply of prime agricultural lands, eventually impacting the nation's ability to supply agricultural output and compete in international markets. Second, that the normal operation of the private land market does not recognize or internalize the positive externalities associated with pastoral activities and open space interspersed in more urban areas. Although we will not attempt to incorporate these two issues into a formal model for evaluation purposes, casual empiricism does permit us to provide some insights into the issues and suggest possible conclusions or outcomes.

Open Space Issues

Urbanization, the conversion of farmland, forestland, and wetland to urban and residential uses, affects less than 800,000 U.S. acres per year out of a total 1.2

billion acres of private, rural land (Vesterby and Heimlich, 1989). But concern continues, especially in high-growth rural-urban fringe areas, about the accumulated decline in open space.

In 1970, there were 6.9 million acres of urban land in the nation's 135 fastest-growing counties (counties that increase by 25,000 people and 25 percent in total population per decade). By 1980, urban land in these counties had increased to 9.3 million acres, a gain of 2.4 million acres. Vasterby and Heimlich (1989) report that of the 2.4 million acres of new urban area, 37 percent was from cropland and pasture. Forestland contributed 24 percent, rangeland 23 percent, and wetlands and land in transition contributed 16 percent. Even through 2.4 million acres shifted out of agriculture during the 1970s in the fast-growth counties, 0.7 million acres shifted into agriculture, mostly from forestland. Combining the fast-growing and slower-growing counties results in an estimate that urban area for the United States grew annually an average of 740,000 acres during the 1970s. This is consistent with previous ERS estimates and below other estimates of farmland conversion, which have ranged from 1.1 to 3 million acres per year. A useful discussion of the economic dimensions of farmland conversion and the competition over land resources at the rural-urban fringe is presented in Fischel (1982).

Moderate rates of population growth can be accommodated without major encroachment on agricultural land. Vesterby and Heimlich (1989), using aerial photography interpretation, show the rate and character of urbanization was fairly consistent in the 1960–70 and 1970–80 periods. Although the marginal rates of land consumption changed little between the two periods, there were important differences in land consumption associated with the stage of urbanization. Less populated, fast-growing counties used more land per household than did more populous, fast-growing and slower-growing counties. Thus, more concerns are likely to arise in areas of recent urbanization. Finally, Vesterby and Heimlich (1989) conclude that there will be less conversion of land to urban uses in the future because of the net effect of changing household numbers, household characteristics, and economic constraints on the demand for land.

Some agricultural areas of the country, however, are in the midst of rapid development that is converting farm land or greatly increasing the price of land and labor, the competition for water, and the efforts of nonfarm residents to restrict agricultural activities (e.g., abatement of smells, noise, spraying). At the same time, 16 of the top 20 counties in the nation in value of agricultural production are metropolitan counties, mostly in the West. These 20 counties alone have 10 percent of the country's total farm output. But from 1980 to 1987, these counties increased in population by 25 percent (2 million people) which is putting pressure on the agricultural use of land in these counties.

Generally, agriculture has adapted to urbanization in the United States with metropolitan areas containing nearly 30 percent of all farms and almost 20 percent of harvested cropland (Heimlich, 1989). The adaptation has come about through smaller farming operations, emphasis on higher-valued products, greater intensity of production, and increased off-farm employment. Heimlich goes on to conclude that a number of factors favor the survival of metro farming including development trends, and more dispersed patterns of settlement in more recently developed metropolitan areas.

Perceived gaps between open space availability and demand have led some State and local governments to develop programs for the preservation of open space near urbanizing areas. Various farmland retention mechanisms, such as preferential farmland taxation, purchase of development rights (PDR) programs, zoning, and fee simple acquisition, have been employed. All 50 states have laws that provide preferential assessment of farmland. Land in a qualifying use is assessed on its value in that use as opposed to its market value. States also vary from having only preferential property tax assessment to deferred taxes to restrictive agreements on future use for tax concessions.

Farmland retention and open space programs, while seemingly complementary, can be in conflict with respect to the land targeted, the uses to which the land may be put, and the mechanisms employed. PDR programs in such States as Massachusetts, New Hampshire, and Maryland have limited resources. Conflicts have arisen over the choice between purchasing inexpensive easements on largely agricultural areas and purchasing expensive easements on small parcels surrounded by development with little future as agriculture but great value as open space.

Zoning can protect both important agricultural land and open space with little monetary outlay during periods of urban growth. However, by the time growth is recognized as a problem, landowners are aware of the unrealized capital gains they stand to lose and may side with developers to oppose zoning.

Despite such state and local efforts, future trends may lead to an undesired distribution of open space, a growing number of property right disputes, and demands for government intervention at a higher level. To capture the economic value of preserving rural areas may require action above the local or state level. For example, there are large, scenic rural areas in Europe, or New England for that matter, that are dependent on recreation and tourism.

There are examples in other countries of government action based on the perception of national interest in a preferred settlement pattern. Britain, for example, has sought to preserve a development-free green belt around London. Land in that belt may be used as in the past, but no new housing or commercial facilities may be built. That arrangement is roughly analogous to our national forest, except that the emphasis is on preserving a variety of rural uses rather than stands of timber. While no European country has set out to block all changes in land uses, most of the wealthier countries, at least, place a high priority on preserving distinct rural areas and invest in this national objective.

Another illustration of national interest in rural topography is Britain's hedgerows. To preserve the rural countryside and to protect tourism for the country as a whole, the British Government is attempting to save the hedgerows that are integral to images of the British countryside. Some farmers object because centuries-old hedgerows restrict field and equipment size, reducing the scale of operation and making farming less profitable. The reaction of these British farmers is not unlike U.S. farmers removing fencerows and restrictive conservation practices, especially in the 1970s, to accommodate the larger farm equipment.

LAND AS A CAPITAL ASSET

Interspatial Model

The previous section considered factors explaining the location of agricultural production activities. This section will develop a general framework for explaining interspatial variations in land prices and illustrate particular applications.

There have been studies of the relationship between farmland values and locational and soil characteristics. The hedonic approach has been used by Miranowski and Hammes (1984), Ervin and Mill (1985), and Gardner and Barrows (1985) to explain cross-sectional variations in land values in terms of soil quality characteristics and the impacts of soil erosion. Miranowski and Hammes found that actual and potential erosion contributed to the explanation of land values, while the other two studies reported mixed results and could not support a relationship between soil erosion and land values. Palmquist and Danielson (1989) related land values to farmland improvements and locational characteristics, including urban concentration, urban growth, and rural amenities. Their estimated coefficients had the expected signs and were statistically significant, leading them to conclude that the hedonic results were reliable and valuable information to individual farmers.

The *hedonic framework* appears to be a potentially useful avenue of land value research. It can be used to address a variety of appraisal (individual) and policy (aggregate) issues. For example, hedonic farmland studies can be used to establish values for particular soil and locational characteristics. Such information can be quite important in appraising the value of a parcel of farmland for sale or purchase as the case may be.

More importantly, such studies can be useful in providing economic information for the policy process. The coefficients from the hedonic model can be used to establish market values for such characteristics as a ton of topsoil, potential erodibility of farmland, climatic characteristics, and water holding capacity. It is then possible to determine if the private benefits of soil conservation practices outweigh the private and public costs of such efforts.

Analytical Framework

A simple intuitive justification of the interspatial land market valuation process can be provided by a soil productivity illustration from the land economics literature. Suppose that we have two identical parcels of farmland except that parcel I has a higher level of soil productivity than parcel II. If soil productivity is valued by farmers, then the price of parcel I should be higher than the price of parcel II by the value placed on the difference in soil productivity. If the price of I exceeds that of II by less than the value of the productivity differential, then purchasers of farmland would increase their bid price for I relative to II, increasing the price differential. Alternatively, if the farmland price differential exceeds the value of the difference in productivity, bid prices would respond to narrow the price differentials between parcels I and II.[1]

Soil productivity is only one of many factors that differ between parcels of land and affect land values. Because parcels of farmland have many factors that differentiate them, land price differentials reflect the values that landowners attach to all relevant components. Because land is sold as a package with a variety of attributes and because the sale price reflects the value of the package, it is difficult to value the individual components determining the package price.

The hedonic technique can be used to determine the effect each characteristic has on the selling price of a parcel of land. A basic assumption of the model is that each parcel may be described by a vector of characteristics

$$L = (l_1, l_2, \ldots, l_n) \tag{36}$$

where l_i is characteristic i of parcel L.

We can express the hedonic price equation as

$$P = P(l_1, \ldots, l_n) \tag{37}$$

where P is the price of a unit of land. If we can estimate Equation (37) from the available data, then the coefficients of the model can be used to determine the *implicit price* associated with each characteristic of a parcel of land, holding all other characteristics constant. For example, if characteristic l_5 measures inches of topsoil, then the price per inch of topsoil is the partial derivative of Equation (37) with respect to characteristic l_5, topsoil,

$$\frac{\partial P}{\partial l_5} = P(l_1, \ldots, l_n) \tag{38}$$

Equation (37) illustrates how the price of a parcel of land is dependent on a particular characteristic, holding all other characteristics fixed.

The hedonic price function for farmland as expressed in Equation (37), can also be interpreted as a rental price function. The equilibrium rental price is determined by the actions of all demanders and suppliers of farmland in a given rental market. Individual market participants can affect the rental price only by altering the set of characteristics they choose when contracting to rent a parcel of farmland, but they cannot influence the equilibrium price, which is determined by the aggregate of renters and landowners interacting in the land rental market.

More formally, following Palmquist (1989), the demand for land to rent can be motivated from the agricultural production function. The implicit production function can be written as

$$h(x, l) = 0 \tag{39}$$

where x is a vector of net outputs exclusive of land, i.e., if $x_i > 0$, then x_i is an output, and if $x_i < 0$, then x_i is an input, and l is a vector of characteristics

---

[1] Because land values are essentially capitalized rents, the differences in values are a measure of the buyers' willingness to pay for the future productivity of the soil.

associated with a given land parcel. Palmquist (1989) now assumes that renters (farmers) maximize variable profits, which are the differences between the value of outputs and the cost of inputs, other than land, on a particular parcel. Maximizing variable profits on a parcel

$$\text{Max } \pi^v = xpx, \text{ subject to } h(x, l) = 0; \pi^v \geq 0 \tag{40}$$

where π^v is variable profits and p is a vector of prices of outputs and nonland inputs. After solving the maximization for output supply and nonland input demand functions, or $x = x(p, l)$, these functions can be substituted into Equation (5) to obtain the variable profit functions

$$\pi^{*v} = \pi^{*v}(p, l) = \sum_p x(p, l) \tag{41}$$

For a parcel of land, the producer will subtract land costs from variable profits to determine actual profits, or π^a. Or the *bid function* can be specified as

$$b(x, p, \pi^a) = \pi^v(p, l) - \pi^a \tag{42}$$

The producer's bid to rent a parcel of land is a function of the prices of output and nonland inputs, actual profits, and the characteristics of the parcel in question.

Given a particular profit level, the bid function can be used to determine the rental payment that a producer would be willing to make to obtain the services of a parcel with a particular set of characteristics. A producer's change in bid for a change in one characteristic of a parcel would equal the change (marginal) in market rental price for a change in that characterisitic under equilibrium conditions.

Likewise, based on the assumption that landowners supplying rental land seek to maximize long-run profits from rental of their parcels, Palmquist (1989) derives a market equilibrium rental schedule. If all characteristics of parcels are beyond the control of landowners, the price of each characteristic and thus the *offer price* would be demand driven (determined). The offer price for exogenously determined characteristics should equal the market price. Otherwise, at an offer price below the market price the landowner would forego profits and at an offer price above the market price there would be no takers. The analysis can be further complicated by specifying some characteristics of a parcel of land that can be altered by the landowner, e.g., drainage. The landowners' profit-maximizing situation can be specified as

$$\text{Max } \pi^0 = R(\bar{l}, \tilde{l}) - C(\bar{l}, \tilde{l}, c) \text{ subject to } \pi^0 \geq, \tilde{l} \tag{43}$$

where π^0 is landowner profits, c is a vector of land improvement costs, $\bar{l}$ are characteristics the landowner cannot control, and $\tilde{l}$ are characteristics the landowner can control. An offer function indicating the prices at which landowners will provide parcels to the market can be specified similar to the bid function

$$Z(\bar{l}, \tilde{l}, \pi^0, c) = \pi^0 + C(\bar{l}, \tilde{l}, c) \tag{44}$$

For characteristics that the landowner cannot control, $\bar{l}$, the characteristic price and offer price would equal the market price. For endogenous characteristics, $\tilde{l}$, that can be controlled by the landowner, the landowner will invest in these characteristics to the point where the marginal cost equals the marginal characteristic price in the market so as to maximize profits on the parcel.

The interaction of producers (bidders) and landowners (offerers) in the rental market determines the market price schedule, but the individual producers and landowners are price takers.

This analytical framework can be used to value land characteristics in the rental market. Given the better availability and quality of data on land value than data on land rental rates, it may be more appropriate to do empirical estimation in terms of land values. Assuming that the value of land as an asset simply depends on the present value of future rents, the discussion that follows will focus on land values as opposed to land rents. Some individuals may argue that producers (renters) are only interested in the current productive capabilities of the land and thus will maximize short-run profits irrespective of what such actions do to the future productivity of the land. But landowners, who have every incentive to maximize long-run profits, can rent their parcels subject to restrictions to protect future productivity. If the discounted present value of more conservation-oriented production exceeds the discounted present value of more profligate resource use, the landowner has every incentive to conserve or restrict use of the land input. To the contrary, if the discounted productivity loses are small and short-term gains outweigh long-term losses, profits will be maximized by more profligate resource use. Thus, using land values rather than rental rates should not alter the outcome of the analysis.

An Empirical Illustration

Iowa county-level land value, locational, and soil characteristic data for 1978 were used to derive coefficient estimates of the value of farmland characteristics. These characteristics were hypothesized to be important factors in the spatial farmland market, especially as they pertain to differences in farmland values and rents.

The empirical model specified for the hedonic farmland price function was

$$P = a_0 + a_1 l_1 + a_2 l_2 + a_3(l_1)(l_2) + a_4 l_3 + a_5 l_4 + a_6 l_5 + a_7 l_6 + a_8 l_7 + a_9 l_8 \quad (45)$$

where P is the price per acre of farmland in the county

l_1 is the country average measure of potential erodibility
l_2 is the average topsoil depth (inches) in the county
l_3 is the cropland share of total farmland in the county
l_4 is the radial distance (miles) to the nearest SMSA
l_5 is population density per square mile in the county
l_6 is the average annual rainfall (inches) in the climate region
l_7 is the average extension expenditure for the county
l_8 is effective real estate tax mill rate on farmland in the county

The coefficient estimate (a_2) implies that as topsoil depth increases, or the amount of soil lost to erosion decreases, the value of farmland increases. The per acre value of an inch of topsoil was close to $60. If on average in Iowa, the loss of an inch of topsoil will reduce corn yields by 1.5 bushels per acre, a $2 per bushel corn price, and assuming no added cost of producing the last increment, then the present value of this yield loss discounted into perpetuity at a 5 percent real rate equals $60. It can be inferred that purchasers of farmland discounted their bid price for cropland based on differences in topsoil depth related to past soil erosion.

The erodibility coefficient had the correct sign and increasing potential erodibility decreased the value of farmland, holding topsoil depth constant. From the interaction term one could conclude that with increased erodibility, depth was less valuable, or deeper topsoils are less valuable when they require additional investment to keep them in place (i.e., prevent them from eroding).

The value of proximity to a SMSA appeared to be overvalued. The effective tax rate undervalued the long-run impacts of property tax obligations. The extension variable indicated that land puchasers were willing to pay more for farmland in counties that spend more on extension activities. Farmland located in counties with higher population densities was higher priced, all other things being equal. Competition from other uses of farmland would support this result. Finally, the share of cropland in total farmland was significant in explaining differences in farmland values, reflecting differences in cropland and noncropland values.

If the analysis could be carried a step further and the productivity impacts of soil characteristics established, the effectiveness of markets in addressing social concerns could be assessed. If participants in the land market "appropriately" value soil characteristics such that the hedonic values approximate the values of the marginal product of soil characteristics, the private farmland market may function to maintain the long-run productivity of farmland. Obviously, the market may fail to account for the off-farm impacts (e.g., sedimentation of streams) of agricultural activities.

Land Acquisition

One of the most important decisions that farmers make is the investment/disinvestment decision in land. Meyer and Robison (1991) presented a model which depicts the land acquisition decision for a competitive firm facing a random output price in an increasing cost industry. They argue that an important component in this decision is the adjustment that firms must make to new equilibrium positions. Two adjustment mechanisms to changes in market equilibrium are examined: entry/exist with changes in the output price level and increases in costs with increases in the production level. Consideration of both mechanisms extends the seminal work of Appelbaum and Katz (1986).

Assume a profit function expressed in terms of input levels rather than in terms of output. Further assume a simple production function of constant returns to scale and the case where one input produces one output. Let

$$\pi = p^*L - \phi^*M^*L \qquad (46)$$

where L is a single input (land), M is the price of the durable asset (land), and ϕ is the interest rate. A per period cost for the land is then $\phi*M$. The demand for land can be calculated using the linear mean-variance utility function, which assumes that the firm maximizes $\mu - ((\lambda/2)\sigma^2)$. λ represents the *risk aversion* of the firm. For the firm in the competitive industry, $\mu = \mu_p^*L - \phi*M*L$. The firm selects L so that the function is maximized where

$$(\mu_p - \phi*M) - \lambda*\sigma_p^2*L = 0 \qquad (47)$$

The optimal size of the firm occurs where

$$L = (\mu_p - \phi*M)/(\lambda*\sigma_p^2) \qquad (48)$$

Hence the demand for land depends upon the mean and variance of the output price, the risk-free rate of return, the price of land, and the risk attitude of the farmer. However, this ignores changes in the industry equilibrium. Aggregating the demand function across n producers in the industry generates

$$L_D = ((\mu_p - \phi*M)/\sigma_p^2)(1/\lambda_1, + \cdots + 1/\lambda_n) \qquad (49)$$

Assuming a fixed supply of land in local markets, L_S, and setting it equal to the aggregate demand produces an equilibrium price.

$$M = (\mu_p/\phi) - (L_S^*\sigma_p^2)/(\phi*(1/\lambda_1 + \cdots + 1/\lambda_n) \qquad (50)$$

The equilibrium price now equals a capitalization of the mean return plus a discount for the risk of agricultural production. The adjustment to the industry equilibrium can be seen by substituting the value of M into the firm level demand equation. The new firm demand is

$$L = \lambda*L_S/(1/\lambda_1 + \cdots + 1/\lambda_n) \qquad (51)$$

Now the firm land acquisition decision depends only on the available supply of land and the farmer's risk aversion relative to the average in the industry. The risk free rate of return and the mean and variance of the output price no longer enter the decision calculus directly.

Meyer and Robison (1991) go on to show in a more general model with additional variable inputs that changes in the mean or variability of output price will change land values, causing wealth effects that alter the firm's demand for land. Only in the case of constant absolute risk aversion will wealth effects not force this adjustment. Obviously the effects will have opposite directions for increasing absolute risk aversion as opposed to decreasing absolute risk aversion.

Intertemporal Model

The determination of agricultural *land values* received a lot of attention in the agricultural economics literature during the 1970s and 1980s. A gradual increase in land values from the 1930s until the 1970s was followed by rapid land value increases during the 1970s and then significant declines during the 1980s.

A number of attempts have been made to explain the large adjustments in national and state farmland values during the 1970s and 1980s. Feldstein (1980) illustrated that rapid inflation could cause large real-land price increases because of related declines in corporate equity. Melichar (1979) argued that capital gains and increased returns to farming largely explained the land value increases of the 1970s. Robison et al. (1985) found that nonfarm demand for land and inflation had major impacts on land values, while Phipps (1984) concluded that urbanization had a minor impact on farmland prices. Alston (1986) and Burt (1986) both concluded that changes in returns to farming were important but inflation was not.

Alternative explanations of land values are both accepted and rejected by the available empirical studies. The conflicting results may be partially attributed to different ad-hoc model specifications and assumptions, different land markets analyzed, and different time periods considered. To provide a more comprehensive assessment of the alternative explanations of land value changes, we will utilize a conceptual model presented in Just and Miranowski (1993) and their empirical results to illustrate a way to evaluate the competing hypotheses or explanations. Their analysis presents a comprehensive theoretical model that maintains plausible economic relationships among variables, utilizes extraneous information coupled with sensitivity analysis to establish several unknown parameters, and estimates the remaining parameters using conventional econometric techniques.

The model structure incorporates not only returns to farming (including government payments) but wealth appreciation and accumulation, the effects of inflation on debt and savings, opportunity rates of savings and debt, discount for risk, credit constraints, tax liabilities, transactions costs, and related economic variables.

A detailed derivation and intuitive description of the development of this land-price model can be found in Just and Miranowski (1993). The land market equilibrium equation for land price is:

$$\bar{P}_t = f_t \frac{xu^{a_t}\bar{P}_t^* + b_t\bar{R}_t + z\bar{A}_t \sum_t}{ua_t + c_t + vd_t + g_t - wf_t d_t} \tag{52}$$

and the variables are defined as follows:

$\bar{P}_t$ = average land price at beginning of t

f_t = 1 plus the rate of inflation at t

a_t = 1 minus the average farm income tax rate times the proportion of capital gains taxed

$\bar{P}_t^*$ = average expected land price at end of period for land held at beginning of t

b_t = 1 minus the average farm income tax rate

$\bar{A}_t$ = average farm size

$\sum_t$ = perceived variance of expected wealth per acre at end of t

c_t = net rate of interest on savings after income taxes

d_t = effective cost of debt

g_t = property tax rate per acre on farmland

u = proportion of land value that is capital gain

v = proportion of farmland subject to a binding savings constraint

w = 1 minus the finance charge rate on new debt times the proportion of farmland financed by debt

x = 1 minus the commission rate on transactions

z = coefficient of absolute risk version

Even though equation (52) may seem complicated, it reduces to the standard discounting formula:

$$\bar{P}_t = \frac{\bar{P}_t^* + \bar{R}_t^*}{1 + r_t} \tag{53}$$

when we assume away transactions costs, risk aversion, taxes, inflation, and credit market imperfections. Further, in equilibrium, $\bar{P}_t = \bar{P}_t^*$, then $\bar{P}_t = \bar{R}_t^*/r_t$.

Just and Miranowski (1993) provide an intuitive explanation of the terms in equation (52). The terms in the numerator are simply (1) the expected value of land appreciation adjusted for selling costs and expected capital gains taxes; (2) the net returns to holding land adjusted for income taxes; and (3) discounting for risk associated with farming and holding land. Likewise, the terms in the denominator are (1) the opportunity cost of investing a dollar; (2) the increased benefit from deferring until sale taxes from land apprecation; (3) the reduced return to savings due to current tax liability; (4) the added borrowing costs associated with debt financing; (5) the real-estate tax rate as an added cost of investment in land; and (6) the adjusted opportunity cost of land associated with a credit constraint. Thus, the key economic components of a theoretically consistent and comprehensive model are incorporated in a relatively straightforward specification.

An Empirical Illustration

Just and Miranowski (1993) used 1963 to 1984 data to estimate the model with results for Iowa being reported. The price changes were decomposed into the effects of various terms in the numerator and denominator. Land price expectations were the most important explanatory force, but the role of other variables was critical in explaining the wide swings in land prices because changes in land price expectations were explained by changes in previous prices and other variables.

With respect to the other variables, the increase in the rate of inflation, the opportunity cost of capital, and the increase in returns to farming were the major factors explaining the predicted 1973 price increase. The predicted 1974 increase was explained by the increase in the rate of inflation and more so by the opportunity cost of capital. Following the 1973 take-off period, much of land price appreciation through 1978 was due to the 1973–74 effects working through the price expectations effects.

In 1979, a second round of increases in the rate of inflation caused another wave of effects resembling 1973, with returns to farming having a comparable effect and the return to savings being another significant explanatory factor. The 1979 shock did not initiate as much land price inflation because rapid movements in land prices had increased perceived risk, thus lower land price expectations.

The model also began to predict a price decline in 1982 explained by the same inflation and opportunity-cost factors.

The results indicated that a consistent theoretical model could be used to explain land price changes, and that decomposing the effects can indicate which factors have been critical in explaining large price swings. In addition to improving our understanding of past land price changes, the framework should be helpful in anticipating future price movements as well as indicating potential periods of farm financial stress.

Land Improvements and Soil Conservation

Another factor that plays an important role in determining farmland values is *land improvements*. Such investments can be designed to improve soil drainage, facilitate cropping and irrigation, maintain or enhance soil productivity through conservation activities, or provide facilities and structures for specialized agricultural activities.

There have been several different approaches suggested to measure the extent of adoption or investment in conservation. Saliba and Bromley (1986) suggest using such measures as reductions in soil loss, proportion of cropland in minimum tillage, proportion of recommended conservation practices adopted, and responses to erosion control surveys. They conclude that the proximity to urban centers and high debt-to-asset ratios have a significant and negative effect on conservation effort. Farm type, farm income, and topography were positively related to adoption of conservation practices.

In another adoption study, Norris and Batie (1989) explored the factors that influence Virginia farmers' decisions to adopt conservation practices. They measured conservation effort in two ways: 1) investments in conservation excluding conservation tillage, and 2) total acres in minimum or no-till systems. Perception of an erosion problem, farm size, income, and existence of a conversion plan were observed to be significantly and positively related to investment. Significant negative influences were off-farm employment, debt level, ratio of rented to owned farmland, and tobacco acreage. A different pattern was detected for adoption of minimum or no-till systems. Significant factors with negative influences on the use of conservation tillage included age, income, off-farm employment, and erosion potential. Significant positive influences were intergenerational expectations and farm size.

On the national policy level, there has long been a concern over the adequacy of our efforts to protect the nation's soil resources. Federal and state conservation programs have been designed to stimulate private investment through cost-sharing and technical assistance for erosion control, drainage, and water conservation. Yet studies (e.g., Strohbehn, 1986; U.S. General Accounting Office, 1983) indicate that some of these programs are not particularly effective and efficient approaches to protecting our soil resources. Provisions of the 1985 Food Security Act and the 1990 Food Agriculture, Conservation and Trade Act are being implemented to enhance existing resource programs.

At the same time, farmers are operating in a more uncertain economic environment characterized by adjustments in input and output prices, domestic and international economic policies, and the move to more market-oriented commodity policies. In the midst of all this uncertainty, little attention has been focused on agricultural investment in general and on conservation and land improvement investment in particular. To provide a more complete understanding of the determinants of conservation investment and the impacts of government conservation programs, it is necessary to go beyond the models of conservation practice adoption (e.g., Ervin and Ervin, 1982; Lee and Stewart, 1983).

In isolating the factors determining conservation investment, it is important to recognize the profound impacts that macroeconomic variables have on the agricultural economy. Only in the last decade, beginning with Schuh's article on "The New Macroeconomics of Agriculture" (1976), has a serious effort been made to identify the role of macroeconomic and international factors in determining the fate of agricultural activity. Traditional theories of agricultural response are now being recast in terms of macroeconomic forces (e.g., Enders and Falk (1984), and the possibility that conservation program incentives are being swamped by macroeconomic variables has been raised (e.g., Miranowski, 1986).

This section draws heavily on work by Nielsen et al. (1989). A conservation and land improvement investment model is presented that is helpful in explaining farmer investment behavior and providing guidance in the national conservation policy arena.

Economic *investment models* suggest that factors such as the interest rates, incomes, and relative prices, influence farmers' decisions to invest in land improvements. Additional factors, such as conservation subsidies, tax incentives, and set-aside programs may also affect decision making by altering the expected value of future returns or costs of the investment project. Also, farm programs may have historically encouraged farmers to clear and drain lands for agriculture (Heimlich, 1988; Heimlich and Langner, 1986).

Government cost-share subsidies for conservation reduce the costs to farmers of installing land improvements. Idling land under Federal farm programs can have a similar effect. If installing a land improvement requires that acreage be temporarily taken out of production, participation in federal set-aside programs can help to reduce or eliminate the costs of foregone production from idling and acreage.[2]

At the margin, farmers will purchase additional land if the expected returns per dollar invested exceed the expected returns from an additional dollar of land improvements and vice versa. An analogous interpretation is Tobin's (1961, 1969) argument that the stock market valuation of firms represents the current assessment of the present discounted value (PDV) of future profits (Tobin, 1961, 1969). A stock price that is higher than the supply price of new capital goods will provide an incentive to invest. Likewise, the farmland price represents the PDV of future rents accruing to the soil resource, and conservation investments augment that soil stock.

As economic theory suggests, macroeconomic factors play potentially important roles. The real interest rate (approximated as the nominal or observed interest rate minus the expected inflation rate over the life of the asset) represents the real cost of borrowing funds. Increases in inflation and inflationary expectations and

---

[2] Farm operators could also take advantage of diversion programs to disinvest in (remove) some improvements, such as soil conservation practices, if the operator believes that profits will be greater without old improvements.

a decrease in the real interest rate reduce the cost of borrowing and should increase external financing of investments.

If productivity losses over a reasonable planning horizon are small (Crosson and Stout, 1983) compared with investment costs and if farmers do not consider off-farm costs in their production decisions, as economic logic suggests, then why do they invest in conservation structures? The farmland market should provide farmers an economic incentive to conserve their soil if the value of future (long-term) productivity losses were capitalized into land values.

Practicing conservation may have other economic incentives. Survey evidence indicates that farmers adopt conservation tillage primarily because it is profitable (Magleby et al. (1984). Similarly, structures such as terraces help to conserve water, thereby reducing irrigation costs in some areas.

Some evidence indicates that *noneconomic factors* may influence a farmer's decisions about soil conservation investment. For instance, Ervin and Ervin (1982) found that stewardship (the belief that farmers have a moral obligation to protect natural resources) is highly associated with the use of conservation practices. This stewardship ethic may be related to what is known as the option value or the bequest value in natural resource economics literature. In the second appraisal of U.S. soil, water, and related resources, in response to the Soil and Water Resources Conservation Act, the U.S. Department of Agriculture (1987) reviewed the literature on the adoption of conservation practices. They concluded that although economic factors are significant in the decision to adopt conservation practices, sociological factors are also important and, for some farmers and landowners, even outweigh economic considerations.

Accounting for the adoption of, and investments in, soil conservation are difficult, and most adoption studies have not explained farmers' behavior well. One major difficulty lies in defining and measuring adoption. For example, sometimes conservation practices are defined in a binary (yes/no) fashion, while at other times, they are measured as the total acreage covered by a particular practice or as actual erosion rates. Also, the types of practices included are inconsistent across studies. Although the adoption of different practices should not be modeled as independent decisions. Most studies were carried out for a particular region and at one point in time (Ervin and Ervin, 1982). Thus, the studies have had a local orientation and do not lend themselves to evaluating the response of conservation investment behavior to changing economic conditions or expectations.

An Empirical Illustration

Nielsen et al. (1989) fitted investments in land improvements to a pooled time-series/cross-sectional regression model of aggregate data.

Assuming that farmers maximize the PDV of future net returns, a simple linear approximation of the investment function was fitted. It incorporated a varying expected cost of capital with expectations of future net returns and other factors hypothesized to influence the investment decision. Although the model is closer to the stock-oriented than to the flow-oriented models of the literature, it explicitly includes expectations and policy variables hypothesized to affect land improvement investment decisions.

More specifically, the model estimated was

$$I_t = b_0 + b_1(_{t-1}Y_t^e) + b_2(_{t-1}r_{t+i}^e) + b_3A_t + b_4P_t + b_5(K_{t-1}) + b_6S_t \qquad (54)$$

where

I_t = land improvement investments
$_{t-1}Y_t^e$ = expected income in the current period
$_{t-1}r_{t+i}^e$ = expected long-term interest rate
A_t = acreage idled under Government programs
P_t = price of land improvements relative to the price of land
K_{t-1} = value of last period's capital stock
S_t = government subsidy for investing in conservation

Expected income was hypothesized to positively influence investment expenditures, including those for land improvements. Idled acreage was hypothesized to be positively associated with investment because structures and drainage can be constructed during the normal growing season. The relative differential over time between the price of investing in improvements and the price of land reflected that the two types of investments were viewed as competing alternatives.

Since investment theories address net investment, conventional capital investment models include a lagged value of the capital stock to compensate for using gross investment rather than net investment as the dependent variable. Because adequate data were not available to measure existing conservation and land improvement capital stock, a variable measuring the need for capital $(1 - K)$ was developed to capture conservation, drainage, and land clearing "needs." Government cost-share programs, including ACP, should promote conservation and positively affect investments in land improvements, but cost-share funds can be used to support conservation tillage and cover crop establishment as well as structures.

If farmers' income expectations were more optimistic, they were slightly more likely to invest in land improvements. The expected interest rate coefficient was negative. The value suggested that a 1-percentage-point increase in the expected real interest rate led to a $9 million decrease in land improvement investments, or about 3 percent of the mean level of investments during the period.

Set-aside acreage appears to be strongly associated with investments in conservation and land improvements. The results support the hypothesis that idling acreage reduces the installation cost and, therefore, encourages land improvements.

The ratio of the price of land improvements to the price of land was also significant in explaining land improvement investments. Thus, land improvements and conservation apparently become more attractive to the farmer as the farmland values increase relative to the price of investment goods. Land characteristics or "needs" also appear to significantly influence conservation and land improvement investments.

From a policy perspective, the results have some important implications. First, the income parameter estimate indicated that farmers invest in land improvements and conservation in response to expected income, although the response appeared to be small. If incomes are expected to rise, then the expected returns to such investments increase and provide incentives for further conservation and land improvement investments and vice versa. Second, the expected real interest rate had the hypothesized inverse effect on land improvement and conservation investments. Third, as farmland prices increase relative to investment costs, farmers and landowners have added incentives to install conservation and land improvements. Fourth, acreage diversion and set-aside programs that idle land during the growing season (the period most suitable for installing practices) apparently provide positive incentives for additional investment, all other things equal, by reducing the opportunity costs of such investments. Finally, a $1 cost-share subsidy induced additional private investment in land improvements.

LAND POLICIES

Following the Homestead Act and related land settlement activities during the 19th century, farmland use and ownership have largely been under the control of state and local entities. Public management of some western rangeland by the U.S. Department of Agriculture's Forest Service and the U.S. Department of Interior's Bureau of Land Management are exceptions to the general rule of state and local control. Although there have been legislative proposals in the U.S. Congress to implement a national land use policy, such efforts have not culminated in new legislation. As discussed elsewhere in this chapter the plethora of state and local policies addressing a wide range of use and ownership issues including open space, foreign ownership, tax preferences, zoning, conservation, and input use practices makes it unfeasible to review or even summarize the alternatives. Rather, this section will focus only on recent land policy issues judged to be of national significance.

Probably the most sweeping "national land use legislation" in recent history is the Conservation Title of the 1985 Food Security Act (FSA) as well as the modifications and extensions included in the Conservation Title of the 1990 Food, Agriculture, Conservation, and Trade Act (FACTA). Even though these titles were not intended specifically as land use policies, in effect, they will be guiding agricultural land use as well as farming practices into the 21st century. Thus, the focus of this section will be on the major provisions of these titles and related policy actions.

Conservation Title

Swampbuster

The *Swampbuster* provision, Title XII C. of the FSA of 1985, was enacted to improve consistency between two goals: farm income and price support and wetland conservation (Heimlich and Langner, 1986). Agricultural activities accounted for 87 percent of wetlands lost between the mid-1950s and mid-1970s, the latest estimates available (Frayer et al., 1983). During the same period, cropland idled under farm programs averaged 20 percent of cropland used for crops.

The "Swampbuster" provision denied farm program benefits to producers who converted wetlands to agricultural production, attempting to improve consistency between government farm program provisions and protecting wetlands from conversion. In other words, eligibility for participation in government farm programs was now contingent on the conservation and use of land resources endowed with particular characteristics.

Heimlich (1988) analyzed the extent to which denial of benefits under the swampbuster provision might influence owners of wetlands highly subject to agricultural conversion. Using data on the extent and location of wetlands, he identified 17 million acres of wetlands highly subject to agricultural conversion out of the 78 million acres of rural nonfederal wetlands inventoried by the Soil Conservation Service. Wetlands highly subject to agricultural conversion were identified based on wetland conversion potential in counties with large percentage increases in cropland. The leverage provided by government payments was proxied by direct government payments relative to net farm income in each country, assuming that the swampbuster provision would be more effective in preventing wetland conversion when government payments constituted a higher proportion of net farm income.

Heimlich (1988) found that only about a third of the wetlands highly subject to agricultural conversion (6 million acres) were located in counties where government payments were more than half of net farm income in 1984. Likewise, temporal cycles in the agricultural economy, as well as definitional, implementation, and enforcement problems, have hampered swampbuster effectiveness to date. For example, farm program participation tends to increase when prices are depressed because market demand is weak, and decrease when prices increase because demand is strong.

Sodbuster

Like the *Swampbuster* provision, the *Sodbuster* provision of the Conservation Title of the FSA denied farm program benefits to participants who broke sod or plowed grass that had been in pastures or range. By the time the legislation was enacted in 1985, there was little economic incentive for landowners or tenants to convert grassland to the production of cultivated crops. Thus, there has been little assessment of the impacts of this provision. Heimlich (1985) did provide an analysis of the potential incentives for "Sodbusting" prior to the enactment of the legislation. The potential impacts of this provision in the future will depend on two factors: 1) market prices for commodities and the incentive to expand production and 2) the attractiveness of participation in commodity programs. If commodity programs continue in the current direction of market-orientation, the benefits of participation may be outweighed by the private benefits of "sodbusting" when world market prices of commodities increase. Thus Sodbuster's effectiveness as a land use policy is highly dependent on the attractiveness of participation in farm commodity programs.

Conservation Compliance

The FSA included another provision, *Conservation Compliance*, in the Conservation Title that could have more far-reaching effects. This provision denies farm program benefits to farmers who are not farming highly erodible land according to an approved conservation plan. Implementation of compliance was to begin in 1990 and be fully implemented by 1995. Conservation plans have been developed for all land requiring such a plan, but many of these plans are now under revision. The expected impacts of Conservation Compliance are difficult to ascertain. First, practices such as conservation tillage will satisfy the requirements of an approved plan in some situations, but certain cases may require withdrawing land from crop production to provide sufficient erosion control. Second, compliance is again tied to denial of farm program benefits. If farm program participation is not sufficiently attractive, the costs of complying may easily exceed the benefits of participation, rendering the provision ineffective in situations where the social benefits of control could be quite large. The FACTA did introduce new provisions that provide for graduated reductions in program benefits in situations where the violators act in good faith, include set aside, diverted, and conserving use land if highly erodible under conservation plans, and extends the implementation period on CRP lands following contract expiration if structures are required. Additionally, the CRP will set aside 1 million acres in 1994 and 1995 for enrollment of highly erodible land that cannot be treated with a conservation plan to satisfy Conservation Compliance requirements.

Conservation Reserve Program

The Conservation Reserve Program (CRP) is a voluntary cropland retirement program established by the FSA of 1985. The USDA pays landowners and operators an annual payment as well as one-half the cost of cover establishment in exchange for placing highly erodible cropland into the CRP for 10 years. The law required the Secretary of Agriculture to place 40–45 million acres into the CRP by the end of the 1990 crop year of which one-eighth was to be planted to trees if practicable. Although the acreage and tree planting goals were not met, nearly 34 million acres were enrolled by the end of 1990. The primary goal of the program was to reduce soil erosion on highly erodible cropland, but there were also secondary objectives including protection of agricultural productivity, reducing sedimentation, improving water quality, fostering wildlife habitat, curbing surplus commodity production, and providing income support to farmers.

The 1990 FACTA established the Environmental Conservation Acreage Reserve Program (ECARP) composed of the CRP and the Wetlands Reserve Program (WRP). The U.S. Department of Agriculture is required to enroll 40 to 45 million acres in ECARP by the end of 1995, including the 34 million acres enrolled in the CRP between 1986 and 1990. The CRP provisions expand the definitions of land to be included. Additionally, the Department has revised the

CRP bidding system to include environmental criteria in addition to highly erodible land. The new WRP is designed to restore and protect wetlands. To the extent practicable, the Secretary will enroll one million acres during 1991 to 1995. Rather than 10-year contracts like the CRP, participants must agree to permanent or 30-year easements. Participants must employ a conservation plan to restore and protect the functional value of the wetland. Landowners will receive technical assistance, cost-sharing payments, and 5 to 20 annual payments in return. The landowner does have the option under a permanent easement to take a single lump-sum payment.

The original intent of the FSA was to use a bidding system to acquire the CRP land on a competitive basis. Ultimately, the bid system became an offer system with maximum acceptable rental rates (MARRs) for each pool or subpool. Naturally, the bids gravitated to the MARRs.

Potential natural resource benefits from the CRP have been estimated by Ribaudo (1989) and Ribaudo et al. (1990). If 45 million acres of highly erodible or environmentally sensitive cropland were removed from crop production, the natural resource benefits were estimated to range from 6 to 14 billion dollars in 1990 present value terms. The potential benefits included soil productivity, water quality, air quality, wildlife, and groundwater supplies. The magnitude of benefits is dependent on the definition of highly erodible land and the regional distribution of CRP lands (see Box 10.2).

The impacts of this set of FSA and FACTA provisions on current and future farmland use are significant. The magnitude of the impacts of the CRP with over 34 million acres retired under 10-year contracts has already been recognized. For example, over 60 percent of the CRP land is located in the Great Plains States, where implementation of the program has had an impact on agricultural land use, rural communities, and farmland values (Young and Osborn, 1990). The post-1990 bid acceptance scheme and the broader ECARP mandate will likely change the distribution of future land enrolled in the program. As noted, the land use impacts of the other provisions will depend on the profitability of expanding the cropland base through "swampbusting" and "sodbusting" coupled with the relative attractiveness of farm program participation, particularly as it applies to conservation compliance.

Technology and Government Programs

Schultz (1951) in his classic article on the declining economic importance of agricultural land concluded that as a country's economy grows, its share of aggregate resources devoted to agricultural production declines. But in developed countries, agriculture is also characterized by pervasive government intervention and efforts to transfer income to the sector, possibly attempting to forstall the inevitable withdrawal of resources from agriculture. Technological change is the predominant factor altering the level and distribution of returns to the factors of production, especially land. Historically, technological change has diminished the share of land in the value of agricultural production. Thus the relative importance of farmland in production has been decreasing over time. Much of the impetus for technological change has come from public sector research supported and undertaken primarily by the U.S. Department of Agriculture and the Land Grant University complex. Simultaneously, government farm programs have attempted to maintain farm incomes (and land values) through acreage controls and price support payments.

Restricting acreage or land as a factor of production has several effects. First, the benefits of commodity programs are transferred to landowners through capitalization into land values (Offutt and Shoemaker, 1988). Second, the substitution of other inputs, including pesticides, fertilizers, higher-yielding varieties, and capital, may be encouraged. Third, the relatively higher price of land further induces the development of land-saving technologies, which further exacerbates the decline in the relative share of land. Finally, the substituted inputs are frequently the source of potential environmental damage through increased residual loadings. Offutt and Shoemaker conclude that farm programs have reduced the rate of decline in land's share of the value of production owing to technological change, but the relative importance of farmland will continue decreasing over time.

REFERENCES

Abel, A.B. "Empirical Investment Equations: An Integrative Framework." *Carnegie Rochester Conference Series on Public Policy* 12:39–91, 1980.

Allen, D. and D. Lueck. "Farmland Leasing in Modern Agriculture." *Choices* 1:30–31, 1992.

Alonso, W. *Location and Land Use*. Cambridge, MA: Harvard University Press, 1964.

Alston, J.M. "An Analysis of Growth of U.S. Farmland Prices, 1963–82." *American Journal of Agricultural Economics* 68:1–9, 1986.

Appelbaum, E. and E. Katz. "Measures of Risk Aversion and Comparative Statistics of Industry Equilibrium." *American Economic Review* 76:524–529, 1986.

Boxley, R.F. "Farmland Ownership and the Distribution of Land Earnings." *Agricultural Economics Research* 37:40–44, 1985.

Brooks, D.H. *Land Use in Economic theory: Principles and Prospects*. ERS Staff Report No. AGE870806, U.S. Dept Agr., Econ. Res. Serv., September 1987.

Burt, O.R. "Econometric Modeling of the Capitalization Formula for Farmland Prices." *American Journal of Agricultural Economics* 68:10–26, 1986.

Castle, E.N., M.M. Kelso, J.B. Stevens and H.H. Stoevener. "Natural Resource Economics, 1946–75." In L.R. Martin (ed): *A Survey of Agricultural Economics Literature, Vol. 3*. Minneapolis: University of Minnesota Press, 1981.

Chueng, S. *The Theory of Share Tenancy*. Chicago: University of Chicago Press, 1969.

Ciriacy-Wantrup, S.V. *Resource Conservation: Economics and Policies. 3rd ed.* Berkeley and Los Angeles: University of California, Div. Agr. Sci. 1968.

Crosson, P. and A. Stout. *Productivity Effects of Cropland Erosion in the United States*. Baltimore: Johns Hopkins University Press, 1983.

Dasgupta, P.S. and G.M. Heal. *Economic Theory and Exhaustible Resources.* Welwyn: Cambridge University Press, 1979.

Daugherty, A.B. *Major Uses of Land in the United States: 1987.* AER-643. U.S. Dept. Agr., Econ. Res. Serv., January 1991.

Dovring, F. *Land Economics.* Boston: Breton Publishing, 1987, 532 pp.

Enders, W. and B. Falk. "A Microeconomic Test of Money Neutrality." *Review of Economics and Statistics* 66:666–669, 1984.

Ervin, C.A. and D.E. Ervin. "Factors Affecting the Use of Soil Conservation Practices: Hypotheses, Evidence and Policy Implications." *Land Economics* 58:256–264, 1982.

Ervin, D.A. and J.W. Mill. "Agricultural Land Markets and Soil Erosion: Policy Relevance and Conceptual Issues." *American Journal of Agricultural Economics* 67:938–942, 1985.

Fischel, W.A. "The Urbanization of Agricultural Land: A Review of the National Agricultural Lands Study." *Land Economics* 58:236–259, 1982.

Feldstein, M. "Inflaton, Portfolio Choice, and the Prices of Land and Corporate Stock." *American Journal of Agricultural Economics* 62:910–916, 1980.

Frayer, W.E., T.J. Monahan, D.C. Bowden, and F.A. Graybill. Status and Trends of Wetlands and Deepwater Habitats in the Coterminous United States, 1950's to 1970's. Colorado State University, Dept. of Forest and Wood Sciences. Fort Collins, CO, 1983.

Gardner, K. and R. Barrows. "The Impact of Soil Conservation Investments on Land Prices." *American Journal of Agricultural Economics* 67:943–947, 1985.

Hallagan, W. "Self-Selection by Contractual Choice and the Theory of Share-cropping." *Bell Journal of Economics* 9:344–354, 1978.

Heimlich, R.E. *Sodbusting: Land Use Change and Farm Programs.* AER-536. U.S. Dept. Agr., Econ. Res. Serv., June 1985.

Heimlich, R. E. The Swampbuster Provision: Implementation and Impact. In P.J. Stuber, coord. *Proceedings of the National Symposium on Protection of Wetlands from Agricultural Impacts.* Biological Report 88(16). Washington, D.C.: U.S. Department of Interior, Fish and Wildlife Service. 1988, pp. 87–94.

Heimlich, R.E. "Metropolitan Agriculture: Farming in the City's Shadow." *APA Journal* 457–466, 1989.

Heimlich, R.E. and L.L. Langner. *Swampbusting: Wetland Conversion and Farm Programs.* AER-551. U.S. Dept. Agr. Agr., Econ. Res. Serv., August 1986.

Hiebert, L.D. "Uncertainty and Incentive Effects in Share Contracts." *American Journal of Agricultural Economics* 60:536–539, 1978.

Hochman, E., E. Pines, and D. Zilberman. "The Effects of Pollution Taxation on the Pattern of Resource Allocation: The Downstream Diffusion Case." *Quarterly Journal of Economics* 91(4):625–638, 1977.

Howe, C.W. *Natural Resource Economics.* New York: John Wiley & Sons, 1979.

Jones, J. and C.H. Barnard. *Farm Real Estate: Historical Series Data 1950–85.* SB-738. U.S. Dept. Agr., Econ. Res. Serv., December 1985.

Just, R.E. and J.A. Miranowski. "Understanding Farmland Price Changes." *American Journal of Agricultural Economics,* 74:(forthcoming), 1993.

Lee, L.K. and W. H. Stewart. "Landownership and the Adoption of Minimum Tillage." *American Journal of Agricultural Economics* 65:256–264, 1983.

Lind, R.C. *Discounting for Time and Risk in Energy Policy.* Washington, DC: Resources for the Future, 1982.

Magleby, R., D. Gadsby, D. Colacicco, and J. Thigpen. "Conservation Tillage: Who Uses It Now?" In *Conservation Tillage: Strategies for the Future.* Conservation Tillage Information Centre, W. Lafayette, 1984.

McConnell, K.E. "An Economic Model of Soil Conservation." *AJAE* 65:83–89, 1983.

Melichar, E. "Capital Gains versus Current Income in the Farming Sector." *American Journal of Agricultural Economics* 61:1085–1092, 1979.

Meyer, J. and L.J. Robison. "The Aggregate Effects of Risk in the Agricultural Sector." *American Journal of Agricultural Economics* 73:18–24, 1991.

Miranowski, J.A. "Macroeconomics of Soil Conservation." In S.B. Lovejoy and T.L. Napier (eds.): *Conserving Soil: Insights from Socioeconomic Research.* Ankeny, IA: Soil Conservation Society of America, 1986.

Miranowski, J.A. "Impacts of Productivity Loss on Crop Production and Management in a Dynamic Economic Model." *American Journal of Agricultural Economics.* 66:61–71, 1984.

Miranowski, J.A. and R.L. Bender. "Impact of erosion control policies on wildlife habitat on private lands." *Journal of Soil and Water Conservation* 37:288–291, 1982.

Miranowski, J.A. and B.D. Hammes. "Implicit Prices for Soil Characteristics in Iowa." *American Journal of Agricultural Economics* 66:379–383, 1984.

Nielsen, E.G., J.A. Miranowski, and M.J. Morehart. *Investments in Soil Conservation and Land Improvements: Factors Explaining Farmers' Decisions.* AER-601. U.S. Dept. Agr., Econ. Res. Serv., January 1989.

Newberry, D.M. "The State Leasing Theory: Conflicts Among Different Models of Decision Making Under Uncertainty." In J. DeBraal and G. Wunderlich (eds.): Rents and Rental Practices in U.S. Agriculture. *Proceedings of a Workshop on Agricultural Rents.* Farm Foundation, Chicago: 1983.

Norris, P.E. and S.S. Batie. "Virginia Farmers' Soil Conservation Decisons: An Appication of TOBIT Analysis." *Southern Journal of Agricultural Economics* 19:79–90, 1987.

Offut, S. and R. Shoemaker. *Farm Programs Slow Technology-Induced Decline in Land's Importance.* TB-1745. U.S. Dept. Agri., Econ. Res. Serv., May 1988.

Palmquist, R.B. "Land as a Differentiated Factor of Production: A Hedonic Model and Its Implications for Welfare Measurement." *Land Economics* 65:23–28, 1989.

Palmquist, R.B. and L.E. Danielson. "A Hedonic Study of the Effects of Erosion Control and Drainage on Farmland Values." *American Journal of Agricultural Economics* 71:55–62, 1989.

Phipps, T.T. "Land Prices and Farm-Based Returns." *American Journal of Agricultural Economics* 66:422–429, 1984.

Randall, A. and E.N. Castle. "Land Resources and Land Markets." In A.V. Kneese and J.L. Sweeney (eds.): *Handbook of Natural Resource and Energy Economics, Vol. II.* New York: North-Holland Press, 1985.

Ribaudo, M., D. Colacicco, L. Langner, S. Piper, and G. Schaible. "Natural Resources and User Benefits from the Conservation Reserve Program." ERS, USDA. Agricultural Economic Report No. 627. 1990.

Ribaudo, M. "Water Quality Benefits from the Conservation Reserve Program." ERS, USDA. Agricultural Economic Report No. 606. 1989.

Robison, L.J. and P.J. Barry. *The Competitive Firm's Response to Risk.* New York: Macmillan Publishing, 1987, pp. 163–174.

Robison, L.J., D.A. Lins, and R. Ven Kataraman. "Cash Rents and Land Values in U.S. Agriculture." *American Journal of Agricultural Economics* 67:794–805, 1985.

Saliba, B. and D. Bromley. "Soil Management Decisions—How Should They Be Compared and What Variables Influence Them?" *North Central Journal of Agricultural Economics* 8(2):305–317, 1986.

Schuh, G.E. "The New Macroeconomics of Agriculture." *American Journal of Agricultural Economics* 58:803–811, 1976.

Schultz, T.W. "The Declining Economic Importance of Agricultural Land." *Economic Journal* 61:725–740, 1951.

Shaffer, J.D. and A.A. Schmid. "Community Economics: A Framework for Analysis of Community Problems." Unpublished Manuscript, Department of Agricultural Economics, Michigan State University, 1985.

Shortle, J.S. and J.A. Miranowski. *J. of Environmental Economics and Management* 14:99–111, 1987.

Shortle, J.S. and J.A. Miranowski. "Dynamic vs. Static Models of Erosion Control Policy Research." *Journal of Northeastern Agricultural Economics Council* 12:7–12, 1983.

Stiglitz, J.E. "A Neoclassical Analysis of the Economics of Natural Resources.' In V.K. Smith (ed.): *Scarcity and Growth Reconsidered.* Baltimore: Johns Hopkins University Press, 1979.

Stiglitz, J.E. "Incentives and Risk Sharing in Sharecropping." *Review of Economic Studies* 42:219–255, 1974.

Strohbehn, R. (ed.). *An Economic Analysis of USDA Erosion Control Programs: A New Perspective.* AER-560. U.S. Dept. of Agri., Econ. Res. Serv., August 1986.

Sutinen, J.G. "The Rational Choice of Share Leasing and Implications for Efficiency." *American Journal of Agricultural Economics* 57:613–621, 1975.

Takayama, T. and G. Judge. *Spatial and Temporal Price and Allocation Models.* Amsterdam: North-Holland Press, 1971.

Tobin, J. "A General Equilibrium Approach to Monetary Theory." *Journal of Money, Credit and Banking* 1:15–29, 1969.

Tobin, J. "Money, Capital and Other Stores of Value." *American Economic Review, Papers and Proceedings* 51:26–37, 1961.

Von Thunen, J.H. *Von Thunen's Isolated State.* Oxford, England: Pergamon Press, 1966.

U.S. Department of Agriculture. *Soil and Water Resources Conservation Act, Second Appraisal. Soil, Water and Related Resources in the United States: Status, Condition, and Analysis of Trends.* Public review draft, July–Aug. 1987.

U.S. Department of Agriculture. *Agricultural Land Values and Markets Situation and Outlook Report.* AR-26. Economic Research Service, Washington D.C., 1992a.

U.S. Department of Agriculture. *Agricultural Resources: Cropland, Water, and Conservation Situation and Outlook Report.* AR-27. Economic Research Service, September 1992b and earlier issues.

U.S. Department of Agriculture. *Agricultural Statistics.* National Agricultural Statistics Service, 1991.

U.S. Department of Commerce. *Statistical Abstract of the United States.* Economics and Statistics Admin. Bureau of Census, Washington D.C., 1991 and earlier years.

U.S. Executive Office of the President. *Environmental Quality*. The Council on Environmental Quality, Washington D.C., 1991 and earlier years.

U.S. General Accounting Office. *Agriculture's Soil Conservation Programs Miss Full Potential in Fight Against Erosion*. GAO/RLED 84-48. November 1983.

Vesterby, M. and R.E. Heimlich. "Land Use and Demographic Change: Results from Fast-Growth Counties." *Land Economics* 67:279–291, 1989.

Young, C.E. and C.T. Osborn. *The Conservation Research Program; An Economic Assessment*. AER-626. U.S. Department of Agriculture, Economic Research Service, Washington, D.C., February 1990.

10

Agricultural Resource Policy

KATHERINE REICHELDERFER AND RANDALL A. KRAMER

When Adam Smith wrote *The Wealth of Nations*, he envisioned a world in which the invisible hand of the marketplace would guide the allocation of resources in the world economy. Two hundred years later, even the Marxist-inspired political systems of Eastern Europe are discovering the advantages of decentralized economic decision making afforded by markets. Yet all of the world's governments continue to intervene in markets in varying ways to influence the allocation of natural and other resources. A "policy" is any intervention of the goverment in the economy, regulation[1] is the outcome of policy, and, for a long laundry list of reasons, agriculture is among the most heavily regulated sectors in developed economies. A variety of the policies employed to achieve intervention in the agricultural sector have as strong or stronger implications for agricultural resource allocation, quality, and value than do independent natural resources and environmental policies. The full set of resource/environmental and agricultural policies affecting agriculture's resource base makes the government's hand highly visible and sufficiently distorts market signals that Smith's "invisible hand" might best be considered *decarnate*.

Taken together, the combination of resource/environmental and agricultural policies affecting agricultural resources often seems (and sometimes is) contradictory. It is easy to question, for example, a set of policies that on the one hand sets aside productive farmland in order to reduce excess commodity supplies and, on the other hand, subsidizes the use of irrigation water to increase agricultural productivity; of policies that concurrently subsidize farmer adoption of soil conservation practices and support the prices of highly erosive crops; or those that link farm income payments to the production of a small number of commodities while funding research and development of "alternative crops." The source, justification, and analysis of implications for natural resources of such paradoxical

---

[1] The term "regulation," is used throughout this chapter in the generic sense, implying government intervention in the economy regardless of the form or effect of policy instruments employed to achieve such intervention.

policy sets and their more straightforward counterparts are the subjects of this chapter.

Our objective is to describe the analytical frameworks that have proved most useful in conducting analysis of policies that mutually affect natural resources and environment and the agricultural sector. We first attempt to explain why the agricultural sectors of developed economies in general, and the United States in particular, tend to be so highly regulated. We then describe the policy processes, adopting public choice theory to explain how decisions are made and where economic analysis can play a role in predicting policy outcomes. The theoretical and analytical linkages between public choice and economic welfare measures are presented to construct the conceptual framework for agricultural resource policy analysis. This background forms the context for a subsequent overview of predominant agricultural and resource policies, their historical objectives, and the range of policy instruments they can or do typically employ. Once both the theoretical and actual policy backgrounds are established, we proceed to apply policy analytical concepts to examine the interrelationships among, and evaluate the implications of, various policies and programs affecting agricultural resources. The chapter concludes with a review of the roles of the economist in the agricultural resource policy process.

THE BASIS FOR GOVERNMENT INTERVENTION IN AGRICULTURE

> Most Americans agree that the unique nature of agriculture—the lengthy production cycle, dependency on the weather, susceptibility to price swings, etc.—justifies a certain level of government involvement.
>
> E. "Kika" de la Garza
> Chairman, House Agriculture Committee
> *Roll Call, 1989*

Is agriculture really that different from most other resource-based industries? Investigative reporter and humorist P.J. O'Rourke has noted that arguments similar to those made by Representative de la Garza for government intervention in agriculture could apply as well to "the unique nature of selling Mazda Miatas," and asks, "Why isn't the government giving (billions of dollars) to car dealerships?" (O'Rourke, 1990). But in fact, the combination of a range of sociological, economic, and political characteristics unique to agriculture has created a situation whereby government intervention is not only more likely than in other industries, but also more tenacious. Retrospection on these factors and their implications for agricultural policy may be found in most reviews of agricultural policy (see, for example: Brandow, 1977; Cochran, 1979; Cochran and Ryan, 1976). Here we briefly note a few with special implications for the interaction between agriculture and resource/ environmental policies.

On the fundamental level, American philosophical thought continues to revere especially the virtues and contribution of the nation's farmers—particularly its "family farmers." The notion of agrarian fundamentalism, what some call "the agrarian myth," (Thompson, 1988), originated in early stages of economic development, depicts agriculture as "a way of life" that is more important socially than other industries and, while increasingly inapplicable in an objective sense to modern agriculture, continues to play a strong role in justifying agricultural support (Bonnen and Browne, 1989). *Agrarian fundamentalism* has relevance to agricultural resource issues in that it provides a socially acceptable rationale for government intervention which preserves human resources in the agricultural sector, even when those resources are unnecessary to meet agricultural demand and even if they result in inefficient use of natural resources. In other words, the "myth" perpetuates political tension between policies that would shrink the size of the agricultural sector and those that would increase sectoral efficiency. It is the fundamental basis for conflict created and intervention justified by the following agricultural economic traits.

Randomness and Uncertainty

As the lead-in quote from de la Garza indicated, agriculture is an industry characterized generally by a high degree of risk associated with climatic, pest, and other natural vagaries. A range of policy interventions, such as government inventory management, subsidized crop insurance, and water reservoir management, have been designed in attempts to reduce risks. Others, such as futures markets, have evolved to help manage inherent randomness and uncertainty. Despite these measures, agricultural prices remain vulnerable to wide variation owing to unpredictable fluctuations in global climate and demand. With particular regard to agricultural resources, the economic insecurity created by such uncertainty may cause farmers to discount heavily the long-term benefits of soil and water conservation.

Rigidities, Asset Fixity, and Imperfect Markets

Agriculture is unique because of the importance of land as its principal capital input. Because the supply of arable land is *fixed* and *lumpy*, "retooling" an agricultural "plant" requires that one either await the availability of land for purchase or change the mix of nonland capital inputs complementing a given quantity of land. Since other agricultural capital, including machinery, equipment, and commodity-specific management skill, is also lumpy and difficult to replace, agriculture as a sector tends to respond less rapidly to economic signals than more adaptable industries. Exacerbating the fixity problem is agriculture's failure to provide timely and even distributed credit and information. The combination of rigidities and imperfect credit and information markets has long been used to justify government intervention aimed at easing adjustment to changing market conditions. This intervention includes rural development policies, the provision of credit, through the farm credit system, and the provision of information through the systems of federal, state, and local extension services.

High Rates of Technical Change and Inelastic Demand

Agriculture has experienced a high rate of technical change, brought about in part by public agricultural research and investment policies. The rate of productivity growth in agriculture, about 2 percent per year through the 1980s, is not in itself unusual relative to other industries. However, the price inelastic demand facing producers of most domestically consumed agricultural goods has meant that the lower prices resulting from productivity gains do not translate into higher revenues. On the contrary, all but the earliest adopters of new agricultural technology are apt to experience income losses. Also, because of income inelasticity of demand for basic foodstuffs, once demand has been saturated, continued increases in per capita income do not result in increased farm revenues. These phenomena contribute to political pressure to maintain farm incomes as technology progresses and nonfarm income rises. With respect to resources, this means that the natural resource adjuncts to excess human resources are also prevented from exiting the sector, even under conditions of oversupply.

Public Goods, Externalities, and Exhaustible Resources

As per capita income rises, rates of growth in the demand for income elastic goods, including, importantly, environmental amenities, are increasingly likely to outstrip any growth in demand for agricultural goods. But the insensitivity of demand for food to farm prices means that consumers have little or no independent market power with respect to the environmental repercussions of farming. One cannot, after all, boycott the very staff of life regardless of the environmental outcome of its production. Thus government is called upon to intervene as a representative of nonmarket demands relating to agriculture; to internalize the external costs of production, to act as caretaker for public goods, and to reconcile private, short-term use of exhaustible resources with public, long-term conservation goals. The nature of modern agricultural externalities—especially those affecting perceived food and drinking water safety—are viewed uniquely by the public as justifying strong government intervention. So, too, is the exhaustible nature of certain soil and water resources seen as a good reason for intervention. But, very unlike the situation describing other industries, where external effects on capital typically are realized by individuals outside of the sector, agricultural landowners possess a legal right to use in any fashion, including degradation or exploitation, the very land and water assets about whose quality the public may be concerned. This means that government has been called upon to arbitrate conflicts between private property right preservation and the felt right by the public to an undegraded but privately owned resource base. Of course, not all agricultural land is privately owned. With around 29 percent of commercial forestland and 37 percent of American range and pastureland publicly owned, with rights leased or concessions for use granted to private producers, government is heavily involved itself as a resource manager.

Heterogeneity

In dealing with all of the previously reviewed agricultural market failures, policy decision makers are faced with a highly diverse set of agricultural producers and market participants. Producers vary by size, management capability, commodity specificity, asset quality, geographic location, and location with respect to the probability and value of external effects of production. This heterogeneity is a problem because it is difficult to design policies, particularly in the area of environmental protection, that are appropriate in meeting the unique circumstances of a majority of producers. Furthermore, it creates immense distributional and equity problems. Because what is "good" for one group of agricultural constituents may hurt another group, new policies are often perceived as required to offset the distributional consequences of initial actions. This explains why agriculture is famous for (and is, in fact, the origin of the term) "pork barreling."

What Form Intervention?

In choosing to deal with the problems described by these characteristics, government intervention can take any number of different forms. In general, policy instruments may operate in the agricultural product market or in factor markets. In any market, regulation may either be directed at the prices of goods or may dictate control over the quality, allocation, or allowable uses of output or factor goods. Each approach and each particular instrument has different implications for the regulated agricultural sector, the legislators who develop the regulations, regulating agencies, and consumers and other actors associated through markets or external effects with the regulated industry. Thus the form that intervention takes is critical in determining which groups gain or lose and by how much from regulatory decisions.

In developed economies whose agricultural sectors share the characteristics previously described, intervention typically takes the general form of subsidies that enhance farm income. Such subsidies may be direct, as in the case of subsidized credit and insurance to resolve the problems of imperfect markets for those important factors, or indirect, as in the case of quotas on commodity supply to enhance market output prices. The particular set of instruments employed to intervene in U.S. agricultural markets is summarized in Box 10.3. While many of the specific mechanisms for carrying out U.S. farm policy are unique, their effect is typical of the agricultural policies of most developed countries—they are highly supportive of income opportunities for producers.

While it is fairly clear that producers gain from the agricultural policy approach taken by the United States and other developed economies, implications for consumers, natural resources and environmental quality vary substantially among the alternative policy instruments available to resolve the market failures and other problems earlier described. How, then, do policy makers and analysts concerned specifically with agricultural resources evaluate regulatory options? The theory of government regulation and agricultural market intervention reviewed in the following section begins to answer this critical question.

A PUBLIC CHOICE VIEW OF THE POLICY PROCESS

> Federal participation in agriculture ... has become entrenched by generations of lawmakers who have devoted large sums of taxpayer money to farm programs and received significant political pay offs in return.
>
> David Rapp (1988)

The preceding section of the chapter provides some rationalization for the observed high degree of government intervention in the agricultural sector. The pressure for policies affecting agriculture and, thus, agricultural resources, is the result of a variety of market failures, including externalities, public goods, and imperfect information, and of unsatisfactory income distribution. Having explained *why* there is a basis for so much intervention in agriculture, we now turn to the questions of *how* such intervention originates, and *what* political and economic factors dictate the form it takes.

The most basic assumption of economics is that people seek to maximize their utility. This is usually presented in terms of consuming a bundle of goods. Of course the utility maximizing bundle can include environmental goods like outdoor recreation, clean air, or bucolic views. Growing income levels since World War II have led to an increase in the demand for environmental amenities because of the high income elasticity for environmental goods. Since environmental goods are not provided by markets, some groups turned to political arenas to seek improved environmental quality. That is, the rise of the environmental movement can be seen as a political manifestation of the growing demand for environmental quality.

This discussion points out that people seek to satisfy certain wants through *collective action*. Both markets and governments are mechanisms for allocating scarce resources. Public choice theory contends that voting is not that different from making food purchases at a store (Buchanan and Tullock, 1974). Public choice takes the most basic assumption of economics—people are utility maximizers—and extends it to politics. This means analyzing political behavior as if each of the sets of actors involved—voters, politicians, and bureaucrats—are maximizing their own utility or self-interest.

Public choice theory views a voter as someone who maximizes utility by voting in his or her own interest. Voters will vote for those candidates who they expect to support things the voter wants whether it be more wilderness areas, more missiles, or more agricultural benefits. One of the earliest findings of public choice theory was that the rational voter will not be informed about the votes he casts (Downs, 1957). This is because he has little incentive to invest much time or effort in obtaining more information because the impact of his one vote will be so small. In fact, many will perceive that the impact of their vote is so small that they will choose not to vote.

The voters' lack of knowledge is not symmetrical (Tullock, 1987). Voters are likely to be better informed about special interests they may have. Furthermore, special interest groups will devote effort to informing voters in such areas. As a result the voter is badly informed, but the information he has will be biased heavily towards his occupation. Thus, farmers are more likely to know a candidate's view on price supports than on defense policy. This creates a situation where special interest groups can have a large impact on political decision making.

Politicians are individuals who make their living by being elected to public office. As a result, according to public choice theory, they are motivated to do things that enhance their reelection chances or attractiveness for higher office. Thus, politicians can be viewed as individuals who seek to maximize their utility by taking public positions that will increase their vote-getting ability.

Potential votes may be increased in several ways. One is by meeting the expressed needs of constituents. Another is by granting the wishes of special interest groups which, by independently influencing constituents' votes, or by supplying financial support for increasingly expensive election campaigns, can have a profound effect on vote-getting ability. Note that this view of politicians' utility downplays elected officials' own, personal views on issues. The fact that they are to vote according to their constituents' wishes instead of their own views is key to representative democracy. At issue is when and how they bow to special interests over constituents, and which special interests predominate—topics to which we soon turn.

In the meantime, it is useful to differentiate bureaucratic behavior from that of voters and politicians. Traditionally, the public administration field viewed bureaucrats as either following the orders of their political superiors, or doing what was right for the public good. Public choice has challenged both of these views. The first view held that bureaucrats were guided by the political process since they had to answer to agency heads who were political appointees. Public choice analysts have argued that this is not true since the civil service system results in little political control over bureaucrats (Tullock, 1987). A political appointee is unable to discipline a bureaucrat by firing him or even reducing his pay, even if he is doing something that contradicts the goals of the party in power.

Public choice theorists also challenged the view of bureaucrats as individuals seeking to achieve the public interest through their activities. They challenged this because the political system does not provide incentives for doing what is in the public good (Mueller, 1989). As an alternative to the traditional views of the bureaucracy, public choice theory argues that bureaucrats seek to maximize utility by increasing their income or power (Niskanen, 1971; Downing, 1984). Both of these are increased through the expansion of the size and scope of their agency. Because agency scope and size is related to the agency's budget, public choice theory often depicts bureaucrats as budget maximizers. Thus, a bureaucrat may favor more stringent pollution regulation, for example, if this means more employees for his department and greater opportunities for advancement.

Public choice theory is not without critics, particularly regarding its treatment of the bureaucracy (McLean, 1987). The assumption of budget maximization ignores the many other arguments of the bureaucrat's utility function such as "ease of managing the agency" and "desire to serve the public good," neither of which may be consistent with increasing the budget of the agency. Furthermore, public choice theory fails to recognize that voter pressure may lead politicians to compete with one another to be the most aggressive cutters of the bureaucracy. Despite its shortcoming, public choice draws attention to the fact that individuals exhibit similar behavior in market and political arenas.

Rent-Seeking

If votes and financial and budgetary support are the currency of political action, then the mechanism for that currency's distribution is rent-seeking by interest groups. Rent-seeking is the activity of influencing the political process to obtain favorable outcomes or avoid unfavorable ones. The term *rent-seeking* is appropriately descriptive since the motivation for rent-seeking behavior is a gain in economic rent (or prevention of a loss of economic rent) to a particular group of potential beneficiaries from policy decisions (Krueger, 1974). In other words, groups seek to provide incentives to the political or bureaucratic decision maker in order to assure that the decision maker's action will retain or increase economic surpluses accruing to the group.

Groups involved in the activity of rent-seeking may be small or large, private, or public. In agriculture, they include a variety of commodity groups and farm organizations, each of which may attempt to influence decision makers to allocate a relatively larger portion of the agricultural budget "pie" to support group income or welfare objectives, or to take policy actions that favor or do not disfavor the relative income position of the group (Hadwiger and Browne, 1978). Since these agricultural interests' goals may directly affect the government controlled allocation of resources utilized in agricultural production, they will indirectly affect the quality and value of agricultural resources. In more direct fashion, a range of public interest groups, including environmental, resource conservation, and consumer groups, attempt to influence agricultural and other policy decision makers to retain, protect, or increase the social and nonmarket values of natural resources used in or affected by agricultural production and marketing. The number of, membership in, resources available to, and political sophistication of, such public interest groups increased dramatically over the decades of the 1970s and 1980s (Reichelderfer and Hinkle, 1989).

Interest groups may use any number of means for influencing the political process: monetary campaign contributions; in-kind support to political decision makers; general lobbying; voter education; and media campaigns, among others. These rent-seeking activities each has some cost. Thus, the process of rent-seeking is, in the political economic context, characterized as the cost associated with the production of various levels of government intervention.

Political Economic Analysis

The public choice approach and rent-seeking are formalized, and their political and economic welfare implications can be estimated, through application of the following generalized model. Consider a policy decision maker who faces multiple policy decisions, some of which fall strictly within the realm of agricultural policy (e.g.: should a drought disaster assistance program be initiated?), some of which concern resource use (should a new irrigation project be approved?), some of which integrate agricultural and resource/environmental concerns (e.g., Should farmers who use more than a fixed amount of fertilizer per acre be denied eligibility for farm program?), and each of which affects the welfare of both agricultural constituents and environmental proponents. The decision maker will attempt to maximize utility across all actions

$$U_g = \sum_{i-1}^{n} w_i U(O_i) \,|\, B \qquad\qquad (1)$$

where U_g is the utility derived by government decision makers from a particular agricultural resource policy action; O_i is a measure of the extent to which objective i is met by the action; w_i is the weight placed by the decision maker on objective i; and B represents a budget constraint. The action considered by the decision maker may concern either the particular policy instruments to be employed to achieve policy objectives, the level(s) of an instrument or instruments (e.g., subsidy rate or quota level), or some combination thereof, Ordeshook (1986) provides detailed explanations of how such multiattribute utility functions affect decision making under budget constraints, uncertainty, and political risk. Here we review more generally their implications for agricultural resource decision making by bureaucrats and elected officials. (See ACP example in Box 10.1.)

In the case of the bureaucratic decision maker, the objectives (O_i) may be described by performance measures and the budget constraint is usually binding. For example, two objectives of an agricultural agency may be to reduce soil erosion by a certain amount and to reduce the supply of a particular commodity by an amount that supports prices at a given level, both within a fixed availability of program funds. In choosing how and to what degrees to achieve these two objectives, the bureaucrat may be assumed to choose actions that will maximize utility by maximizing the probability of continued or increased future program support. Program support comes primarily from politicians—Executive Branch administrators and Congressional fund appropriators. Thus, the weights placed on bureaucratic objectives are a function of politicians' welfare. For an example of bureaucratic decision making according to revealed policy preferences, see Box 10.2 (Reichelderfer and Boggess, 1988). But keep in mind that the weights in the bureaucrat's preference function are derived from those of relevant politicians' preference functions, which take a somewhat more complicated form through extensions of Equation (1).

The politicians' utility is involved with serving constituents and special interests. Thus the objective (O_i) of the political decision maker may be equated with the economic and/or nonmarket surpluses accruing to (or perceived to accrue to) each of the groups influencing political preferences. Equation (1) can thus be expressed for the political decision maker as

$$U_g = \sum_{i=1}^{n} w_i U(\text{CS, PS, ES, etc.}) \qquad\qquad (1a)$$

where: CS is consumers surplus, PS is producers surplus, ES represents

Box 10.1. A Public Choice Interpretation of the Agricultural Conservation Program

The Agricultural Conservation Program (ACP) provides an interesting illustration of evolution of public choice in the making. The ACP began in the 1930s as part of a package of New Deal programs intended to assist farmers. After the Supreme Court struck down the Agricultural Adjustment Act of 1933, which paid farmers to take land out of production, the ACP was established in 1936. Farmers who enrolled in ACP received payments for limiting plantings of soil-depleting crops. The program integrated soil conservation and farm income support objectives, but its major objective was to raise farm income. The link with conservation was one of political expediency (Kramer and Batie, 1985).

The ACP and related programs continued through the 1970s with farm income support as a primary focus. The criterion for distribution of cost-share funding was not related to the severity of a farm's erosion problem. Instead, the program was implemented in such a way as to spread the payments to as many farms as possible.

Over time, as the ACP became more a conservation program and less a production adjustment program, the USDA found itself with two agencies concerned with soil conservation: SCS and ASCS, each with strong clientele and political support (Rasmussen, 1982). The ASCS had major responsibilities for running price support and related programs, but continued to operate the ACP. This led to friction within USDA and Congress. Although arguments were advanced that program effectiveness would be enhanced by placing all conservation programs under SCS control, such a transfer would significantly reduce the ASCS budget. As public choice theory would predict, ASCS vigorously resisted efforts to transfer the ACP to SCS.

Most members of Congress have preferred a program that spreads benefits as widely as possible, since this ensures the greatest support from farmers at election time. Wide distribution of program payments has also ensured the program's longevity. Despite the fact that every president since Truman has tried to reduce or eliminate funding for ACP, Congress has steadfastly maintained appropriations for the program (Rasmussen, 1982).

Not only have members of Congress favored a continuation of the ACP, members of farm interest groups such as the National Association of Conservation Districts have actively lobbied for soil conservation funding (Clarke and McCool, 1985). As a result, ACP cost-share payments to farmers increased from $60 million in 1936 to $233 million in 1979. When adjusted for inflation, this represents a decline, but in its early years ACP was the primary production adjustment program. In 1979, there were 364,000 participating farmers in ACP (Rasmussen, 1982). The benefits of the ACP are concentrated among a small number of the population well informed about the program, while the costs are widely diffused over the taxpaying public, which has little incentive to learn more about the program. Although public opinion polls have consistently showed strong public support for soil conservation, most Americans have never been well informed about conservation policy.

In the 1980s, the ACP began to be redirected. Most payments for production oriented practices were discontinued, and criteria for distribution of cost-share payments were modified to target some of the funds to areas with the most critical erosion problems. These changes in ACP were prompted by public criticism of ACP implementation. Much of the criticism came from environmental organizations. Because of changing perceptions about the relationship between agriculture and the environment, USDA programs including ACP came under close scrutiny. As a result, new constraints were imposed on conservation policy. In the past, the major constraint was how well a program served the interests of agriculture. The question now often asked is, how well does a program conform to the goal of environmental protection (Batie et al., 1986)? Increasingly, the debate about agricultural and resource policy is being framed by those outside the traditional agricultural circles.

environmental surplus, and the surplus measures of the policy objectives each correspond with the welfare of an identifiable group (e.g., ranchers in the politician's home district; an organized group of wildlife supporters who influence public perception of how well the politician is performing; or an agribusiness trade association that contributes to campaign funds). The budget constraint is removed because among the policies open to political decision makers (at least prior to Gramm-Rudman amendments) is an increase in budgeted funds.

More formally, for the political (elected) decision maker, the weights (w_i) placed upon the utility derived from achieving a given policy objective are a function of the votes that can be garnered by the action

$$w_i = f(M) \tag{2}$$

where (after Stigler, 1971)

$$M = nh - (N - n)s \tag{3}$$

and M is the majority the elected official wishes to maximize, n is the number of voters that will benefit from the policy action; h is the probability that a beneficiary will grant political support; N is all voters; and s is the probability that nonbeneficiaries will actively oppose the action.

The degrees of political support and opposition from an action are functions of the expected values of the benefits to beneficiaries and costs to nonbeneficiaries:

$$h = h(b), \tag{4}$$

where

$$b = \frac{T - K - C(n)}{n} \quad \text{and} \tag{5}$$

$$s = g(t, z), \tag{6}$$

where

$$z = \frac{K}{N - n} \tag{7}$$

and b is the per capita net benefit received by beneficiaries; T is the total dollars transferred to the beneficiary group; K is the total amount extracted to lobby the decision maker in support of or opposition to a transfer of T; $C(n)$ is the cost of organization to rent-seek, and exhibits diminishing returns above a certain size, n^*; t is the per capita value of potential loss to nonbeneficiaries, which is, in effect, a tax rate; and z is the per capita cost of effort to oppose the action.

The interactions of the political market for votes thus allocate benefits across consumer, producer, and other interest groups so that total political utility is maximized. In the neoclassical tradition, the political process is viewed as responsible for establishing the weights given to different groups in the determination of income transfer policies. This is a decidedly economic problem. Farm fundamentalism and other philosophical factors enter the economic picture as one means of influencing the political weight of different groups. But, basically, as Gardner (1989) puts it, "policies influence the level of the political preference function only because they influence people's incomes" (p. 1165).

Maximization of the policy makers' objective function (1a) implies that the optimal level of a transfer of wealth or utility from one group to another occurs at the point where the marginal political return from the transfer equals the marginal political cost of the associated tax.[2] (See Peltzman, 1976, for full derivation of the solution.) This can be likened to an economic market, but here the demand function represents constituents' willingness to pay, in votes and political support, for each level of policy action. And the supply function represents the cost, in terms of lost support and new opposition, that the "producer" of the policy, the political decision maker, faces at each level of policy action. Of course the optimal level of intervention will vary across political decision makers since preference functions differ from individual to individual, and the groups forming politicians' constituents vary across voting districts. Rent-seeking groups correspondingly respond with varying degrees of promised support or opposition for different policy decision makers.

Figures 10.1 and 10.2 depict optimizing conditions for use in illustrating hypothesized interactions among agricultural interests, consumers, and environmental interests in two different but related *political markets*. In Figure 10.1, t_1 is the optimal rate of agricultural subsidization as determined by the equivalence of the gains in agricultural producers' surplus achieved, for example, through price support policies, and the loss of political support arising from the subsequent transfer of wealth from consumers to producers.

A similar set of interactions is hypothesized to occur in the political market for environmental regulation (Fig. 10.2), where consumers are taxed to achieve greater surplus in terms of environmental quality. The illustrated, positive optimal tax level (t_3) reflects the results of opinion polls, which find a growing majority of Americans are willing to sacrifice economic growth or pay higher taxes to insure greater environmental protection (Dunlap, 1989). However, in the case where potential environmental regulation unilaterally or especially taxes agricultural producers, the political costs of intervention shift upward as agricultural interests mount opposition to protect their wealth position. In a first best world, starting from the point of zero intervention in either market, it is unlikely that a tax on agricultural producers is feasible within the political market for environmental regulation. Because agricultural interests have a far greater per capita stake ($T/N - n$) in opposing than do environmental interests in generating a tax on agriculture, the addition of agricultural opposition to consumer opposition

---

[2] The word "tax" is used here in a broad sense unrelated to specific instruments. The tax is derived from a transfer of income, which, even if transferred through a direct payment to one group, necessarily means that a loss of real potential income, the "tax," is realized by another group or groups.

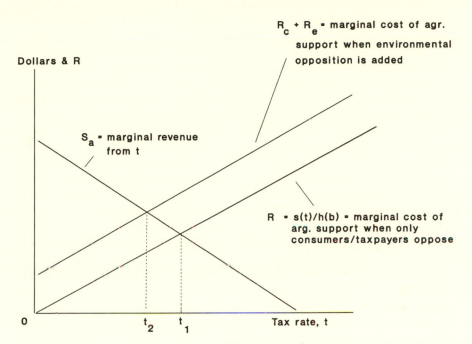

Figure 10.1. Optimal intervention in the political economic market for agricultural support.

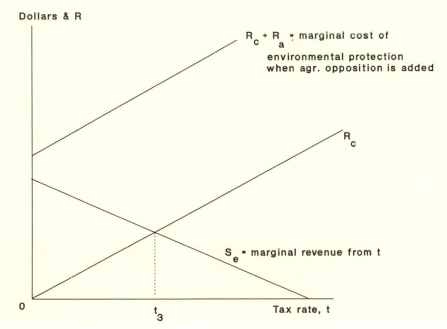

Figure 10.2. Optimal intervention in the political economic market for environmental protection.

453

($R_a + R_c$) precludes *net* taxation of agriculture to buy environmental gains. However, a *reduction* in the level of agricultural subsidization is entirely feasible and is shown in Figure 10.1 as an upward shift (R_c to $R_c + R_e$) in the marginal cost of agricultural support as a result of environmental opposition.

A number of important relationships can be discerned from Equations (1a) through (7) and Figures 10.1 and 10.2. Note first that the optimal income redistributive outcomes of political decision making is, in part, a function of the sizes of the groups that are likely to gain or lose from a policy action. The smaller the size of a a group with common interests, the more likely it is that the group's interests will be favored by political action (Stigler, 1971; Peltzman, 1976). This somewhat counterintuitive result stems from the fact that as interest group size, n, increases, the net gain per member of the group declines, and the cost of organizing effective lobbies rises, both results acting to dilute the net benefits of collective action. A small interest group, on the other hand, can extract high per capita gains because political action that favors its members incurs a small enough per capita tax on the rest of society that opposition to the action will be slight. This goes a long way toward explaining why farmers in developed economies are subsidized.

Since the beginning of the 20th century, the trend in the structure of American farming has been toward fewer and fewer farmers operating larger and larger farms (see Fig. 10.3). This trend lends increasing pressure for intervention on behalf of a small group whose potential benefits from regulation rise as their numbers

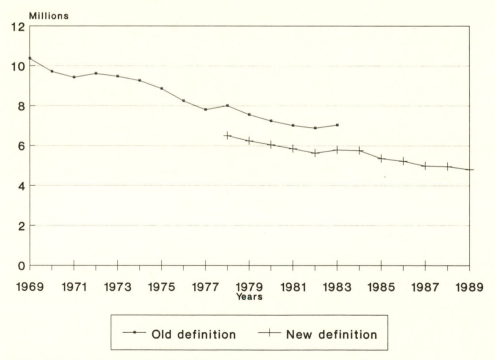

Figure 10.3. Farm population in the United States.

decline. Empirical evidence of this phenomenon is provided by Oehmke and Yao (1990), who found that actions by agricultural decision makers in the 1970s and 1980s implied that the welfare of wheat producers received substantially more weight in the political preference function than did that of the larger groups, taxpayers and wheat consumers. Competition among rent-seeking interest groups for political favor implies that for any set of income redistribution goals, there exists an optimal group size for each interest group in relation to other groups (Becker, 1983).

Second, recalling from Chapter 4 the importance of price elasticities of supply and demand to welfare measures for market participants, consider how market forces enter the political preference function. Because they are important as determinants of the magnitude of welfare changes, they also become important in determining how political demand and supply functions shift. In comparing policies among various agricultural commodities, Gardner (1987) finds that the level of the revealed consumer tax/producer subsidy is primarily affected by commodity supply and demand elasticities, which are critical in that they determine the nature of the economic welfare gains or losses that lead to the strength of political support for or opposition to policy intervention. The illustrated slopes and positions of the marginal benefit (S_a) and marginal cost (R_c) functions in Figure 10.1 are consistent with historical subsidization of producers of food and feed grains, import-competing, and other price-inelastic commodities. So, while regulation may to some degree offset market forces in determining the division of rents among groups, the process of regulation is itself also influenced by market forces.

Third, the political effectiveness of an interest group is determined mainly by its relative efficiency in generating political pressures vis-a-vis that of competing groups. Becker (1983) further shows the strength of influence to be a function of *deadweight losses* incurred in the transformation of taxes into subsidies. He finds, and Gardner (1987) confirms for the case of agricultural subsidies, that an increase in the dead weight cost of a tax encourages pressure by the taxed group because a given reduction in their taxes then has a smaller effect on the amount available as a subsidy. This relationship is the underlying source of Gardner's (1987) finding that commodities with a more price elastic demand receive relatively less support. In the context of agricultural influence relative to environmental influence, it suggests a rising pressure from public interests as a greater proportion of U.S. agricultural production responds to the relative more price-elastic export market.[3]

Of course, as one group gains income in relation to others, all else being equal, the likelihood of further success in rent-seeking declines. This explains the observation that political action tends to favor producer groups during economic recessions and consumer groups during periods of economic expansion (Peltzman, 1989), a finding that has particular relevance to the interaction of agricultural policies with natural resource and environmental policies.

---

[3] Gardner's (1987) contention, that a high export share is positively associated with producer protection in the commodity market because part of the cost of support is absorbed by foreign rather than voting consumers, is assumed not to apply to agricultural influence vis-a-vis environmental, food safety, or related public interests, because the environmental tax associated with producer support is not mitigated through exportation of the output.

Links to Welfare Analysis

Welfare analysis provides quantitative measures of variables that enter into decision makers' objective functions in a political economic framework. In the context of agricultural markets, income redistribution to all or some farmers can be measured as gains in economic rents at the expense of a loss in consumers surplus and taxpayers' income. A political action that favors consumers of environmental amenities may, on the other hand, tax some agricultural producers, resulting in a loss of producers surplus. In other words, the income redistributive outcome of the majority maximizing political process may be translated directly into the framework of economic welfare analysis, thus linking political and economic market factors in a simultaneous system.

The outcome of a policy decision can result in an increase in total economic surplus, a reallocation of surplus among various groups, or both. If there is some equivalence between political interest groups and market participants, the implications of the poitical process can be mapped in multimarket economic welfare space. For example, assume that a political decision concerns the Federal subsidization of irrigation water for western agricultural producers. The politically optimal subsidy rate is equal to the political cost of the decision arising from the imposition of both direct costs on taxpayers and indirect losses to nonirrigators. The subsidy acts to shift the supply curve of irrigated crops to the left, increasing both consumers' surplus in the commodities' markets, and the economic rent gained by producers utilizing subsidized water, but reduces the surplus realized by nonirrigating producers and incurs dead weight losses related to the taxation mechanism. In efficiency analysis, the weights assigned to each group's welfare are assumed equal. In political economic analysis, the political process determines relative weights.

From a policy analytical perspective, the implications of the relationship between economic welfare and political preferences are that 1) the optimal degree of government intervention in a market is, in part, a function of the price elasticity of demand for the relevant good, and the supply schedules faced by different groups of producers, as these functions determine the value of benefits and losses to groups affected by policy action; and 2) optimal changes in economic welfare are a function of political preferences and interest group objectives. Failure to recognize the close links between public choice and economic welfare can lead to inappropriate use of welfare analytics to examine policy options. For instance, using economic efficiency criteria in lieu of political preference for income distribution to judge the relative superiority of alternative policies in an economic welfare framework can limit the utility of the analysis for a political decision maker. After all, if policy decision makers are more concerned with matters of income distribution than economic efficiency, then policies that distort competitive equilibria may achieve their intended distributional effects better than policies that achieve competitive efficiency. Furthermore, if the required (for welfare analysis) assumption of equal welfare weighting among groups fails because the decision maker places higher value on some groups' welfare than on others, welfare analytical results can neither be used to judge the relative merit of alternative policies nor to design better policy options. Finally, recognition of the public choice problem underlying the multimarket welfare issue is needed in order for the analyst to appropriately designate the markets, markets subsets, or regions requiring welfare analysis. Ideally, the market participants whose welfare changes are estimated will coincide with the groups whose potential gains and losses are central to the public choice calculus.

An analytical framework that incorporates the concept of simultaneous political and market interactions will prove most useful to ex ante selection and evaluation of a feasible set of agricultural resource policies as well as in explaining past policy decisions.

U.S. AGRICULTURAL RESOURCE POLICIES

Having shown why there is such a high degree of intervention in agriculture, and described conceptually the process by which policy decisions are made, we now turn to a review of what agricultural resource policy decisions *have* been made in the United States.

Historically, agricultural and resource policies largely have evolved independently. The institutions charged with developing and implementing agricultural policies frequently differ from those with responsibility for resource policies affecting agriculture. Their objectives are often conflicting. There is thus no single, standard set of policies or policy objectives that apply specifically to agricultural resources. On one hand, a vast number of federal, state, and local laws apply generally to the use of land, soil, water, and air as means for meeting a highly diverse set of objectives regarding the development, conservation, and preservation of natural resources, custody of the natural environment, and protection of human health and safety. On the other hand, a set of mostly Federal agricultural policies has been in place since the 1930s to assure a stable and adequate supply of food and fiber at reasonable prices and to maintain farmers' income and well-being. Many resources and environmental policies affect agriculture by creating opportunities or placing constraints on the manner by which resources can be used in production. Likewise, the pattern of production arising from long-standing agricultural policies affects natural resources. To the extent that any sort of "agricultural resource" policy set exists, it is created through the intersections and interaction between agricultural and resource/environmental policies and programs. Because of their close independence in determining resource allocation in agriculture, policies designed specifically for the agricultural sector, and those independently developed to guide natural resource use, need to be examined jointly in order to understand the policy context of agricultural resource use, value, and quality.

Instruments and Goals of Resource and Environmental Policy

The principal objective sought and policy instruments employed in U.S. resource policy have varied significantly over time. In the late 1800s and early 1900s, when natural resources were generally untapped, largely publicly owned, and highly abundant relative to a sparse and regionally concentrated population, policy focus was on the development of resources and resource-based industries. With the drought and depression of the 1930s came widespread recognition of the vulnerability of natural resource-based industries to variation in physical and economic conditions. This hard-learned lesson strengthened incentives for further development of resources to guarantee a more stable supply, and added a new dimension—conservation—to natural resource policy objectives. As demand for the products of agriculture, mining, and forestry rose throughout and following World War II, public concern began to shift toward the accumulating byproducts of those production processes. By the late 1960s it was evident that growing public demand for open space, a clean, safe, and diverse natural environment, and new recreational opportunities were in conflict with the pattern of resource use that evolved as a result of former resource development efforts. Thus, in more recent times, a variety of policy instruments have been developed and applied toward the objective of environmental protection.

This shift in resource policy focus over time is truly evolutionary, and somewhat ironic, in that fulfillment of past policy objectives led directly to conditions that favored policy change. It was partly as a result of successful economic growth through resource development that the predominant view of natural resource value switched from focus on resources as raw materials to the demand by a higher income population for the recreational and amenity services offered by undeveloped resources.

What we are left with in the 1990s is a potpourri of resource and environmental policies affecting agriculture. In reviewing the past and present policy set, it is especially useful to differentiate among those for which the primary objective is 1) resource development, 2) resource conservation, 3) environmental protection, and 4) resource preservation, since these objectives have distinctly different economic implications and may require the use of different policy instruments.

Public Investment in Resource Development

The general goal of *resource development* policies generally is to accelerate economic development by shifting a natural resource to a higher use; one with greater income-generating capabilities. While the government typically provides the capital base for resource development, incentives are often required to encourage private investment in or use of the resource possessing income-generating potential. For example, the Homestead Act of 1862 heavily subsidized private ownership of formerly Federal lands as a means for encouraging population dispersal and creating a base for economic development of the western United States.

Likewise, the Reclamation Act gave authority for Federal subsidization of water resource development by establishing programs under which the government would construct numerous irrigation projects and provide irrigation water at prices below its real values, again with the aim of accelerating economic development. Similar water resource development subsidies are provided for flood control through Army Corps of Engineers projects and for drainage project cost-sharing with the USDA.

Because the aim of resource development policy is to stimulate new income-generating activity, the policy instruments traditionally employed for resource development are positive incentives. These incentives may be provided through direct subsidies, cost-sharing with private investors, or tax breaks to investors.

In examining the success with which resource development projects have generated economic growth, Castle and Goldstein conclude that they have successfully shifted income to individuals using the developed natural resource services, and to consumers of output produced through employment of the resources. While small net income gains were achieved, a significant redistribution of income occurred simultaneously (Castle and Goldstein, 1983). The regions on which resource development efforts have focused gained considerably, but gains have tended to be offset in part by income losses in regions that were placed at a new competitive disadvantage (Haveman, 1972). For example, midcentury development of western water resources was estimated to have displaced 1 in 20 southern farmers who could no longer compete with western irrigated production in meeting fixed demand for cotton and grains (Tolley, 1959).

A consequence of the historical pattern of resource development in the United States has been the shift of resources, particularly water resources, into the agricultural sector. A secondary effect is that technological change in agriculture has evolved with a bias toward complementation of the developed resource. Once investments have been made to establish resource-dependent production patterns, demand for inputs specific to that production pattern rises, inducing technology that is natural resource-using rather than natural resource-saving. Thus, Western agriculture tends to be heavily dependent on irrigation, not just because the water resource was developed for irrigation, but also since subsequent technological change originally focused on enhancing the productivity of factors that are complements to irrigation.

The political economy of resource development involves the transfer of wealth to owners of the developed resources, with associated granting of property rights thereto, while at the same time increasing welfare generally because of increased income generation. So long as there are neither binding budget constraints on nor externalities resulting from resource development policies, little political opposition to them will arise. Thus, utility gains are virtually assured to politicians promoting resource development, particularly for resources owned or used by their constituents.

Incentives for Resource Conservation

Resource conservation programs are intended to improve the management of depletable and renewable resources. From an economic point of view, a desirable goal of resource policy is to improve the efficiency of resource use by encouraging private resource managers to use resources in ways consistent with maximizing net social benefits. As applied in the agricultural sector, resource conservation policy has focused on soil and water resources.

Theoretically, almost any policy instrument could be employed to align private resource use rates with the socially optimal rates of use. Mandated standards could impose socially preferred practices on resource owners. A schedule of taxes, fees, or fines could be devised to raise the private, current cost of resource use to levels reflecting long-run social values. In the United States, however, voluntary behavior in response to positive incentives has been the predominant mechanism for achieving agriculturally related resource conservation policy objectives. From a political economy perspective, this is not surprising. If the political decision maker can achieve simultaneously increases in public welfare and private rents with respect to resource conservation, there is a good probability that political preferences will be accomplished. As in the case of resource development incentives, however, this approach relies strongly on the availability of public funds without severe budget constraints.

In the area of agricultural conservation, an approach employed extensively by the Federal government is the provision of technical assistance, a subsidy for the development of human capital, and improvements in the flow of information to farmers. The primary program has been the Conservation Technical Assistance Program (CTA), authorized by the 1935 Soil Conservation Act and administered by the Soil Conservation Service (SCS) (Rasmussen, 1982). The CTA, operated in cooperation with the nation's nearly 3,000 local soil conservation districts, provides technical support to farmers who voluntarily seek assistance in preparing and implementing soil conservation plans. While the Cooperative Extension Service and Forest Service also provide information and assistance in resource conservation, the CTA accounts for the majority of Federally provided technical assistance. The CTA program, while encouraging soil conservation, may have discouraged conservation of wetlands. Prior to 1977, the program covered technical assistance for drainage and leveling of wetlands for conversion to cropland. After nearly 57 million acres of cropland had been drained under the program, technical assistance was suspended for most wetlands unless the assistance would improve wildlife habitat. The program also has been periodically criticized for its failure to target assistance to areas with the greatest erosion problems.

Direct subsidies for the adoption of soil conservation also have a long history. The Agicultural Conservation Program (ACP), administered by the Agricultural Stabilization and Conservation Service (ASCS), was authorized by the 1936 amendment to the Soil Conservation and Domestic Allotment Act of 1935. The ACP provides cost-sharing assistance to farmers for implementation of approved conservation practices such as contour farming, terrace construction, sod-waterway installation, and irrigation improvements. Similar, though smaller scale programs for on-farm conservation cost-sharing are the ASCS Water Bank Program and the SCS Great Plains Conservation Program. SCS programs providing Federal financial assistance to local organizations include the Small Watershed Program, initiated in 1954 and directed in part to the reduction of soil erosion, sedimentation, and run-off, and the Resource Conservation and Development Program. In addition, ASCS administers the Forestry Incentives Program (FIP), under which cost-sharing is provided by establishment of tree plantings for conservation purposes. At its zenith, between 1978 and 1982, 1.1 million acres of cropland were converted to forestland under FIP.

A heavy investment of public funds was made to agricultural resource development and conservation between 1940 and 1990. In 1988 a total of $2 billion in Federal funds was spent on voluntary conservation incentives programs (ERS, 1988). These funds were supplemented by an estimated $1.8 billion in private, local, and state funds (ERS, 1988). Total annual expenditures, most of which address soil conservation goals, represent around one-half to two-thirds of the $5.8 billion per year value of on- and off-farm losses associated with soil erosion from cropland (ERS, 1988). Programs of this magnitude are subject to intensive scrutiny, and a number of critical evaluations have been conducted over the years. For an evaluation of the Conservation Reserve Program (CRP) see Box 10.2.

An evaluation of all national conservation technical assistance and cost-share programs estimated that the benefit-cost ratio for erosion measures generated by those programs in 1983 ranged from 0.3 to 0.9 in aggregate, and exceeded 1.0 only for the subset of measures implemented on cropland with erosion rates exceeding 15 tons per acre per year (ERS, 1986). Since more than 80 percent of the land treated under these programs was eroding at rates less than 15 tons/acre/year, and 40 percent of treated land was eroding at under 5 tons/acre/year, the evaluation suggests that significant gains in returns to Federal conservation expenditures could be accomplished through program targeting (ERS, 1986). The notion of targeting efforts to lands from which erosion rates and fate incur the highest social cost is straightforward and logical. Its actual implementation is less so since it implies a regional redistribution of Federal funds, with possible political ramifications (See Box. 10.1.)

Other studies suggest a strong influence of macroeconomic factors on the cost-effectiveness of conservation incentive programs. Farmers will be induced to invest in conservation structures or apply new conservation practices only if they can expect the present value of private benefits to exceed private costs. Conservation technical assistance and cost-sharing reduce the private costs of conservation, thus increasing the probability that, other things being equal, private benefits will exceed private costs. However, the present value of expected benefits is not a constant. As the study by Nielsen et al. (1989) (reviewed in Chapter 9), shows, farmer's conservation and land improvement investment decisions appear to be more strongly influenced by real interest rates and farmland values than by the availability of ACP cost-share supplements.

Box 10.2. The Conservation Reserve: Evolution and Implementation of a Multiple-Objective Program

The development of a Conservation Research Program (CRP) was a classic, politically maximizing move. The program's implementation serves as a good example of the problems involved in analysis of multiple-objective policies.

The idea for a CRP arose in 1984–85, during the height of a farm financial crisis. Export demand for U.S. commodities was sluggish, the agricultural sector was plagued by excess capacity, land values were declining, and large numbers of farmers were experiencing a significant loss in wealth. At the same time, environmental interest groups were exerting increasing strength in the farm legislation process. The

CRP, through which highly erodible land would be voluntarily retired in return for acceptable rental payments, could transfer income to farmers, reduce excess supplies, and reduce environmental externalities. Erodible land was identified in many areas, and no farmer would lose rent under CRP compared with the annual acreage reduction programs for which CRP would partially substitute. The CRP was established under the 1985 Food Security Act, which also gave broad discretion to the Secretary of Agriculture in determining how to carry out the program.

CRP legislation cited seven objectives to be met by the program's implementation, including reduce soil erosion; reduce excess commodity supplied; improve water quality; improve farm income; and improve wildlife habitat. No relative weights were attached explicitly to these multiple objectives. The program itself was the sole policy instrument available to achieve the objectives. Administration decisions that would determine the extent to which each objective was met included 1) establishing the characterisitics of land eligible for enrollment; 2) setting procedures by which bids would be solicited and selected for rental payments to eligible landowners; and 3) determining the size of pools from which bids would be selected competitively. These implementation decisions would also determine the magnitude and distribution of transfer payments made through the CRP. The CRP decision problem facing implementors was

$$\text{Max } U(a) = \text{Max } U \sum_{i=1}^{7} (W_i O_i)$$

where $U(a)$ is the utility derived from action a; action a is defined by selection of the set of control variables establishing implementation procedures; O_i are the program objectives; and w_i are the weights associated with the relative priority of those objectives. However, with those weights unrevealed, analysis of implementation options reduces to a determination of which set of control variables would maximize each individual objective. Reichelderfer and Boggess (1988), in simulating a series of implementation alternatives, demonstrated that no one objective could be maximized without forfeiting performance in achieving all other objectives. Analysis revealed, for example, that a) focus on minimization of public cost would result in total program outlay of $11.8 billion, with erosion reduction averaging 28 tons/acre/year and supply reduction on enrolled acres equaling two-thirds of average production potential; but b) maximizing erosion reduction would cost $19.1 billion, with soil savings averaging 37 tons/acre/year and supply control averaging 80 per cent of average production; and c) maximizing supply control would cost $33.3 billion, with soil savings averaging 25 tons/acre/year and supply control from enrolled acres exceeding average production by 13 percent (Reichelderfer and Boggess, 1988).

As eventually implememented, the actual CRP had suboptimal results in achieving its stated objectives. Its net government cost could have been greatly reduced while simultaneously increasing the extent to which erosion and supply control objectives were met. However, the implementation schemes devised for the CRP were successful in meeting a series of unstated political and bureaucratic objectives. The distribution of rents was extensive. Potential loss of rent to agricultural input suppliers was minimized. Rents to farmers exceeded those found to be optimal with respect to achievement of other interest groups' objectives, and administrative costs of the implementors were lower than they would have been if actions had been taken to maximize one or any combination of stated objectives.

In summary, U.S. national conservation incentive programs have transferred significant amounts of income to the agricultural sector and have increased total economic welfare through their influence on the rate of use, particularly, of the soil resource. However, the persistent observation that the programs operate at low levels of cost-effectiveness in achieving conservation objectives suggests that an important though implicit goal of their implementation has been the redistribution of income within the sector.

Environmental Regulation

A range of different strategies has been proposed and could be employed by the Federal government, states, and localities to reduce the level of environmental damage resulting from agricultural activities. But, despite growing recognition and concern with agricultural externalities, few environmental policies or programs are directed exclusively toward agricultural sources. And of those that do directly affect agriculture, most take a quota or standards approach.

That *quotas* and *standards* are the predominant approach to controlling agricultural-source environmental and health risks is not unusual. Recall from Chapter 6 the point that a regulated industry is more likely to earn rents under a system of environmental standards than under the oft-equivalent (in effect) system of effluent or output taxes. Environmental regulatory instrument choice is heavily influenced by interest groups. Regulated groups will seek to implement the instrument that gives the smallest loss (or greatest gain) in welfare to its members while still achieving the level of environmental regulation demanded by competing groups (Hahn, 1990). Not only do quota and standards systems achieve this goal, they are also preferred from the perspective of regulators because of their relative ease of implementation, despite inefficiency implications (Yandle, 1991).

In the United States, the Federal approach has been two-pronged and characterized by 1) absolute restriction of practices judged to pose unreasonable risks to consumers, regardless of geographic location; and 2) provision to States of budgetary incentives to independently design programs that achieve broadly specified Federal standard criteria. The first case is exemplified by pesticide regulation (see Chapter 7). Modern pesticide regulation originated from early agricultural legislation efforts to reduce the transaction costs resulting from imperfect information about the effectiveness of pesticide materials. It evolved slowly into a body of environmental regulations affecting agriculture as the political interests involved in its progression shifted from purely agricultural in focus to those concerned with environmental quality and consumer safety (Reichelderfer and Hinkle, 1989). From a political economy point of view it is interesting that Congressional legislators, in creating modern pesticide regulation mandated the consideration of producer and consumer interests by requiring each action to be based on a benefit-risk decision rule, but shifted the responsibility for setting those rules and their consequential income distributional effects to the EPA, where bureaucratic objective functions are not reliant on distributional impacts. Nevertheless Cropper et al. (1992) found evidence that both public and private interest groups have had a significant influence on the EPA's pesticide regulatory decisions. They found that in the 245 pesticide regulatory decisions made between 1975 and 1989, opposition by environmental interest groups to the continued use of a material increased the probability of the use of being banned by 49 percent over that observed for unopposed (by environmental groups) uses. By the same token, they found that opposition by private, producer interest groups to a material's ban reduced the probability of cancellation by 27 per cent below that observed for unopposed (by producer groups) regulatory actions (Cropper et al., 1992). This finding provides good evidence that direct environmental regulation is inherently a political act.

The more indirect regulatory approach is typified by Federal statutes such as the Clean Water Act, under which states are required to identify nonpoint source water pollution problems and implement management programs to address those problems in order to share in Federal funding opportunities. Under this particular program, most states have identified agriculture as a significant nonpoint source of water pollution.

Proposed and actual state agroenvironmental policy instruments run the gamut from programs providing financial incentives for adoption of beneficial management systems, to laws that limit land use, restrict the use of specific potential water contaminants (fertilizers and pesticides, in particular), or establish liability (limit property rights) of farmers whose practices create negative environmental externalities.

Agricultural chemical taxes and restrictions, required adoption of new production practices, with or without government cost-sharing, and liability for water pollution damages all have one thing in common: They raise the cost of production for some or all farmers, eliciting changes in the allocation of economic surplus between producers and consumers and among producer groups. The distribution of farmers whose costs are increased depends upon the form of the legislation. While fertilizer taxes spread the cost of water protection efforts across all farmers, targeted restrictions on the use of certain farm chemicals near vulnerable water systems raise costs only for those farmers who are located in specific areas and whose agricultural chemical use practices or soil types are among those identified for targeting. Legislation that through voluntary or regulatory action results in reduced use of fertilizers or common pesticides may also reduce crop yields, with additional welfare implications (McSweeney and Kramer, 1986).

The observed proclivity of States to implement taxes, fees, and liability rules in addition to the standards approach employed by the Federal government suggests several things. First, it reflects a difference in the relative influence of interest groups at the State rather than at the national level. Second, it suggests the evolution of state-level regulation as a response to inaction or inefficiency of action at the Federal level.

Resource Implications of Agricultural Support Policies

Although never intended to directly affect resource and environmental quality, the policy instruments employed in the U.S. to support agricultural income (see Box 10.3) can have significant effects on agricultural resource use and its environmental consequences. For example, limited research has shown that increases in commodity

---

Box 10.3. Policy Instruments for Agricultural Support in the United States

American agricultural policy is designed primarily to support farm income. It attempts to accomplish this objective in large part by intervening in the market to raise the prices received by producers.

For grains and cotton, this is done by a combination of market price floors (loan rates), price guarantees to producers (target prices), and deficiency payments that make up the difference between market prices or loan rates and target prices. The target prices stimulate surplus production. To limit the accumulation of surplus stocks, deficiency payments and other program benefits are usually made conditional upon the farmer's cooperation with acreage reduction requirements. When acreage reduction requirements are insufficient, as they have often been in the past, subsidized exports (Export Enhancement Program) and payment-in-kind from government-held stocks to producers (instead of cash) are sometimes utilized.

For commodities of which the United States is a net importer—for example beef, sugar, and dairy—this country relies primarily on import restrictions to boost domestic prices. With milk, the United States also relies on marketing orders and government purchase of surplus stocks to support prices. For peanuts and tobacco, the United States allows producers to form government sponsored cartels that restrict supplies to the domestic market and thus raise prices to domestic consumers. Cartel-like arrangements established by marketing orders for commodities such as California oranges, fluid milk, and walnuts also regulate supplies and generally result in higher prices for consumers.

In addition, goverment-subsidized crop insurance and credit are available to protect U.S. farmers from natural and economic risks; resource conservation is encouraged mainly through income supplementing incentives; and an extensive Federal-state system supplies the results of publicly funded research to farmers for their practical application.

Many of today's agricultural programs evolved from programs initiated during the New Deal at a time of concern about depressed income levels. In 1987–1988, as real farm income approached a record high level, about one-third of all U.S. farms representing one-half of the land in farms received direct support from Federal farm programs. Also in 1987, the 3.6 percent of producers receiving the highest payments received 42 percent of the total direct support (Shaffer and Whittaker, 1990).

---

prices are directly correlated with increases in the use of agricultural chemicals, a not too surprising finding related to the increased marginal value product of fertilizers and pesticides from price support.

To the extent that deficiency payments raise producer returns above equilibrium levels, they too may increase externality problems. The higher returns encourage increased use of agricultural chemical and the cultivation of additional farmland (Miranowski, 1975). The increased cultivation likely increases aggregate soil erosion and reduces wildlife habitat (Reichelderfer, 1990).

However, annual acreage retirement programs and paid land diversion, the supply-control systems implemented in conjunction with deficiency payments, offset the independent effects of direct price-supports. On the one hand, acreage reductions reduce soil erosion and may reduce aggregate use of agricultural chemicals. On the other hand, attempts to control commodity supply by temporarily restricting the quantity of land further reinforce the incentives to intensify production on the land remaining in production. Short-term acreage reduction programs may encourage increased per acre use of agricultural chemicals, eliciting, in effect, a substitution of agricultural chemicals for the constrained fixed factor. Carlson and Shui (1992) have shown that price-induced increases in agricultural chemical demand have been offset by acreage reduction-induced decreases in chemical demand during the 1980 period. They find that the combination of U.S. farm policy instruments used through the early 1990s has *not* led to a net increase in pesticide use.

Over the long run, the historical use of acreage reduction programs as a means of controlling commodity supply has strongly influenced the pattern of resource employment in agriculture. By creating an artificial scarcity of land, the programs induce research, development, and adoption of land-saving agricultural technologies, including improved seed, fertilizers, irrigation, and pesticides.

Agricultural Research and Extension

Farm income also has been affected by public investments in agricultural research and extension. Using a variety of approaches, economists have found high rates of return to public research investments for the U.S. agricultural sector, especially for crop research (Huffman and Evenson, 1989; Norton, 1981). There is also evidence that public investments in extension have yielded very high rates of return (Huffman and Evenson, 1989). In general these studies consider the effects of supply shifts and price changes on economic welfare over time, and compute internal rates of return to the investments.

The *high rates of return* to investments in agriculture suggest that from an economic efficiency perspective, there has been an underinvestment in agricultural research. Economists have turned to political explanations of this phenomenon (Ruttan, 1982; Gardner, 1988). De Gorter and Zilberman (1990) use a political economy framework to examine alternative financing arrangements for agricultural research and other public good inputs, and the effects of those arrangements on the distribution of welfare between consumers, taxpayers, and producers. They conclude that the underinvestment may arise from the political power of farmers, the inelastic demand for agricultural commodities, and the highly productive nature of public good inputs. An empirical study by Oehmke and Yao (1990) uses a policy preference function approach to examine interactions between publicly funded wheat research and other government programs. Their findings show that the main beneficiaries of publicly funded wheat research are consumers. They conclude that if the government assigns a relatively low value to increases in consumer surplus relative to budget savings, then the "policy optimal" level of funding will be low since successful research increases the cost of deficiency payment programs.

The evidence of and reasons for observed agricultural research underinvestment from an efficiency standpoint do not, then, mean that there is underinvestment from societal or political perspectives. In fact, it can be questioned whether the inclusion of nonmarket valued consequences of agricultural research (a formidable task not accomplished as of this writing) might shift the rate of return to investment into the negative range.

An important dimension of the political economy of agricultural research and extension is their indirect effects on farm structure. There is evidence that suggests that both publicly and privately produced agricultural research have encouraged an increase in farm size and specialization (Kramer and Evenson, 1988). Whether this increases or lessens externalities associated with agriculture depends on the relationship between farm structure and pollution, a relationship that has not been adequately studied to date.

The discussion of the effects of agricultural policy on farm structure reminds us that relationships among policies should be viewed from a dynamic perspective. For example, by increasing yields and reducing input use, public research can alleviate some of the long-run exhaustibility problems facing a sector heavily dependent on petroleum-based inputs. However, if other policies intervene to support declining agricultural asset values by supporting prices or incomes, they may in the long run offset the resource-conserving effects of public research by providing incentives to overproduce (Zilberman, 1984). Furthermore, if productivity grows faster than demand, then a policy preference for protecting asset values will result in constant growth in farm program costs (or pressure to reduce public funding for agricultural research).

Coupled Agricultural and Research Policies

Farm bills, which are written every 5 years by the Congress and are the major source of agricultural legislation, typically contain a Conservation Title. It is, in fact, under such titles that soil and water conservation cost-sharing and technical assistance have been authorized. Thus, in a general sense, we can consider such programs to have been coupled with agricultural commodity and income policy, even though their stated objectives have been restricted to achievement of conservation goals. This may explain their revealed use as mechanisms for income distribution.

In addition to such implicit linkages between agricultural and resource policies, are several programs that explicitly have had agricultural commodity, farm income, resource conservation and environmental objectives, as well as a recent set of programs that consciously couple resource/environmental objectives to commodity programs. The instruments used to attempt achievement of coupled policy objectives are 1) long-term acreage retirement programs; and 2) cross-compliance provisions of commodity programs.

Long-term acreage retirement programs: Major, long-term acreage retirement schemes have periodically been implemented to provide commodity supply control while also reducing aggregate soil erosion. Both the Soil Bank Program of 1956 and the Conservation Reserve Program (CRP), authorized by the 1985 Food Security Act, offered landowners an annual rental payment in exchange for converting cropland to grassland or forests for a 10-year contract period. A major difference between these two programs is that participation in the CRP was limited to owners or operators of land that met specific criteria characterizing it as "highly erodible".

The environmental consequences of long-term acreage retirement programs are generally more favorable than for their short-term counterparts. Use of permanent cover, such as grass or trees, prevents annual cultivation of the land and thus avoids periodic disruption of wildlife habitat and exposure of soil to the elements. But long-term acreage retirement, like short-term acreage reduction programs, may stimulate the development and more intensive use of land-saving technologies. This effect is more pronounced for long-term than short-term programs since long-term acreage retirement facilitates the exit of land from the agricultural sector, where short-term acreage reduction, by contrast, encourages the maintenance of excess capacity in the form of land.

A unique characteristic of the particular form of long-term acreage retirement programs employed in the United States is that environmental quality enhancement is explicitly included among the programs' multiple objectives. By targeting highly erodible land for retirement, the CRP increased the soil erosion reduction benefits of land retirement above the levels that would have been realized had any or all land been eligible for CRP enrollment. However, because the CRP has multiple objectives, no one goal (erosion reduction or supply control) can be maximized without trading off performance in meeting the other goal. The productivity of land is not closely correlated with land's erodibility; nor, because of geographic specificity, is the value of damage resulting from sedimentation a constant function of erodibility. Thus, using the CRP to maximize the value of erosion reduction would require giving us some of its supply control. Similarly, maximizing the supply control effects of the CRP would require forfeiture of the program's potential to reduce soil erosion. (See Box 10.2.)

Cross-Compliance Programs

The 1985 Food Security Act also authorized three new cross-compliance programs for conservation purposes: Sodbuster, Swampbuster, and Conservation Compliance. The Sodbuster provisions require that farmers who convert highly erodible native range or woodland to crop production must do so under an approved conservation plan to maintain soil erosion at or below the soil loss tolerance level, or forfeit eligibility for any USDA program payment. In similar fashion, swampbuster provisions require that farmers who convert wetlands to crop production lose eligibility for USDA program benefits unless USDA determines that conversion would have only a minimal effect on wetland hydrology and biology. Conservation Compliance requires that farmers cultivating highly erodible land begin to implement approved conservation plans on such lands by January 1, 1990 and complete implementation by 1995, or lose eligibility for USDA program benefits.

These experiments with programs meant to improve the consistency between agricultural and environmental policy constitute an interesting case for political economic evaluation of policy coordination, a subject to which we now turn.

POLICY CONFLICT AND COORDINATION

> What we have, often, is a farmer lobby working for a higher price, a labor lobby
> working for higher wages, and a business lobby working for higher profits. If these . . .
> efforts are all successful, they result in the multiplication of mutually offsetting
> regulations.
>
> Paarlberg (1971, p. 164)

Many elements of the large set of agricultural, resource, and environmental policies
reviewed in the previous section are implemented simultaneously. Yet, the
objectives and typically employed policy instruments of simultaneously implemented agricultural and resource policies may often appear or actually be
inconsistent with one another. It would not be unusual for an observer to
wonder why, for example, during various periods, American farmers were provided
monetary incentives through commodity programs to expand production of soil
erosion crops while at the same time given subsidies to encourage activities that
reduce soil erosion; why irrigation water subsidies have been provided at the same
time that acreage reduction programs were in place to reduce surplus commodity
production; or why policies that induce land-intensive production are implemented
at the same time that input restrictions (like pesticide regulation) or taxes are
applied. Yet, while there are physical, temporal, and economic bases for actual
conflict between agricultural and resource/environmental policies, there are also
institutional and political rationales for the evolution of paradoxical relationships
between policies that appear to conflict but in fact create a consistent address of
the political preference maximization process. Since the manner by which a set of
policies interacts with one another is central to the choice of the analytical
approach employed to design or evaluate a member of the set, some appreciation
of the underlying conceptual basis for policy interaction is essential.

Sources of Policy Conflict

The compatibility and coordination of agricultural with resource and environmental policies are constrained by basic differences in the temporal and spatial
applicability of the policy sets and by the physical law of conservation of matter,
which results in joint production of agricultural goods and environmental "bads."

One basic reason for some inherent incompatibility between agricultural and
resource policies is the time horizon over which each is directed. Agricultural
policies have a short-term focus, often resulting in the implementation of programs
designed to adjust past production patterns to current, revealed levels of demand.
On the other hand, resource conservation and some environmental policies have
a long-term focus, with programs designed to alter long-run trends in resource
use. Periodic adjustment to short-term conditions will be inconsistent with
long-run change whenever short-run fluctuation proceeds in a direction counter
to long-run trends—a likely situation since economic conditions do not typically
change in continuous, unidirectional fashion. Thus, the comparative static perspec-

tive of agricultural policy design is bound on occasion to conflict with the long-term, dynamic perspective of resource policy design.

Second, the jointness of agricultural processes that lead to production of both agricultural output and environmental externalities fuels the conflict between private, profit-maximizing objectives and societal environmental protection objectives. The joint production situation (see Chapter 6) poses a difficult problem for agricultural and resource policy decision makers. The public demands both a cheap supply of agricultural commodities and a high level of environmental quality. The primary markets for agricultural commodities and derived markets for agricultural inputs recognize only one attribute of the aggregate social utility function, and exclude consideration of the nonmarket good, environmental quality. This particular form of market failure has long been used as a justification for government intervention, but intervention to resolve problems created by the environmental "bads" necessarily means that the markets for jointly produced goods will be affected. The policy conflicts involved in such situations focus on the magnitude of required tradeoffs between environmental quality and agricultural production.

A further problem of consistency between agricultural and resource/environmental policies derives from site-specific variation in the value of agricultural externalities. Environmental "bads" resulting from agricultural production accrue to local or regional populations, but the demand for agricultural goods is expressed by aggregate, national, and international groups of consumers. Thus, a degree of spatial inconsistency arises. Resource or environmental policies targeted to geographically specific problem areas may impose cost on groups located in areas where benefits do not accrue. Likewise, agricultural policies implemented at the national level can have differential local effects on the resource base or environmental quality.

Policy Coordination

At the root of apparent conflict between current patterns of agricultural production and environmental quality is a basic, fundamental inconsistency between the goals and means of historical agricultural and environmental policies. The agricultural policies reviewed in the previous section are not aimed at increasing the efficiency of production, but are designed to enhance agricultural income. Resource conservation and environmental policies are also aimed at protection, but their targets are often inputs to the protected agricultural production sector, creating competition for protection on top of existing competition for use. The problems of resource allocation to competing uses could resolve themselves through the normal functions of efficient resource markets. However, agricultural price and income support and supply control policies create distortions in agricultural markets, including the markets for agricultural resources. Because of these distortions, the markets do not operate efficiently.

Of course, economic efficiency is not necessarily a goal of agricultural policy decision makers or interest groups. Still, when regulation increases efficiency (because it resolves market failure) it increases wealth. Such welfare-expanding policies, referred to by Rausser (1982) as "PERTs" and distinguished from political economic (rent) seeking transfers ("PESTs"), include research, information, conservation subsidies, and provision of other public goods.

Within the framework of a palatable theory of policy evolution, Rausser (1991) suggests that implementing agricultural policies by redistributing income to rent seekers may be a political necessity in order to gain support for resource policies that increase the general welfare. Similarly, the level of political support for resource and environmental programs is believed to rise as the public perceives that the beneficiaries of former income redistributive agricultural programs are thriving. Thus we face a simultaneous system of policy evolution under which political reason to the implementation of policies that enhance resource value or environmental quality increases the probability that policies will be implemented to compensate rent seekers whose relative economic positions are subsequently altered, and vice versa.

Reference to Figures 10.1 and 10.2 and the components of the political preference function [equations (1) through (7)] serves to demonstrate how and why this coevolutionary phenomenon exists. A policy such as a resource development scheme, by subsidizing the use value of a given resource, has the potential to increase the marginal revenue to all or some policy beneficiaries. Thus, it shifts the marginal revenue curve in Figure 10.1 upward to the right. Assuming the political cost function is stable, an upward shift of the marginal revenue curve suggests a greater optimal tax rate on nonbeneficiaries. This rise in t^*, in turn, increases s, the probability of opposition from nonbeneficiaries. The increase in s has a potentially negative effect on political utility. But that effect can be offset by coincidental or subsequent implementation of an income redistributive policy favoring the groups that are taxed by the initial policy.

This form of policy interaction also works in the opposite direction. As taxpayers become aware of the effects of past policies favoring a particular rent-seeking group (e.g, commercial farmers), the marginal political cost of past action begins to rise, creating a politically costly difference between t^* at the time of policy action, and a new, information-induced, lower optimal tax rate. This may occur, for instance, as the relative economic positions of farmers or agribusiness rises, the skewed distribution of agricultural program benefits to larger-sized farms is advertized, and the external effects of past agricultural subsidization become apparent. An effective way to compensate for the difference between actual and eventually optimal tax rates, and thus avoid rising political cost of past actions, is to implement a new welfare expanding policy favoring those who lost wealth or utility from implementation of former policy.

As Rausser and Foster (1990) show, there is in theory an economic surplus possibility frontier that describes for every PERT (welfare expanding) policy the highest possible level of consumers' surplus that can be obtained for each level of producers' surplus in a given economic market. Mapping the surplus transformation associated with alternative welfare-expanding policies or policy instrument levels permits assessment of the optimal level of PEST (rent-seeking) transfers required to maximize political preference as income is simultaneously increased and redistributed. In similar fashion, one may describe the outcome of alternative

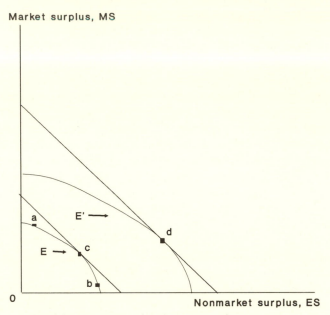

Figure 10.4. Surplus possibility frontiers under alternative policy sets.

agricultural resource policies in terms of the reallocation of surplus between economic market participants (consumers and producers) and those who derive welfare from the nonmarket benefits of natural resources and environmental quality. Figure 10.4 illustrates this relationship. For any given agricultural resource policy or policy instrument level, there are associated levels of market surplus (MS = CS + PS), and of nonmarket surplus (ES), which, together, determine a measure of total (market plus nonmarket) social surplus. A policy that allocates surplus at a point *a* on the surplus transformation curve *E* is one that favors market over nonmarket participants, whereas that at point *b* favors the allocation of nonmarket or environmental benefits over economic surplus. Point *c* on curve *E* represents the equilibrium level of total social welfare as it lies on the point where the surplus transformation curve has a negative slope of unity and any movement from it would decrease the welfare of one group at a greater rate than the increase in welfare of the other group. That we find, in reality, that we tend to operate more closely to point *a* than at the free market equilibrium point *c* is a result largely of producer rent-seeking activity, which, owing to the smaller size of producer groups and the attributes of political preference functions, outcompetes environmental interests in obtaining government intervention, which moves total social welfare away from its nonintervention equilibrium.

Assume now that a welfare-expanding policy, such as an increase in the level of funding for soil conservation and technical and financial assistance, shifts the surplus transformation curve upward (to *E'*) to reflect the higher (nontaxpayer) level of total social surplus possibilities provided by the action. At the new equilibrium level of total social surplus, point *d*, welfare is greater for both market

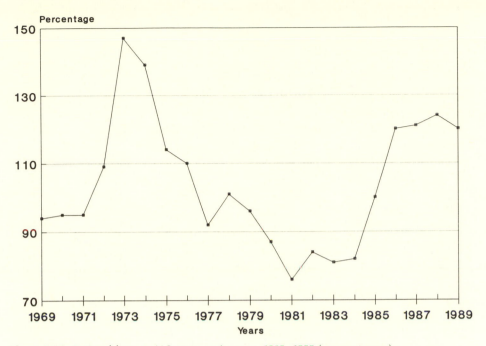

Figure 10.5. Ratio of farm to U.S. average income, 1969–1989 (see next page).

and nonmarket participants than at former equilibrium point c, but market surplus is less than at the more probable former operating point, a. Thus, additional rent-seeking activity will likely take place following welfare expansion in order to reestablish the former allocation favoring market participants.

A simple but concrete historical example of agricultural and resource policy coevolution is provided by the development of U.S. reclamation policy. As originally conceived and implemented, western water resource development programs would expand economic development, increasing the size of the total welfare "pie," and particularly benefit small farmers. As implemented, however, the Reclamation Act of 1902 tends to favor large-scale and established farm interests, limiting the distribution of expanded rents to a small but politically supportive group of beneficiaries. As the difference between the intended and actual effects of the program became increasingly apparent, interest groups brought pressure to legislators to enforce the 160-acre limitation on the size of farms receiving subsidized irrigation water. Still later, in response to the success of these public interest groups, rent-seeking action by the original set of beneficiaries whose benefits had been limited resulted in a 1983 amendment to the original Act, which increased the acre limitation from 160 to 960 acres. As we enter the 1990s, scrutiny and criticism of reclamation policy by public interest groups is again on the rise.

In a broader sense, there is evidence of a similar historical relation between the implementation of agricultural commodity and farm income programs versus resource conservation and environmental programs. Gardner (1987) has demonstrated that farmers receive stronger support during agricultural depressions.

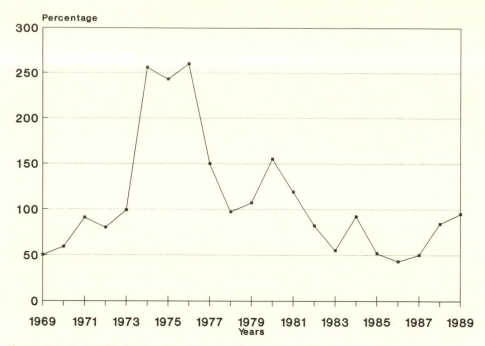

Figure 10.6. Ratio of federal outlays for national resource and environmental programs relative to agricultural programs.

Casual empiricism verifies that farmers more frequently have faced new regulations aimed at consumer price stability, food safety, occupational health, and environmental quality during agricultural expansions. Comparing the trends shown in Figures 10.5 and 10.6 provides some evidence of this relationship. Note that the pattern of Federal government outlays for natural resource and environmental programs, if lagged by about 18 months, virtually duplicates the pattern of farm income relative to U.S. average income over time. This observed correlation illustrates neatly the conceptual relationship between a group's income (or welfare) and political action proffering additional rents. As expected, outlays for agriculture relative to natural resources and environment decline (increase) following increases (decreases) in farm income relative to nonfarm income. Coincidence of sectoral and regulatory cycles may be explained by shifts in the marginal cost of different policy actions that take place as the economic position of farmers relative to the rest of the economy fluctuates, and manifest themselves as different weights in the political preference functon.

Problems of Consistency

Just as some policy sets that appear to be economically inconsistent are, in the political economic context, consistent with one another, other policy sets that appear to impose consistency can prove to be ultimately ineffective. Such is the case, for example, with conservation cross-compliance schemes.

Cross-compliance disincentives perform exceptionally well in assuring that commodity program participants adhere to minimum standards for protection of society's interests in soil conservation. Whether they can lead to successful enhancement of either environmental or agricultural policy goals is an entirely different question. The consistency aspect of compliance schemes may also prove to be their downfall. For example, sodbuster, swampbuster, and conservation compliance were not just made consistent with other farm programs, they were inextricably linked with them by virtue of the fact that the enormity of the penalty for noncompliance is a function of the attractiveness of the other programs' benefits. This relationship works fine, as a coincentive, when there are conditions of surplus and low commodity prices, such as there were when the legislation was formulated. But, as stocks deplete, commodity prices rise, and prospects improve for high, market-determined farm income, the tight linkage between programs will make the cross-compliance provisions ineffective. By tying these programs' incentives to the existence of other farm programs, their success in protecting the environment becomes a direct function of unrelated programs' benefits. Furthermore, disregarding the contribution of program nonparticipants to environmental problems leads to slippage in the achievement of conservation goals even when cross-compliance is an effective disincentive for program participants.

ANALYZING AGRICULTURAL RESOURCE POLICIES

The foregoing sections make it clear (we hope!) that resource and environmental policies cannot be analyzed in isolation from agricultural and commodity policies. Not only do we live in a second-best world, where new policy solutions to current problems are layered upon existing policies enacted to resolve historical problems, but the new and historical policy sets may to some extent be interactively related to each other.

Agricultural resource policies are selected and implemented by utility-maximizing public officials whose political preference weightings are influenced by groups whose concerns may range across such issues as survival of the family farm, profitability of feed grain marketing, and contamination of drinking water by agricultural chemicals. Recognizing that a given policy will benefit some groups and cost others, how does a policy decision maker decide whether the policy is desirable? The answer to this question is central to agricultural resource policy analysis, but is in no way straightforward. The desirability of a policy depends upon the values of the gains and losses that result from its implementation as well as the decision maker's relative valuation of the various groups that gain and lose. Agricultural resource problems, by their very nature, involve agricultural market participants and resource market participants, two sets of groups whose members may overlap little or a lot, and two groups of policy decision makers—agricultural and resource—whose members and objectives may or may not be related to one another. Agricultural policies, by influencing output and input prices, affect private resource allocation decisions and, thus, the level of resulting externalities. Environmental and resource policies can affect the cost of agricultural production. The role of the agricultural resource policy analyst is to sort out for decision makers and evaluate the tradeoffs among the groups affected by alternative policies. A critical question in assessing agricultural resource problems is the extent to which agricultural policies complement or offset the influence of environmental policies, and vice versa.

In what follows we apply and combine two principal policy analytical approaches—welfare analysis and public choice models—which have proved useful in providing information that assists policy makers in deciding whether a given policy is desirable, how it might be used to affect the performance of existing policies and practices, and whether it is preferable to alternative policies.

Evaluating the tradeoffs implicit in a given policy action, either absolutely, or in comparison with other policy options, requires a consistent or standardized measuring stick. The welfare analytic framework employs *economic welfare* as a measure with which the policy impacts in different markets may be aggregated or compared on common grounds. The use of welfare economics does not presume that policy decision makers necessarily wish to maximize social welfare. Rather, it generates welfare measures for society as a whole or for different societal subgroups as an objective benchmark upon which policy decision makers can overlay their own preferences and objectives.

The application of welfare economics to policy analysis (see Just et al., 1982) involves identification of the gainers and losers from a policy action, and determination of the extent to which each affected group gains or loses. Measurement of aggregate gains and losses is typically achieved by estimating the policy-induced changes in producers' and consumers' surplus expected to arise from a multimarket equilibrium shift. The multimarket or general equilibrium context of applied welfare economics has special implications for analysis of agricultural resource policies affecting participants in the markets for agricultural goods as well as those who demand nonmarket goods such as environmental quality.

Once gainers and losers are identified, and the magnitude and distribution of gains and losses are estimated, the impact of the policy action on political preferences may be examined in the framework of public choice. By way of illustrating some policy analytical concepts, we consider qualitatively the example of fertilizer taxation and regulation as policy options for resolving market failure in the form of nitrate contamination of ground water from corn production.

First, assuming perfect competition in fertilizer and corn markets, and recognizing that the demands for fertilizer and land for corn production are derived from the demand for corn, the producers' surplus measure in the market for corn will be the sum of profits in the corn market and its vertically related input and resource markets (Just et al., 1982). The quasi-market for environmental quality with respect to corn production can also be related directly to the market for corn, as shown in Figure 10.7.

The demand for corn is represented by D_y in Figure 10.7. The curve S represents the prepolicy supply curve for corn, and S' is the supply function that results from the addition of a fertilizer tax after the proportions of fertilizer and land in corn production have adjusted to new relative factor prices. If the tax rate is derived from an estimation of willingness to pay for water quality (see Externalities

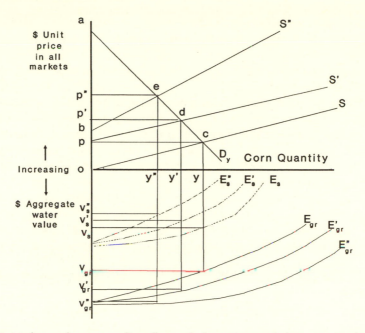

Figure 10.7. Market and water quality effects of alternative regulations on corn fertilizer use.

Chapter 6) then the function S' will equal the sum of the prepolicy supply function and the marginal social cost function for fertilizer, adjusted for factor proportion changes. Because factor proportions would change as a result of the fertilizer tax, corn producers would not face cost increases equivalent to the total social value of the marginal cost of fertilizer use. The resulting adjusted equilibrium level of corn production y' thus reflects a socially optimal level of fertilizer use on corn, but also incorporates the rise in the marginal social cost of land used for corn.

Under pretax equilibrium, corn quantity y is associated with surface water quality (function E_s) equal in value to v_s, and ground water quality (function E_{gr}) of v_{gr}. As the supply function (S') changes to reflect factor proportion changes after the fertilizer tax, the environmental relationships associated with land use (E'_s) and fertilizer use (E'_{gr}) in corn production also change, with associated changes in the values of surface water (v'_s) and ground water (v'_{gr}) quality.

Under a freely operating market for corn, then, the aggregate *welfare economic* effects of the fertilizer tax may be summarized in terms of

A loss of corn consumers' surplus equal to area $pac - p'ad$;

A change in the sum of revenues accruing to producers of corn and fertilizer, and land owners, equal to areas $Opc - Op'd$;

An increase in environmental quality with respect to ground water contamination by corn fertilizers, with value equal to $v'_{gr} - v_{gr}$;

A decrease in environmental quality with respect to land use for corn, with value equal to $v_s - v'_s$;

An increase in government revenues equal to the tax rate times adjusted average per acre fertilizer use times acreage used to produce corn quantity y'.

Individuals and groups that gain utility from improved ground water quality are definite policy gainers who may be located in site-specific problem areas either scattered across or concentrated within particular policy decision makers' voting districts as are those who lose from a decrease in surface water quality. Fertilizer producers and retailers are definite policy losers whose organized political opposition is likely to be strong since their numbers are small and potential per capita losses are high. Secondary and ultimate consumers of corn are clear policy losers, but are unlikely to organize strong policy opposition since per capita losses are small and the population of ultimate corn consumers is large and politically unorganized. On the other hand, primary corn consumers, such as livestock producers, constitute a group of policy losers that is well organized to lobby against the loss of rents that it would realize. Corn producers are also well organized to support or oppose the policy, but the extent to which individual producers stand to gain or lose from a fertilizer tax is not well represented by Figure 10.7.

The gains and/or losses to corn producers are a function of the price elasticity of demand for corn, differences in fertilization requirements across corn production areas, and the influences of Federal corn programs. We will explore the impact of existing commodity programs shortly. First, though, it is important to recognize that when the demand for a commodity is price inelastic, producers as a group will ultimately gain total revenue from policies that increase production cost. However, since a large portion of the U.S. corn crop is exported, its long-run demand is not clearly inelastic, meaning that there is some basis for opposition to the fertilizer tax by corn producers. Furthermore, heavy users of fertilizer will recognize that their relative gain will be less, or relative loss greater, than the aggregate change in revenue, creating a regional bias in support or opposition. The policy decision makers thus must weigh the strength of environmental support against the strength of fertilizer and corn producers' opposition in determining the political utility of a decision to tax fertilizers.

Now consider an alternative policy. What if, instead of taxing fertilizers, the government mandates the manner in which fertilizers can be used in corn production by banning Fall fertilization of corn and also implements an educational program to encourage the use of soil testing to reduce overfertilization during the growing season? Within the joint production context, such a policy would involve several changes. First, it induces a reallocation of variable inputs, in effect requiring reallocation of labor and management (productive, nonexternality generating inputs) to pollution abatement inputs as new complements to fertilizer. Thus, the shape of the production function changes, the slope of the corn supply function changes, and the supply function shifts to the left of the original. Further, because the imposed fertilizer use technology changes the relationship between fertilizer quantity and externality levels, the externality function also changes. The translation of these changes into the corn market might look something like the situation illustrated in Fig. 10.7 by curves S'', E_s'', and E_{gr}''—a distinctly different scenario from that described for the fertilizer tax. The aggregate welfare economic effects of this second policy alternative are

A loss of consumers' surplus equal to area $pac - p''ae$;

A change in producers' surplus equal to area $Opc - Op''e$; and

A net loss in environmental equality with value equal to $(v_{gr} - v'_{gr}) - (v''_s - v_s)$; with

No gain in government revenue, and a taxpayer loss equal to the cost of administrating and enforcing the ban on Fall fertilization plus the cost of the educational program.

Calculation and summarization of the areas depicted by the multimarket relationships tells a policy decision maker several things. Principally, it may be determined for each policy option which large groups gain and lose welfare, and whether aggregate gains in welfare exceed aggregate losses. For example, the estimated value of environmental gains or losses, consumer losses, changes in producer revenues, and additions to or subtractions from Federal revenues under the cases depicted in Figures 10.7 may be directly compared with one another. The political implications of the comparison are thus made transparent to policy decision makers. Furthermore, if the analysis determines that the value of net losses is less than the value of gains in environmental quality, the welfare analytical framework provides a rationale and basis for the design of concurrent or subsequent programs to compensate the losers.

The purely hypothetical example was crafted, as well, to drive home the point that a policy aimed at reducing one environmental problem can worsen another environmental problem, leading, potentially, to a net loss of environmental quality. How this possibility affects the policy decision depends upon whether, for example, groups supporting improved surface water quality are identical with, overlapping with, or distinct from those supporting improved ground water quality, and whether different environmental groups' welfare is valued differently in the political process.

The foregoing analysis assumed a freely operating corn market. But, in fact, the corn market is distorted by government intervention to stabilize corn price and support corn producers' incomes. This distinction is important because the welfare implications of a fertilizer tax or quota policy in a free corn market will differ significantly from those in a price-distorted market.

Resource Policy Analysis with Commodity Market Distortions

Analyzing agricultural resource or environmental policies under an assumption of freely operating, competitive agricultural markets will give inaccurate welfare implications if, in reality, the agricultural market is distorted. Traditional commodity policy can distort a wide variety of agricultural markets through a range of price support and/or supply control options. If average price or aggregate quantity of a commodity is determined in large part by government policy, then resource/environmental policy interventions that are aimed at achieving equilibrium

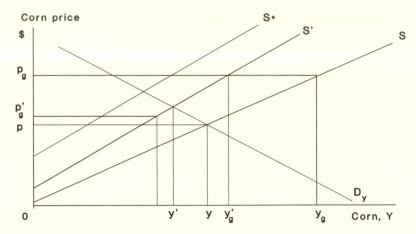

Figure 10.8. Welfare effects of a tax on corn fertilizers with government price support for corn.

conditions from the societal perspective, and are based on adjustments from a competitive equilibrium will over- or undercompensate. The existence of commodity and farm programs thus has important implications with regard to the need for and success of interventions to correct market failure affecting agricultural resources and environmental quality.

The fact that the existence of commodity programs may accelerate resource depletion and stimulate the perceived need for resource policy intervention is illustrated well by studies by Howitt (1990) and Just et al. (1991), both of which link irrigation water use rates directly to the level of price support for irrigated commodities. While consistent with theory and, therefore, not surprising, empirical evidence supports the notion that increases in effective output price raise the demand for inputs. In the case of irrigation water as an input, the situation is further complicated in regions dependent upon water provided through the Bureau of Reclamation. Here, the fixed price of water does not rise to reflect increases in demand and thus magnifies the influence of commodity price support on water use rates.

Employing the welfare analytical framework allows us to draw some general conclusions about the often complex interactions between resource/environmental and commodity/farm policies. Figure 10.8 illustrates a more realistic scenario than does Figure 10.7 for our corn-fertilizer-ground water policy's analysis when the market price for corn is less than the legislated price floor (loan rate) for corn available to corn program participants, or is less than the legislated price level to which corn program participants respond (target price). Let us assume, first, that as a result of corn price support programs, corn producers' decisions are based on a government determined corn price guarantee of p_g. Given the private, unadjusted supply function, S, the aggregate quantity produced will be y_g, a difference of $y_g - y$ from what we would have produced under free market conditions. Under these conditions, adding the marginal social cost of corn fertilizer use to the private cost of corn production to derive S' (as previously illustrated) will not induce the socially optimal level of corn production, y'. Instead, because commodity program provisions maintain corn price above the price that would have been induced by the fertilizer tax in the absence of a corn program, corn production remains above the socially optimal level, underadjusting by an amount equal to $y'_g - y'$. Under a commodity program that guarantees a price higher than the equilibrium price determined when social costs are internalized, the fertilizer tax rate required to generate y' is higher than the free market tax rate. In fact, to achieve the socially desired level of corn production under this sort of corn market distortion, the fertilizer tax would have to be great enough to shift the corn supply curve to S^*, a rate high enough to induce, in effect, an output tax equal to the entire difference between the free market price (p) and the government guaranteed price (p_g).

The existence of commodity programs also affects the cost and welfare implications of environmental regulation. For example, studies of the economic consequences of U.S. pesticide regulation suggest that the welfare losses from regulations are greater than they would have been under free market conditions (Lichtenberg and Zilberman, 1986). Under a free market for commodities that exhibit price inelasticity of demand, pesticide regulation increases production costs and induces an output price rise that tends to increase producers' surplus by more than enough to offset loss in consumer's surplus. However, when output price is fixed at a level such as that represented by p_g in Figure 10.8, the potential for pesticide regulation to increase welfare in the commodity market no longer exists. The effect of pesticide regulation is, instead, a net loss of producers' surplus, with no change in consumers' surplus. The extent of welfare losses in the commodity market is thus greater, for the same increase in environmental quality, than it would have been under a free market (see discussion of Figure 7.13).

Lest one jumps to the conclusion that output price-supportive commodity policies always raise the cost of internalizing agricultural externalities, consider the case (in Fig. 10.8) under which the government guaranteed corn price level is p'_g; a price higher than the free market equilibrium, but lower than the price prescribed by internalization of the external costs of corn fertilization. In this case, application of the standard fertilizer tax would lead to an overadjustment in corn production, with greater losses on consumers' and producers' surplus than would have been the case under a free market.

Several agricultural resource policy implications can be drawn from this comparative exercise: 1) Commodity price support policies (exclusive of acreage-based supply control) may reduce environmental quality to levels below that which would otherwise be associated with market-determined levels of goods whose production generated externalities; 2) Because commodity programs exacerbate externality problems, they may induce a rise in social willingness to pay for environmental quality, thus stimulating a higher degree of political pressure for taxation or regulation of agriculture than would be observed without price-enhancing commodity market distortions; and 3) At the same time, commodity price support programs grant what may be perceived as a property right to the additional producers' surplus they create, making it more costly, from a welfare economic perspective, to alter those rights via environmental policy adjustments.

For the agricultural resource policy analyst, this means that resource and environmental policy options cannot be accurately evaluated exclusive of their interactions with commodity programs. In general, the standard, prescriptive application of a policy action that optimizes production activities under free market conditions will not necessarily lead to optimal behavior under distorted agricultural markets.

Nevertheless, there is no guarantee that reform or removal of government price and income support programs will result in environmentally beneficial change. One study estimates that if the United States was to unilaterally eliminate all its farm programs (as of 1990) except the Conservation Reserve, the intermediate-term results of such reform would include a 33.8 million ton per year increase in soil erosion as land use intensified, but would reduce aggregate domestic nitrogen use by 429,000 tons, herbicide use by 18 million pounds, and insecticide use by 1.4 million pounds (Miranowski, Hrubovcak, and Sutton, 1991). Whether this is an environmental gain or loss depends upon the tradeoffs in value between the damages caused by soil erosion versus the risks reduced through lower use of agricultural chemicals.

Extensions and Limitations of the Analytical Framework

Despite the general usefulness of the standard, static, comparative approach to the welfare economic analysis of alternative resource/environmental policies, the examples developed thus far fail to provide information on a number of important policy implications, some of which can and others of which cannot be considered within the dimensions of standard welfare economics.

First, the multimarket framework for welfare analysis may approximate general equilibrium results, but may not directly represent gains and losses in all related markets. For instance, evaluating the corn-fertilizer-ground water policy alternatives in the corn market incorporates welfare measures for all groups vertically related to corn production, as well as for environmental quality. But the evaluation ignored possible implications for participants in the soybean market—groups likely to be affected by virtue of the close interrelationship between corn and soybean production. This failure can be resolved through an extension of the welfare economic analysis to incorporate related markets (Just et al., 1982). However, when each related market operates under a different commodity program and differentially affects a given resource's use, value, or quality, the extended analysis can be highly complicated.

Second, while evaluation of aggregate economic welfare is useful in a general sense, the results provide no indication of the regional distribution of gains and losses, or of their distribution among various subgroups (e.g. small farmers) of market participants. The welfare analytical approach may be applied at disaggregated levels, so long as data are available to estimate regional or subgroup behavior in the relevant markets. However, the required, disaggregated data often are not available. What this means is that the input to the public choice problem provided through the welfare analysis may be insufficient for political decision making. A political decision maker is less likely to find it useful to know how corn producers, in aggregate, are affected by a fertilizer tax than to learn how corn revenue effects are distributed, particularly within his or her area of representation. It would be of further use in gauging strength of opposition to or support for a particular policy to know the regional locations and size of the subgroups of producers or consumers that gain less or lose more than the aggregate situation suggests. This importance of potential concentration of subgroup opposition is illustrated by current reaction to impending commercialization of bovine somatotropin (bST), a synthetic growth hormone that increases the productivity of dairy operations. While, under dairy programs, dairy producers in aggregate would gain from bST availablity, small dairy operators in the Northeast and Lake States recognize that the availability of bST would increase their competitive disadvantage vis-a-vis larger scale operators in the western United States and have thus organized a highly effective lobby against the hormone's commercialization.

Furthermore, static, comparative welfare analysis does not reflect the influence of random, uncertain events or differences in time horizons for the realization of gains and losses, two problems that can be addressed through dynamic and stochastic extensions of the welfare economic analysis. Also, recall that welfare analysis does not consider the transactions costs associated with different policy options or their political feasibility. Finally, it is important to remember that the "goodness," appropriateness, or desirability of a policy option is not directly apparent from the results of economic welfare analysis. Rather, the results are merely input to the related public choice problem.

ROLE OF THE ECONOMIST IN THE POLICY PROCESS

> The policy analyst, I'm convinced, needs to ... understand not only the economics of the market but to understand the policy process in which the outcome of that analysis is going to be used.
>
>> From an interview with
>> Robert L. Thompson, then USDA
>> Assistant Secretary of Economics, in
>> *Choices*, 1987

As professionals, economists sometimes serve as the principal promoters of efficiency, and, indeed, efficiency may have no other constituency. Is it then possible for economists to prove relevant and useful as policy analysts within the context of a process that runs on rent-seeking, vote maximization, and other economically inefficient influences? Our answer is a resounding "yes." Economists can and do play a variety of important roles in the policy process.

Economists may participate in the policy process by providing analysis (on a voluntary or solicited basis) directed to public policy decision makers at local, state, or federal levels. Or, rather than affecting the decisionmaker directly, economists may influence policy by providing information of analytical results which purposefully or incidentally lend economic arguments that support interest group pressure.

A range of activities by economists have proved useful, to varying degrees, at each of the stages Brewer and deLeon (1983) identify as those through which a policy passes over time, the Initiation, Selection, Implementation, Evaluation, and Termination phases. Among those useful activities are the following.

Providing Information

Information has tremendous value in an uncertain world. Clear, transparent descriptions and explanations of past and current economic phenomena can alter the way that decision makers or interest groups perceive and assess the political, bureaucratic, nonmarket, or other gains or losses from a particular policy action. Likewise, forecasts of economic conditions and the assumptions underlying economic analysis are critical in that they can form or alter policy decision makers' perceptions of the world.

The possibility that economic information can change the way that things are viewed carries with it a great deal of responsibility. An unrealistic assumption that underlies an analysis, or a faulty forecast that is accepted, can have multiplier effects if policy decisions are made on its basis. This suggests that economic input is particularly valuable when it is based on parametric analysis that clearly illustrates the tradeoffs involved under various conditions or assumptions.

Conducting Evaluations

Both ex ante and ex post evaluation of policy options have great potential utility and impact on the policy process. However, living up to that potential requires that such evaluation is conducted with respect to the relevant groups of policy gainers and losers.

Lumping affected groups into highly aggregated categories such as "consumers" and "producers," while often dictated by data availability, ignores the equity focus of policy decision makers and interest groups. Ex ante information is most likely to prove useful if analyses employ a high degree of regional disaggregation and/or disaggregation by type of group (e.g., large farmers, specific commodity groups, low income consumers, etc.).

While the political process is seldom impacted by efficiency analysis alone (Cochrane, 1976), the policy economist may use distributional arguments to advance efficiency concerns. In the political world there is no lobby for efficiency, but it is possible to organize temporary coalitions to oppose a particular inefficiency (Behn, 1981). For example, political pressure to reform inefficient western water policies has been fueled by studies that demonstrate inequitable distributions of benefits (Leman and Nelson, 1981).

Ex post evaluation of past policy decisions is not done too frequently owing to the need to decompose policy-related from unrelated factors affecting policy performance, it is a difficult task. This is a pity, for it can be of great use to decision makers or interest groups seeking a legitimate basis for extending successful programs or eliminating programs that have outlived their usefulness.

Optimization

Economists tend to be well trained in optimization techniques. And as long as an economic analyst knows policy decision makers' objective functions, such techniques may, in theory, be applied to optimize a policy action. In actuality, however, it is highly unlikely that an economist policy analyst will know the nature or attributes of policy decision makers' objective functions. There is a high political cost to clear revelation of political preferences because, by necessity, some groups' welfare is weighted lower than others. Yet, without a clearly articulated objective function, including relative priorities among multiple policy objectives, the task of optimization is impossible. This conundrum may explain why economists' attempts to "optimize" the use of policy instruments often appear to fall on deaf ears.

Economic Expertise in the Political Process

The economist who wishes to truly affect policy through his or her expertise will appropriately conceptualize the issue, ask the "right" questions, and gear presentation of results to the policy audience whose members are to be aided, educated, or influenced (see Aaron, 1980; Leman and Nelson, 1981; Verdier, 1984; Wildavsky, 1979).

Economists who plan to influence policy will undertake analyses of policy options that are relevant to the policy process. A study that shows the welfare gains from eliminating all government intervention in the agriculture sector will have less impact on the policy process than one that considers the budgetary and distributional impacts of decoupling income supports. That does not mean that the former study should not be done. It may be very useful social science research that will advance the state of economic knowledge, but as policy analysis it will have little impact.

Asking the right question requires an understanding of the existing institutional setting for an issue and the history of attempts to address it. For example, cost-sharing for federal water projects has been a part of the water resources institutional setting since the 1930s. Recent debate on reforming cost-sharing has focused on questions of fairness. An understanding of this fairness dimension of the policy debate might lead economists to direct their economic impact studies toward the question of who would pay, rather than who should pay (Shabman, 1984).

The effective analyst will not only conduct the economic analysis, but market it as well. In part, this may mean translating from the technical jargon to the political jargon. This is the big difference between writing for a professional journal and for a decision maker. It may mean presenting findings to lay audiences in addition to professional audiences.

Marketing the analysis also can mean finding a constituency that will support more efficient policies (Leman and Nelson, 1981). In recent years, economists who have studied the losses in economic surplus resulting from the management practices of the Forest Service, have found a receptive audience in environmental organizations, which have used the analyses of below cost timber sales to advance their arguments for reduced harvest rates.

The economist who wishes to market his analysis may need to develop arguments that will change the face of the political debate to make it more amenable to economic considerations (Shabman, 1984). For example, despite nearly two decades of economic studies showing the efficiency advantages of using economic incentives to control pollution, the predominant policy tools used are standards and quotas. Economists might be able to generate greater interest in incentive-based pollution control instruments by shifting the debate to cost-effectiveness. They could argue that because of the budget deficit, environmental protection will be weakened over time unless policy instruments are put into place which are more cost-effective.

Of course there is nothing which requires an economist policy analyst to be a lobbyist for efficiency. The analyst's objectives, like those of policy makers and policy influencers, can vary tremendously as a function of one's employment situation, personal ideology, and political insight. Accordingly, the assumption underlying analyses, the values of variables that initialize analytical models, and other aspects of analysis that require some subjective judgment will vary depending upon the analyst's values and position. Thus, we may often find that a number of different analyses of the same policy issue, all of them "good" by professional standards, arrive at very different conclusions with different implications.

Obtaining different, and even conflicting "correct" conclusions from different analyses of identical agricultural resource policy issues is particularly common. This is due in part to the substantial amount of art and judgment that are required to specify, estimate, operate, and interpret agricultural sector models for policy analysis (Reichelderfer, 1993). In addition, analysis of many of the agricultural resource issues explored in this volume requires some attribution of values to goods that are not valued in the market place; a need that further implies use of the policy analyst's judgment. The challenge to analysts of agricultural resource policies is to balance science (consistency of economic theory and logic) with judgment (e.g., by what method should a life be valued?) and to be clear enough in communicating both scientific and value judgments that users of the analysis know how and under what circumstances conclusions are drawn.

REFERENCES

Aaron, H.J. "Politics and the Professors Revisited." *American Economic Review* 79(2):1–15, 1980.

Batie, S.S., L.S. Shabman, and R.A. Kramer. "U.S. Agricultural and Natural Resource Policy: Past and Future." In K.A. Price (ed.): *The Dilemmas of Choice*. Ames: Iowa State University Press, 1986.

Becker, G.S. "A Theory of Competition Among Pressure Groups for Political Influence," *Quarterly Journal of Economics* 98:371–400, 1983.

Behn, R.D. "Policy Analysis and Policy Politics," *Policy Analysis* 7:199–226, 1981.

Bonnen, J.T. and W.P. Browne. "Why is Agricultural Policy so Difficult to Reform?" In C. Kramer (ed.): *The Political Economy of U.S. Agriculture*: *Challenges for the 1990s*. Washington, DC: Recources for the Future, 1989, pp. 7–33.

Brandow, G.E. "Policy for Commercial Agriculture." In L. Martin (ed.): *A Survey of Agricultural Economics Literature, Vol. 1*. Minneapolis: Univ. of Minnesota Press, 1972, pp. 209–292.

Brewer, G. and P. deLeon. *The Foundations of Policy Analysis*. Homewood IL: Dorsey Press, 1983.

Buchanan, J.M. and G. Tullock. *The Calculus of Consent*. Ann Arbor: The University of Michigan Press, 1974.

Carlson, G.A. and S. Shui. "Farm Programs and Pesticide Demand." Working Paper, North Carolina State University, Raleigh, North Carolina, 1992.

Castle, E.N. and M. Goldstein. "Income Distribution, Poverty, Natural Resources, and Public Policies: Conceptual and Research Issues." Rural Development, Poverty and Natural Resources Workshop Paper Series, Part II., Washington, DC: Resources for the Future, National Center for Food and Agricultural Policy, 1983.

Clarke, J.N. and D. McCool. *Staking Out The Terrain*: *Power Differentials Among Natural Resource Management Agencies*. Albany: State University of New York Press, 1985.

Cochrane, W.W. *The Development of American Agriculture*: *A Historical Analysis*. Minneapols: University of Minnesota Press, 1979.

Cochrane, W.W. and M. Ryan. *American Farm Policy, 1948–1973*. Minneapolis: University of Minnesota Press, 1976.

Cropper, M.L., W.N. Evans, S.J. Berardi, M.M. Ducla-Soares, and P.R. Portney. "The Determinants of Pesticide Regulation: A Statistical Analysis of EPA Decisionmaking." *Journal of Political Economy* 100:175–197, 1992.

de Gorter, H. and D. Zilberman. "On the Political Economy of Public Good Inputs in Agriculture." *American Journal of Agricultural Economics* 72(1): 131–137, 1990.

Downing, P.B. *Environmental Economics and Policy*. Boston MA: Little, Brown and Company, 1984.

Downs, A. *An Economic Analysis of Democracy*. New York: Harper & Row, 1957.

Dunlap, R.E. "Public Opinion and Environmental Policy." In J.P. Lester (ed.): *Environmental Politics and Policy*. Durham: Duke University Press, 1989, pp. 87–134.

Economic Research Service. "Agricultural Resources: Cropland, Water and Conservation Situation and Outlook Report," AR-12, ERS, U.S. Dept. of Agriculture, Washington, DC., Sept., 1988.

Economic Research Service. *An Economic Analysis of USDA Erosion Control Programs*: *A New Perspective*, R. Strohbehn, ed. USDA, ERS, AER-560, Aug., 1986.

Gardner, B. "Price Support and Optimal Agricultural Research." Working Paper #88-1, University of Maryland, 1988.

Gardner, B.L. "Economic Theory and Farm Politics," *American Journal of Agricultural Economics* 71(5):1165–1171, 1989.

Gardner, B.L. "Causes of U.S. Farm Commodity Programs." *Journal of Political Economy* 95(2):290–310, 1987.

Hadwiger, D.F. and W.P. Browne (eds.): *The New Politics of Food*. Lexington, MA: Lexington Books, 1978.

Hahn, R.W. "The Political Economy of Environmental Regulation: Towards a Unifying Framework." *Public Choice* 65:21–47, 1990.

Haveman, R.H. *The Economic Performance of Public Investment: An Ex Post Evaluation of Water Resource Investments*. Baltimore, MD, Johns Hopkins Press for Resources for the Future, 1972.

Howitt, R.E. "Water Policy Effects on Crop Production and Vice Versa: An Empirical Approach." In R. Just and N. Bockstael (eds.): *Commodity and Resource Policies in Agricultural Systems*. New York: Springer Verlag, 1990.

Huffman, W.T. and R.E. Evenson. *The Development of U.S. Agricultural Research and Education: An Economic Perspective*. Part V. Iowa State University, Dept. of Economics, Staff Paper No. 175, December 1989.

Just, R.E., D.L. Hueth, and A. Schmitz. *Applied Welfare Economics and Public Policy*. Englewood Cliffs, NJ: Prentice-Hall, 1982.

Just, R.E., E. Lichtenberg, and D. Zilberman. "The Effects of Feed Grain and Wheat Programs on Irrigation and Groundwater Depletion in Nebraska." In N. Bockstael and R. Just (eds.): *Commodity and Resource Policies in Agricultural Systems*. New York: Springer-Verlag, 1991.

Kramer, R.A. and S.S. Batie, "The Cross-Compliance Concept in Agricultural Programs from the New Deal to the Present." *Agricultural History* 59:307–319, 1985.

Kramer, R.A. and R.E. Evenson. "Public Policy, Technology, and the Structure of U.S. Agriculture: Some Econometric Evidence." Unpublished paper, Economic Growth Center, Yale University, August 1988.

Krueger, A.O. "The Political Economy of the Rent-Seeking Society." *American Economic Review* 64:291–303, 1974.

Leman, C.K. and R.H. Nelson. "Ten Commandments for Policy Economists." *Journal of Policy Analysis and Management* 1:97–117, 1981.

Lichtenberg, E. and D. Zilberman. "The Welfare Economics of Regulation in Revenue Supported Industries: the Case of Price Supports in U.S. Agriculture." *American Economic Review* 76(5):1135–1141, 1986.

McLean, I. *Public Choice: An Introduction*. New York: Blackwell, 1987.

McSweeny, W.T. and R.A. Kramer. "The Integration of Farm Programs for Achieving Soil Conservation and Nonpoint Pollution Control Objectives." *Land Economics* 62:159–173, 1986.

Miranowski, J.A. "The Demand for Agricultural Crop Pesticides under Alternative Farm Programs and Pollution Control Solutions." Ph.D. dissertation, Harvard University, Cambridge, Mass., 1975.

Miranowski, J.A., J. Hrubovak, and J. Sutton. "The Effects of Commodity Programs on Resource Use." In N. Bockstael and R. Just (eds.): *Commodity and Resource Policies in Agricultural Systems*. New York: Springer-Verlag, 1991.

Mueller, D. *Public Choice II*. Cambridge University Press, 1989.

Nielsen, E.G., J.A. Miranowski, and M.J. Morehart. *Investments in Soil Conservation and Land Improvements: Factors Explaining Farmers' Decisions*. USDA, ERS, AER-601, Jan. 1989.

Niskanen, W.A. *Bureaucracy and Representative Government*. Chicago: Aldine, 1971.

Norton, G.W. "The Productivity and Allocation of Research: U.S. Agricultural

Experiment Stations, Revisited." *North Central Journal of Agricultural Economics* 3:1–12, 1981.

Oehmke, J.F. and X. Yao, "A Policy Preference Function for Government Interventions in the U.S. Wheat Market." *American Journal of Agricultural Economics* 72(3):631–640, 1990.

Ordeshook, P.C. *Game Theory and Political Theory: An Introduction.* Cambridge: Cambridge University Press, 1986.

O'Rourke, P.J. "Manuregate." *Rolling Stone* July 12–26: 45–48, 1990.

Paarlberg, D. *Great Myths of Economics.* New York: The New American Library, Inc., 1971.

Peltzman, S. "The Economic Theory of Regulation After a Decade of Deregulation." In M.N. Baily and C. Winston (eds.): *Brookings Papers on Economic Activity, Microeconomics.* Washington, DC: Brookings Inst., 1989, pp. 1–41.

Peltzman, S. "Toward a More General Theory of Regulation." *Journal of Law and Economics* 19:211–240, 1976.

Rapp, D. *How the U.S. Got Into Agriculture ... And Why It Can't Get Out.* Washington, DC: Congressional Quarterly Press, 1988.

Rasmussen, W.D. "History of Soil Conservation, Institutions and Incentives." In H.G. Halcrow et al. (eds.): *Soil Conservation Policies, Institutions, and Incentives.* Ankeny, IA: Soil Conservation Society of America, 1982.

Rausser, G.C. "The Evolution and Coordination of U.S. Commodity and Resource Policies. In N. Bockstael and R. Just (eds.): *Commodity and Resource Policies in Agricultural Systems.* New York: Springer-Verlag, 1991.

Rausser, G.C. "Political Economic Markets: PESTs and PERTs in Food and Agriculture." *American Journal of Agricultural Economics* 64(5):821–833, 1982.

Rausser, G.C. and W.E. Foster, "Political Preference Functions and Public Policy Reform." *American Journal of Agricultural Economics* 72:641–652, 1990.

Reichelderfer, K. "Environmental Protection and Agricultural Support: Are Trade-Offs Necessary?" In K. Allen (ed.): *Agricultural Policies in a New Decade.* Washington, DC: Resources for the Future, 1990, pp. 201–230.

Reichelderfer, K.H. "Utility of Models for Policy Analysis and Decision Making." In C.R. Taylor et al. (eds.): *U.S. Agricultural Sector Models: Description and Selected Policy Applications.* Ames, IA: Iowa State Press, 1993.

Reichelderfer, K. and M.K. Hinkel. "Environmental Interests and Agriculture: The Evolution of Pesticide Policy." In C. Kramer (ed.): *Political Economy of U.S. Agriculture: Challenges for the 1990's.* Washington, DC: Resources for the Future, 1989, pp. 147–173.

Reichelderfer, K. and W.C. Boggess. "Government Decision Making and Program Performance: The Case of the Conservation Research Program." *American Journal of Agricultural Economics* 70(1):1–11, 1988.

Ruttan, V.W. *Agricultural Research Policy.* Minneapolis: University of Minnesota Press, 1982.

Shabman, L.A. "Water Resources Management: Policy Economics for an Era of Transitions." *Southern Journal of Agricultural Economics* 16(1):53–65, 1984.

Shaffer, J.D. and G.W. Whittaker, "Average Farm Incomes: They're Highest Among Farmers Receiving the Largest Direct Government Payments." *Choices,* Second Quarter:30–31, 1990.

Stigler, G.J. "The Theory of Economic Regulation." *Bell Journal of Economics and Management Science* 2:3–22, 1971.

Sutton, J.D. and A.J. Webb, "Trade Policies and the Use and Value of Natural Resources." In J. Sutton (ed.): *Agricultural Trade and Natural Resources: Discovering the Critical Linkages.* Boulder: Lynne Rienner Publishers, Inc., 1988.

Thompson, P.B. "The Philosophical Rationale for U.S. Agricultural Policy." In M.A. Tutwiler (ed.): *U.S. Agriculture in a Global Setting: An Agenda for the Future.* Washington, DC: Resources for the Future, 1988, pp. 34–45.

Tolley, G.S. "Reclamation's Influence on the Rest of Agriculture." *Land Economics* 35(2):176–186, 1959.

Tullock, G. "Public Choice" In J. Eatwell, M. Milgate, and P. Newman (ed.): *The New Palgrave: A Dictionary of Economics.* London: Macmillan Press, 1987.

Verdier, J.M. "Advising Congressional Decision Makers: Guidelines for Economists." *Journal of Policy Analysis and Management* 3:421–438, 1984.

Wildavsky, A. *Speaking Truth to Power: The Art and Craft of Policy Analysis.* Boston: Little, Brown and Co., 1979.

Yandle, B. "Why Environmentalists Should be Efficiency Lovers." Formal publ. no. 195. St. Louis: Center for the Study of American Business, Washington University, 1991.

Zilberman, D. "Technological Change, Government Policies, and Exhaustible Resources in Agriculture." *American Journal of Agricultural Economics* 66(5):634–640, 1984.

11

Emerging Resource Issues
in World Agriculture

GERALD A. CARLSON AND DAVID ZILBERMAN

This book introduces an approach for studying economic, environmental, and resource issues that relies on models that integrate economic principles with specific features (and relationships) of physical and biological systems. This approach has a strong interdisciplinary flavor and suggests that the practitioner should be schooled in economics and the specifics of the problem. Although this general approach was used to address the major environmental and resource problems in the production of North American crops and livestock, it can also be applied to other commodities, and in different countries of the world. Of course each situation requires modification or reformulation of the models and utilization of different policy tools and solutions. This chapter points out several directions for expansion of the approach presented here, indicating the direction of change in the analysis and different policy options.

First, the models in this book are applicable to a broad definition of agricultural and farming activities. Our perspective on agriculture (or farming) is that any output obtained from biological organisms that is managed and controlled by humans is a result of agricultural activity. Thus, the production of corn in Iowa, milk in Wisconsin, and cassava in Nigeria are agricultural activities as are the production of fish in ponds in Ecuador, the raising of cattle on ranches in Guatemala, the cultivation of silkworms in India, and the management of rubber plantations in Malaysia. Thus, aquaculture, animal husbandry, range management, and agroforestry are activities that should be analyzed by the approach presented in this book. Not only is the range of commodities in agriculture broad, but it is changing over time. There is a transition process in food and fiber production from extraction to farming. There are systems in transition today both in developed and developing countries. The economics of this process will be analyzed in the first section of this chapter. This will be followed by a discussion of the possible modification of our methodology to an expanded set of commodities that are likely to be produced by farming activities in the near future.

Second, the modeling approach presented in this book was applied to the agricultural economy of a developed country. To extend the analyses to the environmental and resource management problems of agricultural production systems in developing countries, one has to consider some of the specific institutions and constraints that characterize these countries. Developing countries are likely to have different sets of commercial agricultural policies, and consequently, different farmer incentives than those in developed nations (Schultz, 1968). Their infrastructure, resource base, and research and development (R&D) capabilities are much less advanced than those of industrial countries. Furthermore, their agricultural producers may face completely dissimilar sets of resource scarcities and relative prices of inputs and outputs. Finally, consumer incomes and preferences differ in developing countries. Therefore, resource allocation choices, production patterns, and environmental resource policies in these countries are likely to be different from those in developed countries, and the modeling approach must take these contrasts into account. The second section of this chapter will address some of the modifications to models when applying them to problems of developing countries. We briefly evaluate a set of environmental and resource issues that are of special importance in the agricultural sectors of the developing world.

THE EVOLUTION OF FARMING SYSTEMS

Throughout history, the manipulation of biological systems by humans for their own benefit has evolved. Early men were hunters or gatherers, but slowly they settled and began to raise livestock and field crops; *farming systems* began. The set of commodities produced by farmers has grown continuously through the processes of adaptation and learning. Farming and animal husbandry have evolved to produce food products, fiber for clothing, and oils and energy sources; the transition from hunting/gathering to farming continues. Presently, one of the most striking manifestations of this evolutionary process is the dramatic growth in the farming and ranching of fish and seafood. However, it is not necessarily true that in the long run the entire production of fish will be through farming. We are likely to see an evolving equilibrium where some fish are harvested at sea and some are produced on farms. Economic analysis can identify the forces that establish this equilibrium and its evolution. Such analysis is not only applicable to fish and seafood production but to analysis of the coexistence of farming and harvesting in other commodities. Of course, such analysis will help us to identify situations where, over time, farming becomes the dominant form of production.

Farming has been widely viewed as the cultivation of products of biological processes in a modified environment. Production processes commonly have several stages: the setup stage, breeding, feeding and nurturing, protection and health maintenance, and harvesting. Each of these stages improves over time by trial and error and more formal research and development (R&D) activities. Because of the fragile or dynamic nature of some resources, inputs and R&D will be needed for maintenance as well as improvements.

Farming activities usually entail some form of all these stages of the production processes. In the production of annual field crops, the setup stage includes purchase of inputs and land preparation. Seeding can be viewed as part of the breeding stage, but breeding involves much more than seeding. In entails all the R&D that leads to the introduction of special varieties with unique beneficial properties. One advantage that farming has over direct harvesting is that breeding activities allow the selection away from the propagation of undesirable properties and increases in net yields and qualities of the harvested product. The off-farm R&D activities result in varieties with high yields and other properties amenable to cost-effective production processes given economic conditions.

The use of fertilizers and irrigation are examples of feeding and nurturing activities in field crop farming. Again, this activity benefits from the R&D efforts that lead to efficient irrigation and fertilization practices. Similarly, protection and health maintenance in field crop farming (through pesticides or nonchemical controls) are also improved by new products, new management strategies and development of human capital.

The principal stage performed in traditional fishing/hunting/gathering activities is harvest, and for simplicity we will designate these systems as *harvest systems* in the model below. Hunting and fishing require much search and transportation effort prior to harvest, while harvesting in farming systems does not involve search and requires much less transportation effort. Generally, farming systems also result in products that demand less costly postharvest treatment than fishing and hunting systems.

However, the distinction between farming and harvesting systems is not clear-cut in some cases. There are some agricultural systems where humans control more than one stage of the production process, but not all of them. For example, in some forms of mariculture (farming of fish and seafood at sea), only the breeding (spawning) and feeding are controlled by humans. In some livestock operations, animals eat natural grasses, and producers are minimally involved in breeding— providing mainly protection and health maintenance. In other livestock systems in developed countries (dairy, poultry, and swine), direct human control of every stage of production is the norm, and R&D activities have led to major improvements in genetic stocks, feeding efficiency, animal drugs, and health maintenance. Some production systems for nuts, berries, herbs, lumber, and medicines emphasize harvest with relatively little farming. Systems where hunting and harvest emphasis is dominant are often more prevalent in developing countries

A Modeling Framework of Farming and Harvesting

Here we introduce a simple model to determine the optimum mix of activities for the production of the commodity, say, fish, both by farming and harvesting. The model incorporates a management model of a renewable resource, which is similar to the one introduced in Chapter 3, with a simple production model of an agricultural industry. Following the usual procedure, we first derive socially optimal resource allocation and the optimal shadow price it implies , and then we use it to identify policies (taxes, subsidies, and private entry rules) that will lead to a competitive economy to attain the optimal outcome.

Let Q denote output consumed and $B(Q)$ denote the benefit of consumption.

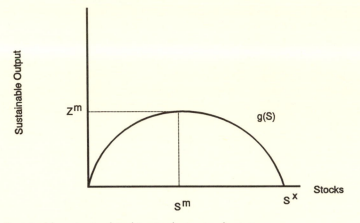

Figure 11.1. Sustainable output related to stocks in steady state.

$B(Q)$ can be interpreted as the area under the compensated demand curve and Q is output produced by farming or harvesting. Equation (1) gives a consumption constraint:

$$Q = Z + Y \tag{1}$$

where $Z =$ amount of output from fishing or harvesting and $Y =$ amount of production from farming.

For simplicity, assume that we are in a steady state (sustainable growth): S is the stock of the resource, say, fish, and $g(S)$ is the growth function denoting the increase of fish stock per unit of time. The sustainable growth constraint is

$$Z = g(S) \tag{2}$$

The stock level, S^m, corresponds to the maximum sustainable yield Z^m (see Fig. 11.1). When the resource stock is smaller than S^m, sustainable yield increases as the stock increases; however, when the stock is greater than S^m, sustainable yield declines and at S^x sustainable yield is zero ($g_s > 0$ when $0 < S < S^m$, $g_s < 0$ when $0 < S < S^x$).

The harvesting cost function is $H(Z, S)$. Marginal costs of harvesting are positive and increasing with the amount harvested, namely, $H_z > 0$, $H_{zz} > 0$, but they are decreasing with the stock of resource, namely, $H_{zs} < 0$. The farming cost is $C(Y)$, and we assume increasing marginal costs of farming, $C_y > 0$, $C_{yy} > 0$. The socially optimal resource allocation will maximize the difference between the benefits from consumption and the costs of harvesting and farming, subject to the sustainable growth constraints. Specifically, the social optimization problem is

$$\underset{S, Q, Z, Y}{\text{Max }} B(Q) - H(Z, S) - C(Y) \tag{3}$$

subject to constraints (1) and (2). Using the Lagrange multiplier approach, this optimization problem can be rewritten

$$L = \max_{S, Q, Z, Y, \lambda, P} B(Q) - H(Z, S) - C(Y) + P[Z + Y - Q] + \lambda[g(S) - Z] \quad (4)$$

where P is the shadow price of output and λ is the shadow price of the resource stock resulting from the sustainable growth constraint. The first optimality condition is

$$L_Q = B_Q - P = 0 \quad (5)$$

With optimal resource allocation, the output price is equal to the marginal benefits of consumption. When benefit measures the area under the compensated demand curve, another condition implies that optimal output price is determined according to the inverse demand curve,

$$L_Z = -H_Z + P - \lambda = 0 \quad (6)$$

Equation (6) implies that the optimal level of harvesting is determined when the marginal cost of fishing is equal to the difference between the fish price and the shadow price of the resource stock. Differentiating (4) for fish stocks one obtains

$$L_S = \lambda g_S - H_S = 0 \quad (7)$$

This condition suggests that the shadow price of stock is equal to the marginal benefit of sustainable resource stock (because of reduced harvesting costs) divided by the marginal cost of sustainable resource stock ($\lambda = H_S/g_S$). Optimal farming intensity is determined at the level where marginal cost of output from farming is equal to the output price:

$$L_y = P - C_y = 0 \quad (8)$$

Conditions (5)–(8) together suggest that an equilibrium with both harvest and farming exists when

$$C_y = H_z + H_s/g_s = B_Q = P \quad (9)$$

Increases in either harvesting costs or the shadow price of stocks will increase the equilibrium level of farming.

The optimal solution can be found for the case of a competitive farming industry and a regulated fishing industry. The regulation can be in the form of a tax, which is equal to λ, or some equivalent output restriction. Over time, the equilibrium outcome may change. For example, with an exogenous increase in the demand for the commodity, equilibrium price (P) increases, the output of farming (Y) increases, and harvesting (Z) increases. However, as the amount harvested gets closer to the maximum sustainable yield (Z is close to Z^m in Fig. 11.1), the possibilities of extending output through harvesting are limited and most of the growth in supply may come from extending farming production. Furthermore, both farming and harvesting techniques may have reductions in costs through technical change; however, the changes are often more rapid in farming. Thus, the share of farming in the production of output may increase over time and may even be the dominant form of production as in the case today of field crops and meat production.

A more general lesson that can be drawn from this analysis is that, when the human population is small and the demand for commodities (food products) is not substantial, harvesting may be the dominant form of production. Over time, human population pressure and increased demand will tend to reduce stocks of resources and make harvesting more costly. Improved technological capabilities make farming less costly; thus, there is a gradual shift from harvesting to farming.

This gradual transition has been documented and analyzed by scholars who studied the impact of increased human population pressure on farming in Africa. Bosrup (1965) studied farming and food production in Africa and documented the transition from harvesting and slash-and-burn agriculture to more continuous forms of farming. Binswanger and McIntire (1987) analyzed the transition from slash-and-burn agriculture to permanent farming. Their analyses suggest that, as food provisions become more dependent on farming, it is essential to establish distinct property rights, or other institutions that will ensure that those who invest in preharvesting stages of production will reap the benefits of the harvest. Thus, the introduction of farming as an alternative to harvesting and production of certain commodities needs to be accompanied by the establishment of incentives and institutions that will make farming worthwhile.

Emerging Agricultural Systems

Aquaculture and agroforestry are expanding forms of biological activities that produce outputs (fish, seafood, and forest products) that are mainly harvested. These *new production activities* share many common features with farming of conventional agricultural commodities, and experiences accumulated in traditional farming activities are useful for development policies and identifying problem areas for the new production processes. These new activities offer other opportunities to address and partially alleviate some of the economic and environmental problems facing existing farming activities, but may aggregate others, especially if they compete with other natural resources activities.

The experience with traditional crops suggests that the key elements for the growth and development of the new farming activities are constant improvement of varieties grown to increase yields and quality and to withstand diseases and other pests. This suggests the need to establish and maintain R&D capacity for breeding the new crops. Furthermore, over time, producers are likely to face pest and disease problems that require a capacity for control through certain cultural practices, disease-resistant varieties, or some form of chemical pesticides. When the new farming industries are envisioned to be competitive in nature (and in many other cases as well), their development and growth may require government expenditures on establishing and maintaining research and extension capacities on breeding and disease and pest control. Public research capacity may be required also for the establishment of economically viable cultural practices and the design of basic machinery to farm the new crops, since the private sector may underinvest in research during the early stages of new farming industries because of uncertainties and the public good nature of this information. On the other hand care is needed to avoid public support of all "infant industries" that cannot compete with existing products.

Research and extension support are not likely to be the only forms of government intervention affecting new farming activities. Their possible usage of chemical pesticides will be the subject of government scrutiny and legislation. The new farming operation may generate waste materials, and their abatement and disposal may be affected by environmental quality control policies.

Furthermore, as Chapter 10 suggests, agricultural industries have the tendency to enter into *excess supply* situations; namely, over time, the supply of agricultural products has tended to grow faster than the demand, that leads to low returns and income of agricultural activities and might justify implementation of government intervention programs. Thus, while the government may play an active part in providing some of the infrastructure for new farming operations, and "infant industry" considerations may argue for some form of direct support in their early stages, it must also provide information to avoid overinvestment or oversupply in new farming operations (especially after viable economic technologies have been developed and seem to provide excellent investment opportunities).

If there is a political or other justification for government intervention, then experience with policies to control excess supply situations for conventional crops may be useful for addressing similar situations if and when they occur with the new farming activities. The new farming activities may also result in different types of risk and policy and institutional experiences with current crops will be useful in designing public and private responses to reduce the negative consequences of these risks. New farming activities may serve to alleviate some of the excess supply problems that tend to plague conventional agriculture. The new activities will compete with conventional crops on the use of existing resources in agriculture which will result in increased returns and value of resources. Thus, new farming activities may serve as new sources of income and value added for agriculture, may allow the sector to grow, and may reduce the need for income and supply-control policies.

While the new farming activities may cause new environmental and resource management problems, they may also contribute much to reduction of some of the existing ones. As the efficiency of farming increases over time, costs of production and commodity prices may decline, and that may lead to a decrease in harvesting activities and a reduction of pressure on species grown in the sea or the forest. Thus, the development of highly productive farming activities capable of producing products that are only harvested today may serve to slow or halt the destruction of environments and the demise of species that may accompany harvesting activities.

Aquaculture

One type of product in which we observe an emergence of farming to complement harvesting is for fish and seafood. Our analysis suggests that as the demand for fish increases and as many fish populations are being depleted, fish farming will grow in importance. A larger variety of fish will be cultivated in farms, and the practice will expand to areas where fish farming is not practiced today. Some of the existing problems with policies that characterize traditional crops may be applicable for domesticated fish and seafood. Thus, the analysis of several of the chapters of the book will be applicable to the emerging fish and seafood farming industries (Anderson, 1986).

While processes of transition occur in many areas, it may not necessarily result in farming practices to which we are accustomed. In fish farming, there may be production of several species that will coexist in the same medium. There are obvious increasing returns to scope and complementarities among species that make multicultural practices very attractive, and we may see an increase in multicultural processes in the future. Furthermore, the transition from fishing to farming may not be complete. We may witness an increase in mariculture activities, namely, activities that provide preharvest support of fish populations at sea. Such activities include the provision of food; management of breeding (hatcheries, genetic development); and protection from disease and predators. Some of these activities may need to be controlled by the government or some local grower organization, especially in cases of open-access fisheries. When access to fisheries is restricted, those with access rights are more likely to support some of the preharvest resource-enhancement activities.

Fish and seafood are not the only commodities produced by aquaculture. New developments in biology may increase the set of commodities produced by farming systems, and algae illustrate one of the important ones. Currently, several varieties of algae are being harvested to provide food, food supplements, and fine chemicals. For example, in the Far East some types of seaweed (macroalgae) are harvested, dried, and used as food products. Agar is the best example of an algae extract with many commercial uses and worldwide sales that approach $500 million annually. Currently, the main sources of agar are seaweeds collected off the shores of Mexico, Italy, and countries in the Far East. However, there is a growing demand for agar derivatives. Some of the natural sources of agar are being overharvested, and there are many experiments in agar farming in the United States and elsewhere.

There are also many microalgae that have large commercial potential. These activites serve to illustrate the wide range of product farming that biological organisms can produce. Spirolina is a microalga that is being harvested (mostly in Mexico) and sold as a health food. Microalgae also have a significant potential in aquaculture activities. There are systems that use microalgae for sewage treatment. Production plants in Hawaii, Australia, and Israel use microalgae to produce fine chemicals such as the food coloring beta carotene ($200 million annual sales). Microalga is a potential source of food coloring, fatty acids (oils that are low in cholesterol), protein-rich feed products, and energy. There is extensive research going on today on the derivation and use of microalga products. As commercial products are created, the developers of the products and policy makers are challenged to establish an industrial structure to farm microalgae and obtain their derivatives. In some cases, microalgae farming may be done by small producers who will sell dried products to a processor by market or via contractors.

In other cases, production at the processing and marketing stages of the final product will be done within one organization. Government policies with respect to research, extension, and resource management can affect the structure and growth of these industries. In particular, the structure will be strongy affected by the degree of involvement of the agricultural research institutions and other public agencies in related technologies, disease control, and production management in microalgae farming.

The growth of the microalgae farming industry and other aquaculture activities will also be strongly affected by water rights, quality, and pricing regulations. Furthermore, the growth of aquaculture will be directly affected by agricultural policies affecting conventional commodities, since aquaculture will compete for resources with conventional farming and aquaculture outputs are substitutes for many products of commercial agriculture. Multiple input, multiple output models that allow for substitution are needed to assess these developments (Chapters 2, 4).

New Animal Husbandry Systems

Unlike fish, which are predominantly obtained by harvesting and whose husbandry is rather recent, farming systems have been the main provider of land animals for human consumption and use. However, the number of species farmed is rather small (cows, pigs, sheep, goats, horses, and poultry), and many of the most critical gains will come from genetic manipulations to gain quality and lower costs of production. As our knowledge of biology, the environment, and international resources increases, it is likely that we will identify other species and animal traits that are appropriate sources of food, clothing, and transportation. Of particular interest in this regard are the tropical forests and the polar zones where farming and cultivation activities have been minimal and where our familiarity with indigenous species is poor. There are several examples of tropical animals that have been efficient sources of food, wool, and other products. We can assume that in the future, utilization of traits for disease resistance, lower fat, and faster rates of growth and reproduction will accelerate. The development and use of synthetic hormones for fast, lean hog production is an important first example of use of biotechnology (Avery, 1991).

As some of the examples of Chapter 3 demonstrate, it is useful to analyze many aspects of animal husbandry as problems of management of renewable resources. Within such a framework, livestock (cattle) are viewed as a growing *renewable resource* that serves as a store of value. Such an outlook is useful in determining the length of animal production cycles and in assessing their values.

Animal farming systems may lead to many public good and externality problems. One important example is open ranges for livestock production. Chapter 3 reviews the *open access* problem associated with grazing and the need for institutions and mechanisms that allow sound management of public range and forest lands. Another externality problem of importance is animal waste management. The chapter on externalities presents some case studies and policies for addressing this issue, but this is an open area for further research—both in terms of management and technology. Animal waste products are being used as inputs for energy, fertilizer, and other activities. One challenge is the development of technologies to make the recycling of these products economically viable given the benefits of reduced external costs.

Some animal farming systems are subject to considerable government intervention. The U.S. dairy program is an obvious example of such policy. Animal farming systems are also influenced by policies affecting the crop sector (corn, soybeans, and fodder). Knutson et al. (1990) estimate that the livestock sector is likely to be the main loser from massive restrictions on pesticide use on feed crops in the United States.

The organization of animal farming takes many forms. Several types of animal farming (raising of hogs and cattle) are performed, to a large extent, by farmers who are also field crop growers and who mix the two types of operations to spread quasifixed resource costs and diversify their risk. Poultry production has become highly integrated with many contract producers linked to large firms providing management, processing, feed and other inputs. Hog production and cattle feeding are following the poultry organization form, but are limited by less rapid technological changes in genetics and feeding systems. Analysis of breeding stock with unique traits requires one to introduce input demand curves that reflect resource differentiation.

Most of the analysis in this book deals with agricultural outputs in perfectly competitive markets. However, many livestock, fish, and forestry products are highly differentiated products. More research is needed to understand trends in these markets and market segments. This will affect infrastructure, resource, and environmental quality demands in the future. Examples include processing plant location, demand for grazing lands, and deforestation rates.

Tree Farming and Agroforestry

Forests provide people with a wide range of fiber products including lumber, pulp, wood fiber, jute, and cane. Forests also provide many recreational benefits and fulfill very important ecological roles, e.g. housing many diverse wildlife species, providing watersheds, and improving air and water quality. There may also be a potential to increase energy production from wood products.

Lumber and other forest products are produced using many types of operations with varying degrees of human involvement at different stages of the production process. Many of the logging operations in the tropical forests, as well as the cutting of old growth forests in the United States, can be considered as direct harvesting operations. In these cases, the forest ecosystems may be viewed as exhaustible resource since forests are more than the wood they contain. In contrast, much of the wood and pulp produced in the United States and Europe are products of renewable systems. In many (mostly coniferous) commercial forests harvesting cycles for lumber last 30 to 50 years, but those for paper are only 15 to 25 years (Deacon, 1985).

The economic situation and market conditions vary across forest products. For some products, there is excessive supply, for others, excessive demand (e.g., high-quality woods). There are growing tendencies to increase forest productivity by expanding the *farming* of forest products. These tree farming operations thus encompass selective breeding, the use of fertilizers and pesticides, efficient irrigation

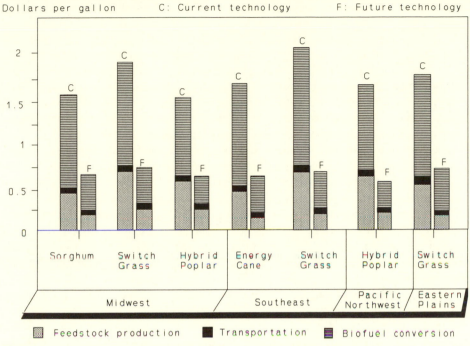

Figure 11.2. Costs of producing ethanol with fuel crops in the United States.

and water management schedules, and the planned management of planting for low-cost harvesting.

In the future, forest farming will play an important role, especially with regard to high-quality wood products and high-volume/high-yield products for pulp and energy production. A major benefit of this type of tree farming is that it may increase the production of certain exotic woods that are today harvested in environmentally sensitive regions (tropical rain forests). The new tree farming operations would increase the supply of these wood products, reduce the incentive for open access harvesting, and thus help to preserve the fragile environments. Hardwood plantations in the southeastern United States are an example of this development. Tree farming could also help in alleviating an "energy crisis" in many regions, mostly in developing nations where wood is being used as a major source of energy for cooking and heating. Existing wood reserves are being depleted, as their rate of growth is outmatched by population growth and wood demands. Higher productivity rates and controlled access that are likely to be obtained by tree farming systems may help to better balance wood availability and needs.

Energy crops are another important development that could influence resource availability and environmental quality. Already sugarcane, food, and fuel wood are important sources of home and industrial energy in many countries. With new genetic and processing developments, agricultural crops may be lower cost sources of energy for transportation and other energy demands. Figure 11.2 from a study by Bhat et al. (1991) summarizes cost of production estimates for ethanol with current and future technology in four parts of the United States with various energy crops. These figures show that technical change in biofuel conversion is a key to making these crops competitive with the private costs of fossil fuel production. Production of energy from biofuels releases about one-tenth the CO_2 to the atmosphere per Btu than coal, natural gas, or oil under current technology, but they often have higher levels of other noxious compounds. When social costs of energy crops are compared with that of fossil fuels, we are likely to see more production of dedicated fuel crops in the future, although not all studies are as positive as the one discussed above (Chapman and Barker, 1991).

One must distinguish between the production of forest products with a monocropping system and an overall forest management strategy that emphasizes multiple products, the coexistence of many species, and the preservation of pristine forest environments. Agroforestry is a new form of farming producing recreation services, lumber, fuel wood, paper, and agricultural products in various setting. Agroforesty is promoted for helping to reverse the decline of forest resources around the world and to take advantage of the increasing returns to scope provided by the joint production of several species in forest and agricultural crop environments.

The development of tree farming and agroforestry methods will be encouraged if society provides monetary incentives for the preservation of unique environments and invests in R&D for renewable wood resources. For farming of wood products, we may be at a point in agricultural history similar to the period just prior to the discovery of hybrid corn. Tree farming is likely to become more economically viable as systematic R&D identifies new varieties of forest products that have valuable properties in terms of rate of growth or product quality.

The development of agroforesty is a much greater challenge, since most farming technologies are geared to produce commodities independently without much emphasis on interdependency of crop systems or recycling possibilities. The development of agroforestry can be linked to the development of sustainable agriculture, which results in integrated farming and resource management systems. Sustainable agriculture (which will be discussed further in the following section) does not necessarily imply a return to the simpler methods of "the good old days." Rather, with increased scientific knowledge and improved computation and transportation technologies, the prospects for modern sustainable systems that produce low-cost, high-quality products that are economically viable and do less damage to the environment are very promising.

EXTENSIONS TO DEVELOPING COUNTRIES

Natural resources and their role in agriculture differ widely as one extends the concepts of this book to various regions of the world. Resource endowments of climate, soils, water, and human skills range from highly productive (with low population levels) to very fragile resources yielding very low levels of food, fiber, and other output. Levels of resource endowments and technology, together with institutions and cultural factors, give rise to very different resource conflicts in developing countries. Sometimes, there are special dimensions to agricultural resource issues in developing countries. While eavesdropping at a meeting of development economists addressing resource problems, one might hear terminology such as *appropriate technology, farming systems, sustainable resource use, infrastructure development, informal markets, germplasm conservation,* or *deforestation.* However, most of the concepts presented in this book can be adapted or modified to interpret these terms. In addition, since institutions, cultural developments, and many government policies evolve slowly, it is often very revealing for those in developed countries to look at resource-use patterns and technologies across countries.

Frequently, relative prices of particular resources are very different in developing countries than in industrial ones. For example, a skilled water engineer, plant pathologist, or other scientist may be available only at very high wages, but workers who plant, protect, and harvest crops are available for only a few dollars per day. Because of transportation and communications costs, reliable supplies of commercial fertilizers at the farm in some parts of South America may be ten times more expensive relative to land costs than they are in North America. In this section we examine some of the current resource issues of developing countries.

Appropriate Technologies and Scale Economies

One of the first lessons learned by scientists traveling to a developing country is that many of the technologies of industrial agriculture do not transfer readily to the small-scale production units of developing countries. There are usually a few *export* or plantation farming operations in many countries, but most households subsist on a few hectares of land utilizing only a few minor implements and high levels of labor. Finding *appropriate* equipment and human resources that fit the scale of operation in developing countries is often a problem, and it is particularly acute as new technologies are introduced.

Development and adoption of appropriate power resources (oxen, tractors, humans) for tillage and harvest operations are good examples of the scale economies concept. It is relatively easy to develop tractors or to introduce oxen to a few literate, large-scale farmers. It is quite difficult to add power resources where cash to purchase, maintain, and fuel the oxen or tractors is quite limited. Spreading the purchase cost over enough units of land partly depends upon how much higher the crop output with high power will be relative to that with hand labor. There will be climatic, crop mix, and soil considerations in how productive the oxen are, how costly it is to maintain them, and how costly the hand labor is. As the next example illustrates, more is involved than merely finding how many hectares of a particular crop it takes to justify an oxen team at average output prices.

Delgado and McIntire (1982) compiled information to evaluate adoption of oxen in Western Africa. Because of scarce feed for maintaining oxen in many locations, herdsmen who could move livestock to locations where feed sources were available were needed to maintain livestock for resident crop farmers. Informal markets for herding services and feed hauling developed. Hiring as well as owning bullocks became an option for crop farmers. The price of bullock power was also influenced by manual sources of power, which were in turn heavily influenced by off-farm wage rates. Different farms and regions used more oxen than others. The benefits of oxen were much greater for farmers owning more irrigated land, and for those growing rice, groundnuts, and cotton rather than sorghum. Crops that have much higher land preparation benefits, such as rice, are more likely to require the use of oxen. In this case study, the cost for maintaining a pair of oxen was a major fixed cost that limited adoption to farmers with larger areas to plant. This seemingly simple system involves the relative costs and productivity of at least five resources: land, oxen services, manual labor on the farms, off-farm labor, and labor and other resources in maintaining oxen. It illustrates that over time relatively complex resource systems evolve even in *low resource* farming situations.

One of the areas where the African experience points to "inappropriate technology" is when subsidized tractors or oxen are introduced into areas with low-intensity farming systems with short tillage periods. Even oxen or tractor rental markets cannot easily develop in areas in which the tillage period per crop season is limited by rainfall or other factors. If manual labor is inexpensive, there will be frequent use of hand hoeing and little incentive to maintain the nonhuman power sources. Size of farms, use per season, and relative benefit per unit of output need evaluation prior to introduction of new power resources.

Evolution of Farming Systems and Land Use

Understanding the causes and consequences of widely differing land-use intensity in different regions is critical for public research and natural resource policy decisions. In a recent study of African agriculture, Pingali et al. (1987) describe farming systems in terms of land use intensity, cultivation techniques, and labor use. They find that the transition from the hand hoe to the plow is closely associated with the evolution in farming systems from low intensity land use (forest-fallow) to intensive, annual cultivation. By examining many different locations with different population densities, they were able to trace agricultural intensification in terms of land use and adoption of mechanization. Studying the effects of population density in rural areas is critical because Africa is now experiencing rapid population growth rates.

Population density, farming systems, and adoption of farming equipment are frequently closely related. Figure 11.3 illustrates how farming intensity increases with population density for the African setting in the 1980s (Pingali et al., 1987). The height of the boxes represents the number of separate locations (villages) corresponding to each of the cross-classifications. Data from the same villages show the association between land-use intensification and the adoption of animal and tractor power sources (Fig. 11.4). Hand tools are associated with short fallow and bush fallow, while animal and tractor traction are used for the more intensive cropping systems. Better access to urban markets also tends to speed farming intensification. This is due to both higher net prices to farmers and more demand for farm labor relative to other regions leading to still more population density.

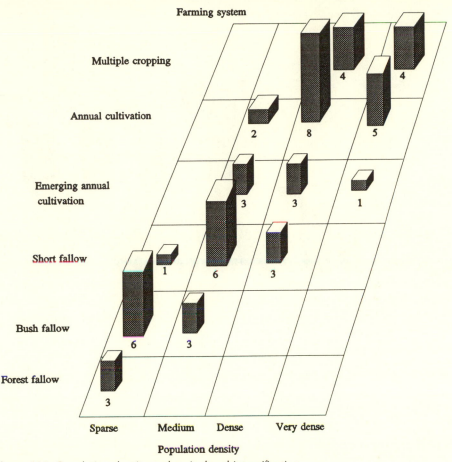

Figure 11.3. Population density and agricultural intensification.

The increased use of more power with farming intensity also lead to more cultivation of heavier soils, which requires more power-intensive land improvements. Africa has large areas of potentially productive land that will need power, improved crop varieties, and many other resources (Avery, 1991).

Intensification in farming systems increases the demand for other agricultural resources. Fertilizers of various types are more profitable as the fallow period is shortened and less leaching occurs. In addition, on the heavier soils there is a demand for irrigation and drainage investments. Labor use will generally increase per unit of land but, as indicated in the Delgado and McIntyre (1982) study, the switch from hand hoe to animal power will only come with high levels of land use. This is so partly because the source of power has only a minimal effect on crop yield. Intensification also increases the benefit from infrastructure developments such as roads, schools, and local agricultural research institutions.

Efficient land use and adoption of improved farming systems are closely linked to farm policies. In many developing countries farm commodity prices are kept

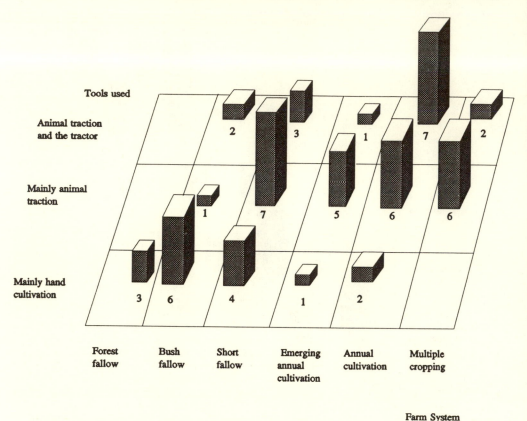

Figure 11.4. The use of tools in the evolution of farming systems.

far below border or world prices. Price ceilings on urban food prices, export taxes on agricultural products, and overvalued currency are frequently used policy instruments. On the other hand inputs such as fertilizer, irrigation, and pesticides are subsidized in some countries. There is concern that expanding agriculture in developing countries will lead to increased deforestation and soil and water degradation. However, others have argued that new technologies to preserve moisture (alley cropping, mulch cropping, tied ridges), increase productivity of soils (acid-soil cropping systems), and reduce losses to pests (pest resistant varieties), together with direct policy intervention to protect forests, will allow expanded output in developing countries without severe environmental damage (Avery, 1991; Anderson, 1992).

Sustainable Soil Resource Use

Maintaining long-term soil productivity is one of the most frequent examples cited for worldwide sustainable resource use in agriculture. Preventing land degradation that is due to erosion, salinity, continuous cropping, or deforestation is a key component of *sustainability* efforts by the World Bank and other development agencies (Anderson and Thampapillia 1990; York, 1988; Lynam and Herdt, 1988).

The McConnell model described in Chapter 9 assumed that soil is a resource that is slowly regenerated. Rational farmers may have soil loss, but they will choose a soil stock that is socially optimal provided there are cost adjustments (subsidies or taxes) for off-farm costs of soil erosion. Because soil depth influences future farm land prices, farmers will manage soil loss to maximize discounted farm income including resale value of the asset. This model depends on farmers knowing various technical relationships, prices, and costs. For example, they must know 1) how soil depth influences yield and land values, 2) how costly soil loss prevention is, and 3) what will be the future time streams of product prices, input costs, and discount rates. In addition, there may be government interventions influencing technology advances, property rights, crop prices, or availablity of inputs. For example, Feder et al. (1988) have show that permanent property rights were important in bringing about long-term soil erosion investment in Thailand. A model with fewer information requirements may fit the developing country situation better.

Consider a physical land degradation process that relates crop yield to soil depth as shown by the solid line in Figure 11.5. Without explicitly considering time, we see that above some soil loss, S_1, crop yield will decline as soil depth declines. However, soil conservation practices to maintain soil depth above (to the left of) S_1 will have a negligible effect on yield. The linkage between yield and topsoil loss is difficult for farmers and researchers to determine because it takes place over long periods, it can be influenced by random weather events, and it is changed by other inputs. For example, the second curve (F) in Figure 11.5, shows that the addition of a substitute input for soil such as fertilizer can increase the range of soil depth changes from S_1 to S_2 before any detectable yield loss occurs.

Technological advances in crop genetics can also influence the consequences of soil loss. Walker and Young (1986) found that new varieties of wheat in northwest United States were very effective replacements for soil depth, and can change the optimal amount of soil conservation. With new germplasm, the yield potential at most soil depths will increase. Such an effect is shown in Figure 11.6 as a shift from the yield curve for the old to a new technology. If farmers are operating at soil depth S_0, introduction of the new genetic technology can increase yield to Y_1, a level above the previous maximum yield.

The optimal level of soil conservation effort depends upon the shape of the soil degradation curve, the yield increase from the new technology, soil conservation costs, and interest costs. Even though fertilizer, water, and new germplasm can change yield levels, it is possible that a new technology can either increase or decrease the demand for soil conservation. For a given package of soil conservation practices and time costs, there is a minimum time until net return with conservation will exceed returns without conservation. This is shown in Figure 11.7 at time t_0. In the analysis of wheat genetic change, Walker and Young (1986) estimated that it takes 60 years before net returns with conservation exceed returns with no conservation. However, with lower discount rates, lower beginning soil depth

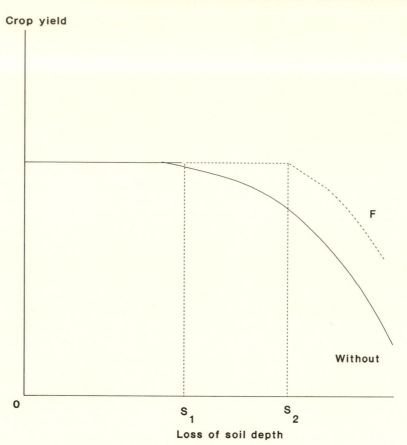

Figure 11.5. Effect of soil loss on yield without and with fertilizer (F).

stocks, or slower technological progress rates it will be only a short time period (t_1) before conservation is the preferred land management option. It is also possible with low starting soil depths that conservation dominates no conservation for all time periods.

This soil conservation evaluation indicates that research and extension efforts directly applicable to the soils, crop prices, discount rates, resource stock levels, and conservation costs of developing countries are needed to recommend particular practices to prevent soil erosion. Another complication comes from scale economies or jointness with other farming operations. On small-scale farms, multifarm conservation practices will often be less expensive and more effective than independent actions of individual farmers. This may require formation of formal conservation districts that can coordinate efforts across farmers. Sometimes, however, the costs of organization and monitoring will not justify undertaking group actions. Free riders and other forms of noncooperation can make joint efforts difficult, and institutions are needed to equate marginal entry costs and benefits (see Chapter 7).

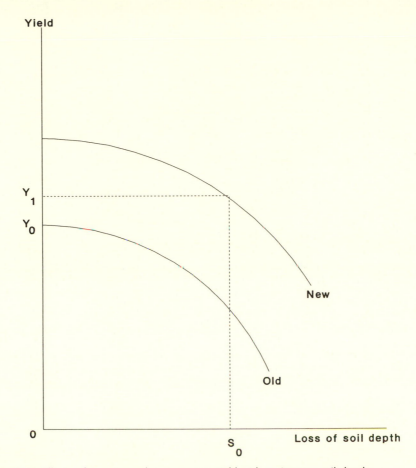

Figure 11.6. Effects of new germplasm on crop yield with various topsoil depths.

There are other sustainability issues besides land degradation in developing countries. Water resources also have important stock changes over time. Reservoirs and canals can be silted up and thereby reduce the storage capacity and delivery capacity of surface irrigation systems. Ground water stocks can be drawn down. Leaching of salts owing to excess irrigation rates can leave soils nonproductive. According to Ruttan (1987), the research and development implications of sustainable systems are often more critical than short-term inefficiencies. To meet the growing population pressures, there must be continuous renewal of research output in the areas of germplasm, new mechanical techniques, and other resources to keep food production levels and incomes from falling.

Spatial Economics and Uncertain Input Supplies

The spatial arrangements of agriculture in developing countries are greatly influenced by the relatively high cost of transportation and communication. This

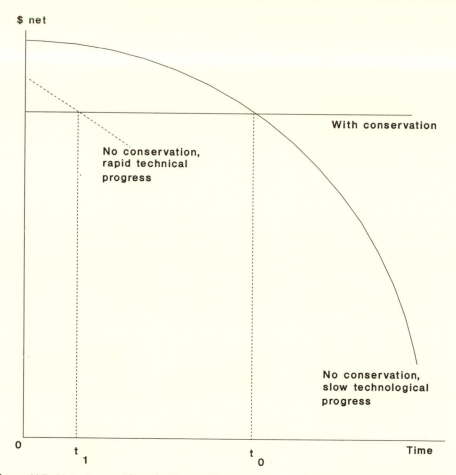

Figure 11.7. Net returns with and without soil conservation and two rates of technical progress.

influences farm level prices of inputs and outputs and restricts use of many
management and information services common to agriculture in developed
countries. One of the manifestations of these high costs that is rarely discussed in
agricultural resource economics in developed countries is uncertain input supplies.
Because farmers in many countries are not assured of having adequate supplies
of purchased inputs, this can lead to lower adoption of advanced technologies.

We can conceptualize the uncertain input supply problem in terms of pest or
fertility management. Training manuals for fertilizer and pesticide evaluation for
developing country settings are available (Perrin et al., 1976; Reichelderfer et al.,
1984). Figure 11.8 shows a crop damage or total revenue (TR) function from
increasing densities of weeds in a crop. The total cost function for achieving various
levels of weed population control using conventional hand weeding is shown as
the function TC_{HW}. This cost is assumed to have a fixed cost component and to
increase at an increasing rate to achieve low levels of weed populations. Net return
is maximized at weed level N_0 giving net returns $a - b$. If a new, effective herbicide

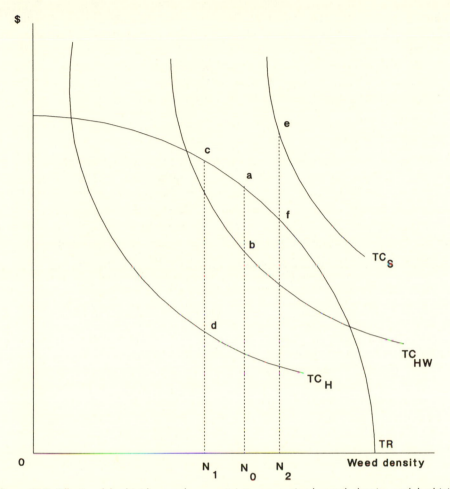

Figure 11.8. Effects of herbicide supply uncertainty on optimal weed density and herbicide adoption.

becomes available, weed control costs are assumed to decline to TC_H. The optimal weed density with the herbicide technology is N_1 yielding net return equal to $c - d$, which is larger than $a - b$. The difference $[(c - d) - (a - b)]$ shows the risk-free net gain to adopting the herbicide technology. However, if a farmer is planning to use a chemical herbicide and his supply of herbicide is disrupted in some periods, then a total cost function that reflects usual production costs plus an unplanned or salvage hand weeding operation to reach equal crop protection can have high costs. This is shown as the total cost function TC_S. In periods when herbicides are not available, net farm income is negative ($e - f$), and losses are minimized by attempting to achieve weed population N_2. It would not take very many short herbicide supply events (probability = p) for the farmer to realize that he could be better off by taking the assured income from hand weeding of $a - b$ rather than the expected herbicide and salvage weeding income $[p(e - f) + (1 - p)(c - d)]$.

When we consider the risk averse nature of most subsistence farmers, it will take an even lower probability of input supply disruption to make hand weeding the preferred choice. This shows that adoption of technologies that depend on deliveries of inputs over long distances can be difficult to introduce in developing countries. It also provides a method to evaluate one of the benefits of improved roads and communication systems in rural areas.

Open Access to Forests

Open-access resources are those that are free to anyone who has the ability to make use of them. Examples such as forests, rangelands, ocean fisheries, and wildlife are common in developing countries. Some lands are also jointly used and managed by groups of farmers or herdsmen. With effective management such as controlled entry on common lands, the resource base can be maintained over long periods. However, there are often high incentives for individuals equipped with chainsaws to invade forests (Prestemon and Laarman, 1989).

Deforestation in developing countries has recently received much worldwide attention. Deforestation rates in open access forests are determined by local costs of utilization, population pressure, and net prices of products *mined* from the forest. If roads are built that lower private transportation costs, marginal revenue of products will increase, and consequently, harvest rates will increase. Logs, minerals, plants, and wildlife are products taken from these forests. Like all resources, tropical forestlands have alternative uses. The profitability of land clearing for livestock pasture, cropland, or other activities will be influenced by prices and costs of production of these alternative products. Government subsidies for crop or livestock inputs, credit, or transportation will usually speed the rate of deforestation. For example in Brazil, Binswanger (1989) showed that general tax policies, special tax incentives, the rules of land allocation, and the agricultural credit system all favored livestock production over forest production in the Amazon Basin.

Deforestation can also lead to local and international costs that are external to private businesses and households. Local external costs would be water quality damage, wildlife losses, and loss of resources such as firewood. International external costs include the (possible) global warming costs and loss of genetic resources. Adding these costs to the private costs of forest product extraction yields social costs of deforestation (see Chapter 6).

Figure 11.9 shows a conceptual framework for thinking about deforestation policy. The optimum deforestation rate for private individuals is at D_1, where private marginal extraction costs, MEC_P, equal the private marginal revenue, MR_P. With a transport cost subsidy, marginal revenue shifts to MR_S and the private deforestation rate will increase to D_2. This type of increase in deforestation could also occur if there were a subsidy for lowering input costs or raising output prices for the use of land following deforestation. The curve labeled MSC includes both the private costs of extraction and external costs described above. This would give an optimal private deforestation rate of D_3 with no transport subsidy, but a rate D_4 similar to D_1 if the transport subsidy is in place.

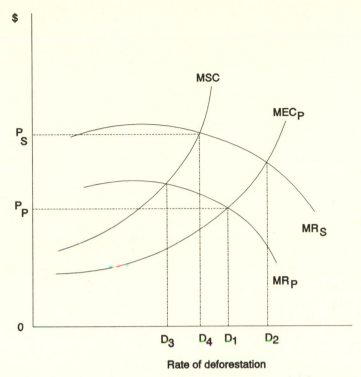

Figure 11.9. Effects of subsidies and external cost on optimal rate of deforestation.

The alternative policies for achieving low rates of deforestation might include changes in subsidies, controlling entry, or changing incentives so that external costs are included in private use decisions. In the above example a user fee equal to $P_S - P_P$ is needed if the transportation subsidy remains. The use of the forest land following deforestation is often changed to crop agriculture. If there is an agricultural output price support or input cost subsidies, then these can also result in increases in deforestation rates. This shows the close link between agricultural policies and incentives to speed or slow deforestation.

The international dimension of external costs is particularly difficult to overcome. If these costs are thought to be large, then actions by developed countries such as financial assistance to countries with large tropical forests (Brazil, Malaysia, Indonesia) may be necessary. Other policies being tried are "debt for nature" swaps and formation of forest reserves financed by user fees (Tietenberg, 1990).

FUTURE RESOURCE USE ISSUES

This book has emphasized the interdependencies among resources in examining resource scarcity. Fertilizer, irrigation water, and pest management resources can often replace scarce land. Labor, management, and equipment can help replace scarce water. Genetic resources combined with more intensive management have helped high-yield agriculture to many parts of the world. There is progress in per capita food production and even a move towards food exports in many developing countries (Avery, 1991).

However, there are always evolving resource constraints. In the developed countries the constraint is more and more frequently that of *environmental quality*. Clean water and air and high levels of human safety have positive income elasticities. Also, demand for outdoor recreation continues to expand. In developing countries limits on human resources, training, and export earnings are often the most obvious constraints. In periods of high energy prices there is a tendency to encourage the "mining" of forests of fuelwood and land for agricultural production with subsidies, tax policies, and free entry. Marginal lands are brought into production as food prices increase. In addition, there is a tendency for middle-income countries to resort to trade restrictions to reduce food imports. The sustainability of these policies and practices is questioned by researchers in environmental and agricultural research organizations (Anderson, 1992; Avery 1991).

The solution to sustainable growth will be reached differently by regions with different endowments of resources. The food demand priorities of individual countries must be recognized. In some cases, the priorities of human health and immediate food production for survival may be higher than that of environmental quality. There is no reason to expect that every resource must be at current stock levels or at some level yielding "maximum sustained yield." The environment and human demands are elastic and can adjust to differing stock levels and prices, respectively. However, this does not mean that food and resource scarcities, degradation, or irreversibilities can be ignored. The models and examples presented in the previous chapters should help in finding an appropriate balance.

As outlined in this book, there is a case for resource enhancement and the development of alternative resources. Research and development must be considered as a key part of sustainable resource use. New genetic materials, new crops and livestock management systems, and improved organization forms will continue to evolve to allow more flexible and efficient resource management. With process innovations many resources can be made renewable and reusable. Both private and public sector agents have roles to play in developed and developing countries.

One must be cautious in hoping that "better management" or research and development can solve major environmental and resource scarcity problems. History is full of examples of major population centers having to adjust to severe resource depletion situations. Development and freedom from poverty depend upon a set of institutional adjustments that are only partially related to agricultural resources. Clearly defined property rights to agricultural and environmental resources must be combined with an extensive set of human and political rights. In most cases the struggle for food and fiber production through the use of water, land, and other inputs will be greatly assisted by a stable political system. In recent years some of the most severe resource depletion and hunger examples have occurred in countries in political turmoil.

Finally, the knowledge base in the science and technology of agriculture and efficient allocation systems continue to expand. There are many challenges for economists to combine the research methods of the social and biological sciences. Government policies, markets for new resources, and new institutional systems will give future generations of economists a full plate of problems to evaluate.

REFERENCES

Anderson, J.R. and J. Thampapillia. "Soil Conservation in Developing Countries: Project and Policy Intervention." Policy and Research Series paper 8, World Bank, Washington, D.C., 1990.

Anderson, K. "Agricultural Trade Liberalization and the Environment: A Global Perspective." *The World Economy* 15(1):153–171, 1992.

Anderson, L.G. *The Economics of Fisheries Management.* Baltimore, MD: Johns Hopkins Press, 1986.

Avery, D.T. *Global Food Progress 1991.* Indianapolis: Hudson Institute, 1991.

Bhat, M.G., B.T. English, and A. Turhollow. "Biofuels from Energy Crops: Economics and Environmental Impact." Dept. of Agri. Econ., Univ. of Tenn., Knoxville, 1991.

Binswanger, H. "Brazilian Policies That Encourage Deforestation in the Amazon." Environment Dept. Working Paper No. 16, World Bank, Washington, D.C., 1989.

Binswanger, H.P. and J. McIntire. "Behavioral and Material Determinants of Production Relations in Land Abundant Tropical Agriculture." *Journal of Economic Development and Cultural Change* 36(1):73–100, 1987.

Bosrup, E. *Conditions of Agricultural Growth.* Chicago: Aldine Pub. Co., 1965.

Chapman, D. and R. Barker. "Environmental Protection, Resource Depletion, and the Sustainability of Developing Country Agriculture." *Journal of Economic Development and Cultural Change* 39(4):723–738, 1991.

Deacon, R.T. "The Simple Analytics of Forest Economics." In R.T. Deacon and M.B. Johnson (eds.): *Forestlands Public and Private.* Pacific Institute of Public Policy Research. Cambridge, MA: Balinger Pub. Co., 1985, pp. 275–302.

Delgado, C.L. and J. McIntire. "Constraints on Oxen Cultivation in the Sahel." *American Journal of Agricultural Economics* 64(2):188–196, 1982.

Feder, G. et al. *Land Policies and Farm Productivity in Thailand.* Baltimore, MD: Johns Hopkins Press.

Knutson, R.D. et al. *Economic Impacts of Reduced Chemical Use.* College Station, TX. Knutson and Associates, 1990.

Lynam, J.K. and R.W. Herdt. "Sense and Sustainability: Sustainability as an Objective in International Agricultural Research." CIP-Rockefeller Conference paper, Rockefeller Foundation, New York, 1988.

Perrin, R.K. et al. From Agronomic Data to Farmer Recommendations: An Economic Training Manual. Information Bulletin, International Maize and Wheat Improvement Center, Mexico City, Mexico, 1976.

Pingali, P. et al. *Agricultural Mechanization and the Evolution of Farming Systems in Sub-Saharan Africa.* Johns Hopkins Univ. Press, Baltimore, Md., 1987.

Prestemon, J.P. and J.G. Laarman. "Should Sawn Wood be Produced With

Chainsaws: Observations in Ecuador." *Journal of World Forest Resource Management* (4):111–120, 1989.

Reichelderfer, K.H, G.A. Carlson, and G. Norton. *Economic Guidelines for Crop Pest Control.* FAO Plant Production and Protection Paper, FAO, Rome, Italy, 1984.

Ruttan, V. "Institutional Requirements for Sustainable Agricultural Development." In T.J. Davis and I.A. Schirmer (eds.): *Sustainability Issues in Agricultural Development.* Proceedings of 7th Ag. Sector Symposium, World Bank, Washington, D.C., 1987.

Schultz, T.W. *Economic Growth and Agriculture.* New York: McGraw-Hill, 1968.

Tietenberg, T.H. "Managing the Transition: The Potential Role for Economic Policies." In J. Matthews (ed.): *Preserving the Global Environment: The Challenge of Shared Leadership.* New York: W. Norton, 1990.

Walker, D.J. and D.L. Young, "Assessing Soil Erosion Productivity Damage." In *Assessing the National Resources Inventory*, Vol. II. National Academy Press, Washington, D.C., 1986, pp. 21–62.

York, E.T. "Improving Sustainability With Agricultural Research." *Environment* 30(19):38–43, 1988.

Author Index

Subject Index